THE BARBOUR
COLLECTION
OF CONNECTICUT TOWN
VITAL RECORDS

THE BARBOUR COLLECTION
OF CONNECTICUT TOWN
VITAL RECORDS

LITCHFIELD 1719–1854

Compiled by

Debra F. Wilmes

General Editor
Lorraine Cook White

INTRODUCTION

As early as 1640 the Connecticut Court of Election ordered all magistrates to keep a record of the marriages they performed. In 1644 the registration of births and marriages became the official responsibility of town clerks and registrars, with deaths added to their duties in 1650. From 1660 until the close of the Revolutionary War these vital records of birth, marriage, and death were generally well kept, but then for a period of about two generations until the mid-nineteenth century, the faithful recording of vital records declined in some towns.

General Lucius Barnes Barbour was the Connecticut Examiner of Public Records from 1911 to 1934 and in that capacity directed a project in which the vital records kept by the towns up to about 1850 were copied and abstracted. Barbour previously had directed the publication of the Bolton and Vernon vital records for the Connecticut Historical Society. For this new project he hired several individuals who were experienced in copying old records and familiar with the old script.

Barbour presented the completed transcriptions of town vital records to the Connecticut State Library where the information was typed onto printed forms. The form sheets were then cut, producing twelve small slips from each sheet. The slips for most towns were then alphabetized and the information was then typed a second time on large sheets of rag paper, which were subsequently bound into separate volumes for each town. The slips for all towns were then interfiled, forming a statewide alphabetized slip index for most surviving town vital records.

The dates of coverage vary from town to town, and of course the records of some towns are more complete than others. There are many cases in which an entry may appear two or three times, apparently because that entry was entered by one or more persons. Altogether the entire Barbour Collection--one of the great genealogical manuscript collections and one of the last to be published--covers 137 towns and comprises 14,333 typed pages.

ABBREVIATIONS

ae.------------age
b.-------------born, both
bd.-----------buried
bp.-----------baptized
B.G.----------Burying Ground
d.-------------died, day, or daughter
decd.---------deceased
f.--------------father
h.-------------hour
J.P.-----------Justice of Peace
m.------------married or month
res.-----------resident
s.--------------son
st.------------stillborn
TM-----------Town Meeting
V.D.M.------Voluns Dias (minister, one who serves god)
w.------------wife
wid.----------widow
wk.-----------week
y.-------------year

THE BARBOUR COLLECTION
OF CONNECTICUT TOWN
VITAL RECORDS

LITCHFIELD VITAL RECORDS
1719 - 1854

	Vol.	Page
AARD, Polly Ann, of Litchfield, m. Edmund **CALKINS,** of Torrington, Aug. 24, 1828, by Rev. Hart Tallcott	2	277
ABBE, Elizabeth Francis, d. Alanson & Eliza W., b. Jan. 3, 1824	2	138
ABBOTT, ABBOT, Antha E., m. Samuel **KILBOURNE,** b. of Litchfield, Feb. 20, 1845, by John F. Norton	TM49	8
Elijah, m. Diany **HALL,** June 4, 1838, by Rev. H. Bryant	2	317
Elijah E., of Southbury, m. J. **BUEL,** of Litchfield, Apr. 9, 1848, by Joseph Henson	TM49	24
Newton B., m. Eliza **WRIGHT,** May 25, 1844, by Rev. D. L. Marks	TM49	4
Palmyra E., m. Reuben **PALMER,** b. of Litchfield, Mar. 10, 1847, by John F. Norton	TM49	18
ABERNATHY, ABERNETHY, Beulah, m. Abner **BEECH,** Apr. 23, 1770, by Rev. Judah Champion	1	167
Elihu S., representative Apr. 1844	2	1557
Lorrin, m. Aaron **BRADLEY,** July 8, 1787	2	68
Pamela, m. Anson **BEACH,** Sept. 20, 1798	2	19
ADAMS, ADAM, Amos, [s. Joseph & Deborah], b. Aug. 13, 1798; d. Sept. [ ],1859, at Baton Rouge, La.	TM49	9
Amos, s. Joseph & Deborah, b. Aug. 13, 1798	2	16
Andrew, representative Oct. 1776, May & Oct. 1777, May & Oct. 1778, May & Oct. 1779, May & Oct. 1780	2	1550
Andrew, Jr., m. Annis **CANFIELD,** Apr. 25, 1785	1	166
Andrew, Jr., m. Annis **CANFIELD,** Apr. 26, 1785, by Rev. Cotton Mather Smith, of Sharon	1	210-11
Betsey, [d. Joseph & Deborah], b. Oct. 31, 1796	TM49	99
Betsey, d. Joseph & Deborah, b. Oct. 31, 1796	2	16
Betsey, d. Joseph & Deborah, b. Oct. 31, 1796	1	166
Charles, [s. Joseph & Deborah], b. May 18, 1805	TM49	99
Charles, s. Joseph & Deborah, b. May 18, 1805	2	16
Charles, m. Jane C. **HINMAN,** Feb. 12, 1827, at New Haven	TM49	99
Charles, m. Julia M. **HINMAN,** Feb. 14, 1830, at New Haven	TM49	99
Charles, [s. Charles & Julia M.], b. Feb. 2, 1845; d. June 11, 1864	TM49	99
Charles, representative Apr. 1845	2	1557
Cornelia, d. Andrew & Annis, b. Feb. 16, 1786	1	166
Cornelia, d. Andrew & Annis, b. Feb. 16, 1786	1	210-11
Deborah, d. July 17, 1857	TM49	99
Eliza, m. Philo C. **SEDGWICH,** Oct. 2, 1833, by Rev. David G. Tomlinson	2	293
Ella Kezia, [d. Charles & Julia M.], b. Feb. 22, 1852	TM49	99
Frances Deborah, [d. Charles & Julia M.], b. Nov. 19, 1847	TM49	99
Frances Scoville, [d. Charles & Julia M.], b. Mar. 24, 1855; d. June 4, 1862	TM49	99
Henry, s. [Joseph & Deborah], b. Aug. 18, 1794; d. Feb. 11, 1842	TM49	99

1

	Vol	Page
ADAMS, ADAM, (cont.),		
Henry, s. Joseph & Deborah, b. Aug. 18, 1794	1	166
Henry, s. Joseph & Deborah, b. Aug. 18, 1794	2	16
Henry William, [s. Charles & Julia M.], b. Dec. 8, 1835, at		
Bath, N.Y.	TM49	99
Jane C., w. Charles, d. June 10, 1828, at New Haven	TM49	99
Jane Deborah, [d. Charles & Julia M.], b. May 19, 1831; d. June 27,		
1832	TM49	99
John Marsh, [s. Joseph & Deborah], b. Apr. 16, 1801; d. Jan. 16, 1853,		
at Augusta, Ga.	TM49	99
John Marsh, s. Joseph & Deborah, b. Apr. 16, 1801	2	16
Joseph, b. July 11, 1767, at Roxbury, Mass.; m. Deborah **MARSH**, Jan.		
26, 1792	TM49	99
Joseph, m. Deborah **MARSH**, Jan. 26, 1792, by Rev. Ashbel Baldwin	1	166
Joseph, b. July 11, 1767, at Roxbury; m. Deborah **MARSH**, Jan. 26,		
1792, by Rev. Ashbel Baldwin	2	16
Joseph, [s. Charles & Julia M.], b. Aug. 19, 1833; d. May 17, 1870	TM49	99
Joseph, d. July 14, 1856	TM49	99
Julia, [d. Charles & Julia M.], b. Oct. 21, 1842	TM49	99
Julia M., w. Charles, d. Sept. 1, 1849	TM49	99
Kezia, [d. Joseph & Deborah], b. Mar. 19, 1811, at Bristol	TM49	99
Kezia, d. Joseph & Deborah, b. Mar. 19, 1811, at Bristol	2	16
Maria Canfield, d. Andrew & Annis, b. Dec. 27, 1787	1	166
Maria Canfield, d. Andrew, Jr. & Annis, b. Dec. 27, 1787	1	210-11
Mary Fairchild, [d. Charles & Julia M.], b. Jan. 29, 1838, at Bath, N.Y.	TM49	99
Sally, d. [Joseph & Deborah], b. Nov. 26, 1792	TM49	99
Sally, d. Joseph & Deborah, b. Nov. 26, 1792	1	166
Sally, d. Joseph & Deborah, b. Nov. 26, 1792	2	16
Sarah Elizabeth, [d. Charles & Julia M.], b. Mar. 25, 1840, at Bath,		
N.Y.; d. May 7, 1842	TM49	99
Sylvia, m. Tobias **CLEAVER**, July 15, 1793, by Rev. Judah		
Champion	2	48
Thomas William, s. Joseph & Deborah, b. Oct. 13, 1814, at Litchfield	2	16
William Thomas, [s. Joseph & Deborah], b. Oct. 14, 1814; d. [ ],		
1847, at Augustus, Ga.	TM49	99
ADDIS, Abigail, d. Thomas & Abigail, b. Oct. 8, 1800	2	137
Abigail, w. Thomas, d. Apr. 14, 1813	2	137
Almira, d. Thomas & Abigail, b. Apr. 11, 1796	2	137
Chester, s. Thomas & Abigail, b. Nov. 16, 1793	2	137
Emily, d. Thomas & Abigail, b. Mar. 28, 1892, [probably intended for		
1792]	2	137
George, s. Thomas & Abigail, b. May 1, 1806	2	137
George, m. Fanny **MOSS**, Nov. 29, 1832, by Rev. Mr. Taylor, of South		
Farms	2	289
George, m. Elizabeth **KING**, b. of Litchfield, Aug. 16, 1846, by Rev.		
Samuel Fuller	TM49	38
Lyman, s. Thomas & Abigail, b. Feb. 8, 1808	2	137
Mary A., m. George **CHURCHILL**, [Dec.] 29, 1830, by Rev. William		
Lucas	2	286
Mary An[n], d. Thomas & Abigail, b. Sept. 14, 1812	2	137
Otis, s. Thomas & Abigail, b. Mar. 26, 1791	2	137
Roxanna M., m. Carl Gustav **BUTTHERST**, b. of Litchfield, May 3,		
1853, by Rev. Benjamin L. Swan	TM49	93

	Vol.	Page
ADDIS, (cont.),		
Sally, m. Hiram **BARNES**, Sept. 21, 1825, Rev. Isaac Jones	2	253
Samuel, s. Thomas & Abigail, b. Apr. 10, 1794	2	137
Samuel, m. Barbara **WEST**, Sept. 3, 1821, by Rev. Isaac Jones	2	104
Sarah, d. Thomas & Abigail, b. Apr. 20, 1801	2	137
Seth, s. Thomas & Abigail, b. Dec. 9, 1810	2	137
Thomas, m. Abigail D. **WOLFF**, Oct. 1, 1790, by Rev. [ ]	2	137
Thomas, s. Thomas & Abigail, b. Mar. 16, 1803	2	137
Thomas, m. Lucy **PELTON**, Nov. 27, 1814, by Rev. Isaac Jones	2	137
William, s. Thomas & Abigail, b. Nov. 8, 1804	2	137
ADSET, Tama M., of Stanford, Dutchess Co., N.Y., m. Thomas M. **COE**, of		
Litchfield, Mar. 3, 1848, at Stanford, N.Y.	TM49	98
AGARD, Abigail, d. James & Elizabeth, d. Mar. 30, 1743	1	0
Anne, d. John & Mary, b. Oct. 17, 1750	1	3
Chloe, d. James & Elizabeth, b. Dec. 21, 1748	1	3
Elizabeth, d. James & Elizabeth, b. Mar. 19, 1746/7	1	3
Hannah, d. John & Mary, b. Aug. 22, 1748	1	3
Hezekiah, m. Abigail **DEMAN**, of Torrington, Dec. 17, 1750, by Rev.		
Nathaniel Robards, of Torrington	1	3
John, m. Mary **HOSFORD**, Nov. 28, 1745, by Rev. Timothy Collins	1	3
Joseph, s. John & Mary, b. Aug. 17, 1746	1	3
Judah, s. John & Mary, b. Aug. 15, 1753	1	3
Maray, wid., d. May 29, 1807, in the 92nd y. of her age	1	42
Mehitable, d. Hezekiah & Abigail, b. Nov. 5, 1752	1	3
Noah, s. John & Mary, b. May 3, 1756	1	3
Sally, w. Samuel, d. June 28, 1813	2	50
Salmon, s. James & Elizabeth, b. Sept. 9, 1744	1	3
Sary, d. James & Elizabeth, b. Apr. 9, 1753	1	3
ALDRIDGE, Daniel, of Troy, m. Rachel **LANDON**, June 23, 1825, by Rev.		
Isaac Jones	2	27
ALFRED, Augustus, m. Edna **MERCHANT**, Apr. 6, 1830, by Rev. William		
Lucas	2	286
ALLEN, ALLIN, [see also **ALLYN**], Azeubah, d. Daniel & Mary, b. May 8,		
1741	1	3
Daniel, m. Mary **GRANT**, Apr. 28, 1737, by Rev. Timothy Collen	1	3
David, m. Ruth **HUMMASTONE**, Nov. 25, 1773, by Rev. Andrew		
Storrs, of Northbury	1	166
Electa, d. Gideon & Rachel, b. Dec. 5, 1806	2	18
Elihu, s. Daniel & Mary, b. May 4, 1739	1	3
Ethan, s. Joseph & Mary, b. Jan. 10, 1737	1	3
Ethan, Gen., was s. of Joseph & Mary (**BAKER**) **ALLEN**. His mother		
was of Woodbury	1	0
Gideon, m. Rachel **HAND**, Oct. 3, 1799, by Rev. Amos Chase	2	18
Henry, twin with Rachal, s. Nathaniel & Esther, b. Jan. 22, 1770	1	3
James, s. Cornelius & Martha, b. Sept. 30, 1735	1	3
John, representative May 1793, Oct. 1793, May & Oct. 1794, May		
1795, May & Oct. 1796	2	1552
Jonah, m. Laura **ROOT**, Jan. 31, 1825, by Rev. George E. Pierce	2	37
Joseph, m. Mary **BAKER**, Mar. 11, 1730, by Rev. Anthony Sladdor, of		
Woodbury	1	3
Loyal W., m. Mary M. **WELMOT**, Jan. 24, 1826, by Rev. Issac Jones	2	260
Lucius D., of Goshen, m. Eliza O. **WHEELER**, of Litchfield, May 30,		
1838, by Rev. Grant Powers, of Goshen	2	317

	Vol.	Page
ALLEN, ALLIN, [see also **ALLYN**], (cont.),		
Lucy, d. Joseph & Anne, b. Dec. 24, 1788	1	210-11
Lucy, d. Gideon & Rachel, b. Oct. 1, 1811	2	18
Maria, d. Gideon & Rachel, b. Nov. 6, 1804	2	18
Mary, w. Nehemiah, d. July 8, 1723	1	3
Mary, d. Daniel & Mary, b. Jan. 24, 1737/8	1	3
Mary, see Mary **BAKER**	1	0
Mercy, wid., d. Feb. 5, 1727/8	1	3
Nelson, s. Gideon & Rachel, b. Sept. 28, 1802	2	18
Orlo, m. Polly **GRISWOULD**, Apr. 18, 1799, by Rev. Judah Champion	1	210-11
Polly, d. Joseph & Anne, b. Apr. 19, 1792	1	210-11
Rachal, twin with Henry, d. Nathaniel & Esther, b. Jan. 22, 1770	1	3
Rufus, s. Gideon & Rachel, b. Mar. 22, 1814	2	18
Sally Birge, d. Orlo & Polly, b. Apr. 23, 1800	1	210-11
Samuel, s. Nehemiah & Mary, b. June 27, 1723	1	3
ALLYN, [see also **ALLEN**], Anne, d. Joseph & Anne, b. Dec. 31, 1783	1	210-11
Elizabeth, d. Joseph & Anne, b. Oct. 23, 1785	1	210-11
Nathan, s. Joseph & Anne, b. Oct. 23, 1781	1	210-11
ALVORD,Thomas Gould, s. Asahel & Rachel, b. Mar. 1, 1741/2	1	3
AMES, Ansel, s. Cheny & Hannah, b. July 16, 1791	1	166
Benjamin, m. Anne **CULVER,** Aug. 2, 1774, by Rev. Judah Champion	1	42
Benjamin, m. Lucy **BUTLER,** June [ ], 1825, by Rev. J. E. Camp	2	265
Chene, m. Hannah **ROWLOSON,** Feb. 23, 1775, by Leah Hart, J.P.	1	166
Cheny, s. Cheny & Hannah, b. Sept. 23, 1792	1	166
David Westover, s. Rufus & Mary, b. Dec. 6, 1832	2	316
Hannah, d. Cheney & Hannah, b. Apr. 16, 1779	1	42
John, s. Cheney & Hannah, b. Feb. 3, 1784	1	210-11
Julia, m. Henry W. **SAWYER,** July 4, 1841, by J. Brace	2	334
Julia Ann, d. Rufus & Olive, b. Feb. 26, 1830; d. Dec. 28, 1830	2	131
Leonard, s. Chene & Hannah, b. Apr. 25, 1776	1	166
Leonard, m. Minerva **PECK,** Jan. 1, 1796, by Rev. Daniel Catlin, of Harwinton	1	210-11
Lydia, m. William **WILLIAMS,** Jan. 10, 1832, by Rev. Mr. Taylor, of South Farms	2	289
Mary Clarinda, d. Rufus & Mary, b. Jan. 25, 1836	2	316
Olive, w. Rufus, d. Apr. 24, 1831	2	131
Orange Barnes, s. Rufus & Olive, b. July 6, 1828	2	131
Orson, s. Leonard & Minerva, b. Oct. 25, 1798	1	210-11
Phebe Burgiss, d. Rufus & Olive, b. Nov. 5, 1826; d. Aug. 14, 1829	2	131
Robert, s. Cheney & Hannah, b. Dec. 20, 1787	1	210-11
Rufus, m. Olive **BARNES,** Dec. 31, 1823, by Rev. Henry Robinson	2	131
Rufus & Olive, had infant d. Apr. 24, 1831	2	131
Rufus, m. Mary **WESTOVER,** Jan. 10, 1832, by Rev. Mr. Taylor of South Farms	2	289
Rufus, m. Mary **WESTOVER,** Jan. 10, 1832, by Rev. Veron D. Taylor	2	316
Rufus, m. Arme **STONE,** Apr. 27, 1851, by Rev. David L. Parmelee	TM49	62
Rufus Smith, s. Rufus & Mary, b. Aug. 7, 1834	2	316
Samuel, s. Cheney & Hannah, b. June 2, 1782	1	42
William Bennet, s. Rufus & Olive, b. Jan. 17, 1825	2	131
ANDREWS, ANDREW, [see also **ANDRUS**], Anne Adalaide, m. William **McKEE,** Nov. 1, 1826, at the house of Jonathan Andrew, by Rev. Seth Higby, of New Hartford & Burlington	2	266
Betsy L., m. John L. **STEWART,** June 30, 1833, by Rev. L. P. Hickok	2	288

	Vol	Page
ANDREWS, ANDREW, [see also **ANDRUS**], (cont.),		
Jerusha, m. Henry **GOSLER**, July 3, 1825, Rev. Isaac Jones	2	141
Lucretia, of Litchfield, m. Edwin **BLAKE**, of Middletown, Mar. 4, 1838, by Rev. Lewis Gunn	2	315
Margarette, m. Luzerne **MOULTHROP**, Nov. 10, 1844, by Rev. D. L. Parmalee	TM49	6
Mary, m. Elijah **GRANT**, Mar. 10, 1755, by Rev. Mr. Woodbridge, of New Haven	1	19
Mary, m. Thomas **SALTONSTALL**, b. of Litchfield, Aug. 10, 1854, by Rev. Lewis Gunn	TM49	111-½
Solomon P., m. Merinda P. **WEED**, Oct. 17, 1844, by Rev. David L. Parmalee	TM49	6
Susanna, m. John **PRESTON**, Nov. 6, 1775, by Rev. Judah Champion	1	155
ANDRUS, ANDROS, [see also **ANDREWS**], Margaret, m. Stephen		
RUSSELL, Dec. 20, 1772, by Rev. Andrew Storrs, of Waterbury	1	74
Susan, m. Matthew B. **BATES**, Feb. 13, 1831, by Rev. Joseph E. Camp, of Northfield	2	292
William, of Hartford, m. Cornelia E. **SPENCER**, of Litchfield, Jan. 19, 1848, by Rev. Benjamin L. Swan	TM49	21
ARCHER, Lucy, m. Friend **GIBBS**, Mar. 5, 1783	1	221
ARUTS, Barzillai, m. Susan **BIDWELL**, Sept. [ ], 1825, by Rev. Joseph E. Camp, of Northfield	2	292
Margaret, m. Austin **LOOMIS**, Jan. 22, 1832, by Rev. L. P. Hickok	2	288
Mary H.*, of Litchfield, m. Frederic **BIDWELL**, of Naugatuck, May 5, 1851, by Benjamin L. Swan *("Mary H. **HARUTS** "?)	TM49	62
ATWATER, Abel, m. Elizabeth **PECK**, May 15, 1776, by Rev. Judah Champion	1	210-11
Almira, d. Abel & Elizabeth, b. Mar. 4, 1796	1	210-11
Bethiah, d. Abel & Elizabeth, b. July 11, 1785	1	210-11
Chauncey, s. Abel & Elizabeth, b. Dec. 14, 1788	1	210-11
Cornelius, s. Abel & Elizabeth, b. Sept. 21, 1777	1	210-11
Edward F., of New Haven, m. Frances W. **SANFORD**, of Litchfield, Oct. 20, 1846, by Rev. William Dixon	TM49	16
Elizabeth, d. Abel & Elizabeth, b. July 21, 1779	1	210-11
Mary, d. Abel & Elizabeth, b. Sept. 16, 1781	1	210-11
Sally, d. Abel & Elizabeth, b. Nov. 23, 1790	1	210-11
Thale Hein (?), d. Abel & Elizabeth, b. Feb. 10, 1793	1	210-11
ATWELL, Fanny, m. Julius **BEACH**, Jan. 10, 1811	2	29
ATWOOD, Belinda, of Litchfield, m. Henry **DANIELS**, of Farmington, Aug. 9, 1832, by Rev. A. B. Goldsmith, of Guilford	2	291
George N., of Bethlem, m. Elizabeth **SMITH**, of Litchfield, Dec. 8, 1847, by Rev. Philo R. Hurd, of Watertown	TM49	20
Mary, m. John **BIRD**, June 20, 1728, by Joseph Minor, J.P.	1	5
Minerva, of Watertown, m. James O. **MARSH**, of Litchfield, July 3, 1846, by Rev. William Dixon	TM49	15
AUSTIN, Mary A., of Litchfield, m. Joseph **GLAUSON**, of Ansonia, May 6, 1849, Rev. S. T. Seelye	TM49	41
Seth, had negro Charlotte, d. Sall, b. Oct. [ ], 1791, at Suffield	1	151
AUTEN, Frederic P., of Haslingen, N.J., m. Eliza **PERKINS**, of Litchfield, Nov. 1, 1837, by R. M. Chipman	2	314
AVERELL, Damaris, m. John **HALL**, Oct. 17, 1776, by Rev. George Beckwith	1	141
AVEREST, Hannah, m. William **TUTTLE**, Sept. 12, 1812, by Rev. Mr.		

	Vol.	Page

AVEREST, (cont.),
   Stone, of Cornwall   2   64
AVERY, Mary M., of Cornwall, m. Charles **CARTER,** of Warren, Dec. 17,
   1848, by John F. Norton   TM49   39
   Nathan, m. Lura **PHILLIPS,** Feb. 22, 1825, by Rev. Isaac Jones   2   86
   William Buel, s. Abel & Elizabeth, b. Apr. 22, 1810   2   3
AYRES, Mary Ensign, d. Benjamin & Mary, b. May 18, 1809   2   19
   Oliver, m. Mary **BARNES,** Dec. 17, 1827, by Daniel L. Carroll   2   276
   Sarah S., of Litchfield, m. Frederick J. **CRANE,** of Bethlem, Jan. 19,
   1832, by Rev. Mr. Taylor, of South Farms   2   289
BACHELOR, Harriet E., m. Albert **HOMER,** Feb. 23, 1843, by Birdsey
   Baldwin, J.P.   2   319
BACKMAN*, Mary, m. David **SMITH,** Jan. 20, 1780, by. Rev. Judah
   Champion *("**BATEMAN**" in Woodruff's "Residents of
   Litchfield")   2   1
BACON, Aurillia, m. Enos **STODDARD,** May 14, 1798, by [   ]   2   100
   Caleb, m. Caty **PECK,** Apr. 17, 1799, by Rev. Dan Huntington   2   4
   Caroline, d. Caleb & Caty, b. July 26, 1804; d. Mar. 22, 1805   2   4
   Caroline Rhoda, d. Caleb & Caty, b. Mar. 8, 1808   2   4
   Daniel Peck, s. Caleb & Caty, b. Jan. 2, 1806   2   4
   E. Thompson, representative Apr. 1840, Apr. 1841   2   1557
   Ebenezer, m. Martha **LEE,** June 28, 1770, by David Welch   1   126
   Henry, s. Caleb & Caty, b. Feb. 16, 1802   2   4
   Irene, d. Aaron & Ruth, b. Aug. 27, 1769   1   128
   Irene, m. Roswell **KILBORN,** [   ]   1   102
   Mary C., d. Caleb & Caty, b. Jan. 17, 1800   2   4
   Sabra, d. Ebenezer & Martha, b. Mar. 11, 1777   1   169
   Thomas, s. Ebenezer & Martha, b. Aug. 21, 1773   1   26
BAILEY, Elisha B., of Goshen, m. Hannah B. **FRISBIE,** of Milton, Oct. 3,
   1843, by Ralph Smith   2   340
BAKER, Conrad, m. Catharine **RING,** b. of Germany, Dec. 19, 1852, by
   Rev. John J. Brandegee   TM49   77
   Jacob, m. Mary **KILBORN,** Mar. 11, 1773, by Rev. Judah Champion   1   167
   Lewis, of LaFayette, N.Y., m. Mrs. Mary Ann **MORSE,** of Milton, Nov.
   23, 1841, by Ralph Smith   2   335
   Mary, m. Joseph **ALLEN,** Mar. 11, 1730, by Rev. Anthony Sladdor, of
   Woodbury   1   3
   Mary, w. Joseph Allen, & mother of Gen. Ethan Allen, was of Woodbury   1   0
   Sarah, m. Josiah **GRANT, Jr.,** Dec. 11, 1735, by Rev. Mr. Stoddard, of
   Woodbury   1   97
BALDWIN, BALDIN, Aaron, of Harwinton, m. Abigail **PLANT,** of
   Litchfield, Feb. 20, 1848, by Rev. Joseph Henson   TM49   23
   Abigail, d. David & Hannah, b. Feb. 8, 1740/1   1   129
   Abigail, m. Lawrence **WESSELLS,** Nov. 10, 1761, by Rev. Judah
   Champion   1   125
   Abigail, m. William **DUDLEY,** May 13, 1785, in Guilford, by Rev.
   Thomas Wells   2   25
   Abigail, d. William & Abigail, b. Dec. 7, 1786   2   38
   Abigail, w. William, d. Mar. [ ], 1787   2   38
   Abigail, m. Gen. Timothy **SKINNER,** May 17, 1801, by Rev. Judah
   Champion   1   122
   Abigail, d. Horace & Rachal, b. Dec. 10, 1808   1   212
   Abigail, m. Jesse **OSBORNE,** b. of Litchfield, July 1, 1827, by Rev.

	Vol.	Page
BALDWIN, BALDIN, (cont.),		
1842	2	127
Jane, d. [Isaac & Rachel], b. Aug. 19, 1832	2	412
Jane, of Milton, m. William M. **WEBSTER**, of Litchfield, May 17,		
1852, by N. C. Lewis, in Milton	TM49	74
John, m. Ann **COLVER**, June 14, 1727, by Rev. Timothy Collens	1	5
John, s. Abner & Anne, b. Jan. 22, 1763	1	126
John, s. Abner & Anne, d. June 3, 1764	1	126
John, s. Abner & Anne, b. Nov. 14, 1764	1	126
John, s. Abner & Achsa, b. Apr. 16, 1789	1	213
John, m. Mary **CHAPEL**, b. of Litchfield, Jan. 31, 1828, by Rev.		
Ebenezer Washburn	2	274
John H., of Goshen, m. Sally P. **BARGE**, of Litchfield, Oct. 14, 1827,		
by D. L. Carroll	2	272
Junius E., of Harwinton, m. Julia W. **CRAWFORD**, of Litchfield, Aug.		
20, 1854, by Rev. H. N. Weed	TM49	101
Lois, m. Isaac **McNEILE**, Jan. 24, 1771, by Rev. Judah Champion	1	24
Lucinda, d. [Isaac & Rachel], b. July 30, 1830	2	412
Lucinda, m. Charles B. **WEBSTER**, b. of Litchfield, Nov. 4, 1849, by		
Rev. William B. Hoyt	TM49	44
Lucinda E., m. Asahel H. **MOSS**, b. of Litchfield, Apr. 19, 1848, by		
Benjamin L. Swan	TM49	24
Lydia, w. Sam[ue]ll, d. Jan. 24, 1734/5, ae 44 y. 3 m.	1	44
Margarett, of Litchfield, m. Jesse **PECK**, of Farmington, Nov. 29, 1826,		
by Rev. Epaprus Goodman	2	267
Maria S., d. Almon & Matilda, b. Mar. 11, 1816	2	64
Martha, m. John **CLEMENS, Jr.**, Dec. 26, 1752	1	46
Mary, m. Alexander **THOMSON**, July 2, 1744, by Rev. Timothy		
Collens	1	27
Mary, d. Isaac & Ann, b. Jan. 20, 1761	1	128
Mary, m. Amos **BARNES**, Dec. 2, 1777	2	86
Mary A., of Litchfield, m. Austin **HINE, Jr.**, of Southbury, Nov. 5,		
1853, by Rev. H. N. Weed	TM49	92
Mary Ann, d. [Isaac & Rachel], b. July 2, 1834	2	412
Mary B., d. William & Mindwell, b. Mar. 11, 1791	2	38
Milo, m. Sophronia H. **CROSSMAN**, Apr. 16, 1849, by Rev. D. L.		
Parmelee	TM49	36
Nab[b]y, d. James & Nab[b]y, b. Aug. 9, 1790	1	248
Nancy, m. Isaac **MOSS, Jr.**, b. of Litchfield, Jan. 7, 1830, by Rev.		
Bradley Sillick	2	284
Nehemiah, of Goshen, m. Arma **GROSS**, of Litchfield, Nov. 26, 1829,		
by Rev. Birdsey Sillick	2	283
Noble D., of Litchfield, m. Ruanna **BOOTH**, of Washington, Oct. 14,		
1834, by Rev. Samuel Fuller	2	289
Noble Doolittle, of Litchfield, m. Ruana **BOOTH**, of Washington, Oct.		
14, 1834, by Rev. Samuel Fuller	TM49	37
Pamela, d. James & Nab[b]y, b. Apr. 17, 1793	1	248
Rachel, d. Nathaniell, b. Sept. 24, 1733	1	45
Rachel, d. Charles & Rachel, b. Sept. 28, 1794	2	56
Rachel, d. Horace & Rachel, b. Mar. 12, 1807	1	212
Rhoda, d. Charles & Rachel, b. July 14, 1793	2	56
Rhoda, m. Charles **DUDLEY**, Jan. 11, 1809, by Rev. Mr. Jordan	2	9
Samuel, of Hunter, N.Y., m. Mary Ann **WOODWORTH**, of Litchfield,		

	Vol.	Page
BARBOUR, BARBER, (cont.),		
John Lyman, s. Norman & Lois, b. Nov. 21, 1818	2	33
Lockwood, s. [Abiel], b. Feb. 21, 1831	2	293
Lois Clarissa, d. Norman & Lois, b. May 30, 1821	2	33
Lois Clarissa, m. Truman **STODDARD**, Sept. 9, 1843, by Rev. William		
Payne	TM49	27
Loyal A., m. Lucinda **BUEL**, June 26, 1833, by Rev. L. P. Hickok	2	288
Lucy, m. Isaac **OSBORN, Jr.**, May 15, 1802, by Rev. Truman Marsh	1	153
Lyman, of Harwinton, m. Amelia **BUELL**, of Litchfield, Aug. 22, 1838,		
by Rev. Jonathan Brace	2	318
Mary, m. Orrin **GILBERT**, Jan. 19, 1807, by Rev. Truman Marsh	2	46
Norman, m. Lois **OSBORN**, Mar. 12, 1805, by Rev. Judah Champion	2	33
Norman Ambrose, s. Norman & Lois, b. May 10, 1823	2	33
Olive, d. Norman & Lois, b. July 19, 1811	2	33
Rachel, d. Norman & Lois, b. Aug. 8, 1813	2	33
Rachel, m. Jerome B. **WOODRUFF**, June 5, 1833, by Rev. David G.		
Tomlinson, of Bradleyville	2	293
Sally Ann, d. [Abiel], b. Aug. 17, 1829	2	293
BARGE, Elijah, [twin with Elisha], s. Joseph & Dorothy, b. June 22, 1731	1	45
Elisha, [twin with Elijah], s. Joseph & Dorothy, b. June 22, 1731	1	45
Sally P., of Litchfield, m. John H. **BALDWIN**, of Goshen, Oct. 14,		
1827, by D. L. Carroll	2	272
BARKER, Jacob, of Buffalo, m. Catharine **MARSH**, of Litchfield, June 4,		
1826, by Rev. Truman Marsh	2	264
BARNARD, Abigail, d. Samuel & Wealthy, b. Oct. 12, 1794	2	62
Ann, of Litchfield, m. John **SANFORD**, of Hartford, Sept. 6, 1837, by		
Rev. Fosdic Harrison, of Bethlehem	2	317
Anna C., d. Samuel & Wealthy, b. May 27, 1806	2	62
Benton, s. Samuel & Marcy, b. June 4, 1786	2	62
Benton, m. Elizabeth **REA**, Jan. 24, 1811, by James Morris, J.P.	2	141
Betsey, d. George & Lois, b. Nov. 3, 1786	1	213
Chauncy, s. Samuel & Mary, b. May 4, 1785	2	62
Elizabeth, d. Samuel & Wealthy, b. Apr. 12, 1802	2	62
George, m. Lois **MANSER**, Jan. 15, 1784, by Rev. Dr. Bellamy	1	213
George, d. Aug. 19, 1787, ae 34 y.	1	212
Henry, s. Benton & Elizabeth, b. Sept. 24, 1819	2	141
Henry, s. Benton & Elizabeth, d. Feb. 14, 1821	2	141
Henry G., s. Samuel & Wealthy, b. Feb. 3, 1790	2	62
Levina, m. Ithamer **HUBBARD**, b. of Litchfield, Dec. 17, 1826, by Rev.		
Henry Robinson, of South Farms	2	267
Lucy G., d. Samuel & Wealthy, b. Apr. 7, 1804	2	62
Mary, m. Burr **GOODWIN**, Nov. 24, 1817, by Rev. Mr. Pettingill	2	69
Mary, w. Samuel, d. [ ]	2	62
Mary B., d. Samuel & Wealthy, b. Apr. 23, 1792	2	62
Mary B., d. Benton & Elizabeth, b. Nov. 17, 1816	2	141
Mary B., m. William **HILL**, July 13, 1836, by Rev. Stephen Hubbell	2	298
Narvina, d. Saumel & Wealthy, b. Dec. 26, 1799	2	62
Sally, d. George & Lois, b. Nov. 1, 1784	1	213
Sally, m. Luman **BEACH**, May 15, 1804, by Rev. Truman Marsh	2	23
Samuel, m. Abigail **GIBBS**, June 22, 1758, by Rev. Judah Champion	1	127
Samuel, m. Mary **BENTON**, Feb. 18, 1784, by Rev. [ ]	2	62
Samuel, Jr., m. Mary **BENTON**, Feb. 19, 1784, by Rev. Judah		
Champion	1	169

	Vol.	Page
BARNARD, (cont.),		
Samuel, m. Wealthy **STEEL**, Sept. 30, 1787	2	62
Samuel, s. Samuel & Wealthy, b. July 17, 1788	2	62
Wealthy, d. Samuel & Wealthy, b. Sept. 22, 1797	2	62
Wealthy S., d. Benton & Elizabeth, b. Jan. 26, 1821	2	141
Wealthy S., m. Alanson **STODDARD**, b. of Litchfield, Aug. 17, 1837, by Enos Stoddard, J.P.	2	313
Wealthy S., m. Alanson **STODDARD**, Aug. 17, 1837, by Enos Stoddard	2	327
William Brainard, s. Benton & Elizabeth, b. June 20, 1818	2	141
William Rea, s. Benton & Elizabeth, b. Sept. 21, 1814	2	141
William Rea, s. Benton & Elizabeth, d. Mar. 27, 1816	2	141
BARNES, BARNS, Abel, m. Abigail **STODDER**, Jan. 19, 1752, by Thomas Harrison, J.P.	1	128
Abel, s. Abel & Abigail, b. Sept. 5, 1754	1	128
Abel, s. Abel & Abigail, d. Sept. 30, 1757	1	4
Abel, m. Gift **GAY**, Aug. 9, 1758, by Rev. Joseph Bellamy	1	128
Abel, s. Abel & Gift, b. May 14, 1759	1	128
Abel, s. Abel & Gift, d. Dec. 4, 1772	1	4
Abigail, w. Abel, d. Oct. 3, 1757	1	4
Abigail, d. Abel & Gift, b. Feb. 8, 1766	1	128
Abigail, m. Moses **STODDOR, Jr.**, Apr. 23, 1766, by Jacob Woodruff	1	120
Abigail, w. Enos, d. June 8, 1768	1	128
Abigail, d. Timothy & Eunice, b. Aug. 29, 1775	1	44
Abigail, w. Norman, d. [ ]	2	87
Abijah, s. Moses & Hepzibah, b. Feb. 3, 1770	1	84
Ama, m. Dan **THROOP**, Apr. 25, 1771, by Rev. Judah Champion	1	121
Ambrose, s. Enos & Abigail, b. May 19, 1757	1	86
Amila, m. Joel **HOUGH**, July [ ], 1825, by Rev. J. E. Camp	2	265
Amos, m. Elizabeth **COLLING**, Mar. 9, 1758, by Rev. Judah Champion	1	126
Amos, s. Amos & Elizabeth, b. Mar. 8, 1762	1	126
Amos, m. Mary **BALDWIN**, Dec. 2, 1777	2	86
Amos, s. Amos & Mary, b. May 28, 1791	2	86
Amos, s. Norman & Abigail, b. July 16, 1809	2	87
Anna, d. Amos & Elizabeth, b. Feb. 16/17, 1769	1	126
Anna, m. Truman **GIBBS**, Feb. 17, 1773, by Rev. George Beckwith	1	140
Anna, m. John **UPSON**, Jan. 14, 1836, by Rev. Charles Chittenden	2	298
Anne, d. Daniel & Anne, b. Feb. 11, 1740	1	87
Anne, d. Enos & Lucy, b. Sept. 19, 1798	1	212
Asa, s. Enos & Abigail, b. May 25, 1768	1	128
Benjamin, s. Daniel & Ann, b. May 25, 1752	1	86
Betsey, d. Amos & Mary, b. Feb. 13, 1779	2	86
Betsey, m. Jonathan **GRISWOULD, Jr.**, May 25, 1801, by Rev. Judah Champion	2	142
Eber, s. Enos, Jr. & Lucy, b. Sept. 27, 1792	1	212
Eliza, d. Norman & Abigail, b. Aug. 31, 1804	2	87
Eliza Ann, d. Norman & Betsey, b. Feb. 8, 1816	2	87
Elizabeth, d. Amos & Elizabeth, b. Apr. 11, 1764; d. Apr. 29, 1764	1	126
Elizabeth, w. Amos, d. Jan. 27, 1777	2	86
Elizabeth, m. Morris **JOHNSON**, Apr. 1, 1792, by Rev. Judah Champion	1	59
Enos, s. Enos & Abigail, b. Sept. 17, 1755	1	85
Enos, s. Abel & Gift, b. Mar. 25, 1761	1	128
Enos, s. Abel & Gift, d. July 1, 1780	1	168

	Vol.	Page
BARNES, BARNS, (cont.),		
1735/6	1	11
Sarah, d. Enos & Abigail, b. Nov. 13, 1759	1	86
Sarah, d. Enos, b. Nov. 13, 1759	1	128
Sarah, d. Timothy & Eunice, b. Aug. 26, 1777	1	169
Sarah, m. James **WICKWIRE**, Aug. 25, 1779, by Rev. George Beckwith	1	165
Sarah Ann, m. John **STEVENS**, b. of Litchfield, Aug. 2, 1846, by Rev.		
Samuel Fuller	TM49	38
Timothy, s. Daniel & Ann, b. Oct. 7, 1745	1	129
Tracy L., m. Lavinia K. **MOORE**, Sept. 11, 1853, by Rev.H. N. Weed	TM49	91
William, s. Enos & Lucy, b. Nov. 11, 1801	1	212
Woodruff, s. Enos & Hannah, b. Dec. 9, 1782	1	213
Zacheas, s. Moses & Hepzibah, b. July 28, 1771	1	84
BARNEY, Charey, m. Alanson **SWAN**, Sept. [ ], 1815, by Ebenezer Tanner	2	129
Mary, m. Ammi **PLANT**, Dec. 7, 1820, by Rev. Isaac Jones	2	97
BARNUM, Julia A., m. David B. **HAWLEY**, Oct. 23, 1831, by Luther Mead	2	290
BARRINGTON, Mary, see Mary **BANINGTON**	TM49	93
BARTHOLOMEW, Anna, m. David **SMITH**, June 2, 1808, by Rev. Mr.		
Camp	2	66
Elizabeth, of Branford, m. Joseph **DARIN, Jr.**, Dec. 14, 1738, by Rev.		
Mr. Robens, of Branford	1	9
Sally, m. James **WOODRUFF**, Aug. 1, 1790, by Rev. Mr. Chase, of		
South Farms Soc.	1	207
Susannah, m. Daniel **HASKIN**, Mar. 23, 1780	1	181
Thankfull, m. Zopher **BASSETT**, Apr. 27, 1794, by Rev. Mr. Williams,		
of Harwinton	2	72
BASSETT, Caroline, d. Zopher & Thankfull, b. Nov. 17, 1802	2	72
Caroline, m. Julius **TODD**, Jan. 10, 1827, by Rev. Jospeh E. Camp, of		
Northfield	2	292
Clarissa, d. Zopher & Thankfull, b. Aug. [ ], 1800	2	72
Clarissa, d. Nathan & Mehetabel, b. Nov. 26, 1801	1	251
Clarrissa, d. Nathan & Mehitabel, b. Nov. 26, 1801	2	8
Clarissa, m. Merret **CLARK**, Nov. 13, 1826, by Rev. Joseph E. Camp,		
of Northfield	2	292
Henry, s. Nathan & Mehitabel, b. June 26, 1809	2	8
Hetty, d. Nathan & Mehitabel, b. Feb. 20, 1796	1	251
Hetty, d. Nathan & Mehitabel, b. Feb. 20, 1796	2	8
Ira, s. Nathan & Mehetabel, b. Apr. 6, 1798	1	251
Ira, s. Nathan & Mehitabel, b. Apr. 6, 1798	2	8
Ira, s. Nathan & Mehetabel, d. Oct. 25, 1799, ae 1 y. 6 m. 20 d.	1	250
Ira, s. Nathan & Mehitabel, d. Oct. 25, 1799	2	8
Ira, s. Nathan & Mehitabel, b. Nov. 28, 1799	1	251
Ira, s. Nathan & Mehitabel, b. Nov. 28, 1700	2	8
Lathrop, s. Zopher & Thankfull, b. May 31, 1795	2	72
Laura, d. Nathan & Mehetabel, b. Aug. 7, 1794	1	251
Laura, d. Nathan & Mehitabel, b. Aug. 27, 1794	2	72
Mary E., m. Chauncey W. **KELLOGG**, b. of Northfield, Oct. 4, 1846,		
by Rev. Jonathan Coe, 2nd, of Northfield	TM49	16
Nathan, m. Mehetabel **BUEL**, Oct. 29, 1793, by Rev. Judah Champion	1	251
Nathan, m. Mehitabel **BUEL**, Oct. 29, 1793, by Rev. Judah Champion	2	8
Ozias, s. Nathan & Mehetabel, b. Mar. 7, 1807	2	8
Pashiah * Ashlee, s. Zopher & Thankfull, b. Aug. 30, 1806		
*("Patrick" in Woodruff's book)	2	72

	Vol.	Page
BASSETT, (cont.),		
Phebe C., d. Zopher & Thankfull, b. Mar. 29, 1798	2	72
Phebe C., d. Zopher & Thankfull, d. Mar. 9, 1822	2	72
Sarah J., of Northfield, m. Albert F. **KELLOGG**, of Adams, Wis., Aug.		
21, 1850, at Northfield, by Rev. Rowel H. Tuttle	TM49	55
Wine*, s. Nathan & Mehitabel, b. July 25, 1805 *("William" in		
Woodruff's book)	2	8
Zopher, m. Thankfull **BARTHOLOMEW**, Apr. 27, 1794, by Rev. Mr.		
Williams, of Harwinton	2	72
Zopher, d. June 11, 1825	2	72
BATCHELOR, Beulah, m. Titus **HUMASTON**, Dec. 20, 1775, by Rev.		
James Nichols, of Farmington	1	141
BATEMAN*, Mary, m. David **SMITH**, Jan. 20, 1780, by Rev. Judah		
Champion *(Arnold Copy has "**BACKMAN**")	2	1
BATES, Ephraim, m. Sarah **GRISWOLD**, May 6, 1773, by Rev. Richard		
Moseley	1	43
Erastus, m. Lucinda H. **HUBBARD**, Sept. 6, 1843, by Rev. David L.		
Marks	2	413
Lorin, m. Almira **HALL**, Aug. 13, 1816, by Rev. Mr. Teal	2	81
Lorin, m. Polly **FANTON**, Feb. 6, 1831, by Rev. Joseph E. Camp, of		
Northfield	2	292
Matthew B., m. Susan **ANDROS**, Feb. 13, 1831, by Rev. Joseph E.		
Camp, of Northfield	2	292
Nathaniel C., of Kent, m. wid. Hannah **KILBORN**, Dec. 7, 1825, by		
Rev. Truman Marsh	2	258
Octavia K., of Litchfield, m. J. Edward **SMITH**, M.D., of Kent, May 2,		
1853, by Rev. Benjamin L. Swan	TM49	93
Octavia Kenyon, d. Nathaniel C. & Hannah, b. Apr. 3, 1829, in		
Salisbury	2	258
William, s. Lorin & Almira, b. May 21, 1817	2	81
Zachariah, d. Mar. 31, 1773	1	4
BEACH, BEECH, Abby C., adopted d. Milo & Rhoda P., b. Sept. 12, 1824,		
in Goshen	2	130
Abby O.*, m. Lorenzo D. **WHITMORE**, b. of Litchfield, Mar. 6, 1843,		
by Rev. Jason Wells *("Abby C.'"?)	2	339
Abigail, d. Miles & Abigail, b. June 11, 1772	1	126
Abigail, d. Miles & Abigail, d. June 12, 1772	1	4
Abigail, w. Capt. Miles, d. Nov. 28, 1781	1	166
Abisher, m. Esther **CLINTON**, Sept. 20, 1750, by Rev. Elisha Kent	1	127
Abner, s. Zopher & Elizabeth, b. Oct. 13, 1748	1	129
Abner, m. Beulah **ABERNATHY**, Apr. 23, 1770, by Rev. Judah		
Champion	1	167
Abner, s. Abner & Beulah, b. Feb. 14, 1788	1	213
Albertine Cecelia, d. Almon J. & Antoinette, b. Dec. 19, 1842	TM49	5
Algaman G., s. Heman, Jr. & Eliza, b. Oct. 23, 1837	2	321
Almeda, d. Enos & Susanna, b. Aug. 14, 1798	2	33
Almada, m. William **TYLER**, May 25, 1824, by Rev. Lyman Beecher	2	136
Almira, d. Oringe & Lydia, b. Feb. 7, 1794	1	212
Almira, d. Anson & Pamela, b. Feb. 22, 1816	2	19
Almond, s. Laban, Jr. & Naomi, b. [ ], 1788; d. June 27, 1805	2	36
Almon J., m. Antoinette **BIRGE**, Oct. 15, 1840, by Rev. Mr. Eastman	TM49	5
Almond J., see Norman **BEACH**	2	331
Almoran, s. Laban, Jr. & Nabon*, b. Nov. 8, 1810 *(Probably		

	Vol.	Page
BEACH, BEECH, (cont.),		
"Naomi")	2	36
Alsida, d. Senier & Rachel, b. Apr. 23, 1794	1	249
Alsida, d. Senior & Rachel, d. Oct. 12, 1795	1	248
Alvin, s. Enos & Susannah, b. July 20, 1807	2	33
Alvin, m. Ursula **BEACH**, Oct. 27, 1831, by Rev. L. P. Hickok	2	288
Amanda, d. Senier & Rachel, b. May 15, 1792	1	249
Amzi, m. Mary **BLAKE**, Nov. 1, 1843, by Rev. D. L. Marks	TM49	1
Andrew Catlin, s. Seymour [& Lucina], b. June 8, 1833	2	116
Ann, d. Senier & Rachel, b. Nov. 30, 1781	1	249
Ann Mariah, d. Seymour [& Lucina], b. June 28, 1828	2	116
Ann Maria, of Litchfield, m. Joseph Henry **BENTON**, of Goshen, Nov. 25, 1847, by Rev. Samuel Fuller	TM49	8
Anna, m. Seth **LANDON**, Dec. 26, 1771, by Rev. Judah Champion	2	25
Anna, d. Enos & Susanna, b. June 20, 1797	2	33
Anna, m. Harvey **DICKINSON**, Aug. 1, 1824, by Rev. Lockwood Dickinson	2	274
Anne, d. Zopher & Elizabeth, b. Apr. 23, 1754	1	129
Anson, s. Laban & Sarah, b. Feb. 11, 1777	1	169
Anson, m. Pamela **ABERNETHY**, Sept. 20, 1798	2	19
Anson B., s. Anson & Pamela, b. May 5, 1804	2	19
Asahel, m. Almeda **OSBORN**, July 4, 1822, by Rev. Lyman Beecher	2	113
Ashbel, s. Samuel, Jr. & Rachal, b. Apr. 4, 1755	1	85
Barnias, m. Chloe **PALMER**, of Branford, May last day, 1759, by Rev. Judah Champion	1	43
Barnier*, s. Senier & Rachel, b. Mar. 2, 1784 *("Bernice" in Woodruff's)	1	249
Benoni, s. Zopher & Elizabeth, b. Aug. 24, 1750	1	129
Betsey, d. Luman & Sally, b. June 7, 1812	2	23
Beulah, d. Enos & Susanna, b. Jan. 6, 1804	2	33
Bula, of Litchfield, m. David **WOOD**, of Warren, June 12, 1822, by Rev. Isaac Jones	2	112
Candice, d. Senier & Rachel, b. Mar. 30, 1786	1	249
Caroline, d. Enos & Susanna, b. June 6, 1806	2	33
Cephas, s. Zopher & Elizabeth, b. June 30, 1752	1	129
Charles, s. Samuel & Rachel, b. May 20, 1768	1	85
Chauncey, s. Luman & Sally, b. Nov. 29, 1810	2	23
Clarissa, d. Lovis & Orilia, b. Apr. 15, 1804	1	166
Clarissa, d. Heman & Clarissa, b. June 25, 1810	2	44
Clarissa, w. Heman, d. Sept. 20, 1818	2	44
Cynthia, d. Senier & Rachel, b. Apr. 26, 1802	1	249
Cynthia, d. Senior & Rachel, d. Oct. 20, 1802	1	248
Daniel, s. Zopher & Elizabeth, b. Dec. 9, 1755	1	85
Daniel S., s. Seymour & Lucina, b. Feb. 3, 1824	2	116
David, m. Lucia **MUCLESTONE***, Jan. 24, 1765, by Rev. Judah Champion *("MUDESTONE" in Woodruff's)	1	126
David, s. Oringe & Lidia, b. Feb. 9, 1796	1	212
David, s. Luman & Sally, b. Mar. 6, 1808	2	23
Dennis, s. Senier & Rachel, b. Jan. 28, 1788	1	249
Dinah, m. Charles **GRANT**, Jan. 25, 1776, by Epaphras Sheldon, J.P.	1	179
Electa, d. [Luman & Sally], b. Aug. 30, 1825	2	23
Electa, m. Leonard Hartwell **NOTT**, Apr. 13, 1848, by Rev. Samuel Fuller	TM49	38

	Vol.	Page
BEACH, BEECH, (cont.),		
Elias, s. Laban, Jr. & Naomi, b. [ ], 1791; d. Nov. 14, 1793	2	36
Elias, s. Laban, Jr. & Naomi, b. Sept. 7, 1793	2	36
Elihu, s. Zopher & Elizabeth, b. Mar. 17, 1758	1	85
Elizabeth, d. Noah & Elizabeth, b. Aug. 7, 1785	2	29
Elizabeth, w. Noah, d. Apr. 8, 1808	2	29
Elmina, m. Samuel G. BEACH, Jan. 17, 1836, by Rev. C. Chittenden	2	298
Emeline, d. Luman & Sally, b. Mar. 5, 1814	2	23
Enos, s. Abner & Beulah, b. Apr. 23, 1771	1	167
Enos, m. Susanna GREEN, Jan. 27, 1796, by Rev. Mr. Farren	2	33
Erastus, s. Noah & Elizabeth, b. Feb. 9, 1795	2	29
Esther, m. Benjamin BIRG, Aug. 23, 1750, by Thomas Harrison, J.P.	1	129
Esther, m. Ezra WEEKS, Dec. 12, 1812, by Rev. Mr. Gillet, of		
Torrington	2	14
Ezekiel, s. Samuel, Jr. & Rachel, b. Mar. 13, 1751	1	129
Fanny Maria, d. James & Fanny, b. Oct. 26, 1814	2	41
Frederick, s. Salmon, Jr. & Lydia, b.Sept. 28, 1797	2	47
Frederick, s. Laban, Jr. & Naomi, b. [ ], 1803; d. Jan. 23, 1805	2	36
Frederick, 2nd, s. Laban, Jr. & Naomi, b. Apr. 7, 1806	2	36
Frederick, m. Amelia STEVENS, Nov. 7, 1828, by Rev. I. Jones	2	278
George B., s. Lyman & Sally, b. Feb. 15, 1806	2	23
George Spencer, m. Louisa BEACH, b. of Litchfield, Sept. 26, 1827,		
by Rev. Isaac Jones	2	272
George W., of Litchfield, m. Sarah M. MINOR, of Litchfield, Nov. 25,		
1852, by Rev. Lewis Jessup	TM49	77
Hannah, m. Abiel SMITH, Jr., Apr. 2, 1758, by Rev. Solomon Palmer	1	76
Hannah, m. Edgar S. VAN WINKLE, of New York, Nov. 11, 1835, by		
Rev. L. P. Hickok	2	296
Hannah M., m. Henry JUDD, Nov. 10, 1850, in Torrington	2	313
Harriet, d. Enos & Susanna, b. Mar. 21, 1801	2	33
Harriet, of Litchfield, m. Martin PRATT, of Cornwall, Dec. 25, 1820,		
by Joseph Harvey	2	98
Heman, s. Abner & Bealah, b. Jan. 23, 1775	1	169
Heman, m. Clarissa KILBORN, Oct. 27, 1794, by Rev. Judah		
Champion	2	44
Heman, s. Heman & Clarissa, b. June 23, 1813	2	44
Heman, m. Phebe LANDON, Feb. 14, 1819, by Seth Landon, J.P.	2	44
Heman, m. Minerva D. GOSLEE, b. of Litchfield, Apr. 2, 1851, by		
Rev. H. L. Vaill	TM49	61
Henry Coleman, s. Jesse & Sally, b. Aug. 21, 1804	1	250
Henry Harrison, s. Noah & Sally, b. May 24, 1809	2	29
Herman Jr., m. Eliza THOMAS, b. of Litchfield, Jan. 16, 1837, by Rev.		
E. Washburn	2	297
Harvey, s. Oringe & Lydia, b. Oct. 11, 1791	1	212
Hiram G., m. Jennet CURTISS, b. of Litchfield, May 11, 1840, by Rev.		
Harvey D. Kitchel	2	327
Horatio, s. Senier & Rachel, b. Mar. 30, 1799	1	249
Irene, d. [Luman & Sally], b. Feb. 26, 1816	2	23
Irene, of Milton, m. Charles D. NOTT, of Hartford, Nov. 28, 1844, by		
Rev. Samuel Tomkins Carpenter, of Milton	TM49	7
James, m. Fanny MERRELS, Sept. [ ], 1810, by Rev. Truman Marsh	2	41
Jesse, s. David & Lucia, b. July 14, 1769	1	128
Jesse, m. Sally COLEMAN, May 17, 1803, by Rev. John Marsh, of		

	Vol.	Page
BEACH, BEECH, (cont.),		
Weathersfield	1	250
John, s. Abner & Beulah, b. Apr. 17, 1779	1	169
John Henry, s. Seymour & Lucina, b. Feb. 14, 1825	2	116
Julius, m. Fanny **ATWELL**, Jan. 10, 1811	2	29
Junor*, s. Samuel & Hannah, b. July 4, 1748 *("Junia" in Woodruff's)	1	129
Laban, s. Samuel & Hannah, b. Sept. 2, 1745	1	44
Laben, m. Sarah **KILBORN**, Feb. 25, 1765, by Timothy Collens	1	126
Laban, s. Laban & Sarah, b. Aug. 25, 1766	1	127
Laban, Jr., m. Naomi **COOK**, [ ], 1787, by Rev. David Welsh	2	36
Laban, s. Laban, Jr. & Naomi, b. Mar. 25, 1801	2	36
Labon, Jr., m. Tryphena **SPENCER**, June 6, 1815, by Morris Woodruff	2	36
Laban, Jr., m. Ann **WEBSTER**, Mar. 9, 1823, by Rev. Isaac Jones	2	118
Lois, d. Samuell, Jr. & Rachel, b. Nov. 6, 1749	1	129
Loisa, d. Noah & Elizabeth, b. June 5, 1805	2	29
Loisa, twin with Lorenzo, d. Julius & Fanny, b. Jan. 6, 1812	2	29
Lorenzo, twin with Loisa, d. Julius & Fanny, b. Jan. 6, 1812	2	29
Louisa, m. George Spencer **BEACH**, b. of Litchfield, Sept. 26, 1827, by Rev. Isaac Jones	2	272
Lovell, s. Senier & Rachel, b. July 26, 1796	1	249
Lovel, m. Harriet Arabella **PRESCOT**, Nov. 5, 1822, by Rev Isaac Jones	2	115
Lovewell, s. Barnias & Chloe, b. May 16, 1765	1	43
Lovis, m. Orilia **KILBORN**, Jan. 27, 1799, by Moses Seymour, J.P.	1	166
Lucinda, d. David & Lucy, b. Apr. 18, 1772	1	213
Lucinda, d. Enos & Susanna, b. July 21, 1802	2	33
Lucinda, m. Ira **TAYLOR**, Dec. [ ], 1823, by Rev. Isaac Jones	2	130
Lucius, s. James & Fanny, b. Sept. 4, 1811	2	41
Lucretia, d. Laban & Sarah, b. May 27, 1774	1	169
Lucretia, m. Ebenezer **CLARK**, Sept. 25, 1802	2	74
Lucy Eliza, d. Seymour [& Lucina], b. Apr. 21, 1836	2	116
Luman, s. Noah & Elizabeth, b. Sept. 9, 1783	2	29
Luman, m. Sally **BARNARD**, May 15, 1804, by Rev. Truman Marsh	2	23
Luna, d. Senier & Rachel, b. Sept. 21, 1804	1	249
Lidia, d. Laban & Sarah, b. June 10, 1771	1	167
Lydia, d. Laban, Jr. & Naomi, b. Apr. 18, 1797	2	36
Lydia, w. Salmon, Jr., d. Oct. [ ], 1808	2	47
Lyman, s. Enos & Susanna, b. Apr. 2, 1796	2	33
Malinda, d. Enos & Susanna, b. Oct. 20, 1799	2	33
Maria, d. Laban, Jr., & Naomi, b. [ ], 1809; d. Sept. 20, 1809	2	36
Mary, d. Enos & Susanna, b. Aug. 26, 1811	2	33
Mary, m. Alonzo **MARVIN**, of Cortright, N.Y., Feb. 8, 1835, by Rev. L. P. Hickok	2	296
Mary A., m. W[illia]m A. **STEPHENS**, Feb. 14, 1844, by Rev. D. L. Marks	TM49	4
Mary Olive, d. Jesse & Sally, b. Sept. 24, 1806	1	250
Melinda, of Litchfield, m. Hiram **TAYLOR**, of Salisbury, June 12, 1831, by Rev. L. P. Hickok	2	287
Mercy, d. Abisher & Esther, b. Aug. 30, 1751	1	127
Mercy, d. Heman & Clarissa, b. June 8, 1801	2	44
Miles, s. Miles & Abigail, b. Aug. 28, 1773	1	126
Miles, s. Miles & Abigail, d. Sept. 4, 1773	1	4
Miles, s. Miles & Abigail, b. Oct. 1, 1774; d. next day	1	167

	Vol.	Page
BEACH, BEECH, (cont.),		
Thomas, s. Samuel, & Jr. & Rachal, b. Mar. 4, 1753	1	85
Ursula, d. Anson & Pamela, b. May 12, 1813	2	19
Ursula, m. Alvin **BEACH**, Oct. 27, 1821, by Rev. L. P. Hickok	2	288
Walter, s. [Luman & Sally], b. Mar. 10, 1823	2	23
Zopher, m. Elizabeth **WOODDAMS***, Dec. 10, 1741, by John Beech,		
J.P. *("**WADHAMS**")	1	129
Zopher, s. Zopher & Elizabeth, b. Feb. 1, 1761	1	128
Zopher, d. May 24, 1779	1	168
Zopher, s. Noah & Elizabeth, b. Nov. 16, 1788	2	29
Zopher, s. [Luman & Sally], b. Jan. 22, 1821	2	23
BEARD, James B., m. Virginia E. **WHEELER**, b. of Litchfield, Oct. 12,		
1851, by N. C. Lewis	TM49	65
BEARDSLEE, Eliza Ann, m. Allen **BUEL**, Jan. 10, 1841, in Goshen	2	338
Milton, m. Susan **CHURCHILL**, Apr. 29, 1829, by Rev. Joseph E.		
Camp, of Northfield	2	292
BECKWITH, Garwood Hawley, m. Delia Maria **RICHARDS**, Jan. 29,		
1826, by Rev. Daniel Coe, of Winchester	2	260
Josiah G., representative Apr. 1852, Apr. 1853, Apr. 1856	2	1558
Sally, m. Eliada **PECK**, Oct. 28, 1798	2	14
Stephen, of Lyme, m. Abby J. **MORSE**, of Litchfield, Nov. 7, 1853, by		
Rev. H. N. Weed	TM49	92
BEEBE, BEEBEE, BEBE, Asael, s. James & Abigail, b. Dec. 18, 1731	1	45
Azuba, d. John & Marth[a], b. Jan. 17, 1736/7	1	87
B[ ], Col., representative Oct. 1781, May1782, May 1783, Oct. 1792,		
Oct. 1793, Oct. 1795	2	1550-2
Bethiah, m. Cornelius **PECK**, Feb. 5, 1748/9, by Rev. Timothy Collens	1	30
Bezaleel, m. Elizabeth **MARSH**, July 11, 1764, by Rev. Judah		
Champion	1	169
Clarissa, d. William & Clarissa, b. Jan. [ ], 1820	2	85
David, s. John & Martha, b. Nov. 29, 1732	1	45
Ebenezer, m. Rebecka **WEBSTER**, Feb. 28, 1735/6, by Rev. Timothy		
Collens	1	87
Ebenezer & Rebecka, had child b. July 8, [1736]; d. July 21, 1736	1	87
Ebenezer, s. Ebenezer & Bethiah, b.Sept. 4, 1743	1	44
Ebenezer, s. Bezaleel & Elizabeth, b. Oct. 27, 1774	1	169
Electa, m. Horace **MARSH**, Sept. 28, 1801, by Rev. Amos Chase	2	133
Eliza, d. William & Clarissa, b. May 9, 1808	2	85
Eliza, m. Dr. John W. **RUSSELL**, June 2, 1828, by Daniel L. Carroll	2	276
Elizabeth, d. John & Martha, b. July 23, 1731	1	45
Elizabeth, d. Bezaleel & Elizabeth, b. Sept. 21, 1768	1	169
Eunice, m. Asher **COLVER**, Sept. 18, 1755	1	89
Ferdinand, m. Amelia A. **MARSH**, Oct. 4, 1841, by Rev. David L.		
Parmelee	2	327
Harriet Maria, d. William & Clarissa, b. Nov. 11, 1814	2	85
James, m. Abigail **COLVER**, June 12, 1727	1	5
Jemyma, d. James & Abigail, b. Nov. 15, 1735	1	87
John, m. Martha **COLVER**, Nov. 24, 1730, by Rev. Timothy Collens	1	45
John, s. John & Martha, b. Apr. 6, 1738	1	87
Laura E., m. Sherman C. **KEELER**, Apr. 9, 1832, by Rev. L. P. Hickok	2	288
Luce, d. James & Abigail, b. Oct. 20, 1737	1	87
Olive, d. William & Clarissa, b. Dec. 14, 1816	2	85
Olive G., m. Sheldon W. **PECK**, Aug. 30, 1841, by Jonathan Brace	2	334

	Vol.	Page
BEEBE, BEEBEE, BEBE, (cont.),		
Phillip S., s. William & Clarissa, b. Mar. 13, 1812	2	85
Philip S., m. Catharine E. **HALL,** Oct. 10, 1838, by Rev. Jonathan		
Brace	2	318
Philip S. representative Apr. 1855	2	1558
Rachal, d. John & Martha, b. July 16, 1734	1	45
Rebecka, w. Ebenezer, d. July 15, 1736	1	86
Rebecca, d. Bezaleel & Elizabeth, b. Aug. 18, 1772	1	169
Rebecca, m. Solomon **STONE,** Jan. 20, 1794, by Rev. Mr. Faren	2	92
Rebecca, d. William & Clarissa, b. June 4, 1810	2	85
Rebecca R., m. Alexander R. **NEWCOMB,** Apr. 6, 1835, by Rev. L. P.		
Hickok	2	296
Sarah, d. Bezaleel & Elizabeth, b. May 10, 1765	1	169
Solomon, s. James & Abigail, b. Apr. 7, 1730	1	45
William, s. John & Elizabeth, b. Dec. 7, 1728	1	5
William, m. Clarissa **SANFORD,** Jan. 17, 1807	2	85
William, representative May & Oct. 1815, May & Oct. 1816, May 1827,		
May 1828, May 1833	2	1554-6
BEECHER, BEACHER, Anson, m. Nancy **BENTON,** b. of Litchfield, Dec.		
5, 1826, by Rev. Henry Robinson, of South Farms	2	267
Fanny, b. Feb. 23, 1782; m. Stephen **DUNING,** July 18, 1802; d. Apr.		
26, 1803	TM49	100
Hannah, of Woodbridge, m. Major **LOUNSBURY,** Sept. 15, 1824, by		
Rev. Isaac Jones	2	113
Nancy, m. Earl **PECK,** Mar. [ ], 1825, by Rev. J. E. Camp	2	265
Philo Mela, m. Orange **HOPKINS,** Jan. 9, 1817, by Rev. Mr.		
Huntington	2	81
Sarah Ann, m. Horace **GREGORY,** Mar. 1, 1821, by Rev. Mr. Terry,		
of Sharon	2	119
BEECHLEY, Julia Maria, of Litchfield, m. George **BOSWORTH,** of Troy,		
Jan. 9, 1839, by Rev. Jonathan Brace	2	318
BEEMAN, Frederick D., m. Maria Hale **BRISBANE,** b. of Litchfield, July		
15, 1851, by Rev. Benjamin W. Stone	TM49	63
BEERS, Ebenezer O., Rev. of the New York Annual Conference, m. Millesent		
Parthenia **SKELTON,** of Watertown, Dec. 27, 1842, by Jason		
Wells	2	337
George Webster, s. Seth P. & Belinda, b. Feb. 18, 1817	2	31
Henry Augustin, s. Seth P. & Belinda, b. Mar. 24, 1823	2	31
Horatio Preston, s. Seth P. & Belinda, b. Mar 24, 1811	2	31
Horatio Preston, s. Seth P. & Belinda, d. Dec. 12, 1824, at Derby,		
ae 13 y. 8 m. 16 d.	2	31
Julia Maria, d. Seth P. & Belinda, b. July 20, 1819	2	31
Seth P., m. Belinda **WEBSTER,** Sept. 12, 1807, by Rev. Truman Marsh	2	31
Seth P., representative May 1820, May 1821, May 1822, May 1823	2	1555
BELDEN, Charles Ogilvie, of Milwaukie, Wis., m. Harriet Buel **WEBSTER,**		
of Brooklyn, N.Y., July 13, 1852, by Rev. John Bandegee	TM49	75
Vincent, of Weathersfield, m. Almira **BUEL,** of Litchfield, Feb. 27,		
1843, by Jonathan Brace	2	337
William, of Milton, m. Esther **BOSTWICK,** of Litchfield, Oct. 13,		
1834, by Rev. Samuel Fuller	TM49	37
William, of Wilton, m. Esther **BOSTWICK,** of Litchfield, Oct. 13,		
1834, by Rev. Samuel Fuller	2	289
BELLAMY, David, m. Rhoda **KILBORN,** Dec. 10, 1821, by Morris		

	Vol.	Page

BELLAMY, (cont.),
Woodruff, J.P. — 2 105
BENEDICT, Andrew, m. Lucy DIBBLE, Nov. 26, 1812, by Rev. Mr.
Crocker, of Reading — 2 253
Andrew Dibble, s. Andrew & Lucy, b. Apr. 28, 1818 — 2 253
Catharine Malissa, d. Eli & Marietta, b. Mar. 25, 1824 — 2 261
Eli, m. Marietta STODDARD, Nov. 29, 1818 — 2 261
Emily, d. Andrew & Lucy, b. Oct. 6, 1814, at Danbury — 2 253
Ira, of Danbury, m. Hannah FARNUM, Mar. 8, 1826, by Rev. Henry
Robinson — 2 261
Levi Stoddard, s. Eli & Marietta, b. July 27, 1822 — 2 261
Matilda Janet, d. Eli & Marietta, b. Dec. 12, 1820 — 2 261
Samuel, s. Andrew & Lucy, b. Sept. 16, 1824 — 2 253
William Gipson, s. Eli & Marietta, b. Dec. 6, 1825 — 2 261
BENHAM, Isaac, m. Jeannette HITCHCOCK, b. of Burlington, Dec. 30,
1829, by L. P. Hickok — 2 283
Martha E., of Watertown, m. Timothy HART, of Litchfield, June 18,
1848, by J. D. Berry — TM49 25
BENNETT, BENNET, Avis, m. Daniel LANDON, May 27, 1821, by Rev.
Isaac Jones — 2 108
Charles G., m. Polly McNEILE, Sept. 21, 1806, by Rev. Truman Marsh — 2 30
Charles G., d. Oct. 2, 1841 — 2 30
Cornelia, d. Charles G. & Polly, b. Apr. 21, 1809 — 2 30
Cornelia J., m. Leonard D. HOSFORD, Oct. 30, 1851, by Rev. David L.
Parmelee — TM49 65
Cornelia M., m. Algenon S. LEWIS, b. of Litchfield, Nov. 10, 1829, by
Isaac Jones — TM49 40
Cornelia M., m. Algernon Sidney LEWIS, Nov. 10, 1829, by Rev. I.
Jones — 2 282
George, s. Charles G. & Polly, b. July 12, 1811 — 2 30
Helen Louisa, d. Charles G. [& Polly], b. Apr. 28, 1825 — 2 30
Mary, d. Charles G. & Polly, b. Oct. 19, 1813 — 2 30
Mary, m. James H. FOSTER, Sept. 17, 1839, by Rev. Jonathan Brace — 2 318
Patty, m. Levi STODDARD, Apr. 27, 1794 — 2 53
BENTON, Abigail, d. Nathaniell & Abigail, b. July 30, 1759 — 1 127
Abraham, s. Nathaniell & Abigail, b. Feb. 19, 1763 — 1 127
Abraham, m. Desire MEADE, Mar. 18, 1790, by John Whittlesey, J.P. — 1 249
Ama, d. Ebenezer & Ama, b. May 4, 1780 — 1 169
Amos, s. Ebenezer & Ama, b. June 13, 1771 — 1 167
Amos, s. Daniel & Margary, b. Mar. 19, 1797 — 1 249
Amos, m. Rachel CATLIN, May 2, 1799, by Moses Seymour, J.P. — 2 122
Amos, of Kingston, O., m. Sarah BENTON, of Litchfield, Nov. 13,
1837, by Joshua Emory, Jr. — 2 314
Amos, m. Sarah FARNUM, Dec. 25, 1843, by Rev. David L. Parmelee — TM49 2
Anna, m. Daniel LAMSON, of Litchfield, June 1, 1833, by Morris
Woodruff, J.P. — 2 293
Anne, d. Nathan & Abigail, b. Mar. [ ], 1779 — 1 166
Bela, s. Nathaniel & Abigail, b. Oct. 24, 1756 — 1 127
Cynthia, d. Ebenezer & Ama, b. Nov. 30, 1783 — 1 169
Daniel, m. Margary FRISBIE, Jan. 28, 1790, by Rev. Judah Champion — 1 249
Daniel L., m. Sally M. STARR, b. of Litchfield, Nov. 30, 1829, by
Morris Woodruff, J.P. — 2 283
Daniel Lamson, s. Ebenezer, Jr. & Lois, b. Jan. 14, 1805 — 2 78

	Vol.	Page
BENTON, (cont.),		
David, s. Nathaniell & Abigail, b. Sept. 11, 1764	1	127
David, s. Ebenezer & Anna, b. Sept. 4, 1768	1	167
David, s. Ebenezer, Jr. & Lois, b. Sept. 20, 1800	2	78
David, m. Sabra **KELLOGG**, Apr. 16, 1826, by Rev. Henry Robinson	2	262
Ebenezer, m. Ama **HOSFORD**, Mar. 19, 1761, by Jacob Woodruff, J.P.	1	127
Ebenezer, s. Ebenezer & Ama, b. Dec. 5, 1766	1	127
Ebenezer, representative May 1767	2	1551
Ebenezer, Jr., m. Lois **FARNAM**, Mar. 31, 1790, by Rev. Amos Chase	2	78
Elias, s. Daniel & Margary, b. Aug. 9, 1794	1	249
Erastus, s. Ebenezer, Jr. & Lois, b. Dec. 20, 1795	2	78
Erastus, m. Anna **REA**, Apr. 22, 1819, by Rev. Amos Pettingill	2	146
Esther, d. Nathaniell & Abigail, b. Feb. 9, 1758	1	127
Esther, m. Benjamin **BISSELL**, Feb. 21, 1779, by Rev. Judah Champion	1	248
Eunice, d. Nathaniel & Abigail, b. Mar. 14, 1768	1	26
Eunice, d. Nathaniel, b. Mar. 14, 1768	1	84
George B., m. Harriet B. **FARNUM**, b. of Litchfield, Sept. 8, 1829, by		
Morris Woodruff, J.P.	2	281
George Baldwin, s. Amos & Rachel, b. July 6, 1805	2	122
Horatio, s. Amos & Rachel, b. Aug. 24, 1811	2	122
Horatio, m. Juliett **WEED**, Oct. 3, 1832, by Rev. Mr. Taylor, of South		
Farms	2	289
Isaac, s. Nathaniel & Abigail, b. Mar. 28, 1772	1	26
Isaac, s. Nathan & Abigail, b. Mar. 28, 1772	1	166
Jane, of Bainbridge, N.Y., m. Sabra **MONGER**, of Litchfield, Mar. 24,		
1849, by Rev. Isaac Jones	TM49	42
Joel, s. Ebenezer, Jr. & Lois, b. Jan. 22, 1794	2	78
John, s. Nathan & Abigail, b. Sept. 12, 1775	1	166
Joseph Henry, of Goshen, m. Ann Maria **BEACH**, of Litchfield, Nov.		
25, 1847, by Rev. Samuel Fuller	TM49	38
Josiah, m. Mehetabel **SMITH**, of Wallingford, Aug. 20, 1765, by Rev.		
James Dana, of Wallingford	1	84
Julia, d. Amos & Rachel, b. Mar. 27, 1800	2	122
Julia, m. Frederick **BUELL**, Oct. 6, 1819, by Rev. Isaac Jones	2	22
Lois, d. Ebenezer & Ama, b. July 2, 1765	1	86
Lois, m. Daniel **LAMSON**, June 17, 1784	2	78
Lucretia, d. Erastus & Anna, b. Nov. 21, 1824	2	146
Lucretia M., m. Thomas W. **GRISWOLD**, Jan. 11, 1849, by Rev.		
David L. Parmelee	TM49	39
Luman, s. Ebenezer, Jr. & Lois, b. Nov. 19, 1790	2	78
Lydia M., m. William **HOTCHKISS**, June 16, 1836, by Rev. R. S.		
Crampton	2	299
Lydia Maria, d. Ebenezer, Jr. & Lois, b. Aug. 23, 1812	2	78
Mary, d. Ebenezer & Ama, b. May 16, 1763	1	127
Mary, m. Samuel **BARNARD**, Feb. 18, 1784	2	62
Mary, m. Samuel **BARNARD, Jr.**, Feb. 19, 1784, by Rev. Judah		
Champion	1	169
Nancy, d. Ebenezer, Jr. & Lois, b. Aug. 17, 1803	2	78
Nancy, m. Anson **BEECHER**, b. of Litchfield, Dec. 5, 1826, by Rev.		
Henry Robinson, of South Farms	2	267
Nathaniel, m. Abigail **GILLET**, Dec. 17, 1755, by Rev. Nathaniell		
Taylor, of New Milford	1	127
Nathaniel, m. Abigail **GILLET**, Dec. 17, 1755, by Rev. Nathaniell		

	Vol.	Page
BENTON, (cont.),		
Taylor, of New Milford	1	128
Nathaniel, s. Nathaniell & Abigail, b. Apr. 11, 1761	1	127
Orange, s. Nathaniel & Abigail, b. May 7, 1766	1	26
Orange, s. Nathaniel, b. May 7, 1766	1	84
Orange, s. Abraham & Desire, b. Jan. 27, 1791	1	249
Orlando, s. Daniel & Margary, b. Sept. 22, 1790	1	249
Polly, d. Ebenezer, Jr. & Lois, b. Mar. 9, 1792	2	78
Polly, m. William **MASON, Jr.**, Mar. 19, 1822, by Morris Woodruff, J.P.	2	110
Polly, m. W[illia]m **MUNSON, Jr.**, Mar. 19, 1822	2	269
Rachal, d. Nathaniel & Abigail, b. May 16, 1770	1	26
Rachel, d. Nathaniel, b. May 16, 1770	1	84
Sarah, d. Ebenezer & Ama, b. Apr. 24, 1773	1	167
Sarah, d. Amos & Rachel, b. June 7, 1816	2	122
Sarah, of Litchfield, m. Amos **BENTON**, of Kingston, O., Nov. 13, 1837, by Joshua Emory, Jr.	2	314
Seth Farnam, s. Ebenezer, Jr. & Lois, b. Nov. 8, 1809	2	78
BESLIN, Ebenezer, of Derby, m. Susan **GREGORY**, of Kent, May 6, 1828, by I. Jones	2	276
BIDWELL, Anna, w. Stephen, d. May 16, 1809, in the 87th y. of her age	1	44
Anne, d. Stephen & Ann, b. Feb. 23, 1763	1	128
Charlotte, d. Stephen & Hannah, b. Mar. 1, 1788	1	213
Cornelia, d. Stephen & Hanah, b. July 12, 1800	1	212
Cornelia, m. Benjamin A. **McCALL**, b. of Litchfield, Mar. 10, 1852, by Benjamin L. Swan	TM49	66
Elijah, s. Stephen & Ann, b. Dec. 9, 1760	1	85
Elijah, m. Lucy **COLE**, Nov. 17, 1785, by Rev. John Trumbull, of Watertown	1	213
Ephraim, m.Clarissa **MORLEY**, Oct. 9, 1825, by Rev. Truman Marsh	2	257
Frederic, of Naugatuck, m. Mary H. **ARUTS***, of Litchfield, May 5, 1851, by Benjamin L. Swan *(Perhaps "HARUTS")	TM49	62
George, s. Stephen & Hannah, b. Dec. 9, 1798	1	212
George, m. Jennett **TUTTLE**, b. of Northfield, Oct. 8, 1848, by J. L. Dickinson	TM49	27
George E., of Terryville, m. Martha A. **WADHAMS**, of Litchfield, Dec. 17, 1749*, by Benjamin L. Swan *(Probably "1849")	TM49	44
Horace, s. Stephen, Jr. & Hannah, b. Feb. 7, 1798	1	212
Joseph Camp, s. Stephen, Jr. & Hannah, b. Sept. 28, 1795	1	212
Linus, s. Stephen, Jr. & Hannah, b. Jan. 16, 1794	1	212
Luce, d. Stephen & Ann, b. Nov. 5, 1754	1	86
Luce, d. Stephen & Anne, d. Jan. 23, 1755	1	86
Lucy, d. Stephen & Anne, d. Apr.23, 1771, in the 15th y. of her age	1	4
Lucy, d. Elijah & Lucy, b. June 4, 1787	1	213
Mabel, d. Stephen & Ann, b. Mar. 15, 1748/9	1	85
Mabel, m. Timothy **WEBSTER, Jr.**, Aug. 23, 1770, by Rev. Judah Champion	1	125
Mabel, d. Stephen, Jr. & Hannah, b. Dec. 13, 1792	1	212
Minerva, d. Stephen, Jr. & Honour, b. Apr. 21, 1790	1	213
Minerva, m. Chauncey **PECK**, Apr. 22, 1812	2	66
Molly, d. Stephen & Ann, b. Nov. 23, 1767	1	128
Patience, d. Stephen & Ann, b. Feb. 15, 1750/1	1	129
Patience, m. Reuben **LEWIS**, Nov. 25, 1773, by Rev. Judah Champion	1	105

	Vol.	Page
BIRGE, BIRG, Albert, s. Joseph & Marietta, b. Aug. 15, 1797	1	250
Albert, s. Joseph & Marietta, b. Aug. 15, 1797	2	252
Albert H., m. Lois **PAGE,** Dec. 28, 1819, by Rev. Isaac Jones	2	255
Antoinette, d. Albert H. & Lois, b. Aug. 13, 1821	2	255
Antoinette, m. Almon J. **BEACH,** Oct. 15, 1840, by Rev. Mr. Eastman	TM49	5
Antoinette, m. Norman* **BEACH,** b. of Litchfield, Oct. 15, 1840, by		
G. C. V. Eastman *(Note says "Almond J. **BEACH**")	2	331
Benjamin, s.Joseph Dorrity, b. Jan. 28, 1726	1	5
Benjamin, m. Esther **BEECH,** Aug. 23, 1750, by Thomas Harrison,		
J.P.	1	129
Benjamin, s. Elisha & Mary, b. Apr. 19, 1761	1	127
Benj[ami]n, s. Joseph & Marietta, b. July 24, 1795	1	250
Benjamin, s. Joseph & Marietta, b. July 24, 1795	2	252
Beriah, s. Benjamin & Esther, b. Nov. 4, 1759	1	128
Chester, s. Joseph & Marietta, b. Oct. 25, 1801	1	250
Chester, s. Joseph & Marietta, b. Oct. 25, 1801	2	252
Chrafts, s. Benjamin & Esther, b. May 24, 1755	1	128
Clarinda F., m. Anson C. **SMITH,** Nov. 27, 1836, by Rev. A. Billings		
Beach	2	299
Clarinda F., d. Harvey & Thankfull, b. Mar. 21, 1812	2	63
Cornelius G., s. Harvey & Thankfull, b. Mar. 7, 1814	2	63
Dorrety, d. Joseph & Dorrety, b. Dec. 18, 1723	1	5
Dorothy, m. Benjamin **OSBORN,** Sept. 27, 1758, by Rev. Judah		
Champion	1	29
Elias, s. Joseph & Marietta, b. July 11, 1793	1	250
Elias, s. Joseph & Marietta, b. July 11, 1793	2	252
Elias, [s. Albert H. & Lois], [ ]	2	255
Elijah, m. Lydia **DIEBELL**(?), Sept. 12, 1751, by Rev. Stephen Heaton,		
of Goshen	1	129
Hannah, m. Joshua **PHELPS,** July 8, 1752, by Rev. Mr. Russell, of		
Windsor	1	71
Hannah, L., d. Harvey & Thankfull, b. Apr. 27, 1810	2	63
Harriet, d. Joseph & Marietta, b. Aug. 27, 1791; d. Feb. 4, 1794, ae 2 y.		
5 m.	1	250
Harriet, d. Joseph & Marietta, b. Aug. 27, 1791; d. Feb. 4, 1794, ae 2 y.		
5 m.	2	252
Harriet, d. James & Sally, b. Mar. 2, 1797	2	145
Harriet, d. Joseph & Marietta, b. Oct. 8, 1799	1	250
Harriet, d. Joseph & Marietta, b. Oct. 8, 1799	2	252
Harriet J., m. Ruel **SEDGWICK,** b. of Litchfield, Nov. 15, 1853, by		
Rev. John J. Brandegee	TM49	94
Harvey, s. James & Sally, b. June 9, 1782	2	145
Harvey, m. Thankfull **GRISWOULD,** Apr. 12, 1806, by Rev. Truman		
Marsh	2	63
Harvey, m. Anna **WADHAMS,** b. of Litchfield, Sept. 28, 1840, by Seth		
W. Scofield	2	327
James, s. Elisha & Mary, b. Oct. 16, 1758	1	127
James, m. Sally **PALMER,** Oct. 29, 1780, by Rev. James Nichols	2	145
James, Jr., s. James & Sally, b. Sept. 4, 1789	2	145
Jane, d. Albert H. & Lois, b. May 20, 1824	2	255
Jane, of Litchfield, m. Truman Leander **JENNINGS,** of Warren, Oct.		
27, 1847, by Rev. Samuel Fuller	TM49	38
Jenette, d. Joseph & Marietta, b. Sept. 26, 1809	1	250

	Vol.	Page
BIRGE, BIRG, (cont.),		
Jenette, d. Joseph & Marietta, b. Sept. 26, 1809	2	252
Jenette, m. Ithamer PAGE, Feb. 10, 1828, by E. B. Kellogg	2	275
John Ward, s. Joseph & Marietta, b. Dec. 9, 1807	1	250
John Ward, s. Joseph & Marietta, b. Dec. 9, 1807	2	252
Joseph, m. Doroty KILBORN, Nov. 8, 1721, by David Goodrich, J.P.	1	5
Joseph, s. Joseph & Dorothy, b. Sept. 29, 1722	1	5
Joseph, s. Benjamin & Esther, b. May 21, 1753	1	85
Joseph, m. Marietta WARD, Apr. 2, 1786, by Rev. Ashbel Baldwin	2	252
Joseph, m. Marietta WARD, Apr. 2, 1789, by Rev. Ashbel Baldwin	1	250
Joseph, s. Joseph & Marietta, b. Nov. 18, 1805	1	250
Joseph, s. Joseph & Marietta, b. Nov. 18, 1805	2	252
Lemuel, s. James & Sally, b. Feb. 14, 1787	2	145
Mary, d. Joseph & Dorothy, b. Nov. 24, 1729	1	45
Mary, w. Elisha, d. Dec. 9, 1786	1	168
Mary, d. Joseph & Marietta, b. Jan. 28, 1790	1	250
Mary, d. Joseph & Marietta, b. Jan. 28, 1790	2	252
Mary, [d. Albert H. & Lois], [ ]	2	255
Orrin, s. James & Sally, b. July 4, 1784	2	145
Rhoda, d. Elijah & Lydia, b. Aug. 12, 1751	1	129
Sally Palmer, d. Harvey & Thankfull, b. Jan. 22, 1808	2	63
Sarah, d. Elisha & Mary, b. Nov. 27, 1763	1	127
Selina, d. James & Sally, b. Mar. 6, 1792	2	145
Salina, d. Harvey & Thankfull, b. Apr. 25, 1816	2	63
S[e]lina, m. Norman WETMORE, Feb. 21, 1836, by Rev. Isaac Jones	2	298
Susan, [d. Albert H. & Lois], [ ]	2	255
Thankful, d. Benjamin & Esther, b. May 19, 1751	1	129
Tryphena, d. Elisha & Mary, b. July 18, 1757	1	127
BISHOP, Almira, d. Amos & Lois, b. Oct. 13, 1800	2	24
Amos, [s. Noah & Anne], b. Oct. 24, 1769	2	24
Amos, m. Lois CORNWALL, Mar. 8, 1792, by David Welch	2	24
Amos Curtiss, s. Amois & Lois, b. June 14, 1810	2	24
Anne, [d. Noah & Anne], b. July 7, 1766	2	24
Anne, d. Silvanus & Molly, b. Aug. 23, 1766	1	127
Anne, m. Jeremiah KILBORN, Apr. 28, 1785	1	145
Anne, d. Amos & Lois, b. Aug. 19, 1799	2	24
Anne, d. Amos & Lois, d. Feb. 26, 1807	2	24
Annis, d. Amos & Lois, b. Dec. 22, 1792	2	24
Charles s. Solon & Julian, b. Sept. 13, 1815	2	43
Cyrenia, d. Jonathan, Jr. & Submit, b. Sept. 15, 1764	1	127
Elizabeth, d. Silvanus & Molly, b. Apr. 26, 1770	1	127
Elizabeth, d. Sylvanus & Mary, d. Aug. 28, 1776	1	168
Eunice, d. Amos & Lois, b. Jan. 28, 1798	2	24
Eunice, d. Amos & Lois, d. Mar. 6, 1801	2	24
Frederick, s. Solon & Julian, b. Apr. 16, 1813	2	43
Hannah, d. Jonathan & Submit, b. Jan. 22, 1746	1	44
Henry Fowler, s. Jonathan & Submit, b. Apr. 9, 1800	1	249
Hiram Levi, s. Sylvanus & Clarinda, b. Apr. 26, 1838	2	109
Jane, m. Gad FARNUM, May 14, 1760, by Rev. Judah Champion	1	13
Jane, d. Samuel [& Mary Ann], b. Sept. 5, 1829	2	24
John, m. Eliza BOLLES, Dec. 23, 1831, by Truman Kilborn, J.P.	2	290
John Sylvanus, s. Sylvanus, b. Dec. 10, 1833	2	109
Jonathan, Jr., m. Submit SMITH, Dec. 18, 1753, by Rev. Mr. Mansfield	1	44

	Vol.	Page
BISHOP, (cont.),		
Jonathan, Jr., d. Mar. 2, 1765	1	4
Jonathan, s. Silvanus & Molly, b. Mar. 24, 1768	1	127
Julia, m. Bateman SMITH, Nov. 25, 1816, by Ephraim Depew, J.P., of		
Rochester, N.Y.	2	113
Lamon*, s. Jonathan, Jr. & Submit, b. Aug. 25, 1757 *("Luman" in		
Woodruff's book)	1	44
Lois, [d. Noah & Anne], b. May 16, 1774	2	24
Lois, m. Eliphaz PARSONS, Jr., May 6, 1797, by Rev. Mr. Butler	2	23
Luce, m. Benjamin KILBORN, Mar. 20, 1757	1	61
Lucretia, m. Daniel STODDARD, Apr. 29, 1797	2	66
Lucy, [d. Noah & Anne], b. Mar. 6, 1772	2	24
Lucy, m. Friend Hezekiah FRISBIE, Feb. 1, 1795, by Rev. Mr. Butler	2	143
Luman, s. Solon & Julian, b. Nov. 7, 1809	2	43
Luman, m. Mary WILLMOT, Sept. 25, 1831, by Rev. Mr. Taylor, of		
South Farms	2	289
Luman, see also Lamon		
Mary, d. Jonathan & Submit, b. June 7, 1748	1	44
Mary A., of Litchfield, m. Walstein C. WADHAMS, of Goshen, Dec.		
29,1850, by Rev. H. L. Vaill	TM49	40
Medad Dudley, s. Jonathan & Submit, b. Feb. 16, 1798	1	249
Mehitabel, [d. Noah & Anne], b. Aug. 28, 1762	2	24
Mercy, m. Joel BISSELL, Nov. 7, 1750, by Rev. Thomas Ruggles, of		
Guilford	1	129
Noah, m. Anne PALMERLY, May [ ], 1762, by Rev. Judah Champion	2	24
Noah, [s. Noah & Anne], b. Apr. 6, 1776	2	24
Noah, d. Sept. 6, 1777	2	24
Noah, s. Amos & Lois, b. Jan. 6, 1807	2	24
Olive, d. Jonathan, Jr. & Submit, b. Dec. 18, 1754	1	44
Osander, s. Solon & Julian, b. May 19, 1811	2	43
Osander, m. Julia WILLMOT, Sept. 15, 1833, by Rev. John Dowdney	2	294
Rhoda, d. Silvanus & Molly, b. July 10, 1763	1	127
Sabra, d. Jonathan, Jr. & Submit, b. Nov. 6, 1761	1	129
Sabra, m. Frederick STANLEY, Sept. 25, 1781	1	162
Samuel, d. June 25, 1778, ae 79 y. 3 m.	1	168
Samuel, s. Amos & Lois, b. Nov. 11, 1794; d. June 2, 1796	2	24
Samuel, s. Amos & Lois, b. June 2, 1804	2	24
Samuel, m. Mary Ann NEAL, Oct. 30, 1828, by W. Clark, in New York		
State	2	24
Sarah, d. Seth & Hannah, b. July 4, 1758	1	85
Sarah, m. George DARE, Dec. 2, 1778, by Rev. Judah Champion	1	49
Seth, m. Hannah BRADLEY, Nov. 2, 1757, by Rev. Amos Fowler	1	85
Seth, s. Seth & Hannah, b. Mar. 5, 1761	1	85
Silvanus, m. Molly LANDON, Nov. 25, 1762, by Solomon Palmer	1	127
Silvanus, s. Jonathan & Ruth, b. July 24, 1792	1	249
Solon, m. Julia Ann KILBORN, Feb. [ ], 1809	2	43
Submit, m. John JOY, Sept. 23, 1766, by Timothy Collens, J.P.	1	58
Submit, m. John JOY, Sept. 23, 1766, by Timothy Collens, J.P.	1	101
Sylvanus, m. Clarinda WESTOVER, Dec. 16, 1830, by Rev. William		
Lucas	2	286
Thankfull, d. Amos & Lois, b. Sept. 15, 1802	2	24
Thankfull, m. Ethan KILBURN, b. of Litchfield, May 31, 1830, by		
Rev. L. P. Hickok	2	285

	Vol.	Page
BISSELL, BESSELL, Abel, s. John & Mary, b. Aug. 26, 1796	2	73
Abigail, m. Thomas **CATLING**, May 8, 1732, by Rev. Timothy Colens	1	7
Abigail, d. Benj[ami]n, & Esther, b. Feb. 19, 1792	1	248
Albert, s. Reuben & Huldah, b. Aug. 24, 1801	2	2
Almira, d. John & Mary, b. Jan. 22, 1784	2	73
Almira, m. Elizur B. **SMITH**, Jan. [ ], 1821, by Rev. Lyman Beecher	2	100
Amanda, d. John & Mary, b. Apr. 22, 1793	2	73
Amanda, d. John & Mary, d. Nov. 27, 1795	2	73
Amanda Gennet, d. John & Ruby, b. Apr. 20, 1811	2	73
Amanda Joannette, of Milton m. William **BISSELL**, of Kent, Nov. 3, 1831, by Rev. H. S. Atwater, of New Preston	2	290
Ameranda, d. Reuben & Huldah, b. Nov. 5, 1803	2	2
Amos, s. John & Mary, b. Jan. 14, 1786	2	73
Amos, s. Benjamin & Esther, b. July 15, 1799	1	248
Amos, s. John & Mary, d. Nov. 20, 1807	2	73
Amos, m. Lydia **HALL**, b. of Litchfield, Mar. 15, 1827, by Rev. Henry Robinson, of South Farms	2	269
Anne, d. Benjamin & Esther, b. Dec. 14, 1784	1	248
Arcolos*, s. Isaac & Sarah, b. Aug. 14, 1758 *("Archelaus")	1	129
Arilla, d. John & Mary, b. June 18, 1782	2	73
Augustus, s. Benjamin [& Melissa], b. [ ]	2	148
Benjamin, m. Leah **PECK**, Nov. 6, 1740, by Rev. Timothy Collens	1	129
Benjamin, d. Jan. 11, 1747/8	1	128
Benjamin, s. Benjamin & Leah, b. Dec. 12, 1748	1	129
Benjamin s. Zebulon & Abigail, b. Jan. 15, 1754	1	129
Benjamin, m. Esther **BENTON**, Feb. 21, 1779, by Rev. Judah Champion	1	248
Benjamin, s. Benjamin & Esther, b. Dec. 26, 1788	1	248
Benjamin, s. Hiram [& Beatia], b. May 5, 1807	2	114
Benjamin, Jr., m. Melissa **POST**, Feb. 6, 1822, by Rev. Charles Prentice	2	148
Benjamin, s. Benjamin, Jr. & Melissa, b. Dec. 16, 1824	2	148
Benjamin, m. Betsey A. **BROOKER**, b. of Litchfield, Oct. 24, 1849, by Rev. S. T. Seelye	TM49	43
Betsey Elizabeth, d. Zebulon & Sarah, b. Dec. 10, 1781	1	213
Calvin, s. Isaac & Sarah, b. Apr. 21, 1753	1	85
Caroline Eliza, d. Henry & Belinda, b. Aug. 14, 1837	2	324
Charles Leonard, s. Herman & Anna, b. Oct. 24, 1821	2	99
Charles Oliver, s. Reuben & Huldah, b. July 13, 1815	2	2
Clarissa, d. John & Mary, b. Feb. 22, 1789	2	73
Cornelia Eliza, d. John & Ruby, b. Aug. 13, 1812	2	73
Cornelia Eliza, of Milton, m. John **MORGAN**, of Kent, Nov. 3, 1831, by Rev. H. S. Atwater, of New Preston	2	290
David, s. George & Lydia, b. Jan. 17, 1742/3	1	87
David, s. John & Mary, b. May 26, 1791	2	73
David Ozias, s. Herman & Anna, b. May 2, 1823	2	99
Diantha, m. Garwood **SANFORD**, [ ], 1820, by Lyman Beecher	2	98
Diantha, m. Garwood **SANFORD**, [ ], 1820, by Rev. Lyman Beecher	2	103
Dotha, d. Benj[ami]n & Esther, b. Oct. 18, 1795	1	248
Edward, s. Amos & Lydia, b. Dec. 16, 1827	2	323
Elisha Smith, s. Reuben & Huldah, b. May 3, 1809	2	2
Elizabeth, wid. Lieut. Isaac, d. Jan. 13, 1761	1	4
Elizabeth, d. Amos & Lydia, b. Feb. 26, 1832	2	323

	Vol.	Page
BISSELL, BESSELL, (cont.),		
Emily Frances, d. Henry & Belinda, b. Feb. 23, 1840	2	324
Erastus, s. Nathaniel & Anna, b. Apr. 18, 1812	2	148
Eunice, d. Benj[ami]n & Esther b. Feb. 10, 1790	1	248
Evlyn Lyman, s. Lyman & Theresa, b. Sept. 10, 1836	2	114
Frances Jennet, d. Herman [& Anna], b. Sept. 28, 1831	2	99
Frederick, s. Nathaniel & Anna, b. May 12, 1821	2	148
Garry, s. Hiram [& Beatia], b. Mar. 28, 1806	2	114
Garry, m. Sally **HALL,** b. of Litchfield, June 23, 1831, by Rev. William Lucas	2	287
George, m. Lydia **GAY,** Oct. 1, 1740, by Rev. Timothy Collens	1	85
George C., m. Susan **KILBORN,** May 1, 1826, by Rev. Trumas	2	263
George Post, s. Benjamin, Jr. & Melissa, b. May 4, 1826	2	148
Harriet, m. Curtiss **HALLOCK,** b. of Litchfield, Nov. 25, 1845, by Rev. William Dixon	TM49	12
Harriet Ann, d. Herman & Anna, b. Feb. 26, 1828	2	99
Heman, s. Zebulon & Sarah, b. Apr. 6, 1778	1	213
Heman, s. Benjamin & Esther, b. Jan. 16, 1797	1	248
Henry, s. Nathaniel & Anna, b. Apr. 10, 1814	2	148
Henry, m. Patience **McNEILE,** b. of Litchfield, Sept. 20, 1835, by Rev. Samuel Fuller, Jr.,	2	296
Herman, m. Anna **PECK,** Dec. [ ], 1820, by Rev. Lyman Beecher	2	99
Hiram, s. Benjamin & Mabel, b. Apr. 28, 1783	1	210-11
Hiram, m. Beatia **WETMORE,** [ ], 1805	2	114
Hiram, s. Hiram [& Beatia], b. Sept. 27, 1808	2	114
Isaac, Lieut., d. Nov. 6, 1744	1	4
Isaac, m. Sarah **STONE,** Oct. 1, 1746, by Rev. Timothy Collens	1	85
Isaac, s. Isaac & Sary, b. Aug. 5, 1747	1	85
Isaac, Jr., m. Allithea **WAY,** Dec. 13, 1770, by Rev. Judah Champion	1	44
Jehiel, s. George & Lydia, b. Feb. 18, 1740/1	1	85
Joel, m. Mercy **BISHOP,** Nov. 7, 1750, by Rev. Thomas Ruggles, of Guilford	1	129
Joel, d. Feb. 1, 1761	1	4
John, s. Roger & Sarah, b. July 25, 1744	1	85
John, b. Dec. 28, 1761	2	73
John, s. Isaac, Jr. & Allithea, b. Nov. 15, 1771	1	44
John, s. Zebulon, Jr. & Sarah, b. Feb. 10, 1776	1	167
John, m. Mary **DICKINSON,** Nov. [ ], 1781	2	73
John, m. Ruby **CHAPEL,** Dec. 20, 1807	2	73
Joseph, m. Esther **SMITH,** Sept. 5, 1774, by David Welch, J.P.	1	43
Joseph, m. Esther **SMITH,** Sept. 5, 1774, by David Welch, J.P.	1	167
Joseph J., s. Hiram [& Beatia], b. Sept. 3, 1814	2	114
Julia, m. Lyman V. **SMITH,** Feb. 23, 1825, by Rev. Lyman Beecher	2	139
Julia, d. Amos & Lydia, b. Feb. 13, 1837	2	323
Juliana, d. Nathaniel & Anna, b. July 5, 1823	2	148
Julina, d. Benjamin & Esther, b. May 12, 1801	1	248
Julius, s. Herman & Anna, b. Aug. 14, 1825	2	99
Julius, s. Herman & Anna, d. Sept. 17, 1826	2	99
Julius Peck, s. Herman & Anna, b. Jan. 25, 1834	2	99
Kilborn, s. Hiram [& Beatia], b. July 11, 1809 [1810]	2	114
Lawrence, s. Benjamin [& Melissa], b. [ ]	2	148
Leah, d. Benjamin & Leah, b. Nov. 16, 1746	1	129
Leah, m. Jonathan **WRIGHT,** Apr. 6, 1767, by Rev. Judah Champion	1	165

	Vol.	Page
BISSELL, BESSELL, (cont.),		
Leonard, m. Charlotte **KINNEY**, b. of Litchfield, Oct. 24, 1844, by		
Rev. George H. Hastings	TM49	8
Lucy, d. Hiram [& Beatia], b. May 14, 1811	2	114
Lucy, m. Alva **SHARP**, Nov. 15, 1830, by Rev. William Lucas	2	286
Luther, s. Isaac & Sarah, b. Mar. 28, 1751	1	85
Luther, s. Isaac, Jr. & Allithea, b. June 17, 1773	1	44
Luther, d. June 29, 1776, at Crown Point	1	168
Lyman, s. Hiram [& Beatia], b. Oct. 19, 1812	2	114
Lyman, m. Thresa Maria **SKEELES**, [ ]	2	114
Maranda, m. Abram D. **STONE**, b. of Litchfield, Feb. 27, 1828, by Rev.		
John S. Stone	2	275
Maria, m. Lyman **PALMER**, Oct. 16, 1825, by Rev. Truman Marsh	2	257
Mary, w. John, d. Apr. 14, 1807	2	73
Mary Theoddard, d. Reuben & Huldah, b. Aug. 6, 1807	2	2
Melissa, d. Benjamin [& Melissa], b. [ ]	2	148
Molly, m. Ebenezer **KELLOGG**, Dec. 9, 1779, by Rev. Judah		
Champion	1	103
Nabby, m. John **GRISWOLD, Jr.**, [ ]	2	280
Nancy, d. Hiram [& Beatia], b. May 30, 1816	2	114
Nathaniel, s. Benjamin & Esther, b. Dec. 31, 1786	1	248
Nathaniel, m. Anna **SMITH**, Jan. 2, 1811, by Rev. Mark Mead, of		
Middlebury	2	148
Nathaniel, m. Sally **MARSH**, b. of Litchfield, Oct. 6, 1852, by		
Benjamin L. Swan	TM49	76
Olive, d. Isaac & Sarah, b. Aug. 13, 1755	1	85
Oscar, s. Benjamin, Jr. & Melissa, b. Dec. 20, 1822	2	148
Ozias, s. Joel & Mercy, b. Aug. 6, 1751	1	129
Ozias, m. Temperance **COLVER**, Nov. 12, 1769, by Rev. Judah		
Champion	1	84
Rachel, d. Benjamin & Leah, b. June 6, 1741	1	129
Rachel, d. Benjamin & Leah, d. Apr. 3, 1749	1	4
Rachel, d. Benj[ami]n & Esther, b. Sept. 18, 1793	1	248
Ralph, s. Nathaniel & Anna, b. Sept. 17, 1816	2	148
Rebecca, d. Benjamin & Esther, b. Feb. 9, 1782	1	248
Reuben, s. Joseph & Esther, b. June 30, 1775	1	167
Reuben, m. Huldah **TILFORD**, [ ], by Rev. Truman Marsh	2	2
Renold, s. Simeon & Lura, b. Jan. 1, 1804	1	212
Rhoda, d. Zebulon & Abigail, b. Apr. 5, 1760	1	85
Roger, m. Sarah **STOUGHTON**, Oct. 25, 1743, by Rev. Jonathan		
Marsh, of Windsor	1	85
Rufus M., s. Hiram [& Beatia], b. Sept. 24, 1820	2	114
Sarah, m. James **KILLBORN**, Sept. 12, 1733	1	21
Sarah, d. Isaac & Sarah, b. Apr. 23, 1749	1	85
Sarah, m. Heber **STONE**, Jan. 1, 1772, by Timothy Collens, J.P.	1	34
Sarah, m. Job **PALMER**, Nov. 13, 1788, by Rev. Judah Champion	1	112
Sarah, m. George **COOK**, b. of Litchfield, Aug. 29, 1838, by Rev. Gad		
N. Smith	2	319
Sideriss Lorania, d. John & Ruby, b. Feb. 16, 1815	2	73
Simeon, s. Joseph & Esther, b. July 18, 1777	1	167
Simeon, m. Lura **GATES**, Mar. 20, 1803, by Rev. Truman Marsh	1	212
Stephen, representative May & Oct. 1818	2	1555
William, s. John & Mary, b. June 18, 1803	2	73

	Vol.	Page

BISSELL, BESSELL, (cont.),

	Vol.	Page
William, s. Amos & Lydia, b. Mar. 15, 1830	2	323
William, of Kent, m. Amanda Joanette BISSELL, of Milton, Nov. 3, 1831, by Rev. H. S. Atwater, of New Preston	2	290
Zebulon, m. Abigail SMITH, May 21, 1749, by Rev. Mr. Gibbs	1	83
Zebulon, s. Zebulon & Abigail, b. "3rd, 10th, 1751" (Date is "Oct. 30, 1751", in Woodruff's)	1	129
Zebulon, Jr., m. Sarah WATKINS, Jan. 13, 1774, by Rev. Andrew Bartholomew	1	167
BLACKMAN, Angeline, d. Jacob S. & Rebecca, b. Jan. 30, 1825	2	256
Dimeann, m. Henry BRYON, of Saugatuck, May 13, 1822, by Datus Ensign, Elder	2	111
Emma, of Litchfield, m. Minas SMITH, of Watertown, Jan. 24, 1828, by Rev. Henry Robinson, of South Farms	2	275
George Beecher, s. Charles A. & Lurinda, b. Oct. 11, 1837	2	316
Jacob S., m. Rebecca WRIGHT, May 10, 1823, by Rev. Reuben Sherwood, of Norwalk	2	256
Mary Eliza, d. Charles A. & Lurinda, b. Apr. 24, 1835	2	316
Mary L., m. Thomas McLOYD, Oct. 19, 1851, by Rev. David L. Parmalee	TM49	65
Nancy, m. William REA, Jan. 29, 1816, by Rev. Lyman Beecher	2	82
Nancy, m. William RAY, Jan. 29, 1816, by Rev. Lyman Beecher	2	258
Patron M., m. Mrs. Samantha HAZARD, Apr. 20, 1846, by Rev. William Dixon	TM49	14
Samantha Hazzard, wid. of Patron M., of Litchfield, m. Eden JOHNSON, of Bethany, Aug. 27, 1851, by Oliver A. G. Todd, J.P.	TM49	63
Sarah, m. Joseph PARKER, July 12, 1809, by Rev. Azel Backus, of Bethlem	2	84
BLAKE, Albert, s. James & Dorcas, b. May 22, 1796	2	74
Albert, m. Ada GARNER, Feb. 12, 1845, by Rev. D. L. Marks	TM49	8
Albert, of Cornwall, m. Hannah MONROE, of Warren, Sept. 5, 1854, by Rev. H. N. Weed	TM49	103
Buel, s. James & Dorcas, b. Sept. 29, 1809	2	74
Buel, m. Sally E. TUTTLE, May 8, 1842	TM49	75
Buel, of Cornwall, m. Sally E. TUTHILL, of Milton, May 8, 1842, by Ralph Smith	2	410
Catharine, d. James & Dorcas, b. Sept. 29, 1812	2	74
Cicero, s. [Buel & Sally E.], b. Aug. 4, 1849	TM49	75
Demaris, d. Richard & Demaris, b. Aug. 31, 1778	1	169
Dorcas L., d. James & Dorcas, b. Oct. 14, 1817, in Cornwall	2	74
Edwin, of Middletown, m. Lucretia ANDREWS, of Litchfield, Mar. 4, 1838, by Rev. Lewis Gunn	2	315
Flora, d. James & Dorcas, b. Nov. 20, 1807	2	74
James, s. Richard & Damaris, b. Oct. 8, 1769	1	127
James, m. Dorcas BUEL, Apr. 1, 1793, by Rev. Judah Champion	2	74
James, s. James & Dorcas, b. May 18, 1798	2	74
James, d. Nov. 17, 1817	2	74
Jesse, s. Richard & Damaris, b. Aug. 31, 1771	1	127
Julia Catharine, d. [Buel & Sally E.], b. Sept. 5, 1851	TM49	75
Julius, s. James & Dorcas, b. Jan. 27, 1805	2	74
Lewis, s. Buel & Sally E., b. May 26, 1846	TM49	75
Mary, m. Amzi BEACH, Nov. 1, 1843, by Rev. D. L. Marks	TM49	1

	Vol.	Page
BOARDMAN, BORDMAN, (cont.),		
Oliver, m. Sarah **DANFORTH**, May 1, 1781, by Rev. Enoch		
Huntington	1	213
Oliver, s. Oliver & Sarah, b. Aug. 23, 1785	1	213
Polly Frothingham, d. Oliver & Sarah, b. Mar. 28, 1796	1	213
Sally, d. Oliver & Sarah, b. Feb. 21, 1782	1	213
Sherman, s. Oliver & Sarah, b. July 10, 1787	1	213
Thomas Danforth, s. Oliver & Sarah, b. Jan. 21, 1784	1	213
BOLLES, BOLLS, Abigail, wid. [Ebenezer], d. Dec. 29, 1844	2	26
Asa, m. Lidena **FRISBIE**, Sept. 2, 1821, by Rev. Asa Tallmadge	2	104
Asa H., m. Sedena **FRISBIE**, Sept. 2, 1821	2	268
Caroline Amelia, d. George & Clarissa, b. May 17, 1825	2	108
Charley, s. Eben[eze]r W. & Lucretia, b. Dec. 19, 1825	2	136
Eben W., m. Lucretia M. **LEWIS**, Sept. 21, 1823, by Rev. Mr. Howe	2	136
Ebenezer, m. Abigail **PENFIELD**, Dec. 20, 1789, by Rev. Mr. Austin	2	26
Ebenezer, had negro Laura, d. Mille **HIND**, b. Apr. 12, 1797	2	27
Ebenezer, d. Aug. 28, 1826	2	26
Ebenezer W. & Lucretia, had d. [ ], b. Oct. 31, 1827	2	136
Ebenezer W., m. Lydia A. **STRONG**, Oct. 18, 1832, by Rev. L. P.		
Hickok	2	288
Ebenezer Williams, s. Ebenezer & Abigail, b. Feb. 2, 1793	2	26
Eliza, m. John **BISHOP**, Dec. 23, 1831, by Truman Kilborn, J.P.	2	290
George, s. Ebenezer & Abigail, b. Nov. 27, 1799	2	26
George, m. Clarissa M. **KILBORN**, Nov. 29, 1821, by Rev. Lyman		
Beecher	2	108
Henry, s. Ebenezer & Abigail, b. Mar. 4, 1802	2	26
Henry, [s. Ebenezer & Abigail], d. Mar. 5, 1849, at Burlington, Carroll		
Cty., Ind.	2	26
Henry A., s. Asa H. & Sedena, b. [ ] 8, 1827	2	268
Joshua, s. Ebenezer & Abigail, b. Aug. 20, 1797	2	26
Joshua, s. Ebenezer & Abigail, d. Jan. 15, 1799	2	26
Julia Mariah, d. George & Clarissa, b. Oct. 14, 1822	2	108
Margerette C., m. Joshua **GARRETT**, Nov. 4, 1828	2	329
Margeret Cowan, d. Ebenezer & Abigail, b. Jan. 2, 1806	2	26
Mary A., d. Eben W. & Lucretia, b. Sept. 9, 1824	2	136
Mary P., [d. Samuel P. & Roxana], b. May 4, 1842; d. Nov. 13, 1843	2	136
Mary R., [d. Samuel P. & Roxana], b. Mar. 16, 1846	2	136
Penfield, s. [Samuel P. & Roxana], b. May 24, 1831; d. Apr. 12, 1835	2	136
Phebe, m. Gross **GATES**, of Harwinton, Feb. 24, 1832, by Rev. L. P.		
Hickok	2	288
Roxana C., d. Samuel P. & Roxana, b. May 6, 1826	2	136
Roxana C., [d. Samuel P. & Roxana], d. Nov. 5, 1846	2	136
Sam[ue]l P., representative Apr. 1848, Apr. 1854	2	1558
Samuel Penfield, s. Ebenezer & Abigail, b. Feb. 25, 1791	2	26
Samuel Penfield, s. Ebenezer & Abigail, d. Sept. 18, 1792	2	26
Samuel Penfield, 2nd, s. Ebenezer & Abigail, b. June 2, 1795	2	26
Samuel Penfield, m. Roxana P. **CLARK**, May 27, 1824, by Rev. Lyman		
Beecher	2	136
Sarah Margaret, d. [Samuel P. & Roxana], b. July 8, 1836	2	136
William, s. Ebenezer & Abigail, b. Apr. 12, 1808	2	26
William R., s. Asa H. & Sedena, b. Mar. 13, 1824	2	268
BONNEY, John T., s. Thomas & Polly, b. Oct. 28, 1821	2	273
Marinda, d. [Thomas & Polly], b. July 9, 1824	2	273

	Vol.	Page

BONNEY, (cont.),

Marinda, m. Philip **SALISBURY**, b. of Litchfield, Oct. 18, 1839, by
Rev. H. Bryant — 2 — 325

BOOTH, BOOTHE, Ann C. ,of Litchfield, m. Theron **KENT**, of Sharon,
[Oct.] 7, 1849, by Rev. Herman L. Vaill — TM49 — 43

Charles, of Plymouth, m. Vanilla **HALL**, of Litchfield, Sept. 22, 1824,
by Rev. Rodney Rosseter — 2 — 102

David, m. Lydia **SHEPARD**, Mar. 4, 1821, by Rev. Lyman Beecher — 2 — 251

David, m. Anna C. **GOODWIN**, b. of Litchfield, Dec. 5, 1838, by
Rev. H. Bryant — 2 — 325

Emeline C., d. David & Lydia, b. May 23, 1824 — 2 — 251

George, m. Emeline **MARTINS**, b. of Litchfield, Apr. 4, 1831, by Rev.
David Miller — 2 — 287

Lucinda, m. Ariel **JOHNSON**, b. of Torrington, June 5, 1842, by
Jonathan Brace — 2 — 410

Ruana, of Washington, m. Nobel Doolittle **BALDWIN**, of Litchfield,
Oct. 14, 1834, by Rev. Samuel Fuller — TM49 — 37

Ruanna, of Washington, m. Nobel D. **BALDWIN**, of Litchfield, Oct.
14, 1834, by Rev. Samuel Fuller — 2 — 289

BORDEN, Louisa, m. David **KILBORN**, Apr. 20, 1763, by Rev. Judah
Champion — 1 — 61

BOSTWICK, Esther, of Litchfield, m. William **BELDEN**, of Milton, Oct.
13, 1834, by Rev. Samuel Fuller — TM49 — 37

Esther, of Litchfield, m. William **BELDEN**, of Wilton, Oct. 13, 1834,
by Rev. Samuel Fuller — 2 — 289

Joel, m. Mrs. Mabel **McNEILE**, Dec. 4, 1842, by Jonathan Brace — 2 — 411

Mary Jones, of Litchfield, m. Rev. Fred D. **HARRIMAN**, of
Crowfordsville, Ind., Aug. 27, 1851, by Rev. Benjamin W. Stone,
at Bantam Falls — TM49 — 63

Sally, m. Benjamin **GRISWOLD**, b. of Litchfield, May 20, 1839, by
Rev. H. Bryant — 2 — 325

W[illia]m W., Rev. of Bath, Steuben Co., N.Y., m. Mary **LEWIS**, of
Litchfield, Apr. 10, 1828, by Rev. John S. Stone — 2 — 276

Zachariah, m. Polly **STONE**, May 16, 1826, by Rev.Truman Marsh — 2 — 264

BOSWORTH, George, of Troy, m. Julia Maria **BEECHLEY**, of Litchfield,
Jan. 9, 1839, by Rev. Jonathan Brace — 2 — 318

BOWKER, Mary Ann, of Sudbury, Mass., m. Edward E. **CULVER**, of
Litchfield, Nov. 1, 1849, by Benjamin L. Swan — TM49 — 44

BRACE, Abel, s. James & Susan, b. Oct. 29, 1794 — 2 — 87

Anna Pierce, d. James & Susan, b. Dec.19, 1797 — 2 — 87

Charles Loring, s. John P. [& Lucy E.], b. June 19, 1826 — 2 — 108

Emma Potter, d. John P. [& Lucy E.], b. Apr. 21, 1828 — 2 — 108

James, m. Susan **PIERCE**, Jan. 11, 1792, by Rev. Judah Champion — 2 — 87

John Pierce, s. James & Susan, b. Feb. 10, 1793 — 2 — 87

Mary E., of Litchfield, m. John W. **SKINNER**, of St. Louis, Mo., Dec.
8, 1852, by Rev. Benjamin L. Swan — TM49 — 77

Mary Elizabeth, d. John P. & Lucy E., b. Oct. 11, 1820 — 2 — 108

Rachel, m. Jesse **GOODWIN**, Apr. 30, 1760, by Rev. Andrew
Bartholomew, of Harwinton — 1 — 139

Susan Mary, d. James & Susan, b. July 30, 1800; d. Sept. 22, 1802 — 2 — 87

Thomas Kimberley, of New York, m. Mary Jane **BUEL**, of Litchfield,
Jan. 18, 1853, by Benjamin L. Swan — TM49 — 78

Timothy Pierce, s. James & Susan, b. July 25, 1803 — 2 — 87

	Vol.	Page
BRACE, (cont.),		
Uriel Holmes, s. John P. [& Lucy E.], b. Dec. 13, 1822; d. Apr. 21, 1828	2	108
BRADLEY, BRADLYE, Aaron, s. Leaminf* & Anna, b. Aug. 27, 1762		
*(Leaming)	2	68
Aaron, m. Lorrin **ABERNETHY,** July 8, 1787	2	68
Aaron, representative Oct. 1806, May & Oct. 1807, May 1808, May &		
Oct. 1810	2	1553-4
Abraham, m. Hannah **BALDWIN,** May 26, 1763, by Rev. Judah		
Champion	1	126
Abraham, s. Abraham & Hannah, b. Feb. 21, 1767	1	126
Abraham, representative Oct. 1775, May 1776, Oct. 1783, May 1785	2	1550-1
Alfred, m. Clarrissa J. **BRISCO,** Dec. 30, 1827, by E. B. Kellogg	2	273
Amanda, m. Erastus **BANCROFT,** Sept. 21, 1820, at Wolcottville, by		
Rev. Isaac Jones	2	100
Amy, Mrs. of Bantam, ae 37, m. Isaac **MASON,** of South Britain, ae 25,		
Dec. 26, 1853, by Rev. Daniel E. Brown, of Bantam. Witnesses		
Marcelus Judd, of Litchfield, H. M. Pratt, of Bantam	TM49	97
Anna, m. Levi **KILBORN,** Nov. 27, 1794	2	65
Ariel, m. Polly Matilda **SHERMAN,** Jan. 26, 1809, by Rev. Judah		
Champion	2	42
Aseneth, m. Seth **FARNUM, Jr.,** Nov. 25, 1802, by Rev. Dan		
Huntington	2	62
Augustus B., m. Julia Ann **CLEMONS,** May 22, 1832, by Fred		
Holcomb	2	290
Betsey, m. Edward **WILLIAMS,** Nov. 26, 1820, by James Birge, J.P.	2	101
Catharine Elizabeth, d. Isaac & Catharine, b. July 23, 1815	2	90
Chester Porter, s. Isaac & Catharine, b. May 19, 1806	2	90
Clarissa, d. Joseph & Lucy, b. Nov. 27, 1807	2	68
Comfort, m. Sally **JOY,** Dec. 31, 1788, by Rev. Ashbel Baldwin	2	27
Comfort, m. Sally **JOY,** Dec. 31, 1788, by Rev. Ashbel Baldwin	2	261
Comfort, s. Leaming & Anna, b. [ ]	2	68
Cornelia, d. Joseph & Lucy, b. Sept. 11, 1805	2	68
Dan Augustus, s. Horace & Hannah, b. Oct. 20, 1812	2	68
Daniel, m. Sophronia **LANDON,** Aug. 12, 1832, by Rev. David E.		
Tomlinson, of Bradleyville	2	291
Dinnis, m. Mabel **ROOT,** [ ], 1796, by Rev. Noah Benedict	2	94
Electa, d. Thomas & Martha, b. Jan. 20, 1742/3	1	129
Elihu, m. Ruth **HOSFORD,** Mar. 5, 1805, by Rev. Dan Huntington	2	70
Elihu, m. Anna **CATLIN,** Oct. 28, 1816, by Rev. Lyman Beecher	2	70
Elizabeth, m. Augustus F. **HULL,** Apr. 14, 1816, by Rev. Joseph E.		
Camp	2	44
Elizabeth S., d. Dinnis & Mabel, b. Jan. 19, 1802, in Woodbury	2	94
Emeline, m. William E. **RUSSELL,** b. of Torrington, May 24, 1827, by		
Rev. John J. Stone	2	270
Erastus, s. Phenias & Martha, b. Apr. 18, 1741	1	129
Erastus, s. Erastus & Lydia, b. July 30, 1777	1	168
Erastus, s. Comfort & Sally, b. Apr. 26, 1790	2	27
Erastus, s. Comfort & Sally, b. Apr. 26, 1790	2	261
Fred Abernethy, s. Horace & Hannah, b. Oct. 10, 1810	2	68
George, m. Louisa Maria **GRISWOLD,** b. of Litchfield, Apr. 25, 1847,		
by Rev. Samuel Fuller	TM49	38
Hannah, m. Seth **BISHOP,** Nov. 2, 1757, by Rev. Amos Fowler	1	85
Hannah, d. Abraham & Hannah, b. Oct. 20, 1771	1	126

	Vol.	Page
BRADLEY, BRADLYE, (cont.),		
Hannah, m. James **WAUGH**, Oct. 10, 1786, by Rev. Mr. Damins, of		
Salisbury	1	207
Hannah, w. Horace, b. Oct. 1, 1792	2	68
Hannah, m. Samuel **DARE**, Sept. 15, 1799, by Rev. Dan Huntington	1	90-1
Harriet M., m. Albert **DUNBAR**, Jan. 13, 1850, by Rev. David L.		
Parmelee	TM49	44
Horace, s. Aaron & Lorrin, b. June 8, 1788	2	68
Horace, m. Hannah **HAWKINS**, Feb. 7, 1808	2	68
Isaac, m. Catharine Colson **MARCH**, [ ], 11, 1802, by Rev. Nathan		
Strong, of Hartford	2	90
Isaac Blakesley, s. Isaac & Catharine, b. May 26, 1810	2	90
John R., s. Dinnis & Mabel, b. Mar. 5, 1798, in Woodbury	2	94
John R., m. Julia Ann **ROBERTS**, Dec. 27, 1824, by Rev. Lyman		
Beecher	2	139
John R., m. Julia Ann **ROBERTS**, Dec. 27, 1823, by Rev. Lyman		
Beecher	2	278
John R., s. John R. & Julia Ann, b. June 18, 1827	2	278
Joseph, s. Leaming & Anna, b. Sept. 6, 1770	2	68
Joseph, m. Lucy **STODDARD**, May 24, 1798	2	68
Julia Angeline, d. Ariel & Polly M., b. May 3, 1812	2	42
Julia Angeline, d. John R. & Julia Ann [Roberts], b. Nov. 3, 1825	2	278
Julian, d. Horace & Hannah, b. Oct. 12, 1814	2	68
Leaming, b. June 11, 1737; m. Anna [ ], Nov. 15, 1759	2	68
Leaming, s. Aaron & Lorrin, b. Mar. 8, 1790	2	68
Leaming Hawkins, s. Horace & Hannah, b. Oct. 10, 1808	2	68
Lewis Bliss, s. Isaac & Catharine, b. June 29, 1804	2	90
Lois, d. Abraham & Hannah, b. Feb. 18, 1765	1	126
Lorenzo, m. Amy M. **GIBBS**, b. of Litchfield, June 19, 1831, by Rev.		
Mr. Taylor, of South Farms	2	289
Louisa, d. Joseph & Lucy, b. July 29, 1802	2	68
Louisa, m. Leonard **KENNY**, June 14, 1819, by Rev. Lyman Beecher	2	127
Lucy, w. Joseph, b. May 24, 1772	2	68
Lucy, m. Jacob **KILBORN**, Sept. 12, 1789, by Rev. A. Baldwin	2	70
Mabel L., m. Benjamin **DART**, June 4, 1854, by Rev. David L.		
Parmelee	TM49	101
Maria T., m. William **COE**, b. of Litchfield, June 14, 1826, by Rev.		
C. S. Boardman, of Preston	2	265
Mariah Tallmadge, d. Aaron & Lorrin, b. Dec. 29, 1805	2	68
Marilla, d. Comfort & Sally, b. Mar. 3, 1792	2	27
Marilla, m. Elisha **HORTON**, Apr. [ ], 1825, by Rev. Lyman Beecher	2	140
Martha, d. Comfort & Sally, b. Mar. 3, 1792	2	261
Mary Abigail, d. Isaac & Catharine, b. July 20, 1808	2	90
Mary Ann, d. Aaron & Lorrin, b. Mar. 19, 1795	2	68
Mary Ann, m. Henry **WADSWORTH**, Mar. 19, 1811, by Rev. Truman		
Marsh	2	69
Mary Ann, m. Curtiss **HULL**, Jan. 5, 1840, by Rev. Thomas Ellis	2	320
Matilda Ann, d. Ariel & Polly M., b. Feb. 5, 1816	2	42
Olive, m. Lewis K. **CHURCHILL**, b. of Litchfield, Apr. 20, 1829, by		
Rev. Henry Robinson, of South Farms	2	280
Olive M., d. Dinnis & Mabel, b. Aug. 15, 1804, in Southbury	2	94
Phenias, m. Martha **SHERMAN**, Apr. 24, 1740, by Rev. Joseph Noyce,		
of New Haven	1	129

	Vol.	Page
BRADLEY, BRADLYE, (cont.),		
Phineas, s. Phineas & Martha, b. May 17, 1745	1	129
Phineas, s. Abraham & Hannah, b. July 17, 1769	1	126
Rhoda, m. Timothy **HAND**, Nov. 24, 1768, by Rev. Joseph Bellamy, of Bethlem	1	99
Ruth, w. Elihu, d. June 2, 1816	2	70
Ruth Ann, d. Elihu & Anna, b. Oct. 9, 1817	2	70
Sally M., m. Wilmot N. **DAMES**, b. of Litchfield, Apr. 17, 1831, by Hugh P. Welch	2	290
Seyming, m. Mary **SIMONS**, b. of Litchfield, Sept. 19, 1830, by Rev. Bradley Sillick	2	286
William C., s. Isaac & Catharine, b. May 8, 1812	2	90
Zina, s. Phineas & Martha, b. Dec. 23, 1747	1	129
BRAINARD, Gilbert, of Bristol, m. Almira **GOODWIN**, of Litchfield, Oct. 16, 1837, by Rev. David G. Tomlinson, of Bradleyville	2	314
BRAMAN, BRAMIN, BRAYMAN, Caroline M., m. Chauncey M. **HOOKER**, Sept. 30, 1850, by Benjamin L. Swan	TM49	55
Catharine, m. Chester **GOSLEE**, [ ], 1820, by Lyman Beecher	2	98
Frederick J., m. Lois L. **WOOD**, b. of Litchfield, Oct. 11, 1849, by Rev. William B. Hoyt	TM49	43
Samuel G., m. Mary **PALMS**, b. of Litchfield, Oct. 15, 1827, by Rev. John S. Stone	2	272
BRAMHALL, Edmond, of New York, m. Easther **LORD**, of Litchfield, Sept. 6, 1842, by G. C. V. Eastman	2	411
BRAYMAN, [see under **BRAMAN**]		
BRICKLEY, Emeline F., of Briston, m. Herman C. **HINE**, of Washington, Sept. 13, 1842, by Rev. David L. Parmelee	2	410
BRISBANE, Maria Hale, m. Frederick D. **BEEMAN**, b. of Litchfield, July 15, 1851, by Rev. Benjamin W. Stone	TM49	63
Mary Susan, m. Gideon Hiram **HOLLISTER**, b. of Litchfield, June 3, 1847, by Rev. Samuel Fuller	TM49	38
BRISCO, Clarrissa J., m. Alfred **BRADLEY**, Dec. 30, 1827, by E. B. Kellogg	2	273
BRISTOL, BRISTOLL, Alva M., m. Mary A. **JUDD**, Dec. 31, 1846, by Rev. David L. Parmelee	TM49	16
Esther, m. Franklin **NEWELL**, Mar. 18, 1846, by Rev. David L. Parmelee	TM49	14
Eunice, d. Levi & Martha, b. Apr. 20, 1794	1	212
Henry, s. Levi & Martha, b. July 13, 1792	1	212
Isaac, m. Julia Ann **WAUGH**, June 12, 1848, by Rev. David L. Parmelee	TM49	22
Loley, of Cornwall, m. Punderson **MANSFIELD**, of Plymouth, May 6, 1846, by John F. Norton	TM49	14
Martha, m. John M. **DOWNS**, Sept. 7, 1834, by Rev. Joseph E. Camp	2	297
Reuben, s. Levi & Martha, b. July 12, 1803	1	212
Sally C., of Torrington, m. Arvi **DAYTON**, of Wolcottville, Jan. 7, 1840, by Jonathan Brace	2	318
BRONSON, BRUNSON, Charles Phinehas*, s. [Silas N. & Almira E.], b. June 13, 1849 *(Note says, "the above name is wrong, should be Phinehas Miner **BRONSON**")	TM49	18
Laura E., d. [Silas N. & Almira E.], b. Apr. 18, 1852	TM49	18
Lydia, m. Ezekiel **BUCK**, Dec. 15, 1724, by Rev. Daniel Bordman, of New Milford	1	5

	Vol.	Page
BRONSON, BRUNSON, (cont.),		
Phinehas Miner, see Charles Phinehas **BRONSON**	TM49	18
Sarah Almira, d. Silas N. & Almira E., Feb. 7, 1846	TM49	18
Sena, m. David **WETTMORE**, May 5, 1805	2	286
William Henry, [s. Silas N. & Almira E.], b. Apr. 13, 1848	TM49	18
William Hooker, [s. Silas N. & Almira E.], b. July 27, 1855	TM49	18
BROOKER, BROOKEIR, Betsey A., m. Benjamin **BISSELL**, b. of		
Litchfield, Oct. 24, 1849, by Rev. S. T. Seelye	TM49	43
Chester, m. Huldah D. **SMITH**, Mar. 27, 1831, by I. Jones	2	288
John Chester, s. Samuel & Polly, b. Sept. 26, 1810	2	141
Martin, s. Samuel & Polly, b. Apr. 5, 1816	2	141
Mary, d. Samuel & Polly, b. July 16, 1807	2	141
Russell, s. Samuel & Polly, b. Dec. 29, 1802	2	141
Samuel, m. Polly **COOK**, Apr. 20, 1797, by Rev. Joshua Williams,		
of Harwinton	2	141
Samuel, s. Samuel & Polly, b. Apr. 13, 1813	2	141
Samuel, Jr., representative Apr. 1855	2	1558
Ursula, d. Samuel & Polly, b. Oct. 17, 1804	2	141
Ursula, m. Silah **FROST**, of Torrington, Aug. 21, 1823, by Rev.		
Epaphras Goodman, of Torrington	2	50
Warren, s. Samuel & Polly, b. July 27, 1799	2	141
Warren, m. Mary Ann **KEYES**, Apr [ ], 1825, by Rev. Lyman Beecher	2	140
BROOKS, George, of Harwinton, m. Clarissa M. **GRISWOLD**, of		
Southbury, Sept. 16, 1838, by Rev. Gad N. Smith	2	319
Hiram, m. Eliza **SUTLEFF**, Jan. 4, 1835, by Rev. Joseph E. Camp	2	297
BROWN, Abraham, of Hartford, Vt., m. Lucy Maria **HARRISON**, of		
Litchfield, Oct. 18, 1826, by Rev. Henry Robinson, of South Farms	2	101
Alanson, s. Richard & Sally, b. Mar. 10, 1824	2	89
Amanda E., d. Ira & Elizabeth, b. Feb. 18, 1812	2	39
Amanda Elizabeth, of Litchfield, m. Milton Andrews **PATMOR**, of		
Penn., June 23, 1836, by Rev. Samuel Fuller, Jr.	2	296
Anna, m. Oliver **EM[M]ONS**, Mar. 7, 1787, by James Morris	1	11
Annis H., d. Richard & Sally, b. Feb. 13, 1817	2	89
Calista, d. Richard & Sally, b. Jan. 12, 1814	2	89
Caroline, d. Richard & Sally, b. July 9, 1805	2	89
Caroline, of Litchfield, m. Alonzo **MOULBECBIER**, of Batavia, N.Y.,		
Apr. 25, 1830, by Rev. L. P. Hickok	2	285
Catharine, d. Ira & Catherine, b. Nov. 21, 1809	2	39
Catherine, w. Ira, d. Nov. 27, 1809	2	39
Daniel Ebenezer, Rev. of Painted (?) Post (?), N.Y., m. Harriet Jones		
LEWIS, of Litchfield, Oct. 12, [1834], by Rev. Samuel Fuller	TM49	37
Daniel Ebenezer, Rev. of Tamtece (?) Port (?), N.Y., m. Harriet Jane		
LEWIS, of Litchfield, Oct. 12, 1834, by Rev. Samuel Fuller	2	289
Elizabeth, d. Richard & Sally, b. Aug. 28, 1803	2	89
Elsay B., d. Richard & Sally, b. Apr. 26, 1807	2	89
George, m. Mary A. **SMITH**, b. of Litchfield, June 25, 1848, by [Joseph		
Henson]	TM49	27
Harriet, d. Richard & Sally, b. Nov. 9, 1811	2	89
Henry Shelton, s. Richard & Sally, b. May 17, 1819, in Bethlem	2	89
Ira, b. Mar. 24, 1778, in Goshen; m. Catherine **SMITH**, Sept. 30, 1807	2	39
Ira, m. Elizabeth **TOMKINS**, Nov. 27, 1810	2	39
Ira, s. Ira & Elizabeth, b. June 21, 1813	2	39
Julia Ann, d. Ira & Catherine, b. July 26, 1808	2	39

	Vol.	Page
BROWN, (cont.),		
Lydia, m. Ozias SANFORD, May 24, 1810, by Isaac Aliton	2	88
Richard, m. Sally PARMELEE, [ ], 1801, by David Whittlesey	2	89
Samuel, m. Sarah MOORE, Oct. 13, 1847, by Joseph Henson	TM49	23
Shelton J., m. Ann KIMBERLEY, Oct. 15, 1844, by Rev. David L. Parmelee	TM49	6
Shelton Perry, s. Richard & Sally, b. Aug. 18, 1821	2	89
Susan, of Litchfield, m. Darius TURRELL, of Winchester, May 25, 1829, by Rev. Henry Robinson of South Farms	2	281
Susan C., d. Richard & Sally, b. July 27, 1809	2	89
BRYAN, BRYON, [see also **BRYANT**], Henry, of Saugatuck, m. Dimeann BLACKMAN, May 13, 1822, by Datus Ensign, Elder	2	111
Ira, of Oxford, m. Mary HILLS, of Litchfield, Dec. 4, 1836, by Rev. Samuel Fuller, Jr.	2	296
BRYANT, [see also **BRYAN**], John S., of Sheffield, Mass., m. Phebe JACKSON, Nov. 29, 1821, by Rev. Isaac Jones	2	105
M., of South Farms, m. C. F. SMITH, of Woodbury, May 30, 1852, by Lewis Jessup, of Northfield	TM49	75
BUCK, Abisha, s. Ezekiel & Lydia, b. Nov. 10, 1725	1	5
Ezekiel, m. Lydia BRUNSON, Dec. 15, 1724, by Rev. Daniel Bordman, of New Milford	1	5
Ezekiel, d. Feb. 3, 1726/7	1	4
Joseph, s. Abishia & Esther, b. Feb. 4, 1754	1	85
Sarah, of New Milford, m. Thomas TREADWAY, of Litchfield, Oct. 8, 1735, by Roger Brownson, J.P.	1	39
BUCKLAND, William, of Bolton, m. Maria CLARK, of Litchfield, Jan. 10, 1839, by Rev. Gad N. Smith	2	319
BUCKLEY, [see also **BULKLEY**], David C., m. Mary Ann STODDARD, May 2, 1831, by Rev. William Lucas	2	287
Eunice, m. John WARD, May 21, 1833, by Rev. L. P. Hickok	2	288
Eunice Robins, d. Henry & Betsey, b. Aug. 12, 1814	2	15
Harry, m. Betsey DODD, July 14, 1812, by Rev. Abel Flint	2	15
Susanna Dodd, d. Henry & Betsey, b. Nov. 9, 1812	2	15
BUELL, BUEL, Abbe, [twin with Rachel], d. Jonathan & Abigail, b. Apr. 12, 1810	1	251
Abigail, d. Peter, Jr. & Abigail, b. May 3, 1770	1	43
Abraham, m. Sarah STONE, May 20, 1759, by Rev. Judah Champion	1	85
Alban, twin with Albert, s. Truman & Nancy, b. Oct. 20, 1814	2	11
Albert, twin with Alban, s. Truman & Nancy, b. Oct. 20, 1814	2	11
Albert Hallar, s. Solomon, Jr. & Mary, b. Apr. 16, 1779	1	169
Alexander McNeile, s. David & Rachal, b. July 7, 1782	1	169
Allen, m. Eliza Ann BEARDSLEE, Jan. 10, 1841, in Goshen	2	338
Almira, d. Obed & Honor, b. Feb. 11, 1803	2	52
Almira, of Litchfield, m. Vincent BELDEN, of Weathersfield, Feb. 27, 1843, by Jonathan Brace	2	337
Amelia, d. Norman & Marina, b. Feb. 24, 1818	2	127
Amelia, of Litchfield, m. Lyman BARBER, of Harwinton, Aug. 22, 1838, by Rev. Jonathan Brace	2	318
Andrew, s. Obed & Honor, b. Mar. 8, 1794	2	52
Andrew, m. Louisa CATLIN, Feb. 19, 1822, by Rev. Lyman Beecher	2	111
Angelina, d. Truman & Nancy, b. Nov. 2, 1817	2	11
Angeline, of Litchfield, m. Benjamin KNAPP, of Norfolk, Dec. 24, 1833, by I. Marsh	2	294

Vol.   Page

BUELL, BUEL, (cont.),
Ann, d. Dea. Peter & Avis, b. Apr. 24, 1750   1   86
Ann, d. Dea. Peter & Avis, d. Sept. 10, 1753   1   86
Ann, d. Arcalos & Mary, b. Mar. 27, 1759   1   85
Ann Eliza, twin with Eliza Ann, d. [Allen & Eliza Ann], b. Mar. 22,
1842   2   338
Anna, m. Reuben WEBSTER, June 2, 1781, by Rev. Judah Champion   1   204-5
Anne, d. Salmon & Margaret, b. Nov. 3, 1763   1   43
Anne, m. Stephen RUSSELL, Dec. 25, 1820, by Rev. Isaac Jones   2   98
Annis, d. Abraham & Sarah, b. Dec. 3, 1767   1   128
Arkelos, s. Peter & Avis, b. Apr. 14, 1737   1   87
Arcalos, m. Mary LANDON, May 3, 1758, by Rev. Judah Champion   1   85
Asahel, s. Abraham & Sarah, b. Dec. 18, 1761   1   128
Ashbel, s. Dea. Peter & Avis, b. Apr. 29, 1747; d. Sept. 6, 1753   1   86
Ashbel, s. Archelos & Mary, b. Jan. 10, 1765   1   169
Augustus C., m. Margaret Ann WARREN, Jan. 12, 1829, by Rev.
Joseph E. Camp, of Northfield   2   292
Avis, d. Peter & Avis, b. Jan. 26, 1744/5   1   86
Avis, w. Dea. Peter, d. Nov. 1, 1754   1   86
Avis, m. Thomas CATLIN, Dec. 25, 1763, by Rev. Judah Champion   1   88
Azubah, d. Ebenezer & Dorothy, b. Aug. 27, 1740   1   86
Azubah, m. John GARNSEY, Jr., Mar. 24, 1757, by Rev. Judah
Champion   1   139
Belinda, d. Obed & Honour, b. Dec. 13, 1789   1   213
Belinda, d. Obed & Honor, b. Dec. 13, 1789   2   52
Belinda, d. Obed & Honor, d. Sept. 25, 1791   1   212
Belinda, d. Obed & Honor, d. Sept. 19, 1791   2   52
Betsey, d. Ira & Sally, b. Sept. 30, 1822   2   125
Bordem*, s. Dea. Peter & Avis, b. Dec. 18, 1752   *("Dan" in
Woodruff's book)   1   86
Candace, d. Archelos & Mary, b. Dec. 12, 1772   1   169
Candice, d. Ashbel & Huldah, b. Apr. 2, 1791   1   213
Charles, s. Peter, Jr. & Abigail, b. Oct. 1, 1778   1   169
Charles, m. Susan BULL, Jan. 2, 1804, by Rev. Menzes Royner   2   61
Charles C., s. Cromwell & Sally, b. Apr. 15, 1806   2   56
Charles H., s. Obed & Honor, b. Nov. 28, 1809   2   52
Charles S., m. Eliza BARBER, b. of Litchfield, Apr. 23, 1828, by Rev.
John S. Stone   2   276
Charles Seymour, s. Charles & Susan, b. Feb. 12, 1805   2   61
Cloe, d. Ebenezer & Dorothy, b. Aug. 10, 1742   1   86
Chloe, d. Ebenezer & Dorothy, d. Oct. 21, 1742   1   86
Chloe, d. Ebenezer & Dorothy, b. Apr. 12, 1745   1   86
Cordelia M., m. Alva STONE, Nov. 1, 1840, by William Payne   2   331
Cromwell, s. Archelos & Mary, b. May 14, 1779   1   169
Cromwell, m. Sally CHASE, Jan. 17, 1805, by Rev. Truman Marsh   2   56
Cyrus E., s. Elisha L. & Julia, b. Jan. 14, 1819   2   95
Dan*, s. Dea. Peter & Avis, b. Dec. 18, 1752   *(Arnold copy has
"Bordem")   1   86
David, m. Mrs. Rachel McNEILE, Oct. 3, 1771, by Rev. Judah
Champion   1   167
David, s. Archelos & Mary, b. Feb. 24, 1776   1   169
David, s. Salmon & Margaret, b. Sept. 17, 1781   1   43
David, m. Polly ROGERS, Mar. 22, 1800, by Rev. Dan Huntington   2   148

	Vol.	Page
BUELL, BUEL, (cont.),		
David, s. Truman & Nancy, b. Oct. 6, 1824	2	11
Deborah, m. Ebenezer **MARSH**, Nov. [ ], 1725, by Rev. Timothy Collins	1	25
Dorcas, d. Solomon & Eunice, b. July 14, 1742	1	86
Dorcas, d. Abraham & Sarah, b. Dec. 10, 1765	1	86
Dorcas, d. Solomon, Jr. & Mary, b. Feb. 13, 1777	1	167
Dorcas, m. James **BLAKE**, Apr. 1, 1793, by Rev. Judah Champion	2	74
Dorothy, d. Ebenezer & Dorothy, b. May 19, 1739	1	87
Dorothy, w. Ebenezer, d. June 24, 1767, ae 56 y. 5 m. 14 d.	1	4
Ebenezer, of Litchfield, m. Dorothy **GELLET**, of Hartford, Oct. 19, 1736, by Rev. Benjamin Colton	1	87
Ebenezer & Dorothy, had s. [ ], b. Apr. 13, 1745; d. same day	1	86
Ebenezer, s. Ebenezer & Dorothy, b. Mar. 26, 1747	1	86
Ebenezer, Jr., m. Hannah **PLUMBE**, Nov. 24, 1768	1	169
Ebenezer & Hannah, had s. [ ], b. Feb. 28, 1769; d. same day	1	169
Ebenezer, 2nd, s. Ebenezer, d. May 26, 1823, ae 76	1	86
Edward, s. Samuel & Minerva, b. May 26, 1824	2	119
Elias, s. Obed & Honor, b. Nov. 16, 1790	2	52
Elias, s. Obed & Honour, b. Nov. 16, 1790	1	213
Elisha L., s. Obed & Honor, b. Nov. 14, 1792	2	52
Elisha L., m. Julia **CATLIN**, Feb. 2, 1818, by Rev. Lyman Beecher	2	95
Eliza, b. June 9, 1809; m. Peleg **WHEELER**, Oct. 12, 1829	2	338
Eliza, of Litchfield, m. Peleg **WHEELER**, of Goshen, Oct. 12, 1829, by Rev. L. P. Hickok	2	282
Eliza Ann, twin with Ann Eliza, d. [Allen & Eliza Ann], b. Mar. 22, 1842	2	338
Eliza M., m. Arthur D. **CATLIN**, b. of Litchfield, Apr. 26, 1853, by Benjamin L. Swan	TM49	78
Elizabeth, m. Ezra **PLUMBE**, Mar. 29, 1739, by Rev. Timothy Collens	1	113
Elizabeth, d. Ebenezer & Hannah, b. June 7, 1770	1	169
Emeline, d. Cromwell & Sally, b. Sept. 10, 1812	2	56
Emeline, of Litchfield, m. David **TALLMADGE**, of Torringford, Nov. 28, 1833, by Rev. Aaron S. Hill	2	294
Enos, s. Abraham & Sarah, b. Mar. 11, 1772	1	126
Esther, d. Ebenezer & Esther, b. Feb. 1, 1772	1	167
Eunice, w. Capt. Solomon, d. Aug. 7, 1771, in the 51st y. of her age	1	4
Eunice, d. Salmon & Margaret, b. Aug. 8, 1771	1	43
Ezra, s. Abraham & Sarah, b. Sept. 18, 1769	1	128
Ezra, s. Truman & Nancy, b. Apr. 20, 1812	2	11
Fayette, s. Cromwell & Sally, b. Dec. 5, 1819	2	56
Ferdinand, s. Cromwell & Sally, b. Oct. 25, 1817	2	56
Ferdinand, m. Almeda Mariah **OSBORN**, b. of Litchfield, Feb. 14, 1843, by Rev. Jason Wells	2	337
Fred, Gen. representative Apr. 1840, Apr. 1841, Apr. 1854	2	1557-8
Frederick, m. Julia **BENTON**, Oct. 6, 1819, by Rev. Isaac Jones	2	22
George, s. Truman & Nancy, b. Oct. 10, 1809	2	11
George Decanter, s. Charles & Susan, b. Sept. 6, 1814	2	61
George Marsh, s. Salmon, Jr. & Lydia, b. Aug. 2, 1794	2	47
George Seymour, s. Jonathan & Abigail, b. Dec. 5, 1804	1	251
Hannah, m. Joseph **WALLER**, Dec. 8, 1726, by Rev. Timothy Collens	1	41
Hannah, d. Ebenezer & Dorothy, b. July 19, 1743	1	86
Hannah, m. Ebenezer **SMITH**, Sept. 9, 1762, by Rev. Judah Champion	1	139

	Vol.	Page
BUELL, BUEL, (cont.),		
Han[nah], m. Ebenezer **SMITH**, Sept. 9, 1762	1	157-8
Hannah, w. Ebenezer, 2nd, d. Sept. 6, 1835, ae 86 y.	1	86
Henry, s. Samuel & Minerva, b. Apr. 7, 1820	2	119
Honor, d. Obed & Honor, b. June 17, 1801	2	52
Huldah, d. Abraham & Sarah, b. Feb. 10, 1764	1	128
Hyman, s. Cromwell & Sally, b. Nov. 15, 1809	2	56
Ira, s. Solomon & Eunice, b. Feb. 20, 1744/5	1	86
Ira, m. Prudence **DEMING**, Jan. 27, 1767, by Rev. Stephen Johnson,		
of Lyme	1	86
Ira, m. Sally **NORTH**, Oct. 1, 1809, by Rev. Truman Marsh	2	125
J., of Litchfield, m. Elijah E. **ABBOTT**, of Southbury, Apr. 9, 1848, by		
Joseph Henson	TM49	24
James, s. Salmon & Margaret, b. June 16, 1784	1	43
James Harry, s. Ira & Sally, b. Aug. 3, 1820	2	125
Jane, d. Jonathan & Abigail, b. June 5, 1812	1	251
Jane, m. James H. **COOK**, Dec. 9, 1835, by Rev. L. P. Hickok	2	296
John, s. Ebenezer & Dorothy, b. June 25, 1737	1	87
John, s. Ebenezer & Dorothy, d. Nov. 6, 1737	1	86
John, Capt. representative Oct. 1740, May 1741	2	1545
John, s. Ebenezer & Dorothy, b. Oct. 11, 1751	1	86
John, s. Salmon & Margaret, b. Sept. 10, 1777	1	43
John, s. Ebenezer, the Elder, d. June 12, 1824, ae 73	1	86
John B. B., s. David & Polly, b. Sept. 28, 1801	2	148
John W., s. Samuel & Ann, d. Feb. 20, 1818	2	135
John W., s. Samuel & Ann, b. May 13, 1821	2	135
John Wellington, s. Samuel & Ann, b. Jan. 14, 1816	2	135
Jonathan, s. Peter, Jr. & Abigail, b. May 8, 1776	1	167
Jonathan, m. Abigail **BUCH**, Feb. 7, 1802, by Rev. E. Judson, of		
Sheffield	1	251
Jonathan, representative Oct. 1815, May & Oct. 1816, May & Oct. 1817	2	1554-5
Jos. H., of Holley, N.Y., m. Sophia P. **CHURCHILL**, of Litchfield, Oct.		
20, 1839, by William Payne	2	328
Juliann, d. Ira & Sally, b. Feb. 3, 1816	2	125
Juia Ann, of Litchfield, m. Clark **NEWCOMB**, of Williamstown, Vt.,		
Apr. 22, 1833, by Rev. Samuel Fuller	TM49	37
Julia Ann, m. Clark **NEWCOMB**, Apr. 22, 1833, by Rev. Samuel		
Fuller	2	289
Katharine, d. Solomon, Jr. & Mary, b. Mar. 5, 1775	1	167
Katharine, d. Aug. 10, 1777, in the 3rd y. of her age	1	166
Katharine, d. Solomon, Jr. & Mary, b. Mar. 25, 1781	1	169
Levi Man*, s. Ashbel & Huldah, b. Apr. 22, 1794 *("Loveman" in		
Woodruff's)	1	213
Lowese, m. Supply **STRONG**, Jan. 16, 1722/3, by John Marsh, J.P.	1	37
Lois, d. Salmon & Margaret, b. Dec. 22, 1774	1	43
Lois Ann, d. Samuel, 2nd & Ann, b. Feb. 27, 1812	2	135
Loiza, d. Ira & Sally, b. Mar. 9, 1813	2	125
Lorain, d. Ebenezer & Hannah, b. Oct. 16, 1776	1	169
Lorania, d. Truman & Nancy, b. Sept. 26, 1805	2	11
Lorana, of Litchfield, m. Jonathan **MERVIN**, of Cornwall, Nov. 7,		
1822, by Rev. Joseph Harvey, of Goshen	2	115
Lucinda, m. Loyal A. **BARBER**, June 26, 1833, by Rev. L. P. Hickok	2	288
Lucius L., s. David & Polly, b. Nov. 30, 1810	2	148

	Vol.	Page
BUELL, BUEL, (cont.),		
Lucretia, d. Peter & Avis, b. Apr. 26, 1742	1	86
Lucretia, d. Norman & Marina, b. Apr. 25, 1814	2	127
Lydia, d. Samuel & Ann, b. Feb. 13, 1819	2	135
Lydia, d. Samuel & Ann, d. Jan. 22, 1820	2	135
Margret, d. Salmon & Margaret, b. July 9, 1769	1	43
Margaret, m. Claudiaus **WEBSTER**, Feb. 1, 1795, by Rev. Judah Champion	1	204-5
Maria, d. Jonathan & Abigail, b. Feb. 3, 1815	1	251
Maria C., m. William G. **TUTTLE**, Sept. 16, 1832, at Bradleyville, by Rev. D. E. Tomlinson	2	291
Maria L., d. Samuel & Minerva, b. June 15, 1831; d. Aug. 16, 1831	2	119
Marian, d. Jonathan & Abigail, b. Feb. 18, 1807	1	251
Marian C., d. Andrew & Louisa, b. Dec. 17, 1822	2	111
Mariana, d. William, 2nd & Lucretia, b. Apr. 8, 1818	2	126
Marina, b. Apr. 8, 1818; m. Royal A. **FORD**, Nov. 13, 1839, by Rev. Jonathan Brace	TM49	3
Marina, m. Royal A. **FORD**, Nov. 13, 1839, by Rev. Jonathan Brace	2	318
Mary, d. Ebenezer & Dorothy, b. June 16, 1738	1	87
Mary, d. Ebenezer & Dorothy, d. Nov. 12, 1738	1	86
Mary, d. Arcolos & Mary, b. Apr. 16, 1761	1	127
Mary, d. Truman & Nancy, b. Oct. 16, 1807	2	11
Mary, of Litchfield, m. Ransby **SCOVILL**, of Cornwall, Mar. 9, 1831, by Rev. L. P. Hickok	2	287
Mary Ann, m. Merret **HEMINGWAY**, of Watertown, Mar. 7, 1832, by Rev. L. P. Hickok	2	288
Mary Catharine, d. Ira & Sally, b. Oct. 10, 1810	2	125
Mary Hervey, d. David & Rachal, b. Aug. 11, 1778	1	169
Mary Jane, d. Samuel & Minerva, b. Dec. 11, 1827	2	119
Mary Jane, of Litchfield, m. Thomas Kimberley **BRACE**, of New York, Jan. 18, 1853, by Benjamin L. Swan	TM49	78
Mehetabel, m. Nathan **BASSETT**, Oct. 29, 1793, by Rev. Judah Champion	1	251
Mehitabel, m. Nathan **BASSETT**, Oct. 29, 1793, by Rev. Judah Champion	2	8
Melinda, d. Obed & Honor, b. Mar. 28, 1798	2	52
Melinda, d. Obed & Honor, d. Aug. 27, 1819	2	52
Malinda Louisa, d. Andrew & [Louisa], b. Nov. 30, 1829	2	111
Miles, s. Ebenezer, Jr. & Hannah, b. Aug. 28, 1772	1	169
Molly, d. Salmon & Margaret, b. Aug. 5, 1765	1	43
Norman, s. Archelos & Mary, b. Apr. 9, 1767	1	169
Norman, representative May 1806	2	1553
Norman, m. Marina **WEBSTER**, Dec. 28, 1812, by Rev. Lyman Beecher	2	127
Obed*, s. Ebenezer & Hannah, b. Apr. 25, 1769 *(A note reads "Error Obed was son of Dorothy")	1	85
Obed, m. Honour **MA[R]SH**, Dec. 25, 1788	1	213
Obed, m. Honor **MARSH**, Dec. 25, 1788	2	52
Obed A., s. Obed & Honor, b. Feb. 10, 1805	2	52
Olive, d. Archelos & Mary, b. Dec. 9, 1769	1	169
Olive, m. Reuben **CULVER**, Mar. 22, 1792, by Rev. Judah Champion	1	133
Peter, m. Avis **COLLINS**, Dec. 26, 1734, by Rev. Timothy Collens	1	87
Peter, s. Peter & Avis, b. Oct. 12, 1739	1	86

	Vol.	Page
BUELL, BUEL, (cont.),		
Peter, Capt. representative May 1755, May & Oct. 1756, May 1757	2	1547
Peter, Jr., m. Abigail **SEYMOUR**, Dec. 25, 1766, by Rev. Judah		
Thompson	1	43
Polly, w. David, d. June 6, 1824	2	148
Polly Teresa, d. Samuel, 2nd & Ann, b. Feb. 14, 1814	2	135
Rachel, m. Thomas **GRANT**, Dec. 6, 1738, by Capt. John Buell, J.P.	1	19
Rachel,d. Salmon & Margaret, b. Oct. 16, 1761	1	43
Rachal, d. Peter, Jr. & Abigail, b. May 17, 1773	1	43
Rachal, d. Peter, Jr. & Abigail, b. May 17, 1773	1	44
Rachel, m. Daniel **STAR**, Apr. 20, 1784, by Rev. Judah Champion	1	201
Rachel, [twin with Abbe], d. Jonathan & Abigail, b. Apr. 12, 1810	1	251
Rachel Bread (?), d. John & Mary, b. May 22, 1723	1	5
Rhoda, d. William, 2nd & Lucretia, b. July 11, 1822	2	126
Ruth, 2nd w. Ebenezer, d. Sept. 19, 1796, ae 67 y.	1	4
Sally, d. David & Rachal, b. Mar. 12, 1780	1	169
Sally, d. Ira & Sally, b. June 3, 1818	2	125
Salmon, s. Solomon & Eunis, b. Oct. 14, 1739	1	87
Salmon, s. Salmon & Margaret, b. June 9, 1767	1	43
Salmon, Jr., m. Lydia **MARSH**, [ ], 1793, by Rev. Judah		
Champion	2	47
Samuel, s. Peter, Jr. & Abigail, b. Sept. 27, 1782	1	169
Samuel, s. John & Lydia, b. Mar. 28, 1783	1	213
Samuel, 2nd, m. Ann **WADHAMS**, Jan. 30, 1811, by Rev. Joseph		
Harvey	2	135
Samuel, m. Minerva **WADHAM**, June 29, 1819, by Rev. Joseph		
Harvey, of Goshen	2	119
Sam[ue]l, Dr. representative Apr. 1838, Apr 1839	2	1557
Samuel Bush, s. Jonathan & Abigail, b. Jan. 26, 1803	1	251
Samuel D., s. [Samuel & Minerva], b. June 15, 1832	2	119
Sarah, d. Ebenezer & Dorothy, b. Mar. 11, 1749/50	1	86
Sarah, b. June 7, 1784; m. Stephen **DUNING**, Oct. 23, 1804	TM49	100
Sarah, m. Walter S. **FRANKLIN**, Sept. 25, 1821, by Rev. Joseph E.		
Camp	2	106
Sarah A., m. William L. **BURGESS**, b. of Litchfield, Oct. 8, 1849, by		
Benjamin L. Swan	TM49	43
Silas, s. Obed & Honor, b. June 25, 1795	2	52
Silas, s. Obed & Honor, d. Dec. 3, 1795	2	52
Solomon, m. Eunis **GRISWOLD**, Jan. 19, 1737/8, by Rev. Timothy		
Collens	1	87
Solomon, s. Solomon & Eunice, b. Jan. 7, 1754	1	87
Solomon, Capt., had negro Cato, b. May 7, 1784	1	214
Susan, d. Charles & Susan, b. Apr. 30, 1812	2	61
Truman, s. Ebenezer, Jr. & Hannah, b. Apr. 21, 1786	1	212
Truman, m. Nancy **HENMAN**, Aug. 14, 1805, by Rev. Asahel Hooker,		
of Goshen	2	11
Ursula Bull, d. Charles & Susan, b. July 16, 1809	2	61
Ward, s. Archelos & Mary, b. Nov. 1, 1782	1	213
Ward, s. Ashbel & Huldah, b. Sept. 4, 1788	1	213
William, s. Peter, Jr. & Abigail, b. Nov. 27, 1767	1	43
William, 2nd, m. Lucretia **WEBSTER**, Nov. 27, 1816, by Rev. Lyman		
Beecher	2	126
William E., s. Obed & Honor, b. Mar. 12, 1807	2	52

	Vol.	Page
BUELL, BUEL, (cont.),		
William Nelson, s. Charles & Susan, b. Mar. 6, 1807	2	61
William R., s. David & Polly, b. Aug. 10, 1806	2	148
William R., m. Dotha L. **STONE,** May 2, 1832, by Rev. L. P. Hikcok	2	288
BULKLEY, BULKELEY, [see also **BUCKLEY**], David Collins, m. Harriet Abigail **MILLER,** b. of Litchfield, Apr. 12, 1848, by Rev. Samuel Fuller	TM49	38
Edwin A., of New Haven, m. Mary A. **SANFORD,** of Litchfield, Feb. 5, 1850, by Rev. William B. Hoyt	TM49	53
Susan D., m. Abiather **CHADWICK,** b. of Litchfield, Nov. 19, 1840, by William Payne	2	332
BULL, Asa, m. Tamer **LITTLE,** June 17, 1773, by Rev. Judah Champion	1	167
Elizabeth, d. Asa & Tamar, b. Sept. 25, 1773	1	26
Elizabeth, d. Asa & Tamer, b. Sept. 25, 1773	1	169
Eunice, d. George & Ruth, b. May 25, 1787	1	166
George Macknish*, m. Ruth **COLLENS,** Apr. 11, 1771, by Rev. Judah Champion *("George McKnight BULL, m. Ruth CATLIN" in Woodruff's)	1	167
Hosea, s. George McNish* & Ruth, b. Dec. 24, 1771 *(McKNIGHT"?)	1	167
Huldah, d. George & Ruth, b. Mar. 16, 1780	1	166
Jabez L., of Buffalo, m. Sarah M. **BUTLER,** of Litchfield, Apr. 12, 1841, by William Payne	2	333
Ruth, w. George, d. Aug. 13, 1789, ae 39 y.	1	166
Senne*, d. Asa & Tamar, b. Nov. 13, 1774, *("Serina" in Woodruff's)	1	169
Susan, m. Charles **BUEL,** Jan. 2, 1804, by Rev. Menzes Royner	2	61
Susanna, d. George & Ruth, b. Apr. 7, 1778	1	166
Susanna, m. Uriah **TRACY,** May 1, 1782, by Rev. Judah Champion	1	203
William, s. George & Ruth, b. Mar. 20, 1784	1	166
BUMAN, Harriet, m. William **MOORE,** of Plymouth, Jan. 11, 1848, by Joseph Henson	TM49	23
BUMP, Philip, m. Mary **HORSFORD,** Feb. 4, 1722/3, by John Marsh, J.P.	1	5
Phillip, m. Mary **HORSFORD,** Feb. 4, 1722/3, by John Marsh, J.P.	1	31
BUNCE, Jonas, s. Jacob & Martha, b. May 18, 1740	1	87
BUNNELL, BUNNEL, Alva, m. Hannah **WHEELER,** May 2, 1823, by Rev. Isaac Jones	2	120
Dotha, of Litchfield, m. Joseph H. **TOOLEY,** of Mereden, Nov. 27, 1834, by Rev. David G. Tomlinson, of Milton	2	295
Elijah, m. Lucy **STONE,** May 28, 1826, by Rev. Truman Marsh	2	263
Emily, m. David **KINNEY,** Oct. 30, 1851, by Rev. David L. Parmalee	TM49	65
Ephraim K., m. Roena **GRISWOULD,** Dec. 31, 1823, by Rev. Josiah L. Dickinson	2	257
Ephraim R., m. Cornelia **STONE,** Mar. 6, 1828, by I. Jones	2	274
Matilda, b. July 14, 1817; m. Harry **STONE,** Feb. 13, 1842	TM49	15
Samuel, of Litchfield, m. Amanda **HULL,** of Waterbury, Oct. 12, 1840, by F. Chittenden, J.P.	2	330
BURCH, Lyman, m. Hannah **FRISBIE,** Jan. 13, 1822, by James Birge, J.P.	2	108
Mercey, m. James C. **NEWCOMB,** July 4, 1819, by Rev. Isaac Jones	2	146
BURGE, [see under **BIRGE**]		
BURGESS, BURGISS, BURGEES, Abby, of Litchfield, m. Albert S. **COHAN,** of Woodbury, Jan. 1, 1840, by Richard Woodruff	2	318
Ebenezer, m. Olive **SMEDLEY,** Mar. 20, 1804, by Rev. Amos Chase	2	54
Ezra, m. Rosanna **SMITH,** Sept. 8, 1771, by Increase Moseley, J.P.	1	84
Ezra, m. Nabby **HOWE,** Feb. 11, 1798, by James Morris	2	38

	Vol.	Page
BURGESS, BURGISS, BURGEES, (cont.),		
Fanny, d. Ezra & Nabby, b. July 26, 1803	2	38
Fanny, of Litchfield, m. Grandison LOOMIS, of Torrington, Nov. 7,		
1827, by Morris Woodruff, J.P.	2	273
Fanny, m. Grandison LOOMIS, Nov. 7, 1827, by Morris Woodruff,		
J.P.	2	326
Gideon S., s. Eben & Olive, b. Sept. 11, 1817	2	54
Henry, s. Ebben & Olive, b. Oct. 18, 1810	2	54
Junius, s. Ezra & Nabby, b. Aug. 19, 1801	2	38
Junius, m. Sally TREAT, Nov. 19, 1821, by Rev. John Langdon, of		
Bethlem	2	110
Lucy, d. Ebben & Olive, b. May 20, 1806	2	54
Lucy V., m. Elam LUDDINGTON, Jr., of Bristol, Oct. 26, 1831, by		
Enos Stoddard, J.P.	2	290
Mary, m. Benjamin THROOP, Nov. 16, 1775, by Increase Moseley,		
J.P.	1	121
Mary J., of Litchfield, m. William Bennett JUDD, of Watertown, Oct. 7,		
1851, by N. C. Lewis	TM49	65
Nabby, d. Ezra & Nabby, b. May 10, 1809	2	38
William L., m. Sarah A. BUEL, b. of Litchfield, Oct. 8, 1849, by		
Benjamin L. Swan	TM49	43
William Lewis, s. Junius & Sally, b. Jan. 26, 1823	2	110
BURLEY, Clarissa, of Derby, m. John P. FRANCIS, of Lisbon, May 6,		
1828, by I. Jones	2	276
BURNHAM, Eliza, m. David STAMFORD, Dec. 12, 1812, by Rev. Isaac		
Jones	2	117
BURR, Sally, m. Tapping REEVE, June 24, 1773, by Rev. Mr. Hubbard, of		
Farifield	1	117
BURRUS, Hannah, of Windsor, m. Josiah STONE, Jr., Sept. 14, 1738, by		
Rev. Timothy Collens	1	77
BURTON, Ephraim, m. Mary ORTON, July 10, 1788	1	213
BUSH, Abigail, m. Jonathan BUEL, Feb. 7, 1802, by Rev. E. Judson, of		
Sheffield	1	251
BUSHNELL, Aaron, s. Elijah & Eunice, b. Nov. 12, 1774	1	167
Zerviah, d. Elijah & Eunice, b. Dec. 12, 1772	1	167
BUTLER, Charles, m. Mary THOMSON, May 9, 1790, by Rev. Stephen		
Stebbins	1	249
Harriet, d. Charles & Mary, b. July 27, 1799	1	249
Lucy, m. Benjamin AMES, June [ ], 1825, by Rev. J. E. Camp	2	265
Maria, d. Charles & Mary, b. Sept. 8, 1791	1	249
Martha, m. Isaac HART, Mar. 19, 1812, in Harwinton, by Rev. Joseph		
E. Camp	2	249
Mary, d. Charles & Mary, b. June 3, 1797	1	249
Mary W., m. Henry E. LORD, May 8, 1836, by Rev. L. P. Hickok	2	296
Mindwell, m. William BALDWIN, [ ], by Rev. Ashbel		
Baldwin	2	38
Nancy, d. Charles & Mary, b. Aug. 9, 1793	1	249
Robert C., of Rockport, Pa., m. Louisa A. CLEMONS, of Litchfield,		
Dec. 28, 1854, by Rev. H. N. Weed	TM49	105
Sarah*, m. Reeve PECK, Jr., Apr. 14, 1774 *(Arnold Copy has		
"Sarah BUTTES" m. Apr. "17")	1	155
Sarah M., of Litchfield, m. Jabez L. BULL, of Buffalo, Apr. 12, 1841,		
by William Payne	2	333

	Vol.	Page
BUTLER, (cont.),		
Silas G., b. [ ], in New York City; d. Mar. 25, 1864, at the		
Mansion House, Hick St., Brooklyn, N.Y. ae 34	TM49	105
William, s. Charles & Mary, b. June 18, 1795	1	249
BUTTES*, Sarah, m. Reeve **PECK, Jr.**, Apr. 17*, 1774 *("BUTLER" in		
Woodruff's) *("14" in Woodruff's)	1	155
BUTTHERST, Carl Gustav, m. Roxanna M. **ADDIS**, b. of Litchfield, May 3,		
1853, by Rev. Benjamin L. Swan	TM49	93
BUTTON, Caroline N., m. Julius **SCOVILLE**, Sept. 17, 1845, by Rev. Jno		
Morrison Ried, of Wolcottville	TM49	11
Minerva W., m. Virgil **WILSON**, of Harwinton, Apr. 19, 1848, by Rev.		
S. T. Seeley	TM49	24
CABLE, CABLES, Daniel S., of Plymouth, m. Maria G. **CANFIELD**, of		
Litchfield, Apr. 21, 1835, by R. S. Crampton	2	298
Emily, m. Henry **BALDWIN**, May 2, 1852, by Rev. David L. Parmelee	TM49	74
Esther, m. John A. **MERRIMAN**, Jan. 25, 1821, by Moses Woodruff,		
J.P.	2	98
Hannah, m. Henry **BALDWIN**, July 1, 1827	2	127
Hannah, m. Henry **BALDWIN**, b. of Litchfield, July 1, 1827, by Rev.		
John S. Stone	2	271
James, m. Lucy **MALLORY**, July 4, 1833, by Rev. Joseph E. Camp, of		
Northfield	2	292
James T., m. Louisa **PERKINS**, b. of Litchfield, Apr. 1, 1838, by Enos		
Stoddard, J.P.	2	317
Mary, m. George **MERRIMAN**, b. of Litchfield, Nov. 30, 1820, by,		
Morris Woodruff, J.P.	2	97
Sally, m. Charles **STEEL**, Jan. 15, 1822, by Morris Woodruff, J.P.	2	109
CADY, Alexander, m. Maria **WARD**, Aug. 28, 1849, by Rev. David L.		
Parmelee	TM49	42
Cyrel, of Torringford, m. Cordelia E. **FISHER**, of Litchfield, May 12,		
1839, by William Payne	2	328
CAHILL, Ellen, m. W[illia]m **KEAVELY**, b. of South Cornwall, Aug. 20,		
1854, by Rev. Thomas Hendriken	TM49	85
CALHOUN, Frederick F., of Cornwall, m. Mary S. **MARSH**, of Litchfield,		
Sept. 11, 1844, by Rev. David L. Parmelee	TM49	5
CALKINS, Edmund, of Torrington, m. Polly Ann **AARD**, of Litchfield, Aug.		
24, 1828, by Rev. Hart Tallcott	2	277
CAMP, A. P. P., m. Caroline **CARRINGTON**, b. of Litchfield, Jan. 27,		
1840, by Willliam Payne	2	328
Abel, m. Sabra **MARSH**, Jan. 9, 1769, by Rev. Judah Champion	1	46
Abel, m. Sabra **MARSH**, Jan. 9, 1769, by Rev. Judah Champion	2	48
Abel, s. Abel & Sabra, b. Dec. 28, 1787	2	48
Abel, Jr., m. Deziah **PEASE**, Feb. 22, 1808, by Nathaniel Stepens	2	47
Abel, m. Milecent **PORTER**, May 29, 1808	2	48
Albert Barlow, s. Joseph E. & Rhoda, b. Feb. 16, 1797	2	264
Ann Eliza, m. Robert **SIMESON**, b. of Litchfield, Oct. 16, 1851, by		
Rev. Benjamin L. Swan	TM49	66
Augustus Pearse Pettebone, s. Abel, Jr. & Desire, b. Mar. 31, 1818	2	47
Charlotte, m. John **REA**, Dec. 19, 1816, by Rev. Amos Pettingill	2	81
David Beechwood Washington, s. Joseph E. & Rhoda, b. Feb. 9, 1804	2	264
Deziah, m. Augustus **PHELPS**, Nov. 22, 1848, by Rev. David L.		
Parmelee	TM49	39
Elizabeth, m. Rev. Erastus **COLES**, of Hunter, N.Y., Sept. 28, 1823,		

	Vol.	Page
CAMP, (cont.),		
by Rev. Henry Robinson	2	126
Elizabeth Selenda, d. Joseph E. & Rhoda, b. Mar. 3, 1807	2	264
Eunice, d. Abel & Sarah*, b. Jan. 30, 1775 *("Sabra")	1	171
Eunice, d. Abel & Sabra, b. Jan. 30, 1775	2	48
Eunice, m. Hezekiah MURRY, May 29, 1796, by Rev. Amos Chase	2	85
Harriet M., of Litchfield, m. Richard TIBBALS, of Norfolk, Mar. 6, 1837, by B. Y. Messenger, V.D.M.	2	313
Harriet Maria, d. Abel, Jr. & Deziah, b. Apr. 15, 1811	2	47
Harvey, Rev. of Sandusky City, O., m. Harriet A. GREGORY, of New York, Mar. 6, 1850, by Rev. William B. Hoyt	TM49	53
Jabez McCall, s. Joseph E. & Rhoda, b. June 26, 1811	2	264
John, s. Abel & Sarah*, b. Mar. 19, 1773 *("Sabra")	1	171
John, s. Abel & Sabra, b. Mar. 19, 1773	2	48
John Pierpoint, s. Joseph E. & Rhoda, b. June 15, [25], 1801; d. Dec. 3, 1817	2	264
Joseph E., Rev., m. Rhoda TURNER, Dec. 3, 1795, by Rev. Judah Champion	2	264
Joseph William, s. Joseph E. & Rhoda, b. Mar. 12, 1809	2	264
Lydia, d. Abel & Sarah, b. June 9, 1780	1	171
Lydia, d. Abel & Sabra, b. June 9, 1780	2	48
Phineas, s. Abel & Sarah, b. Jan. 11, 1777	1	171
Phinehas, s. Abel & Sabra, b. Jan. 11, 1777	2	48
Phinehas, s. Abel & Sabra, d. Nov. 18, 1794	2	48
Phinehas W., m. Louisa B. McNEILE, Mar. 18, 1835, by Rev. L. P. Hickok	2	296
Phinehas William, s. Abel, Jr. & Deziah, b. June 9, 1809	2	47
Ralph Garwood, s. Joseph E. & Rhoda, b. June 14, 1799	2	264
Rebecca, d. Abel & Sabra, b. Mar. 24, 1769	1	46
Rebecca, d. Abel & Sabra, b. May 24, 1769	1	171
Rebecca, d. Abel & Sabra, b. May 29, 1769	2	48
Sabra, d. Abel & Sabra, b. June 6, 1771	2	48
Sabra, d. Abel & Sabra, b. June 6, 1771	1	171
Sabra, w. Abel, d. May 19, 1807	2	48
Sarah, m. David GIBBS, Mar. 12, 1770, by Rev. Judah Champion	1	18
Sarah*, d. Abel, b. June 6, 1771; m. Isaac ENSIGN, s. Samuel, June 5, 1790 *(Probably "Sabra")	2	95
Sarah, m. Samuel STODDARD, Apr. 13, 1815, by Rev. Roger Searl	2	93
Susan, d. Abel & Sabra, b. May 8, 1782	2	48
CANDACE, David Merritt, m. Helen Almeda WOODIN, b. of Litchfield, Jan. 3, 1854, by Rev. Benjamin L. Swan	TM49	101
CANDEE, Polly, m. Phinehas LORD, Dec. 25, 1797, by Rev. Mr. Williams	2	65
CANFIELD, Annis, m. Andrew ADAMS, Jr., Apr. 25, 1785	1	166
Annis, m. Andrew ADAMS, Jr., Apr. 26, 1785, by Rev. Cotton Mather Smith, of Sharon	1	210-11
Caroline A., m. William P. KILBORN, Apr. 26, 1832, by Rev. Mr. Taylor, of South Farms	2	289
James, of Litchfield, m. Mary J. WILLIAMS, of Bethlem, Apr. 21, 1835, by R. S. Crampton, V.D.M.	2	298
Maria G., of Litchfield, m. Daniel S. CABLES, of Plymouth, Apr. 21, 1835, by R. S. Crampton	2	298
CARISH*, Jabez M., m. Mary HEATON, Apr. 17, 1833, by Rev. Joseph E. Camp, of Northfield *("PARISH"?)	2	292

	Vol.	Page

CARPENTER, Enos, of Litchfield, m. Jane WYANT, of New Milford, Aug.
23, 1852, by Rev. Lewis Gunn — TM49 — 77
William F., m. Ruth Ann JUDSON, b. of Litchfield, Sept. 30, 1844, by
Rev. Silas Hall — TM49 — 5
CARRIER, John, of Canton, m. Annah MATHEWS, of Bristol, July 21,
1830, by Rev. L. P. Hickok — 2 — 285
CARRINGTON, Caroline, m. A. P. P. Camp, b. of Litchfield, Jan. 27, 1840,
by William Payne — 2 — 328
Caroline Amelia, d. Jonathan & Nabby, b. Oct. 5, 1820 — 2 — 32
Chester, s. Jonathan & Nabby, b. Apr. 14, 1811 — 2 — 32
Clark, m. Ruth HART, Nov. 26, 1805, at Bristol, by Rev. Giles Cowles — 2 — 254
Cyrus, s. Jonathan & Nabby, b. Oct. 23, 1808 — 2 — 32
Dornelia M., d. Clark & Ruth, b. Dec. 10, 1806, in Bristol — 2 — 254
Edwin Andrew, s. Jonathan & Nabby, b. June 5, 1813 — 2 — 32
Elizabeth Ann, d. Leonard [& Ann], b. Oct. 4, 1846 — TM49 — 40
Emeline Maria, d. Jonathan & Nabby, b. Aug. 21, 1815 — 2 — 32
Emeline Maria, m. Benjamin Hart MORSE, b. of Litchfield, Apr. 20,
1836, by Rev. Samuel Fuller, Jr. — 2 — 296
Freeman Dodd, s. Leonard [& Ann], b. Sept. 9, 1848 — TM49 — 40
George Dodd, s. Leonard & Ann, b. Aug. 10, 1842 — TM49 — 40
John Hart, s. Clark & Ruth, b. Jan. 22, 1823 — 2 — 254
Jonathan, m. Nabby McNEILE, Sept. 29, 1807, by [   ] — 2 — 32
Jonathan, m. Mrs. Cynthia TURNER, b. of Litchfield, Apr. 18, 1838,
by G. C. V. Eastman — 2 — 317
Leonard, s. Jonathan & Nabby, b. Apr. 27, 1818 — 2 — 32
Leonard, m. Ann DODD, Jan. 26, 1841, in Hartford, by Rev. Mr. Moore — TM49 — 40
Leonard John, s. Leonard [& Ann], b. Nov. 30, 1844 — TM49 — 40
Loviza, d. Clark & Ruth, b. Apr. 28, 1810, in Bristol — 2 — 254
Maria, d. Clark & Ruth, b. May 23, 1808, in Bristol — 2 — 254
Martha, m. Ezekiel LEWIS, Oct. 14, 1804 — 2 — 49
Sabra, d. Clark & Ruth, b. Mar. 16, 1815, in Bristol — 2 — 254
Walter Kellogg, s. Cyrus & Milla Ann, b. Nov. 5, 1839 — 2 — 326
CARROLL, Ellenor, m. W[illia]m MURPHY, Sept. 24, 1854, by Thomas
H. Hendricken — TM49 — 100
CARTER, Ann*, m. Lucius TOMPKINS, b. of Litchfield, Aug. 5, 1827, by
Rev. John S. Stone *(Arnold Copy says "Betsy Ann CARTER
was name by which she was baptized") — 2 — 271
Betsey, m. Amos PALMALEE, Jr., Sept. 12, 1814, by [   ] — 2 — 135
Betsey Ann, b. June 5, 1807; m. Lucius TOMPKINS, Aug. 5, 1827 — TM49 — 3
Betsey Ann, m. Lucius TOMPKINS, b. of Litchfield, Aug. 5, 1827 — TM49 — 3
Betsey Ann, see Ann CARTER — 2 — 271
Charles, m. Elizabeth CLARK, June 11, 1844, by Rev. D. L. Marks — TM49 — 4
Charles, of Warren, m. Mary M. AVERY, of Cornwall, Dec. 17, 1848,
by John F. Norton — TM49 — 39
John, m. Mary Ann RIGGS, of Milton, June 16, 1831, by Rev. William
Lucas — 2 — 287
Lyman, m. Lucretia PARSONS, July 7, 1822, by Rev. Isaac Jones — 2 — 113
Mahitabel, m. Abel CLEMONS, Aug. 4, 1784, by James Morris — 2 — 147
CASE, Elias W., m. Emeline M. LUDDINGTON, Aug. 19, 1832, by Rev.
L. P. Hickok — 2 — 288
Mary, d. David & Sarah, b. Apr. 13, 1752 — 1 — 89
Sarah, had s. James Lee, b. Mar. 31, 1773 — 1 — 130
Sarah, had s. James Lee, b. Mar. 31, 1773 — 1 — 47

	Vol.	Page
CASKEY, Jane, m. Sheldon MUNGER, b. of Litchfield, July 8, 1849, by Samuel Fuller	TM49	42
CATCHPOLE, Cornelius Gibson, of Albany, N.Y., machinist, ae 31, m. Catharine FANNING, of Litchfield, ae 25, Feb. 19, 1854, by Rev. Daniel E. Brown. Witnesses, Fred Gibbs & Elijah M. Peck	TM49	97
CATLIN, CATLING, Abba, m. Asahel PECK, Jr., Feb. 18, 1816 by, Rev. Mr. Beecher	2	80
Abby, m. Lester N. SMITH, Apr. 26, 1826, by Rev. Henry Robinson	2	262
Abel, s. Thomas & Abigail, b. Feb. 25, 1746/7	1	89
Abel, s. Thomas & Avis, b. Mar. 16, 1770	1	88
Abel, m. Dorothy SEYMOUR, Nov. 20, 1776	1	132
Abel, 2nd, Dr., m. Mary PECK, Mar. 20, 1808, by Rev. Dan Huntington	2	33
Abigail, d. Thomas & Abigail, b. Nov. 5, 1744	1	47
Abigail, m. Michael DICKINSON, Feb. 3, 1765, by Rev. Judah Champion	1	9
Abigail, d. Isaac & Desire, b. July 19, 1767	1	6
Achsah, d. Levi & Anna E., b. Sept. 13, 1816	2	112
Alexander, s. John & Margret, b. Jan. 6, 1738/9	1	47
Ama, d. Samuel & Hepzibah, b. July 28, 1768	1	130
Ann, d. John & Margret, b. Oct. 12, 1743	1	47
Anna, d. Thomas, Jr. & Mary, b. Mar. 21, 1788	1	133
Anna, m. Elihu BRADLEY, Oct. 28, 1816, by Rev. Lyman Beecher	2	70
Anne, m. Jesse STODDARD, May [ ], 1791, by Rev. Ashbel Baldwin	1	201
Arthur D., m. Eliza M. BUELL, b. of Litchfield, Apr. 26, 1853, by Benjamin L. Swan	TM49	78
Arthur Darwin, s. [Cyrus & Anna Emeline], b. June 17, 1830	2	112
Ashbel, s. John & Margret, b. Sept. 10, 1745	1	47
Avis, d. Levi & Anna E., b. Feb. 8, 1809; d. Feb. 19, 1809	2	112
Avis, d. Levi & Anna E., b. Feb. 10, 1810	2	112
Avis, m. Levi HEATON, Jr., Dec. 10, 1832, by Rev. Joseph E. Camp, of Northfield	2	292
Bradley, s. Isaac & Desire, b. Oct. 12, 1758	1	6
Candace, m. Morris WOODRUFF, Nov. 21, 1804, by Rev. Joshua Williams	2	77
Caroline, d. Isaac & Desire, b. Apr. 1, 1760	1	6
Caroline, twin with Catharine, d. Robert & Sally, b. Jan. 28, 1810	2	6
Caroline, m. Moses MOSS, Feb. 18, 1818, by Rev. Elisha P. Jacobs	2	134
Caroline, m. Israel SMITH, Nov. 21, 1832, by Rev. L. P. Hickok	2	288
Catharine, twin with Caroline, d. Robert & Sally, b. Jan. 28, 1810	2	6
Catharine*, m. Sidney PECK, b. of Litchfield, Dec. 2, 1829, by Morris Woodruff, J. P. *(Perhaps "Catharine COLLIN"?)	2	283
Clara, m. Epaphras WADSWORTH, Mar. 23, 1780, by Rev. Judah Champion	1	165
Clarinda Maria, d. [Cyrus & Anna Emeline], b. June 17, 1825	2	112
Clarinda Maria, d. Cyrus & Emeline Ann, b. June 17, 1825	2	275
Cyrus, s. Thomas, Jr. & Mary, b. July 17, 1801	1	133
Cyrus, m. Emeline WETMORE, Sept. [ ], 1824, by Rev. Joseph E. Camp	2	265
Cyrus, m. Anna Emeline WETMORE, Sept. 14, 1824	2	112
Cyrus, m. Emeline Anna WETMORE, Sept. 14, 1824, by Rev. Joseph E. Camp	2	275
Dan, s. Levi & Anna E., b. Nov. 24, 1806	2	112

	Vol.	Page

CATLIN, CATLING, (cont.),

	Vol.	Page
Dan, representative Apr. 1844, Apr. 1845	2	1557
David, s. John & Margret, b. Apr. 21, 1747	1	47
Dennis, s. Abel & Dorothy, b. Mar. 16, 1777	1	132
Dianthe, d. David & Anne, b. June 15, 1782	2	21
Dianthe, m. Orange WEBSTER, June 17, 1801, by Rev. Judah		
Champion	2	21
Eleanora Seymour, d. [Cyrus & Anna Emeline], b. Apr. 12, 1834; d.		
May 3, 1837	2	112
Eli, s. John & Margret, b. Jan. 22, 1733/4	1	47
Eliza, d. Thomas, Jr. & Mary, b. Aug. 31, 1791	1	133
Elizabeth, d. Thomas & Abigail, b. May 1, 1733	1	47
Elizabeth, m. Eaton JONES, May 5, 1756, by Rev. Judah Champion	1	59
Elizabeth, d. Roger & Elizabeth, b. May 12, 1764	1	88
Ellen, d. [Cyrus & Anna Emeline], b. Apr. 16, 1838	2	112
Ellis, d. Levi & Anna E., b. Mar. 4, 1812	2	112
Emily, m. Birdsey GIBBS, b. of Litchfield, Sept. 11, 1829, by Rev.		
Harry Frink	2	281
Emma, d. [Cyrus & Anna Emeline], b. [ ]; d. Apr. 30, 1837	2	112
Frances Amanda, d. [Truman] M. [& Rhoda], b. Feb. 21, 1830	2	248
Guy, s. Levi & Anna E., b. Oct. 9, 1818	2	112
Guy, m. Julia Ann GARNSEY, b. of Northfield, May 23, 1843, by Rev.		
Albert B. Camp	2	339
Hannah, d. Isaac & Desire, b. Oct. 14, 1762	1	6
Heman, s. Uriah & Rebecka, b. Mar. 4, 1773	1	88
Henry, s. Robert & Sally, b. July 7, 1816	2	6
Horace, s. Uriah & Rebecca, b. Apr. 29, 1768	1	131
Horace, s. Uriah & Rebecca, b. Aug. 24, 1771	1	46
Israel, s. Theordore & Mary, b. Sept. 15, 1762	1	6
Jane, d. Pierce & Philana, b. Oct. 19, 1815; d. Mar. 17, 1816	2	24
John, m. Margaret SEYMORE, Aug. 25, 1731, by Nathaniell Stanley	1	7
John, s. John & Margaret, b. July 30, 1732	1	7
John, m. Sarah PARMELE, Jan. 8, 1769, by Cyrus Marsh, J.P.	1	130
John, s. Levi & Anna E., b. May 23, 1814	2	112
Julia, d. Thomas, Jr. & Mary, b. July 25, 1793	1	133
Julia, m. Elisah L. BUEL, Feb. 2, 1818, by Rev. Lyman Beecher	2	95
Lamira, d. Thomas, Jr. & Mary, b. Apr. 11, 1799	1	133
Lanura*, of Milton, m. Truman GUILD, of Warren, Feb. 21, 1830, in		
Milton, by Rev. I. Jones, of [ ] *("Lamira"?)	2	284
Levis, s. Thomas, b. Nov. 11, 1772; m. Anna Elizabeth LANDON,		
d. Seth, Aug. 31, 1803, by Rev. Truman Marsh	2	112
Levis, s. Thomas & Avis, b. Nov. 11, 1772	1	130
Levi, Jr., s. Levi & Anna E., b. Nov. 1, 1821	2	112
Luissa, m. Ithamar FERRIS, June 3, 1821, by Rev. Isaac Jones	2	103
Louisa, m. Andrew BUEL, Feb. 19, 1822, by Rev. Lyman Beecher	2	111
Lucina, d. Thomas & Abigail, b. Aug. 19, 1749	1	89
Lucina, d. Uriah & Rebecca, b. Jan. 12, 1777	1	88
Lucina, m. Seymour BEACH, Nov. 28, 1822, by Rev. Isaac Jones	2	116
Lucretia, m. James WOODRUFF, Nov. 17, 1812, by Rev. Joseph E.		
Camp	2	56
Margret, d. John & Margret, b. Nov. 4, 1741	1	47
Margaret, d. Theodore & Mary, b. Nov. 16, 1764	1	6
Marian, d. Samuel & Hephzibah, b. Aug. 21, 1789	1	130

	Vol.	Page
CATLIN, CATLING, (cont.),		
Marian, m. Hiram J. **HAND**, Feb. 20, 1814, by Rev. Isaac Jones	2	13
Mary, m. Girdon **GRANNISS**, Mar. 3, 1791	2	71
Mary Cordelia, d. [Cyrus & Anna Emeline], b. Sept. 8, 1828	2	112
Millecent, m. Jonathan **ROSSETTER**, Nov. 15, 1757, by Rev. Andrew Bartholomew, of Harwington	1	75
Nabbe, d. Samuel & Hepzibah, b. Apr. 30, 1771	1	130
Nabby, d. Robert & Sally, b. July 24, 1806	2	6
Olive, d. Uriah & Rebeckah, b. Nov. 20, 1774	1	88
Persis, d. Uriah & Rebecca, b. Aug. 19, 1789	1	133
Philana, w. Pierce, d. May 13, 1816	2	24
Phineas, s. [Theodore & Mary], b. Nov. 27, 1758; d. Jan. 7, 1759	1	6
Phineas, s. Theodore & Mary, b. Oct. 22, 1760	1	6
Pierce, m. Philana **LEE**, Nov. 27, 1814, by Rev. Truman Marsh	2	24
Polly, m. John **McNEILE**, Aug. 9, 1802, by Rev. Dan Huntington	2	130
Rachel, d. Samuel & Hephzibah, b. Nov. 6, 1775	1	130
Rachel, m. Amos **BENTON**, May 2, 1799, by Moses Seymour, J.P.	2	122
Rebecca, d. Uriah & Rebecca, b. Oct. 31, 1769	1	131
Rebecca, w. Uriah, d. Sept. 14, 1806, ae 61 y.	1	130
Richard, s. Samuel & Hepzibah, b. July 31, 1766	1	130
Robert, s. Samuel & Hepzibah, b. Mar. 29, 1773	1	46
Robert, m. Sally **MERIAM**, Nov. 9, 1800, by Rev. Truman Marsh	2	6
Roger, s. Thomas & Abigail, b. Apr. 19, 1742	1	47
Roger, m. Elizabeth **McNIELE**, Oct. 13, 1763, by Rev. Judah Champion	1	88
Roswell, s. John & Margaret, b. July 30, 1752	1	89
Ruth, m. George McKnight **BULL**, Apr. 11, 1771, by Rev. Judah Champion *(Arnold copy has "George MacKnish **BULL**, m. Ruth **COLLENS**")	1	167
Sabra, m. Samuel Wilkinson **BALDWIN**, Nov. 25, 1773, by Rev. Andrew Bartholomew, of Harwinton	1	167
Sally, d. Samuel & Hephzibah, b. Aug. [ ], 1783	1	130
Sally, m. Seth **LANDON, Jr.**, May 1, 1802	2	44
Samuel, s. Thomas & Abigail, b. Nov. 6, 1739	1	47
Samuel, s. Isaac & Desire, b. Dec. 6, 1764	1	6
Samuel, m. Hepzibah **MARSH**, Feb. 16, 1766, by Ebenezer Marsh, J.P.	1	130
Samuel, s. Robert & Sally, b. Feb. 1, 1804	2	6
Samuel, of Harwinton, m. Sally **SCOVIL**, Dec. 8, 1824, by Rev. George E. Dumas	2	34
Samuel, m. Lucy **WICKWIRE**, May 1, 1825, by Morris Woodruff	2	139
Sarah A., m. William **JACKSON**, Oct. 21, 1844, by Rev. David L. Parmelee	TM49	6
Seth, s. Levi & Anna E., b. Dec. 10, 1804	2	112
Seth, m. Caroline **GURNEY**, Dec. 21, 1825, by Rev. J. E. Camp	2	265
Theodor, s. John & Margret, b. Oct. 16, 1735	1	47
Theodore, m. Mary **GOODWIN**, Nov. 12, 1758, by Rev. Judah Champion	1	6
Thomas, m. Abigail **BISSELL**, May 8, 1732, by Rev. Timothy Colens	1	7
Thomas, s. Thomas & Abigail, b. June 18, 1737	1	47
Thomas, m. Avis **BUELL**, Dec. 25, 1763, by Rev. Judah Champion	1	88
Thomas, s. Thomas & Avis, b. Nov. 28, 1764	1	88
Thomas, s. Thomas & Avis, b. May 7, 1767	1	131
Thomas, Jr., m. Mary **COE**, Mar. 1, 1787	1	133

	Vol.	Page

CATLIN, CATLING, (cont.),
Truman, s. [Cyrus & Anna Emeline], b. Apr. 22, 1842   2   112
Truman M., m. Rhoda **POND**, Apr. 12, 1829, at Camden, Oneida Cty,
   N.Y.   2   248
Truman Merit, s. Thomas, Jr. & Mary, b. July 10, 1803   1   133
Uriah, s. Thomas & Abigail, b. June 15, 1735   1   47
Uriah, m. Rebecca **KILBORN**, Dec. 29, 1765, by Rev. Thomas Davies   1   88
CEASER, Minor Sherman, m. Eliza **JACKSON**, Mar. 27, 1834, by Rev.
   L. P. Hickok   2   288
CHADWICK, Abiather, m. Susan D. **BULKLEY,** b. of Litchfield, Nov. 19,
   1840, by William Payne   2   332
CHAMBERLAIN, Jemima, m. Amos **JOHNSON,** Oct. 16, 1762, by Jacob
   Woodruff, J.P.   1   59
Lidia, d. Moses & Jemima, b. Jan. 30, 1745/6   1   89
Remembrance, s. Moses & Jemima, b. Dec. 19, 1747   1   89
Sarah, m. Hubbel **WEST,** June 8, 1814, at Colebrook, by Rev. Rufus
   Babcock   2   149
Susanna, m. Aaron **SHEPARD,** Nov. 1, 1759, by Jacob Woodruff, J.P.   1   118
CHAMPION, Anna, m. John R. **LANDON,** Jan. 10, 1796, by Rev. Judah
   Champion   1   187
Dorothy, m. Julius **DEMING,** Aug. 7, 1781, by Rev. Robert Robbins,
   of Colchester   1   49
Dorothy, m. Julius **DEMING,** Aug. 7, 1781, by Rev. Mr. Robins   2   90
Elizabeth, d. Rev. Judah & Elizabeth, b. Sept. 1, 1759   1   131
Judah, Rev. of Litchfield, m. Mrs. Elizabeth **WELCH,** of New Milford,
   Jan. 4, 1758, by Rev. Nathaniel Taylor, of New Milford   1   131
CHAPIN, Henry B., of Sheffield, Mass., m. Margaret **PENDLETON,** of
   Litchfield, Jan. 26, 1848, by Joseph Henson   TM49   23
CHAPMAN, Deliverance, m. Stephen **STONE,** May 12, 1768, by Jacob
   Woodruff, J.P.   1   120
James D., m. Abby J. **SMITH,** b. of Litchfield, Aug. 24, 1828, by Rev.
   Henry Robinson, of South Farms   2   277
Phebe, m. Daniel **STEWARD,** Jan. 11, 1762, by Rev. Joseph Fowler, of
   East Haddam   1   159
[CHAPPELL], CHAPELL, CHAPEL, Deborah, of Lebanon, m. Joseph
   GILLET, of Litchfield, Nov. 9, 1732, by Rev. Jacob Eliot   1   97
Mary, m. John **BALDWIN,** b. of Litchfield, Jan. 31, 1828, by Rev.
   Ebenezer Washburn   2   274
Ruby, m. John **BISSELL,** Dec. 20, 1807   2   73
CHASE, CHACE, Amanda, m. Jones B. **GILBERT,** Aug. 10, 1834, by Rev.
   David G. Tomlinson, of Milton   2   295
Amos, Rev., m. Joanna **LANGMAN,** June 27, 1792, by Rev. Mr. King,
   of Norwich   1   215
Ann Maria, of Milton, m. Erwin **STONE,** of Bradleyville, Sept. 27,
   1843, by Ralph Smith   2   340
Charles, s. Lot & Rhoda, b. Aug. 30, 1785   2   40
Harriet, m. Moses **STODDARD,** Jan. 4, 1837, by Rev. A. Billings
   Beach   2   299
Hellen R., m. Edwin **STONE,** Sept. 30, 1846, by John F. Norton   TM49   15
Joanna, d. Amos & Joanna, b. June 29, 1796   1   215
Lot, m. Rhoda **PECK,** Apr. 3, 1783, by Rev. Judah Champion   2   40
Mary Ann, of Litchfield, m. Lemuel D. **MORSE,** of Harwinton, Oct. 10,
   1837, by Rev. Lewis Gunn   2   315
Philo, s. Lot & Rhoda, b. Apr. 30, 1791   2   40

	Vol.	Page
CHASE, CHACE, (cont.),		
Rebecca Hart, d. Rev. Amos & Joanna, b. Apr. 17, 1793	1	215
Sally, d. Lot & Rhoda, b. Dec. 27, 1783	2	40
Sally, m. Cromwell **BUEL**, Jan. 17, 1805, by Rev. Truman Marsh	2	56
Semantha, of Milton, m. George **HOLLISTER**, of Glastonbury, Dec.		
26, 1841, by Ralph Smith	2	336
CHENEY, Charlotte M., d. Silas E. & Polly, b. Apr. 24, 1809	2	12
Mary G., d. Silas E. & Polly, b. Oct. 20, 1811	2	12
Silas E., m. Polly **YOUNG**, May 18, 1807, by Rev. Mr. Barber	2	12
CHRISSEY, Abigail, m. Abel **HARRISON**, Mar. 26, 1756, by Increase		
Moseley, J.P.	1	17
CHURCH, Jerusha, m. William **CLARK**, June 27, 1771, by Rev. Judah		
Champion	1	130
Rodman, of Bethlem, m. Lydia **DEAN**, of Litchfield, Oct. 18, 1829, by		
Mr. Jones	2	282
CHURCHILL, Almira, d. William & Ketura, b. Dec. 3, 1800	2	3
Almira, d. William & Keturah, b. Dec. 3, 1806	2	7
Almira, m. Joseph **HINE**, Aug. 6, 1826, by Joseph E. Camp	2	266
Anna, d. John, Jr. & Ruamy, b. Aug. 28, 1809	2	11
Ashbel Wessells, s. William & Keturah, b. Jan. 28, 1823	2	7
Canfield, m. Esther **TURNER**, Apr. 14, 1834, by Rev. Joseph E. Camp	2	297
Charles, s. John, Jr. & Ruamy, b. Nov. 11, 1806	2	11
Chloe E., of Northfield, m. Henry **DAVIS**, of Wolcottville, Oct. 1, 1848,		
by Rev. J. L. Dickinson, of Northfield	TM49	26
Cloe Elizabeth, d. William & Keturah, b. Sept. 21, 1827	2	7
Daniel, s. Jonathan & Comfort, b. N[ov.] 14, 1798	1	133
Daniel Canfield, s. John, Jr. & Ruamy, b. Feb. 17, 1813	2	11
David Moore, s. William & Keturah, b. Sept. 26, 1804	2	7
David Moss, s. William & Ketura, b. Sept. 26, 1804	2	3
Edward, of Canojahary, m. Patty **MORSE**, of Litchfield, Oct. 31, 1822,		
by Rev. William Bentley	2	116
Emeline, d. Timothy & Dothy, b. July 11, 1823	2	125
Emily, d. William & Ketura, b. Apr. 22, 1813	2	3
Emela, d. William & Keturah, b. Apr. 22, 1813	2	7
Emily, m. Asaph **BLAKESLEE**, Feb. 8, 1835, by Rev. Joseph E. Camp	2	297
Eunice, d. William & Ketura, b. Dec. 27, 1808	2	3
Eunice, d. William & Keturah, b. Dec. 27, 1808	2	7
Ezra H., s. Hull & Huldah, b. May 1, 1818	2	144
Ezra H., m. Lurena E. **MORSE**, b. of Litchfield, May 11, 1845, by Joel		
L. Dickinson, of Northfield	TM49	10
George, s. Timothy & Dothy, b. Apr. 7, 1806	2	125
George, m. Mary A. **ADDIS**, [Dec.] 29, 1830, by Rev. William Lucas	2	286
Hannah, d. Hull & Huldah, b. Feb. 11, 1814	2	144
Hannah, of Litchfield, m. John S. **PRESTON, Jr.**, of Harwinton,		
[, 1832], by Rev. Levi Peck	2	291
Hiram, s. John, Jr. & Ruamy, b. Dec. 30, 1804	2	11
Hiram, m. Naomi **NETTLETON**, Nov. 25, 1830, by Rev. Joseph E.		
Camp, of Northfield	2	292
Huldah, w. Hull, d. Oct. [ ], 1818	2	144
Huldah, d. Hull & Polly, b. Apr. 26, 1820	2	144
Hull, m. Huldah **MORSE**, Mar. 11, 1807, by Daniel Potter, J.P.	2	144
Hull, m. Polly **MOSS**, Feb. 11, 1819	2	144
Irene, d. Jonathan & Sarah, b. Feb. 14, 1786	1	133

	Vol.	Page
CHURCHILL, (cont.),		
Jennet, d. John, Jr. & Ruamy, b. Apr. 8, 1803	2	11
John, Jr., b. Aug. 23, 1770; m. Ruamy **ORTON,** Dec. 16, 1801	2	11
John, s. John, Jr. & Ruamy, b. Feb. 15, 1811	2	11
Jonah, s. Jonathan & Sarah, b. Jan. 11, 1777	1	133
Jonathan, m. Comfort **WOODCOCK,** [ ]	1	132
Julia, d. Timothy & Dothy, b. Aug. 27, 1820	2	125
Julia, m. Jesse **TYLER,** Apr. 28, 1832, by Rev. George E. Pierce	2	291
Ketura, d. William & Ketura, b. Aug. 18, 1811	2	3
Keturah Julia, d. William & Keturah, b. Aug. 18, 1811	2	7
Leman, s. Jonathan & Sarah, b. Dec. 6, 1780	1	133
Lewis K., s. Timothy & Dothy, b. Dec. 14, 1803	2	125
Lewis K., m. Olive **BRADLEY,** b. of Litchfield, Apr. 20, 1829, by Rev. Henry Robinson, of South Farms	2	280
Lucy, d. Jonathan & Sarah, b. May 6, 1779	1	133
Lucy, d. William & Ketura, b. Sept. 7, 1816	2	3
Lucy, d. William & Keturah, b. Sept. 7, 1816	2	7
Maria, d. Timothy & Dothy, b. Mar. 10, 1818	2	125
Mariah, of Litchfield, m. Nelson **TOMLINSON,** of Plymouth, [ ] 25, 1841, by G. C. V. Eastman	2	335
Maria Buel, d. William & Keturah, b. Jan. 5, 1821	2	7
Marian, d. Timothy & Dothy, b. July 20, 1811	2	125
Mary A., of Watertown, m. Orange A. **HUBBELL,** of Plymouh, Oct. 13, 1853, by Rev. Benjamin L. Swan	TM49	92
Mary Ann, of Litchfield, m. Elliot **HITCHCOCK,** of Plymouth, Nov. 12, 1832, by Rev. Samuel Fuller	TM49	37
Mary Ann, m. Elliott **HITCHCOCK,** Nov. 12, 1832, by Rev. Samuel Fuller	2	289
Minerva, d. Oliver & Eunice, b. Nov. 5, 1796	1	133
Nabbe, d. Jonathan & Comfort, b. Jan. 26, 1806	1	133
Patty Emily, d. Jonathan & Comfort, b. May 13, 1808	1	132
Phebe, d. Jonathan & Sarah, b. Feb. 28, 1791	1	133
Polly, d. Jonathan & Sarah, b. Apr. 8, 1784	1	133
Sally, d. Jonathan & Sarah, b. June 18, 1775	1	133
Sally, d. William & Ketura, b. Apr. 26, 1802	2	3
Sally, d. William & Keturah, b. Apr. 26, 1802	2	7
Sally, m. Sylvester **HINE,** Dec. 31, 1828	TM49	64
Sally Ann, d. John, Jr. & Ruamy, b. July 27, 1815	2	11
Samuel B., s. William & Ketura, b. Aug. 3, 1818	2	3
Samuel Buel, s. William & Keturah, b. Aug. 3, 1818	2	7
Samuel Buel, s. William & Keturah, d. Mar. 3, 1819	2	7
Sarah, d. Oct. 8, 1795	1	132
Sarah, m. Sylvester **HINE,** Dec. 31, 1828, by Rev. Joseph E. Camp, of Northfield	2	292
Sophia P., d. Timothy & Dothy, b. Dec. 17, 1814	2	125
Sophia P., of Litchfield, m. Jos. H. **BUELL,** of Holley, N.Y., Oct. 20, 1839, by William Payne	2	328
Susan, d. Hull & Huldah, b. Aug. 4, 1807	2	144
Susan, m. Milton **BEARDSLEE,** Apr. 29, 1829, by Rev. Joseph E. Camp, of Northfield	2	292
Timothy, m. Dothy **KILBORN,** Feb. 24, 1808, by Rev. Judah Champion	2	125
William, m. Ketura **MOSS,** Dec. 24, 1800, by Rev. Joseph E. Camp	2	3

	Vol.	Page
CHURCHILL, (cont.),		
William, m. Keturah **MOORE**, Dec. 24, 1800, by Rev. Joseph E. Camp	2	7
William, s. Timothy & Dothy, b. Apr. 20, 1808	2	125
William, d. Sept. 10, 1828	2	7
CLAP, Emily, m. James **WINSHIP**, Feb. 14, 1813, by Rev. Abel Flint	2	38
CLARK, [see also **CLOCK**], Aaron, s. Peck & Polly, b. May 28, 1811	2	80
Adotha, m. Abiel **BARBER**, of Harwinton, Feb. 5, 1823, by Ozias Lewis, J.P.	2	117
Albert, s. Peck & Polly, b. Nov. 8, 1809	2	80
Alfred, s. Peck & Polly, b. Apr. 20, 1813	2	80
Alvah, m. Mary M. **ENSIGN**, b. of Litchfield, June 13, 1827, by Rev. Henry Robinson, of South Farms	2	271
Benjamin, s. James & Rhoda, b. Nov. 5, 1769	1	46
C. E., m. H. A. **OVIATT**, May 31, 1847, by Rev. David L. Parmelee	TM49	19
Charles F., of Bethany, m. Anna **PERKINS**, of Litchfield, Dec. 25, 1853, by S. T. Seelye	TM49	94
Cyrus, [s. Ebenezer & Sally], b. Feb. 20, 1819	2	30
Daniel Watson, s. [Ebenezer & Sally], b. Nov. 4, 1832	2	30
Ebenezer, b. Dec. 4, 1786	2	30
Ebenezer, m. Mary **TOMKINS**, Nov. 10, 1790, in Waterbury	2	74
Ebenezer, m. Elizabeth **PRITCHARD**, Mar. 15, 1795, in Waterbury	2	74
Ebenezer, s. Ebenezer & Elizabeth, b. June 4, 1797, in Waterbury	2	74
Ebenezer, m. Lucretia **BEACH**, Sept. 25, 1802	2	74
Ebenezer, s. Ebenezer & Elizabeth, d. Mar. 26, 1820	2	74
Edward, s. Peck & Polly, b. June 16, 1814	2	80
Elizabeth, m. Michael **WEBSTER**, July 10, 1774, by Rev. Judah Champion	1	124
Elizabeth, d. Ebenezer, Jr., b. Aug. 9, 1820	2	293
Elizabeth, m. Charles **CARTER**, June 11, 1844, by Rev. D. L. Marks	TM49	4
Elizabeth Fowler, d. Merit & Lydia, b. Feb. 8, 1818	2	146
Emily, [d. Ebenezer & Sally], b. May 17, 1817	2	30
Franklin, [s. Ebenezer & Sally], b. Sept. 8, 1825	2	30
Frederick, s. Peck & Polly, b. Sept. 18, 1817	2	80
Horace, m. Rhoda **STONE**, Nov. 1, 1831, by Rev. L. P. Hickok	2	288
Huldah, m. Roswell **McNEILE**, July 4, 1844, by Rev. D. L. Marks	TM49	4
James, m. Rhoda **GIBBS**, Dec. 21, 1762	1	46
James, s. James & Rhoda, b. Sept. 11, 1767	1	46
Job, m. Rhoda Ann **THOMAS**, Apr. 25, 1841, by Rev. David L. Parmelee	2	333
John, s. Ebenezer & Mary, b. Nov. 10, 1792, Waterbury	2	74
John, of Brooklyn, N.Y., m. Nancy **ROGERS**, of Litchfield, Sept. 4, 1828, by Rev. John S. Stone	2	278
Joseph A., m. Elvira **HOTCHKISS**, Sept. 14, 1833, by Rev. Joseph E. Camp, of Northfield	2	292
Julia, d. Peck & Polly, b. July 16, 1808	2	80
Julietta, of Litchfield, m. Hiram E. **HALE**, of New Berlin, Wis., July 3, 1849, by Rev. William B. Hoyt	TM49	42
Laura, b. Aug. 8, 1794; m. Jeremiah **GUILD**, Jr., Sept. 1, 1813, Rev. Truman Marsh	2	254
Laura Elizabeth, [d. Ebenezer & Sally], b. Sept. 7, 1822	2	30
Lewis, s. Ebenezer & Lucretia, b. Apr. 29, 1812	2	74
Lewis S., m. Naomi M. **HAYDEN**, b. of New Britain, Apr. 28, 1844, by Rev. Isaac Jones	TM49	4

	Vol.	Page
CLARK, [see also **CLOCK**], (cont.),		
Lois, d. James & Rhoda, b. Aug. 10, 1763	1	46
Lucian Ebenezer, [s. Ebenezer & Sally], b. July 5, 1814	2	30
Mabel, d. Ebenezer & Mary, b. Sept. 27, 1791, in Waterbury	2	74
Mabel, m. Isaac **McNEILE, 2nd**, Dec. [ ], 1810, by Rev. Lyman		
Beecher	2	88
Maria, of Litchfield, m. Willliam **BUCKLAND**, of Bolton, Jan. 10,		
1839, by Rev. Gad N. Smith	2	319
Martha, d. Lemuel & Lois, b. Sept. 6, 1772	1	46
Martha, m. Elijah **WEBSTER**, Oct. 18, 1780	1	165
Mary, m. Phares S. **PALMER**., b. of Litchfield, Oct. 23, 1826, by John		
Welch, J.P.	2	266
Merit, m. Lydia **KELLOGG**, May 7, 1817, by Rev. Joseph E. Camp	2	146
Merret, m. Clarissa **BASSETT**, Nov. 13, 1826, by Rev. Joseph E. Camp,		
of Northfield	2	292
Merrett A., m. Anna A. **SMITH**, b. of Northfield, Sept. 6, 1847, by Rev.		
J. L. Dickinson	TM49	19
Peck, m. Polly **KELLOGG**, May 12, 1805, by Rev. T. Marsh	2	80
Rhoda, d. James & Rhoda, b. July 1, 1765	1	46
Roxanna, d. Stephen & Roxana, b. Aug. 28, 1803	1	133
Roxana P., m. Samuel Penfield **BOLLES**, May 27, 1824, by Rev.		
Lyman Beecher	2	136
Sally, b. Oct. 6, 1792	2	30
Samuel, s. William & Jerusha, b. Feb. 2, 1772	1	130
Sarah, m. Noah **STONE**, Dec. 24, 1758, by Rev. Judah Champion	1	118
Sarah, d. Lemuel & Lois, b. July [ ], 1770	1	46
Sarah G., d. Stephen & Roxana, b. Apr. 16, 1808	1	133
Sarah G., m. Jason **WHITING**, June 5, 1828, by Daniel L. Carroll	2	276
Susanna, m. Ambrose **PALMER**, Sept. 15, 1774, by Thomas Matthews,		
J.P., of Waterbury	1	113
William, m. Jerusha **CHURCH**, June 27, 1771, by Rev. Judah		
Champion	1	130
William F., of Orange, m. Mary J. **PENFIELD**, of Northfield, Sept. 1,		
1852, by Rev. Lewis Jessup	TM49	76
William Mather, s. Stephen & Roxana, b. Mar. 26, 1805	1	133
[CLAUSON], [see under **GLAUSON**]		
CLEAVER, Amelia, d. Tobias & Sylvia, b. Dec. 5, 1803	2	48
Amelia B., of Litchfield, m. John B. **COPELAND**, of Middlebury, Vt.,		
June 12, 1826, by Rev. Truman Marsh	2	140
Caroline, d. Tobias & Sylvia, b. July 30, 1806	2	48
Cecelia, d. Tobias & Sylvia, b. July 12, 1794	2	48
Clarissa, d. Tobias & Sylvia, b. Nov. 1, 1796	2	48
Eliza, d. Tobias & Sylvia, b. Apr. 9, 1798	2	48
Maria Adams, d. Tobias & Sylvia, b. Apr. 21, 1800	2	48
Sylvia, w. Tobias, d. Aug. 25, 1816, in the 53rd y. of her age	2	48
Tobias, m. Sylvia **ADAMS**, July 15, 1793, by Rev. Judah Champion	2	48
CLEMENCE, [see under **CLEMONS**]		
CLEMONS, CLEMENS, CLEMON, CLEMMENS, CLEMENCE, Abel,		
s. John & Rachal, b. May 6, 1764	1	46
Abel, m. Mahitabel **CARTER**, Aug. 4, 1784, by James Morris	2	147
Abel, s. Abel & Mahetabel, b. Jan. 5, 1802	2	147
Abel, of Litchfield, m. Eunice **HULL**, of Waterbury, Oct. 12, 1840, by		
Frederick Chittenden, J.P.	2	330

Vol. Page

CLEMONS, CLEMENS, CLEMON, CLEMMENS, CLEMENCE,
(cont.),

Abel H., m. Mahola STONE, b. of Litchfield, Feb. 13, 1828, by Rev.
John S. Stone   2   275
Abigail, d. John & Martha, b. Aug. 14, 1753   1   46
Anna, d. Abel & Mahitabel, b. Dec. 26, 1805   2   147
Clarissa, d. Abel & Mahetabel, b. Sept. 9, 1792   2   147
Delia, d. Abel & Mehetabel, b. Jan. 8, 1800   2   147
Desire, m. Aaron GIBBS, Aug. 10, 1758, by Rev. Judah Champion   1   139
Dotha, d. Abel & Mahetable, b. Aug. 17, 1789   2   147
Harriet M., see under Harriet McCLEMON
Harvey, s. Abel & Mahetable, b. Oct. 6, 1786   2   147
Joel, m. Sary PETTIBONE, Mar. 23, 1757, by Rev. Abel Newell, of
Goshen   1   46
John, Jr., m. Martha BALDWIN, Dec. 26, 1752   1   46
John, s. John & Martha, b. Aug. 12, 1757   1   46
John, Jr., m. Rachel NORTHROP, Nov. 20, 1759, by Bushnel
Bostwick, J.P.   1   46
Julia Ann, m. Augustus B. BRADLEY, May 22, 1832, by Fred
Holcomb   2   290
Louisa A., of Litchfield, m. Robert C. BUTLER, of Rockport, Pa., Dec.
28, 1854, by Rev. H. N. Weed   TM49 105
Lucina, d. John & Rachal, b. Aug. 20, 1760   1   46
Lucina, d. John, Jr. & Rachel, b. Aug. 20, 1760   1   46
Lucy, d. Abel & Mahetabel, b. Dec. 16, 1798   2   147
Lucy, m. John Thompson PETERS, June 25, 1828, by I. Jones   2   277
Mabel, d. John & Rachal, b. Nov. 6, 1769   1   46
Martha, d. John & Martha, b. June 10, 1755   1   46
Martha, w. John, Jr., d. Jan. 8, 1759   1   46
Oren, s. Abel & Mahetabel, b. Sept. 19, 1790   2   147
Pamala, d. John, Jr. & Rachal, b. May 14, 1762   1   46
Permala, m. Ebenezer LANDON, Aug. 6, 1783, by Rev. Judah
Champion   1   104
Sabarina, d. Joel & Sary, b. Feb. 6, 1758   1   46
Samuel Pettibone, s. Joel, b. May 31, 1769   1   131
[CLEVELAND], CLEAVELAND, Sibel, m. Azariah ORTON, Feb. 3,
1780, by Rev. George Beckwith   1 110-11
CLINTON, Anna Parmelia, d. Truman & Rhoda, b. Oct. 10, 1799   1   215
Esther, m. Abisher BEECH, Sept. 20, 1750, by Rev. Elisha Kent   1   127
Truman, m. Rhoda PECK, June 22, 1797, by Rev. Amos Chase   1   215
CLOCK, [see also CLARK], Harriet M., of Litchfield, m. William LINES,
of Naugatuck, Dec. 25, 1849, by Benjamin L. Swan   TM49   44
Mary A., of Litchfield, m. Rodman PILGRIM, of Brooklyn, Conn.,
Jan. 24, 1848, by Benjamin L. Swan   TM49   21
Samuel, of Poundridge, N.Y., m. Harriet M. GIBBS, of Litchfield, June
10, 1827, by Rev. Henry Robinson, of South Farms   2   271
COE, Asaph, s. Thomas & Mary, b. Aug. 16, 1763   1   131
Asaph, s. Thomas & Mary, d. Aug. 17, 1763   1   130
Charles (?) Ida, d. [Thomas M. & Tama M.], b. May 2, 1852   TM49   98
Charles Van Loon, s. [Thomas M. & Tama M.], b. Sept. 14, 1849 TM49   98
Clarissa B., of Litchfield, m. Franklin A. CURTIS, of Warren, Nov. 1,
1847, by John F. Norton   TM49   20
Debby, d. Levi & Debby, b. July 10, 1812   2   45

	Vol.	Page
COE, (cont.),		
Debby M., d. Levi & Debby, b. [ ]. "Entered wrong"	2	45
Dier, s. Levi & Debby, b. June 2, 1794	2	45
Elizabeth, d. Levi & Debby, b. Jan. 18, 1805	2	45
Elizabeth, of Litchfield, m. John A. **OVIATT**, of Washington, Jan. 11, 1837, by Gordon Hayes	2	297
Emeline, d. Levi & Debby, b. Feb. 2, 1801	2	45
Emeline, m. Truman **KILBORN**, Sept. 27, 1819, by Rev. Lyman Beecher	2	70
Eunice, d. Thomas & Mary, b. July 24, 1766	1	131
Ira, s. Levi & Debby, b. Apr. 9, 1796	2	45
Levi, m. Olive **MARSH**, May [ ], 1786, by Rev. Judah Champion	2	45
Levi, m. Debby **McCALL**, Sept. [ ], 1789	2	45
Levi, s. Levi & Debby, b. Sept. 14, 1810	2	45
Levi, m. Lavinia M. **McNEILE**, May 23, 1838, by Rev. Stephen Hubbell	2	320
Levi, m. Frances **LANDON**, b. of Bantam, May 7, 1854, by Rev. Daniel E. Brown, of Bantam	TM49	103
Lois, d. Thomas & Mary, b. Mar. 24, 1762	1	131
Louisa, of Litchfield, m. J. D. **ROBERTS**, of Pardeeville, Wis., Oct. 13, 1851, by Rev. Benjamin L. Swan	TM49	66
Maria D., m. Daniel B. **STODDARD**, May 31, 1831, by Rev. L. P. Hickok	2	287
Mary, d. Thomas & Mary, b. Jan. 4, 1765	1	131
Mary, m. Thomas **CATLIN, Jr.**, Mar. 1, 1787	1	133
Olive, w. Levi, d. May [ ], 1788, in the 22nd y. of her age	2	45
Olive M. W., d. Levi & Debby, b. Oct. 29, 1806	2	45
Persis, d. Thomas & Mary, b. Aug. 24, 1768	1	131
Rhoda, m. David **WARD**, Jan. 14, 1788, by Rev. Mr. Huntington, of Middletown	2	145
Thomas, s. Thomas & Mary, b. May 23, 1772	1	130
Thomas M., s. Levi & Debby, b. Jan. 4, 1815	2	45
Thomas M., of Litchfield, m. Tama M. **ADSET**, of Stanford, Dutchess Co., N.Y., Mar. 3, 1848, at Stanford, N.Y.	TM49	98
Thomas M., representative Apr. 1851	2	1558
Walter, s. Levi & Debby, b. Feb. 10, 1798	2	45
Walter, m. Marina **KILBORN**, Dec. 15, 1824, by Rev. Henry Robinson	2	137
William, s. Levi & Debby, b. Nov. 28, 1802	2	45
William, m. Maria T. **BRADLEY**, b. of Litchfield, June 14, 1826, by Rev. C. S. Boardman, of Preston	2	265
COGSWELL, Charles, m. Asenath **HUBBARD**, Dec. 22, 1824, by Rev. Henry Robinson	2	138
George W., of New Preston, m. Lydia A. **POTTER**, of Litchfield, Sept. 7, 1846, by Rev. William Dixon	TM49	15
Louisa M., of Washington, m. Rollin F. **KILBORN**, of Litchfield, Nov. 13, 1844, by Rev. G. C. V. Eastman	TM49	8
Stephen, m. Rachel **SEYMOUR**, Dec. 21, 1823, by Rev. Lyman Beecher	2	133
Stephen, Jr., m. Lucy **WHITTLESEY**, Apr. 12, 1824, by Rev. Henry Robinson, of South Farms Soc.	2	85
Zerviah, m. Thomas **LITTLE**, June 9, 1752, by Timothy Hatch, J.P., of Kent	1	63
COHAN, [see also CONE], Albert S., of Woodbury, m. Abby **BURGESS**, of		

	Vol.	Page
COHAN, [see also CONE], (cont.),		
Litchfield, Jan. 1, 1840, by Richard Woodruff	2	318
COLBY, COLEBEY, John, m. Sally MORSE, Sept. 2, 1832, by Truman		
Kilborn, J.P.	2	292
John T., of Norwalk, m. Mary A. PERKINS, of Litchfield, Apr. 7, 1845,		
by Rev. D. L. Marks	TM49	9
COLDBREATH, Mary, m. Timothy PLANT, May 10, 1771, by Rev. Job		
Prudden, of Milford	1	30
COLEMAN, Sally, m. Jesse BEACH, May 17, 1803, by Rev. John Marsh, of		
Weathersfield	1	250
COLES, COLE, [see also COWLES], Ann, of Plymouth, m. Hiram HILLS,		
of Litchfield, Feb. 10, 1828, by Rev. John S. Stone	2	299
Catharine, m. Reuben M. GIBBS, June 6, 1819, by Rev. Benjamin		
Norris, of Weston	2	256
Erastus, Rev. of Hunter, N.Y., m. Elizabeth CAMP, Sept. 28, 1823, by		
Rev. Henry Robinson	2	126
Lucy, m. Elijah BIDWELL, Nov. 17, 1785, by Rev. John Trumbull, of		
Watertown	1	213
COLLIER, COLLYER, Cynthia, d. Joseph & Jemima, b. Jan. 17, 1764	1	131
Joseph, s. Joseph & Jemima, b. June 1, 1762	1	131
Polly, m. David MOORE, May 6, 1784, by Rev. Mr. Strong,of		
Norwich	1	108
COLLINS, COLLENS, COLLING, Almira, d. William & Esther, b. July		
10, 1790	1	171
Ambrose, s. Timothy & Elizabeth, b. Mar. 30, 1737	1	47
Ambrose, s. Cyprian & Azubah, b. Mar. 28, 1756	1	89
Amos Morris, s. William & Esther, b. Mar. 30, 1788	1	171
Ann, m. Isaac BALDWIN, Mar. 7, 1750/1, by Rev. Timothy Collens	1	128
Anna, d. Charles & Anna, b. Oct. 10, 1759	1	89
Anne, d. Timothy & Elizabeth, b. Aug. 24, 1725; [m.] Isaac BALDWIN,		
[ ]	1	7
Anne, d. John & Lidia, b. May 17, 1768	1	6
Anson, s. William & Esther, b. Feb. 2, 1795	1	171
Augustus, s. William & Esther, b. Jan. 13, 1793	1	171
Avis, m. Peter BUELL, Dec. 26, 1734, by Rev. Timothy Collens	1	87
Betsey, d. William & Esther, b. Jan. 13, 1784	1	171
Catharine*, m. Sidney PECK, b. of Litchfield, Dec. 2, 1829, by Morris		
Woodruff, J.P. *("Catharine CATLIN"?)	2	283
Charles, s. Timothy & Elizabeth, b. Aug. 5, 1727	1	7
Charles, m. Ann HUNTINGTON, June 18, 1752, by Rev. Solomon		
Williams, of Lebanon	1	89
Charles, s. Charles & Anna, b. Aug. 14, 1761	1	130
Cyprian, s. Timothy & Elizabeth, b. Mar. 4, 1732/3	1	47
Cyprian, m. Azubah GIBBS, Jan. 9, 1756, by Timothy Collens, J.P.	1	89
Darius, s. Charles & Anna, b. Nov. 8, 1769	1	130
David, s. Charles & Anne, b. May 1, 1772	1	88
Eliza, of Litchfield, m. Sanford HANNAHS, of Bethlem, Oct. 30, 1821,		
by Rev. Isaac Jones	2	104
Elizabeth, d. Charles & Ann, b. Sept. 25, 1755	1	89
Elizabeth, m. Amos BARNES, Mar. 9, 1758, by Rev. Judah Champion	1	126
Elisabell, d. John & Lidia, b. Aug. 5, 1766	1	6
Elizabeth, m. James PIERPOINT, Sept. 28, 1782, by Rev. Judah		
Champion	2	144

	Vol.	Page
COLLINS, COLLENS, COLLING, (cont.),		
Elizabeth, m. Daniel Wadsworth **LEWIS**, July 25, 1791	1	164
Eunice, [twin with Lois], d. Charles & Anna, b. Oct. 11, 1757	1	89
Frederick, s. William & Esther, b. Feb. 24, 1804	1	171
Hiram, s. [John & Lydia], b. Nov. 9, 1781	1	6
James, s. Oliver & Sarah, b. Apr. 26, 1766	1	131
John, s. Timothy & Elizabeth, b. June 1, 1739	1	47
John, s. John & Lydia, b. Mar. 5, 1776	1	6
Lewis, s. Rev. Timothy & Elizabeth, b. Aug. 8, 1729	1	7
Lewis, s. Charles & Ann, b. Oct. 29, 1753	1	89
Lois, [twin with Eunice], d. Charles & Anna, b. Oct. 11, 1757	1	89
Lois, d. Eli & Elizabeth, b. Mar. 25, 1758	1	89
Lorain, d. Charles & Anna, b. May 1, 1767	1	130
Lucina, d. Thomas, d. Aug. 30. 1758, ae 9 y.	1	6
Lucretia, d. John & Lydia, b. Jan. 20, 1779	1	6
Lydia, d. John & Lydia, b. Jan 5, 1772	1	6
Maria, d. William & Esther, b. June 9, 1799	1	171
Michael, s. William & Esther, b. May 17, 1797	1	171
Norman, s. John & Lidia, b. Dec. 13, 1769	1	6
Olliver, s. Rev. Timothy & Elizabeth, b. Mar. 7, 1723/4	1	7
Oliver, m. Sarah **HIDE**, June 22, 1746, by Rev. Solomon Williams, of Lebanon	1	89
Oliver, s. Oliver & Sarah, b. June 5, 1763	1	131
Polly, d. John & Lydia, b. June 5, 1774	1	6
Rhoda, d. Timothy & Elizabeth, b. May 3, 1731	1	7
Rhoda, d. Charles & Anna, b. Oct. 5, 1764	1	130
Ruth*, m. George Macknish* **BULL**, Apr. 11, 1771, by Rev. Judah Champion *("Ruth **CATLIN**" in Woodruff's)		
*("**McKNIGHT**"in Woodruff's)	1	167
Thomas, d. Nov. 14, 1754, in the 49th y. of his age	1	6
Timothy, Rev., m. Mrs. Elizabeth **HIDE**, of Lebanon, Jan. 16, 1722/3, by Henry Willes	1	7
Timothy, s. Oliver & Sary, b. Apr. 16, 1748	1	89
William Burrage, s. William & Esther, b. Nov. 6, 1807	1	171
William Morris, s. William & Esther, b. Mar. 18, 1786	1	171
William Morris, d. Feb. 26, 1788, ae 23 m.	1	170
COLT, John R., m. Eliza M. **SPERRY**, May 21, 1854, by Rev. David L. Parmelee	TM49	101
COLVER, [see under **CULVER**]		
COMSTOCK, Calvin, m. Elizabeth **WATKINS**, Nov. 27, 1771, by Daniel Catlin, J.P.	1	88
Calvin, had negro Jenny, b. June 4, 1784	1	151
CONARD, Jane C*., m. Oliver S. **WOLCOTT**, Mar. 9, 1820, by Lyman Beecher *("Law" written over "C.")	2	98
CONE, [see also **COHAN**], Elizabeth A., d. Warren, m. Payne Kenyon **KILBURN**, s. Chauncey, Aug. 3, 1842, at Norfolk, by Rev. Joseph Eldredge	TM49	98
Hubbel B., of Wetumpka, Ala., m. Mary M. **SKELTON**, of Litchfield, Nov. 17, 1836, by Rev. Alpheas Geer, of Hebron	2	299
COOK, COOKE, Augustus, b. Dec. 8, 1799; m. Mary N. **COOPER**, Mar. 22, 1821	2	27
Augustus, m. Mary **COOPER**, Mar. 25, 1821, by Rev. Isaac Jones	2	101
Charles N., m. Jane M. **HAND**, Dec. 1, 1847, by Rev. David L.		

	Vol.	Page
COOK, COOKE, (cont.),		
Parmelee	TM49	20
Charles W., 2nd s. [Augustus & Mary N.], b. Oct. 31, 1825	2	27
Elizabeth, m. Richard W. STILES, Aug. 31, 1824, by Rev. Lyman		
Beecher	2	13
Esther C., 1st d. [Augustus & Mary N.], b. May 23, 1824	2	27
George, m. Susan C. HUMPERVILLE, Dec. 7, 1825, by Rev.		
Frederick Holcomb	2	259
George, m. Sarah BISSELL, b. of Litchfield, Aug. 29, 1838, by Rev.		
Gad N. Smith	2	319
George Albro, s. George [& Susan], b. Dec. 18, 1833	2	259
George B., of Winsted, m. Cornelia TROWBRIDGE, of Litchfield,		
Nov. 24, 1851, by Benjamin L. Swan	TM49	66
George H., 3rd s. [Augustus & Mary N.], b. Dec. 21, 1827	2	27
Hannah, m. Joshua COLVER, b. of Litchfield, Aug. 3, 1741, by Rev.		
Timothy Collens	1	89
Hiram M., 1st s. [Augustus & Mary N.], b. Aug. 19, 1822	2	27
Homer E., of Plymouth, m. Hannah W. GRANNISS, of Warren, Feb.		
28, 1853, by Rev. John J. Brandegee	TM49	78
James C., 4th s. [Augustus & Mary N.], b. Feb. 21, 1832	2	27
James H., m. Jane BUEL, Dec. 9, 1835, by Rev. L. P. Hickok	2	296
Joab, [twin with Job], s. Nathaniel & Mary, b. Aug. 27, 1740	1	47
Job, [twin with Joab], s. Nathaniel & Mary, b. Aug. 27, 1740	1	47
John William, of New York City, m. Sarah Ann SPERRY, of Litchfield,		
July 19, 1848, by Rev. Samuel Fuller	TM49	38
Joseph W., of Chicago, Ill., m. Electa C. HALL, of Litchfield, May 1,		
1854, by Rev. Daniel E. Brown	TM49	101
Julia, m. Othniel IVES, Oct. 28, 1833, by Rev. L. P. Hickok	2	288
Louisa A., d. George [& Susan], b. Dec. 22, 1830	2	259
Lidia, m. John MASON, Jan. 20, 1743/4, by Rev. Timothy Collens	1	107
Naomi, m. Laban BEACH, Jr., [ ], 1787, by Rev. David Welsh	2	36
Phinehas G., s. George & Susan, b. Jan. 15, 1827	2	259
Polly, m. Samuel BROOKER, Apr. 20, 1797, by Rev. Joshua Williams,		
of Harwinton	2	141
Sally W., m. Frederick WOLCOTT, June 21, 1815, by Rev. William		
Andrews, of Danbury	2	17
Susan S., 2nd d. [Augustus & Mary N.], b. Nov. 11, 1829	2	27
Virgillius G., m. Elizabeth S. WASHBURN, Sept. 23, 1840, by		
Jonathan Brace	2	327
COOPER, Mary, m. Augustus COOK, Mar. 25, 1821, by Rev. Isaac Jones	2	101
Mary N., b. Oct. 23, 1797; m. Augustus COOK, Mar. 22, 1821	2	27
COPELAND, John B., of Middlebury, Vt., m. Amelia B. CLEAVER, of		
Litchfield, June 12, 1826, by Rev. Truman Marsh	2	140
CORNING, Elisha P., m. Sally T. POST, June 14, 1820, by Lyman Beecher	2	95
CORNWALL, Lois, m. Amos BISHOP, Mar. 8, 1792, by David Welch	2	24
COUCH, Mehetabel, m. Joel G. ROBERTS, Oct. 28, 1802	2	12
COWLES, [see also COLES], Clarinda Sanford, d. Edward & Wealthy M.,		
b. Sept. 27, 1822	2	17
Edward, m. Welthy Maria DOWNS, Feb. 28, 1816, by Morris Woodruff	2	17
Edward, m. Mrs. Rhoda S. HARRISON, b. of Litchfield, Sept. 22,		
1839, by Rev. Richard Woodruff	2	324
Mary E., m. Memory (?) J. A. KEITH, July 27, 1845, by Rev. David L.		
Parmelee	TM49	10

	Vol.	Page
COWLES, (cont.),		
Mary Elizabeth, d. Edward & Wealthy M., b. Dec. 27, 1818	2	17
COYLE, John, m. Mary **BANINGTON** or **BARRINGTON,** b. of Ireland,		
Apr. 8, 1853, by Rev. John J. Brandegee	TM49	93
CRAMER, George, m. Abby E. **LOOMIS,** Mar. 26, 1850, by Rev. David L.		
Parmelee	TM49	53
CRAMPTON, CRAMTON, Anne, d. Elen & Avis, b. May 19, 1783	1	171
Augustus, s. Neri & Abigail, b. June 10, 1769	1	131
Avis, d. Elen & Avis, b. Sept. 21, 1794	1	171
Avis, m. Caleb **PICKET,** June 21, 1818	2	21
Benjamin, s. Elon & Avis, b. Aug. 4, 1783	1	171
Elizabeth, d. Elon & Avis, b. June 22, 1806	1	171
Elon, m. Avis **WEBSTER,** Jan. 1, 1783, by Rev. Judah Champion	1	171
Elon, s. Elon & Avis, b. Apr. 21, 1790	1	171
James, s. Elon & Avis, b. June 16, 1788	1	171
Mabel, d. Miles & Rhoda, b. Mar. 1, 1772	1	130
Miles, m. Rhoda **KIRYES,** Mar. 12, 1770, by John Cooke, J.P.	1	130
Molly, m. James **KILBORN,** May 15, 1771, by Timothy Collens, J.P.	1	103
Neri, m. Abigail **FIELD,** July 18, 1758, by Rev. Jonathan Todd, of		
East Guilford	1	131
Polly, d. Elon & Avis, b. Nov. 11, 1796	1	171
Polly, m. Gurdon **PHILLEY,** Feb. 1, 1818, by Rev. Lyman Beecher	2	109
Rachel, d. Miles & Rhoda, b. Aug. 29, 1770	1	130
CRANDALL, Reynold C., m. Julia A. **STONE,** Sept. 13, 1838, by Rev. Gad		
N. Smith	2	319
Reynolds C., m. Eliza A. **STONE,** b. of Litchfield, Dec. 13, 1840, by		
Rev. Thomas Ellis	2	331
CRANE, Frederick J., of Bethlem, m. Sarah S. **AYRES,** of Licthfield, Jan. 19,		
1832, by Rev. Mr. Taylor, of South Farms	2	289
Orlando F., of Litchfield, m. Esther **MURRAY,** of Litchfield, Feb. 22,		
1832, by Rev. Mr. Taylor, of South Farms	2	289
CRAWFORD, Julia W., of Litchfield, m. Junius E. **BALDWIN,** of		
Harwinton, Aug. 20, 1854, by Rev. H. N. Weed	TM49	101
Oliver, of Newburgh, N.Y., m. Rebecca **MATTHEWS,** Jan. 18, 1835,		
by Rev. L. P. Hickok	2	296
CROSBY, CROSBIE, Alonzo O., s. Thomas W. & Harriet, b. Jan. 9, 1825	2	256
Amanda, m. Noah **GARNSEY, Jr.,** Apr. 25, 1816, by Rev. Joseph E.		
Camp	2	86
Amasay L., s. Thomas W. & Harriet, b. Nov. 7, 1818	2	256
Bansly*, s. Simon & Huldah, b. May 11, 1793　　*("Ransley" in		
Woodruff's")	1	171
Charles M., s. Thomas W. & Harriet, b. Sept. 30, 1821	2	256
Ebenezer, s. Timothy & Ruth, b. Aug. 26, 1782	1	171
Eliakim, s. Timothy & Ruth, b. Mar. 2, 1779	1	171
Elizabeth, d. Timothy & Ruth, b. Aug. 20, 1784	1	171
Erastus, s. Simon & Huldah, b. May 30, 1784	1	171
Harriet, d. Thomas W. & Harriet, b. Dec. 26, 1822	2	256
Mary Ann, d. Thomas W. & Harriet, b. May 25, 1820	2	256
Orris, s. Simon & Huldah, b. Jan. 2, 1792	1	171
Simon, m. Huldah **GILLET*,** Sept. 17, 1783, by Rev. Andrew Storrs,		
of Northbury　　*("GIBBS" in Woodruff's book)	1	171
Thomas W., m. Harriet **THOMAS,** Oct. 4, 1814, by Amasa Porter, of		
Darby	2	256

	Vol.	Page
CROSBY, CROSBIE, (cont.),		
Timothy, m. Ruth **GIBBS**, Nov. 20, 1777, by Rev. George Beckwith	1	171
Truman E., s. Thomas W. & Hariet, b. Apr. 20, 1815	2	256
William E., s. Thomas W. & Hariet, b. Nov. 29, 1816	2	256
CROSS, Susanna J., of Litchfield, m. David **HAMLIN, Jr.**, of Clay, N.Y.,		
Oct. 8, 1827, by Rev. Henry Robinson, of South Farms	2	273
CROSSMAN, Laura M., m. John P. **TROWBRIDGE**, b. of Litchfield, July		
3, 1851, by Benjamin L. Swan	TM49	63
Lucy, m. James **PIERPOINT**, Dec. 16, 1817, at Salsbury, by Rev. John		
Langdon	2	144
Lucy W., m. Joseph N. **MARSH**, b. of Litchfield, June 11, 1828, by		
Rev. Henry Robinson, of South Farms	2	277
Sophronia H., m. Milo **BALDWIN**, Apr. 16, 1849, by Rev. D. L.		
Parmelee	TM49	36
CULVER, COLVER, Aaron, s. Joshua & Hannah, b. Apr. 7, 1749	1	89
Abel, s. Ebenezer & Mary, b. May 7, 1760	1	131
Abigail, m. James **BEEBE**, June 12, 1727	1	5
Abigail, d. Jonathan & Sarah, b. Sept. 16, 1750	1	89
Abner, s. Azariah & Elizabeth, b. Feb. 24, 1778	1	130
Adah, w. Ebenezer, d. Nov. 22, 1765	1	130
Ann, m. John **BALDWIN**, June 14, 1727, by Rev. Timothy Collens	1	5
Ann, d. Zebulon & Eleanor, b. Sept. 1, 1749	1	89
Anne, m. Benjamin **AMES**, Aug. 2, 1774, by Rev. Judah Champion	1	42
Ashbel, s. Ebenezer & Mary, b. Mar. 15, 1755	1	131
Asher, s. Daniel & Deborah, b. Mar. 19, 1734	1	7
Asher, m. Eunice **BEEBE**, Sept. 18, 1755	1	89
Avis, d. Joshua & Avis, b. Apr. 10, 1761	1	131
Avise, w. Joshua, d. Feb. 2, 1796, in the 63rd y. of her age	1	88
Azariah, s. Zebulon & Eleanor, b. Sept. 23, 1751	1	89
Azariah, m. Elizabeth **BALDWIN**, Feb. 29, 1776, by John Hubbard, of		
Mereden	1	171
Benjamin, m. Mary **HORSFORD**, b of Litchfield, Apr. 20, 1738, by		
Rev. Timothy Collens	1	47
Benjamin, s. Ebenezer & Mary, b. July 28, 1747	1	89
Benjamin, s. Ebenezer & Mary, b. July 28, 1747	1	131
Benjamin, m. Abigail **ELSWORTH**, July 18, 1770, by Rev. Judah		
Champion	1	46
Charles, of Litchfield, m. Mary E. **ROOT**, of Litchfield, July 1, 1853, by		
Rev. H. N. Weed	TM49	91
Daniel, m. Deborah **GOODRICH**, Feb. 12, 1723/4, by Rev. Timothy		
Collens	1	7
Daniel, d. Apr. 9, 1734, ae 36 y.	1	6
Daniel, s. Azariah & Elizabeth, b. Dec. 20, 1785	1	133
Diana, d. Ebenezer & Mary, b. Sept. 2, 1757	1	131
Ebenezer, m. Mary **STONE**, Oct. 24, 1745, by Rev. Timothy Collens	1	131
Ebenezer, s. Ebenezer & Mary, b. Sept. 20, 1752	1	131
Ebenezer, m. Adah **GRAY**, Dec. 5, 1762, by Rev. Judah Champion	1	131
Edward, Lieut., d. Apr. 7, 1732	1	6
Edward, s. Jonathan & Sarah, b. Apr. 20, 1753	1	89
Edward E., of Litchfield, m. Mary Ann **BOWKER**, of Sudbury, Mass.,		
Nov. 1, 1849, by Benjamin L. Swan	TM49	44
Eleanor, d. Zebulon & Eleanor, b. June 3, 1747	1	89
Eleanor, m. Amasa **MOSS**, Nov. 17, 1768	1	107

	Vol.	Page
CULVER, COLVER, (cont.),		
Elner, w. Zebulon, d. Mar. 29, 1805, in the 82nd y. of her age	1	130
Elizabeth, d. Nathaniel & Ruth, b. Jan. 15, 1755	1	6
Emily, m. Silas **NICHOLS**, July 3,1835, by Rev. L. P. Hickok	2	296
Ephraim, d. Feb. 10, 1728/9	1	6
Ephraim, m. Hannah **MASON**, b. of Litchfield, Jan. 24, 1739/40, by		
[ ]	1	47
Eunice, d. Zebulon & Eleanor, b. Dec. 31, 1762	1	88
Frances, s. Daniel & Deborah, b. Jan. 22, 1726/7	1	7
Hannah, d. Samuel & Hannah, b. Apr. 20, 1724	1	7
Hannah, d. Joshua & Hannah, b. Sept. last day, 1743	1	89
Hannah, w. Joshua, d. July 3, 1753, ae about 35 y.	1	88
Hannah, d. Zebulon & Eleanor, b. May 2, 1761	1	6
Hannah, w. Samuel, d. July 16, 1770	1	6
Hannah, m. Stephen **BIDWELL, Jr.**, Sept. 26, 1786, by Rev. Judah		
Champion	1	213
Hyman, s. Reuben & Olive, b. June 14, 1795	1	133
Irene, d. Zebulon & Eleanor, b. Mar. 28, 1757	1	89
Joel, s. Daniel & Deborah, b. Dec. 4, 1731	1	7
Joel, s. Zebulon & Eleanor, b. May 13, 1745	1	89
Jonathan, s. Samuel & Hannah, b. Mar. 5, 1725/6	1	7
Jonathan, m. Sarah **HENMAN**, Nov. 16, 1749, by Rev. Stephen Heaton,		
of Goshen	1	89
Jonathan, s. Jonathan & Sarah, b. Mar. 31, 1758	1	88
Joshua, m. Hannah **COOK**, b. of Litchfield, Aug. 3, 1741, by Rev.		
Timothy Collens	1	89
Joshua, s. Joshua & Hannah, b. Oct. 30, 1746	1	89
Joshua & Avis, had s. [ ], b. Aug. 1, [1757]; d. Aug. 11, 1757	1	6
Levi, s. Azariah & Elizabeth, b. Sept. 17, 1787	1	133
Lois, d. Joshua & Avis, b. Oct. 16, 1758	1	131
Lois, d. Zebulon & Eleanor, b. Aug. 4, 1765	1	88
Lucia, d. Joshua & Hannah, b. Jan. [ ], 1752	1	88
Lucretia, d. Azariah & Elizabeth, b. Nov. 30, 1776	1	171
Lucretia, d. Mar. 18, 1778, ae 15 m.	1	130
Martha, m. John **BEBE**, Nov. 24, 1730, by Rev. Timothy Collens	1	45
Mary, d. Ebenezer & Mary, b. July 1, 1762	1	131
Mary, w. Ebenezer, d. July 17, 1762	1	130
Mary, w. Benjamin, d. May 30, 1770* *("Dec. 30" precedes this date)	1	6
Molly, d. Reuben & Olive, b. Aug. 7, 1793	1	133
Nathaniel, s. Samuel & Hannah, b. June 29, 1728	1	7
Nathaniel, m. Ruth **KILBORN**, Nov. 23, 1752, by Ebenezer Marsh, J.P.	1	89
Philomelee, d. Nathaniel & Ruth, b. Mar. 11, 1760	1	6
Rachal, d. Zebulon & Eleanor, b. Dec. 16, 1753	1	89
Rachel*, m. Amos **MOSS**, Dec. 13, 1777 *(In the births of her		
children the name is given "Elizabeth")	2	19
Reuben, m. Olive **BUEL**, Mar. 22, 1792, by Rev. Judah Champion	1	133
Rhoda, d. Joshua & Avis, b. Oct. 2, 1763	1	131
Ruth, m. John **HAMASTON**, Dec. 29, 1742, by Rev. Samuell Todd,		
of Northbury	1	16
Ruth, d. Zebulon & Eleanor, b. Sept. 22, 1748	1	89
Sabra, d. Daniel & Deborah, b. Oct. 16, 1729	1	7
Sabra, d. Zebulon & Eleanor, b. Mar. 16, 1768	1	88
Samuel, representative Oct. 1741	2	1545

	Vol.	Page
CULVER, COLVER, (cont.),		
Sarah, d. Jonathan & Sarah, b. Apr. 5, 1755	1	88
Sarah, d. Joshua & Avis, b. Apr. 19, 1766	1	131
Sarah, m. Jonathan WOODWORTH, Nov. 27, 1788, by Rev. Judah		
Champion	1	206
Silphina, d. Ebenezer & Adah, b. Aug. 8, 1764	1	131
Stephen, s. Zebulon & Eleanor, b. Mar. 15, 1759	1	6
Susanna, d. Nathaniel & Ruth, b. Apr. 16, 1754	1	6
Tamor, d. Joshua & Hannah, b. Jan. 14, 1744/5	1	89
Temperance, d. Ebenezer & Mary, b. Jan. 6, 1750	1	131
Temperance, m. Ozias BISSELL, Nov. 12, 1769, by Rev. Judah		
Champion	1	84
Zebulon, m. Alaner* TAYLOR, July 30, 1740, by Rev. Timothy		
Collens *("Eleanor")	1	47
Zebulon, Lieut., d. Dec. 14, 1806, in the 91st y. of his age	1	130
Zerviah, m. Ebenezer TAYLER, Jr., Jan. 17, 1749/50, by Capt. Joseph		
Bird, J.P.	1	79
CUMMINGS, CUMINGS, CUMINS, Clarissa Ann, m. Lester		
GRISWOULD, Sept. 21, 1823, by Rev. Isaac Jones	2	126
Heman Lewis, m. Caroline HARD, Dec. 29, 1822, by Rev. Isaac Jones	2	116
CURTIS, CURTISS, Belinda Maria, [d. Orson], b. Mar. 10, 1838	2	323
Charles, [s. Orson], b. Aug. 2, 1840	2	323
Eli, s. Daniel & Lois, b. Sept. 5, 1786	1	171
Eliakim, m. Lucy HART, Mar. 29, 1819, by Rev. Joseph E. Camp	2	255
Elmira, of Sheffield, m. Truman McNEILE, Mar. 2, 1823, by Ozias		
Lewis, J.P.	2	117
Franklin A., of Warren, m. Clarissa B. COE, of Litchfield, Nov. 1, 1847,		
by John F. Norton	TM49	20
George, s. Eliakim & Lucy, b. June 3, 1821	2	255
Gideon, s. Gideon & Zerviah, b. May 11, 1792	1	171
Gilbert, s. Gideon & Zerviah, b. June 28, 1794	1	171
Hannah, m. Benjamin HART, Dec. 15, 1775, at Wallingford, by Rev.		
Simeon Waterman	2	249
Huldah, d. Gideon & Zerviah, b. Apr. 26, 1789	1	171
Jason, m. Phebe TURNER, [ ], 1820, by Lyman Beecher	2	98
Jennet, m. Hiram G. BEACH, b. of Litchfield, May 11, 1840, by Rev.		
Harvey D. Kitchel	2	327
Joseph, [s. Orson], b. Mar. 20, 1830	2	323
Joseph, s. Eliakim & Lucy, b. June 8, 1831	2	255
Laura, of Litchfield, m. Isaac C. FENN, of Wolcottville, Oct. 4, 1843,		
by Rev. H. D. Kitchel	2	340
Levi, s. Eliakim & Lucy, b. Oct. 14,1824	2	255
Orson, m. Hepzibah WESTOVER, Mar. 23, 1825, by Rev. Seth Higbey	2	139
Phebe, d. Eliakim & Lucy, b. Nov. 9, 1822	2	255
Philena, d. Daniel & Lois, b. Oct. 2, 1779	1	133
Philena, m. Bille TURNER, Jan. [ ], 1796, by Daniel Potter, J.P.	2	5
Polly, d. Daniel & Lois, b. Sept.13, 1782	1	133
Polly, m. Isaac NEWTON, Nov. 2, 1800, by Daniel Potter	2	132
Russell, [s. Orson], b. Oct. 2, 1834	2	323
Sheldon C., m. Harriet E. LOVELAND, Oct. 2, 1854, by Rev. David		
L. Parmelee, at South Farms	TM49	103
Warren Hotchkiss, s. Gideon & Zerviah, b. Apr. 14, 1790	1	171
William, [s. Orson], b. Mar. 11, 1826	2	323

	Vol.	Page
CURTIS, CURTISS, (cont.),		
William, m. Mary **WESTOVER**, Jan. 11, 1846, by Rev. David L.		
Parmelee	TM49	13
DALEY, Julia M., m. William H. **TURKINGTON**, Oct. 8, 1854, by Rev.		
David L. Parmelee	TM49	105
DAMES, Aurelia, of Litchfield, m. W[illia]m B. **FROST**, of Waterbury,		
Oct. 5, 1841, by Jonathan Brace	2	320
Wilmot N., m. Sally M. **BRADLEY**, b. of Litchfield, Apr. 17, 1831, by		
Hugh P. Welch	2	290
DAMMON, [see also **DEMAN & DEMING**], Thankful, d. Feb. 5, 1762	1	8
DANFORTH, Sarah, m. Oliver **BORDMAN**, May 1, 1781, by Rev. Enoch		
Huntington	1	213
DANIELS, Henry, of Farmington, m. Belinda **ATWOOD**, of Litchfield, Aug.		
9, 1832, by Rev. A. B. Goldsmith, of Guilford	2	291
DARE, Electa, d. Samuel & Hannah, b. Aug. 24, 1800	1	90-1
George, m. Sarah **BISHOP**, Dec. 2, 1778, by Rev. Judah Champion	1	49
Samuel, s. George & Sarah, b. Sept. 13, 1779	1	49
Samuel, m. Hannah **BRADLYE**, Sept. 15, 1799, by Rev. Dan		
Huntington	1	90-1
DARIN, Arauna, s. Joseph, Jr. & Elizabeth, b. Jan. 9, 1739/40	1	9
Joseph, Jr., m. Elizabeth **BARTHOLOMEW**, of Branford, Dec. 14,		
1738, by Rev. Mr. Robens, of Branford	1	9
Joseph, m. Deliverance **HILL***, Feb. 8, 1743/4, by Rev. Thomas		
Ruggles, of Guilford *("HALL" in Woodruff's book)	1	9
Uzziel, s. Joseph & Elizabeth, b. Nov. 30, 1741	1	9
DARROW, Leverett, m. Betsey **SMITH**, Oct. 18, 1821, by Rev. Mr.		
Pettingill	2	104
Leverett, of Plymouth, m. Betsey **SMITH**, of Litchfield, Oct. 18, 1821,		
by Rev. Amos Pettingill	2	111
DART, Benjamin, m. Mabel L. **BRADLEY**, June 4, 1854, by Rev. David L.		
Parmelee	TM49	101
DAVIS, DAVICE, Anthony G., m. Helen A. **STONE**, Mar. 15, 1831, by		
Rev. W. Lucas	2	287
George Whitfield, of Springfield, Mass., m. Cornelia Elvira **FISHER**, of		
Litchfield, July 2, 1846, by Rev. Samuel Fuller	TM49	38
Grace, m. Roderic C. **DEMINS**, May 19, 1851, by Rev. David L.		
Parmalee	TM49	62
Henry, of Wolcottville, m. Chloe E. **CHURCHILL**, of Northfield, Oct.		
1, 1848, by Rev. J. L. Dickinson, of Northfield	TM49	26
Joel, d. Mar. 25, 1777, in his 21st y.	1	48
Polly J., m. Jeremiah **LINSLEY**, Jan. 13, 1802, by David Judson	2	53
Sarah, m. Norman **PERKINS**, b. of Litchfield, Nov. 25, 1847, by		
Joseph Henson	TM49	23
Welles D., of Portland, m. Phila M. **SKELTON**, of South Farms, Jan.		
18, 1853, by Rev. Alpheas Geers, of North Guilford	TM49	78
DAY, Eunice P., m. Riley **WARREN**, Apr. 29, 1849, by Rev. David L.		
Parmelee	TM49	36
DAYTON, Arvi, of Wolcottville, m. Sally C. **BRISTOL**, of Torrington, Jan.		
7, 1840, by Jonathan Brace	2	318
Benjamin Gibbs, s. Zadock & Amy, b. Dec. 20, 1823	2	132
Lydia, d. Zadock & Amy, b. Mar. 3, 1812	2	132
Olive, m. William **MUNSON**, Mar. 30, 1790, by Rev. Mr. Gridley	2	86
Polly Ann, d. Zadock & Amy, b. Aug. 11, 1810	2	132

	Vol.	Page
DEMING, [see also **DEMAN & DUNNING**], (cont.),		
Frederick Ray, s. Stephen & Sarah, [formerly of Sharon], b. Sept. 4, 1820	2	133
Henry B., [s. Stephen & Sarah], b. May 27, 1812; d. July 4, 1837	TM49	100
Henry Burnam, s. Stephen & Sarah, [formerly of Sharon], b. May 27, 1812	2	133
James L., s. Benjamin & Almena, b. Dec. 3, 1813	2	69
Julius, m. Dorothy **CHAMPION,** Aug. 7, 1781, by Rev. Robert Robbins, of Colchester	1	49
Julius, m. Dorothy **CHAMPION,** Aug. 7, 1781, by Rev. Mr. Robins	2	90
Julius, s. Julius & Dorothy, b. July 28, 1782	1	49
Julius, s. Julius & Dorothy, b. July 28, 1782	2	90
Julius, representative Oct. 1790, May 1791, May 1798	2	1551-2
Julius, s. Julius & Dorothy, d. Aug. 8, 1799	2	90
Legrand L., s. Benjamin & Almena, b. Oct. 29, 1812	2	69
Louisa, d. Frederick & Mary, b. Oct. 23, 1822	2	125
Lucretia, d. Julius & Dorothy, b. Aug. 13, 1804	2	90
Mary, d. Julius & Dorothy, b. Oct. 16, 1798	2	90
Mary G., d. Frederick & Mary, b. May 8, 1815	2	125
Minor R., [s. Stephen & Sarah], b. Feb. 24, 1810; d. Sept. 10, 1845, at Carthage, Ill.	TM49	100
Prudence, m. Ira **BUELL,** Jan. 27, 1767, by Rev. Stephen Johnson, of Lyme	1	86
Roderic C., s. Benjamin & Almena, b. Jan. 9, 1815	2	69
Roderic C., m. Grace **DAVICE,** May 19, 1851, by Rev. David L. Parmalee	TM49	62
Sarah, of Litchfield, m. Dr. Thomas T. **SEELEY,** of Woodbury, Jan. 13, 1846, by Rev. Jno Churchill, of Woodbury	TM49	13
Sarah A., d. [Stephen & Sarah], b. Jan. 6, 1824	TM49	100
Sarah Ann, d. Stephen & Sarah, [formerly of Sharon], b. Jan. 6, 1824,	2	133
Stephen, b. Dec. 19, 1780; m. Fanny **BEECHER,** July 18, 1802	TM49	100
Stephen, m. Sarah **BUEL,** Oct. 23, 1804	TM49	100
William, s. Julius & Dorothy, b. Mar. 1, 1792	2	90
DENISON, DENNISON, Aruna, d. Chauncey & Sarah, b. Sept. 17, 1782	2	145
Chauncey, m. Sarah **GRANNISS,** Jan. 1, 1782, by Rev. Nicholas Street, of East Haven	2	145
John, s. Chauncey & Sarah, b. June 6, 1789	2	145
John, s. Chauncey & Sarah, d. Aug. 5, 1793	2	145
Joseph, of Newton, Mass., m. Sarah Jane **WOODRUFF,** of Litchfield, July 8, 1845, by Rev. William Dixon	TM49	11
Sally, d. Chauncey & Sarah, b. Mar. 4, 1792	2	145
DENNY, Lucy, m. John **HEMINWAY,** of Watertown, July 28, 1847, by Joseph Henson	TM49	23
DERWIN, Ann, d. Sept. 2, 1734, ae 48 y. 1 m. 5 d.	1	8
DEWEY, DEWY, George, ae 25, m. Sabra **JOHNSON,** ae 20, Sept. 10, 1815	2	78
John, m. Mary P. **MARSH,** Dec. 27, 1821, by Rev. Isaac Jones	2	105
DeWOLF, DeWOLFE, Honor, m. Abraham **PECK,** [ ], 1787, by Rev. Judah Champion	1	195
Maria, m. Kasson **GOODWIN,** b. of Litchfield, Nov. 29, 1827, by Rev. Henry Robinson, of South Farms	2	274
DEWS, William, of Wakefield, York Cty., m. [ ] **WORKMAN,** of Winton Hampton Gloucestershire, Eng., Sept. 9, 1849, by Rev. Isaac Jones	TM49	42

	Vol.	Page
DIBBLE, DIBBALL, DIEBELL, Lucy, m. Andrew **BENEDICT,** Nov. 26, 1812, by Rev. Mr. Crocker, of Reading	2	253
Lydia, m. Elijah **BIRGE,** Sept. 12, 1751, by Rev. Stephen Heaton, of Goshen	1	129
Silas, s. Silas & Rachal, b. Feb. 7, 1772	1	9
Silas, m. Rachel J. **KILBORN,** May 15, 1772, by Timothy Collens, J.P.	1	9
DICKERSON, Sarah, of Weathersfield, m. Jonathan **KILBORN,** of Litchfield, Oct. 27, 1737, by Rev. Daniel Russel	1	21
DICKINSON, Abigail, m. Daniel **LORD,** Jan. 10, 1788, by Rev. Judah Champion	2	65
Ambrose, s. Oliver & Anna, b. May 10, 1783	1	49
Amos, m. Sally **PERRY,** Aug. 6, 1819, by Rev. Mr. Hubbard	2	141
Anna, d. Oliver & Anna, b. Jan. 2, 1793	1	49
Anna, d. Oliver & Anna, d. Sept. 13, 1793	1	48
Anson, s. Oliver & Anna, b. Apr. 19, 1779	1	49
Asa, s. Michael & Abigail, b. Apr. 12, 1772	1	9
David Clinton, of Torrington, m. Sally **RICHARDS,** Sept. 14, 1823, by Rev. Epaphras Goodman, of Torrington	2	51
Desire, m. Daniel **HALL,** Nov. 21, 1802, by Rev. Mr. Judd	2	73
Edwin P., s. Amos & Sally, b. Jan. 4, 1821	2	141
Edwin P., m. Harriet E. **GILBERT,** b. of Litchfield, July 3, 1848, by J. D. Berry	TM49	25
Hannah, d. William & Ruth, b. Aug. 20, 1775	1	49
Harvey, b. Nov. 30, 1797	2	274
Harvey, m. Anna **BEACH,** Aug. 1, 1824, by Rev. Lockwood Dickinson	2	274
Henry, s. Oliver & Anna, b. June 29, 1790	1	49
Hezekiah, of Albany, N.Y., m. Mrs. Louisa **KINGSLEY,** of Northfield; Nov. 29, 1846, by Rev. Albert B. Camp	TM49	15
Ithamer, s. Amos & Sally, b. Nov. 7, 1821	2	141
Joel, s. Michael & Abigail, b. Nov. 25, 1776	1	9
John, s. Michael & Abigail, b. Dec. 29, 1769	1	9
Lanord, s. Oliver & Anna, b. June 18, 1788	1	49
Lois, d. Michael & Abigail, b. Mar. 3, 1782	1	9
Lucinda, d. Oliver & Anna, b. Aug. 25, 1785	1	49
Mary, b. Mar. [ ], 1762	2	73
Mary, m. John **BISSELL,** Nov. [ ], 1781	2	73
Michael, m. Abigail **CATLIN,** Feb. 3, 1765, by Rev. Judah Champion	1	9
Michael, s. Michael & Abigail, b. Aug. 26, 1774	1	9
Moses, s. Michael & Abigail, b. July 23 1779	1	9
Nabbe, d. Michael & Abigail, b. Oct. 22, 1765	1	9
Nabbe, d. Michael, d. Nov. 26, 1766	1	8
Nabbe, d. Michael & Abigail, b. July 26, 1767	1	9
Nab[b]y, m. James **BALDWIN,** Aug. 16, 1785, by Rev. Judah Champion	1	248
Oliver, m. Anna **LANDON,** June 11, 1778	1	49
Rappael, s. Oliver & Anna, b. Feb. 6, 1781	1	49
Roxana, m. Alban **GUILD,** July 19, 1807, by Rev. Truman Marsh	2	145
Susanna, d. Michael & Abigail, b. Jan. 6, 1785	1	9
William, m. Ruth **STURTEVANT,** May 19, 1774, by Daniel Lee, J.P.	1	49
William E., of Ontenagon, Mich., ae 39, m. Delia E. **WELCH,** of Litchfield, ae 24, Sept. 8, 1853, by Rev. David E. Brown, of Milton. Witnesses Hon. O. P. Seymour, Mrs. Delia Barnes, of Buffalo, N.Y.	TM49	91

	Vol.	Page
DIEBELL, [see under **DIBBLE**]		
DODD, Ann, m. Leonard **CARRINGTON,** Jan. 26, 1841, in Hartford, by Rev. Mr. Moore	TM49	40
Betsey, m. Harry **BUCKLEY,** July 14, 1812, by Rev. Abel Flint	2	15
Mary W., of Hartford, m. George F. **LORD,** of Litchfield, Dec. 12, 1847, by J. D. Berry	TM49	20
DOOLITTLE, Almedia, m. Horace **PECK,** b. of Litchfield, Apr. 30, 1837, by Rev. Samuel Fuller	TM49	37
Bethiah, m. Jonathan **SMITH, Jr.,** Apr. 25, 1765, by Rev. Judah Champion	1	157-8
Damaris, m. Benjamin **HALL,** Jan. 28, 1760, by Rev. Mr. Hall, of Wallingford	1	57
Mehetable, m. Isaac **KILBORN,** May 8, 1757, by Rev. Solomon Palmer	1	103
Phebe, m. Nathan **SMEDLEY,** [, 17] by Rev. Judah Champion	1	122
Sarah J., of Northfield, m. Franklin J. **FOOT,** of Bennington, N.H., Feb. 12, 1854, by Rev. Lewis Jessup	TM49	97
William, of Northeast Penn., m. Rebecca **HALL,** of Litchfield, Oct. 30, 1822, by Morris Woodbury	2	115
DOUBLEDAY, Anna, m. Amos **DEAN,** Oct. 19, 1803, at Lebanon, by Rev. Zebulon Eli	2	77
DOUGLASS, Sam[ue]ll, s. Sam[ue]ll & Mary, b. Dec. 27, 1733	1	9
Sarah, d. Samuell & Mary, b. June 12, 1732	1	9
DOWNS, DOWNE, John M., m. Martha **BRISTOLL,** Sept. 7, 1834, by Rev. Joseph E. Camp	2	297
Louisa A., of Northfield, m. Franklin H. **FROST,** of Waterbury, Dec. 17, 1851, by Lewis Jessup, of Northfield	TM49	75
Thomas, s. James & Rachal, b. May 17, 1771	1	9
Welthy Maria, m. Edward **COWLES,** Feb. 28, 1816, by Morris Woodruff	2	17
DUBOIS, William Augustus, s. Hiram & Anna Maria, b. July 19, 1838	2	119
DUDLEY, Alexander C., s. William & Abigail, b. Sept.10, 1801	2	25
Augustus B., s. William & Abigail, b. June 17, 1793; d. May 1, 1807	2	25
Charles, m. Ruth **HART,** Nov. [ ], 1798, by Rev. Thomas W. Bray	2	9
Charles, m. Rhoda **BALDWIN,** Jan. 11, 1809, by Rev. Mr. Jordan	2	9
Charles A., m. Louisa M. **KINNEY,** May 18, 1842, by Jonathan Brace	2	410
Frederick, s. Charles & Ruth, b. Sept. [ ], 1806	2	9
Lois, d. Charles & Ruth, b. Jan. 29, 1802	2	9
Lois, m. Frederick **GIBBS,** b. of Litchfield, May 5, 1829, by Rev. L. P. Hickock	2	281
Marian, d. Charles & Rhoda, b. Nov. 7, 1809	2	9
Mary Ann, m. Eliada **KILBORN,** b. of Litchfield, Nov. 1, [1843], by Ralph Smith	2	340
Nabby, d. William & Abigail, b. Dec.11, 1789	2	25
Nabbe, m. Levi **FRISBIE,** Oct. 17, 1811, by Rev. Abraham Fowler	2	250
Ruth, d. Charles & Ruth, b. Aug. 24, 1808	2	9
Ruth, w. Charles, d. Aug. 27, 1808	2	9
Ruth, of Litchfield, m. James **LANDON,** of Brimfield, O., Oct. 15, 1840, by Rev. Jonathan Brace	2	331
Samuel Hart, s. Charles & Ruth, b. June [ ], 1804	2	9
Susannah, d. Charles & Ruth, b. Dec. 19, 1799	2	9
William, m. Abigail **BALDWIN,** May 13, 1785, in Guilford, by Rev. Thomas Wells	2	25
William H., m. Lydia **KILBORN,** b. of Litchfield, Nov. 20, 1843, by		

	Vol.	Page
DUDLEY, (cont.),		
Ralph Smith	TM49	1
William N., s. William & Abigail, b. Jan. 16, 1797	2	25
DUNBAR, Albert, m. Harriet M. **BRADLEY,** Jan. 13, 1850, by Rev. David		
L. Parmelee	TM49	44
Martha, m. Garrett **THOMPKINS,** Aug. 14, 1825, by Rev. J. E. Camp	2	265
DUNNING, [see also **DEMING**], Ruth, of Litchfield, m. Samuel H.		
GUENSEY, of Plymouth, Oct. 26, 1848, by Joseph Henson		
*("**DEMING**"?)	TM49	27
Sarah M., of Litchfield, m. Rufus J. **LYMAN,** of New Hartford, Oct.		
26, 1848, by [Joseph Henson] *("**DEMING**"?)	TM49	27
DURKEE, Daniel, s. Abijah & Sibel, b. Jan. 11, 1756	1	9
Elizabeth, d. Abijah & Sibel, b. Feb. 11, 1753	1	9
Lidia, d. Abijah & Sibel, b. Mar. 14, 1760	1	9
DUTTON, Reuben, s. Amasa & Sarah, b. Feb. 3, 1771	1	9
Susanna, d. Amasa & Sarah, b. Nov. 25, 1767	1	9
EADON, [see under **EATON**]		
EASTON, Mabel, m. Daniel **ROBERTS,** July 7, 1794, by Rev. Mr. Wathams	2	59
EATON, EADON, John, m. Sarah **PARMER,** of Sheffield, Cty., of		
Yorkshire, Eng., Jan. 25, 1829, by Isaac Jones	2	279
John Curtus, of Bristol, m. Henrietta Lorain **HINMAN,** of Litchfield,		
Apr. 23, 1848, by Rev. Samuel Fuller	TM49	38
EDWARDS, Daniel S., of Roxbury, m. Mary Ann **WEBSTER,** of Litchfield,		
Apr. 15, 1829, by Rev. Isaac Jones	2	280
Mary A., m. Frederick L. **MERWIN,** b. of Litchfield, Oct. 10, 1849, by		
Benjamin L. Swan	TM49	43
Nehemiah C., m. Ann Maria **MILLER,** b. of Litchfield, Apr. 8, 1845,		
by George H. Hastings. Int. Pub.	TM49	9
Nehemiah Clark, m. Cynthia Ann **WEBSTER,** Oct. 1, 1823, by Rev.		
Isaac Jones	2	124
ELIOTT, George Wheaton, s. W[illia]m & Cynthia, b. Jan. 7, 1828	2	274
Julia Arvilla, d. W[illia]m & Cynthia, b. Feb. 9, 1825	2	274
Stephen Randolph, s. W[illia]m & Cynthia, b. June 25, 1826	2	274
William, m. Cynthia **SHERWOOD,** Mar. 13, 1824, at Southbury, by		
John Pearce	2	274
ELLIS, Mary J., of Naugatuck, m. Joseph S. **HUBBARD,** of Litchfield, Sept.		
17, 1850, by Rev. Herman L. Vaill	TM49	55
ELSWORTH, Abigail, m. Benjamin **COLVER,** July 18, 1770, by Rev.		
Judah Champion	1	46
Ann, d. Joseph & Abigail, b. Nov. 10, 1731	1	11
Joseph, s. Joseph & Abigail, b. Jan. 30, 1738	1	11
Tryphena, d. Joseph & Abigail, b. June 30, 1741	1	11
EMMONS, EMONS, Abner, b. Dec. 2, 1761	1	11
Alice, m. William **MUNSON, Jr.,** Sept. 5, 1815	2	269
Almond, s. Oliver & Anne, b. Aug. 22, 1793	1	172-5
Almond, m. Julian **LOUNSBERY,** Nov. 3, 1813, by James Morris	2	18
Alson, s. Russel & Jemima, b. May 10, 1788	1	50-1
Ama, d. William & Thankful, b. Feb. 29, 1772	1	50-1
Ann Lovisa, d. Almond & Julian, b. Feb. 14, 1817	2	18
Anna, d. William & Thankful, b. Nov. 24, 1777	1	50-1
Arthur, s. Arthur & Sarah, b. June 14, 1757	1	11
Arthur, Jr., m. Elizabeth **PALMER,** Nov. 6, 1777, by Jacob Woodruff,		
J.P.	1	50-1

	Vol.	Page
EMMONS, EMONS, (cont.),		
Asenath, d. Phinehas & Kezia, b. Mar. 18, 1781	1	50-1
Chibar, s. Phinehas & Kezia, b. Mar. 24, 1792	1	50-1
Chebor, m. Nancy **PECK**, Nov. 17, 1814	2	21
Edmond, s. Arthur & Elizabeth, b. Sept. 2, 1782	1	50-1
Eli, s. William, Jr. & Sarah, b. Mar. 20, 1737/8	1	11
Eli, s. William & Thankful, b. Feb. 10, 1781	1	50-1
Eliza, d. Enos & Sally, b. Feb. 20, 1813	2	57
Eliza, m. John C. **GRISWOLD**, Nov. 22, 1832, by Rev. Mr. Taylor, of South Farms	2	289
Elizabeth, d. William & Thankful, b. Feb. 5, 1770	1	50-1
Enos, s. Arthur, Jr. & Elizabeth, b. Apr. 6, 1780	1	50-1
Enos, m. Sally **WEEKS**, Apr. 29, 1800	2	57
Esquire, s. Russel & Jemima, b. Apr. 5, 1784	1	50-1
Ethel, s. Anos & Sally, b. July 6, 1802	2	57
Hannah, m. Silus **RICHMOND**, Dec. 19, 1733, by Capt. John Buel, J.P.	1	37
Heman, s. William & Thankfull, b. Nov. 4, 1791	1	50-1
Henry Brown, s. Almond & Julian, b. Aug. 14, 1814	2	18
Irene, d. Russel & Jemima, b. Sept. 5, 1780	1	50-1
Isaac, s. Arthur & Sarah, b. Sept. 19, 1759	1	11
Jesse, s. Jesse & Sarah, Dec. 18, 1753	1	11
Jesse, s. Russel & Jemima, b. Aug. 2, 1782	1	50-1
John, s. William, Jr. & Sarah, b. May 5, 1750	1	11
John, s. William & Thankful, b. May 2, 1784	1	50-1
Laura, d. Enos & Sally, b. Sept. 12, 1804	2	57
Laura, m. Orson **MOSS**, Jan. 16, 1837, by Dan Catlin	2	297
Lois, d. William & Thankfull, b. Oct. 8, 1788	1	50-1
Lovice, d. Russel & Jemima, b. June 1, 1776	1	50-1
Lucia A., m. James M. **MORSE**, b. of Litchfield, Mar. 25, 1839, by Rev. Richard Woodruff	2	324
Lydia, d. William & Thankful, b. Jan. 30, 1774	1	50-1
Lydia, d. Phinehas & Kezia, b. July 4, 1777	1	50-1
Maria A., of South Farms, m. Nicholas H. **FOGG**, of Watertown, Mar. 7, [1852], by N. C. Lewis	TM49	74
Mary, d. William, Jr. & Sarah, b. Apr. 17, 1754	1	11
Mary, d. William & Thankful, b. Mar. 16, 1783	1	50-1
Nancy, d. Chebor & Nancy, b. Sept. 12, 1815	2	21
Olive, d. William, Jr. & Thankfull, b. May 2, 1769	1	11
Olive, d. William & Thankful, b. May 2, 1769	1	50-1
Oliver, s. Arthur & Sarah, b. Sept. 6, 1768	1	11
Oliver, m. Anna **BROWN**, Mar. 7, 1787, by James Morris	1	11
Oringe, s. Arthur & Sarah, b. Apr. 5, 1763	1	11
Orson, s. Ethiel, b. Aug. 14, 1828	2	105
Pamela, m. Herman **POTTER**, Feb. 24, 1813, by Nathan Bassett	2	46
Pede, d. Phinehas & Kezia, b. May 4, 1785	1	50-1
Phineas, s. Arthur & Sarah, b. Oct. 1, 1756	1	11
Phinehas, m. Kezia **PALMER**, July 18, 1776	1	50-1
Phinehas, d. June 13, 1825, in the 69th y. of his age	1	10
Phinehas B*, s. Phinehas & Kezia, b. Mar. 26, 1790 *("Phinehas R" in Woodruff's)	1	50-1
Reuben, s. Phinehas & Kezia, b. Dec. 6, 1787	1	50-1
Rhoda, m. Orrin **POTTER**, Sept. 24, 1812, by Rev. Amos Chase	2	46

	Vol.	Page
EMMONS, EMONS, (cont.),		
Russell, s. Arthur & Sarah, b. Aug. 18, 1752	1	11
Russel, m. Jemima PALMER, Sept. 21, 1774, by Rev. Mr. Knap, of		
Winchester	1	50-1
Samuel, s. Enos & Sally, b. Dec. 25, 1809	2	57
Sarah, d. William, Jr. & Sarah, b. July 16, 1747	1	11
Sarah, d. Arthur & Sarah, b. Nov. 20, 1761	1	11
Sarah, d. William & Thankful, b. Nov. 17, 175	1	50-1
Tabitha, m. Benjamin GALLUP, May 29, 1767, by Rev. Judah		
Champion	1	136-8
Urania, d. William & Thankful, b. May 28, 1779	1	50-1
Ursula, of Litchfield, m. William PAGE, of Salisbury, June 7, 1835, by		
Rev. Samuel Fuller	TM49	37
Ursula, of Litchfield, m. William PAGE, of Salisbury, June 7, 1835, by		
Rev. Samuel Fuller	2	289
William, Jr., of Litchfield, m. Sarah BARNS, of Farmington, Jan. 4,		
1735/6	1	11
William, Jr. & Sarah, had child b. Mar. 26, 1736/7; d. same day	1	11
William, s. William, Jr. & Sarah, b. Oct. 6, 1744	1	11
William, Jr., m. Thankfull LEE, Apr. 4, 1768, by Rev. Judah Champion	1	11
William, m. Thankful LEE, Apr. 4, 1768, by Rev. Judah Champion	1	50-1
William, s. Russel & Jemima, b. July 27, 1778	1	50-1
ENDERTON, John, m. Clarissa GOODWIN, Nov. 25, 1823, by Rev. Isaac		
Jones	2	122
ENSIGN, Abigail A., d. Samuel, Jr. & Abigail, b. Sept. 18, 1799	2	129
Catharine M., d. Isaac & Sabra, b. Dec. 31, 1791	2	95
Catharine M., m. Enoch J. WOODRUFF, Dec. 31, 1808, by Rev. Amos		
Chase	2	140
Charles, s. Samuel, Jr. & Abigail, b. June 27, 1811	2	129
Emily, d. Isaac & Sabra, b. Apr. 25, 1812	2	95
Esther G., d. Samuel, Jr. & Abigail, b. May 12, 1806	2	129
Frederick, s. Samuel, Jr. & Abigail, b. June 2, 1795	2	129
George, s. Jesse & Electa, b. Nov. 12, 1803	2	76
Harmon, s. Samuel, Jr. & Abigail, b. Feb. 17, 1793	2	129
Harriet E., m. Harley MORSE, Oct. 21, 1845, by Rev. David L.		
Parmelee	TM49	11
Harriet Eliza, d. Jesse & Electa, b. Jan. 4, 1802	2	76
Henry Pierpoint, s. Jesse & Electa, b. Sept. 20, 1808	2	76
Isaac, s. Samuel, b. Sept. 10, 1769; m. Sabra CAMP, d. Abel, June 5,		
1790	2	95
Jesse, m. Electa GOODWIN, May 9, 1798, by Rev. Judah Champion	2	76
Jesse Ensign, s. Samuel & Mary, b. Sept. 15, 1771	2	76
John N., of Watertown, m. Amelia P. NEGUS, of Litchfield, Nov. 1,		
1853, by Rev. H. N. Weed	TM49	92
Lavina, d. Samuel, Jr. & Abigail, b. Oct. 10, 1791	1	172-5
Lavina, d. Samuel, Jr. & Abigail, b. Oct. 14*, 1791 *(Probably "Oct.		
10")	2	129
Lavina, m. Salmon WOODRUFF, Oct. 10, 1811, by Rev. Amos Chase	2	62
Lemuel, s. Samuel, Jr. & Abigail, b. Oct. 18, 1808	2	129
Lewis Grant, s. Jesse & Electa, b. May 6, 1806	2	76
Lucius Bird, s. Jesse & Electa, b. Apr. 7, 1822	2	76
Lucy S., d. Samuel, Jr. & Abigail, b. Sept. 25, 1801	2	129
Mary M., m. Alvah CLARK, b. of Litchfield, June 13, 1827, by Rev.		

	Vol.	Page
FARNUM, FARNAM, FARNHAM, (cont.),		
David, s. Nathan & Rosamond, b. July 20, 1776	1	13
David, d. Sept. 7, 1802, ae 26	1	12
Dinah, w. Seth, d. Jan. 2, 1816, ae 75 y.	1	12
Edwin Pickett, s. [William H. & Marinda H.], b. Feb. 21, 1849	TM49	98
Emely C., m. James W. **HARRISON,** Oct. 11, 1825, by Rev. Henry		
Robinson	2	257
Emily Collins, d. Seth, Jr. & Aseneth, b. Dec. 10, 1803	2	62
Ethel T., s. John & Hannah, b. May 5, 1798	2	63
Ethel T., s. John & Hannah, d. Oct. 9, 1815	2	63
Gad, m. Jane **BISHOP,** May 14, 1760, by Rev. Judah Champion	1	13
Gad, had child b. Dec. 25, 1762; d. Jan. 1, 1763	1	12
Hannah, d. John, Jr. & Lidia, b. July 26, 1755	1	13
Hannah, d. Gad & Jane, b. July 3, 1771	1	13
Hannah, d. Sept. 9, 1777, in her 75th y.	1	52
Hannah, m. Asa **PECK,** June 15, 1786, by Rev. Judah Champion	1	195
Hannah, m. Simeon **HARRISON,** June 2, 1796, by Rev. Amos Chase	2	8
Hannah, m. Ira **BENEDICT,** of Danbury, Mar. 8, 1826, by Rev. Henry		
Robinson	2	261
Harriet, d. Seth, Jr. & Asenath, b. Sept. 8, 1809	2	62
Harriet B., m. George B. **BENTON,** b. of Litchfield, Sept. 8, 1829, by		
Morris Woodruff, J.P.	2	281
James, s. Gad & Jane, b. June 15, 1778	1	92-5
John, Jr., d. Aug. 5, 1756, in the 30th y. of his age	1	12
John, s. Gad & James, b. May 30, 1761	1	13
John, d. July 22, 1780	1	12
John, m. Hannah **TAYLOR,** Nov. 29, 1795, by James Morris	2	63
Joseph, s. Seth & Dinah, b. July 10, 1773	1	13
Joseph, d. Aug. 21, 1777, in his 5th y.	1	52
Joseph, s. Seth & Dinah, b. Aug. 10, 1779	1	53
Joseph, m. Merian **HICKOX,** Dec. 3, 1803	2	67
Leman, s. Seth & Dinah, b. May 8, 1775	1	53
Leman, d. Aug. 28, 1777, in his 3rd y.	1	52
Leman Henry, s. Joseph & Merian, b. July 12, 1812	2	67
Lemira P., d. John & Hannah, b. Mar. 22, 1804	2	63
Lemira P., d. John & Hannah, d. Apr. 28, 1812	2	63
Lemira P., d. John & Hannah, b. Mar. 26, 1813	2	63
Lois, d. Seth & Dinah, b. Dec. 13, 1766	1	13
Lois, m. Ebenezer **BENTON, Jr.,** Mar. 31, 1790, by Rev. Amos Chase	2	78
Luce, m. Ens. Jacob **WOODRUFF,** May 22, 1755, by Rev. Judah		
Champion	1	83
Lucy, d. Gad & Jane, b. Sept. 18, 1773	1	13
Lucy, d. David & Keziah, b. June 7, 1798	1	13
Lidia, m. Jospeh **LINLEY,*** Apr. 17, 1758, by Thomas Harrison		
*("LINSLEY")	1	63
Nathan, m. Rosamond **STEEL,** Dec. 22, 1762, by Rev. Joseph Bellamy,		
of Woodbury	1	13
Nathan, m. Mehetable **ROBINSON,** Dec. 14, 1796, by Rev. Mr. Collin,		
of Lanesborough	1	92-5
Olive, d. Gad & Jane, b. June 3, 1776	1	92-5
Pamela Hickox, d. Joseph & Merian, b. July 14, 1808	2	67
Pamela Hickox, d. Joseph & Marian, d. Oct. 8, 1809	2	67
Pamelia M., m. Homer S. **KEELER,** b. of Litchfield, Jan. 21, 1840, by		

	Vol.	Page
FARNUM, FARNAM, FARNHAM, (cont.),		
Richard Woodruff	2	324
Peter, s. Gad & Jane, b. July 6, 1769	1	13
Phebe Maria, d. Seth, Jr. & Asenath, b. Dec. 22, 1805	2	62
Rebecca, of Litchfield, m. Alanson **TAYLOR**, of Danbury, Oct. 9, 1822,		
by Morris Woodruff	2	114
Rebeckah B., d. John & Hannah, b. Mar. 30, 1800	2	63
Rhoda, d. Gad & Jane, b. May 20, 1780	1	92-5
Rhoda, m. James **MORRIS**, Mar. 6, 1815, by Rev. Lyman Beecher	2	22
Rosemond, w. Nathan, d. July 7, 1796, in the 60th y. of her age	1	12
Rosamond Dudley, d. David & Keziah, b. Jan. 6, 1803	1	13
Rosetta Marinda, d. William H. & Marinda H., b. Apr. 12, 1840	TM49	98
Ruth, d. Gad & Jane, b. Dec. 12, 1765	1	13
Sally, d. Seth & Dinah, b. Oct. 10, 1786	1	53
Sarah, m. Amos **BENTON**, Dec. 25, 1843, by Rev. David L. Parmelee	TM49	2
Sarah J., of Monteray, Mass., m. Charles C. **GREGORY**, of New		
Milford, Feb. 3, 1851, by Rev. William B. Hoyt	TM49	61
Seth, m. Dinah **GIBBS**, Jan. 23, 1766, by Jacob Woodruff, J.P.	1	13
Seth, s. Seth & Dinah, b. May 17, 1777	1	53
Seth, Jr., m. Aseneth **BRADLEY**, Nov. 25, 1802, by Rev. Dan		
Huntington	2	62
Seth Taylor, s. [William H. & Marinda H.], b. Aug. 20, 1847	TM49	98
Thankfull, d. Nathan & Rosamond, b. May 1, 1767	1	13
William H., m. Marinda H. **PICKETT**, Sept. 6, 1837	TM49	98
William Henry, s. Seth, Jr. & Asenath, b. Aug. 22, 1811	2	62
FENN, Frederic, of Washington, m. Betsey **LANDON**, of Litchfield, Oct.		
24, 1837, by Rev. H. Bryant	2	314
Isaac C., of Wolcottville, m. Laura **CURTISS**, of Litchfield, Oct. 4,		
1843, by Rev. H. D. Kitchel	2	340
Phillip C., m. Mary **TRYON**, Sept. 1, 1824, by Rev. Isaac Jones	2	134
Polly, m. Levi **SMITH**, Dec. 7, 1809, by Rev. Joseph E. Camp	2	126
FERNOLD, Mary Ann, of Penfield, Charlotte Cty., N.B., m. Lucius Denman		
WOODRUFF, of Litchfield, Oct. 7, 1846, by Rev. Samuel Fuller	TM49	38
FERRIS, Abigail Julia, [twin with Charles William], d. [Charles &		
Mehetable], b. Apr. 11, 1836	TM49	17
Charles, m. Mehetable **PARSONS**, b. of Litchfield, Mar. 16, 1831	TM49	17
Charles, m. Mahitabel **PARSONS**, Mar. 28, 1831, by I. Jones	2	288
Charles William, [twin with Abigail Julia], s. [Charles & Mehetable], b.		
Apr. 11, 1836	TM49	17
Harriet Lucretia, d. [Charles & Mehetable], b. Jan. 25, 1832	TM49	17
Ithamar, m. Luissa **CATLIN**, June 3, 1821, by Rev. Isaac Jones	2	103
Robert, of New Milford, m. Alice **WRIGHT**, of Milton, Sept. 13, 1843,		
by Rev. E. M. Porter	2	412
FERVER, Chester, m. Rhoda **PARMELEY**, Mar. 13, 1831, by Rev. William		
Lucas	2	286
FIELD, Abigail, m. Neri **CRAMPTON**, July 18, 1768, by Rev. Jonathan		
Todd, of East Guilford	1	131
FILER*, Hannah, m. Charles **KELCEY**, Nov. 8, 1770 *(Arnold Copy has		
"TILER"),	1	103
FILLEY, Benjamin, m. Marian **WINSHIP**, b. of Litchfield, Dec. 24, 1845,		
by Rev. Joel Dickinson, of Northfield	TM49	12
Walter, m. Cornelia A. **WINSHIP**, b. of Litchfield, June 12, 1854, by		
Rev. Benjamin L. Swan	TM49	101

	Vol.	Page
FISH, Elizabeth R., m. George R. **PRESCOTT**, Dec. 13, 1842, by J. Brace	2	411
George Washington, m. Elvira Menarch **POWERS**, b. of Litchfield, Aug. 31, 1845, by Rev. Samuel Fuller	TM49	37
John W., m. Amy **WESTOVER**, b. of Litchfield, Apr. 22, 1838, by Rev. Lewis Gunn	2	317
FISHER, Charles C., s. William & Mary K., b. Dec. 16, 1822	2	0
Clarissa M., d. William & Mary K., b. Aug. 19, 1811	2	0
Cordelia E., of Litchfield, m. Cyrel **CADY**, of Torringford, May 12, 1839, by William Payne	3	328
Cornelia E., d. William & Mary K., b. Apr. 7, 1824	2	0
Cornelia Elvira, of Litchfield, m. George Whitfield **DAVIS**, of Springfield, Mass., July 2, 1846, by Rev. Samuel Fuller	TM49	38
Edward D., of Litchfield, m. Fanny **EVERETT**, of London, Eng., Feb. 18, 1849, by Joseph Henson	TM49	40
Edward Edwin, s. William & Mary K., b. Dec. 20, 1825	2	0
George Frederick Stanton, s. William S. & [ ], b. Oct. 15, 1831	2	0
Hannah R., d. William & Mary K., b. July 1, 1814	2	0
Hannah Roxana, of Litchfield, m. William Elijah **MUNSON**, of New Haven, June 15, 1835, by Rev. Samuel Fuller, Jr.	2	296
Harriet E., d. William & Mary K., b. Mar. 15, 1820	2	0
Mary A., m. W. W. **TYRRELL**, b. of Litchfield, Jan. 6, 1839, by William Payne	2	328
Mary Ann, d. William & Mary K., b. July 6, 1812	2	0
Sabra E., d. William & Mary K., b. Jan. 4, 1817	2	0
William, m. Mary Kerwin **MUNGER**, June 3, 1810, by Rev. Truman Marsh	2	0
William L., s. William & Mary R., b. June 15, 1818	2	0
FISKE, Henry B., of Waterbury, m. Finette **SMITH**, of Litchfield, Aug. 22, 1849, by Rev. William B. Hoyt	TM49	42
FITCH, Harry, colored, m. Harriet **SEYMOUR**, Mar. 13, 1826, by Rev. Seth Higby	2	27
Henry, of Litchfield, m. Pina **WELLS**, of Cornwall (colored), Nov. 5, 1835, by Rev. Samuel Fuller, Jr.	2	296
Maria, m. Henry **GARDINER**, (colored), Jan. 2, 1822, by Rev. Isaac Jones	2	105
Rhoda, m. Abijah **PECK**, June 6, 1773, by Rev. Judah Champion	1	113
FLINT, Augustus, of Amenia, N.Y., m. Julia **LORD**, of Litchfield, Mar. 4, 1847, by Rev. Samuel Fuller	TM49	38
FLOWERS, **FLOWER**, Sarah J., m. John L. **MARVIN**, b. of Litchfield, Sept. 6, 1854, by Rev. H. N. Weed	TM49	103
Susanna, m. Joseph **ROGERS**, Jan. 31, 1759, by Rev. Elnathan Whitman, of Hartford	1	74
FLOYD, Mary, m. Col. Benjamin **TALLAND***, Mar. 16, 1784, in Brookline, N.Y., by Rev. B. Tallmadge *("TALLMADGE" in Woodruff's book)	1	242-3
FOGG, Nicholas H., of Watertown, m. Maria A. **EMMONS**, of South Farms, Mar. 7, [1852], by N. C. Lewis	TM49	74
FOOTE, **FOOT**, Franklin J., of Bennington, N.H., m. Sarah J. **DOOLITTLE**, of Northfield, Feb. 12, 1854, by Rev. Lewis Jessup	TM49	97
Lucy M., m. Alanson H. **KIMBERLY**, Jan. [ ], 1818, by Rev. Amos Pettingill	2	99
Lucy Maria, d. Timothy & Abigail, b. June 19, 1795	1	176-7
Mary, m. David **BALDWIN**, Nov. 20, 1818, at New Haven, by Rev.		

	Vol.	Page
FOOTE, FOOT, (cont.),		
Sam[ue]ll Merwin	2	264
Naby Caroline, d. Timothy & Abigail, b. Nov. 22, 1796	1	176-7
Roxanna, m. Joshua **GARRETT**, May 14, 1823	2	329
Sally Garnsey, d. Timothy & Abigail, b. July 10, 1802	1	176-7
Timothy, m. Abigail **STODDARD**, Oct. 2, 1791, by Rev. Amos Chase	1	176-7
William S., s. Timothy & Abigail, b.Mar. 23, 1809	1	176-7
William S., of Litchfield, m. Adaline T. **FRENCH**, of Bethlem, Jan. 10, 1836, by Rev. R. S. Crampton	2	299
FORBES, Hannah, m. Hick **SMITH**, Sept. 11, 1799, by Rev. Joshua Knap	1	62
Hannah, m. Hick **SMITH**, Sept. 11, 1799, by Rev. Joshua Knap	2	59
Lavinia, m. Edward **PHELPS**, Jan. 3, 1806, by Rev. Mr. Backus	2	41
FORD, Anner, m. Truman **WOOSTER**, b. of Litchfield, Mar. 31, 1850, by Rev. William B. Hoyt	TM49	53
Elizabeth, m. William **MONSON**, Sept. 6, 1835, by Rev. Rufus Babcock	2	86
Elizabeth, of Litchfield, m. Wiliam **MONSON**, of New York State, Sept. 22, 1835, by Rev. Rufus Babcock	2	298
Royal A., b. Aug. 31, 1818; m. Marina **BUELL**, Nov. 13, 1839, by Rev. Jonathan Brace	TM49	3
Royal A., m. Marina **BUEL**, Nov. 13, 1839, by Rev. Jonathan Brace	2	318
Sally, m. George **PETTIS**, Sept. 7, 1828, by Rev. Joseph E. Camp, of Northfield	2	292
Sarah M., d. [Royal A. & Marina], b. May 28, 1846	TM49	3
William B., s. Royal A. & Marina, b. Apr. 25, 1841, at Watertown	TM49	3
FOSTER, Almira, m. Luman O. **PECK**, b. of Watertown, Sept. 26, 1854, by Rev. H. N. Weed	TM49	103
Charles, of Bethlem, m. Catharine L. **WICKWIRE**, of Litchfield, Dec. 17, 1829, by Rev. Abraham Browne	2	283
James H., m. Mary **BENNETT**, of Litchfield, Sept. 17, 1839, by Rev. Jonathan Brace	2	318
Mary Jane, m. Robert D. **SIMPSON**, Nov. 24, 1853, by Rev. David L. Parmelee	TM49	94
FOWLER, Richard, of New Haven, m. Lueza **SANFORD**, of Litchfield, Sept. 14, 1847, by Joseph Henson	TM49	23
FOX, A. Watson, m. Sally **WEBSTER**, July 1, 1832, by Rev. Joseph E. Camp, of Northfield	2	292
Abner G., m. Anna **WEBSTER**, Mar. 2, 1829, by Rev. Joseph E. Camp, of Northfield	2	292
Eliza, of Northfield, m. Merrett **MARKS**, of Harwinton, Jan. 17, 1848, by Rev. Joel L. Dickinson	TM49	22
Fanny, m. Jacob **TURNER**, July 1, 1827, by Fred Holcomb	2	272
Henry H., of Woodbury, m. Julia **WEBSTER**, of Litchfield, Nov. 8, 1835, by R. S. Crampton	2	298
Julia A., m. Truman **SMITH**, Nov. 4, 1833, by Rev. Joseph E. Camp, of Northfield	2	292
Nancy E., m. Lucius J. **TURNER**, July 28, 1833, by Rev. Joseph E. Camp, of Northfield	2	292
FRANCIS, John P., of Lisbon, m. Clarissa **BURLEY**, of Derby, May 6, 1828, by I. Jones	2	276
FRANKLIN, Walter S., m. Sarah **BUEL**, Sept. 25, 1821, by Rev. Joseph E. Camp	2	106
FREAY, Harvay*, s. Rosier & Huldah, b. July 4, 1790 *("Horace" in		

	Vol.	Page
FREAY, (cont.),		
Woodruff's book)	1	176-7
Rosier*, m. Huldah **WRIGHT**, d. Jonathan, May [ ], 1789, by Rev.		
Judah Champion *("Roger **FRY**" corrected by Mrs. Bissell)	1	176-7
Sina*, d. Rosier & Huldah, b. May 29, 1793 *("Sina **FRY**"?)	1	176-7
FREEMAN, Charles, of Litchfield, m. Sarah Ann **NICHOLS**, of Sharon,		
Aug. 9, 1848, by Benjamin L. Swan	TM49	24
Fred, Rev., m. Hannah H. **WOLCOTT**, Apr. 21, 1834, by Rev. L. P.		
Hickok	2	288
FRENCH, Adaline T., of Bethlem, m. William S. **FOOTE**, of Litchfield, Jan.		
10, 1836, by Rev. R. S. Crampton	2	299
Asa J., of Plymouth, m. Julia C. **WINSHIP**, of Litchfield, Feb. 7, 1844,		
by Rev. Isaac Jones	TM49	2
Asa J., m. Lucretia **McNEILE**, Mar. 18, 1852, by Rev. David L.		
Parmelee	TM49	67
Delia, m. David **MORSE**, Sept. 1, 1833, by Rev. Joseph E. Camp, of		
Northfield	2	292
Ebenezer, s. John & Content, b. Dec. 1, 1735	1	13
Martha S., of New Hampshire, m. John **PHELPS, 2nd**, of Litchfield,		
Mar. 6, 1842, at Charlestown, N.H.	TM49	25
Nathan, m. Susan **MORSE**, Dec. 27, 1826, by Rev. Joseph E. Camp, of		
Northfield	2	292
FRINK, Elias, of Cornwall, m. Harriet **TUTTLE**, of Litchfield, Nov. 27,		
1844, by Rev. John F. Norton	TM49	7
FRISBIE, Almira, d. Sherman & Abby, b. Mar. 21, 1828	2	321
Augustus Baldwin, s. Levi & Nabbi, b. Aug. 22, 1812	2	250
Betsey, d. Friend H. & Lucy, b. Jan. 21, 1811	2	143
Betsey, d. Levi & Nabbe, b. Feb. 24, 1820	2	250
Betsey M., m. Henry **FRISBIE**, b. of Milton, [, 1843], by Ralph		
Smith	2	340
Caroline C., d. Levi & Nabbe, d. Dec. 28, 1816	2	250
Caroline C., of Litchfield, m. George **LEAVENWORTH**, of Roxbury,		
Sept. 11, 1844, by Rev. David L. Parmelee	TM49	5
Caroline Collins, d. Levi & Nabbe, b. Mar. 24, 1814	2	250
Caroline Collins, 2nd, d. Levi & Nabbe, b. Apr. 18, 1818	2	250
Eleanor L., of Washington, m. Henry **NASH**, of Canton, Oct. 15, 1834,		
by Rev. Samuel Fuller	2	289
Eleanora Louisa, of Washington, m. Henry **NASH**, of Canton, Oct. 15,		
1834, by Rev. Samuel Fuller	TM49	37
Eliza A., m. Sidney H. **GRANNISS**, b. of Litchfield, Jan. 16, 1848, by		
John F. Norton	TM49	21
Elizabeth, d. Sherman & Abbey, b. July 16, 1822	2	321
Elizabeth, m. Walter C. **PALMER**, b. of Litchfield, Apr. 20, 1847, by		
John F. Norton	TM49	19
Frederick, m. Freelove C. **FRISBIE**, b. of Milton, [, 1843], by		
Ralph Smith	2	340
Frederick, m. Jane **EVERITT**, Oct. 3, 1853, by Rev. James Noyes, of		
Milton Soc.	TM49	92
Freelove, d. Levi & Nabbe, b. July 20, 1823	2	250
Freelove C., m. Frederick **FRISBIE**, b. of Milton, [, 1843], by		
Ralph Smith	2	340
Friend Hezekiah, m. Lucy **BISHOP**, Feb. 1, 1795, by Rev. Mr. Butler	2	143
Hannah, d. Friend H. & Lucy, b. Aug. 20, 1802	2	143

	Vol.	Page
FRISBIE, (cont.),		
Hannah, m. Lyman **BURCH**, Jan. 13, 1822, by James Birge, J.P.	2	108
Hannah B., of Milton, m. Elisha B. **BAILEY**, of Goshen, Oct. 3, 1843,		
by Ralph Smith	2	340
Harriet Burnham, d. Levi & Nabbe, b. June 19, 1816	2	250
Hayston*, s. Friend H. & Lucy, b. Oct. 13, 1804 *("Hastings")	2	143
Henry, m. Betsey M. **FRISBIE**, b. of Milton, [, 1843], by Ralph		
Smith	2	340
Levi, m. Nabbe **DUDLEY**, Oct. 17, 1811, by Rev. Abraham Fowler	2	250
Lidena, m. Asa **BOLLS**, Sept. 2, 1821, by Rev. Asa Tallmadge	2	104
Lucinda, m. James **TRYON**, Jan. 11, 1814	2	31
Margary, m. Daniel **BENTON**, Jan. 28, 1790, by Rev. Judah Champion	1	249
Margary, d. Friend H. & Lucy, b. July 5, 1808	2	143
Margary, m. Noah **STONE**, b. of Litchfield, Jan. 21, 1829, by Rev. Hart		
Talcott	2	279
Mary, m. Benjamin **PECK**, Oct. 22, 1755, by Rev. Judah Champion	1	71
Noah, s. Friend H. & Lucy, b. Nov. 23, 1795	2	143
Orlando Benton, s. Sherman & Abby, b. July 2, 1824	2	321
Ozias Sherman, s. Sherman & Abby, b. Jan. 27, 1831	2	321
Sedena, m. Asa H. **BOLLES**, Sept. 2, 1821	2	268
Sheldon, s. Friend H. & Lucy, b. Oct. 26, 1799	2	143
Sherman, s. Friend H. & Lucy, b. Dec. 3, 1797	2	143
Sherman, s. Friend H., b. Dec. 3, 1797; m. Abbey **PARMELEE**, d.		
Amos, Oct. 14, 1821, by Rev. Asa Tallmadge	2	321
Sherman, m. Abbe **PALMETER**, Oct. 14, 1821, by Rev. Asa Tallmadge	2	104
Theaon, m. Ann **HALL**, Jan. 1, 1834, by Rev. L. P. Hickok	2	288
FROST, Abner, s. Joel & Mary, b. May 29, 1770	1	13
Franklin H., of Waterbury, m. Louisa A. **DOWNS**, of Northfield, Dec.		
17, 1851, by Lewis Jessup, of Northfield	TM49	75
Lois, d. Joel & Mary, b. Dec. 3, 1772	1	13
Mary, d. Joel & Mary, b. Sept. 19, 1774	1	13
Silah, of Torrington, m. Ursula **BROOKER**, Aug. 21, 1823, by Rev.		
Epaphras Goodman, of Torrington	2	50
W[illia]m B., of Waterbury, m. Aurelia **DAMES**, of Litchfield, Oct. 5,		
1841, by Jonathan Brace	2	320
FRY, [see also **FREAY**], Roger*, m. Huldah **WRIGHT**, d. Jonathan, May [ ],		
1789, by Rev. Jonathan Champion *(Arnold Copy has "Rosier		
FREAY". Corrected by Mrs. Bissell)	1	176-7
FULLER, Abigail, m. Stephen **SANFORD**, Jan. 6, 1774, by Rev. Andrew		
Storrs, of Waterbury	1	161
Alice, m. Elias **SANFORD**, Jan. 23, 1776, by Rev. Mr. Backues	1	161
John C., m. Abigail E. **MUNGER**, b. of Litchfield, Mar. 1, 1841, by		
Rev. Thomas Ellis	2	333
GALLUP, Benjamin, m. Tabitha **EMONS**, May 29, 1767, by Rev. Judah		
Champion	1	136-8
Hannah, d. Benjamin & Tabitha, b. Oct. 6, 1770	1	179
Molly, d. Benjamin & Tabitha, b. May 28, 1769	1	136-8
GALPIN, Amos, m. Sybel **TALLMADGE**, Jan. 31, 1785, by Rev. Mr. Foot,		
of Cheshire	1	221
Betsey, d. Amos & Sybel, b. Nov. 8, 1785	1	221
Clarisa, d. Amos & Sybel, b. Feb. 2, 1791	1	221
Clarissa Smith, w. Sylvester, d. July 8, 1840	2	324
Fanny, d. Amos & Sybel, b. Dec. 18, 1796	1	221

	Vol.	Page
GALPIN, (cont.),		
Frances Smith, d. Sylvester & Clarissa, b. May 13, 1834	2	324
Marian, d. Amos & Sybel, b. Dec. 2, 1798	1	221
Mary Ann, m. Leonard **GOODWIN**, Oct. 15, 1817, by Rev. Lyman		
Beecher	2	123
Mary Tallmadge, d. Sylvester & Clarissa, b. Feb. 4, 1836	2	324
Robert Erwin, s.Amos & Sybel, b. Jan. 6, 1795	1	221
Sylvester, s. Amos & Sybel, b. Jan. 13, 1793	1	221
Sylvester, m. Clarissa **SMITH**, Oct. 9, 1831, at West Haven, by Rev. S.		
William Stebbins	2	324
Sylvester, m. Cynthia J. **SMITH**, May 2, 1841, at New Haven, by Rev.		
T. B. Truesdale	2	324
William Dwight, s. Sylvester & Clarissa, b. Mar. 21, 1838	2	324
GARDINER, [see also **GARNER**], Henry, m. Maria **FITCH**, (colored), Jan.		
2, 1822, by Rev. Isaac Jones	2	105
GARNER, [see also **GARDINER**], Ada, m. Albert **BLAKE**, Feb. 12, 1845,		
by Rev. D. L.Marks	TM49	8
GARNSEY, [see under **GUERNSEY**]		
GARRETT, GARRITT, GARRIT, Abba, d. Daniel & Huldah, b. Mar. 6,		
1805	2	94
Anna, d. Daniel & Huldah, b. Dec. 16, 1799	2	94
Anna Maria, d. Joshua & Margarett C., b. Aug. 20, 1830	2	329
Charles, s. Joshua & Margarett C., b. June 21, 1841	2	329
Daniel, m. Huldah **SMITH**, Nov. 12, 1794	2	94
Daniel, s. Daniel & Huldah, b. June 28, 1815	2	94
Daniel, Jr., m. Mary Ann **SMITH**, Sept. 24, 1841, by Jonathan Brace	2	335
George, s. Daniel & Huldah, b. June 17, 1810	2	94
George M., m. Clarissa **MARSH**, Apr. 17, 1842, by Frederick Holcomb	2	410
Huldah Maria, m. Enoch J. **WOODRUFF**, May 4, 1826, by Joseph E.		
Camp	2	266
Joshua, m. Anne **TAYLOR**, Dec. 11, 1735, by Rev. Timothy Collens	1	97
Joshua, s. Joshua & Anne, b. Jan. 26, 1740; d. Feb. 3, 1740	1	96
Joshua, s. Joshua & Anne, b. Jan. 20, 1742/3	1	96
Joshua, s. Daniel & Huldah, b. Oct. 1, 1801	2	94
Joshua, m. Roxanna **FOOTE**, May 14, 1823	2	329
Joshua, m. Margerette C. **BOLLES**, Nov. 4, 1828	2	329
Joshua Bolles, s. Joshua & Margarett, b. Jan. 23, 1832	2	329
Joshua F., s. Joshua & Roxanna, b. Apr. 30, 1824; d. Aug. 30, 1824	2	329
Lewis, s. Daniel & Huldah, b. July 14, 1807	2	94
Olive Maria, m. Henry **WOOSTER**, Sept. 2, 1809, by Rev. Truman		
Marsh	2	31
Roxana, w. Joshua, d. June 13, 1824	2	329
William, s. Daniel & Huldah, b. Apr. 13, 1813	2	94
William Penfield, s. Joshua & Margarett, b. Dec. 16, 1836	2	329
GARTHONE, James, m. Mary **GOODWIN**, Apr. 29, 1823, by Rev. Isaac		
Jones	2	119
GATES, GATE, [see also **GATTE**], Abby, m. Israel **STONE**, June 23, 1795	2	58
Gross, of Harwinton, m. Phebe **BOLLES**, Feb. 24, 1832, by Rev. L. P.		
Hickok	2	288
Isaac, s. Clarrissa Tryon, b. June 4, 1809	1	203
Lura, m. Simeon **BISSEL**, Mar. 20, 1803, by Rev. Truman Marsh	1	212
Rachel, m. Henry **SPENCER**, Oct. 31, 1797, by Rev. Mr. Blakeslee	2	61
GATTE, [see also **GATES**], Charlotte, m. Lyscomb **PALMER**, Nov. 5,		

	Vol.	Page
GATTE, [see also **GATES**],		
1819, by Rev. Isaac Jones	2	83
GAY, Ann, d. John & Lidia, b. Nov. 3, 1729	1	15
David, s. John & Lydia, b. Sept. 8, 1741; d. Oct. 2, 1741	1	96
Ebenezer, s. John & Lydia, b. Dec. 26, 1725	1	15
Eleony, d. John & Lydia, b. Apr. 17, 1738	1	97
Fisher, s. John & Lydia, b. Oct. 9, 1733	1	55
Gift, m. Abel **BARNES**, Aug. 9, 1758, by Rev. Joseph Bellamy	1	128
John, s. John & Lidia, b. Jan. 28, 1727/8	1	15
Lettes, d. John & Lidia, b. Jan. 29, 1739/40; d. Feb. 26, 1739/40	1	96
Lidia, d. John & Lidia, b. Mar. 11, 1724	1	15
Lydia, m. George **BISSELL**, Oct. 1, 1740, by Rev. Timothy Collens	1	85
Mary, d. John & Lidia, b. Oct. 3, 1722	1	15
Peres, s. John & Lidia, b. Jan. 5, 1735/6	1	97
Sary, d. John & Lydia, b. July 20, 1731	1	55
GAYLORD, Patience, m. Julian **GUITTEAU**, Oct. 27, 1774, by Rev. Mr. Newell, of New Cambridge	1	140
Susan, m. William **NORTON**, May 1, 1845, by George Hastings	TM49	10
GIBBS, Aaron, s. Zebulon & Euenis, b. Mar. 1, 1736	1	54
Aaron, m. Desire **CLEMENS**, Aug. 10, 1758, by Rev. Judah Champion	1	139
Aaron, s. Solomon & Honor, b. Apr. 17, 1807	2	43
Abigail, d. Henry & Abigail, b. Aug. 23, 1742	1	19
Abigail, m. Samuel **BARNARD**, June 22, 1758, by Rev. Judah Champion	1	127
Abigail, w. Benjamin, d. Jan. 19, 1767, ae about 80 y.	1	18
Abigail, d. Lemuel & Esther, b. Jan. 15, 1769	1	178
Abigail, d. Lemuel & Esther, b. Jan. 16, 1769	1	179
Abigail, d. Zadock & Lydia, b. Oct. 13, 1773	1	140
Abigail, m. Samuel **ENSIGN, Jr.**, Jan. 6, 1791, by Rev. Amos Chase	1	172-5
Abigial, m. Samuel **ENSIGN, Jr.**, Jan. 6, 1791, by Rev. Amos Chase	2	129
Achsah, d. Caleb & Margaret, b. Aug. 15, 1770	1	139
Amon, s. Henry, d. Mar. 23, 1756	1	14
Amos Alric, s. Moore & Patience, b. Apr. 4, 1787	2	15
Amy, d. William, Jr. & Amy, b. Sept. [ ], 1770	2	7
Amy, m. Zadock **DAYTON**, Jan. 10, 1808, by Rev. Amos Chase	2	132
Amy M., m. Lorenzo **BRADLEY**, b. of Litchfield, June 19, 1831, by Rev. Mr. Taylor, of South Farms	2	289
Anna, d. Medad & Betsey, b. Oct. 5, 1810	2	126
Anne, d. Aaron & Desire, b. July 25, 17[ ]	1	97
Anne, m. Ephraim **SMEDLEY, Jr.**, Jan. 28, 1767, by Rev. Judah Champion	1	76
Anne, d. William, Jr. & Dolly, b. June 24, 1816	2	73
Anthy*, d. Zadock & Sarah, b. June 14, 1790 *("Anthony, a son" in Woodruff's)	1	221
Arthur Foot, s. Willis & Eunice, b. Dec. 3, 1844	TM49	26
Azubah, d. Benjamin, Jr. & Dinah, b. Dec. 13, 1734	1	55
Azubah, m. Cyprian **COLLENS**, Jan. 9, 1756, by Timothy Collens, J.P.	1	89
Benjamin, m. Rachal **WARD** (?), May 18, 1729	1	15
Benjamin, s. Benjamin & Dinah, b. Oct. 12, 1747	1	96
Benjamin, s. Lemuel & Esther, b. Sept. 14, 1773	1	140
Benjamin, s. Lemuel & Esther, b. Sept. 14, 1773	1	178
Birdsey, s. Moore & Patience, b. Feb. 10, 1798	2	15

	Vol.	Page
GIBBS, (cont.),		
Birdsey, s. Reuben M. & Catharine, b. Aug. 2, 1824	2	256
Birdsey, m. Emily **CATLIN**, b. of Litchfield, Sept. 11, 1829, by Rev.		
Harry Frink	2	281
Caleb, s. Benjamin & Abigail, b. Nov. 13, 1729	1	54
Caleb, m. Marjory **STEWARD**, June 30, 1757, by Rev. Judah		
Champion	1	139
Caleb, s. Caleb & Margaram, b. Mar. 11, 1758	1	96
Candace, d. Caleb & Margaram, b. Dec. 27, 1759	1	96
Charles Baldwin, s. Willis & Eunice, b. May 29, 1839	TM49	26
Chauncey, s. Ithamer & Elizabeth, b. May 28, 1784	1	221
Clarissa, d. Ithamer & Elizabeth, b. June 24, 1787	1	221
Clark, s. Zadock & Sarah, b. May 7, 1788	1	221
Cyrenius, s. Caleb & Margary, b. Apr. 30, 1766	1	136-8
Cyrenius, s. Caleb, d. Feb. 1, 1768	1	14
Cyrenius, s. Caleb & Marjory, b. Apr. 17, 1768	1	136-8
Daniel, s. Justus & Hannah, b. Jan. 20, 1775	1	178
Daniel, s. Justus & Hannah, b. Jan. 20, 1775	1	179
Darius, s. Warham & Eunice, b. Feb. 9, 1759	1	139
David, s. Henry & Abigail, b. July 9, 1744	1	19
David, s. Henry & Abigail, d. June 3, 1747	1	18
David, s. Henry & Abigail, b. Oct. 4, 1748	1	19
David, s. Henry & Abigail, b. Oct 14, 1750	1	19
David, s. Henry & Abigail, b. Oct. 14, 1750	1	96
David, s. Henry & Abigail, b. May 16, 1753	1	19
David, m. Sarah **CAMP**, Mar. 12, 1770, by Rev. Judah Champion	1	18
David, 2nd, m. Mary **KNAP**, Feb. 27, 1817, by Morris Woodruff, J.P.	2	97
Dinah, d. Benjamin, Jr. & Dinah, b. Jan. 12, 1740/1	1	54
Dinah, m. Seth **FARNUM**, Jan. 23, 1766, by Jacob Woodruff, J.P.	1	13
Dolly, d. Zadock & Sarah, b. Apr. 12, 1786	1	221
Dorcas, d. Warham & Eunice, b. July 15, 1763	1	139
Eldad, s. Remembrance & Rachel, b. June 5, 1764	1	136-8
Eli, s. Solomon & Honor, b. Nov. 2, 1796	2	43
Eliakim, s. Zebulon & Eunice, b. Mar. 29, 1745	1	96
Eliakim, m. Ruth **HALL**, Jan. 29, 1765, by Jacob Woodruff	1	14
Elias, s. Truman & Anna, b. Feb. 23, 1774	1	140
Elias, s. Solomon & Honor, b. Apr. 22, 1792	2	43
Elizabeth, d. Benjamin & Abigail, b. Feb. 3, 1725	1	54
Elizabeth, d. Zadock & Lidia, b. May 7, 1759	1	96
Elizabeth, d. Zadock & Lidia, d. Oct. 25, 1759	1	18
Elizabeth, d. Zadock & Lidia, b. Dec. 2, 1760	1	139
Elizabeth, d. Lemuel & Esther, b. June 10, 1771	1	178
Elizabeth, d. Lemuel & Esther, b. June 17, 1771	1	179
Emma Eliza, d. Willis & Eunice, b. Apr. 16, 1848	TM49	26
Esther, d. Lemuel & Esther, b. Nov. 6, 1775	1	178
Eunis, d. Zebulon & Eunis, b. Nov. 2, 1739	1	54
Eunice, d. Henry & Eunice, b. Aug. 17, 1784	1	178
Frederick, s. Solomon & Honor, b. Feb. 20, 1803	2	43
Frederick, s. Medad & Betsey, b. July 10, 1806	2	126
Frederick, m. Lois **DUDLEY**, b. of Litchfield, May 5, 1829, by Rev.		
L. P. Hickock	2	281
Friend, m. Lucy **ARCHER**, Mar. 5, 1783	1	221
Gershom, s. Benjamin & Abigail, b. July 28, 1721. "Said to be the first		
male child born in Litchfield".	1	55

	Vol.	Page
GIBBS, (cont.),		
Gideon, s. Simeon & Hannah, b. Sept. 12, 1780	1	179
Gideon, s. David, 2nd & Mary, b. Sept. 20, 1820	2	97
Hannah, m. Jeremiah **GRISWOLD**, Jan. 30, 1734/5, by Capt. John		
Buel, J.P.	1	55
Hannah, d. Justus & Hannah, b. Sept. 27, 1768	1	178
Hannah, m. William **REA***, Nov. 9, 1780, by Esquire Averit, J.P.		
*("**RHEA**" in Woodruff's)	2	5
Hannah, d. Ithamer & Elizabeth, b. Feb. 6, 1782	1	221
Harriet M., d. William, Jr. & Dolly, b. Apr. 7, 1811	2	73
Harriet M., of Litchfield, m. Samuel **CLOCK**, of Poundridge, N.Y.,		
June 10, 1827, by Rev. Henry Robinson, of South Farms	2	271
Henry, of Litchfield, m. Abigail **MARTIN**, of Woodbury, Nov. 8, 1739,		
by Capt. Joseph Minor, J.P.	1	19
Henry, d. Jan. 22, 1769	1	14
Henry, m. Eunice **WOODRUFF**, Dec. 25, 1772	1	136-8
Herman, s. Aaron & Desire, d. Feb. 13, 1771	1	96
Herman, s. Aaron & Desire, b. Nov. 2, 1771	1	97
Hervey, s. Remembrance & Rachel, b. June 14, 1766	1	96
Huldah, d. Eliakim & Ruth, b. Sept. 15, 1765	1	14
Huldah, d. Zadock & Lidia, b. Mar. 13, 1771	1	136-8
Huldah*, m. Simon **CROSBY**, Sept.17, 1783, by Rev. Andrew Storrs,		
of Northbury *(Arnold Copy has "Huldah **GILLET**")	1	171
Ida*, d. Solomon & Honor, b. Jan. 7, 1798 *("Idea" in Woodruff's		
book)	2	43
Irene, d. Justus & Hannah, b. Aug. 20, 1770	1	178
Irene, d. Remembrance & Rachel, b. Aug. 19, 1780	1	140
Isaac, s. Gershom & Tabitha, b. May 18, 1759	1	139
Isaac, s. Justus & Hannah, b. Nov. 14, 1781	1	178
Ithamer, s. Lieut. Benjamin & Dinah, b. June 5, 1756	1	19
Jane, d. William & Mary, b. Jan. 6, 1753	1	96
Jane, m. Jonathan **JOHNSON**, Jan. 12, 1775, by Rev. Judah Champion	1	58
Jerusha, d. Justus & Hannah, b. June 23, 1779	1	178
Justice, s. Benjamin & Abigail, b. July 10, 1731	1	54
Justus, m. Hannah **LINSLEY**, Jan. 13, 1757, by Thomas Harrison, J.P.	1	139
Justus, s. Justus & Hannah, b. Nov. 21, 1766	1	178
Leman*, s. Warham & Eunice, b. Mar. 17, 1765 *("Luman" in		
Woodruff's book)	1	136-8
Leman, s. Remembrance & Rachel, b. Sept. 16, 1776	1	140
Lemuel, m. Esther **JOHNSON**, Mar. 12, 1761	1	139
Lemuel, s. Lemuel & Esther, b. Oct. 4, 1776	1	136-8
Lemuel, s. Lemuel & Esther, b. Oct. 4, 1776	1	178
Levi, s. Justus & Hannah, b. June 25, 1763	1	139
Levi, s. Justus & Hannah, b. June 25, 1763	1	178
Lina*, d. Solomon & Honor, b. Sept. 15, 1788 *("Line" in Woodruff's		
book)	2	43
Line, d. Solomon & Honor, d. Dec. 13, 1812, ae 24 y.	2	43
Lois, d. Remembrance & Rachel, b. Dec. 1, 1770	1	136-8
Lois, m. Aruna **ORTON**, Sept. 1, 1793	2	10
Lorain, d. Justus & Margaret, b. Feb. 5, 1765	1	136-8
Lorain, d. Justus & Hannah, b. Feb. 5, 1765	1	178
Lovell, s. Gershom & Tibatha, b. Aug. 23, 1763	1	18
Lucy, d. Remembrance & Rachel, b. Oct. 16, 1773	1	140

	Vol.	Page
GIBBS, (cont.),		
Lydia, d. Zadock & Lydia, b. Feb. 25, 1754	1	96
Lydia, d. Eliakim & Ruth, b. Mar. 4, 1770	1	179
Lydia, m. Timothy **GIBBS**, Feb. 20, 1782, by Rev. Judah Champion	1	179
Lydia, d. Zadock, Jr. & Sarah, b. Mar. 15, 1784	1	221
Lidia, m. Miles **ORTON**, Jan. 22, 1795	2	10
Marshall Cole, s. Reuben M. & Catharine, b. Oct. 20, 1820	2	256
Mary, d. William & Mary, b. May 17, 1747	1	19
Mary, wid. William, d. Sept. 6, 1806, ae 87	1	220
Medad, s. Lemuel & Esther, b. Oct. 21, 1762	1	139
Medad, s. Lemuel & Esther, b. Oct. 21, 1762	1	178
Medad, m. Betsey **OSBORN**, June 20, 1805, by Rev. Truman Marsh	2	126
Meriam, d. Warham, d. Feb. 17, 1766	1	54
Meriam, d. Warham, d. Apr. 29, 1767	1	54
More, s. Gershom & Tabitha, b. Jan. 12, 1757	1	139
Moore, m. Patience **SKEEL**, June 29, 1786, by Rev. John Miner, of South Britain	2	15
Nathan, s. Zadock, d. Apr. 23, 1765, ae 1 y. 8 m. 13 d.	1	18
Nathan, [twin with Thankful], s. Zadock & Lidia, b. May 11, 1766	1	136-8
Nathan, s. Zadock & Lidia, b. Aug. 10, 1768	1	19
Nathan, m. Anne **GRANGER**, Nov. 15, 1789	1	221
Newton, s. Moore & Patience, b. Apr. 20, 1809	2	15
Newton, m. Sally Ann **PALMS**, b. of Litchfield, Jan. 4, 1830, by Rev. Isaac Jones	2	283
Norvina, d. Truman & Anna, b. Nov. 11, 1775	1	140
Obed, s. Eliakim & Ruth, b. Sept. 16, 1772	1	179
Oliver, s.Garshom & Tabitha, b. May 23, 1762	1	96
Ozias, s. Justus & Hannah, b. Mar. 7, 1758	1	139
Ozias, s. Justus & Hannah, b. Mar. 7, 1758	1	178
Ozias, d. Apr. 2, 1776, at Dedham	1	140
Ozias, d. Apr. 2, 1776, at Dedham	1	178
Ozias, s. Justus & Hannah, b. Sept. 16, 1777	1	178
Phebe, d. Caleb & Margaret, b. Feb. 1, 1775	1	140
Phebe, d. Moore & Patience, b. May 18, 1803	2	15
Phebe, m. Charles **STONE**, Sept. 17, 1822, by Rev. Isaac Jones	2	114
Philo, s. Lemuel & Esther, b. Sept. 15, 1764	1	178
Phinehas, s. Aaron & Desire, b. Oct. 15, 1764	1	139
Preserved, s. Justus & Hannah, b. Jan. 21, 1773	1	178
Rebecca, d. Henry & Eunice, b. Dec. 9, 1779	1	179
Remembrace, s. Benjamin & Abigail, b. Feb. 4, 1734	1	54
Remembrance, s. Benjamin & Abigail, d. Feb. 20, 1738/9	1	18
Remembrance, m. Rachel **HALL**, July 18, 1763, by Jacob Woodruff, J.P.	1	139
Reuben M., m. Catharine **COLES**, June 6, 1819, by Rev. Benjamin Norris, of Weston	2	256
Reuben Marshall, s. Moore & Patience, b. Mar. 14, 1794	2	15
Rhoda, d. Benjamin, Jr. & Dinah, b. Jan. 10, 1742/3	1	54
Rhoda, m. James **CLARK**, Dec. 21, 1762	1	46
Rhoda, d. Eliakim & Ruth, b. Nov. 2, 1767	1	136-8
Rhoda, d. Henry & Eunice, b. Sept. 13, 1775	1	179
Rhoda, d. Benjamin & Thankfull, b. Sept. 18, 1778; m. David **PAGE**, Jr., s. David & Anna, Mar. 12, 1801	2	96
Rhoda, d. Moore & Patience, b. Mar. 17, 1807	2	15

	Vol.	Page
GIBBS, (cont.),		
Rhoda, m. Warham **HARVEY**, Mar. 19, 1823, by Rev. Josiah L.		
Dickerson	2	119
Ruth, d. Zebulon & Eunice, b. May 9, 1751	1	96
Ruth, d. Gershom & Tabitha, b. May 25, 1752	1	96
Ruth, m. Timothy **CROSBY**, Nov. 20, 1777, by Rev. George Beckwith	1	171
Sally Eliza, d. Reuben M. & Catharine, b. Aug. 15, 1822	2	256
Sally O., of South Farms, m. Willis **WILMOT**, of Waterbury, Sept. 25,		
1843, by Rev. Fosdic Harrison, of Bethleham	2	340
Sarah, d. Benjamin & Abigail, b. Jan. 28, 1727	1	54
Sarah, d. Henry & Abigail, d. June 10, 1747	1	18
Sarah, m. Gideon **SMEDLEY**, Nov. 17, 1768, by Rev. Judah Champion	1	34
Sarah, d. Zadock, Jr. & Sarah, b. Aug. 31, 1781	1	178
Sarah, w. Zadock, Jr., d. Dec. 21, 1791	1	220
Sarah, of Litchfield, m. Samuel **SHERWOOD**, of Manchester, Aug. 3,		
1845, by Rev. William Dixon	TM49	11
Sheldon, s. Warham & Eunice, b. Mar. 27, 1768	1	136-8
Simeon, s. Henry, b. Apr. 12, 1755	1	14
Simeon, s. Justus & Hannah, b. Sept. 3, 1759	1	139
Simeon, s. Justus & Hannah, b. Sept. 3, 1759	1	178
Simeon, m. Hannah **MARTIN**, Nov. 18, 1778, by Daniel Everitt, J.P.	1	179
Simeon Martin, s. Simeon & Hannah, b. July 22, 1782	1	179
Solomon, s. William & Mary, b. July 15, 1760	1	96
Solomon, s. Aaron & Desire, d. Oct. 12, 1763	1	14
Solomon, m. Honor **MARSH**, Dec. 27, 1787, by Rev. Judah Champion	2	43
Spencer, s. Warham & Eunice, b. Jan. 26, 1762	1	54
Statira, d. Caleb & Marjeram, b. Mar. 27, 1762	1	18
Thankful, [twin with Nathan], d. Zadock & Lidia, b. May 11, 1766	1	136-8
Tilletson, s. Moore & Patience, b. May 2, 1796	2	15
Timothy, s. Justus & Hannah, b. Dec. 18, 1761	1	139
Timothy, s. Justus & Hannah, b. Dec. 18, 1761	1	178
Timothy, m. Lydia **GIBBS**, Feb. 20, 1782, by Rev. Judah Champion	1	179
Truman, m. Anna **BARNES**, Feb. 17, 1773, by Rev. George Beckwith	1	140
Tryphene, d. Lemuel & Esther, b. June 10, 1779	1	178
Wareham, s. Zebulon & Eunis, b. May 4, 1734	1	55
Warham, m. Eunice **SPENCER**, Mar. 4, 1756, by Rev. John Graham,		
of Suffield	1	139
Warren, s. Zebulon, Jr. & Lidia, b. Aug. 10, 1767	1	136-8
William, of Litchfield, m. Mary **NICHOLS**, of Woodbury, Dec. 4,		
1745, by Rev. Anthony Stoddard, of Woodbury	1	19
William, s. William & Mary, b. May 12, 1755	1	19
William, Jr., m. Amy **PECK**, Sept. [ ], 1769, by Mr. Hart, J.P.	2	7
William, s. William, Jr. & Amy, b. Aug. [ ], 1775	2	7
William, Jr., m. Dolly **JUDD**, Nov. 22, 1808, by Rev. Mr. Chase	2	73
William Augustus, s. William, Jr. & Dolly, b. June 1, 1818	2	73
William Herbert, s. Willis, & Eunice, b. Apr. 26, 1836	TM49	26
Wyllys, s. Moore & Patience, b. Aug. 13, 1804	2	15
Willis, of Litchfield, m. Eunice Maria **BALDWIN**, of New York, Sept.		
22, 1834, by Rev. David G. Tomlinson	TM49	26
Willis, m. Emma Maria **BALDWIN**, Sept. 21, 1834, by Rev. David G.		
Tomlinson, of Milton	2	295
Zadock, s. Benjamin & Abigail, b. Apr. 9, 1727	1	55
Zadock, Jr., m. Lydia **HODGE**, Jan. 8, 1777, by William Cogswell, J.P.	1	179

	Vol.	Page
GIBBS, (cont.),		
Zadock, Jr., m. Sarah **STONE,** Apr. 22, 1779, by Rev. Judah Champion	1	179
Zadock, d. Dec. 12, 1789, ae 67 y.	1	220
Zebulon, m. Eunis **WOODRUFF,** Jan. 22, 1733/4, by Capt. John Buel, J.P.	1	55
Zebulon, s. Zebulon & Eunis, b. Oct. 10, 1737	1	54
Zebulon, s. Remembrance & Rachel, b. June 4, 1768	1	136-8
Zebulon, s. Friend & Lucy, b. Apr. 7, 1784	1	221
GIBSON, William, of New Marlborough, Mass., m. Mary Ann **STANTON,** of Litchfield, Nov. 23, 1842, by Jonathan Brace	2	411
GILBERT, GELBERT, Aaron C., m. Betsey **NOBLE,** Nov. 22, 1802, by Rev. Joseph E. Camp	2	147
Abner, s. Orman & Polly Maria, b. Apr. 29, 1816	2	49
Abner, m. Roxana **GUILD,** b. of Litchfield, Sept. 2, 1838, by Rev. H. Bryant	2	325
Albert Lewis, s. Orrin & Mary, b. June 29, 1809	2	46
Ann, d. Abner & Lydia, b. May 18, 1783	1	216
Anna, d. Orman & Polly, b. Apr. 29, 1819	2	49
Burton, of Warren, m. Thalia **MILLER,** of Litchfield, Feb. 21, 1848, by Rev. Samuel Fuller	TM49	38
Calvin, m. Sally **BEACH,** May 24, 1789, by Rev. Ashbel Baldwin	2	28
Caroline, d. James & Abigail, b. Apr. 15, 1802	2	147
Emily Lemira, d. Orrin & Mary, b. Oct. 27, 1807	2	46
George Gilbert, s. Linus & Maria, b. Jan. 21, 1822	2	148
Harriet, d. James & Abigail, b. Mar. 4, 1809	2	147
Harriet E., m. Edwin P. **DICKINSON,** b. of Litchfield, July 3, 1848, by J. D. Berry	TM49	25
Harriet Lucretia, d. Orrin & Mary, b. July 4, 1817	2	46
Harris, of New Haven, m. Harriet D. **JACKSON,** of Litchfield, Dec. 25, 1843, by Jonathan Brace	TM49	1
Henry Seymour, s. Orrin & Mary, b. June 10, 1811	2	46
Huldah*, m. Solomon **MOSS, Jr.,** Dec. 31, 1800, by Daniel Catlin *("Hannah" in some of the birth records of the children)	2	6
James, m. Abigail **KENNEY** Apr. 9, 1801, by Rev. Jeremiah Day	2	147
Jonathan, s. Orman & Polly Maria, b. Nov. 5, 1817	2	49
Jones B., m. Amanda **CHASE,** Aug. 10, 1834, by Rev. David G. Tomlinson, of Milton	2	295
Lewis T., m. Lydia G. **LOVELAND,** Sept. 16, 1850, by Rev. David L. Parmelee	TM49	44
Linus, of Litchfield, m. Maria **TOLLES,** of Woodbury, Feb. 9, 1821, by Rev. Frederick Holcomb, of Watertown	2	148
Lucretia, m. Jacob **MOSS,** Nov. 8, 1813, by Rev. Mr. Wheeler, of Watertown	2	40
Mary Goodale, d. Orrin & Mary, b. July 20, 1813	2	46
Orin, s. Abner & Lydia, b. Nov. 17, 1785	1	216
Orrin, m. Mary **BARBER,** Jan. 19, 1807, by Rev. Truman Marsh	2	46
Orman, s. Abner & Lydia, b. Nov. 2, 1789	1	216
Orman, m. Polly Maria **TERRIL,** Mar. 12, 1815, by Rev. Isaac Jones	2	49
Polly, m. Samuel **MARSH,** Jan. 6, 1825, by Rev. Isaac Jones	2	138
Sarah, d. James & Abigail, b. July 16, 1818	2	147
Sarah Ann, of Litchfield, m. Isaac B. **WOODRUFF,** of Watertown, Oct. 7, 1841, by Rev. Philo R. Hurd, of Watertown	2	328
William Lewis, s. James & Abigail, b. Dec. 3, 1806	2	147

	Vol.	Page
GILBERT, GELBERT, (cont.),		
William Wallace, s. Orrin & Mary, b. Oct. 23, 1815	2	46
GILES, Anna Idia, of Milton, m. David **JOHNSON,** of Bethlem, Mar. 14,		
1841, by G. C. V. Eastman	2	333
Elizabeth, m. Charles **WHEELER,** b. of Litchfield, Nov. 10, 1841, by		
G. C. V. Eastman	2	335
GILLETT, GILLET, GELLET, GELET, GILLOT, Abigail*, m. Abial		
SMITH, Sept. 24, 1729, by Rev. Benjamin Alton *("Abigail		
PELET" in Woodruff's book)	1	37
Abigial, m. Nathaniel **BENTON,** Dec. 17, 1755, by Rev. Nathaniell		
Taylor, of New Milford	1	127
Abigail, m. Nathaniel **BENTON,** Dec. 17, 1755, by Rev. Nathaniell		
Taylor, of New Milford	1	128
Amos, s. Joseph & Deborah, b. Feb. 23, 1735	1	97
Ann, d. Joseph & Ann, b. June 16, 1731	1	55
Asa, Jr., s. Asa, b. June [ ], 1764	1	221
Asa, m. Naomi **HOLISTER*,** Aug. 9, 1787 *("HOSFORD" in		
Woodruff's)	1	221
Asa, s. Asa & Naomi, b. Oct. 16, 1789	1	221
Deborah, d. Joseph & Deborah, b. Sept. 28, 1738	1	97
Dorothy, of Hartford, m. Ebenezer **BUEL,** of Litchfield, Oct. 19, 1736,		
by Rev. Benjamin Colton	1	87
Huldah*, m. Simon **CROSBY,** Sept. 17, 1783, by Rev. Andrew Storrs,		
of Northbury *("Huldah GIBBS" in Woodruff's book)	1	171
Irene, d. Nathaniell & Mercy, b. Jan. 14, 1736/7	1	97
John, s. Nathaniell & Mercy, b. Feb. 9, 1733/4	1	55
Jonathan, s. Nathaniell & Mercy, b. June 30, 1731	1	55
Jonathan, s. Nathaniell & Mercy, b. June last, 1731	1	55
Joseph, m. Ann **MERELL,** Jan. 23, 1727/8, by Rev. Benjamin Catlin	1	15
Joseph, of Litchfield, m. Deborah **CHAPELL,** of Lebanon, Nov. 9,		
1732, by Rev. Jacob Eliot	1	97
Lydia, d. Joseph & Deborah, b. Oct. 11, 1737	1	97
Mary, d. Nathaniell & Mercy, b. Nov. 19, 1728	1	55
Mary, d. Nathaniell & Mercy, b. Nov. 28, 1728	1	55
Mary, d. Asa & Naomi, b. Mar. 15, 1788	1	221
Naomi, d. Asa & Naomi, b. Jan. 17, 1791	1	221
Naomi, m. Denman **WOODRUFF,** Feb. 1, 1813, by Asa Tallmadge	2	32
Naomi, w. Asa, d. Jan. 30, 1828	2	2
Nathaniel, of Litchfield, m. Mercy **SMITH,** Apr. 6, 1727, by Rev.		
Timothy Collens	1	15
Nathaniel, s. Nathaniel & Mercy, b. Aug. 15, 1739	1	97
Rebecca, m. Lemuel **WOOSTER,** Jan. [ ], 1782, by Rev. Judah		
Champion	2	124
Sary, d. Joseph & Anna, b. Sept. 25, 1728	1	15
Sarah, d. Joseph & Deborah, b. Sept. 10, 1733	1	97
Sarah, m. Isaac **BALDWIN,** Sept. 24, 1823, by Rev. Isaac Jones	2	127
GITTEAU, GUITTEAU, Benjamin, s. Judson & Patience, b. July 4, 1783	1	178
Benjamin, s. Judson & Patience, b. July 4, 1783	1	221
David, s. Judson & Patience, b. Dec. 5, 1775	1	179
David, d. Apr. 1, 1776, ae about 4 m.	1	140
Jerusha, d. Judson & Patience, b. Apr. 7, 1777	1	140
Jerusha, d. Judson & Patience, b. Apr. 7, 1777	1	179
Jonathan, s. Judson & Patience, b. Jan. 14, 1781	1	179

	Vol.	Page
GITTEAU, GUITTEAU, (cont.),		
Julian, m. Patience **GAYLORD**, Oct. 27, 1774, by Rev. Mr. Newell, of		
New Cambridge	1	140
Minerva, d. Judson & Patience, b. Oct. 24, 1786	1	221
Patience, d. Judson & Patience, b. Apr. 1, 1777	1	140
Patience, d. May 12, 1783, ae 24 y.	1	220
Patience, d. Judson & Patience, b. Feb. 11, 1785	1	221
Ruth, of Bethlem, m. Robert **WAUGH**, Nov. 28, 1758, by Daniel		
Everest, J.P.	1	82
GLASS, David, s. James & Hannah, b. July 5, 1780	1	179
Susanna, d. James & Hannah, b. Feb. 9, 1779	1	179
GLAUSON, [see also **GLEASON**], Joseph, of Ansonia, m. Mary A.		
AUSTIN, of Litchfield, May 6, 1849, by Rev. S. T. Seelye	TM49	41
GLEASON, [see also **GLAUSON**], Mary, m. Frederick **DEMING**, July 19,		
1813, by Rev. Noah Porter	2	125
GLOVER, Elisha, m. Ruthy **WEDGE**, Apr. 27, 1815, by E. Tanner	2	45
Lucinda, d. Elisha & Ruthy, b. June 11, 1816	2	45
Nancy F., m. Darling **PRITCHARD**, May 28, 1809, by Rev. Truman		
Marsh	2	45
GOFF, Ruth, d. June 26, 1742	1	14
GOLD, [see also **GOULD**], Joel, s. William & Huldah, b. Dec. 29, 1767	1	136-8
John, s. William & Huldah, b. July 21, 1769	1	136-8
William, m. Huldah **STONE**, Mar. 5, 1767, by Rev. Judah Champion	1	136-8
GOODELL, Eleanor, of Pomfret, m. Joel **TAYLOR**, of Litchfield, July 5,		
1758, by Timothy Sabin, J.P.	1	79
Mary, of Pomfret, m. Zachariah **KEYES**, of Litchfield, Sept. 20, 1750,		
by Rev. William Ebenezer Williams	1	61
GOODRICH, Anne, d. William & Margaret, b. Mar. 20, 1722	1	15
Deborah, m. Daniel **CULVER**, Feb. 12, 1723/4, by Rev. Timothy		
Collens	1	7
Elisha, s. William & Margaret, b. Jan. 5, 1724/5	1	15
Lucy, d. William & Margret, b. July 18, 1729	1	15
Solomon, s. William & Margret, b. Mar. 7, 1726/7	1	15
GOODWIN, Abi, d. Thomas & Anne, b. Nov. 7, 1758	1	140
Abigail, d. Ozias & Hannah, b. Nov. 15, 1771	1	140
Abigail, m. John **OSBORN, 2nd**, Oct. 16, 1822, by Rev. Isaac Jones	2	115
Abraham, m. Mary **BIRD**, Apr. 13, 1726, by Rev. Sam[ue]ll Whitman	1	55
Abraham, s. Charles & Thankful, b. Oct. 13, 1754	1	14
Almira, of Litchfield, m. Gilbert **BRAINARD**, of Bristol, Oct. 16, 1837,		
by Rev. David G. Tomlinson, of Bradleyville	2	314
Ama, [child of Thomas & Ann], b. July 10, 1753	1	96
Amy, d. Thomas & Anne, b. July 10, 1753	1	140
Ann, d. Thomas & Ann, b. July 10, 1753	1	89
Ann Eliza, d. Erastus & Phebe, b. Aug. 25, 1822, at Salisbury	2	262
Ann Eliza, m. Elijah W. **GARNSEY**, Oct. 6, 1841, by Rev. David L.		
Parmelee	2	327
Anna, d. Thomas & Olive, b. May 23, 1807	2	42
Anna C., m. David **BOOTH**, b. of Litchfield, Dec. 5, 1838, by Rev. H.		
Bryant	2	325
Burr, s. Nathaniel & Rhoda, b. Oct. 10, 1794	2	42
Burr, m. Mary **BARNARD**, Nov. 24, 1817, by Rev. Mr. Pettingill	2	69
Catharine, d. Nathaniel & Rhoda, b. May 24, 1789	2	42
Catharine, m. Whiting P. **SMITH**, Feb. 20, 1839, by Rev. Jonathan		

	Vol.	Page
GOODWIN, (cont.),		
Brace	2	318
Charles, s. Abraham & Mary, b. May 5, 1731	1	55
Charles, m. Thankful RUSSELL, Mar. 7, 1754, by Rev. Mr.		
Hemingway, of East Haven	1	14
Chloe, d. Nathaniel & Elizabeth, b. Aug. 14, 1766	1	136-8
Chloe, m. Joseph SANFORD, 2nd, Jan. 1, 1784, by Rev. Judah		
Champion	1	163
Chloe E., d. Erastus & Olive, b. June 16, 1805; d. Nov. 10, 1806	2	262
Clarissa, d. Ozias & Hannah, b. May 24, 1785	1	221
Clarissa, m. Caleb PHELPS, of Troy, Sept. 22, 1806, by Rev. Dan		
Huntington	1	195
Clarissa, m. John ENDERTON, Nov. 25, 1823, by Rev. Isaac Jones	2	122
Clarissa B., d. Erastus & Olive, b. June 26, 1813	2	262
Cromwell, m. Irene THOMPSON, Sept. 24, 1804, by Rev. Dan		
Huntington	1	220
David, s. Charles & Thankful, b. Feb. 28, 1739	1	97
David C., m. Olive Jane MARSH, June 12, 1850, by Rev. Benjamin W.		
Stone	TM49	54
Dorcas, d. Nathaniel & Elizabeth, b. Jan. 8, 1770	1	14
Edmond G.*, s. Erastus [& Olive], d. Nov. 24, 1806, ae 3 y.		
*(Probably "Edward S.")	2	262
Edward S., s. Erastus & Olive, b. Sept. 2, 1803	2	262
Electa, d. Ozias & Hannah, b. Nov. 26, 1773	2	76
Electa, d. Ozias & Hannah, b. Nov. 26, 1773	1	140
Electa, m. Jesse ENSIGN, May 9, 1798, by Rev. Judah Champion	2	76
Eliza, d. Ozias & Hannah, b. Dec. 27, 1775	1	178
Elizabeth, d. Nathaniel & Elizabeth, b. Aug. 2, 1752	1	14
Elizabeth, d. Nathaniell & Elizabeth, d. Sept. 8, 1753	1	14
Elizabeth, m. Samuel WAUGH, Dec. [ ], 1784, by Rev. Mr. Brinsmade	2	55
Elizabeth, m. Samuell WAUGH, Dec. 2, 1784, by Rev. Mr. Brinsmade	1	245
Elizabeth, d. Erastus & Olive, b. May 18, 1811	2	262
Elizabeth, of Litchfield, m. Charles G. IVES, of Bristol, Jan. 27, 1841,		
by Rev. H. D. Kitchel, of South Farms	2	332
Elizabeth Church, d. Leonard & Mary Ann, b. June 5, 1820	2	123
Emeline, d. Erastus & Olive, b. Sept. 25, 1800	2	262
Emeline, m. Myron OSBORN, Dec. 22, 1824, by Rev. Henry Robinson	2	138
Emily, m. Frederick McNEIL, b. of Litchfield, Mar. 26, 1828, by Rev.		
John S. Stone	2	275
Erastus, m. Olive SANFORD, Jan. 30, 1799, by Rev. Judah Champion	2	262
Erastus, m. Theba THOMAS, Mar. 21, 1821, at Salisbury, by Rev. Mr.		
Hide	2	262
Esther, d. Cromwell & Irene, b. Sept. 18, 1805	1	220
Ethan, s. James & Abigail, b. July 31, 1780	1	179
Frederick, s. Leonard & Mary Ann, b. Oct. 5, 1822	2	123
Frederick, of Stockbridge, m. Maria H. TROWBRIDGE, d. Stephen, of		
Litchfield, May 18, 1848, by Rev. Truman Marsh	TM49	24
Hannah, d. Ozias & Hannah, b. Jan. 16, 1769	1	136-8
Harley, s. Thomas & Olive, b. Sept. 29, 1794	2	42
James, s. Nathaniel & Elizabeth, b. Apr. 18, 1757	1	14
James, m. Abigail HARRISON, Oct. 11, 1779, by Rev. Mr. Allen, of		
Pittsfield	1	179
Jesse, s. Abraham & Mary, b. Sept. 3, 1737	1	19

	Vol.	Page

GOODWIN, (cont.),

	Vol.	Page
Ozias, Ens., d. Mar. 1, 1788	1	178
Ozias, of Plymouth, m. Mary Ann JOHNSON, Sept. 30, 1835, by Rev. L. P. Hickok	2	296
Phinehas, s. Abraham & Mary, b. June 8, 1733	1	19
Phinehas, s. Thomas & Anne, b. Jan. 7, 1756	1	19
Phinehas, s. Thomas & Anne, b. Jan. 7, 1756	1	140
Phinehas, s. Ozias & Hannah, b. June 3, 1764	1	139
Polly, d. Ozias & Hannah, b. Dec. 26, 1780	1	178
Rachel, d. Jesse & Rachel, b. June 15, 1763	1	139
Rhoda, d. Ozias & Hannah, b. Jan. 30, 1766	1	136-8
Rhoda, w. Nathaniel, d. Oct. 27, 1796	2	42
Rhoda O., d. Nathaniel & Rhoda, b. Oct. 18, 1796	2	42
Ruth, m. Moses STODDER, May 18, 1732, by Capt. John Marsh, J.P., of Hartford	1	37
Ruth, d. Abraham & Mary, b. Aug. 5, 1743	1	19
Sally, m. Elihu BARBER, Dec. [ ], 1821, by Rev. Lyman Beecher	2	108
Samuel, s. Ozias & Hannah, b. Mar. 22, 1782; d. Mar. 24, 1782	1	178
Samuel Birdsy, s. Ozias & Hannah, b. Aug. 14, 1788	1	221
Sarah, d. Ozias & Hannah, b. Feb. 18, 1779	1	178
Solomon, s. Nathaniel & Elizabeth, b. Apr. 26, 1755	1	14
Solomon, s. Thomas & Olive, b. May 31, 1800	2	42
Tallmadge, s. Leonard & Mary Ann, b. Aug. 31, 1818	2	123
Tallmadge, s. Leonard & Mary Ann, d. Dec. 12, 1820	2	123
Thomas, s. Abraham & Mary, b. June 30, 1729	1	55
Thomas, m. Ann KILBORN, Nov. 23, 1752, by Ebenezer Marsh, J.P.	1	89
Tho[ma]s, m. Ann KILBORN, Nov. 23, [17]52	1	96
Thomas, s. Thomas & Anne, b. Apr. 9, 1765	1	140
Thomas, Jr., m. Olive KILBORN, Nov. 14, 1793, by Rev. Judah Champion	2	42
Uri, s. Thomas & Anne, b. Dec. 13, 1763	1	140
GOSLEE, GOSLIE, Chester, m. Catharine BRAYMAN, [ ], 1820, by Lyman Beecher	2	98
Chester Clark, s. Solomon & Lydia, b. June 3, 1798	2	60
Helen S., m. Henry S. KENNEY, b. of Litchfield, Oct. 26, 1852, by Rev. Benjamin L. Swan	TM49	77
Henry, m. Jerusha ANDREWS, July 3, 1825, by Rev. Isaac Jones	2	141
Henry Rowley, s. Solomon & Lydia, b. Oct. 19, 1800	2	60
Lucretia, d. Solomon & Lydia, b. Feb. 2, 1795	2	60
Minerva, d. Solomon & Lydia, b. Jan. 4, 1791	2	60
Minerva D., m. Heman BEACH, b. of Litchfield, Apr. 2, 1851, by Rev. H. L. Vaill	TM49	61
Sally, d. Solomon & Lydia, b. Aug. 14, 1786	2	60
Samuel Clark, of Litchfield, m. Polly C. WESTON, of Woodville, May 2, 1849, at Woodville, by Rev. F. D. Harriman, of Bantam Falls & Milton	TM49	41
Solomon, m. Lydia STONE, June 10, 1784	2	60
GOULD, [see also GOLD], Charles, s. James & Sally M. C., b. Sept. 11, 1811	2	115
Edward S., s. James & Sally M. C., b. May 11, 1805	2	115
Emeline Letitia, m. Seymour STEVENS, b. of Litchfield, Feb. 19, 1829, by Rev. Harry Finch	2	280
George, s. James & Sally M. C., b. Sept. 2, 1807	2	115
Henry Guy, s. James & Sally M. C., b. Sept. 16, 1801	2	115

	Vol.	Page
GOULD, [see also **GOLD**], (cont.),		
James, m. Sally M. C. **TRACY**, Oct. 21, 1798	2	115
James K., s. James & Sally M. C., b. Nov. 2, 1803	2	115
John, s. James & Sally M. C., b. Nov. 5, 1814	2	115
Julia, d. James & Sally M. C., b. Nov. 7, 1809	2	115
Robert H., s. James & Sally M. C., b. Mar 29, 1818	2	115
William Tracy, s. James & Sally M. C., b. Oct. 25, 1799	2	115
GRACE*, Elizabeth, m. Amos **PALMELEE, Jr.**, May 27, 1786, by Rev.		
Judah Champion *("GROCE" in Woodruff's)	2	135
GRANGER, GRAINGER, Anne, m. Nathan **GIBBS**, Nov. 15, 1789	1	221
Phebe, m. Asa **HOPKINS, Jr.**, Oct. 28, 1765, by Rev. John Graham	1	17
GRANNIS, GRANNISS, Army, m. Alvah **STONE**, b. of Litchfield, Oct. 5,		
1834, by Truman Kilborn, J.P.	2	295
Arme, d. Girdon & Mary, b. June 30, 1803	2	71
Asa L., m. Sally J. **POTTER**, b. of Litchfield, Mar. 11, 1849, by John F.		
Norton	TM49	36
Asahel Lyman, s. Thomas & Ruth, b. Jan. 1, 1814	2	54
Desire G., teacher, ae 28, m. Lucius **GRISWOLD**, farmer, ae 42, b. of		
Milton, Jan. 1, 1854, by Rev. Daniel E. Brown, of Milton	TM49	97
Eliza, m. Eli C. **STONE**, Apr. 2, 1832, by Rev. David S. Tomlinson, of		
Bradleyville	2	290
Frederick Augustus, m. Mary Charlotte **WARD**, b. of Litchfield, Dec.		
24, 1845, by Rev. Samuel Fuller	TM49	37
George, s. Girdon & Mary, b. Dec. 22, 1800	2	71
Girdon, m. Mary **CATLIN**, Mar. 3, 1791	2	71
Girdon & Mary, had s. [ ], b. Aug. 9, 1791; d. [Aug.] 15, 1791	2	71
Girdon, m. Anner **SMITH**, Mar. 3, 1808	2	71
Hannah W., of Warren, m. Homer E. **COOK**, of Plymouth, Feb. 28,		
1853, by Rev. John J. Brandegee	TM49	78
Laury, d. Thomas & Ruth, b. Jan. 11, 1801	2	54
Levina, m. Zerah **KOELER**, June 12, 1823, by Rev. Isaac Jones	2	120
Lois, d. Girdon & Mary, b. Mar. 22, 1798	2	71
Mary, d. Girdon & Mary, b. Oct. 30, 1792	2	71
Mary, w. Girdon, d. June 18, 1804	2	71
Mary Ann, of Litchfield, m. Zenas **TAYLOR**, of Warren, Oct. 25, 1832,		
by Rev. Hart Talcott, of Warren	2	291
Sarah, m. Chauncey **DENNISON**, Jan. 1, 1782, by Rev. Nicholas		
Street, of East Haven	2	145
Sarah, d. Girdon & Mary, b. Oct. 2, 1795	2	71
Sidney H., m. Eliza A. **FRISBIE**, b. of Litchfield, Jan. 16, 1848, by		
John F. Norton	TM49	21
Thomas, m. Ruth **STONE**, Nov. 21, 1799	2	54
Thomas Sheldon, s. Thomas & Ruth, b. July 28, 1807	2	54
Thomas Sheldon, m. Clarissa Irene **SEIMMAY**, June 29, 1828, by I.		
Jones	2	277
GRANT, Ambrose, s. Increase & Ann, b. Sept. 14, 1747	1	96
Ambrose, m. Hannah **MASON**, Nov. 20, 1771, by Rev. Judah Champion	1	136-8
Anne, d. Josiah & Sarah, b. May 30, 1730	1	15
Anne, d. Charles & Dinah, b. Mar. 27, 1779	1	179
Asenath, d. Josiah & Sarah, b. Nov. 1, 1749	1	96
Augustus, m. Elizabeth H. **BARBER**, Nov. 9, 1847, by Rev. David L.		
Parmelee	TM49	20
Bethia M., of Litchfield, m. A. H. **IVES**, of Fairfax Co., Va., Feb. 3,		

	Vol.	Page
GRANT, (cont.),		
1852, by Lewis Jessup, of Northfield	TM49	75
Billy, s. Ambrose & Hannah, b. Feb. 26, 1776	1	179
Charles, s. Increase & Ann, b. July 14, 1749	1	96
Charles, m. Dinah BEACH, Jan. 25, 1776, by Epaphras Sheldon, J.P.	1	179
Charles, s. Charles & Dinah, b. Nov. 15, 1784	1	179
Charles, m. Hannah McNEILE, June 12, 1809, by Rev. Judah		
Champion	2	37
Charles, d. Mar. [ ], 1821, ae 38 y.	2	37
Charles William, s. Charles & Hannah, b. Apr. 28, 1810	2	37
Charlotte, d. Jesse & Anne, b. Jan. 19, 1768	1	179
Chauncey Lewis, s. Jesse & Anne, b. May 8, 1769	1	179
David, s. Josiah, Jr. & Sarah, b. Sept. 4, 1744	1	96
David, s. Ambrose & Hannah, b. Feb. 25, 1778	1	179
David McNeile, s. Charles & Hannah, b. Aug. 11, 1812	2	37
Ebenezer, m. Martha HILL, Nov. 18, 17[4]7	1	19
Elihu, s. Ebenezer & Martha, b. Oct. 11, 1756	1	18
Elijah, s. Josiah & Sarah, b. Apr. 28, 1728	1	15
Elijah, m. Mary ANDREWS, Mar. 10, 1755, by Rev. Mr. Woodbridge,		
of New Haven	1	19
Frederick L., s. Lewis F. & Emma, b. Feb. 2, 1841, in Litchfield	2	325
Frind, s. Thomas & Rachel, b. Sept. 19, 1740	1	19
Hannah, d. Charles & Dinah, b. Aug. 6, 1781	1	179
Harriet Lucretia, d. Charles & Hannah, b. Sept. 9, 1814	2	37
Huldah, d. Ebenezer, b. Mar. 19, 1763	1	139
Huldah, d. Ebenezer & Martha, d. Sept. 8, 1764	1	54
Huldah, d. Ambrose & Hannah, b. Oct. 16, 1774	1	179
Increase, m. Ann HOSFORD, Feb. 19, 1745/6, by Ebenezer Marsh, J.P.	1	96
Isaac, s. Ebenezer & Martha, b. Apr. 3, 1760	1	18
Jeheil, m. Abigail PHELPS, Feb. last day, 1743/4, by Rev. Mr. Tudor,		
of Windsor	1	99
Gerusha, d. Josiah & Sary, d. Nov. 21, 1736	1	54
Jerusha, d. Josiah, Jr. & Sarah, b. Jan. 1, 1736/7	1	97
Jesse, s. Josiah, Jr. & Sarah, b. Dec. 10, 1742	1	96
Jesse, m. Anne LEWIS, Jan. 1, 1767, by Rev. Mr. Rexford	1	179
Joel, s. Elijah & Mary, b. Feb. 21, 1756	1	14
John, s. Josiah, Jr. & Sarah, b. Apr. 23, 1738	1	97
John Mason, s. Charles & Hannah, b. June 14, 1817	2	37
Josiah, Jr., m. Sarah BAKER, Dec. 11, 1735, by Rev. Mr. Stoddard, of		
Woodbury	1	97
Josiah, d. Feb. 26, 1762, in the 81st y. of his age	1	54
Josiah, d. Nov. 15, 1789, ae 79 y.	1	220
Lois, d. Elijah & Mary, b. Nov. 5, 1757	1	14
Lidia, d. Ebenezer & Martha, b. Sept. 18, 1753	1	96
Lidia, d. Ambrose & Hannah, b. Dec. 28, 1772	1	179
Martha, d. Eben & Martha, b. May 4, 1761	1	19
Martha, w. Ebenezer, d. May 20, 1764	1	14
Martha, w. Ebenezer, d. May 26, 1764	1	54
Mary, m. Daniel ALLEN, Apr. 28, 1737, by Rev. Timothy Collen	1	3
Phebe, d. Charles & Dinah, b. Nov. 11, 1776	1	140
Rachal, d. Thomas & Rachal, b. Feb. 26, 1747/8	1	19
Rhoda, d. Josiah, Jr. & Sary, b. June 13, 1746	1	96
Rhoda, m. Zebulon TAYLOR, Jan. 19, 1775, by Rev. Judah Champion	1	121

	Vol.	Page
GRANT, (cont.),		
Rhoda, m. Nathaniel **GOODWIN**, Oct. 3, 1797, by Rev. Judah		
Champion	2	42
Roswel, s. Elijah & Mary, b. Aug. 18, 1762	1	18
Sary, d. Thomas & Rachel, b. Aug. 7, 1745	1	19
Sary, d. Eben & Martha, b. Oct. 24, 1748	1	19
Sarah, m. Elisha **PECK**, Jan. [ ], 1770*, by Rev. Timothy Collens		
*("1730/1")	1	31
Sarah, wid. Josiah, d. Feb. 28, 1777, ae 86 y.	1	178
Sip*, s. Josiah, Jr. & Sarah, b. Nov. 24, 1739 *(Arnold Copy has		
"Tip")	1	96
Thomas, m. Rachel **BUELL**, Dec. 6, 1738, by Capt. John Buell, J.P.	1	19
Thomas, Capt., d. Aug. 16, 1753	1	18
Thomas, s. Capt. Thomas & Rachal, b. Mar. 26, 1754	1	14
Tip*, s. Josiah, Jr. & Sarah, b. Nov. 24, 1739 *("Sip" in Woodruff's)	1	96
Zelotes C., of East Winsor, m. Bethiah J. **MORSE**, of Litchfield, Apr.		
30, 1832, by Levi Peck	2	290
GRAVES, [see also **GREEVES**], Matilda, m. Pompe **LEOPEON**, [ ],		
1806, by Rev. [ ] Romain	2	101
Sarah, d. Asahel & Sarah, b. Aug. 14, 1776; d. Sept. 17, 1777, ae 13 m.	1	140
Si Remembrance*, s. Asahel & Sarah, b. July 12, 1770 *("Remington"		
in Woodruff's)	1	140
GRAY, GREY, Adah, m. Ebenezer **COLVER**, Dec. 5, 1762, by Rev. Judah		
Champion	1	131
Frances A., of Ledyard, m. Ethan O. **BARBER**, of Litchfield, Feb. 24,		
1839, at Ledyard	TM49	22
Polly, m. Minor **POTTER**, Feb. 26, 1817, by Rev. Lyman Beecher	2	128
GREEN, Jacob, of Warren, m. Betsey A. **BLAKESLEE**, July 1, 1832, by		
Rev. L. P. Hickok	2	288
Susanna, m. Enos **BEACH**, Jan. 27, 1796, by Rev. Mr. Farren	2	33
[ ], m. Mrs. Lucina **LUMA**, wid. Minnis (colored), Nov. 12,		
1837, by Truman Marsh	2	315
GREEVES, [see also **GRAVES**], Alexander, s. William & Deliverance, b.		
Sept. 5, 1760	1	139
Elisha, s. William & Deliverance, b. May 28, 1762	1	139
Elisha, s. William & Dolle, d. Jan. 31, 1765, ae 2 y. 8 m. 3 d.	1	18
Huldah, d. William & Dille, b. Jan. 17, 1765	1	18
Lucia, d. William & Deliverance, b. May 5, 1768	1	136-8
William, m. Deliverance **PECK**, June 14, 1759, by Ebenezer Marsh	1	139
GREGORY, Charles C., of New Milford, m. Sarah J. **FARNHAM**, of		
Monteray, Mass., Feb. 3, 1851, by Rev. William B. Hoyt	TM49	61
Harriet A., of New York, m. Rev. Harvey **CAMP**, of Sandusky City, O.,		
Mar. 6, 1850, by Rev. William B. Hoyt	TM49	53
Harriet Maria, d. Horace & Sarah Ann, b. Mar. 13, 1823	2	119
Horace, m. Sarah Ann **BEECHER**, Mar. 1, 1821, by Rev. Mr. Terry, of		
Sharon	2	119
Myron Beecher, s. Horace & Sarah Ann, b. Feb. 24, 1825	2	119
Susan, of Kent, m. Ebenezer **BESLIN**, of Derby, May 6, 1828, by I.		
Jones	2	276
GRIFFIS, GRIFFICE, GRIFFUS, Daniel, s. Thomas & Sarah, b. Apr. 9,		
1737	1	97
James, s. Thomas & Sarah, b. Aug. 29, 1739	1	97
Jonathan, s. Thomas & Sarah, b. Sept. 7, 1734	1	55

	Vol.	Page
GRISWOLD, GRISWOULD, Abigail, d. Asahel & Hannah, b. Dec. 27, 1771	1	18
Abigail, d. Asahel & Hannah, b. Dec. 27, 1772	2	269
Abigail, m. Norman **BARNES**, Dec. 25, 1799	2	87
Abigail E., of Litchfield, m. Albert **BALDWIN**, of Bethlem, Feb. 7, 1843, by Enos Stoddard, J.P.	2	337
Almira, d. John & Rhoda, b. Jan. 6, 1793	2	6
Alvira, d. Julius & Asenath, b. Nov. 2, 1814	2	66
Amanda, d. Midian & Annis, b. July 4, 1792	2	58
Ann, d. Jacob & Comfort, b. June 11, 1723	1	15
Anne, m. Jacob **WOODRUFF**, Dec. 31, 1741, by Rev. Mr. Collens	1	83
Asahel, b. Jan. 23, 1744, at Newtown	2	269
Asahel, m. Hannah **LEE**, July 16, 1760, by Timothy Collins, J.P. ("Feb. 16, 1765" in Woodruff's)	1	18
Asahel, s. Asahel, b. Dec. 22, 1775	2	3
Asahel, s. Asahel & Hannah, b. Dec. 22, 1775	2	269
Asahel, Jr., m. Desire [ ], Aug. 17, 1797	2	3
Balinda, of Washington, m. Charles **WICKWIRE**, Nov. 10, 1828, by Rev. I. Jones	2	278
Benjamin, s. Asahel & Hannah, b. Oct. 13, 1779	2	269
Benjamin, m. Sally **WRIGHT**, Aug. 5, 1799, by Rev. Dan Huntington	2	72
Benjamin, s. Benjamin & Sally, b. Sept. 26, 1810	2	72
Benjamin, m. Sally **BOSTWICK**, b. of Litchfield, May 20, 1839, by Rev. H. Bryant	2	325
Betsey, d. John & Rhoda, b. Aug. 30, 1798	2	6
Betsey, d. Jonathan, Jr. & Betsey, b. Sept. 1, 1808	2	142
Betsey, w. Julius, d. Dec. 20, 1809, ae 26 y.	2	66
Betsey, d. Jonathan, Jr. & Betsey, d. June 10, 1810	2	142
Betsey, m. Jonathan **WRIGHT, 2nd**, Jan. 25, 1824, by Rev. Isaac Jones	2	132
Caroline Mary, d. [Lyman L. & Rachel], b. Oct. 1, 1851	TM49	67
Caty, d. Midian & Annis, b. Nov. 2, 1786	2	58
Chapman, s. Midian & Annis, b. June 13, 1794	2	58
Charles, m. Mary **SLOCUM**, Oct. 15, 1852, by Rev. David L. Parmelee	TM49	76
Chester, s. Elizur & Tryphena, b. Sept. 8, 1782	1	221
Clarissa, d. Midian & Annis, b. June 22, 1785	2	58
Clarissa, d. Asahel & Hannah, b. July 6, 1788	2	39
Clarissa, m. Lyman **HOTCHKISS**, Nov. 13, 1804, by Rev. Amos Chase	2	81
Clarissa, m. Jesse **OSBORNE**, Sept. 22, 1822, by Rev. Isaac Jones	2	4
Clarissa, m. Jesse **OSBORN**, Sept. 22, 1822, by Rev. Isaac Jones	2	114
Clarissa, m. F. T. **JENNINGS**, b. of Milton, Dec. 25, 1848, by Rev. F. D. Harriman	TM49	39
Clarissa M., of Southbury, m. George **BROOKS**, of Harwinton, Sept. 16, 1838, by Rev. Gad N. Smith	2	319
Cornelia A., m. Charles **VAILL**, Apr. 19, 1832, by Rev. L. P. Hickok	2	288
Cornelia Ann, d. John, Jr. & Nabby, b. Mar. 8, 1813	2	280
Daniel, s. Elijah, b. Aug. 1, 1744	1	19
Deborah, m. Edward **PHELPS**, June 18, 1723, by Rev. Mr. Marsh, of Windsor	1	31
Deborah, m. Edward **PHELPS**, June 18, 1723, by Rev. Mr. Marsh, of Windsor	1	112
Deborah, d. Elijah & Elizabeth, b. May 6, 1740	1	19
Deborah, m. Ebenezer **PLUMB**, Mar. 24, 1768, by Rev. Solomon		

	Vol.	Page
GRISWOLD, GRISWOULD, (cont.),		
John C., m. Eliza **EMONS**, Nov. 22, 1832, by Rev. Mr. Taylor, of South Farms	2	289
Jonathan, Jr., m. Betsey **BARNES**, May 25, 1801, by Rev. Judah Champion	2	142
Joseph, Capt. representative May 1742	2	1545
Judd, s. Midian & Annis, b. Sept. 26, 1802	2	58
Judd, m. Polly **PRITCHARD**, b. of Litchfield, Jan. 31, 1830, by Enos Stoddard, J.P.	2	284
Julia E., m. Henry A. **POTTER**, Oct. 3, 1853, by Rev. David L. Parmelee	TM49	92
Julius, s. John & Rhoda, b. Jan. 23, 1784	2	6
Julius, m. Betsey **STEWART**, June 1, 1808	2	66
Julius, m. Asenath **HALL**, Nov. [ ], 1812	2	66
Leman, s. Jonathan, Jr. & Betsey, b. June 20, 1818	2	142
Lester, m. Clarissa Ann **CUMINGS**, Sept. 21, 1823, by Rev. Isaac Jones	2	126
Lewis, s. Benjamin & Sally, b. Apr. 21, 1812	2	72
Linus, s. Midian & Annis, b. Jan. 13, 1804	2	58
Louisa Maria, m. George **BRADLEY**, b. of Litchfield, Apr. 25, 1847, by Rev. Samuel Fuller	TM49	38
Lucius, of Milton, farmer, ae 42, m. Desire G. **GRANNISS**, of Milton, teacher, ae 28, Jan. 1, 1854, by Rev. Daniel E. Brown, of Milton	TM49	97
Lyman L., of Litchfield, m. Rachel **PRINDLE**, of Cornwall, Mar. 24, 1844	TM49	67
Malinda, m. Eli K. **PICKET**, Sept. 22, 1811, by Rev. Truman Marsh	2	57
Mary, d. Jacob & Comfort, b. Mar. 22, 1726	1	15
Mary, d. Benjamin & Sally, b. May 14, 1802	2	72
Melinda, d. John & Rhoda, b. June 16, 1804	2	6
Midian, m. Annis **WADKIER***, [ ], 1784, by David Catlin *("WADKINS" in Woodruff's)	2	58
Midian, s. Midian & Annis, b. Aug. 5, 1800	2	58
Minerva, d. John & Rhoda, b. Dec. 2, 1795	2	6
Morgan, s. Midian & Annis, b. July 10, 1796	2	58
Morgan, of Washington, m. Flora **HAMASTON**, of Litchfield, Sept. 13, 1820, by Moses Woodruff, J.P.	2	96
Myron, s. Jonathan, Jr. & Betsey, b. Oct. 28, 1803	2	142
Nathan Stewart, s. Julius & Betsey, b. July 28, 1809	2	66
Orra, d. Midian & Annis, b. Oct. 15, 1788	2	58
Polly, d. Elizur & Tryphena, b. June 24, 1779	1	221
Polly, m. Orlo **ALLEN**, Apr. 18, 1799, by Rev. Judah Champion	1	210-11
Rachel, d. Elijah & Elizabeth, b. Oct. 18, 1740	1	99
Rhoda, d. John & Rhoda, b. Nov. 28, 1789	2	6
Roena, d. Midian & Annis, b. July 18, 1798	2	58
Roena, m. Ephraim K. **BUNNELL**, Dec. 31, 1823, by Rev. Josiah L. Dickinson	2	257
Sally Maria, d. Benjamin & Sally, b. June 13, 1806	2	72
Sarah, d. Elijah & Elizabeth, b. July 27, 1752	1	96
Sarah, d. Jeremiah & Hannah, b. Aug. 30, 1753	1	18
Sarah, m. Ephraim **BATES**, May 6, 1773, by Rev. Richard Moseley	1	43
Sarah, m. Ezra **PLUMBE, Jr.**, Dec. 4, 1783, by Rev. Judah Champion	1	155
Seth, s. Elijah & Elizabeth, b. May 8, 1757	1	19
Seth, s. Asahel & Hannah, b. Feb. 27, 1770	1	18

	Vol.	Page
GRISWOLD, GRISWOULD, (cont.),		
Seth, s. Asahel & Hannah, b. Feb. 27, 1770	2	269
Stanley, s. Benjamin & Sally, b. May 12, 1804	2	72
Sylvester, s. Benjamin & Sally, b. May 21, 1814	2	72
Thankfull, d. Asahel & Hannah, b. Dec. 11, 1784	2	269
Thankfull, m. Harvey **BIRGE**, Apr. 12, 1806, by Rev. Truman Marsh	2	63
Thomas W., m. Lucretia M. **BENTON**, Jan. 11, 1849, by Rev. David		
L. Parmelee	TM49	39
Timothy, m. Mary **NEWELL**, Mar. 18, 1771, by Rev. Mr. Hawley, of		
Farmington	1	136-8
Welthy, d. Midian & Annis, b. Sept. 5, 1790	2	58
Wealthy, m. Thomas **MOON***, [ ], 1820, by Lyman Beecher		
*("**MOORE**"?)	2	98
William, s. [Lyman L. & Rachel], b. Nov. 21, 1847	TM49	67
William, s. Timothy & Mary, b. [ ]	1	136-8
William Lewis, s. Julius & Asenath, b. Jan. 2, 1817	2	66
GRITMAN, Hiram, of Warren, m. Julia A. **WETMORE**, of Litchfield, July		
2, 1843, by Rev. Ralph Smith	2	412
GROCE, [see also GROSS], Elizabeth*, m. Amos **PALMALEE, Jr.**, May		
27, 1786, by Rev. Judah Champion *(Arnold Copy has		
"Elizabeth **GRACE**")	2	135
GROSS, [see also GROCE], Arma, of Litchfield, m. Nehemiah **BALDWIN**,		
of Goshen, Nov. 26, 1829, by Rev. Birdsey Sillick	2	283
GUERNSEY, GARNSEY, GUENSEY, GURNEY, Anna, m. Abel		
HARRISON, Mar. 21, 1759, by Rev. Judah Champion	1	17
Anne, d. Noah & Hannah, b. Aug. 12, 1779	1	221
Azubah, d. John & Azubah, b. July 6, 1759	1	14
Carolina, d. Noah & Hannah, b. Feb. 18, 1797	1	221
Caroline, d. Noah & Hannah, d. Oct. 31, 1801	1	220
Caroline, m. Seth **CATLIN**, Dec. 21, 1825, by Rev. J. E. Camp	2	265
Clarissa, d. Noah & Hannah, b. Mar. 18, 1782	1	221
Daniel, s. John, b. May 31, 1749	1	18
Dorcas, d. John, b. Feb. 23, 1744	1	18
Egbert, s. Noah & Amanda, b. July 8, 1823	2	86
Elijah W., m. Ann Eliza **GOODWIN**, Oct. 6, 1841, by Rev. David L.		
Parmelee	2	327
Eunice, d. John, b. Nov. 17, 1754	1	18
Hannah, d. Noah & Hannah, b. May 10, 1771	1	140
Hannah Holister, d. John & Laura, b. Aug. 21, 1820	2	88
Isaac, s. John, Jr. & Azubah, b. Jan. 26, 1758	1	96
John, Jr., m. Azubah **BUELL**, Mar. 24, 1757, by Rev. Judah Champion	1	139
John, s. Noah & Hannah, b. Mar. 20, 1789	1	221
John, m. Laura **MOSS**, May 28, 1817, by Rev. Joseph E. Camp	2	88
John & Laura, had s. [ ], b. Mar. 12, 1818	2	88
John Jenkinson, of Watertown, m. Mary Jane **POTTS**, of Stamford,		
June 25, 1837, by Rev. Charles Rockwell	2	313
Joseph H., m. Elizabeth C. **TURNER**, Nov. 26, 1829, by Fred Holcomb	2	283
Julia Ann, d. Noah & Amanda, b. Feb. 11, 1820	2	86
Julia Ann, m. Guy **CATLIN**, b. of Northfield, May 23, 1843, by Rev.		
Albert B. Camp	2	339
Lois, d. John, b. June 15, 1751	1	18
Noah, s. John, b. Aug. 18, 1746	1	18
Noah, s. Noah & Hannah, b. Apr. 10, 1793	1	221

	Vol.	Page

GUERNSEY, GARNSEY, GUENSEY, GURNEY, (cont.),

Noah, Jr., m. Amanda CROSBY, Apr. 25, 1816, by Rev. Joseph E. Camp	2	86
Noah, s. Noah [& Amanda], b. Sept. 11, 1828	2	86
Polly, d. Noah & Hannah, b. May 27, 1785	1	221
Rachal, d. Noah & Hannah, b. Sept. 3, 1773	1	140
Samuel, s. Noah & Hannah, b. Aug. 31, 1775	1	221
Samuel H., m. Frances M. GRISWOLD, b. of Litchfield, Mar. 26, 1845, by Rev. Joel E. Dickinson, of Northfield	TM49	8
Samuel H., of Plymouth, m. Ruth DUNNING*, of Litchfield, Oct. 26, 1848, by Joseph Henson *("DEMING"?)	TM49	27
Sarah, d. John & Azubah, b. Aug. 30, 1760	1	14
William Holister, s. Noah, Jr. & Amanda, b. Apr. 28, 1817	2	86

GUILD, GUILDS, [see also GUILE], Alban, m. Roxana DICKINSON, July

19, 1807, by Rev. Truman Marsh	2	145
Anna Idia, d. Alban & Roxana, b. Oct. 13, 1812	2	145
Clark O., m. Gennet PARMELEE, b. of Litchfield, Sept. 1, 1837, by Rev. H. Bryant	2	314
Clark Osborn, s. Jeremiah, Jr. & Laura, b. June 10, 1815	2	254
David, s. Alban & Roxana, b. Aug. 17, 1808	2	145
David Dickinson Osborn, s. Alban & Roxana, b. Aug. 17, 1808	1	68
David D., m. Eunice THOMAS, Dec. 24, 1834, by Rev. David G. Tomlinson, of Milton	2	295
Disdamona, m. Samuel WRIGHT, May 29, 1814, by Rev. Isaac Jones	2	17
Edmund, m. Maria A. WOOD, b. of Litchfield, May 19, 1850, by Rev. William B. Hoyt	TM49	54
Gad, of Litchfield, m. Sarah TAYLOR, of London, Eng., Nov. 4, 1810, by Rev. Truman Marsh	TM49	27
Gad, m. Sarah TAYLOR, Nov. 4, 1810, by Rev. Truman Marsh	2	146
Jedediah, m. Phebe NEWCOMB, Aug. 31, 1823, by Rev. Isaac Jones	2	122
Jeremiah, Jr., b. Apr. 15, 1792, in Middletown; m. Laura CLARK, Sept. 1, 1813, by Rev. Truman Marsh	2	254
Jeremiah, Jr., b. Apr. 15, 1792, in Middletown	2	254
Leman Andrew, s. Jeremiah, Jr. & Laura, b. Oct. 1, 1823	2	254
Letitia Emeline, d. Alban & Roxana, b. June 7, 1810	2	145
Lewis Hale, s. Jeremiah, Jr. & Laura, b. Oct. 1, 1817	2	254
Louisa, d. Jeremiah, Jr. & Laura, b. Feb. 6, 1821	2	254
Louisa, of Litchfield, m. Albert B. JUDD, of New Milford, Nov. 10, 1845, by Rev. Isaac Jones, of Milton	TM49	12
Mary Elizabeth, d. Alban & Roxana, b. Feb. 26, 1821	2	145
Mary Irene, d. [Gad & Sarah], b. Mar. 3, 1816	TM49	27
Mary Irene, m. James STEVENS, Feb. 1, 1837, by Rev. A. Billings Beach	2	299
Mary Jane, d. Gad & Sarah, b. Mar. 3, 1816	2	146
Penfield Gould, s. [Gad & Sarah], b. Jan. 31, 1831	TM49	27
Roxana, m. Abner GILBERT, b. of Litchfield, Sept. 2, 1838, by Rev. H. Bryant	2	325
Roxana Osborn, d. Alban & Roxana, b. Feb. 29, 1816	2	145
Sally, m. John JENNING, of Cornwall, Dec. 5, 1824, by Rev. Isaac Jones	2	56
Truman, of Waren, m. Lanura CATLIN, of Milton, Feb. 21, 1830, by Rev. I. Jones, in Milton	2	284
William, s. Gad & Sarah, b. Feb. 28, 1812	2	146

	Vol.	Page
GUILD, GUILDS, [see also GUILE], (cont.),		
William Gould, s. [Gad & Sarah], b. Feb. 28, 1812	TM49	27
GUILE, [see also GUILD], Lydia, d. Joshua & Jane, b. May 21, 1774	1	40
GUITTEAU, [see under GITTEAU]		
GUNN, GUANN, James, m. Harriet NUTON, b. of Litchfield, Jan. 1, 1851,		
by Rev. Benjamin W. Stone	TM49	61
Nancy Matilda, d. Samuel & Betsey, b. Mar. 1, 1802	2	55
Polly Betsey, d. Samuel & Betsey, b. Oct. 17, 1794 in Washington	2	55
Ralph Rockwell, s. Samuel & Betsey, b. Dec. 9, 1804	2	55
Samuel, m. Betty ROCKWELL, Nov. 26, 1793, by David Whittlesey	2	55
Samuell Northrop, s. Samuel & Betsey, b. Mar. 15, 1797	2	55
Susan, m. Charles SMITH, b. of Litchfield, Feb. 23, 1844, by Charles		
S. Webb, J.P.	TM49	2
Thomas John, s. Samuel & Betsey, b. July 25, 1799	2	55
Thomas John, m. Phebe MALLORY, Apr. 4, 1824, by Morris		
Woodruff, J.P.	2	80
GUY, Henry, of Middlefield, N.Y., m. Emeline STONE, of Litchfield, Sept.		
25, 1831, by Rev. William Lucas	2	287
HADSELL, Lewis, of Burlington, m. Irene KEELER, of Bantam Falls, Mar.		
21, 1843, at Bantam Falls, by Rev. E. M. Porter, of Milton Soc.	2	412
HALE, [see also HALL], Frances G., of Wallingford, m. Linus MARSH, of		
Northfield, Mar. 7, 1852, by Lewis Jessup, of Northfield	TM49	75
Hiram E., of New Berlin, Wis., m. Julietta CLARK, of Litchfield, July		
3, 1849, by Rev. William B. Hoyt	TM49	42
Mary, d. William & Mary Ann, b. Aug. 31, 1843	TM49	5
William, of Weathersfield, m. Nancy MATHEWS, of Bristol, July 21,		
1830, by Rev. L. P. Hickok	2	285
HALIN, James, of Harwinton, m. Emily WOODRUFF, d. John A., of		
Litchfield, May 2, 1849, by Benjamin L. Swan	TM49	41
HALL, [see also HALE], Aaron, s. Gilbert & Hannah, b. Oct. 15, 1759	1	99
Alandon, m. Elizabeth C. MARSH, Nov. 17, 1825, by Rev. Henry		
Robinson	2	258
Alice, d. Samuel & Anne, b. Apr. 16, 1777	1	141
Almira, d. Linus & Hannah, b. Aug. 26, 1794	1	181
Almira, m. Lorin BATES, Aug. 13, 1816, by Rev. Mr. Teal	2	81
Amanda, d. Joseph & Dorcas, b. Aug. 3, 1792	1	181
Andras, s. Erastus & Polly, b. Sept. 9, 1797	1	181
Andrew, s. Erastus & Polly, b. Sept. 9, 1797	2	76
Ann, m. Theaon FRISBIE, Jan. 1, 1834, by Rev. L. P. Hickok	2	288
Annis, d. Ephraim S. & Sarah, b. Aug. 21, 1790	2	55
Asenath, m. Julius GRISWOULD, Nov. [ ], 1812	2	66
Benjamin, m. Damaris DOOLITTLE, Jan. 28, 1760, by Rev. Mr. Hall,		
of Wallingford	1	57
Benjamin C., m. Harriet PAYNE, Jan. 9, 1822, by Rev. Rodney		
Rossiter, of Plymouth	2	110
Benjamin Cook, s. Linus & Hannah, b. Sept. 14, 1796	1	181
Calvin, s. Joseph & Dorcass, b. Mar. [ ], 1812	1	181
Caroline, d. Linus & Hannah, b. Dec. 13, 1798	1	181
Catharine E., m. Philip S. BEEBEE, Oct. 10, 1838, by Rev. Jonathan		
Brace	2	318
Cordella, d. Erastus & Polly, b. May 12, 1810	2	76
Daniel, s. John & Damaris, b. Aug. 8, 1777	1	141
Daniel, m. Desire DICKINSON, Nov. 21, 1802, by Rev. Mr. Judd	2	73

	Vol.	Page
HALL, [see also **HALE**], (cont.),		
David, s. William, Jr. & Mary, b. Mar. 27, 1777	1	141
David, m. Phebe **SMEDLEY**, Mar. 4, 1802, by James Morris	2	72
David Lumin, s. David & Phebe, b. May 7, 1822	2	72
Delila, d. Erastus & Polly, b. Mar. 31, 1815	2	76
Deliverance*, m. Joseph **DARIN**, Feb. 8, 1743/4, by Rev. Thomas		
Ruggles, of Guilford *(Arnold copy has "Deliverance **HILL**")	1	9
Diana, d. David & Phebe, b. Jan. 3, 1807	2	72
Diany, m. Elijah **ABBOT**, June 4, 1838, by Rev. H. Bryant	2	317
Dorcas, d. Joseph & Dorcas, b. Sept. 27, 1799	1	181
Electa C., of Litchfield, m. Joseph W. **COOK**, of Chicago, Ill., May 1,		
1854, by Rev. Daniel E. Brown	TM49	101
Ephraim, s. Joseph & Dorcas, b. June 13, 1794	1	181
Ephraim S., m. Sarah **SANFORD**, [ ], 1785, by Rev. Joseph		
Bellamy	2	55
Eph[rai]m S., representative May & Oct. 1817, May 1818	2	1555
Ephraim Smedley, s. William Jr. & Mary, b. May 19, 1761	1	141
Erastus, m. Polly **MOSS**, [ ], 1796, by Rev. James Noyes	2	76
Erastus, s. Erastus & Polly, b. Feb. 15, 1808	2	76
Esther Bier, d. Linus & Hannah, b. Mar. 30, 1792	1	181
Gideon, s. William, Jr. & Mary, b. June 20, 1774	1	141
Hannah, d. David & Hannah, b. Jan. 24, 1768	1	98
Hannah, d. David & Hannah, d. Feb. 16, 1769	1	98
Hannah, d. David & Hannah, b. Nov. 26, 1769	1	98
Henry, m. Jane **NORTON**, Dec. 23, 1838, by Rev. Stephen Hubbell	2	320
Huldah, d. Joseph & Dorcas, b. Jan. 5, 1805	1	181
Ithamer, s. William & Jerusha, b. Sept. 23, 1768	1	141
James Lawrence, s. David & Phebe, b. Apr. 15, 1815	2	72
Jennet, d. Daniel & Desire, b. Dec. 7, 1824	2	73
Joel, s. Joseph & Desire, b. Jan. 11, 1808	1	181
John, s. William & Mercy, b. Feb. 26, 1754	1	17
John, s. David & Hannah, b. Jan. 11, 1766	1	98
John, m. Damaris **AVERELL**, Oct. 17, 1776, by Rev. George Beckwith	1	141
Jonathan, m. Clarissa **HEATON**, Sept. [ ], 1829, by Rev. Joseph E.		
Camp, of Northfield	2	292
Joseph, s. William & Jerusha, b. Sept. 14, 1766	1	141
Joseph Catlin, s. Joseph & Dorcas, b. Apr. 27, 1802	1	181
Julia, d. Ephraim S. & Sarah, b. Sept. 6, 1797	2	55
Julia, of Litchfield, m. William H. **McCORD**, of Penn., Feb. 22, 1825,		
by Rev. Henry Robertson	2	74
Lanson, s. Erastus & Polly, b. Sept. 15, 1799	1	181
Lanson, s. Erastus & Polly, b. Sept. 15, 1799	2	76
Linus, s. Linus & Hannah, b. Dec. 13, 1790	1	181
Lucy, d. Daniel & Desire, b. Dec. 10, 1814	2	73
Lucy D., of Milton, m. Frederick D. **PECK**, of "Banbury", Dec. 28,		
1836, by Rev. P. Teller Babbit	2	298
Lidia, m. Stephen **SMITH**, Mar. 26, 1764, by Jacob Woodruff, J.P.	1	118
Lydia, d. David & Phebe, b. Aug. 26, 1802	2	72
Lydia, m. Amos **BISSELL**, b. of Litchfield, Mar. 15, 1827, by Rev.		
Henry Robinson, of South Farms	2	269
Manson, s. Ephraim S. & Sarah, b. Dec. 21, 1802	2	55
Mary, d. Ephraim S. & Sarah, b. Sept. 28, 1788	2	55
Mary, d. David & Phebe, b. Apr. 30, 1817	2	72

	Vol.	Page
HALL, [see also **HALE**], (cont.),		
Mary, d. Daniel & Desire, b. May 1, 1822	2	73
Mary, m. Charles D. **WADHAMS**, b. of Milton, Sept. 14, 1843, by Rev.		
E. M. Porter	2	412
Mehetable, m. John **MOSS**, May 14, 1773, by Rev. Mr. Waterman	1	189
Mercy, d. William & Jerusha, b. June 25, 1764	1	17
Milecent, d. Erastus & Polly, b. Feb. 8, 1803	2	76
Morris, s. Joseph & Dorcas, b. Feb. 15, 1797	1	181
Norman, s. Daniel & Desire, b. Apr. 18, 1805	2	73
Norman, m. Emily **MERRIMAN**, b. of Litchfield, Dec. 6, 1829, by		
Rev. Birdsey Sillick	2	283
Phebe, d. David & Phebe, b. May 12, 1810	2	72
Phebe, of Litchfield, m. Erasmus **JUDD**, of Loraine, O., Nov. 24, 1840,		
by Rev.Thomas Ellis	2	331
Phila, d. Erastus & Polly, b. Nov. 29, 1816	2	76
Polly, d. Erastus & Polly, b. Jan. 31, 1805	2	76
Rachel, m. Remembrance **GIBBS**, July 18, 1763, by Jacob Woodruff,		
J.P.	1	139
Rebecca, d. William, Jr. & Mary, b. Feb. 13, 1768	1	141
Rebecca, d. Ephraim S. & Sarah, b. Dec. 4, 1794	2	55
Rebecca, of Litchfield, m. William **DOOLITTLE**, of Northeast Penn.,		
Oct. 30, 1822, by Morris Woodbury	2	115
Reuben Doolittle, s. Benjamin & Damaris, b. June 14, 1762	1	141
Rhoda, d. Samuel & Anne, b. Mar. 10, 1779	1	141
Ruth, m. Eliakim **GIBBS**, Jan. 29, 1765, by Jacob Woodruff	1	14
Sally, m. Ezekiel **WOODRUFF**, June 30, 1782, by Rev. Enoch		
Huntington	1	207
Sally, d. Ephraim S. & Sarah, b. Sept. 20, 1792	2	55
Sally, d. Daniel & Desire, b. Mar. 17, 1819	2	73
Sally, m. Garry **BISSELL**, b. of Litchfield, June 23, 1831, by Rev.		
William Lucas	2	287
Salmon C., s. Daniel & Desire, b. Nov. 9, 1809	2	73
Samuel, s. William & Mercy, b. May 25, 1750	1	17
Salina, d. Erastus & Polly, b. Sept. 1, 1801	2	76
Selina, d. Erastus & Polly, b. Sept. 1, 1801	1	181
Susan, m. Harley **MORSE**, Feb. 15, 1817, by Rev. James Noyce	2	134
Vanilla, d. Linus & Hannah, b. Sept. 3, 1803	1	181
Vanilla, of Litchfield, m. Charles **BOOTHE**, of Plymouth, Sept. 22,		
1824, by Rev. Rodney Rosseter	2	102
Webster, s. William & Jerusha, b. Mar. 22, 1762	1	17
William, Jr., m. Mary **SMEDLEY**, Feb. 9, 1758, by Thomas Harrison,		
J.P.	1	17
William, s. William, Jr. & Mary, b. Oct. 23, 1758	1	141
William, m. Jerusha **MARTIN**, Feb. 18, 1759, by Rev. Solomon		
Williams, of Lebanon	1	17
William, s. Gilbert & Hannah, b. Mar. 19, 1762	1	99
William, d. July 8, 1779, ae 19 y.	1	180
William s. Ephraim S. & Sarah, b. Mar. 9, 1786	2	55
William, s. Daniel & Desire, b. Sept. 3, 1803	2	73
William Lumin, s. David & Phebe, b. Feb. 10, 1820	2	72
Serviah*, m. Roswell **HARRISON**, [ ], 1821, by Rev. Erastus		
Ripley *("Zerviah")	2	139
HALLOCK, Almira, Mrs., m. Leavitt **MUNSON**, Jan. 4, 1852, by Rev.		

	Vol.	Page
HALLOCK, (cont.),		
David L. Parmelee	TM49	66
Curtiss, m. Harriet **BISSELL,** b. of Litchfield, Nov. 25, 1845, by Rev.		
William Dixon	TM49	12
Edward J., of Castleton, Vt., m. Mary **LANDON,** of Litchfield, Aug. 25,		
1840, by Jonathan Brace	2	319
Jarvis, of Kent, m. Harriet M. **LANDON,** 2nd d. of Abner, of Bantam		
Falls, Jan. 19, 1848, at Bantam Falls, by J. D. Berry	TM49	21
Loran, m. Maria A. **WEDGE,** b. of Litchfield, Dec. 26, 1852, by Rev.		
Charles R. Adams, of West Goshen	TM49	77
HALLOT, Lavina, m. Jeremiah **WILLIAMS,** Jan. 16, 1823, by Rev.		
Ananias Dathick	2	80
HAMIAKS, Abel, of Columbia, N.Y., m. Mary Ann **WADSWORTH,** Dec.		
10, 1834, by Rev. L. P. Hickok	2	296
HAMLIN, Anna, m. John **WETMORE,** [ ], 1795, by Rev. Mr.		
Grann	1	208
Anna, m. John **WETMORE,** [ ], 1795, at Middletown, by Rev.		
Mr. Graves	2	61
David, Jr., of Clay, N.Y., m. Susanna J. **CROSS,** of Litchfield, Oct. 8,		
1827, by Rev. Henry Robinson, of South Farms	2	273
HAMMILL, William, m. Esther R. **SANFORD,** Oct. 8, 1824, by Rev.		
Lyman Beecher	2	136
HAMMOND, Isaac, Dr., of Pleasant Valley, Dutchess Cty., N.Y., m. Dorcas		
BARBER, of Litchfield, Nov. 9, 1837, by Rev. E. Washburn	2	314
HANCOCK, Amasa, s. Abner & Rachel, b. Feb. 15, 1775	1	98
Uriah, s. Abner & Rachel, b. Dec. 7, 1771	1	141
HAND, HANDS, Cornelia, d. Hiram J. & Marian, b. July 16, 1817	2	13
Cornelia, m. Simeon **STONE,** b. of Litchfield, May 17, 1838, by Rev.		
Fosdic Harrison, of Bethlehem	2	317
Cyrus, s. Timothy & Rhoda, b. Oct. 19, 1769	1	57
David Wessells, m. Rebecca Beebe **STONE,** b. of Litchfield, Mar. 1,		
1836, by Rev. Samuel Fuller, Jr.	2	296
Eunice, m. Ozias **SANFORD,** Feb. 4, 1816, by Rev. Isaac Jones	2	88
Frederick **BUEL,** s. Hiram J. & Mary Ann, b. Oct. 26, 1827	2	13
Guy, m. Eunice **STODDARD,** Dec. 26, 1812, by Rev. Truman Marsh	2	15
Guy, d. Sept. 10, 1813, in the 32nd y. of his age	2	15
Guy Stoddard, s. Guy & Eunice, b. Oct. 25, 1813	2	15
Hiram J., m. Marian **CATLIN,** Feb. 20, 1814, by Rev. Isaac Jones	2	13
Jane, d. Hiram J. & Maryann, b. July 25, 1825	2	13
Jane M., m. Charles N. **COOK,** Dec. 1, 1847, by Rev. David L.		
Parmelee	TM49	20
Julia B., m. Israel H. **SMITH,** Nov. 21, 1848, by Rev. David L.		
Parmelee	TM49	39
Julia Benton, d. Hiram J. & Marian, b. Jan. 1, 1815	2	13
Loisa, d. Hiram J. & Marian, b. Aug. 11, 1822	2	13
Rachel, m. Gideon **ALLEN,** Oct. 3, 1799, by Rev. Amos Chase	2	18
Rhoda, d. Timothy & Rhoda, b. Apr. 1, 1773	1	98
Sarah, m. William **THROOP,** Nov. 19, 1767, by Rev. Jonathan Todd	1	121
Timothy, m. Rhoda **BRADLEY,** Nov. 24, 1768, by Rev. Joseph		
Bellamy, of Bethlem	1	99
HANK, Truman, s. Benjamin & Ellis, b. June 11, 1782	1	141
HANNAH, HANNA, Agnis, d. Hugh & Anne, b. Nov. 12, 1773	1	141
Daniel Miller, s. Hugh & Anne, b. Oct. 17, 1766	1	99

	Vol.	Page
HANNAH, HANNA, (cont.),		
Hugh, m. Anne **WATSON**, Apr. 18, 1765	1	99
Jonas, s. Hugh & Anne, b. Apr. 8, 1771	1	141
Medad, s. Hugh & Anne, b. Nov. 20, 1769	1	141
Medad, s. Hugh & Anne, d. Mar. 25,1776	1	180
Rosanna, d. Hugh & Anne, b. Aug. 30, 1776	1	141
Sanford, of Bethlem, m. Eliza **COLLINS**, of Litchfield, Oct. 30, 1821,		
by Rev. Isaac Jones	2	104
Urania, d. Hugh & Anne, b. Jan. 29, 1768	1	99
HARD, Caroline, m. Heman Lewis **CUMMINS**, Dec. 29, 1822, by Rev.		
Isaac Jones	2	116
HARRIMAN, Fred D., Rev., of Crowfordsville, Ind., m. Mary Jones		
BOSTWICK, of Litchfield, Aug. 27, 1851, by Rev. Benjamin W.		
Stone, at Bantam Falls	TM49	63
Louisa, m. Horace **BALDWIN**, Feb. 12, 1824, by Rev. Lyman Beecher	2	133
HARRIS, Abigail, m. Asa **HOPKINS**, Oct. 1, 1741, by Rev. Benjamin		
Colton, of Hartford	1	57
Merian, m. Asahel **HARRISON**, Apr. 28, 1808, by Rev. Charles		
Prentice, of Canaan	2	128
HARRISON, Abel, m. Abigail **CHRISSEY**, Mar. 26, 1756, by Increase		
Moseley, J.P.	1	17
Abel, m. Anna **GARNSEY**, Mar. 21, 1759, by Rev. Judah Champion	1	17
Abel & Anna, had d. [ ], b. Jan. 9, 1760	1	17
Abigail, m. James **GOODWIN**, Oct. 11, 1779, by Rev. Mr. Allen, of		
Pittsfield	1	179
Alexander Hamilton, s. Simeon & Hannah, b. Sept. 1, 1804	2	8
Almon, s. Titus & Ann, b. June 2, 1761	1	17
Ann, d. Gideon & Sary, b. July 28, 1754	1	57
Ann, d. Gideon & Sary, d. Sept. 22, 1754	1	56
Ann, d. Elihu & Theda, b. Dec. 11, 1764	1	99
Anna, w. Roswell, d. Dec. 17, 1819, ae 48	2	139
Asahel, m. Merian **HARRIS**, Apr. 28, 1808, by Rev. Charles Prentice,		
of Canaan	2	128
Charles Lewis, s. John & Mahola, b. Mar. 19, 1801	1	181
Charles William, s. Roswell & Merian, b. Aug. 18, 1811	2	128
Clarinda, d. Elihu & Miranda, b. Nov. 15, 1824	2	101
Clarissa Woodruff, d. John & Mahola, b. Dec. 7, 1802	1	181
Dan, s. Elihu & Theda, b. Sept. 14, 1770	1	99
David, s. Ephraim & Hannah, b. Nov. 9, 1753	1	57
Electa, d. Levi & Electa, b. Apr. 12, 1770	1	99
Elihu, m. Theda **WOODRUFF**, Jan. 19, 1764, by Rev. Judah		
Champion	1	99
Elihu, m. Miranda **WARNER**, Apr. 20, 1820, by Rev. Frederick		
Holcomb	2	101
Elihu, representative May 1832, May 1835	2	1556
Eliza, m. Thaddeus **RUSSELL**, b. of North Bremford, Mass., [May] 28,		
1843, by Jonathan Brace	2	339
Elizabeth, d. Jacob & Elizabeth, b. July 4, 1764	1	99
Elizabeth, m. Noah **BEACH**, Jan. 1, 1783, by Rev. Judah Champion	2	29
Elizabeth, d. Roswell & Serviah, b. June 13, 1822	2	139
Elizabeth, m. Abram C. **SMITH**, b. of Litchfield, Dec. 5, 1838, by Rev.		
Richard Woodruff, of South Farms	2	316
Ephraim, m. Hannah **SANFORD**, Feb. 15, 1751, by Thomas Harrison,		

	Vol.	Page
HARRISON, (cont.),		
J.P.	1	57
Ephraim, m. Lydia P. **STODDARD**, Oct. 6, 1833, by Rev. L. P. Hickok	2	288
Frances, d. William & Clarinda, b. Feb. 6, 1825	2	130
Gideon, m. Sary **WOODRUFF**, Feb. 11, 1746/7, by Timothy Collens	1	57
Gideon & Mary, had d. [ ], b. July 28, 1754	1	16
Hannah, d. Ephraim & Hannah, b. Mar. 20, 1757	1	57
Henry Sanford, s. William H. & Rhoda, b. Sept. 25, 1830	2	115
Jacob, m. Elizabeth **PLUMB**, Feb. 3, 1762, by Rev. Judah Champion	1	141
James, s. Lemuel & Lois, b. July 23, 1767	1	99
James W., m. Emely C. **FARNUM**, Oct. 11, 1825, by Rev. Henry Robinson	2	257
John, s. Levi & Electa, b. July 25, 1772	1	141
John, m. Mahola **PECK**, June 23, 1800, by Rev. Amos Chase	1	181
John S., m. Polly **TODD**, Oct. 16, 1822, by Rev. Joseph E. Camp, of Northfield	2	292
Joseph, s. Gideon & Mary, b. Oct. 28, 1752	1	16
Julia, d. William & Clarinda, b. May 1, 1829	2	130
Lemuel, m. Lois **BARNES**, Feb. 18, 1762, by Jacob Woodruff, J.P.	1	99
Lemuel, s. Lemuel & Lois, b. Nov. 17, 1765	1	99
Levi, m. Electa **WOODRUFF**, Oct. 21, 1766, by Rev. Judah Champion	1	99
Levi, his child, d. Apr. 12, 1769	1	56
Levina, d. Ephraim & Hannah, b. May 17, 1767	1	17
Levina, d. Ephraim & Hannah, d. Aug. 7, 1777	1	56
Lois, d. Titus & Anne, b. Nov. 6, 1756	1	57
Lois, d. Lemuel & Lois, b. Aug. 29, 1776	1	141
Lucinda, d. Roswell & Merian, b. Oct. 27, 1815	2	128
Lucinda, of Litchfield, m. James **McDANIEL**, of Bethlem, May 11, 1836, by Rev. Fosdic Harrison, of Bethlem	2	297
Luce, d. Ephraim & Hannah, b. Mar. 29, 1762	1	99
Lucy Maria, d. Simeon & Hannah, b. Nov. 18, 1800	2	8
Lucy Maria, of Litchfield, m. Abraham **BROWN**, of Hartford, Vt., Oct. 18, 1826, by Rev. Henry Robinson, of South Farms	2	101
Lidia, d. Elihu & Theda, b. Jan. 8, 1766	1	99
Lydia, m. Dr. Joseph **PARKER**, Jan. 2, 1786, by James Morris	2	84
Mary, d. Gideon & Sary, b. Nov. 29, 1747	1	57
Mary, d. Ephraim & Hannah, b. Dec. 13, 1754	1	57
Mary, m. Obed **STODDARD**, Mar. 4, 1767, by Rev. Judah Champion	1	159
Mary Ann, d. Thomas & Sibel, b. June 18, 1769	1	99
Maryan, d. Roswell & Anna, b. Sept. 29, 1798	2	139
Marian, m. Nathan D. **SMITH**, Mar. 19, 1818	2	121
Melinda, d. Roswell & Merian, b. Aug. 23, 1820	2	128
Malinda L., m. Wilson D. **WAGONER**, Oct. 18, 1843, by Rev. David L. Parmelee	2	340
Meriam, d. Roswell & Merian, b. Jan. 5, 1810	2	128
Minerva, d. Elihu & Miranda, b. Feb. 10, 1821	2	101
Noah, s. Titus & Ann, b. July 12, 1759	1	17
Olive, d. Levi & Electa, b. June 17, 1767	1	99
Olney, s. Lemuel & Lois, b. Nov. 24, 1774	1	141
Olney, s. Lemuel & Lois, d. Nov. 16, 1776	1	56
Phebe, d. Lemuel & Lois, b. June 6, 1769	1	99
Rachal, d. Ephraim & Hannah, b. Feb. 15, 1751	1	57
Reuben, s. Abel & Anah, b. Jan. 1, 1762	1	99

	Vol.	Page

HARRISON, (cont.),

Rhoda S., Mrs., m. Edward **COWLES**, b. of Litchfield, Sept. 22, 1839,
   by Rev. Richard Woodruff | 2 | 324
Rollin Hamilton, s. William H. & Rhoda, b. Sept. 14, 1823 | 2 | 115
Roswell, m. Anna **SPERRY**, May [ ], 1796, by Rev. Nathaniel Taylor | 2 | 139
Roswell, m. Serviah **HALL**, [   ], 1821, by Rev. Erastus Ripley | 2 | 139
Roswell, m. Sarah **MERRIMAN**, Dec. 1, 1841, by J. Brace | 2 | 335
Samuel, s. Jacob & Elizabeth, b. Nov. 20, 1763 | 1 | 141
Sarah, d. Gideon & Sary, b. Feb. 20, 1749/50 | 1 | 57
Sila M., m. James M. **PIERPOINT**, Nov. 5, 1823, by Rev. Henry
   Robinson | 2 | 130
Sila Mitchel, d. Roswell & Anna, b. Aug. 16, 1801 | 2 | 139
Simeon, s. Elihu & Theda, b. Oct. 8, 1768 | 1 | 99
Simeon, m. Hannah **FARNUM**, June 2, 1796, by Rev. Amos Chase | 2 | 8
Simon Gibson, s. Roswell & Merian, b. Oct. 27, 1813 | 2 | 128
Solomon, s. Ephraim & Hannah, b. Apr. 17, 1760 | 1 | 57
Stephen Sperry, s. Roswell & Anna, b. Oct. 7, 1804 | 2 | 139
Thomas, representative May & Oct. 1747, Oct. 1749, May & Oct. 1750,
   May & Oct. 1751, Oct. 1753, May 1752, Oct. 1754 | 2 | 1546-7
Thomas, m. Sibel **SHUMWAY**, Sept. 20, 1764, by Elisha Stoddard | 1 | 99
Thomas, s. Thomas & Sibel, b. Aug. 18, 1765 | 1 | 99
Thomas, s. Thomas & Elizabeth, b. May 14, 1781 | 1 | 56
Timothy, s. Lemuel & Lois, b. Oct. 31, 1763 | 1 | 99
Titus, m. Anna **PECK**, Feb. 18, 1756, by Thomas Harrison, J.P. | 1 | 57
William, m. Clarissa **SANFORD**, Nov. 12, 1823, by Rev. Henry
   Robinson | 2 | 130
William Henry, s. Simeon & Hannah, b. Sept. 29, 1797 | 2 | 8
William Henry, m. Rhoda **SANFORD**, b. of Litchfield, Nov. 6, 1822,
   by Morris Woodruff, J.P. | 2 | 115
Wooster, s. Lemuel & Lois, b. June 18, 1772 | 1 | 141

HART, Abiel W., s. William A. & Mary, b. Nov. 7, 1804 | 2 | 7

Benjamin, m. Hannah **CURTISS**, Dec. 15, 1775, at Wallingford, by
   Rev. Simeon Waterman | 2 | 249
Charles, s. Lorenzo & Amelia, b. Apr. 20, 1823 | 2 | 252
Fanny, m. Moses **MOORE**, Mar. 30, 1835, by Rev. L. P. Hickok | 2 | 296
Isaac, s. Benjamin & Hannah, b. Apr. 1, 1788 | 2 | 249
Isaac, m. Martha **BUTLER**, Mar. 19, 1812, in Harwinton, by Rev.
   Joseph E. Camp | 2 | 249
Isaac, d. Mar. 6, 1834, ae 46 | 2 | 249
Isaac Phinehas, s. Isaac & Martha, b. July 16, 1834 | 2 | 249
Jonathan, s. Benjamin & Hannah, b. Aug. 11, 1786 | 2 | 249
Lamira, d. Isaac & Martha, b. Dec. 31, 1822 | 2 | 249
Lorenzo, s. William A. & Margaretta, b. May 9, 1792 | 2 | 7
Lorenzo, m. Amelia **WORDEN**, Nov. 11, 1821, by Rev. Isaac Jones | 2 | 105
Lorenzo, m. Amelia **WARDEN**, Oct. [Nov.] 11, 1821, by Rev. Isaac
   Jones | 2 | 252
Lucy, [twin with Phebe], d. Benjamin & Hannah, b. Aug. 28, 1784 | 2 | 249
Lucy, m. Eliakim **CURTISS**, Mar. 29, 1819, by Rev. Joseph E. Camp | 2 | 255
Lucy Ann, d. Isaac & Martha, b. June 7, 1816 | 2 | 249
Lurany, twin with Nancy, d. William A. & Margaretta, b. Sept. 9, 1795 | 2 | 7
Luraney, m. George **MATTHEWS**, Dec. 21, 1834 | TM49 | 13
Lurania, m. George **MATTHEWS**, Dec. 21, 1834, by Rev. L. P.
   Hickok | 2 | 296

	Vol.	Page
HART, (cont.),		
Luther Butler, s. Isaac & Martha, b. Mar. 9, 1821	2	249
Lydia, d. Benjamin & Hannah, b. Sept. 30, 1794	2	249
Margaritte, w. W[illia]m, d. Sept. 7, 1803, ae 36 y.	1	180
Margaritta, w. William A., d. Sept. 7, 1803, ae 36 y.	2	7
Margaretta L., d. William A. & Margaretta, b. July 22, 1797	2	7
Martha, w. Isaac, d. Apr. 8, 1839, ae 52	2	249
Martha Sophia, d. Isaac & Martha, b. June 30, 1828	2	249
Mary Ann, d. Lorenzo & Amelia, b. Aug. 11, 1825	2	252
Mary Ann, of Litchfield, m. Alanson Lewis **MORRIS**, of Torringford, Sept. 17, 1835, by Rev. Samuel Fuller, Jr.	2	296
Mary Jane, d. Isaac & Martha, b. June 19, 1831	2	249
Nancy, twin with Lurany, d. William A. & Margaretta, b. Sept. 9, 1795	2	7
Phebe, [twin with Lucy], d. Benjamin & Hannah, b. Aug. 28, 1784	2	249
Phebe, m. Aaron **SACKETT**, July 6, 1786	1	201
Phebe, m. White **WEBSTER**, Jan. 6, 1803, by Rev. Joseph E. Camp, of Northfield	1	164
Philela S., d. William A. & Margaretta, b. Apr. 8, 1788	2	7
Roswell, of Winchester, m. Lavina **KILBORN**, Jan. 6, 1825, by Rev. Isaac Jones	2	15
Ruth, m. Charles **DUDLEY**, Nov. [ ], 1798, by Rev. Thomas W. Bray	2	9
Ruth, m. Clark **CARRINGTON**, Nov. 26, 1805, at Bristol, by Rev. Giles Cowles	2	254
Sophrona, d. Isaac & Martha, b. July 9, 1813	2	249
Sophronia, m. Sylvester **SAXTON**, June 24, 1840, at Wolcottville	2	249
Timothy, s. Isaac & Martha, b. Oct. 27, 1825	2	249
Timothy, of Litchfield, m. Martha E. **BENHAM**, of Watertown, June 18, 1848, by J. D. Berry	TM49	25
William A., m. Margaretta **SMITH**, July 5, 1787, by Judah Holcomb, J.P.	2	7
William A., s. William & Margaretta, b. Jan. 23, 1790	2	7
William A., m. Mary **MORRIL**, Nov. 26, 1803, by Rev. Judah Champion	2	7
HARTSHORN, Mary, m. John G. **TITUS**, Apr. 8, 1852, by Rev. David L. Parmelee	TM49	67
Phebe, m. Joshua **MOORE**, Aug. 18, 1791	1	228
HARUTS (?), Mary, of Litchfield, m. Frederic **BIDWELL**, of Naugatuck, May 5, 1851, by Benjamin L. Swan	TM49	62
HARVEY, Henry, s. Warham & Rhoda, b. June 13, 1824	2	119
Warham, m. Rhoda **GIBBS**, Mar. 19, 1823, by Rev. Josiah L. Dickerson	2	119
HASKELLS, C. W., of New York, m. Charlotte **BARBER**, of Litchfield, Nov. 15, 1848, by Joseph Henson	TM49	27
HASKIN, HASKINS, Abraham, s. Elkanah & Lois, b. Sept. 20, 1755	1	98
Abraham, m. Hannah **STOCKWELL**, Feb. 10, 1774, by Rev. Judah Champion	1	17
Anne, d. Daniel & Susannah, b. Dec. 4, 1782	1	181
Anne, d. Daniel & Susannah, d. Sept. 25, 1793	1	180
Daniel, s. Elkanah & Lois, b. July 13, 1759	1	98
Daniel, m. Susannah **BARTHOLOMEW**, Mar. 23, 1780	1	181
Dorcas, d. Elkanah & Lois, b. Jan. 30, 1765	1	98
Elisha, s. Daniel & Susannah, b. Oct. 27, 1780	1	181
Elkanah, m. Lois **KILBORN**, Sept. 18, 1754	1	98

	Vol.	Page
HASKIN, HASKINS, (cont.),		
Lidia, d. Elkanah & Lois, b. Apr. 6, 1757	1	98
Polly, d. Daniel & Susannah, b. Feb. 6, 1787	1	181
Solomon, s. Daniel & Susannah, b. Sept. 1, 1790	1	181
Solomon, s. Daniel & Susannah, d. July 20, 1793	1	180
Truman, s. Daniel & Susannah, b. Apr. 20, 1785	1	181
Whitman, s. Daniel & Susannah, b. Oct. 11, 1792	1	181
HASTINGS, George Henry, Rev., m. Catharine Ward **SWIFT,** b. of New		
York City, Aug. 26, 1847, by Rev. Samuel Fuller	TM49	38
HATCH, H. E., m. E. P. **HILL,** Oct. 18, 1843, by Rev. D. L. Marks	TM49	1
HAWKINS, Hannah, m. Horace **BRADLEY,** Feb. 7, 1808	2	68
HAWLEY, Andrew, of Philadelphia, m. Hannah **LAW,** of Litchfield, July 25,		
1838, by Rev. Jonathan Brace	2	318
Anne, d. Enos & Mary, b. Apr. 11, 1759	1	99
David B., m. Julia A. **BARNUM,** Oct. 23, 1831, by Luther Mead	2	290
Luce, d. Enos & Mary, b. Dec. 12, 1760	1	99
HAYDEN, HAYDON, Flora Ann, of Litchfield, m. John **McMAHON,** of		
Goshen, Feb. 3, 1841, by Gad N. Smith	2	333
Lois M., of Litchfield, m. Henry B. **MIDDLEBROOKS,** of Bridgeport,		
Nov. 29, 1849, by Rev. William B. Hoyt	TM49	44
Naomi M., m. Lewis S. **CLARK,** b. of New Britain, Apr. 28, 1844, by		
Rev. Isaac Jones	TM49	4
Ursula, m. James **MARSH,** Dec. [ ], 1790, by Rev. Joshua Williams	2	257
HAYES, HAYS, David L., m. Emma **KELLY,** July 24, 1833, by Rev. David		
G. Tomlinson, of Bradleyville	2	294
Ephraim, of Bethlem, m. Cynthia **WICKWIRE,** Dec. 21, 1820, by Rev.		
John Langman, of Bethlem	2	102
Julia E., m. George **STODDARD,** Apr. 9, 1854, by Rev. David L.		
Parmelee	TM49	85
HAZARD, Samantha, Mrs., m. Patron M. **BLACKMAN,** Apr. 20, 1846, by		
Rev. William Dixon	TM49	14
HAZEN, HAZZON, Lydia Ann, of Warren, m. Rufus **HOTCHKISS,** of		
Naugatuck, July 2, 1851, by Nathaniel C. Lewis	TM49	63
Samuel, s. Samuel, b. Apr. 5, 1749	1	16
HEALY, Hannah, of Killingsworth, m. Nathan **MITCHELL,** of Litchfield,		
Aug. 30, 1738, by Rev. Timothy Collens	1	65
HEATH, Aaron, s. Joseph & Mercy, b. Nov. 19, 1780	1	98
Jacob, s. Joseph & Mercy, b. Aug. 19, 1764	1	17
Joseph, s. Joseph & Mercy, b. Feb. 14, 1766	1	17
Lois, d. Joseph & Mercy, b. Mar. 30, 1770	1	17
Susana, d. Joseph & Mercy, b. Jan. 4, 1768	1	17
Sibel, d. Joseph & Mercy, b. May 29, 1774	1	98
Waitstill, d. Joseph & Mercy, b. Sept. 7, 1776	1	98
Waitstill, d. Joseph & Mercy, b. Sept. 4, 1778	1	98
HEATON, Clarissa, m. Jonathan **HALL,** Sept. [ ], 1829, by Rev. Joseph E.		
Camp, of Northfield	2	292
Levi, Jr., m. Avis **CATLIN,** Dec. 10, 1832, by Rev. Joseph E. Camp, of		
Northfield	2	292
Mary, m. Jabez M. **CARISH,** Apr. 17, 1833, by Rev. Joseph E. Camp,		
of Northfield	292	2
HEBBARD, HEBIRD, HEBARD, [see also **HUBBARD**], Christian, d.		
Reuben & Rachal, b. Sept. 2, 1742	1	57
Margret, d. Reuben & Rachal, b. Mar. 6, 1741	1	57

	Vol.	Page
HEBBARD, HEBIRD, HEBARD, [see aso **HUBBARD**], (cont.),		
Miranda, d. Nathaniell & Elizabeth, b. Mar. 6, 1776	1	141
Nathan, s. Nathan & Elizabeth, b. Feb. 6, 1774	1	98
Rachal, d. Ruben, decd. & Rachal, b. Mar. 21, 1752	1	16
Reuben, m. Rachal **PECK**, b. of Litchfield, Oct. 14, 1740, by Rev. Timothy Collens	1	57
Reuben, s. Nathan & Elizabeth, b. June 19, 1770	1	98
HEMINGWAY, HEMINWAY, John, of Watertown, m. Lucy **DENNY**, July 28, 1847, by Joseph Henson	TM49	23
Merret, of Watertown, m. Mary Ann **BUEL**, Mar. 7, 1832, by Rev. L. P. Hickok	2	288
HEMSTED, Elisha, m. Elizabeth **LEWIS**, Oct. 24, 1824, by Rev. Isaac Jones	2	136
Fanny Aurelia, d. Elisha & Eliza, b. Aug. 15, 1825	2	136
HENDRICK, Abel, s. Abel & Lois, b. Oct. 7, 1789	1	141
Lucy*, d. Abel & Lois, b. June 30, 1787 *(Arnold Copy has "Sally")	1	141
Sally*, d. Abel & Lois, b. June 30, 1787 *("Lucy" in Woodruff's)	1	141
HEWITT, Lucretia, of Litchfield, m. George **HINMAN**, of Derby, Sept. 6, 1846, by Rev. William Dixon	TM49	15
HICKEY, Mary, m. John **QUANN**, b. of Ireland, Feb. 29, [1852], by N. C. Lewis	TM49	74
HICKOX, Merian, m. Joseph **FARNAM**, Dec. 3, 1803	2	67
HICKS, Hannah, m. Philo **PECK**, Feb. 26, 1778, by Rev. Judah Champion	2	49
HIDE, Elizabeth, Mrs., of Lebanon, m. Rev. Timothy **COLLINS**, Jan. 16, 1722/3, by Henry Willes	1	7
Joshua, s. Joshua & Rhoda, b. July 27, 1758	1	57
Lewis Collens, s. Joshua & Rhoda, b. July 3, 1755	1	57
Luther, s. Joshua & Rhoda, b. Sept. 25, 1751	1	57
Sarah, m. Oliver **COLLENS**, June 22, 1746, by Rev. Solomon Williams, of Lebanon	1	89
HILL, HILLS, Deliverance*, m. Joseph **DARIN**, Feb. 8, 1743/4, by Rev. Thomas Ruggles, of Guilford *("Deliverance **HALL**" in Woodruff's)	1	9
E. P., m. H. E. **HATCH**, Oct. 18, 1843, by Rev. D. L. Marks	TM49	1
Harriet, m. John H. **MILLER**, June 20, 1832, by Rev. Mr. Taylor, of South Farms	2	289
Hiram, of Litchfield, m. Ann **COLES**, of Plymouth, Feb. 10, 1828, by Rev. John S. Stone	2	299
Lucy A., of Litchfield, m. Theodore J. **KEELER**, of Albany, July 28, 1841, by Jonathan Brace	2	334
Martha, m. Ebenezer **GRANT**, Nov. 18, 17[4]7	1	19
Mary, of Litchfield, m. Ira **BRYAN**, of Oxford, Dec. 4, 1836, by Rev. Samuel Fuller, Jr.	2	296
William, m. Mary B. **BARNARD**, July 13, 1836, by Rev. Stephen Hubbell	2	298
HINE, Adaline Clarinda, [d. Sylvester & Sally], b. June 15, 1844	TM49	64
Albert Jotham, [s. Sylvester & Sally], b. May 12, 1832	TM49	64
Austin, Jr., of Southbury, m. Mary A. **BALDWIN**, of Litchfield, Nov. 5, 1853, by Rev. H. N. Weed	TM49	92
Catharine Emily, [d. Sylvester & Sally], b. July 13, 1841	TM49	64
Eliada Osborn, [s. Sylvester & Sally], b. Feb. 19, 1834	TM49	64
Herman C., of Washington, m. Emeline F. **BRICKLEY**, of Bristol, Sept. 13, 1842, by Rev. David L. Parmelee	2	410
Joseph, m. Almira **CHURCHILL**, Aug. 6, 1826, by Joseph E. Camp	2	266

	Vol.	Page
HINE, (cont.),		
Julia Tyler, [d. Sylvester & Sally], b. June 21, 1839	TM49	64
Polly Sarah, [d. Sylvester & Sally], b. Aug. 26, 1836	TM49	64
Samuel David, [s. Sylvester & Sally], b. Oct. 15, 1846	TM49	64
Sylvester, m. Sally CHURCHILL, Dec. 31, 1828	TM49	64
Sylvester, m. Sarah CHURCHILL, Dec. 31, 1828, by Rev. Joseph E. Camp, of Northfield	2	292
William Churchill, [s. Sylvester & Sally], b. Nov. 29, 1829	TM49	64
HINMAN, HENMAN, Eliza A., m. Theodore J. STRONG, Apr. 28, 1847, by John R. Keep	TM49	19
George, of Derby, m. Lucretia HEWITT, of Litchfield, Sept. 6, 1846, by Rev. Willliam Dixon	TM49	15
Harriet, m. Levi STONE, b. of Litchfield, Nov. 19, 1840, by William Payne	2	332
Henrietta Lorain, of Litchfield, m. John Curtus EATON, of Bristol, Apr. 23, 1848, by Rev. Samuel Fuller	TM49	38
Jane C., m. Charles ADAMS, Feb. 12, 1827, at New Haven; d. June 10, 1828, at New Haven	TM49	99
Julia M., m. Charles ADAMS, Feb. 14, 1830, at New Haven; d. Sept. 1, 1849	TM49	99
Nancy, m. Truman BUEL, Aug. 14, 1805, by Rev. Asahel Hooker, of Goshen	2	11
Nathan B., m. Julia A. RAY, Apr. 14, 1852, by Rev. David L. Parmelee	TM49	74
Sarah, m. Jonathan COLVER, Nov. 16, 1749, by Rev. Stephen Heaton, of Goshen	1	89
HINSDALE, Rosamond, of Litchfield, m. Dr. Josiah MILLARD, of Manlius, N.Y., Jan. 7, 1822, by Rev Amos Pettingill	2	106
HITCHCOCK, Elliot, of Plymouth, m. Mary Ann CHURCHILL, of Litchfield, Nov. 12, 1832, by Rev. Samuel Fuller	TM49	37
Elliot, m. Mary Ann CHURCHILL, Nov. 12, 1832, by Rev. Samuel Fuller	2	289
Jeanette, m. Isaac BENHAM, b. of Burlington, Dec. 30, 1829, by L. P. Hickok	2	283
HOAR, James, m. Mary T. WHEELER, of Bantam Falls, May 18, 1851, by J. D. Berry	TM49	62
HODGE, HODGEE, Joseph, m. Nancy SPALDEN, July 10, 1825, by Rev. Isaac Jones	2	143
Lydia, m. Zadock GIBBS, Jr., Jan. 8, 1777, by William Cogswell, J.P.	1	179
HOLLEY, Anne, d. Elnathan & Anne, b. Mar. 5, 1792	1	181
Elnathan, m. Anne MATTOCKS, Sept. 28, 1783, by Rev. Mr. Nichols	1	181
Martha Brown, d. Elnathan & Anne, b. June 11, 1787	1	181
Ruhamah, d. Elnathan & Anne, b. May 5, 1784	1	181
Walter, s. Elnathan & Ann, b. Aug. 4, 1785	1	181
William, s.Elnathan & Anne, b. Jan. 11, 1790	1	181
HOLLISTER, HOLISTER, George, of Glastonbury, m. Semantha CHASE, of Milton, Dec. 26, 1841, by Ralph Smith	2	336
Gideon Hiram, m. Mary Susan BRISBANE, b. of Litchfield, June 3, 1847, by Rev. Samuel Fuller	TM49	38
Horace, of Farmington, m. Ursula B. NIVINS, of Litchfield, Feb. 18, 1823, by Rev. Truman Marsh	2	118
Naomi, b. [ ] 13, 1770	1	141
Naomi*, m. Asa GILLET, Aug. 9, 1787 *("Naomi HOSFORD" in Woodruff's book)	1	221

	Vol.	Page
HOLMES, Albert, b. May 27, 1799	2	83
Thomas Stevenson, s. Thomas, b. May 22, 1773	1	98
Urial, representative Oct. 1803, May & Oct. 1804, May & Oct. 1805, Oct. 1806, May & Oct. 1807, Oct. 1814	2	1553-4
HOMER, Albert, m. Maria **HUBBARD**, July 31, 1823, by Rev. Isaac Jones	2	121
Albert, m. Harriet E. **BACHELOR**, Feb. 23, 1843, by Birdsey Baldwin, J.P.	2	319
Frederick, of Southbury, m. Mary Ann **JACKLIN** (colored), Oct. 20, 1830, by Rev. Isaac Jones	2	286
Maria, d. Albert [& Maria], b. Feb. 12, 1824	2	121
HOOKER, Chauncey M., m. Caroline M. **BRAMAN**, of Litchfield, Sept. 30, 1850, by Benjamin L. Swan	TM49	55
HOPKINS, Abigail, d. Harris & Margaret, b. Aug. 12, 1770	2	78
Anna, d. Harris & Margaret, b. Nov. 16, 1776	2	78
Asa, m. Abigail **HARRIS**, Oct. 1, 1741, by Rev. Benjamin Colton, of Hartford	1	57
Asa, s. Asa & Abigail, b. Nov. 13, 1742	1	57
Asa, s. Asa & Phebe, b. Sept. 28, 1761	1	17
Asa, Jr., m. Phebe **GRAINGER**, Oct. 28, 1765, by Rev. John Graham	1	17
Asa, Lieut., d. Sept. 18, 1766	1	16
Asa, Lieut., d. Sept. 18, 1766	1	56
Asa, Lieut., d. Sept. 18, 1766. "Error"	1	98
Asa, s. Harris & Margaret, b. Feb. 2, 1779	2	78
Asa, m. Laura **NETTLETON**, Nov. 7, 1811, by Rev. Luke Wood	2	80
Asa, representative May 1833	2	1556
Edward, s. Joseph H. & Phebe, b. Jan. 31, 1797	2	79
Edward Harris, s. Orange & Phila Mela, b. Dec. 7, 1817	2	81
George Washington, s. William & Thankfull, b. Jan. 27, 1800	2	79
Harris, s. Asa & Abigail, b. Mar. 1, 1744/5	1	57
Harris, m. Margaret **PECK**, Apr. 4, 1764, by Rev. [ ]	2	78
Joseph Harris, s. Harris & Margaret, b. Nov. 4, 1764	2	78
Joseph Harris, m. Phebe **TURNER**, Mar. 3, 1790, by Daniel Potter, J.P.	2	79
Nery Matilda, d. William & Thankfull, b. Oct. 25, 1807	2	79
Nicy M., m. John A. **WOODRUFF**, b. of Litchfield, June 9, 1853, by Rev. Lewis Jessup	TM49	91
Orange, s. Joseph H. & Phebe, b. May 28, 1791	2	79
Orange, m. Phila Mela **BEECHER**, Jan. 9, 1817, by Rev. Mr. Huntington	2	81
Or[r]a, m. Asa **BLAKESLEE**, Sept. [ ], 1833, by Rev. Joseph E. Camp, of Northfield	2	292
Orra Emila, d. William & Thankfull, b. Mar. 20, 1812	2	79
Pamela, d. Joseph H. & Phebe, b. May 29, 1799	2	79
Rhoda, d. Alva & Rhoda, b. Nov. 1, 1759	1	99
Rhoda, d. Asa & Rhoda, b. Nov. 1, 1759	1	206
Rhoda, d. Harris & Margaret, b. Mar. 26, 1773	2	78
Rhoda, m. Elijah **WADSWORTH**, Feb. 16, 1780, by Rev. Judah Champion	1	165
Rhoda, m. Elijah **WADSWORTH**, Feb. 16, 1780	1	206
Sally, d. Harris & Margaret, b. Jan. 29, 1785	2	78
Sarah, m. Mark **HOTCHKISS**, June [ ], 1829, by Rev. Joseph E. Camp, of Northfield	2	292
Sarah Turner, d. Joseph H. & Phebe, b. Jan. 31, 1803	2	79
William, s. Harris & Margaret, b. Dec. 15, 1766	2	78

	Vol.	Page
HOPKINS, (cont.),		
William, m. Thankfull **BALDWIN**, Apr. 25, 1798, by Rev. Mr. Waterman	2	79
William Lyman, s. William & Thankfull, b. Sept. 17, 1803	2	79
William S., m. Mariana **MERWIN**, Aug. 13, 1830, by Frederick Holcomb	2	285
HOPPIN, James Mason, Rev. of Salem, Mass., m. Mary Deming **PERKINS**, of Litchfield, June 13, 1850, by Benjamin L. Swan	TM49	54
HORNBECK, Jane, m. Henry **PRATT**, Jan. 12, 1824, by Rev. Isaac Jones	2	131
HORTON, Elisha, m Marilla **BRADLEY**, Apr. [ ], 1825, by Rev. Lyman Beecher	2	140
HOSFORD, HORSFORD, HOSBORN, Aaron, s. Isaac & Mindwell, b. Dec. 27, 1751	1	16
Ame, d. William & Mary, b. Dec. 2, 1738	1	56
Ama, m Ebenezer **BENTON**, Mar. 19, 1761, by Jacob Woodruff, J.P.	1	127
Ann, m. Increase **GRANT**, Feb. 19, 1745/6, by Ebenezer Marsh, J.P.	1	96
Asael, s. Benjamin & Experience*, b. Mar. 8, 1728 *("Experience is written over Deborah")	1	16
Benjamin, m. Experience **SMITH**, May 9, 1723, by Capt. John Marsh, J.P.	1	16
Betsey, d. John & Mary, b. Aug. 20, 1800	2	75
Eli, s. Jesse & Elizabeth, b. Aug. 22, 1754	1	57
Elijah, s. Jesse & Elizabeth, b. Mar. 13, 1749/50	1	16
Elizabeth, d. Jesse & Elizabeth, b. Feb. 9, 1752	1	16
Ezekiel, s. Benjamin & Experience, b. Dec. 2, 1729	1	16
Gideon, s. Benjamin & Experience, b. Nov. 20, 1733	1	16
Harriet, d. John & Mary, b. Aug. 17, 1805	2	75
Isaac, s. Isaac & Mindwell, b. Aug. 28, 1758	1	17
Isaac, d. Jan. 8, 1761	1	17
Jeremiah, s. Jess & Elizabeth, b. Nov. 2, 1758	1	57
John, s. Nathaniel & Mary, d. Dec. 3, 1724	1	17
John, s. Benjamin & Experience*, b. June 6, 1726 *("Experience is written over Deborah")	1	16
John, s. Willliam & Mary, b. Sept. 16, 1740	1	56
John, Jr., m. Mary **MANSFIELD**, Oct. [ ], 1794	2	75
Lavina, b. Sept. 14, 1802; m. John A. **WOODRUFF**, Apr. 16, 1823	2	293
Lavina, b. Sept. 14, 1802; m. John A. **WOODRUFF**, Apr. 16, 1823	2	325
Levina, d. John & Mary, b. Nov. 14, 1802	2	75
Lavina, m. John A. **WOODRUFF**, Apr. 16, 1823, by Rev. Isaac Jones	2	120
Leonard D., s. Dudley, b. July 1, 1829	2	46
Leonard D., m. Cornelia J. **BENNETT**, Oct. 30, 1851, by Rev. David L. Parmelee	TM49	65
Mary, m. Philip **BUMP**, Feb. 4, 1722/3, by John Marsh, J.P.	1	5
Mary, m. Phillip **BUMP**, Feb. 4, 1722/3, by John Marsh, J.P.	1	31
Mary, m. Benjamin **COLVER**, b. of Litchfield, Apr. 20, 1738, by Rev. Timothy Collens	1	47
Mary, m. John **AGARD**, Nov. 28, 1745, by Rev. Timothy Collens	1	3
Mary, w. Dea. Nathaniell, d. Jan. 3, 1750/51	1	17
Mary, d. John & Mary, b. Sept. 19, 1798	2	75
Naomi*, m. Asa **GILLET**, Aug. 9, 1787 *(Arnold Copy has "Naomi **HOLISTER**")	1	221
Naomi, d. John & Mary, b. Oct. 26, 1810	2	75
Nathaniel, m. Martha **STRONG**, Oct. 2, 1746, by Rev. Jonathan Marsh,		

	Vol.	Page
HOSFORD, HORSFORD, HOSBORN, (cont.),		
of Windsor	1	17
Nathaniel, Dea., d. Apr. 3, 1748	1	17
Nathaniel, d. Oct. 11, 1781	1	56
Neri, s. John & Mary, b. Feb. 14, 1797	2	75
Noah, s. Benjamin & Experience, b. Oct. 9, 1731	1	16
Pamela, d. John & Mary, b. Mar. 7, 1795	2	75
Philomela, m. Roswell **SAGE**, of Cornwall, Feb. 5, 1824, by Rev. Isaac Jones	2	132
Ruben, s. Benjamin & Experience*, b. Apr. 13, 1724 *("Experience is written over Deborah")	1	16
Reuben, s. Isaac & Mindwell, b. Oct. 13, 1758	1	17
Ruth, d. W[illia]m & Mary, b. Dec. 16, 1736	1	56
Ruth, m. Elihu **BRADLEY**, Mar. 5, 1805, by Rev. Dan Huntington	2	70
Sarah, m. Zebulon **TAYLOR**, Dec. 20, 1727, by Rev. Timothy Collen	1	39
Sarah, d. Jesse & Elizabeth, b. Nov. 26, 1756	1	17
Timothy, d. Jan. 7, 1740/1, in the 79th y. of his age	1	57
William, m. Mary **MASON**, Mar. 14, 1736	1	56
William, s. William & Mary, b. Sept. 7, 1742	1	57
William, d. June 7, 1743	1	56
William, s. John & Mary, b. Feb. 19, 1808	2	75
HOTCHKISS, Elihu, m. Lydia **ROBINSON**, [ ], 1769, by Rev. Mr. Halley	2	79
Elihu, s. Lyman & Clarissa, b. Apr. 21, 1814	2	81
Elihu, m. Eliza Ann **PERKINS**, b. of Litchfield, Oct. 10, 1838, by Rev. Gad N. Smith	2	319
Elivra, m. Joseph A. **CLARK**, Sept. 14, 1833, by Rev. Joseph E. Camp, of Northfield	2	292
Hiram, s. Lyman & Clarissa, b. May 8, 1819	2	81
Huldah, m. Hezekiah **MURRY**, [ ], 1815	2	85
Lavis*, s. Lyman & Clarissa, b. Aug. 29, 1811 *("Lewis"?)	2	81
Lewis, m. Maria **WESTOVER**, Mar. 23, 1834, by Rev. James F. Warner, of South Farms	2	289
Lyman, s. Elihu & Lydia, b. May 26, 1781	2	79
Lyman, m. Clarissa **GRISWOULD**, Nov. 13, 1804, by Rev. Amos Chase	2	81
Mark, m. Sarah **HOPKINS**, June [ ], 1829, by Rev. Joseph E. Camp, of Northfield	2	292
Mary, d. Elihu & Lydia, b. Dec. 26, 1776	2	79
Mary S., of Litchfield, m. Calvin H. **STUDLEY**, of Sharon, Apr. 13, 1854, by Rev. Horatio N. Weed	TM49	85
Rachel, d. Elihu & Lydia, b. Feb. 28, 1779	2	79
Rufus, of Naugatuck, m. Lydia Ann **HAZEN**, of Warren, July 2, 1851, by Nathaniel C. Lewis	TM49	63
Ruth, m. David **KENNEY**, [ ], 1793	2	64
Sheldon, s. Lyman & Clarissa, b. June 19, 1808	2	81
Sheldon, m. Lucena **MERCHANT**, Dec. 26, 1831, by Rev. L. P. Hickok	2	288
William, s. Lyman & Clarissa, b. Oct. 24, 1805	2	81
William, m. Lydia M. **BENTON**, June 16, 1836, by Rev. R. S. Crampton	2	299
HOUGH, Joel, m. Amila **BARNES**, July [ ], 1825, by Rev. J. E. Camp	2	265
HOULBUD, Rachall, m. Thomas **LEE**, Sept. 19, 1723, by Joseph Minor, J.P	1	23.

	Vol.	Page
HOWE, HOW, David, of Warren, m. Harriet **LAMPSON**, of Litchfield, Jan. 25, 1830, by Rev. Bradley Sillick	2	284
Levi Scovil, of Cornwall, m. Ercintha **SPENCER**, Oct. 27, 1823, by Rev. Isaac Jones	2	94
Nabby, m. Ezra **BURGESS**, Feb. 11, 1798, by James Morris	2	38
HOYT, Francis C., m. Betsey M. **HUBBARD**, May 2, 1842, by Rev. David L. Parmalee	2	410
Rollin, m. Abigail **ROCKWELL**, Apr. 8, 1830, by Rev. William Lucas	2	286
Sarah M., m. Charles **MATTHEWS**, Mar. 12, 1829	2	322
HUBBARD, [see also **HEBBARD**], Abigail, of Middletown, m. Reuben **SMITH**, of Litchfield, Oct. 23, 1770, by Rev. Enoch Huntington	1	36
Abigail, Mrs., m. Dr. Reuben **SMITH**, Oct. 23, 1770, by Rev. Mr. Huntington, of Middletown	1	163
Amos, s. Lewis & Lovisa, b. Jan. 11, 1820	2	121
Angeline H., m. Linus G. **MOSS**, b. of Litchfield, Feb. 26, 1838, by Rev. Lewis Gunn	2	315
Ann Eliza, d. [Benjamin & Polly], b. Feb. 14, 1850	TM49	54
Anson, m. Elizabeth **MANSFIELD**, Sept. 6, 1818, by Rev. Amos Pettingill	2	251
Asahel, s. Joseph, Jr. & Hannah, b. July 16, 1814	2	51
Asal, of Warren, m. Susan **TRACY**, of Washington, Feb. 4, 1839, by Rev. H. Bryant	2	325
Asenath, m. Charles **COGSWELL**, Dec. 22, 1824, by Rev. Henry Robinson	2	138
Benjamin, of Litchfield, m. Polly **PARMELEE**, of Bristol, Aug. 24, 1841, in Watertown	TM49	54
Betsey M., m. Francis C. **HOYT**, May 2, 1842, by Rev. David L. Parmelee	2	410
Caroline, d. Lewis & Lovisa, b. Jan. 29, 1817	2	121
Charles Punderson, s. Anson & Elizabeth, b. Apr. 4, 1819	2	251
Charlotte, d. Lewis & Lovisa, b. Sept. 6, 1821	2	121
Charlotte, of Litchfield, m. Leman **OSBORN**, of Utica, N.Y., Feb. 24, 1839, by Rev. Gad N. Smith	2	319
Cornelia Louisa, twin with Cornelius Lewis, d. Lewis & Louisa, b. Oct. 18, 1827	2	121
Cornelius Lewis, twin with Cornelia Louisa, d. Lewis & Louisa, b. Oct. 18, 1827	2	121
Eliza L., m. William D. **MEAD**, b. of New Haven, Sept. 14, 1836, by Isaac Jones	2	299
Elizabeth, m. James **MORRIS**, Jr., Dec. 20, 1781, by Hon. Jabez Hamlin	1	149
Elziva Zuletta, [d. Benjamin & Polly], b. Sept. 10, 1846	TM49	54
Henry Downs, s. Jacob & Lucetta, b. Jan. 16, 1822	2	254
Hiram W., of Plymouth, m. Clarissa **WHEELER**, of Litchfield, Oct. 4, 1840, by Jonathan Brace	2	330
Hiram Warner, s. Jacob &Lucetta, b. Oct. 4, 1819	2	254
Horace, m. Ann **MANSFIELD**, Feb. 20, 1834, by Rev. James F. Warner, of South Farms	2	289
Horace, of Watertown, m. Mary J. **WOODWARD**, of Litchfield, Dec. 31, 1854, at the house of H. B. Woodward, by Rev. Frederick Holcomb	TM49	105
Hortensia, m. Nicholas **MASTERS**, b. of Litchfield, Oct. 11, 1846, by Rev. Samuel Fuller	TM49	38

	Vol.	Page
HUBBARD, [see also **HEBBARD**], (cont.),		
Ithamer, m. Levina **BARNARD**, b. of Litchfield, Dec. 17,1826, by Rev.		
Henry Robinson, of South Farms	2	267
Jacob, b. Dec. 23, 1783; bp. [ ], 1803, by Rev. D. Huntek; m.		
Lucetta **WARNER**, Nov. 8, 1815, by Rev. Luther Hart	2	254
James Morris, s. Anson & Elizabeth, b. Jan. 19, 1823	2	251
Jesse Dwight, s. Benjamin & Polly, b. Feb. 14, 1843	TM49	54
John Mansfield, s. Anson & Elizabeth, b. Apr. 1, 1824,	2	251
Joseph, Jr., m. Hannah **TALLMADGE**, Aug. 7, 1813, by Rev. Mr. Ives	2	51
Joseph S., of Litchfield, m. Mary J. **ELLIS**, of Naugatuck, Sept. 17,		
1850, by Rev. Herman L. Vaill	TM49	55
Lewis, m. Lovisa **SMITH**, Jan. 10, 1813, by Rev. Mr. Ives, of Cheshire	2	121
Lucinda H., m. Erastus **BATES**, Sept. 6, 1843, by Rev. David L. Marks	2	413
Mahola, m. Ozias **PECK**, Oct. 21, 1823, by Rev. Henry Robinson, of		
South Farms,	2	129
Malissa, d. Lewis & Lovisa, b. Dec. 26, 1818	2	121
Maria, m. Albert **HOMER**, July 31, 1823, by Rev. Isaac Jones	2	121
Mary Jane, d. Jacob & Lucetta, b. Aug. 14, 1824	2	254
Mary Newell, d. [Benjamin & Polly], b. Aug. 10, 1844	TM49	54
Otensa, d. Lewis & Lovisa, b. Nov. 17, 1815	2	121
Phillip, of Litchfield, m. Jane **TANNER**, of Poughkeepsie, Dec. 25,		
1827, by Rev. John S. Stone	2	273
Rosette, d. Joseph, Jr. & Hannah, b. Mar. 2, 1816	2	51
Sally, m. Amos **JOHNSON**, May 6, 1802, by Rev. Dan Huntington	2	250
Sally, m. Jeremiah **PAGE**, Aug. 26, 1822, by Rev. Lyman Beecher	2	113
Sophia, m. Jasper **STODDARD**, July 11, 1813, by Rev. Amos Chase	2	251
William Morris, s. Joseph & Lydia, b. Nov. 20, 1808	2	64
HUBBELL, Orange A., of Plymouth, m. Mary A. **CHURCHILL**, of		
Watertown, Oct. 13, 1853, by Rev. Benjamin L. Swan	TM49	92
HUGHES, Charlotte S., m. Joseph W. **SHEARES**, Mar. 28, 1852, by Rev.		
David L. Parmelee	TM49	67
Margaret, m. George **TETHER**, b. formely of England, now of		
Litchfield, Aug. 28, 1853, by Rev. Horatio N. Weed	TM49	91
HULL, Amanda, of Waterbury, m. Samuel **BUNNELL**, of Litchfield, Oct. 12,		
1840, by F. Chittenden, J.P.	2	330
Augustus F., m. Elizabeth **BRADLEY**, Apr. 14, 1816, by Rev. Joseph		
E. Camp	2	44
Curtiss, m. Mary Ann **BRADLEY**, Jan. 5, 1840, by Rev. Thomas Ellis	2	320
Eben, m. Mary Ann **TRYON**, b. of Litchfield, Apr. 7, 1839, by Rev.		
Gad N. Smith	2	319
Eunice, of Waterbury, m. Abel **CLEMENS**, of Litchfield, Oct. 12,		
1840, by Frederick Chittenden, J.P.	2	330
HUMASTON, HAMASTON, HUMMISTON, HAMISTON,		
HUMMASTONE, Amos, s. John & Ruth, b. May 30, 1749	1	16
Belinda W., d. Sherman & Polly, b. Jan. 1, 1820	2	69
Comfort, d. Aug. 5, 1781	1	140
Content, d. Titus & Beulah, b. Dec. 24, 1777	1	141
Content, d. Aug. 5, 1781	1	180
Damaris, d. John & Ruth, b. Feb. 10, 1746	1	16
Elisha, s. Titus & Beulah, b. Nov. 5, 1776	1	141
Enos, s. John & Ruth, b. Nov. 27, 1756	1	17
Ezra, s. John & Ruth, d. Sept. 12, 1760	1	16
Flora, of Litchfield, m. Morgan **GRISWOULD**, of Washington, Sept.		

	Vol.	Page
HUMASTON, HAMSTON, HUMMISTON, HAMISTON,		
HUMMASTONE, (cont.),		
13, 1820, by Moses Woodruff, J.P.	2	96
Hannah, m. Daniel **LORD**, Dec. 25, 1766, by Rev. Mr. Storrs, of		
Northbury	1	105
Hannah, m. Daniel **LORD**, Dec. 25, 1766, by Rev. Andrew Storrs, of		
Northbury Soc.	2	65
Huldah, m. John **KILBORN**, b. of Litchfield, June 23, 1833, by Rev.		
Samuel Fuller	TM49	37
Huldah, m. John **KILBORN**, June 23, 1833, by Rev. Samuel Fuller	2	289
Isaac, s. Titus & Beulah, b. June 14, 1783	1	141
John, of Litchfield, m. Mary **SANFORD**, of New Haven, June 5, 1738,		
by Rev. Isaac Hilles	1	16
John, s. John & Mary, b. Feb. 25, 1741/2	1	16
John, m. Ruth **COLVER**, Dec. 29, 1742, by Rev. Samuell Todd, of		
Northbury	1	16
John, Jr., m. Hannah **SANFORD**, Dec. 14, 1769, by Timothy Collens,		
J.P.	1	98
John, m. Thankful **TILER**, June 21, 1770, by Rev. Mr. Steeres, of		
Northbury	1	16
John, s. Sherman & Polly, b. July 11, 1815	2	69
Laura, d. Sherman & Polly, b. Oct. 1, 1813	2	69
Lois, d. John & Ruth, b. May 30, 1755	1	17
Love, d. Titus & Beulah, b. Aug. 17, 1780	1	141
Lyman, s. Titus & Beulah, b. Jan. 14, 1782	1	141
Martha, d. John & Ruth, b. Jan. 9, 1760	1	16
Martha, d. John & Ruth, b. Jan. 9, 1760	1	57
Martha, d. John & Ruth, d. Nov. 10, 1760	1	16
Mary, d. John & Mary, b. May 10, 1739	1	16
Mary, w. John, d. Mar. 8, 1742	1	16
Noah, s. John & Ruth, b. Dec. 20, 1745	1	16
Phebe B., d. Sherman & Sally, b. May 3, 1823	2	69
Polly, d. Titus & Beulah, b. Aug. 24, 1784	1	141
Ruth, d. John & Ruth, b. May 29, 1755	1	57
Ruth, d. John & Ruth, b. June 91st [sic], 1755	1	16
Ruth, w. John, d. Dec. 31, 1769	1	56
Ruth, m. David **ALLEN**, Nov. 25, 1773, by Rev. Andrew Storrs, of		
Northbury	1	166
Sherman, s. John, b. Sept. 24, 1789	1	98
Sherman, m. Polly **TOMPKINS**, Dec. 28, 1812, by Rev. Joseph E.		
Camp	2	69
Sidney, m. Sherman **PIERPOINT**, Dec. 1, 1807, by Rev. Joseph E.		
Camp	2	133
Silas, m. Mary **BLAKESLEE**, Jan. 6, 1794, by Daniel Potter, J.P.	2	143
Thankful, d. John & Ruth, b. Nov. 26, 1748	1	16
Titus, s. John & Ruth, b. Nov. 30, 1751	1	17
Titus, m. Beulah **BATCHELOR**, Dec. 20, 1775, by Rev. James		
Nichols, of Farmington	1	141
William L., of Winsted, m. Laura **MOORE**, of Bradleyville, Nov. 24,		
1845, by Rev. William Dixon	TM49	12
HUMPHREY, John, of Norfolk, m. Maria **TURNER**, of Litchfield, Oct. 30,		
1845, by Rev. Samuel Fuller	TM49	37
HUMPHREVILLE, HUMPHERVILLE, HUMPERVILLE, Albra		

	Vol.	Page
HUMPHREVILLE, HUMPHERVILLE, HUMPERVILLE, (cont.),		
Madison, s. Lemuel & Ursula, b. June 12, 1810	2	142
Deborah, d. Lemuel & Ursula, b. Feb. 8, 1817	2	142
Harriet, d. Lemuel & Ursula, b. May 19, 1812	2	142
Lemuel, m. Ursula **PRESTON**, Jan. 1, 1800, by Daniel Catlin, J.P.	2	142
Lemuel Garner, s. Lemuel & Ursula, b. Mar. 15, 1805	2	142
Loisa, d. Lemuel & Ursula, b. Nov. 7, 1800	2	142
Louisa, m. Smith **LAW**, Feb. 26, 1821, by Rev. Frederick Holcomb	2	142
Mary, d. Lemuel & Ursula, b. Jan. 3, 1808	2	142
Mary, m. Newton **PERKINS**, Aug. 13, 1832, by Frederick Holcomb	2	291
Susan C., d. Lemuel & Ursula, b. Feb. 26, 1803	2	142
Susan C., m. George **COOK**, Dec. 7, 1825, by Rev. Frederick Holcomb	2	259
HUNGERFORD, Carlos C., m. Rhoda **BLAKESLEE**, Apr. 13, 1828, by F. Holcomb	2	276
Lucina, m. Eliada **ORTON**, Jan. 10, 1770, by Rev. Mr. Chapman, of Farmington	1	69
Philinda, of Litchfield, m. Norman **WADAMS**, of Goshen, Aug. 17, 1822, by Rev. Isaac Jones	2	113
Rhoda, see Rhoda **SMITH**	2	130
Thaddeus, b. Apr. 11, 1783, in Bristol	2	41
Thaddeus, m. Polly **KING**, Dec. 25, 1805, by Rev. Ashbel Backas	2	41
HUNTER, Ann, m. George **STEWARD**, Sept. 10, 1843, by Rev. David S. Marks	2	413
HUNTINGTON, Ann, m. Charles **COLLENS**, June 18, 1752, by Rev. Solomon Williams, of Lebanon	1	89
Betsey, m. Frederick **WOLCOTT**, Oct. 12, 1800, by Rev. Mr. Strong, of Norwich	1	245
Betsey, m. Frederick **WOLCOTT**, Oct. 12, 1800, by Rev. Mr. Strong, of Norwich	2	17
Charles Phelps, s. Rev. Dan & Elizabeth, b. Mar. 24, 1802	1	222-3
Dan, Rev., m. Elizabeth Whiting **PHELPS**, Jan. 1, 1800, by Rev. Dr. Parsons	1	222-3
Elizabeth Porter, d. Rev. Dan & Elizabeth, b. May 8, 1803	1	222-3
Gurdon, Dr., of Cairo, m. Mary **PRUDEN**, Nov. 10, 1821, by Rev. Amos Pettingill, of South Farms Soc.	2	104
Israel, m. Ama **PECK**, June 7, 1764, by Rev. Judah Champion	1	98
Jabez W., representative May 1828	2	1556
HURD, HUIRD, Adaline M., Mrs., m. Selah W. **TALLMADGE**, of Southwick, Mass., July 2, 1854, by Rev. H. A. Weed	TM49	85
Ann, m. John Gould **PARMELE**, July 25, 1766, by Increase Mosely, J.P.	1	30
Bostwick, of Marlborough, m. Avis **WAY**, of Goshen, Jan. 14, 1827, by Hugh P. Welch	2	268
[HURLBURT], [see under **HOULBUD**]		
INGRAHAM, Hanna, m. Joel **MUNGER**, Mar. 1, 1812, by William Cogswell, J.P.	2	263
ISAAC, Henry, s. Joseph & Clarissa, b. Dec. 4, 1814	2	101
Joseph, m. Clarissa **TUMA** (colored), May 10, 1812, by Rev. Truman Marsh	2	101
ISBELL, ISBEL, Barbara, Mrs., m. Israel **STONE**, Feb. 16, 1830, by Enos Stoddard, J.P.	2	284
Polly L., m. Chester L. **NORTHROP**, b. of Litchfield, Oct. 31, 1841, by Rev. Jason Wells	2	335

	Vol.	Page
IVES, A. H., of Fairfax Co., Va., m. Bethia M. **GRANT**, of Litchfield, Feb. 3, 1852, by Lewis Jessup, of Northfield	TM49	75
Charles G., of Bristol, m. Elizabeth **GOODWIN**, of Litchfield, Jan. 27, 1841, by Rev. H. D. Kitchel, of South Farms	2	332
Othniel, m. Julia **COOKE**, Oct. 28, 1833, by Rev. L. P. Hickok	2	288
JACKLIN, Harvey, s. John & Violet, b. May 17, 1800 (Probably colored)	1	151
Mary Ann, of Litchfield, m. Frederick **HOMER**, of Southbury, (colored), Oct. 20, 1830, by Rev. Isaac Jones	2	286
JACKSON, Caroline, of Litchfield, m. Rensellaer **PEASE**, of Bridgeport, (colored), Oct. 10, 1850, by Benjamin L. Swan	TM49	55
Charles, m. Amy **RAYMOND**, b. of Bethleman, Oct. 9, 1836, by Rev. Fosdic Harrison, of Bethleham	2	297
Eliza, m. Minor Sherman **CEASER**, Mar. 27, 1834, by Rev. L. P. Hickok	2	288
Harriet D., of Litchfield, m. Harris **GILBERT**, of New Haven, Dec. 25, 1843, by Jonathan Brace	TM49	1
John P., of Newark, N.J., m. Elizabeth **WOLCOTT**, of Litchfield, May 22, 1827, by Rev. John J. Stone	2	270
Phebe, m. John S. **BRYANT**, of Sheffield, Mass., Nov. 29, 1821, by Rev. Isaac Jones	2	105
Phebe, m. William **WOODIN**, Dec. 31, 1823, by Rev. Isaac Jones	2	131
Sarah, m. Leonard **STONE**, b. of Litchfield, Oct. 22, 1849, by Rev. W. B. Hoyt	TM49	43
William, m. Sarah A. **CATLIN**, Oct. 21, 1844, by Rev. David L. Parmelee	TM49	6
JAMES, Laban & Cloe, had negro Minnias, b. May 12, 1796	1	151
JELET, [see under **GILLET**]		
JENKINS, Abigail, w. Joseph, d. Jan. 20, 1752, ae about 29 y.	1	24
Abigail, d. Joseph & Hannah, b. Jan. 28, 1756	1	59
Dorcas, d. Joseph & Hannah, b. Dec. 19, 1757	1	59
Joseph, s. Joseph & Hannah, b. Nov. 18, 1761	1	59
Mary, d. Joseph & Hannah, b. Oct. 31, 1759	1	59
Patience, m. Roswell **KILBORN**, Jan. [ ], 1769, by Rev. Judah Champion	1	102
Sam, s. Joseph & Hannah, b. Oct. 4, 1753	1	20
Samuel, s. Joseph & Hannah, b. Oct. 4, 1756	1	19
JENNINGS, JENNING, F. T., m. Clarissa **GRISWOLD**, b. of Milton, Dec. 25, 1848, by Rev. F. D. Harriman	TM49	39
Henry S., of Fairfield, m. Laura C. **THOMAS**, of Litchfield, May 6, 1827, by Rev. Henry Robinson, of South Farms	2	270
John, of Cornwall, m. Sally **GUILDS**, Dec. 5, 1824, by Rev. Isaac Jones	2	56
Truman Leander, of Warren, m. Jane **BIRGE**, of Litchfield, Oct. 27, 1847, by Rev. Samuel Fuller	TM49	38
JOHNSON, Abbe, d. Amos & Sally, b. Nov. 23, 1812	2	250
Abigail, d. Edward & Abigail, b. Mar. 30, 1764	1	59
Abigail, m. Joseph **MERRIMAN**, June 16, 1833, by Rev. L. P. Hickok	2	288
Addison, m. Cornelia **TUTTLE**, Feb. 8, 1838, by Rev. Stephen Hubbell	2	320
Amaziah, s. Amos & Jemima, b. Apr. 1, 1769	1	59
Amos, m. Jemima **CHAMBERLAIN**, Oct. 16, 1762, by Jacob Woodruff, J.P.	1	59
Amos, d. Dec. 21, 1776, "in captivity in New York", ae 38	1	100
Amos, s. Luther & Betsey, b. Dec. 6, 1794	2	142
Amos, m. Sally **HUBBARD**, May 6, 1802, by Rev. Dan Huntington	2	250

	Vol.	Page

JOHNSON, (cont.),

Amos, of Watertown, m. Betsey **BALDWIN**, of Milton, Sept. 22, 1845, by Rev. William Dixon	TM49	12
Amey Jane, d. George & Amey, b. Oct. 28, 1839	2	326
Anne, d. Amos & Jemima, b. July 25, 1763	1	59
Antoinette E., d. [Horace & Harriet], b. May 1, 1833	2	120
Ariel, m. Lucinda **BOOTH**, b. of Torrington, June 5, 1842, by Jonathan Brace	2	410
Asa, s. Lambert & Matilda, b. Mar. 15, 1788	2	7
Benjamin, m. Lucretia **KILBORN**, Feb. [ ], 1785, by Rev. Judah Champion	2	43
Benjamin, s. Benjamin & Lucretia, b. July 13, 1794	2	43
Benjamin H., s. Horace & Harriet, b. Nov. 17, 1822	2	120
Broughton [ ], of Suffield, in Boston Colony, m. Mary **PEARS**, of Litchfield, Dec. 31, 1740, by Capt. John Buell, J.P.	1	58
Caroline, m. John **WILLMOTT, Jr.**, Oct. 18, 1797	2	54
Caroline, d. [Horace & Harriet], b. Oct. 24, 1844; d. Mar. 29, 1849	2	120
Clarissa, d. Lambert & Matilda, b. Feb. 24, 1786	2	7
Clarissa, d. Amos & Sally, b. Aug. 29, 1806	2	250
Clarississa [sic], m. Edwin **MASON**, b. of Litchfield, Dec. 13, 1826, by Rev. Henry Robinson, of South Farms	2	267
Clarissa, d. Morris [& Amanda], b. Nov. 22, 1831	2	60
Cynthia, d. [George & Amy], b. Oct. 6, 1833	2	326
Daniel, m. Elizabeth **TRUMAN**, b. of Torrington, Nov. 18, 1840, by William Payne	2	332
David, of Bethlem, m. Anna Idia **GILES**, of Milton, Mar. 14, 1841, by G. C. V. Eastman	2	333
David, m. Eliza **McGARRY**, Mar. 9, 1851, by Rev. David L. Parmelee	TM49	61
Dotha, d. Benjamin & Lucretia, b. Dec. 14, 1786	2	43
Eben S., of Litchfield, m. Sarah C. **THOMAS**, of South Farms, Nov. 28, 1844, by Gordon Hayes	TM49	6
Ebenezer, m. Betsey **STOCKER**, June 20, 1821, by Ozias Lewis, J.P.	2	103
Eden, of Bethany, m. Samantha Hazzard **BLACKMAN**, wid., of Patron M., of Litchfield, Aug. 27, 1851, by Oliver A. G. Todd, J.P.	TM49	63
Edward, Jr., m. Abigail **STODDARD**, Nov. 13, 1760	1	59
Edward., s. Edward & Abigail, b. July 15, 1773	1	58
Elijah, s. Zacharias & Sarah, b. Oct. 4, 1770	1	59
Elijah, d. Aug. 7, 1777, ae 6 y. 10 m.	1	100
Eliza, d. Jonathan & Jane, b. Nov. 2, 1775	1	58
Elizabeth, d. Zacharias & Sarah, b. Mar. 1, 1764	1	58
Elizabeth, d. Zacharias & Sarah, d. Dec. 6, 1766	1	58
Elizabeth, m. John **KELLY, 2nd**, Oct. [ ], 1769	1	103
Elvin, s. Zacharias & Sarah, b. June 18, 1776	1	58
Elvin, d. Aug. 6, 1777, ae 13 m.	1	100
Emela, d. Luther & Betsey, b. Oct. 9, 1798	2	142
Esther, m. Lemuel **GIBBS**, Mar. 12, 1761	1	139
Esther, m. Alvin **MORSE**, May 29, 1810, by Rev. Joseph E. Camp	2	54
Eunice, d. Amos & Sally, b. Oct. 16, 1808	2	250
Eunice, m. George **MARCHANT**, b. of Litchfield, Nov. 27, 1828, by Rev. Henry Robinson, of South Farms	2	279
Experience, m. Thomas **LANDON**, Apr. 4, 1774, by Rev. George Beckwith	1	147
Frances, d. [George & Amy], b. May 4, 1836	2	326

	Vol.	Page
JOHNSON, (cont.),		
George, s. Luther & Betsey, b. Nov. 2, 1810	2	142
George, m. Amy **MOSS**, Dec. 7, 1831, by Rev. Mr. Taylor, of South Farms	2	289
George, m. Amy **MOSS**, Dec. 7, 1831, by Rev. Mr. Taylor, of South Farms	2	326
Harriet, of Bristol, m. Edward **SEYMOUR**, of Torrington, Nov. 26, 1829, by Isaac Jones	2	282
Henry M., m. Phebe Ann **NEGUS**, b. of Litchfield, Sept. 1, 1844, by Rev. Johnson Howard, of Northfield & South Dover, N.Y.	TM49	55
Horace, s. Benjamin & Lucretia, b. Oct. 24, 1797	2	43
Horace, s. Benjamin & Lucretia, b. Oct. 24, 1797; m. Harriet **MOORE**, d. David & Polly, June 13, 1819, by Rev. Isaac Jones	2	120
Huldah, d. Amos & Jemima, b. Jan. 23, 1765	1	59
Irene, d. Zephaniah & Sarah, Dec. 21, 1782	1	59
Isaac, s. Zacharias & Sarah, b. Aug. 9, 1773	1	58
Isaac, d. July 26, 1777, in the 4th y. of his age	1	100
James Helleger, m. Artemesia **THOMPSON**, b. of Litchfield (colored), July 4, 1833, by Rev. Samuel Fuller	TM49	38
Jane, m. Rev. Joseph S. **MORSE**, b. of Litchfield, May 6, 1845, by Rev. D. L. Marks	TM49	9
Jemima, d. Amos & Jemima, b. Aug. 21, 1773	1	58
Jemima, d. Mar. 7, 1828, ae 84 y.	2	85
Jeremiah, of Norfolk, m. Caroline **LEAVENWORTH**, of Litchfield, Oct. 30, 1848, by John F. Norton	TM49	39
Jerome, m. Abigail **STONE**, b. of Ltichfield, Oct. 29, 1838, by Rev. Jonathan Brace	2	318
Joel, s. Amo & Sally, b. Mar. 15, 1818	2	250
John, s. Lambert & Matilda, b. Oct. 4, 1793	2	7
Jonathan, m. Jane **GIBBS**, Jan. 12, 1775, by Rev. Judah Champion	1	58
Lambert, m. Matilda **SMITH**, Sept. 20, 1785	2	7
Leonard, s. Amos & Sally, b. Jan. 5, 1823	2	250
Lewis, s. Luther & Betsey, b. May 16, 1796	2	142
Lois, d. Edward & Abigail, b. Apr. 15, 1761	1	59
Lucretia, d. Edward & Abigail, b. Feb. 25, 1766	1	59
Lucy, d. Luther & Betsey, b. Feb. 2, 1802	2	142
Luther, s. Amos & Jemima, b. Feb. 14, 1767	1	59
Luther, s. Benjamin & Lucretia, b. Oct. 25, 1791	2	43
Luther, m. Betsey **PERKINS**, [ ], by Mr. Bronson, of Waterbury	2	142
Lydia, d. Amos & Jemima, b. July 7, 1771	1	58
Maria, d. Amos & Sally, b. Sept. 29, 1810	2	250
Marinda, 3rd d. [George & Amy], b. Aug. 28, 1837	2	326
Martha, m. James **KELLOGG**, [ ], 1795, by Thomas Mitchell, J.P.	2	91
Martha E., m. Henry **MORSE**, Nov. 27, 1850, by Rev.David L. Parmelee	TM49	55
Martin, s. George & Amy, b. Aug. 28, 1842	2	326
Mary, d. Horace & Harriet, b. July 23, 1820	2	120
Mary, m. Samuel A. **MERRIMAN**, b. of Litchfield, Apr. 16, 1843, by Rev. Jason Wells	2	339
Mary Ann, d. Amos & Sally, b. Mar. 26, 1816	2	250
Mary Ann, m. Ozias **GOODWIN**, of Plymouth, Sept. 30, 1835, by Rev.		

	Vol.	Page
JOHNSON, (cont.),		
L. P. Hickok	2	296
Minerva, d. Zacharias & Sarah, b. July 7, 1768	1	59
Morris, m. Elizabeth **BARNS**, Apr. 1, 1792, by Rev. Judah Champion	1	59
Morris, s. Amos & Sally, b. Sept. 3, 1804	2	250
Morris, m. Amanda **MERCHANT**, Apr. 9, 1828, by Rev. J. E. Camp	2	60
Morris, m. Amanda **MERCHANT**, Apr. 16, 1828, by Rev. Joseph E. Camp, of Northfield	2	292
Mortimer L., s. [Horace & Harriet], b. Aug. 30, 1828	2	120
Nabby, d. Lambert & Matilda, b. Aug. 12, 1791	2	7
Olive, d. Amos & Jemima, b. Oct. 26, 1775	1	101
Olive, d. Amos & Jemima, d. Aug. 7, 1777	1	100
Olive, d. Luther & Betsey, b. Feb. 13, 1792	2	142
Oringh, s. Edward & Abigail, b. July 14, 1762	1	59
Phebe, m. Hezekiah **ORTON, Jr.**, July 25, 1767, by Rev. Judah Champion	1	69
Polly, d. Luther & Betsey, b. June 13, 1804	2	142
Polly, m. Augustus **THOMPSON**, Dec. 14, 1834, by Rev. Joseph E. Camp	2	297
Rhoda, of Harwinton, m. Chauncey **EVANS**, of Litchfield, Jan. 4, 1830, by Jonathan Buel, J.P.	2	283
Sabra, ae 20, m. George **DEWY**, ae 25, Sept. 10, 1815	2	78
Sally, d. Benjamin & Lucretia, b. Dec. 20, 1802	2	43
Samuel, m. Polly Esther **WALKER**, b. of Litchfield, Apr. 27, 1828, by David Bird, J.P.	2	276
Sarah, m. Samuel **WOODRUFF**, Jan. 10, 1776, by Rev. Judah Champion	1	124
Sarah, d. Zephaniah & Sarah, b. June 4, 1778	1	101
Sarah, d. Amos & Sally, b. Jan. 2, 1814	2	250
Seymour, s. Edward, Jr. & Abigail, b. Apr. 30, 1771	1	59
Stephen, s. Luther & Betsey, b. Mar. 7, 1800	2	142
Silvia, d. Edward, Jr. & Abigail, b. June 4, 1769	1	59
William, m. Cornelia A. **LOOMIS**, Mar. 26, 1850, by Rev. David L. Parmelee	TM49	53
Zacharias, m. Sarah **PECK**, July 20, 1765, by Jacob Woodruff, J.P.	1	59
JONES, Abigail, d. Eaton & Mary, b. Apr. 20, 1793	1	101
Charles, s. Eaton & Elizabeth, b. Nov. 20, 1774	1	101
Charles, s. Eaton & Mary, b. Apr. 26, 1797	1	101
Charles, m. Clarisa **BLIN**, Aug. 12, 1804	2	2
Charles, s. Charles & Clarissa, b. July 26, 1814	2	2
Clarissa, d. Charles & Clarissa, b. Mar. 15, 1811	2	2
Eaton, m. Elizabeth **CATLING**, May 5, 1756, by Rev. Judah Champion	1	59
Eaton, s. Eaton & Elizabeth, b. Nov. 9, 1762	1	101
Eaton, m. Mary **McNEILE**, May 1, 1788, by Rev. Judah Champion	1	101
Edwin, s. Charles & Clarissa, b. July 2, 1805	2	2
Harriet N., d. Eliakim & Hannah, b. Mar. 16, 1789	1	101
Harris, d. Sept. 2, 1824, ae 90 y.	1	58
Homer, s. Eaton & Elizabeth, b. Sept. 29, 1767	1	101
Homer, s. Eaton & Elizabeth, d. Oct. 1, 1767	1	100
Isaac, Rev., m. Tabitha **THOMAS**, Oct. 17, 1804, by Rev. James Dana, D.D., at New Haven	2	93
Isaac, Rev., d. Mar. 1, 1850, ae 75	2	93
James, s. Eaton & Elizabeth, b. June 19, 1765	1	101

	Vol.	Page
JONES, (cont.),		
Julia Henrietta, d. Isaac & Tabitha, b. Dec. 14, 1805, at Woodbridge; d.		
Nov. [ ], 1851	2	93
Julius [twin with Marick*], s. Eaton & Mary, b. Jan. 1, 1791		
*("Marcus" in Woodruff's book)	1	101
Katharine, d. Eaton & Elizabeth, b. May 6, 1777	1	101
Liza, d. Eaton & Elizabeth, b. Sept. 29, 1768	1	101
Liza, d. Eaton & Elizabeth, b. Mar. 10, 1771	1	101
Liza, d. Eaton & Elizabeth, d. [ ]	1	100
Luvina*, d. Eaton & Elizabeth, b. Sept. 12, 1758 *("Lucina" in		
Woodruff's book)	1	59
Lucina, d. Eaton & Elizabeth, b. Sept. 12, 1758	1	101
Maria, d. Eaton & Elizabeth, Mar. 4, 1795	1	101
Marian, d. Charles & Clarissa, b. May 9, 1808	2	2
Marick*, [twin with Julius], s. Eaton & Mary, b. Jan. 1, 1791		
*("Marcus" in Woodruff's book)	1	101
Mary, d. Harris & Anne, b. Nov. 28, 1760	1	59
Mary, d. Eaton & Mary, b. Oct. 25, 1789	1	101
Mary, m. Ozias **LEWIS, Jr.**, Jan. 19, 1801, by Rev. Mr. Gammel, of		
New Haven	1	147
Mary, m. Ozias **LEWIS, Jr.**, Jan. 19, 1801, by Rev. Mr. Gammel, of		
New Haven	2	47
Nancy, b. May 25, 1778; m. Lemuel **SMITH**, s. Jacob & Mary, Nov.		
17, 1797	2	92
Samuel, s. Eaton & Elizabeth, b. Oct. 15, 1756	1	59
Samuel, s. Eaton & Elizabeth, b. Oct. 15, 1756	1	101
Samuel, s. Eaton & Elizabeth, d. Dec. [ ], 1759	1	100
Samuel, s. Eaton & Elizabeth, b. Oct. 25, 1760	1	59
Samuel, s. Eaton & Elizabeth, b. Oct. 25, 1760	1	101
Tabitha, wid. [Rev. Isaac], d. Oct. 9, 1852, ae 65	2	93
William Edwin, s. Isaac & Tabitha, b. May 31, 1817; d. Mar. [ ], 1851,		
at Chicago	2	93
JORDAN, Edmund, of Waterbury, m. Emeline A. **TODD**, of Northfield, Jan.		
26, 1851, in Northfield, by Rev. Ruel H. Tuttle	TM49	61
JOY, John, m. Submit **BISHOP**, Sept. 23, 1766, by Timothy Collens, J.P.	1	58
John, m. Submit **BISHOP**, Sept. 23, 1766, by Timothy Collens, J.P.	1	101
John, s. John & Submit, b. Jan. 7, 1773	1	58
Nabby, d. John & Submit, b. Mar. 15, 1770	1	58
Sally, m. Comfort **BRADLEY**, Dec. 31, 1788, by Rev. Ashbel Baldwin	2	27
Sally, m. Comfort **BRADLEY**, Dec. 31, 1788, by Rev. Ashbel Baldwin	2	261
Sarah, d. John & Submit, b. Oct. 23, 1767	1	101
Walter, of Buffalo, N.Y., m. Jane Ellen **RADCLIFFE**, of Litchfield, Jan.		
22, 1833, by Rev. Samuel Fuller	TM49	37
Walter, m. Jane Ellen **RADCLIFFE**, Jan. 22, 1833, by Rev. Samuel		
Fuller	2	289
JUDD, Albert B., of New Milford, m. Louisa **GUILD**, of Litchfield, Nov. 10,		
1845, by Rev. Isaac Jones, of Milton	TM49	12
Caroline B., d. [Henry & Hannah M.], b. Aug. 8, 1831, in Torrington	2	313
Clarissa, d. Orrin & Asenath, b. Jan. 17, 1825	2	252
Dan J., m. Ursula **STEVENS**, Apr. 23, 1828, by Rev. Joseph E. Camp,		
of Northfield	2	292
Dolly, m. William **GIBBS, Jr.**, Nov. 22, 1808, by Rev. Mr. Chase	2	73
Elizabeth Ann, d. Orrin & Asenath, b. Dec. 31, 1808	2	252

	Vol.	Page

JUDD, (cont.),

Erasmus, of Loraine, O., m. Phebe **HALL**, of Litchfield, Nov. 24, 1840

    by Rev. Thomas Ellis   2   331

Harriet C., d. Orrin & Asenath, b. July 2, 1813   2   252

Harriet Clarissa, of Litchfield, m. William **LORD, Jr.**, of East Winsor,

    Apr. 11, 1833, by Rev. Samuel Fuller   TM49   37

Harriet Clarissa, m. William **LORD**, of East Windsor, Apr. 11, 1833, by

    Rev. Samuel Fuller   2   289

Henry, s. Orrin & Asenath, b. Mar. 10, 1805   2   252

Henry, m. Hannah M. **BEACH**, Nov. 10, 1850, in Torrington, by [   ]   2   313

Huldah, d. Jesse & Mary, b. Dec. 18, 1779   1   59

Jesse, s. Orrin & Asenath, b. June 1, 1815   2   252

Louisa C., of Litchfield, m. Josiah L. **STEARNS**, of New York City,

    May 1, 1839, by Rev. Richard Woodruff   2   324

Marinda, d. Orrin & Asenath, b. Aug. 18, 1811   2   252

Mary, d. Orrin & Asenath, b. Oct. 12, 1806   2   252

Mary A., m. Alva M. **BRISTOL**, Dec. 31, 1846, by Rev. David L.

    Parmelee   TM49   16

Orrin, m. Asenath **LANDON**, Nov. 15, 1801, by Truman Marsh   2   252

Orrin, d. June 5, 1830   2   252

William Bennett, of Watertown, m. Mary J. **BURGESS**, of Litchfield,

    Oct. 7, 1851, by N. C. Lewis   TM49   65

JUDSON Eben, m. Polly **TAYLOR**, Nov. 23, 1807, by Rev. Dan Huntington   2   75

Jane, d. Eben & Polly, b. June 13, 1821   2   75

Joel Taylor, s. Eben & Polly, b. Oct. 15, 1813   2   75

Levina, m. Lemuel **WOOSTER**, July 20, 1789   2   124

Levina, m. Samuel **McNEILE**, Jan. 26, 1807, by Rev. Dan Huntington   2   51

Mary Caroline, m. Harry **KILBORN**, Apr. 3, 1822, by Rev. Mr.

    Harrison   2   123

Phebe, m. Lemuel **KILBORN**, Mar. 17, 1762, by Rev. Jedediah Mills   1   61

Ruth Ann, m. William F. **CARPENTER**, b. of Litchfield, Sept. 30,

    1844, by Rev. Silas Hall   TM49   5

Truman H., of Woodbury, m. Sarah **PATTERSON**, of Litchfield, [June]

    16, 1841, by G. C. V. Eastman   2   334

JUNE, Sally Ann, of New Fairfield, m. Nathan **PALMER**, of Stamford, Mar.

    23, 1834, by Daniel Wooster, Dea.   2   294

KEAVELY, W[illia]m, m. Ellen **CAHILL**, b. of South Cornwall, Aug. 20,

    1854, by Rev. Thomas Hendriken   TM49   85

KEELER, Daniel, m. Hannah **STOCKER**, Oct. [ ], 1809, by Rev. Truman

    Marsh   2   48

Hannah, ae 29, m. Enos **STODDARD**, farmer, ae 39, b. of Litchfield,

    May 31, 1853, by Rev. Daniel E. Brown, of Bantam. Witnesses,

    Daniel Keeler & Sherman Keeler   TM49   94

Homer S., m. Pamelia M. **FARNUM**, b. of Litchfield, Jan. 21, 1840, by

    Richard Woodruff   2   324

Irene, d. Daniel & Hannah, b. July 30, 1812   2   48

Irene, of Bantam Falls, m. Lewis **HADSELL**, of Burlington, Mar. 21,

    1843, at Bantam Falls, by Rev. E. M. Porter, of Milton Soc.   2   412

Mary, [d. Daniel & Hannah], [   ]   2   48

Rosanna, m. James B. **NEWCOMB**, b. of Litchfield, Apr. 17, 1849,

    by Rev. F. D. Harriman, of Bantam Falls   TM49   36

Sherman, s. Daniel & Hannah, b. July 8, 1810   2   48

Sherman C., m. Laura E. **BEEBEE**, Apr. 9, 1832, by Rev. L. P. Hickok   2   288

	Vol.	Page
KEELER, (cont.),		
Theodore J., of Albany, m. Lucy A. **HILLS**, of Litchfield, July 28, 1841, by Jonathan Brace	2	334
William R., [s. Daniel & Hannah], [ ]	2	48
William R., m. Elizabeth M. **THROOP**, b. of Litchfield, May 12, 1847, by Rev. William Dixon	TM49	19
KEITH, Memory (?) J. A., m. Mary E. **COWLES**, July 27, 1845, by Rev. David L. Parmelee	TM49	10
KELLOGG, Abigail, d. James & Lydia, b. Jan. 5, 1789, in Norwalk, Conn.	2	91
Albert F., of Adams, Wis., m. Sarah J. **BASSETT**, of Northfield, Aug. 21, 1850, at Northfield, by Rev. Rowel H. Tuttle	TM49	55
Anna Weed, d. James & Martha, b. Mar. 26, 1803	2	91
Charles, s. James & Martha, b. Aug. 14, 1798, in York State	2	91
Chauncey W., m. Mary E. **BASSETT**, b. of Northfield, Oct. 4, 1846, by Rev. Jonathan Coe, 2nd, of Northfield	TM49	16
Clark, s. James & Martha, b. Oct. 14, 1800 , in York State	2	91
Ebenezer, m. Molly **BISSELL**, Dec. 9, 1779, by Rev. Judah Champion	1	103
Edward, s. James & Lydia, b. Oct. 18, 1790, in Norwalk, Conn.	2	91
Elijah, s. James & Lydia, b. Oct. 18, 1784, in Norwalk, Conn.	2	91
Frederick, s. James & Lydia, b. Aug. 11, 1792, in Norwalk, Conn.	2	91
Hulda, of Litchfield, m. Stephen **SHARPLESS**, of Connelsville, Pa., Aug. 21, 1828, by D. L. Carroll	2	278
Isaac, s. Ebenezer & Molly, b. Nov. 6, 1782	1	103
James, m. Lydia **NASH**, Nov. [ ], 1779, by Mr. Mather	2	91
James, s. James & Lydia, b. July 17, 1781, in Norwalk, Conn.	2	91
James, m. Martha **JOHNSON**, [ ], 1795, by Thomas Mitchell, J.P.	2	91
Julia, d. James & Martha, b. Mar. 26, 1805	2	91
Julia, of Litchfield, m. Ogden **SMITH**, of Elizabethtown, N.J., Nov. 5, 1828, by Frederick Holcomb	2	278
Lorain, d. Ebenezer & Molly, b. Sept. 25, 1780	1	103
Lydia, d. James & Lydia, b. Apr. 28, 1794, in Franklin, N.Y.	2	91
Lydia, w. James, d. Aug. [ ], 1794	2	91
Lydia, m. Merit **CLARK**, May 7, 1817, by Rev. Joseph E. Camp	2	146
Merret, s. James & Martha, b. Dec. 17, 1808	2	91
Polly, d. James & Lydia, b. Dec. 29, 1782, in Norwalk, Conn.	2	91
Polly, m. Peck **CLARK**, May 12, 1805, by Rev. T. Marsh	2	80
Rufus, s. James & Lydia, b. Dec. 13, 1786, in Norwalk, Conn.	2	91
Sabra, m. David **BENTON**, Apr. 16, 1826, by Rev. Henry Robinson	2	262
KELLY, Daniel, s. John, 2nd & Elizabeth, b. Mar. 3, 1770	1	102
Emma, m. David L. **HAYES**, July 24, 1833, by Rev. David G. Tomlinson, of Bradleyville	2	294
Frederick H., m. Artavia L. **LAMSON**, Sept. 15, 1852, by Rev. David L. Parmelee	TM49	76
Gad, s. John, 2nd & Elizabeth, b. Nov. 16, 1771	1	102
John, 2nd, m. Elizabeth **JOHNSON**, Oct. [ ], 1769	1	103
John, s. John, 2nd & Elizabeth, b. Oct. 15, 1773	1	102
Joseph Johnson, s. John & Elizabeth, b. [ ]	1	102
Olive, d. John & Elizabeth, b. Aug. 7, 1775	1	102
Phebe, d. John & Elizabeth, b. [ ]	1	102
KELSEY, KELCEY, KELLSY, Charles, m. Hannah **TILER***, Nov. 8, 1770 *("FILER" in Woodruff's book)	1	103
Charles, s. Charles & Hannah, b. May 31, 1773	1	103

	Vol.	Page
KELSEY, KELCEY, KELLSY, (cont.),		
Mabel, d. Charles & Hannah, b. Feb. 7, 1772	1	103
KENNEY, KENNY, Abigal, m. James **GILBERT**, Apr. 9, 1801, by Rev.		
Jeremiah Day	2	147
Charles, s. David & Ruth, b. July 17, 1804	2	64
Charlotte Ann, d. Leonard & Louisa, b. May 7, 1822	2	127
Chester, s. David & Ruth, b. Mar. 4, 1795	2	64
Cornelia, of Litchfield, m. Leonard **RUSSELL**, of Ton-du-Lac, Wis.,		
Oct. 24, 1853, by Rev. Benjamin L. Swan	TM49	92
David, m. Ruth **HOTCHKISS**, [ ], 1793	2	64
George, s. Leonard & Louisa, b. Nov. 28, 1824	2	127
George, m. Caroline M. **OSBORN**, b. of Litchfield, Oct. 12, 1846, by		
Rev. Benjamin L. Swan	TM49	16
Hariet, d. David & Ruth, b. Feb. 7, 1794	2	64
Hariet, d. David & Ruth, d. [ ]	2	64
Henry S., m. Helen S. **GOSLEE**, b. of Litchfield, Oct. 26, 1852, by Rev.		
Benjamin L. Swan	TM49	77
Joseph, m. Helen M. **WESTOVER**, b. of Litchfield, Oct. 3, 1849, by		
B. L. Swan	TM49	43
Joseph M., s. David & Ruth, b. Mar. 23, 1813	2	64
Juan*, d. David & Ruth, b. Sept. 17, 1799 *("Jan" in Woodruff's)	2	64
Lemuel Hotchkiss, s. David & Ruth, b. Jan. 16, 1810	2	64
Leonard, s. David & Ruth, b. Feb. 23, 1797	2	64
Leonard, m. Louisa **BRADLEY**, June 14, 1819, by Rev. Lyman		
Beecher	2	127
Louisa Maria, d. Leonard & Louisa, b. Mar. 14, 1820	2	127
Murray, m. Abigail E. **WOODRUFF**, Aug. 25, 1835, by Rev. L. P.		
Hickok	2	296
Polly A., d. David & Ruth, b. Apr. 16, 1807	2	64
Ranslear, s. David & Ruth, b. Mar. 19, 1802	2	64
KENT, Darius, s. Seth & Lois, b. Dec. 18, 1758	1	61
Theron, of Sharon, m. Ann C. **BOOTH**, of Litchfield, [Oct.] 7, 1849, by		
Rev. Herman L. Vaill	TM49	43
KENYON, Hannah, m. Chauncey **KILBORN**, June 30, 1811, by Lebius		
Armstrong	2	52
KERBY, [see under **KIRBY**]		
KEYES, KIYES, KIRYES, David, s. Zachariah & Mary, b. Aug. 24, 1751	1	61
David, s. Zachariah & Mary, d. Aug. 25, 1751	1	60
Luce, d. Zachariah & Mary, b. Sept. 21, 1752	1	61
Mary Ann, m. Warren **BROOKER**, Apr. [ ], 1825, by Rev. Lyman		
Beecher	2	140
Rhoda, m. Miles **CRAMTON**, Mar. 12, 1770, by John Cooke, J.P.	1	130
Zachariah, of Litchfield, m. Mary **GOODELL**, of Pomfret, Sept. 20,		
1750, by Rev. William Ebenezer Williams	1	61
KILBORN, KILLBORN, KILBURN, KILBOURNE, Aaron, s. Joseph &		
Elizabeth, b. Jan. 30, 1773	1	21
Abel, s. James & Molly, b. Sept. 4, 1776	1	102
Abigail, d. Joseph & Abigail, b. May 20, 1744	1	61
Abigail, w. Joseph, d. May 20, 1748	1	20
Abigail, m. James **WALLON**, Sept. 11, 1823, by Rev. Truman Marsh	2	131
Abraham, s. Abraham & Rebecca, d. Sept. 3, 1747	1	60
Abraham, s. Isaac & Mahetable, b. Nov. 15, 1759	1	103
Abraham, representative May & Oct. 1769, May & Oct. 1770	2	1549

	Vol.	Page
KILBORN, KILLBORN, KILBURN, KILBOURNE, (cont.),		
Abraham, d. Feb. 25, 1776	1	20
Alice, d. Solomon & Anne, b. Jan. 25, 1769	1	60
Almira, d. Jeremiah & Anne, b. Sept. 29, 1795	1	145
Amanda, d. Whitman & Thala, b.Sept. 26, 1811	2	42
Amanda, m. James B. **PECK,** Sept. 9, 1840, by Jonathan Brace	2	319
Ann, d. Joseph & Abigail, b. Mar. 7, 1731	1	61
Ann, d. Samuell & Mary, b. July 2, 1743	1	61
Ann, m. Thomas **GOODWIN,** Nov. 23, 1752, by Ebenezer Marsh, J.P.	1	89
Ann, m. Tho[ma]s **GOODWIN,** Nov. 23, [17]52	1	96
Ann, m. Darius **TERRIL,** of Winchester, Feb. 6, 1823, by Ozias Lewis, J.P.	2	117
Anna, m. Gideon **STODDARD,** Feb. 28, 1790	2	87
Anne, d. Solomon & Anne, b. July 12, 1767	1	60
Anne, d. Jeremiah & Anne, b. Apr. 12, 1793	1	145
Anthony, s. Isaac & Mehetable, b. Mar. 17, 1764	1	103
Appleton, s. James & Sarah, b. Sept. 12, 1731	1	21
Benjamin, s. Joseph & Abigail, b. Apr. 4, 1728	1	21
Benjamin, m. Hannah **STODDAR,** Dec. 5, 1751, by Rev. Timothy Collens	1	61
Benjamin, m. Luce **BISHOP,** Mar. 20, 1757	1	61
Benjamin, s. Benjamin & Lucy, b. Jan. 27, 1765	1	60
Benjamin, s. Lewis & Anne, b. June 17, 1799	1	145
Benjamin, m. Amanda **MILLARD,** July 1, 1821, at Cornwall, by Rev. Walter Smith	2	272
Billy, twin with Polly, s. Benjamin & Lucy, b. May 6, 1778	1	60
Catharine, d. Joseph & Abigail, b. Apr. 19, 1742	1	61
Catharine, m. Putnum **KILBORN,** Jan. 12, 1814, by Rev. Truman Marsh	2	19
Charles, s. Joseph & Abigail, b. Feb. 24, 1740	1	61
Charles, s. Benjamin & Luce, b. Mar. 3, 1758	1	61
Charles, s. Lewis & Anne, b. May 28, 1783	1	145
Charles J., s. Truman & Emeline, b. July 11, 1820	2	70
Chauncey, m. Hannah **KENYON,** June 30, 1811, by Lebius Armstrong	2	52
Chauncey, Sr., d. June [ ], 1819	2	52
Clarissa, m. Heman **BEACH,** Oct. 27, 1794, by Rev. Judah Champion	2	44
Clarissa, d. James & Diantha, b. Oct. 15, 1798	2	16
Clarissa Amanda, d. Harry & Mary Caroline, b. Jan. 5, 1825	2	123
Clarissa M., m. George **BOLLS,** Nov. 29, 1821, by Rev. Lyman Beecher	2	108
David, s. Abraham & Rebecca, b. Apr. 28, 1742	1	61
David, m. Louisa **BORDEN,** Apr. 20, 1763, by Rev. Judah Champion	1	61
David, s. Benjamin & Lucy, b. Feb. 21, 1767	1	60
David, m. Deidamia **KILBORN,** June 15, 1769, by Rev. Salomon Palmer	1	103
Deidamia, m. David **KILBORN,** June 15, 1769, by Rev. Solomon Palmer	1	103
Doroty, m. Joseph **BIRG,** Nov. 8, 1721, by David Goodrich	1	5
Dotha, d. Lewis & Anne, b. July 24, 1785	1	145
Dothy, m. Timothy **CHURCHILL,** Feb. 24, 1808, by Rev. Judah Champion	2	125
Eliada, s. Whitman & Thala, b. Feb. 20, 1809	2	42
Eliada, m. Mary Ann **DUDLEY,** b. of Litchfield, Nov. 1, [1843], by		

	Vol.	Page
KILBORN, KILLBORN, KILBURN, KILBOURNE, (cont.),		
Ralph Smith	2	340
Elijah, s. Jonathan & Sarah, b. Jan. 17, 1742/3	1	21
Elijah, s. Jonathan & Sarah, d. Jan. 27, 1742/3	1	20
Elisha, s. Joseph & Abigail, b. Oct. 16, 1726	1	21
Elisha, s. James & Diantha, b. July 10, 1803	2	16
Elizabeth, d. Roswell & Irene, b. Jan. 4, 1765	1	102
Elizabeth, d. Joseph & Elizabeth, b. June 7, 1770	1	103
Elizabeth, m. Philander **WESTOVER,** Dec. 10, 1795, by Rev. [ ]		
Butler	2	135
Elizabeth D., d. Truman & Emeline, b. Aug. 19, 1835; d. July 18, 1841	2	70
Esther, m. Sam[ue]ll **SMEDLE, Jr.,** Feb. 1, 1729, by Rev. Timothy		
Collens	1	37
Ethan, s. Whitman & Thala, b. Aug. 18, 1803	2	42
Ethan, m. Thankfull **BISHOP,** b. of Litchfield, May 31, 1830, by Rev.		
L. P. Hickok	2	285
Eunice, d. Abraham & Rebecka, b. Nov. 7, 1735	1	21
George, s. Norman & Lucy, b. Dec. 27, 1815	2	67
Giles, s. Samuel & Mary, b. Jan. 25, 1728/9	1	61
Giles Chauncey, s. [Chauncey & Hannah], b. July 3, 1817; d. Apr. 1,		
1826, in Kent	2	52
Hannah, d. Solomon & Anne, b. Mar. 6, 1760	1	60
Hannah, wid., m. Nathaniel C. **BATES,** of Kent, Dec. 7, 1825, by Rev.		
Truman Marsh	2	258
Hannah, d. Norman, m. Edward **WOODRUFF,** b. of Bantam Falls, Sept.		
28, 1846, by Joshua D. Berry, at his house	TM49	16
Hannah, [d. Norman & Lucy], [ ]	2	67
Harry, m. Mary Caroline **JUDSON,** Apr. 3, 1822, by Rev. Mr. Harrison	2	123
Henry, s. John & Lois, b. Sept. 12, 1798	2	60
Henry, s. Norman & Lucy, b. July 30, 1813	2	67
Hephsibah, d. Isaac & Mehetabel, b. May 8, 1771	1	103
Hiram, m. Harriet **MOULTHROP,** b. of Litchfield, [Dec.] 24, [1840],		
by G. C. V. Eastman, in Milton Soc.	2	332
Hiram G., s. Putnam & Catharine, b. Oct. 19, 1814	2	19
Honor, [d. Norman & Lucy], [ ]	2	67
Huldah, m. Charles **WILLIAMS,** Oct. 27, 1805, by Rev. Amos Chase	2	92
Irene, w. Roswell, d. Feb. [ ], 1768	1	102
Irene, d. Roswell & Patience, b. June 19, 1769	1	102
Isaac, s. Abraham & Rebecka, b. Jan. 16, 1739	1	21
Isaac, m. Mehetable **DOOLITTLE,** May 8, 1757, by Rev. Solomon		
Palmer	1	103
Isaac, s. Isaac & Mehetabel, b. Jan. 31, 1762	1	103
Jacob, s. Jesse & Sarah, b. Sept. 10, 1767	1	103
Jacob, m. Lucy **BRADLEY,** Sept. 12, 1789, by Rev. A. Baldwin	2	70
James, m. Sarah **BISSELL,** Sept. 12, 1733	1	21
James, s. James & Sarah, b. Jan. 3, 1750	1	61
James, d. Mar. 9, 1762	1	20
James, m. Molly **CRAMTON,** May 15, 1771, by Timothy Collens, J.P.	1	103
James, s. David, b. Sept. 18, 1771; m. Diantha **SMITH,** Dec. 25, 1795,		
by Rev. Mr. Botts	2	16
James, s. David & Deidamia, b. Sept. 21, 1771	1	61
James, s. David, d. May 20, 1809	2	16
James, s. Whitman & Thala, b. May 27, 1816	2	42

	Vol.	Page
KILBORN, KILLBORN, KILBURN, KILBOURNE, (cont.),		
Jeremiah, s. Joseph & Abigail, b. July 17, 1733	1	21
Jeremiah, s. Joseph & Abigail, d. July 30, 1733	1	20
Jeremiah, s. Solomon & Anne, b. Apr. 8, 1762	1	60
Jeremiah, m. Anne **BISHOP,** Apr. 28, 1785	1	145
Jeremiah, m. Rachel **WESTOVER,** b. of Litchfield, [Mar.] 14, 1844, by		
G. C. V. Eastman	TM49	2
Jerusha, m. Supreme **SMITH,** Nov. 25, 1764, by Rev. Thomas Davies	1	118
Jesse, s. Abraham & Rebecca, b. Jan. 2, 1744	1	61
Jesse, m. Sarah **MATTOCKS,** Feb. 24, 1765, by Rev. Judah Champion	1	61
John, s. Samuel & Mary, b. Apr. 15, 1735	1	61
John, s. Giles, b. Mar. 16, 1766; m. Lois **STODDARD,** Apr. 26, 1790	2	60
John, s. Roswell & Patience, b. May 19, 1775	1	102
John, s. Chauncey & Hannah, b. Nov. 1, 1812	2	52
John, m. Huldah **HUMMISTON,** b. of Litchfield, June 23, 1833, by		
Rev. Samuel Fuller	TM49	37
John, m. Huldah **HUMASTON,** June 23, 1833, by Rev. Samuel Fuller	2	289
Jonathan, of Litchfield, m. Sarah **DICKERSON,** of Weathersfield, Oct.		
27, 1737, by Rev. Daniel Russel	1	21
Jonathan, s. Jonathan & Sarah, b. Mar. 28, 1739	1	21
Jonathan, m. Sarah **BLISS,** b. of Litchfield, Sept. 17, 1740, by Capt.		
John Buel, J.P.	1	21
Joseph, Jr., m. Abigail **STOCKWELL,** Nov. 12, 1723	1	21
Joseph, Jr. & Abigail, had 1st s. [ ], b. July 25, 1724; d. July 25,		
1724	1	21
Joseph, Jr. & Abigail, had 2nd s. [ ], b. June 8, 1725; d. June 8,		
1725	1	21
Joseph, representative Oct. 1752, May 1753	2	1547
Joseph, s. Jonathan & Sarah, b. Mar. 5, 1764/5	1	21
Joseph, m. Elizabeth **MARSH,** Nov. 30, 1765, by Ebenezer Marsh, J.P.	1	103
Joseph, s. Benjamin & Lucy, b. Feb. 15, 1771	1	60
Joseph, s. Roswell & Patience, b. Feb. 15, 1777	1	102
Joseph, s. Roswell & Patience, d. Aug. 24, 1777	1	102
Julia, d. James & Diantha, b. Jan. 6, 1797	2	16
Julia Ann, m. Solon **BISHOP,** Feb. [ ], 1809	2	43
Julia Elizabeth, d. Payne Kenyon & Elizabeth A., b. Aug. 9, 1843	TM49	98
Julia Maria, d. James & Diantha, b. Oct. 25, 1809; d. July 15, 1797	2	16
Julia Maria, d. James & Diantha, d. Dec. [ ], 1819	2	16
Lavina, m. Roswell **HART,** of Winchester, Jan. 6, 1825, by Rev. Isaac		
Jones	2	15
Lelia Kenyon, d. Payne Kenyon & Elizabeth A., b. May 1, 1850	TM49	98
Lemuel, m. Phebe **JUDSON,** Mar. 17, 1762, by Rev. Jedediah Mills	1	61
Lemuel Judson, s. Lemuel & Phebe, b. Apr. 3, 1763	1	61
Levi, s. David & Diedamia, b. Apr. 15, 1773	1	60
Levi, m. Anna **BRADLEY,** Nov. 27, 1794	2	65
Lewis, s. Benjamin & Hannah, b. May 22, 1755	1	61
Lewis, s. Whitman & Thala, b. May 31, 1806	2	42
Lois, m. Elkanah **HASKIN,** Sept. 18, 1754	1	98
Lois, d. Harry & Mary Caroline, b. July 2, 1823	2	123
Louis, m. Anne **PALMALEE,** Jan. 30, 1782, by Rev. James Nichols	1	145
Louisa, w. David, d. Nov. 2, 1768	1	60
Lovina, d. Jeremiah & Anne, b. Apr. 21, 1804	1	145
Lucretia, d. Jesse & Sarah, b. Dec. 13, 1765	1	103

	Vol	Page
KILBORN, KILLBORN, KILBURN, KILBOURNE, (cont.),		
Lucretia, m. Benjamin **JOHNSON**, Feb. [ ], 1785, by Rev. Judah		
Champion	2	43
Lucretia, d. Jeremiah & Anne, b. Jan. 29, 1786	1	145
Lucy, d. Benjamin & Lucy, b. Mar. 17, 1773	1	60
Lydia, m. Benjamin **PALMER**, Mar. 25, 1779, by Rev. Judah		
Champion	1	112
Lydia, m. William H. **DUDLEY**, b. of Litchfield, Nov. 20, 1843, by		
Ralph Smith	TM49	1
Lydia Ann, d. Benjamin & Amanda, b. Jan. 6, 1824	2	272
Lydia Ann, m. Henry Roland **RAY**, b. of Litchfield, May 4, 1846, by		
Rev. Samuel Fuller	TM49	37
Mahala, d. John & Lois, b. Mar. 18, 1801	2	60
Maria, twin with Mariana, d. Levi & Anna, b. Jan. 28, 1800	2	65
Maria, d. Benjamin & Amanda, b. Nov. 14, 1822	2	272
Mariana, twin with Maria, d. Levi & Anna, b. Jan. 28, 1800	2	65
Marina, m. Walter **COE**, Dec. 15, 1824, by Rev. Henry Robinson	2	137
Mary, d. Samuel & Mary, b. Jan. 17, 1730/1	1	61
Mary, m. Nathaniel **WOODRUFF**, Nov. 5, 1749	1	83
Mary, m. Jacob **BAKER**, Mar. 11, 1773, by Rev. Judah Champion	1	167
Mary, d. John & Lois, b. Dec. 2, 1803	2	60
Mary Ann, d. Levi & Anna, b. June 2, 1807	2	65
Mary Ann, m. Lucius **WILLMOT**, Sept. 15, 1833, by Rev. David G.		
Tomlinson, of Bradleyville	2	294
Mary M., m. Henry **BALDWIN**, b. of Litchfield, Oct. 29, 1846, by Rev.		
William Dixon	TM49	16
Mehetabel, d. Isaac & Mehetabel, b. Mar. 25, 1773	1	103
Mehetabel, m. Joseph **WESTOVER**, Sept. [ ], 1796, by Rev. Amos		
Chase	2	149
Mercy, d. Isaac & Mehetable, b. June 13, 1769	1	103
Muna*, m. Henry P. **TROWBRIDGE**, b. of Litchfield, July 12, 1841,		
by William Payne *("Maria"?)	2	334
Myron, s. Whitman & Thala, b. Oct. 10, 1801	2	42
Nabby, d. Jacob & Lucy, b. Aug. 3, 1792	2	70
Nancy, d. Jeremiah & Anne, b. May 9, 1799	1	145
Nancy, m. Herman **STODDARD**, Jan. 3, 1819, by Rev. Isaac Jones	2	259
Nancy D., m. Curtiss L. **OSBORN**, June 4, 1839, by William Payne	2	328
Noah, s. Jeremiah & Anne, b. Nov. 11, 1787	1	145
Norman, s. Jacob & Lucy, b. Apr. [ ], 1790	2	70
Norman, s. Lewis & Anne, b. July 15, 1790	1	145
Norman, m. Lucy **PECK**, Sept. 12, 1810, by Rev. Truman Marsh	2	67
Olive, m. Thomas **GOODWIN**, Jr., Nov. 14, 1793, by Rev. Judah		
Champion	2	42
Orange, s. David & Deidamia, b. Feb. 23, 1770	1	61
Orilia, m. Lovis **BEACH**, Jan. 27, 1799, by Moses Seymour, J.P.	1	166
Orrin S., s. James & Diantha, b. Oct. 18, 1806	2	16
Orrin T.*, s. James & Diantha, d. Mar. 5, 1809 *("S."?)	2	16
Payne Kenyon, s. Chauncey & Hannah, b. July 26, 1815	2	52
Payne Kenyon, s. Chauncey, m. Elizabeth A. **CONE**, d. Warren, Aug. 3,		
1842, at Norfolk, by Rev. Joseph Eldredge	TM49	98
Philo, s. Lemuel & Phebe, b. Nov. 12, 1769	1	61
Polly, twin with Billy, d. Benjamin & Lucy, b. May 6, 1778	1	60
Polly, m. Elisha S. **MUNGER**, Oct. 29, 1783, by Rev. James Nichols	1	189

	Vol.	Page
KILBORN, KILLBORN, KILBURN, KILBOURNE, (cont.),		
Putnam, s. Jeremiah & Anne, b. June 10, 1791	1	145
Putnam, m. Catharine **KILBORN**, Jan. 12, 1814, by Rev. Truman		
Marsh	2	19
Rachal, d. James & Sarah, b. July 22, 1753	1	61
Rachal, d. Solomon & Anne, b. Aug. 18, 1757	1	60
Rachel J., m. Silas **DIBBALL**, May 15, 1772, by Timothy Collens, J.P.	1	9
Rebecca, d. Abraham & Rebecca, b. Jan. 26, 1746	1	61
Rebecca, m. Uriah **CATLIN**, Dec. 29, 1765, by Rev. Thomas Davies	1	88
Rebecca, w. Abraham, d. June 16, 1767, in the 63rd y. of her age	1	20
Rebecca, d. Isaac & Mehetabel, b. July 27, 1767	1	103
Rebecca, d. Roswell & Patience, b. Nov. 5, 1770; d. Dec. 24, 1770	1	102
Rebecca, d. Roswell & Patience, b. Aug. 21, 1772	1	102
Rebecca, m. Joseph **WESTOVER**, Sept. [ ], 1787, by Rev. Ashbel		
Baldwin	2	149
Reuben, s. David & Diedamia, b. June 15, 1775	1	60
Rhoda, d. James & Sarah, b. May 9, 1744	1	61
Rhoda, d. Roswell & Irene, b. May 4, 1761	1	102
Rhoda, m. Elisha **MARSH**, [ ], 1802, by Rev. Judah Champion	2	52
Rhoda, m. David **BELLAMY**, Dec. 10, 1821, by Morris Woodruff, J.P.	2	105
Rollin F., of Litchfield, m. Louisa M. **COGSWELL**, of Washington,		
Nov. 13, 1844, by Rev. G. C. V. Eastman	TM49	8
Rosel, s. James & Sarah, b. June 29, 1734	1	21
Roswel, s. Roswel & Irene, b. Apr. 7, 1763	1	102
Roswell & Irene, had d. [ ], b. Aug. 6, 1767; d. next day	1	102
Roswell, m. Patience **JENKINS**, Jan. [ ], 1769, by Rev. Judah		
Champion	1	102
Roswell, d. Feb. 8, 1777	1	102
Roswell, m. Irene **BACON**, [ ]	1	102
Ruth, d. Joseph & Abigail, b. May 9, 1734	1	21
Ruth, d. Benjamin & Hannah, b. Oct. 17, 1752	1	61
Ruth, m. Nathaniel **COLVER**, Nov. 23, 1752, by Ebenezer Marsh, J.P.	1	89
Sally, d. Jacob & Lucy, b. June 24, 1797	2	70
Sally, m. John **PALMER**, Aug. 16, 1801, by Rev. Truman Marsh	2	105
Samuel, d. Dec. 12, 1748	1	20
Samuel, s. Joseph & Anna, b. Mar. 12, 1752	1	61
Samuel, s. Benjamin & Lucy, b. Feb. 21, 1769	1	60
Samuel, m. Antha E. **ABBOTT**, b. of Litchfield, Feb. 20, 1845, by John		
F. Norton	TM49	8
Sary, d. Samuel & Mary, b. Jan. 31, 1726/7	1	61
Sarah, w. Jonathan, d. Apr. 6, 1739	1	20
Sarah, d. James & Sarah, b. Nov. 27, 1746	1	61
Sarah, m. Laben **BEECH**, Feb. 25, 1765, by Timothy Collens	1	126
Sarah, d. James & Molly, b. May 20, 1772	1	103
Solomon, s. Joseph & Abigail, b. Mar. 1, 1736	1	21
Solomon, m. Anne **PALMER**, Apr. 8, 1756, by Rev. Judah Champion	1	60
Solomon, s. Solomon & Anne, b. Dec. 17, 1764	1	60
Susan, d. James & Diantha, b. Nov. 14, 1800	2	16
Susan, m. George C. **BISSELL**, May 1, 1826, by Rev. Mr. Trumas	2	263
Susanna, d. Joseph & Elizabeth, b. July 4, 1766	1	103
Sybel, d. Samuel & Mary, b. Jan. 31, 1732/3	1	61
Sibbel, d. Solomon & Anne, b. Nov. 8, 1774	1	60
Temperance, d. Samuell & Mary, b. Oct. 18, 1739	1	61

	Vol.	Page
KILBORN, KILLBORN, KILBURN, KILBOURNE, (cont.),		
Theral, s. David & Louisa, b. Oct. 19, 1767	1	61
Thirza, d. John & Lois, b. Aug. 26, 1796	2	60
Timothy, s. Joseph & Elizabeth, b. June 11, 1768	1	103
Truman, s. Jeremiah & Anne, b. May 28, 1789	1	145
Truman, s. Jacob & Lucy, b. Jan. 1, 1795	2	70
Truman, m. Emeline **COE**, Sept. 27, 1819, by Rev. Lyman Beecher	2	70
Truman C., s. Truman & Emeline, b. May 21, 1831	2	70
Whitman, s. Solomon & Anne, b. Apr. 12, 1772	1	60
Whitman, m. Thala **OSBORN**, Apr. 7, 1800, by Rev. Judah Champion	2	42
William, s. Norman & Lucy, b. July 27, 1811	2	67
William L., s. Truman & Emeline, b. Nov. 2, 1823	2	70
William P., m. Caroline A. **CANFIELD**, Apr. 26, 1832, by Rev. Mr. Taylor, of South Farms	2	289
KIMBERLY, KIMBERLEY, Alanson H., m. Lucy M. **FOOT**, Jan. [ ], 1818, by Rev. Amos Pettingill	2	99
Ann, m. Shelton J. **BROWN**, Oct. 15, 1844, by Rev. David L. Parmelee	TM49	6
Lucy Ann, d. Alanson H. & Lucy M., b. Oct. 28, 1819	2	99
KING, David, m. Sarah **MARSH**, June 29, 1773, by Rev. Judah Champion	1	103
David, s. David & Sarah, b. Oct. 19, 1773	1	102
David, m. Hannah **PECK**, Jan. 25, 1821, by Rev. Amos Pettingill	2	98
Elizabeth, m. George **ADDIS**, b. of Litchfield, Aug. 16, 1846, by Rev. Samuel Fuller	TM49	38
Julia Elizabeth, of Litchfield, m. William Franklin **NOYES**, of Stonington, Apr. 9, 1837, by Rev. Samuel Fuller	TM49	37
Polly, b. [ ], 1784, in Reading	2	41
Polly, m. Thaddeus **HUNGERFORD**, Dec. 25, 1805, by Rev. Ashbel Backas	2	41
KINGSLEY, Louisa, Mrs. of Northfield, m. Hezekiah **DICKINSON**, of Albany, N.Y., Nov. 29, 1846, by Rev. Albert B. Camp	TM49	15
KINNEY, Charlotte, m. Leonard **BISSELL**, b. of Litchfield, Oct. 24, 1844, by Rev. George H. Hastings	TM49	8
David, m. Emily **BUNNELL**, Oct. 30, 1851, by Rev. David L. Parmelee	TM49	65
Louisa M., m. Charles A. **DUDLEY**, May 18, 1842, by Jonathan Brace	2	410
KIRBY, Abraham, s. Abraham & Eunice, b. Apr. 3, 1764	1	102
Anna, d. Abraham & Eunice, b. July 21, 1775	1	102
Catharine, d. Ephraim & Ruth, b. Oct. 11, 1802	1	145
Edmond, s. Ephraim & Ruth, b. Apr. 8, 1794	1	145
Ephraim, s. Abraham & Eunice, b. Feb. 23, 1757	1	21
Ephraim, m. Ruth **MARVIN, Jr.**, Mar. 17, 1784, by Rev. Judah Champion	1	145
Ephraim, representative Oct. 1791, May 1792, May & Oct. 1794, May 1795, Oct. 1799, May & Oct. 1797, Oct. 1798, May 1799, May & Oct. 1800, May 1801, Oct. 1802	2	1551-3
Ephraim, s. Ephraim & Ruth, b. Jan. 25, 1796	1	145
Ephraim, had negro Chloe, d. Violet, b. Sept. 23, 1796	1	151
Eunice, d. Abraham & Eunice, b. Mar. 20, 1766	1	102
Fanny, d. Ephraim & Ruth, b. Apr. 6, 1785	1	145
Harriet, d. Ephraim & Ruth, b. Mar. 20, 1788	1	145
Harriet, d. Aug. 25, 1789	1	142-4
Harriet, d. Ephraim & Ruth, b. May 23, 1798	1	145
Helen, d. Ephraim & Ruth, b. Nov. 18, 1800	1	145
James, s. Abraham & Eunice, b. July 15, 1758	1	102

	Vol.	Page
KIRBY, (cont.)		
John Starkweather, s. Abraham & Eunice, b. Sept. 20, 1762	1	102
Joseph, s. Abraham & Eunice, b. Apr. 28, 1768	1	102
Martha, d. Abraham & Eunice, b. Feb. 10, 1760; d. Mar. 25, 1760	1	102
Martha, d. Abraham & Eunice, b. Dec. 3, 1760	1	102
Mary, d. Abraham & Eunice, b. Aug. 1, 1771	1	102
Rachel, d. Joseph & Rachel, b. Mar. 4, 1759	1	103
Reuben, s. Joseph & Rachel, b. Nov. 17, 1760	1	103
Reynolds Marvin, s. Ephraim & Ruth, b. Mar. 10, 1790	1	145
Sabra, d. Abraham & Eunice, b. Feb. 27, 1773	1	102
Sarah, d. Joseph & Rachel, b. Feb. 18, 1765	1	103
Sinta*, d. Joseph & Rachel, b. July 18, 1762 *("Seula" in Woodruff's)	1	103
KIRYES, [see under **KEYES**]		
KNAPP, KNAP, Ambrose, of North Canaan, m. Jane A. **MAXHY**, of		
Litchfield, July 20, 1841, by William Payne	2	334
Annis, m. Oliver **WOODRUFF**, Dec. 5, 1785	1	245
Benjamin, of Norfolk, m. Angeline **BUEL**, of Litchfield, Dec. 24, 1833,		
by I. Marsh	2	294
Betsey Jane, d. Jared & Caty, b. May 30, 1808	2	128
Catharine, d. Jared & Caty, b. Feb. 23, 1804	2	128
Charles Harlois, s. Jared & Caty, b. Mar. 19, 1802	2	128
Elizabeth A., m. Ira **PAGE**, b. of Litchfield, Oct. 29, 1854, by Rev. H.		
N. Weed	TM49	103
George Washington, s. Jared & Caty, b. July 22, 1806	2	128
Jared, m. Caty **BALDWIN**, June 9, 1795, by Rev. Mr. Smith	2	128
Julia Beach, d. Jared & Caty, b. May 3, 1817	2	128
Lucy Maria, d. Jared & Caty, b. May 22, 1813	2	128
Mary, d. Jared & Caty, b. Feb. 23, 1798	2	128
Mary, m. David **GIBBS, 2nd**, Feb. 27, 1817, by Morris Woodruff, J.P.	2	97
Sophia, d. Jared & Caty, b. Apr. 5, 1796	2	128
William Riley, s. Jared & Caty, b. Jan. 6, 1800	2	128
KOELER, Zerah, m. Levina **GRANNISS**, June 12, 1823, by Rev. Isaac		
Jones	2	120
LAMPMAN, Harriet, m. Miles **NICHOLS**, b. of Litchfield, Dec. 17, 1850,		
by Benjamin L. Swan	TM49	53
LAMPSON, LAMSON, [see also **LANSON**], Artavia L., m. Frederick H.		
KELLY, Sept. 15, 1852, by Rev. David L. Parmelee	TM49	76
Daniel, m. Lois **BENTON**, June 17, 1784	2	78
Daniel, m. Anna **BENTON**, b. of Litchfield, June 1, 1833, by Morris		
Woodruff, J.P.	2	293
Harriet, of Litchfield, m. David **HOWE**, of Warren, Jan. 25, 1830, by		
Rev. Bradley Sillick	2	284
LANDON, [see under **LANGDON**]		
LANGDON, LANDON, Abigail, d. Benjamin & Abigail, b. Nov. 4, 1765	1	63
Abener, s. Daniell & Martha, b. Mar. 10, 1739/40	1	23
Abner, s. Remembrance & Sally, b. Dec. 1, 1795	1	147
Abner, m. Minerva **STONE**, Apr. 24, 1822, by Rev. Isaac Jones	2	111
Almeda, m. William J. **LOVELAND**, Apr. 20, 1842	2	336
Ambrose, s. James & Sarah, b. Sept. 9, 1744	1	23
Ann B., m. John C. **LASCY**, Oct. 26, 1834, by Rev. L. P. Hickok	2	288
Ann E., of Litchfield, m. Benjamin F. **LANGDON**, of Vt., Feb. 18,		
1839, by Rev. Jonathan Brace	2	318
Anna, m. Oliver **DICKINSON**, June 11, 1778	1	49

	Vol.	Page
LANGDON, LANDON, (cont.),		
Anna, w. Seth, d. Nov. 10, 1800	2	25
Anna, m. Chester **SMEDLEY**, Feb. 6, 1805	2	89
Anna Beach, d. Seth, Jr. & Sally, b. Apr. 6, 1804	2	44
Anna Elizabeth, d. Seth, b. Jan. 6, 1779; m. Levi **CATLIN**, s. Thomas,		
Aug. 31, 1803, by Rev. Truman Marsh	2	112
Anna Elizabeth, d. John R. & Anna, b. July 10, 1804	1	187
Anne, d. Daniel, Jr. & Chloe, b. Apr. 19, 1760	1	105
Anne, m. Chester **SMEDLEY**, Feb. 6, 1805	2	4
Anne Elizabeth, d. Seth & Anna, b. [ ]	2	25
Asa, s. James & Sarah, b. July 27, 1736	1	23
Asahel, s. David, Jr. & Chloe, b. Aug. 6, 1772	1	62
Asenath, m. Orrin **JUDD**, Nov. 15, 1801, by Truman Marsh	2	252
Aseneth, d. Seth & Anna, b. [ ]	2	25
Benjamin, s. David & Mary, b. Mar. 8, 1744	1	23
Benjamin F., of Vt., m. Ann E. **LANDON**, of Litchfield, Feb. 18, 1839,		
by Rev. Jonathan Brace	2	318
Benjamin Franklin, m. Caroline **LANDON**, May 4, 1822, by Rev.		
Lyman Beecher	2	120
Betsey, of Litchfield, m. Frederic **FENN**, of Washington, Oct. 24, 1837,		
by Rev. H. Bryant	2	314
Caroline, d. Daniel, Jr. & Chloe, b. Dec. 31, 1757	1	105
Caroline, d. John R. & Anna, b. Mar. 22, 1802	1	187
Caroline, m. Benjamin Franklin **LANGDON**, May 4, 1822, by Rev.		
Lyman Beecher	2	120
Charlot, d. John R. & Anne, b. June 16, 1798	1	187
Charlotte, d. Ebenezer & Permala, b. July 31, 1800; d. Sept. 9, 1801	1	104
Charlotte, m. James R. **LIVINGSTONE**, [ ], 1820 by Lyman		
Beecher	2	98
Charlotte, A., m. Sidney D. **MOORE**, b. of Bantam Falls, May 9, 1849,		
by J. D. Berry	TM49	41
Chloe, d. David, Jr. & Cloe, b. Mar. 8, 1775	1	62
Clarissa, d. Remembrance & Sally, b. July 5, 1790	1	147
Clarissa, d. Ebenezer & Permala, b. Sept. 12, 1793	1	104
Clarissa, m. Chester **SMEDLEY**, Mar. 22, 1810	2	89
Daniel, m. Martha **YOUNGS**, May 22, 1736, by Rev. Jared Elliot	1	23
Daniel, s. Daniel & Martha, b. Feb. 11, 1737	1	23
Daniel, Jr., m. Chloe **SMITH**, Nov. 9, 1755	1	105
Daniel, s. Daniel, Jr. & Chole, b. Feb. 25, 1765	1	105
Daniel, m. Avis **BENNEL**, May 27, 1821, by Rev. Isaac Jones	2	108
David, s. David & Mary, Oct. 13, 1741	1	23
David, s. David, Jr. & Chloe, b. Apr. 6, 1769	1	63
Diana, m. Raphael **POTTER**, b. of Litchfield, May 22, 1834, by Enos		
Stoddard, J.P.	2	295
Dorcas, d. Benjamin & Jerusha, b. Apr. 25, 1774	1	105
Ebenezer, m. Permala **CLEMON**, Aug. 6, 1783, by Rev. Judah		
Champion	1	104
Edmond, s. Thomas & Experience, b. Apr. 3, 1781	1	147
Elizabeth, d. Benjamin & Jerusha, b. Nov. 6, 1769	1	105
Elizabeth, d. Seth, Jr. & Sally, b. Apr. 21, 1813	2	44
Emeline, d. Seth, Jr. & Sally, b. Mar. 13, 1816	2	44
Erastus, m. Julia **STONE**, May 20, 1832, by Rev. Luther Mead	2	290
Ethan, s. Thomas & Experience, b. June 15, 1779	1	147

	Vol.	Page
LANGDON, LANDON, (cont.),		
Ezekiel, s. James & Sarah, b. Aug. 31, 1738	1	23
Francis, m. Levi **COE**, b. of Bantam, May 7, 1854, by Rev. Daniel E. Brown, of Bantam	TM49	103
Harriet M., 2nd d. Abner, of Bantam Falls, m. Jarvis **HALLOCK**, of Kent, Jan. 19, 1848, at Bantam Falls, by J. D. Berry	TM49	21
Horace, s. Thomas & Experience, b. Nov. 16, 1783	1	147
Huldah H., m. Frederick W. **PLUMB**, b. of Litchfield, Dec. 8, 1828, by Rev. John S. Stone	2	279
Huldah Seymour, d. Seth, Jr. & Sally, b. Oct. 21, 1806	2	44
Isaac, s. Thomas & Experience, b. Aug. 4, 1776	1	147
James, s. Abner & Eunice, b. Jan. 13, 1761	1	63
James, s. Remembrance & Sally, b. May 5, 1808	1	147
James, of Brimfield, O., m. Ruth **DUDLEY**, of Litchfield, Oct. 15, 1840, by Rev. Jonathan Brace	2	331
Jane Fidelia, of Litchfield, m. David **DeFORREST**, of Plymouth, Sept. 14, 1842	TM49	17
Jane Fidelia, of Litchfield, m. David **DeFOREST**, of Plymouth, Sept. 14, 1842, by G. C. V. Eastman	2	410
Jarvis, s. Ebenezer & Permala, b. Apr. 13, 1798	1	104
Jeremiah, s. Daniel, Jr. & Chloe, b. May 31, 1769	1	105
Jess, s. Ebenezer & Permala, b. Oct. 22, 1795	1	104
Jesse, s. Benjamin & Jerusha, b. Nov. 30, 1767	1	105
John, s. Daniel & Mary, b. May 14, 1747	1	23
John, Rev., m. Abby **PIERPOINT**, Dec. 9, 1824, by Rev. Henry Robinson	2	134
John R., m. Anna **CHAMPION**, Jan. 10, 1796, by Rev. Judah Champion	1	187
Joseph, s. Daniel & Martha, b. Feb. 3, 1758	1	63
Judah Champion, s. John R. & Anna, b. July 27, 1800	1	187
Julius, s. Ebenezer & Permala, b. Sept. 23, 1786	1	104
Lemira, d. Seth, Jr. & Sally, b. May 21, 1810	2	44
Lois, d. James & Sarah, b. July 11, 1746	1	23
Lois, d. James & Sarah, d. July 31, 1746	1	22
Louisa, m. Everett H. **WRIGHT**, b. of Litchfield, Sept. 22, 1852, by Rev. John J. Brandegee	TM49	76
Lidia, d. Abner & Eunice, b. Apr. 15, 1759	1	63
Martha, m. Aaron **MARSH**, Dec. 24, 1809, by Rev. Truman Marsh	2	249
Martha, d. Seth & Anna, b. [ ]	2	25
Mary, d. David & Mary, b. Nov. 22, 1739	1	23
Mary, m. Arcalos **BUELL**, May 3, 1758, by Rev. Judah Champion	1	85
Mary, d. Benjamin & Jerusha, b. July 27, 1771	1	105
Mary, of Litchfield, m. Edward J. **HALLOCK**, of Castleton, Vt., Aug. 25, 1840, by Jonathan Brace	2	319
Mehetabel, d. Abner & Eunice, b. June 5, 1767	1	105
Molly, d. Daniell & Martha, b. Apr. 6, 1743	1	23
Molly, m. Silvanus **BISHOP**, Nov. 25, 1762, by Solomon Palmer	1	127
Molly, d. Daniel, Jr. & Chloe, b. Jan. 11, 1763	1	105
Nancy, d. Remembrance & Sally, b. Oct. 26, 1792	1	147
Nancy, d. Remembrance & Sally, b. Aug. 31, 1793	1	146
Nathan, s. David & Mary, b. Aug. 7, 1748	1	23
Nathan, s. Daniel & Martha, b. June 8, 1752	1	63
Nathan, m. Sarah **SMITH**, Feb. 13, 1788, by Rev. Judah Champion	2	88

	Vol.	Page
LANGDON, LANDON, (cont.),		
Nobel, s. Ebenezer & Permala, b. Nov. 22, 1783	1	104
Norman, s. Remembrance & Sally, b. Oct. 15, 1800	1	147
Oliver, s. Daniel & Martha, b. Mar. 12, 1753	1	63
Orin, s. Ebenezer & Permala, b. Oct. 8, 1790	1	104
Ozias, s. David, Jr. & Chloe, b. Oct. 28, 1764	1	63
Phebe, m. Heman **BEACH**, Feb. 14, 1819, by Seth Landon, J.P.	2	44
Rachel, m. Samuel **MO[O]RE**, Oct. 9, 1735, by Rev. Nathaniell Mather	1	65
Rachal, d. James & Sarah, b. Oct. 11, 1742	1	23
Rachel, m. Daniel `ALDRIDGE`, of Troy, June 23, 1825, by Rev. Isaac		
Jones	2	27
Remembrance, s. Abner & Eunice, b. Sept. 20, 1765	1	105
Remembrance, m. Sally **ENSIGN**, Mar. 26, 1789, by Rev. Ashbel		
Baldwin	1	147
Samuel, s. Seth & Anna, b. [ ]	2	25
Sarah, d. Daniel, Jr. & Chloe, b. Mar. 10, 1756	1	105
Seth, s. Daniel & Mary, b. Dec. 18, 1749	1	23
Seth, m. Anna **BEACH**, Dec. 26, 1771, by Rev. Judah Champion	2	25
Seth, s. Seth & Anne, b. Apr. 13, 1777	1	62
Seth, s. Seth & Anna, b. Apr. 13, 1777	2	25
Seth, m. Eunice **SEYMOUR**, Nov. 23, 1801, by Rev. Truman Marsh	2	25
Seth, Jr., m. Sally **CATLIN**, May 1, 1802	2	44
Sherman, s. Remembrance & Sally, b. Oct. 10, 1798	1	147
Sophronia, m. Daniel **BRADLEY**, Aug. 12, 1832, by Rev. David E.		
Tomlinson, of Bradleyville	2	291
Stephen, s. Daniel, Jr. & Chloe, b. Dec. 18, 1766	1	105
Stephen, s. Daniel, Jr., d. Feb. 14, 1768	1	104
Sylva, d. Seth & Anne, b. Jan. 6, 1773	1	62
Silvia, d. Seth & Anna, b. Jan. 6, 1773	2	25
Sylva, m. Benjamin **VAILL**, Nov. 11, 1793, by Rev. Judah Champion	2	9
Sylvia M., of Litchfield, m. Thaddeus **SPERRY**, of Goshen, Dec. 28,		
1826, at the house of Heman Beach, by Rev. Frances H. Case, of		
Goshen	2	268
Temperance, d. David, Jr. & Chloe, b. Dec. 9, 1762	1	63
Thaddeus, s. David, Jr. & Chloe, b. Dec. 1, 1760	1	63
Thankful, d. David & Thankful, b. Aug. 31, 1756	1	63
Thankful, d. David, m. Jonathan **WRIGHT**, May 15, 1788, by David		
Welch	1	209
Thomas, s. James & Sarah, b. Sept. 10, 1740	1	23
Thomas, s. David & Mary, b. Jan. 14, 1745/6	1	23
Thomas, m. Experience **JOHNSON**, Apr. 4, 1744, by Rev. George		
Beckwith	1	147
Thomas, s. Thomas & Experience, b. Mar. 10, 1775	1	147
Timothy, Dr., of Naugatuc, m. Mary Ann **MORSE**, of Litchfield, Dec.		
21, 1841, by Jonathan Brace	2	320
Verona, of Litchfield, m. Henry **RICHARDSON**, of Somers, Mar. 27,		
1836, by Rev. Samuel Fuller, Jr.	2	296
William, s. Ebenezer & Permala, b. Aug. 22, 1802	1	104
Zopher, s. Seth & Anne, b. Oct. 3, 1774	1	62
Zopher, s. Seth & Anna, b. Oct. 3, 1774	2	25
LANGMAN, Joanna, m. Rev. Amos **CHASE**, June 27, 1792, by Rev. Mr.		
King, of Norwich	1	215
LANSON, [see also **LAMPSON**], Jobeas, m. Sarah **SEELEY**, (colored), b.		
of Litchfield, Feb. 3, 1828, by Rev. John S. Stone	2	274

	Vol.	Page
LASCY, John C., m. Ann B. **LANDON**, Oct. 26, 1834, by Rev. L.P. Hickok	2	288
LATCHFORD, Mary Catharine, m. Amos M. **THORPE**, Feb. 9, 1851, by		
Rev. Benjamin W. Stone	TM49	61
LAW, Abbey L., d. [Benedict A. & Thankfull], b. Aug. 10, 1824	2	294
Abby L., of Litchfield, m. Henry M. **PRATT**, of Bradleyville, Jan. 28,		
1846, by Rev. J. L. Dickinson, of Northfield	TM49	13
Andrew, s. [Benedict A. & Thankfull], b. Sept. 24, 1806	2	294
Andrew Monroe, s. Smith & Louisa, b. May 17, 1825	2	142
Benedict, s. [Benedict A. & Thankfull], b. Feb. 8, 1802; d. Oct. 17, 1810	2	294
Benedict, s. [Benedict A. & Thankfull], b. July 12, 1815	2	294
Benedict A., b. Dec. 21, 1775, at Milford; m. Thankfull **SMITH**, Apr. 6,		
1797	2	294
Emily, d. [Benedict A. & Thankfull], b. Jan. 27, 1817	2	294
Garry, s. Benedict A. & Thankfull, b. Apr. 17, 1800	2	294
Hannah, d. [Benedict A. & Thankfull], b. Dec. 26, 1811	2	294
Hannah, of Litchfield, m. Andrew **HAWLEY**, of Philadelphia, July 25,		
1838, by Rev. Jonathan Brace	2	318
Lyman, s. [Benedict A. & Thankfull], b. July 26, 1813	2	294
Oliver G., s. [Benedict A. & Thankfull], b. Mar. 1, 1810	2	294
Sally, d. [Benedict A. & Thankfull], b. May 19, 1804	2	294
Sally, of Litchfield, m. David **MATTHEWS**, of Bristol, Dec. 4, 1836,		
by Rev. Samuel Fuller, Jr.	2	296
Smith, s. Benedict A. & Thankfull, b. Mar. 13, 1798	2	294
Smith, m. Louisa **HUMPHERVILLE**, Feb. 26, 1821, by Rev.		
Frederick Holcomb	2	142
Willys, s. [Benedict A. & Thankfull], b. May 21, 1819	2	294
Willis, m. Susan M. **BEACH**, b. of Litchfield, [Jan.] 23, 1844, by		
Jonathan Brace	TM49	2
LAWRENCE, William H., m. Aphelia M. **SMEDLEY**, Oct. 26, 1854, by		
Rev. David L. Parmelee	TM49	105
LEACH, LEECH, Abigail, d. Richard & Amity, b. Dec. 6, 1745	1	23
Caleb, [twin with Joshua], s. Richard & Amity, b. Apr. 11, 1748	1	63
Joshua, [twin with Caleb], s. Richard & Amity, b. Apr. 11, 1748	1	63
Marjory, m. Allorn **McNIGHT**, Feb. 11, 1768, by Timothy Collens	1	106
Tabitha, d. Richard & Amity, b. Dec. 20, 1750	1	23
LEAVENWORTH, Caroline, of Litchfield, m. Jeremiah **JOHNSON**, of		
Norfolk, Oct. 30, 1848, by John F. Norton	TM49	39
George, of Roxbury, m. Caroline C. **FRISBIE**, of Litchfield, Sept. 11,		
1844, by Rev. David L. Parmelee	TM49	5
John H., m. Mary A. **PECK**, Apr. 13, 1852, by Rev. David L. Parmelee	TM49	74
LEE, Edward, d. Jan. 30, 1747/8	1	22
Elizabeth, d. Thomas, Jr. & Martha, b. Dec. 19, 1749	1	63
Elizabeth, m. James **WRIGHT**, Dec. 13, 1768, by Rev. Judah		
Champion	1	125
Elizabeth, w. Thomas, d. Apr. 17, 1774	1	22
Hannah, m. Asahel **GRISWOLD**, July 16, 1760, by Timothy Collins,		
J.P. (Feb. 16, 1765 in Woodruff's)	1	18
James, s. Sarah Case, b. Mar. 31, 1773	1	130
James, s. Sarah Case, b. Mar. 31, 1773	1	147
Mabel, d. Thomas & Rachal, b. July 4, 1724	1	23
Martha, d. Thomas, Jr. & Martha, b. Mar. 16, 1754	1	63
Martha, m. Ebenezer **BACON**, June 28, 1770, by David Welch	1	126
Mary, d. Thomas & Rachal, b. Nov. 18, 1727	1	23

	Vol.	Page

LEE, (cont.)

	Vol.	Page
Mary, m. Samuel **RIPNER**, Feb. 7, 1771	1	75
Noah, s. Thomas & Rachell, b. May 10, 1726 (The first child christened in the new Meeting House	1	23
Philana, m. Pierce **CATLIN**, Nov. 27, 1814, by Rev. Truman Marsh	2	24
Thankfull, m. William **EMMONS, Jr.**, Apr. 4, 1768, by Rev. Judah Champion	1	11
Thankful, m. William **EMONS**, Apr. 4, 1768, by Rev. Judah Champion	1	50-1
Thomas, m. Rachall **HOULBUD**, Sept. 19, 1723, by Joseph Minor, J.P.	1	23
Thomas, Jr., m. Martha **DEAN**, Mar. 9, 1748/9, by Rev. Solomon Palmer, of Cornwal	1	63
Thomas, Jr., d. June 10, 1755	1	62

LEECH, [see under **LEACH**]

	Vol.	Page
LEOPEON, Adelia, d. Pompe [& Matilda], b. Feb. [ ], 1828	2	101
Cintha Metilda, d. Pompe & Matilda, b. Feb. [ ], 1819	2	101
George, s. Pompe & Matilda, b. Dec. [ ], 1815	2	101
Harvey, s. Pompe & Matilda, b. June 20, 1824	2	101
Manda, d. Pompe & Matilda, b. May 18, 1822	2	101
Pompe, m. Matilda **GRAVES**, [ ], 1806, by Rev. [ ] Romain	2	101
LEOVELL, Clarissa, m. Oliver **GOODWIN**, Apr. 20, 1818, by Rev. John Langdon	2	102
LESCHER, J. J., of Mt. Carmel, Ill., m. Eliza E. **SMITH**, of Litchfield, Nov. 12, 1851, by Rev. Benjamin L. Swan	TM49	66
LEWIS, Albert Parmelee, s. Algenon S. & Cornelia M., b. Mar. 26, 1836	TM49	40
Algenon S., m. Cornelia M. **BENNETT**, b. of Litchfield, Nov. 10, 1829, by Isaac Jones	TM49	40
Algernon Sidney, s. Ozias, Jr. & Mary, b. Dec. 10, 1807	2	47
Algernon Sidney, m. Cornelia M. **BENNET**, Nov. 10, 1829, by Rev. I. Jones	2	282
Ambrose, s. William & Bathsheba, b. Feb. 15, 1783	1	105
Amelia, d. Ozias, Jr. & Mary, b. Sept. 25, 1810	2	47
Amelia, of Litchfield, m. Elijah **PECK**, of Flushing, L.I., Mar. 31, 1845, by William Payne	TM49	9
Amelia C., d. Luke & Mary H., b. Oct. 27, 1799	2	34
Anne, m. Jesse **GRANT**, Jan. 1, 1767 by Rev. Mr. Rexford	1	179
Charles Sidney, s. Ozias, Jr. & Mary, b. Dec. 2, 1802	1	147
Charles Sidney, s. Ozias, Jr. & Mary, b. Dec. 2, 1802	2	47
Charles Sidney, s. Ozias, Jr. & Mary, d. June 18, 1804	2	47
Cornelia Bennett, d. Algenon S. & Cornelia M., b. Dec. 10, 1831, in Bethlem	TM49	40
Daniel Wadsworth, m. Elizabeth **COLLENS**, July 25, 1791	1	164
Dudley Saltonstall, s. Daniel W. & Elizabeth, b. Aug. 14, 1792	1	164
Eli Todd, s. Ezekiel & Martha, b. July 3, 1813	2	49
Elizabeth, d. Nathaniell & Esther, b. Nov. 20, 1767	1	63
Elizabeth, d. Ozias, Jr. & Mary, b. Nov. 1, 1801	1	147
Elizabeth, d. Ozias, Jr. & Mary, b. Nov. 1, 1801	2	47
Elizabeth, m. Elisha **HEMSTED**, Oct. 24, 1824, by Rev. Isaac Jones	2	136
Ezekiel, m. Martha **CARRINGTON**, Oct. 14, 1804	2	49
George Sidney, s. [Algenon S. & Cornelia M.], b. Oct. 7, 1833, in Bethlem; d. Dec. 17, 1838, in Litchfield	TM49	40
George Sidney, s. Algenon S. & Cornelia M., b. Sept. 16, 1838	TM49	40

	Vol.	Page
LEWIS, (cont.),		
Garshem, d. Oct. 18, 1766, in 62nd y. of his age	1	20
Gershom, d. Oct. 18, 1766, in his 62nd y.	1	22
Harriet Jane, of Litchfield, m. Rev. Daniel Ebenezer **BROWN**, of		
Tamtece Port, N.Y., Oct. 12, 1834, by Rev. Samuel Fuller	2	289
Harriet Jones, d. Ozias, Jr. & Mary, b. Mar. 18, 1806	2	47
Harriet Jones, of Litchfield, m. Daniel Ebenezer **BROWN**, of Painted		
Post, N.Y., Oct. 12, [1834], by Rev. Samuel Fuller	TM49	37
James, s. Edward & Rebecca, b. Dec. 10, 1746	1	23
Jane R., d. Luke & Mary H., b. Jan. 14, 1806	2	34
Jennet, d. Ozias, Jr. & Mary, b. Dec. 25, 1820	2	47
Jennet Lynde, d. Ozias, Jr. & Mary, b. Apr. 6, 1813	2	47
Jenette Lynde, d. Ozias, Jr. & Mary, d. Oct. 22, 1819	2	47
John, s. Gershom, d. Oct. 30, 1758, in the 23rd y. of his age	1	22
John, d. Oct. 30, 1758, in the 23rd y. of his age	1	62
John, s. Ozias, Jr. & Mary, b. Nov. 4, 1815	2	47
Jonathan Thomas, s. Ezekiel & Martha, b. June 18, 1808	2	49
Julia, d. Ozias, Jr. & Mary, b. Jan. 19, 1817; d. Nov. 16, 1819	2	47
Louisa C., of Litchfield, m. Henry **PHELPS**, of Albany, Sept. 16, 1829,		
by Rev. L. P. Hickok	2	281
Lovisa C., d. Luke & Mary H., b. Nov. 7, 1802	2	34
Lucretia M., m. Eben W. **BOLLS**, Sept. 21, 1823, by Rev. Mr. Howe	2	136
Lucy, d. Ozias & Lucy, b. Nov. 29, 1773	2	44
Lucy, m. David **PALMETER**, Jan. 22, 1795	2	44
Lucy Bigelow, d. Ozias, Jr. & Mary, b. Dec. 18, 1804	2	47
Luke, m. Mary H. **ROOT**, Dec. 27, 1795, by Rev. Mr. Cowles	2	34
Lydia, d. Reuben & Patience, b. Oct. 30, 1776	1	147
Martha Derrington, d. Ezekiel & Martha, b. Aug. 8, 1815	2	49
Mary, m. Jacob **SMITH, Jr.**, Jan. 13, 1763, by Rev. Judah Champion	1	118
Mary, d. Ozias, Jr. & Mary, b. May 1, 1809	2	47
Mary, of Litchfield, m. Rev. W[illia]m W. **BOSTWICK**, of Bath		
Steuben Co., N.Y., Apr. 10, 1828, by Rev. John S. Stone	2	276
Mary Ann R., d. Luke & Mary H., b. Feb. 1, 1797	2	34
Nancy, d. William & Bathsheba, b. Jan. 27, 1777	1	105
Nathaniel, m. Esther **TUTTLE**, Jan. 16, 1767, by Timothy Collens, J.P.	1	63
Ozias, m. Lucia **BIGELOW**, Jan. 7, 1773, by Rev. Mr. Judah Champion	1	105
Ozias, m. Lucy **BIGELOW**, Jan. 7, 1773, by Rev. Judah Champion	2	44
Ozias, s. Ozias & Lucy, b. Dec. 16, 1774* *(Date corrected, "Dec. 16,		
1777")	2	44
Ozias, Jr., m. Mary **JONES**, Jan. 19, 1801, by Rev. Mr. Gammel, of		
New Haven	1	147
Ozias, Jr., m. Mary **JONES**, Jan. 19, 1801, by Rev. Mr. Gammel, of		
New Haven	2	47
Ozias, s. Ozias, Jr. & Mary, b. Feb. 6, 1812	2	47
Patience, w. William, d. Mar. 3, 1773	1	22
Polly, m. William **TUTTLE**, Oct. 6, 1805, by Rev. Uriel Gridley	2	64
Reuben, s. Gershom & Mary, b. Mar. 22, 1753	1	105
Reuben, m. Patience **BIDWELL**, Nov. 25, 1773, by Rev. Judah		
Champion	1	105
Rufus, of Hartford, m. Rosetta **TURNER**, of Litchfield, Sept. 13, 1829,		
by Rev. L. P. Hickok	2	281
Sarah Azubah, d. Ezekiel & Martha, b. Aug. 28, 1805	2	49
Thomas, f. of Ezekiel, d. Sept. 2, 1815, in the 76th y. of his age	2	49

	Vol.	Page
LEWIS, (cont.),		
Truman, s. Reuben & Patience, b. Mar. 24, 1774	1	147
William, m. Bathsheba **PALMER,** Dec. [ ], 1773, by Rev. Judah		
Champion	1	104
William, s. William & Bathsheba, b. Sept. 15, 1779	1	105
William Henry, s. Ozias, Jr. & Mary, b. Dec. 22, 1803	2	47
LIDDECOTT, William, of Northampton, m. Louisa P. **ROOTS,** of		
Litchfield, Dec. 26, 1852, by Rev. Charles R. Adams, of West		
Goshen	TM49	78
LINES, William, of Naugatuck, m. Harriet M. **CLOCK,** of Litchfield, Dec.		
25, 1849, by Benjamin L. Swan	TM49	44
LINSLEY, LINLEY, Abiel, s. Abiel, Jr. & Thankful, b. Dec. 26, 1757	1	63
Daniel, s. Solomon & Mindwell, b. May 15, 1764	1	63
David, s. Solomon & Mindwell, b. Nov. 11, 1772	1	62
Dothy, d. Jeremiah & Polly J., b. Mar. 27, 1811	2	53
Edmund, s. Jeremiah & Polly J., b. Dec. 20, 1809	2	53
Edward, m. Lidia **PAGE,** Sept. 27, 1771	1	62
Edward, m. Tryphena **PAGE,** Apr. 12, 1778, by Rev. Samuel Ellis, of		
Branford	1	105
Electa, d. Joseph & Lidia, b. June 1, 1766	1	63
Eunice, d. Solomon & Mindwell, b. June 4, 1769	1	105
Hannah, m. Justus **GIBBS,** Jan. 13, 1757, by Thomas Harrison, J.P.	1	139
Jeremiah, m. Polly J. **DAVIS,** Jan. 13, 1802, by David Judson	2	53
Joel, s. Abiel, Jr. & Thankful, b. Feb. 7, 1756	1	63
John, s. Joseph & Lidia, b. Oct. 4, 1761	1	63
Joseph, m. Lidia **FARNUM,** Apr. 17, 1758, by Thomas Harrison	1	63
Lucy, d. Jeremiah & Polly J., b. Aug. 28, 1807	2	53
Lucy, m. Homer B. **STONE,** b. of Litchfield, Mar. 2, 1828, by Enos		
Stoddard, J.P.	2	275
Lidia, d. Joseph & Lidia, b. Feb. 14, 1764	1	63
Mary N., of Litchfield, m. John **STONE,** of Bethlem, Sept. 27, 1829, by		
Rev. Henry Robinson, of South Farms	2	282
Mary Nelson, d. Jeremiah & Polly J., b. Mar. 21, 1805	2	53
Oliver, s. Solomon & Mindwell, b. July 20, 1766	1	105
Polly, d. Jeremiah & Polly J., b. May 11, 1813	2	53
Rhoda, d. Joseph & Lidia, b. Aug. 7, 1769	1	105
Simeon, s. Solomon & Mindwell, b. Sept. 21, 1761	1	63
Solomon, s. Solomon & Mindwell, b. July 21, 1759	1	63
Statira, m. Simeon **PALMER, Jr.,** Nov. 24, 1803, by Rev. Mr. Chase	2	37
Timothy, s. Joseph & Lidia, b. Nov. 6, 1759	1	105
LITTLE, James, s. Thomas & Zerviah, b. Aug. 16, 1758	1	63
Julia, of Northfield, m. Rufus C. **THORPE,** Nov. 11, 1849, by Rev.		
Benjamin W. Stone	TM49	54
Nathaniel, s. Thomas & Zerviah, b. June 10, 1753	1	63
Samuel, s. Thomas & Zerviah, b. Jan. 5, 1763	1	63
Tamar, d. Thomas & Zeruiah, b. July 16, 1756	1	63
Tamer, m. Asa **BULL,** June 17, 1773, by Rev. Judah Champion	1	167
Thomas, m. Zerviah **COGSWELL,** June 9, 1752, by Timothy Hatch,		
J.P., of Kent	1	63
Thomas, s. Thomas & Zerviah, b. Aug. 11, 1754	1	63
William, s. Thomas & Zerviah, b. Oct. 27, 1760	1	63
LIVINGSTONE, James R., m. Charlotte **LANDON,** [ ], 1820, by		
Lyman Beecher	2	98

	Vol.	Page
LOCKWOOD, George W., m. Francis M. **WOODRUFF**, Nov. 10, 1842, by		
Jason Wells	2	337
Stanley G., of New Milford, m. Luisa **SEYMOUR**, of Litchfield, Feb. 9,		
1823, by Rev. Truman Marsh	2	118
LONG, Cybel, m. Ambrose **PALMER**, Jan. 14, 1766, by Timothy Collens,		
J.P.	1	73
LOOMIS, Abby E., m. George **CRAMER**, Mar. 26, 1850, by Rev. David L.		
Parmelee	TM49	53
Abby Elizabeth, d. Grandison & Fanny, b. Apr. 30, 1833	2	326
Austin, m. Margaret **ARUTS**, Jan. 22, 1832, by Rev. L. P. Hickok	2	288
Charles Grandison, s. Grandison & Fanny, b. June 30, 1836	2	326
Cornelia A., m. William **JOHNSON**, Mar. 26, 1850, by Rev. David L.		
Parmelee	TM49	53
Cornielia Ann, d. Grandison, b. Apr. 21, 1831	2	134
Emily W., m. Perry **ODELL**, Nov. 28, 1849, by Rev. D. L. Parmelee	TM49	44
Grandison, of Torrington, m. Fanny **BURGISS**, of Litchfield, Nov. 7,		
1827, by Morris Woodruff, J.P.	2	273
Grandison, m. Fanny **BURGISS**, Nov. 7, 1827, by Morris Woodruff,		
J.P.	2	326
LORD, Abigail Lyman, d. Lynde & Mary, b. Aug. 6, 1804	2	16
Belinda, d. Phinehas & Polly, b. Dec. 27, 1807	2	65
Belinda, d. Phinehas & Polly, d. May 21, 1808	2	65
Belinda, d. Phinehas & Polly b. July 1, 1809	2	65
Bennet, s. David C. & Mary, b. July 24, 1829	2	322
Daniel, m. Hannah **HUMASTON**, Dec. 25, 1766, by Rev. Mr. Storrs,		
of Northbury	1	105
Daniel, m. Hannah **HUMASTON**, Dec. 25, 1766, by Rev. Andrew		
Storrs, of Northbury Soc.	2	65
Daniel, m. Abigail **DICKINSON**, Jan. 10, 1788, by Rev. Judah		
Champion	2	65
Daniel, s. Phinehas & Polly, b. Aug. 6, 1798; d. Nov. 21, 1798	2	65
Daniel, s. Phinehas & Polly, b. Jan. 9, 1800	2	65
David C., of Litchfield, m. Mary **WARREN**, of Plymouth, Apr. 28,		
1828, at Plymouth	2	322
David Candee, s. Phinehas & Polly, b. Dec. 28, 1803	2	65
Elizabeth, d. Daniel & Elizabeth*, b. Apr. 4, 1768 *("Elizabeth"		
written in original. Probably "Hannah"?)	2	65
Elizabeth, d. Daniel & Hannah, b. Apr. 24, 1768	1	105
Elizabeth, m. Ives **MOSS**, Dec. 20, 1787, by Rev. Judah Champion	1	189
Emily, d. Phinehas & Polly, b. Feb. 1, 1802	2	65
Emily, m. John S. **WARNER**, of Plymouth, Feb. 18, 1824, by Rev.		
Isaac Jones	2	132
Emily Frances, d. David C. & Mary, b. July 30, 1835	2	322
Erastus Aurielius, s. Lynde, Jr. & Mary, b. Oct. 16, 1792	2	16
Easther, of Litchfield, m. Edmond **BRAMHALL**, of New York, Sept. 6,		
1842, by G. C. V. Eastman	2	411
Esther Maria, d. Phinehas & Polly, b. Nov. 25, 1816	2	65
Francis Maria, d. Lynde & Mary, b. Nov. 7, 1798	2	16
George, s. Lynde, Jr. & Mary, b. Oct. 29, 1800	2	16
George F., of Litchfield, m. Mary W. **DODD**, of Hartford, Dec. 12,		
1847, by J. D. Berry	TM49	20
Hannah, d. Daniel & Elizabeth*, b. Dec. 14, 1786 *("Elizabeth"		
written in original. Probably "Hannah"?)	2	65

	Vol.	Page
LORD, (cont.),		
Hannah, w. Daniel, d. Dec. 16, 1786, in the 42nd y. of her age	2	65
Hannah, m. Wyllys **POND**, Dec. 29, 1811, by Rev. Truman Marsh	2	63
Harriet, d. [Phinehas & Polly], b. [ ]	2	65
Harriet M., m. William F. **BALDWIN**, b. of Litchfield, May 5, 1841, by		
William Payne	2	334
Henry E., m. Mary W. **BUTLER**, May 8, 1836, by Rev. L. P. Hickok	2	296
Henry Edwin, s. Lynde, Jr. & Mary, b. Feb. 13, 1797	2	16
Huldah, d. Daniel & Hannah, b. May 27, 1770	1	105
Huldah, d. Daniel & Elizabeth*, b. [ ], 1770 *("Elizabeth"		
written in original. Probably "Hannah"?)	2	65
Huldah, d. Daniel & Hannah, d. Dec. 14, 1786	2	65
Huldah, d. Daniel & Abigail, b. [ ], 1789; d. [ ],		
ae 4 m.	2	65
John M. Henry, s. Erastus A. & Charlotte, b. Jan. 1, 1824	2	134
Joseph Lynde, s. Lynde, Jr. & Mary, b. Sept. 2, 1788	1	147
Joseph Lynde, s. Lynde, Jr. & Mary, b. Sept. 2., 1788	2	16
Joseph Lynde, 2nd, s. Lynde, Jr. & Mary b. Aug. 25, 1790	2	16
Joseph Lynde, m. Maria **TRYON**, May 10, 1812, by Rev. Lyman		
Beecher	2	17
July, d. Phinehas & Polly, b. Apr. 10, 1814	2	65
Julia, of Litchfield, m. Augustus **FLINT**, of Amenia, N.Y., Mar. 4,		
1847, by Rev. Samuel Fuller	TM49	38
Lynde, m. Lois **SHELDON**, July 7, 1757, by Rev. Judah Champion	1	63
Lynde, s. Lynde & Lois, b. Oct. 21, 1761	1	63
Lynde, representative Oct. 1771, May 1772	2	1549
Lynde, had negro Jenny, d. Barley, b. Dec. 4, 1784	1	151
Lynde, Jr., m. Mary **LYMAN**, Jan. 30, 1786	1	147
Lynde, Jr., m. Mary **LYMAN**, Jan. 30, 1786	2	16
Lynde, d. Feb. 12, 1813, ae 52 y.	2	16
Maria Thersa, d. Joseph L. & Maria, b. Feb. 20, 1813, at Boston	2	17
Mary, d. Phinehas & Polly, b. Jan. 29, 1812	2	65
Mary Elizabeth, d. David C. & Mary, b. July 6, 1831	2	322
Mary L., m. John **PIERPOINT**, Sept. 23, 1810, by Rev. Lyman		
Beecher	2	16
Mary Sheldon, d. Lynde, Jr. & Mary, b. Jan. 31, 1787	1	147
Mary Sheldon, d. Lynde, Jr. & Mary, b. Jan. 31, 1787	2	16
Patty, d. Daniel & Elizabeth*, b. [ ], 1773 *("Elizabeth"		
written in original. Probably "Hannah"?)	2	65
Patta, d. Daniel & Hannah, b. Feb. 21, 1774	1	62
Patty, d. Daniel & Hannah, d. Nov. [ ], 1778, in her 5th y.	2	65
Patty, 2nd, d. Daniel & Elizabeth*, b. Sept. 2, 1782 *("Elizabeth"		
written in original. Probably "Hannah"?)	2	65
Phinehas, s. Daniel & Hannah, b. Feb. 10, 1777	1	62
Phinehas, s. Daniel & Elizabeth*, b. Feb. 10, 1777 *("Elizabeth"		
written in original. Probably "Hannah"?)	2	65
Phinehas, m. Polly **CANDEE**, Dec. 25, 1797, by Rev. Mr. Williams	2	65
Phinehas, representative Oct. 1818, May 1818, May 1836, May 1837,	2	1555-7
William, Jr., of East Winsor, m. Harriet Clarissa **JUDD**, of Litchfield,		
Apr. 11, 1833, by Rev. Samuel Fuller	TM49	37
William, of East Windsor, m. Harriet Clarissa **JUDD**, Apr. 11, 1833, by		
Rev. Samuel Fuller	2	289
William Rufus, s. Lynde, Jr. & Mary, b. Aug. 14, 1794	2	16

	Vol.	Page
LOUNSBURY, LOUNSBERY, Julian, m. Almond **EMONS,** Nov. 3, 1813, by James Morris	2	18
Major, m. Hannah **BEACHER,** of Woodbridge, Sept. 15, 1824, by Rev. Isaac Jones	2	113
LOVELAND, Clark, m. Lydia **GOODWIN,** Mar. 31, 1811	2	74
Harriet E., m. Sheldon C. **CURTISS,** Oct. 2, 1854, by Rev. David L. Parmelee, of South Farms	TM49	103
James Lewis, s. Clark & Lydia, b. Jan. 9, 1812	2	74
Lydia G., m. Lewis T. **GILBERT,** Sept. 16, 1850, by Rev. David L. Parmelee	TM49	44
Nathaniel G., m. Sarah J. **STONE,** Nov. 29, 1838, by Rev. Jonathan Brace	2	318
Nathaniel Goodwin, s. Clark & Lydia, b. Aug. 9, 1815	2	74
William J., s. Clark & Lydia, b. June 15, 1817	2	74
William J., m. Almeda **LANDON,** Apr. 20, 1842	2	336
Wyllys Wheeler, s. Clark & Lydia, b. Sept. 7, 1813	2	74
LUDDINGTON, Elam, Jr., of Bristol, m. Lucy V. **BURGESS,** Oct. 26, 1831, by Enos Stoddard, J.P.	2	290
Emeline M., m. Elias W. **CASE,** Aug. 19, 1832, by Rev. L. P. Hickok	2	288
LUMA, Lucina, wid. Minnis, m. [ ] **GREEN** (colored), Nov. 12, 1837, by Truman Marsh	2	315
LUWIN (?), Sally, m. John **MOSS, Jr.,** Mar. 20, 1810, by [ ] Patterson	2	39
LYMAN, Elijah, m. Lorinda **SMITH,** Nov. 18, 1798, by John Welch, J.P.	1	62
John, d. Feb. [ ], 1777, in captivity New York	1	146
Martha, m. Isaac **MARSH, Jr.,** Nov. 24, 1776, by Rev. Judah Champion	1	106
Mary, d. David & Mary, d. Mar. 21, 1776	1	62
Mary, m. Lynde **LORD, Jr.,** Jan. 30, 1786	1	147
Mary, m. Lynde **LORD, Jr.,** Jan. 30, 1786	2	16
Rufus J., of New Hartford, m. Sarah M. **DUNNING*,** of Litchfield, Oct. 26, 1848, by [Joseph Henson] *("DEMING")	TM49	27
Sarah, m. Eli **PARDEE,** Feb. 24, 1791, by Samuel Darrow, J.P.	1	156
LYNUS, Eunice, d. Nathaniell & Anna, b. Aug. 11, 1744	1	23
Freelove, d. Nathaniell & Anna, b. May 23, 1742	1	23
Nathaniel, s. Nathaniel & Anna, b. Jan. 1, 1740/1; d. Jan. 20, 1740/1	1	23
LYON, Elizabeth, m. Oliver **SANFORD,** Feb. 8, 1762, by Jacob Woodruff, J.P.	1	161
McCALL, Benjamin A., m. Cornelia **BIDWELL,** b. of Litchfield, Mar. 10, 1852, by Benjamin L. Swan	TM49	66
Debby, m. Levi **COE,** Sept. [ ], 1789	2	45
Delia E., m. Albert **STODDARD,** b. of Litchfield, May 21, 1851, by William B. Hoyt	TM49	63
McCLEMON, Harriet, d. Rhoda Simmons, b. Jan. 16, 1810	2	3
McCONNELL, Bernard, m. Abigail **SAUNDERS,** Sept. 6, 1847, by Rev. Benjamin L. Swan	TM49	19
McCORD, David A., m. Sarah J. **PICKETT,** Jan. 1, 1845, by Rev. David L. Parmelee	TM49	7
William H., of Penn., m. Julia **HALL,** of Litchfield, Feb. 22, 1825, by Rev. Henry Robertson	2	74
McDANIEL, James, of Bethlem, m. Lucinda **HARRISON,** of Litchfield, May 11, 1836, by Rev. Fosdic Harrison, of Bethlem	2	297
McEWEN, David J., m. Frances J. **WOOSTER,** Mar. 16, 1829, by Mr. Jones	2	280
McGARRY, Eliza, m. David **JOHNSON,** Mar. 9, 1851, by Rev. David L.		

	Vol.	Page
McGARRY, (cont.)		
Parmelee	TM49	61
McKEE, William, m. Anne Adalaide **ANDREW,** Nov. 1, 1826, at the house		
of Jonathan Andrew, by Rev. Seth Higby of New Hartford &		
Burlington	2	266
McKNIGHT, McNIGHT, Allom, m. Marjory **LEECH,** Feb. 11, 1768, by		
Timothy Collens	1	106
Archibald, s. Allem & Marjory, b. Jan. 14, 1769	1	106
Mary, d. Allen & Marjory, b. Jan. 10, 1770	1	107
McLOYD, Thomas, m. Mary L. **BLACKMAN,** Oct. 19, 1851, by Rev.		
David L. Parmelee	TM49	65
McMAHON, John, of Goshen, m. Flora Ann **HAYDEN,** of Litchfield, Feb. 3,		
1841, by Gad N. Smith	2	333
McNEILE, McNIELE, McNEIL, Abigail, d. Archibald & Jemima, b. Feb.		
22, 1768	1	24
Abigail, d. John & Polly, b. Dec. 19, 1814	2	130
Alexander, m. Deborah **PHELPS,** Oct. 28, 1747, by Timothy Collens	1	107
Alexander, s. Roswell & Elizabeth, b. Aug. 29, 1770	1	64
Amanda, d. [Elias & Catharine], b. Oct. 4, 1817	TM49	18
Amanda, d. Elias & Catharine, b. Oct. 4, 1817	1	109
Amanda B., of Litchfield, m. Jeremiah **ENSWORTH,** of Hartford, May		
4, 1841, by William Payne	2	334
Anna, m. Moses **WHEELER,** Mar. [ ], 1805	2	123
Anne, d. Archibald & Jemima, b. Jan. 27, 1776	1	149
Anne, d. Charles & Thankful, b. July 21, 1781	1	189
Archibald, s. Archibald & Sarah, b. July 17, 1738	1	64
Archibald, Jr., m. Jemima **ORTON,** Dec. 31, 1764, by Rev. Judah		
Champion	1	24
Archibald, s. John & Polly, b. Dec. 20, 1813	2	130
Archibald, s. John & Polly, d. Jan. [ ], 1814, ae 2 m.	2	130
Belinda, d. John & Polly, b. Jan. 22, 1809	2	130
Benjamin, s. Charles & Thankful, b. Dec. 19, 1779	1	189
Charles, s. Archibald & Sarah, b. June 30, 1751	1	64
Charles, m. Thankful **WOOSTER,** Feb. 3, 1773, by Rev. Judah		
Champion	1	189
Charles, s. Isaac & Lois, b. Feb. 16, 1774	1	64
Charles, s. John & Polly, b. May 3, 1819	2	130
Charles, s. [Elias & Catharine], b. Feb. 23, 1829	TM49	18
Charles, m. Matilda **WHEELER,** b. of Litchfield, Apr. 25, 1841, by		
William Payne	2	333
David, s. Charles & Thankful, b. Jan. 3, 1774	1	189
David, s. Capt. Isaac & Lois, b. Feb. 21, 1788	1	229
Elias, s. Samuel & Sina, b. May 15, 1791	1	108
Elias, s. Samuell & Sina, b. May 15, 1791; m. Catharine **SANFORD,**		
Oct. 11, 1813 (Chenango Broome Cty., N.Y.)	1	109
Elias, m. Catharine **SANFORD,** b. of Litchfield, Oct. 11, 1813	TM49	18
Eliza, d. John & Polly, b. July 8, 1807	2	130
Elizabeth, m. Roger **CATLIN,** Oct. 13, 1763, by Rev. Judah Champion	1	88
Elizabeth, d. Roswell & Elizabeth, b. Dec. 2, 1773	1	64
Emily, d. John & Polly, b. Dec. 20, 1811	2	130
Emily, m. John **O'BRIEN,** Feb. 7, 1836, by Rev. L. P. Hickok	2	296
Emory, s. Isaac, 2nd & Mabel, b. Nov. [ ], 1813	2	88
Frederick, s. Roswell & Olive, b. June 24, 1803	2	89

	Vol.	Page
McNEILE, McNIELE, McNEIL, (cont.)		
Frederick, m. Emily **GOODWIN**, b. of Litchfield, Mar. 26, 1828, by		
Rev. John S. Stone	2	275
Hannah, d. Capt. Isaac & Lois, b. July 8, 1785	1	229
Hannah, m. Charles **GRANT**, June 12, 1809, by Rev. Judah Champion	2	37
Harriet, d. Roswell & Olive, b. Jan. 28, 1810	2	89
Harriet, m. Henry **PERKINS**, Mar. 12, 1834, by Rev. L. P. Hickok	2	288
Henry, s. Elias & Catharine, b. May 30, 1815	TM49	18
Henry, s. Elias & Catharine, b. May 30, 1815	1	109
Henry, m. Martha J. **ODELL**, b. of Litchfield, Oct. 21, 1840, by Rev.		
William Payne	TM49	18
Henry L., m. Martha J. **ODELL**, Oct. 21, 1840, by William Payne	2	331
Huldah, of Litchfield, m. Amos **SANFORD**, of Goshen, Apr. 29, 1852,		
by H. L. Vaill	TM49	74
Isaac, s. Archibald & Sarah, b. May 16, 1748	1	64
Isaac, m. Lois **BALDWIN**, Jan. 24, 1771, by Rev. Judah Champion	1	24
Isaac, s. Isaac & Lois, b. Jan. 14, 1772	1	24
Issac, 2nd, m. Mabel **CLARK**, Dec. [ ], 1810, by Rev. Lyman Beecher	2	88
Isaac Horace, s. Samuel & Levina, b. Nov. 14, 1807	2	51
James, s. Samuel & Sina, b. May 15, 1786	1	108
John, s. Archibald & Sarah, b. Feb. 14, 1741	1	64
John, s. Archibald, Jr. & Jemima, b. Sept. 26, 1773	1	24
John, s. Archbald & Jemima, b. Sept. 27, 1773	1	149
John, s. Samuel & Sina, b. Sept 24, 1782	1	108
John, m. Polly **CATLIN**, Aug. 9, 1802, by Rev. Dan Huntington	2	130
John, s. John & Polly, b. Mar. 2, 1816	2	130
John, Jr., m. Ferebe **TRACY**, Feb. 27, 1837, by Rev. Charles Chittenden	2	297
Lavinia M., m. Levi **COE**, May 23, 1838, by Rev. Stephen Hubbell	2	320
Levina Maria, d. Samuel & Levina, b. Sept. 29, 1815	2	51
Lewis Judson, s. Samuel & Levina, b. Nov. 19, 1809	2	51
Lois, d. Capt. Isaac & Lois, b. July 29, 1776	1	229
Lois, d. Capt. Isaac & Lois, d. July 29, 1776	1	228
Lois, d. Capt. Isaac & Lois, b. Dec. 5, 1779	1	229
Lois, m. Miles **NORTON**, June 1, 1797, by Rev. Judah Champion	1	67
Loiza, d. Samuel & Levina, b. Jan. 14, 1812	2	51
Lorinda, [d. Roswell & Olive], [ ]	2	89
Louisa B., m. Phinehas W. **CAMP**, Mar. 18, 1835, by Rev. L. P. Hickok	2	296
Lucinda, m. Sidney **TERRELL**, Apr. 9, 1838, by Rev. Stephen Hubbell	2	320
Lucretia, d. Isaac, 2nd & Mabel, b. Jan. [ ], 1815	2	88
Lucretia, m. Asa J. **FRENCH**, Mar. 18, 1852, by Rev. David L.		
Parmelee	TM49	67
Mabel, Mrs., m. Joel **BOSTWICK**, Dec. 4, 1842, by Jonathan Brace	2	411
Mary, d. Archibald, Jr. & Jemima, b. Aug. 27, 1770	1	24
Mary, m. Eaton **JONES**, May 1, 1788, by Rev. Judah Champion	1	101
Mary, d. John & Polly, b. Nov. 14, 1805	2	130
Mary, d. Isaac & Mabel, b. Oct. [ ], 1811	2	88
Mary, m. James **O'BRIEN**, Oct. 28, 1832, by Rev. L. P. Hickok	2	288
Mary Ann, m. Rufus **SMITH**, May 13, 1845, by George Hastings	TM49	10
Mary Antoinette, d. [Elias & Catharine], b. Jan. 11, 1820	TM49	18
Mary Antoinette, d. Elias & Catharine, b. Jan. 11, 1820	1	109
Mary C., m. Lyman **WOOSTER**, June 4, 1834, by Rev. L. P. Hickok	2	288
Myron, s. [Elias & Catharine], b. Mar. 22, 1822	TM49	18
Myron, s. Elias & Catharine, b. Mar. 22, 1822	1	109

	Vol.	Page
McNEILE, McNIELE, McNEIL, (cont.)		
Nabby, d. Samuel & Sina, b. Feb. 8, 1781	1	108
Nabby, m. Jonathan **CARRINGTON**, Sept. 29, 1807	2	32
Olive, d. Archibald & Jemima, b. Feb. 10, 1779	1	149
Olive, m. Roswell **McNEILE**, Mar. 16, 1802, by Rev. Dan Huntington	2	89
Orello, d. Samuel & Sina, b. Feb. 11, 1788	1	108
Patience, m. Henry **BISSELL**, b. of Litchfield, Sept. 20, 1835, by Rev. Samuel Fuller, Jr.	2	296
Polly, d. Samuel & Sina, b. May 11, 1784	1	108
Polly, m. Charles G. **BENNET**, Sept. 21, 1806, by Rev. Truman Marsh	2	30
Rachel, Mrs., m. David **BUELL**, Oct. 3, 1771, by Rev. Judah Champion	1	167
Rachel, d. Charles & Thankful, b. Apr. 25, 1776	1	189
Rachel, d. John & Polly, b. Feb. 16, 1804	2	130
Rachel, m. Loomis **ROWLEY**, Mar. 2, 1825	TM49	12
Rachel, m. Loomis **ROWLEY**, Mar. 2, 1825, by Rev. Lyman Beecher	2	139
Rhoda, d. Alexander & Deborah, b. Nov. 27, 1750	1	107
Rhodah, m. John **MARSH, 3rd**, Sept. 14, 1769, by Timothy Collens, J.P.	1	149
Rhoda, d.[ ] & Deborah, b. Nov. 27, 1750; m. John **MARSH, 3rd**, s. Col. Ebenezer & Deborah, Sept. 15, 1769	2	93
Rosel, s. Alexander & Deborah, b. Sept. 21, 1748	1	107
Roswel, m. Elizabeth **MARSH**, Sept. 13, 1769, by Timothy Collens, J.P.	1	24
Roswell, m. Olive **McNEILE**, Mar. 16, 1802, by Rev. Dan Huntington	2	89
Roswell, m. Huldah **CLARKE**, July 4, 1844, by Rev. D. L. Marks	TM49	4
Samuel, m. Sina **STONE**, Jan. 4, 1776, by Rev. Judah Champion	1	108
Samuel, s. Capt. Isaac & Lois, b. Aug. 21, 1777	1	229
Samuel, s. Capt. Isaac & Lois, d. Sept. 30, 1777	1	228
Samuel, s. Capt. Isaac & Lois, b. Jan. 31, 1782	1	229
Samuel, s. Samuel & Sina, b. Apr. 2, 1797	1	108
Samuel, m. Levina **JUDSON**, Jan. 26, 1807, by Rev. Dan Huntington	2	51
Samuel, s. [Elias & Catharine], b. Oct. 14, 1824	TM49	18
Samuel, s. Elias & Catharine, b. Oct. 14, 1824	1	109
Samuel, 2nd, m. Julia L. **MERIMAN**, b. of Litchfield, Mar. 14, 1849, by Joseph Henson	TM49	36
Sarah, d. Archibald & Jemima, b. Nov. 16, 1765	1	64
Sarah, m. James **MARSH, 2nd**, May 10, 1785, by Rev. Judah Champion	1	229
Truman, s. Samuel & Sina, b. Aug. 27, 1793	1	108
Truman, m. Elmira **CURTISS**, of Sheffield, Mar. 2, 1823, by Ozias Lewis, J.P.	2	117
William Henry, s. Henry & Martha, b. May 13, 1842	TM49	18
MALLORY, MALORY, Fanny, m. Heman **BARNES**, Jan. 1, 1827, by Amael Catlin, J.P.	2	268
Lucy, m. James **CABLE**, July 4, 1833, by Rev. Joseph E. Camp, of Northfield	2	292
Phebe, m. Thomas John **GUNN**, Apr. 4, 1824, by Morris Woodruff, J.P.	2	80
MANSER, Lois, m. George **BARNARD**, Jan. 15, 1784, by Rev. Dr. Bellamy	1	213
MANSFIELD, Ann, m.Horace **HUBBARD**, Feb. 20, 1834, by Rev. James F. Warner, of South Farms	2	289
Anna, m. Chandler **SWIFT**, of Cornwall, May 28, 1822, by Morris Woodruff, J. P.	2	111
Anna Thompson, d. [John T. & Dolly], b. Aug. 12, 1802	2	270
Daniel Punderson, s. [John T. & Dolly], b. June 7, 1820	2	270

	Vol.	Page
MANSFIELD, (cont.),		
Edward D., of Cincinnati, O., m. Mary **PECK**, of Litchfield, Apr. 25,		
1827, by Rev. John J. Stone	2	269
Elizabeth, d. John T. & Dolly, b. June 29, 1799	2	270
Elizabeth, m. Anson **HUBBARD**, Sept. 6, 1818, by Rev. Amos Pettingill		
Hannah, d. [John T. & Dolly], b. Dec. 8, 1824	2	270
Harriet Smith, d. [John T. & Dolly], b. Aug. 27, 1812	2	270
John Todd, s. [John T. & Dolly], b. Apr. 22, 1818	2	270
Joseph Punderson, s. [John T. & Dolly], b. Feb. 26, 1808	2	270
Lemuel Steel, s. [John T. & Dolly], b. May 8, 1810	2	270
Mary, m. John **HOSFORD**, Jr., Oct. [ ], 1794	2	75
Mary, d. [John T. & Dolly], b. Apr. 19, 1814	2	270
Punderson, of Plymouth, m. Loley **BRISTOL**, of Cornwall, May 6,		
1846, by John F. Norton	TM49	14
Sally Maria, d. [John T. & Dolly], b. Aug. 7, 1816	2	270
Susan, d. [John T. & Dolly], b. Sept. 22, 1805	2	270
Susan, m. Asa **SLADE**, May 17, 1826, by Rev. Henry Robinson	2	262
MARCHANT, MERCHANT, Amanda, m. Morris **JOHNSON**, Apr. 9,		
1828, by Rev. J. E. Camp	2	60
Amanda, m. Morris **JOHNSON**, Apr. 16, 1828, by Rev. Joseph E.		
Camp, of Northfield	2	292
Anna, m. Thomas **TURNER**, July [ ], 1791, by David Potter, J.P.	2	85
Edna, m. Augustus **ALFRED**, Apr. 6, 1830, by Rev. William Lucas	2	286
George, m. Eunice **JOHNSON**, b. of Litchfield, Nov. 27, 1828, by Rev.		
Henry Robinson, of South Farms	2	279
Lucena, m. Sheldon **HOTCHKISS**, Dec. 26, 1831, by Rev. L. P.		
Hickok	2	288
Sara, m. Allison **TURNER**, June 22, 1820, by Frederick Holcomb	2	96
MARK, MARKS, Julia C., m. William L. **SMEDLEY**, May 9, 1836, by		
Rev. R. S. Crampton	2	299
Merrett, of Harwinton, m. Eliza **FOX**, of Northfield, Jan. 17, 1848, by		
Rev. Joel L. Dickinson	TM49	22
MARSH, MARCH, Aaron, m. Martha **LANDON**, Dec. 24, 1809, by Rev.		
Truman Marsh	2	249
Abby P., m. Myron **MARWIN**, Apr. 8, 1851, by Rev. David L.		
Parmelee	TM49	62
Abigail, d. Elisha & Honor, b. Nov. 15, 1769	1	64
Abigail, m. Eliada **OSBORN**, May 31, 1794/5, by Rev. Judah		
Champion	1	153
Abigail Pierpoint, d. Horace & Electa, b. July 10, 1815	2	133
Almira, d. Daniel & Seneth, b. Aug. 8, 1812	2	14
Ambrose, s. George & Lydia, b. Feb. 27, 1731/2	1	65
Amelia A., m. Ferdinand **BEEBE**, Oct. 4, 1841, by Rev. David L.		
Parmelee	2	327
Amelia Ann, d. Horace & Electa, b. Feb. 26, 1809	2	133
Andrew* W., s. Daniel & Seneth, b. Oct. 17, 1808 *(Arnold Copy		
says "Andros" as well as "Andrew")	2	14
Andros, see Andrew W. **MARSH**		
An[n], d. William & Susannah, b. June 23, 1735	1	25
Ann, of Litchfield, m. Isaac B. **REDFIELD**, of Fairfield, Apr. 8, 1827,		
by Rev. John J. Stone	2	270
Ann, w. Ormond, d. Mar. 29, 1829	2	262
Anna, d. Edward & Deborah, b. May 25, 1738	1	25

	Vol.	Page
MARSH, MARCH, (cont.),		
Anna, d. John, 3rd & Rhoda, b. Apr. 14, 1779, m. Andrew **ROWLAND**,		
[ ]; d. Feb. 18, 1819, in her 40th y.	2	93
Anna, d. John, 3rd & Rhoda, b. Apr. 14, 1779	2	93
Anna, m. Asahel **PECK**, Feb. [ ], 1789	2	82
Anna, w. David, d. Sept. 3, 1824	2	32
Anna M., d. Daniel & Seneth, b. Sept. 21, 1805	2	14
Anne, m. Abner & Baldwin, Jan. 10, 1754	1	126
Anne, d. John, Jr. & Anne, b. Mar. 25, 1768	1	107
Anne, d. John & Anne, b. Mar. 25, 1768	1	149
Anne, of Litchfield, m. Andrew **ROWLAND, Jr.**, of Fairfield, Mar. 26,		
1799, by Rev. Judah Champion	1	117
Appleton, s. Roger & Lucy, b. Mar. 22, 1770	1	106
Appleton, m. Betsey [ ], Feb. [ ], 1801, by James Morris, J.P.	2	258
Archi, s. James & Sarah, b. May 23, 1794	1	229
Asa Kiah*, s. John, of Hartford, b. Apr. [ ], 1720, *("Hezekiah" in		
Woodruff's)	1	24
Ashbel, s. Ebenezer, Jr. & Lucy, b. Nov. 12, 1767* *(Written "1766		
mistake" underneath)	1	149
Benjamin, s. Daniel & Seneth, b. Sept. 21, 1803	2	14
Caroline, d. Charles & Charlotte, b. May 12, 1794	1	229
Caroline, d. Daniel & Seneth, b. Feb. 12, 1802	2	14
Caroline, m. Samuel **WAUGH, JR.**, b. of Litchfield, Jan 28, 1829, by		
Rev. Henry Robinson, of South Farms	2	279
Catharine, d. Truman & Clarissa, b. Mar. 20, 1807	2	20
Catharine, d. Truman & Clarissa, b. Mar. 20, 1807	2	67
Catharine, d. Daniel & Seneth, b. Jan. 15, 1814	2	14
Catharine, of Litchfield, m. Jacob **BARKER**, of Buffalo, June 4, 1826,		
by Rev. Truman Marsh	2	264
Catharine C., m. Enos **STODDARD, Jr.**, Mar. 24, 1837, by Rev. A.		
Billings Beach	2	299
Catharine Colson, m. Isaac **BRADLEY**, [ ] 11, 1802, by Rev. Nathan		
Strong, of Hartford	2	90
Charles, s. John, 3rd & Rhoda, b. Dec. 23, 1771	2	93
Charles, m. Charlotte **ROBERTS**, June 16, 1793, by Rev. David Butler	1	229
Charles, s. Charles & Charlotte, b. Mar. 5, 1799	1	229
Clarissa, d. Truman & Clarissa, b. Apr. 29, 1802	2	20
Clarissa, d. Truman & Clarissa, b. Apr. 29, 1802	2	67
Clarissa, m. Garret P. **WELCH**, Sept. 10, 1823, by Rev. Truman Marsh	2	131
Clarissa, m. George M. **GARRETT**, Apr. 17, 1842, by Frederick		
Holcomb	2	410
Daniel, s. John & Anne, b. May 5, 1774	1	149
Daniel, m. Seneth **WOODRUFF**, Dec. 23, 1798, by James Morris	2	14
Daniel, representative May 1824	2	1555
David, m. Anna **MARDOCK**, Jan. 19, 1809, by Rev. William Andrews	2	32
David, m. Rachel **OSBORN**, Mar. 3, 1825, by Rev. Isaac Jones	2	32
David, representative May 1825, Apr. 1846, Apr. 1847	2	1555-7
Deboro, d. Ebenezer & Deboro, b. Nov. 9, 1726	1	25
Deborah, b. July 18, 1773, at Litchfield; m. Joseph **ADAMS**, Jan. 26,		
1792, by Rev. Ashbel Baldwin	2	16
Deborah, d. John, 3rd & Rhoda, b. July 18, 1773	2	93
Deborah, b. July 18, 1773; m. Joseph **ADAMS**, Jan. 26, 1792	TM49	99
Deborah, wid. Col. Ebenezer, d. July [ ], 1784, ae 77 y.	1	148

	Vol.	Page
MARSH, MARCH, (cont.)		
Deborah, m. Joseph **ADAMS**, Jan. 26, 1792, by Rev. Ashbel Baldwin	1	166
Delia, d. Truman & Clarissa, b. Dec. 23, 1804	2	20
Delia, d. Truman & Clarissa, b. Dec. 23, 1804	2	67
Delia, d. Truman & Clarissa, d. July 30, 1807	2	20
Delia, d. Truman & Clarissa, d. July 30, 1807	2	67
Delia, 2nd, d. Truman & Clarissa, b. Sept. 12, 1809	2	20
Delia, d. Truman & Clarissa, b. Sept. 12, 1809	2	67
Ebenezer, [twin with Elizabeth], s. John, of Hartford, b. Nov. [ ], 1701	1	24
Ebenezer, m. Deborah **BUEL**, Nov. [ ], 1725, by Rev. Timothy Collins	1	25
Ebenezer, s. Ebenezer & [Deborah], b. Mar. 4, 1737	1	65
Ebenezer, s. Ebenezer & Deborah, d. May 12, 1737	1	64
Ebenezer, representative May 1740, May & Oct. 1741, May & Oct. 1742, May & Oct. 1743, May 1744, May 1745, May & Oct. 1746, May & Oct. 1748, May & Oct. 1749, May & Oct. 1750, May & Oct. 1751, May 1752, May & Oct. 1754, Oct. 1755, May & Oct. 1756, May & Oct. 1757, May & Oct. 1758, Oct. 1759, May & Oct. 1760, May & Oct. 1761, May & Oct. 1762	2	1545-8
Ebenezer, s. Ebenezer & Deborah, b. Oct. 7, 1740	1	65
Ebenezer, Jr., m. Lucy **PHELPS**, Apr. 15, 1763, by Ebenezer Marsh, J.P.	1	149
Ebenezer, representative May & Oct. 1763, May & Oct. 1764, May & Oct. 1765, May & Oct. 1766, Oct. 1767, May 1768, May & Oct. 1769, May 1771, May & Oct. 1784, Oct. 1785, May & Oct. 1786, May & Oct. 1787, May & Oct. 1788, May 1790	2	1548-51
Ebenezer, s. Ebenezer, Jr. & Lucy, b. Jan. 17, 1764	1	149
Ebenezer, Col., d. Apr. [ ], 1773, ae 71 y. 5 m.	1	148
Ebenezer, s. Col. Ebenezer & Deborah, d. Oct. 9, 1807, in the 68th y. of his age	1	148
Elias, s. Elisha & Rhoda, b. Sept. 18, 1812	2	52
Elisha, s. Isaac & Susanna, b. Nov. 4, 1742	1	64
Elisha, s. Elisha & Honor, b. Aug. 27, 1772	1	64
Elisha, m. Rhoda **KILBORN**, [ ], 1802, by Rev. Judah Champion	2	52
Elisha, s. Elisha & Rhoda, b. Apr. 4, 1808	2	52
Elizabeth, [twin with Ebenezer], d. John, of Hartford, b. Nov. [ ], 1701	1	24
Elizabeth, d. John, of Hartford, b. Nov. [ ], 1703	1	24
Elizabeth, d. Ebenezer & Deboro, b. Feb. 10, 1729/30	1	25
Elizabeth, w. Capt. Solomon & d. Benjamin Webster, b. Jan. 23, 1741/2; d. June 29, 1835	1	148
Elizabeth, m. Bezaleel **BEEBE**, July 11, 1764, by Rev. Judah Champion	1	169
Elizabeth, m. Joseph **KILBORN**, Nov. 30, 1765, by Ebenezer Marsh, J.P.	1	103
Elizabeth, m. Roswel **McNEILE**, Sept. 13, 1769, by Timothy Collens, J.P.	1	24
Elizabeth, d. James & Sarah, b. Mar. 10, 1786	1	229
Elizabeth, d. Horace & Electa, b. Feb. 9, 1807	2	133
Elizabeth, m. Abraham **MOSS**, Nov. 10, 1807, by Rev. J. E. Camp	2	35
Elizabeth Ann, d. David & Anna, b. Mar. 28, 1815	2	32
Elizabeth C., m. Alanson **HALL**, Nov. 17, 1825, by Rev. Henry Robinson	2	258
Elizabeth Eliza, of Litchfield, m. Birdsey **WADSHAMS**, of Goshen, Oct. 9, 1820, by Lyman Beecher	2	97
Emela, d. Linus & Philena, b. May 13, 1825	2	107

	Vol.	Page
MARSH, MARCH, (cont.),		
Frederick, s. Horace & Electa, b. Apr. 12, 1803	2	133
Frederick, s. Appleton & Betsey, d. Jan. 21, 1804	2	258
Frederick, s. Appleton & Betsey, b. Sept. [ ], [ ]	2	258
George, s. John, of Hartford, b. Feb. [ ], 1708	1	24
George, m. Lydia **BIRD**, June 16, 1731	1	65
George & Lydia, had d. [ ], b. Aug. 4, 1735	1	65
George & Lydia, had d. [ ], d. Aug. 6, 1735	1	64
George, s. George & Lydia, b. Sept. 25, 1736	1	25
George, s. James & Ursula, b. Sept. 8, 1794	2	257
George, s. Ormond & Ann, b. Dec. 6, 1821	2	46
Hannah, d. Ebenezer & Deborah, b. Mar. 24, 1733	1	25
Hannah, m. Edward **PHELPS, Jr.**, Dec. 21, 1752, by Ebenezer Marsh, J.P.	1	71
Harriet Ann, d. Ormond & Ann, b. Mar. 2, 1818	2	46
Hariet Soprena, d. Horace & Electa, b. Mar. 8, 1811	2	133
Hepzibah, d. Maj. Ebenezer & Deborah, b. Aug. 29, 1745	1	65
Hepzibah, m. Samuel **CATLIN**, Feb. 16, 1766, by Ebenezer Marsh, J.P.	1	130
Hezekiah*, s. John, of Hartford, b. Apr. [ ], 1720 *(Arnold Copy has "Asa Kiah")	1	24
Honor, d. Roger & Lucy, b. Aug. 12, 1760	1	106
Honor, d. Elisha & Honor, b. July 23, 1766	1	64
Honor, m. Solomon **GIBBS**, Dec. 27, 1787, by Rev. Judah Champion	2	43
Honour, m. Obed **BUEL**, Dec. 25, 1788	1	213
Honor, m. Obed **BUEL**, Dec. 25, 1788	2	52
Horace, s. John & Anne, b. July 10, 1772	1	149
Horace, m. Electa **BEEBEE**, Sept. 28, 1801, by Rev. Amos Chase	2	133
Horace Clark, s. Horace & Electa, b. Apr. 13, 1805	2	133
Horatio, s. Charles & Charlotte, b. May 3, 1796	1	229
Huldah, d. James & Sarah, b. July 27, 1799	1	229
Irene, d. William & Susanah, b. Oct. 4, 1738	1	65
Irene, m. David **WELCH**, Dec. 6, 1758, by Judah Champion, V.D.M.	1	83
Isaac, s. John, of Hartford, b. Nov. [ ], 1710	1	24
Isaac, m. Susannah **PRAT[T]**, Dec. 23, 1735, by Rev. Mr. Wadsworth	1	64
Isaac, s. Isaac & Susannah, b. Sept. 11, 1736	1	64
Isaac, Jr., m. Martha **LYMAN**, Nov. 24, 1776, by Rev. Judah Champion	1	106
Isaac, s. Isaac, Jr. & Martha, b. Feb. 18, 1777	1	149
Isaac, Jr., d. Aug. 9, 1779	1	148
Isaac, m. Sally **MARSH**, Oct. 2, 1803, by Rev. Dan Huntington	1	229
Isaac, s. Isaac & Polly, b. Dec. 15, 1803	1	229
James, s. Roger & Lucy, b. Sept. 22, 1762	1	106
James, 2nd, m. Sarah **McNEILE**, May 10, 1785, by Rev. Judah Champion	1	229
James, m. Ursula **HAYDEN**, Dec. [ ], 1790, by Rev. Joshua Williams	2	257
James Erwin, s. Aaron & Martha, b. Dec. 20, 1817	2	249
James M., s. Daniel & Seneth, b. Apr. 5, 1811	2	14
James O., of Litchfield, m. Minerva **ATWOOD**, of Watertown, July 3, 1846, by Rev. William Dixon	TM49	15
James Ormond, s. Ormond & Ann, b. Mar. 29, 1824	2	46
Jared, s. James & Sarah, b. June 10, 1788	1	229
Jerusha, d. John & Sarah, b. Oct. 23, 1735	1	65
Jerusha, m. Salmon **BEACH, Jr.**, Mar, [ ] 1809, by Rev. Dan		

	Vol.	Page
MARSH, MARCH, (cont.),		
Huntington	2	47
John, s. John, of Hartford, b. Oct. [ ], 1712	1	24
John, s. John & Sarah, b. Oct. 17, 1733	1	65
John, 3rd, s. Col. Ebenezer & Deborah, b. Jan. 24, 1749, m. Rhoda		
McNEILE, d. [ ] & Deborah, Sept. 15, 1769	2	93
John, representative Oct. 1766, May & Oct. 1767, May 1768, May		
1771, Oct. 1772, May 1774	2	1548-9
John, 3rd, m. Rhoda McNEILE, Sept. 14, 1769, by Timothy Collens,		
J.P.	1	149
John, s. John & Anne, b. June 17, 1770	1	149
John, s. John, 3rd & Rhoda, b. Aug. 4, 1781	2	93
John, 2nd, d. Dec. 3, 1806, ae 73	1	64
John, m. Sarah Ann SMITH, Apr. 19, 1853, by Rev. David L. Parmelee	TM49	93
John P., s. Daniel & Seneth, b. July 14, 1800	2	14
John W. S., s. Ormond & Ann, b. Apr. 6, 1814	2	46
John W. S., s. Ormond & Ann, d. Feb. 11, 1815	2	46
John W. S., s. Ormond & Ann, d. Feb. 11, 1815	2	262
Joseph N., m. Lucy W. CROSSMAN, b. of Litchfeild, June 11, 1828,		
by Rev. Henry Robinson, of South Farms	2	277
Julia Camp, d. Horace & Electa, b. May 14, 1813	2	133
Katy, d. Ebenezer & Rhoda, b. July 18, 1778	1	149
Kirby, s. James & Sarah, b. Feb. 17, 1808	1	229
Kirby, m. Emily WEBSTER, Apr. 29, 1833, by Rev. L. P. Hickok	2	288
Laura, d. James & Ursula, b. July 10, 1792	2	257
Laura, m. Amos OSBORN, May 23, 1821, by Rev. Joseph E. Camp	2	106
Lewis, s. Elisha & Rhoda, b. Nov. 28, 1810	2	52
Linus, s. Appleton & Betsey, b. Dec. 2, 1802	2	258
Linus, m. Philena MORSE, Nov. 28, 1821, by Rev. Joseph E. Camp	2	107
Linus, of Northfield, m. Frances G. HALE, of Wallingford, Mar. 7,		
1852, by Lewis Jessup, of Northfield	TM49	75
Lois, d. Ebenezer & Deboro, b. Mar. 3, 1731	1	25
Lois, m. Mark PRINDLE, Nov. 3, 1755, by Ebenezer Marsh	1	113
Lucy, d. Roger & Lucy, b. Apr. 10, 1768	1	106
Lucy, d. Ebenezer & Rhoda, b. Aug. 21, 1781	1	149
Lucy, d. James & Ursula, b. Jan. 9, 1801	2	257
Lucy, m. Noah PRESTON, May [ ], 1823, by Rev. Joseph E. Camp	2	265
Lucy, d. Aaron & Martha, b. July 4, 1823	2	249
Lydia, m. Salmon BUEL, Jr., [ ], 1793, by Rev. Judah		
Champion	2	47
Maranda, d. Daniel & Seneth, b. Feb. 9, 1810	2	14
Maria, d. Truman & Clarissa, b. Jan. 14, 1797	2	20
Maria, d. Truman & Clarissa, b. Jan. 14, 1797	2	67
Martha, m. Eli PARDEE, Apr. 24, 1781, by Rev. Judah Champion	1	155
Mary Ann, d. Daniel & Seneth, b. Mar. 7, 1818	2	14
Mary P., m. John DEWEY, Dec. 27, 1821, by Rev. Isaac Jones	2	105
Mary R., d. Ormond & Ann, b. Oct. 3, 1816	2	46
Mary R., d. Ormond & Ann, d. July 4, 1817	2	46
Mary R. I., d. Ormond & Ann, d. Feb. 4, 1817	2	262
Mary S., of Litchfield, m. Frederick F. CALHOUN, of Cornwall, Sept.		
11, 1844, by Rev. David L. Parmelee	TM49	5
Miron, s. Elisha & Rhoda, b. Mar. 2, 1814	2	52
Molly, d. Ebenezer & Deborah, b. Nov. 24, 1752	1	200

	Vol.	Page
MARSH, MARCH, (cont.),		
Molly, m. Moses **SEYMOUR**, Nov. 7, 1771, by Rev. Judah Champion	1	159
Molly, m. Moses **SEYMOUR**, Nov. 7, 1771, by Rev. Judah Champion	1	200
Molly, m. Moses **SEYMOUR**, Nov. 7, 1771, by Rev. Judah Champion	2	248
Molly, d. John, 3rd & Rhoda, b. Nov. 13, 1774	2	93
Morris, s. Appleton & Betsey, b. May 13, 1807	2	258
Moses Seymour, s. Truman & Clarissa, b. Dec. 30, 1792	2	20
Moses Seymour, s. Truman & Clarissa, b. Dec. 30, 1792	2	67
Olive, m. Levi **COE**, May [ ], 1786, by Rev. Judah Champion	2	45
Olive Jane, m. David C. **GOODWIN**, June 12, 1850, by Rev. Benjamin W. Stone	TM49	54
Ormond, m. Ann **WHISTLER**, Jan. 6, 1812, by James Abbott, of Detroit	2	46
Orson, s. James & Sarah, b. Nov. 23, 1790	1	229
Ozias, s. Maj. Ebenezer & Deborah, b. Apr. 5, 1743	1	65
Ozias, d. Apr. 5, 1815, ae 53 y.	1	148
Polly, d. Elisha & Rhoda, b. Dec. 9, 1804	2	52
Rachel, d. John, 3rd & Rhoda, b. Dec. 17, 1770	1	149
Rachel, d. John, 3rd & Rhoda, b. Dec. 17, 1770	2	93
Rachel, m. Horace **BALDWIN**, June 24, 1791	1	212
Rachel, d. Daniel & Seneth, b. Nov. 27, 1821	2	14
Rhoda, d. John, 3rd & Rhoda, b. June 24, 1777	2	93
Rhoda, d. Elisha & Rhoda, b. Aug. 14, 1806	2	52
Roger, s. George & Lydia, b. Oct. 31, 1733	1	65
Roger, s. Roger & Lucy, b. Dec. 19, 1765	1	106
Ruth, d. Isaac & Susanna, b. May 14, 1738	1	64
Sabra, m. Abel **CAMP**, Jan. 9, 1769, by Rev. Judah Champion	1	46
Sabra, m. Abel **CAMP**, Jan. 9, 1769, by Rev. Judah Champion	2	48
Sally, d. Elisha & Rhoda, b. Apr. 25, 1803	2	52
Sally, m. Isaac **MARSH**, Oct. 2, 1803, by Rev. Dan Huntington	1	229
Sally, m. Elihu **WEBSTER**, Nov. [ ], 1823, by Rev. Joseph E. Camp	2	265
Sally, m. Nathaniel **BISSELL**, b. of Litchfield, Oct. 6, 1852, by Benjamin L. Swan	TM49	76
Samuel, s. Ebenezer, Jr. & Lucy, b. June 17, 1765	1	149
Samuel, m. Polly **GELBERT**, Jan. 6, 1825, by Rev. Isaac Jones	2	138
Sarah, d. John, Jr. & Anne, b. Jan. 8, 1766	1	107
Sarah, d. John, Jr. & Anne, b. Jan. 8, 1766	1	149
Sarah, m. David **KING**, June 29, 1773, by Rev. Judah Champion	1	103
Sarah, d. James & Sarah, b. Jan. 1, 1803	1	229
Sarah Jane, d. Ormond & Ann, b. Dec. 23, 1819	2	46
Solomon, s. Ebenezer & Deborah, b. Feb. 10, 1735	1	65
Solomon, representative Oct. 1792	2	1552
Solomon, Capt., d. May 30, 1804 in the 70th y. of his age	1	148
Solomon, s. David & Anna, b. Nov. 18, 1813	2	32
Susan, d. Daniel & Seneth, b. Mar. 7, 1816	2	14
Susanna, d. William & Susannah, b. Jan. 16, 1736/7	1	25
Susanna, d. Isaac & Susanna, b. Aug. 20, 1746	1	64
Susanna, m. Timothy **SKINNER**, Nov. 15, 1770	1	120
Sylva Ann, d. Aaron & Martha, b. Oct. 30, 1815	2	249
Thale*, d. Ebenezer, Jr. & Lucy, b. Mar. 11, 1770 *("Kate" in Woodruff's book)	1	149
Thale, d. Ebenezer, Jr. & Lucy, d. Dec. 10, 1770	1	148
Timothy, s. John, of Hartford, b. Oct. [ ], 1714	1	24

	Vol.	Page
MARSH, MARCH, (cont.),		
Tracy, s. James & Sarah, b. Oct. 27, 1796	1	229
Truman, s. Ebenezer, Jr. & Lucy, b. Feb. 22, 1768	1	149
Truman, m. Clarissa **SEYMOUR**, Oct. 22, 1791, by Rev. Ashbel Baldwin	2	20
Truman, Rev., m. Clarissa **SEYMOUR**, Oct. 22, 1791, by Rev. Ashbel Baldwin	2	67
Truman, s. Truman & Clarissa, b. July 3, 1799	2	20
Truman, s. Truman & Clarissa, b. July 3, 1799	2	67
Truman, s. Truman & Clarissa, d. Mar. 9, 1800	2	20
Truman, s. Truman & Clarissa, d. Mar. 9, 1800	2	67
William, s. John, of Hartford, June [ ], 1706	1	24
William, m. Susanah **WEBSTER**, Nov. 9, 1733, by Rev. Daniel Wadsworth	1	25
William, s. William & Susanah, b. Sept. 14, 1740	1	65
William B., s. Ormond & Ann, d. Mar. 24, 1829	2	262
William Bishop, s. Ormond & Ann, b. Mar. 8, 1829	2	46
William Murdock, s. David & Anna, b. Dec. 24, 1809	2	32
MARSHALL, Almeron, s. Gad & Mary, b. May 1, 1765	1	107
Desdemony, d. Gad & Mary, b. July 16, 1763	1	107
MARTIN, MARTEN, MARTINS, Abigail, of Woodbury, m. Henry **GIBBS**, of Litchfield, Nov. 8, 1739, by Capt. Joseph Minor, J.P.	1	19
Emeline, m. George **BOOTH**, b. of Litchfield, Apr. 4, 1831, by Rev. David Miller	2	287
Eunis, of Woodbury, m. Benjamin Woodruff, of Litchfield, Nov. 20, 1739, by Capt. Joseph Miner, J.P.	1	83
Hannah, m. Simeon **GIBBS**, Nov. 18, 1778, by Daniel Everitt, J.P.	1	179
Jerusha, m. William **HALL**, Feb. 18, 1759, by Rev. Solomon Williams, of Lebanon	1	17
MARVIN, Alonzo, of Cortright, N.Y., m. Mary **BEACH**, Feb. 8, 1835, by Rev. L. P. Hickok	2	296
Harriet, m. Daniel M. **PECK**, Nov. 7, 1843	TM49	93
Harriet, of Litchfield, m. Daniel M. **PECK**, of Woodbury, [Nov.] 7, [1843]*, by Jonathan Brace *(Note says "Nov. 10, 1843")	2	413
John L., m. Sarah J. **FLOWERS**, b. of Litchfield, Sept. 6, 1854, by Rev. H. N. Weed	TM49	103
Reynold, m. Mrs. Ruth **WELCH**, Feb. 23, 1763, by Rev. Nathaniel Taylor	1	107
Reynold, had negroes Violet, b. Apr. 15, 1777; Pero, b. Nov. 20, 1782; Lettice, b. June 1, 1791	1	151
Reynold, d. July 20, 1802, ae 78	1	148
Ruth, d. Reynold & Ruth, b. Dec. 20, 1763	1	107
Ruth, Jr., m. Ephraim **KIRBY**, Mar. 17, 1784, by Rev. Judah Champion	1	145
Ruth, w. Reynold, d. May 12, 1793, ae 53 y.	1	148
MASON, Abigail, d. Joseph & Mary, b. Mar. 19, 1723	1	25
Abigail, d. John & Lidia, b. Jan. 21, 1753	1	64
Abigail, m. William **BALDWIN**, [,17], by Rev. Judah Champion	2	38
Almira, d. Jonathan & Sally, b. Aug. 3, 1791	2	22
Ashbel, s. Joseph, Jr. & Rebecca, b. Apr. 27, 1757	1	64
Benjamin, s. Elisha & Lucretia, b. May 22, 1805	2	261
Caroline, d. Elisha & Lucretia, b. Dec. 22, 1792	1	229
Caroline, d. Elisha & Lucretia, b. Dec. 22, 1792	2	261
Caroline, m. John A. **OVIAT**, Nov. [ ], 1821, by Rev. Lyman Beecher	2	107

	Vol.	Page
MASON, (cont.),		
Charles, s. Jonathan & Sally, b. May 9, 1806	2	22
Charles Hubert, s. [Benjamin W. & Susan], b. Apr. 7, 1835	2	316
Sintha*, d. Elisha & Lucretia, b. July 24, 1785 *("Cynthia")	1	189
Cinthia, d. Elisha & Lucretia, b. July 24, 1786	2	261
Cynthia, m. Isaac TURNER, Jan. 15, 1810, by Rev. Joseph E. Camp	2	38
Edwin, s. Elisha & Lucretia, b. Aug. 17, 1803	2	261
Edwin, m. Clarississa JOHNSON, b. of Litchfield, Dec. 13, 1826, by		
Rev. Henry Robinson, of South Farms	2	267
Elijah, s. Elisha & Lucretia, b. June 7, 1797	1	229
Elijah, s. Elisha & Lucretia, b. June 7, 1797; d. [ ], 1798*		
*(Note says "d. Apr. 14, 1799")	2	261
Elijah, s. Elisha &Lucretia, d. Apr. 14, 1799	1	188
Elijah, 2nd, s. Elisha & Lucretia, b. May 25, 1799	1	229
Elijah, 2nd, [s. Elisha & Lucretia, b. May 25, 1799]* *(This entry in		
note)	2	261
Eliot, s. Jonathan & Sally, b. Nov. 28, 1799	2	22
Eliot, m. Harriet SANFORD, Jan. 28, 1822, by Rev. Isaac Jones	2	109
Elisha, s. Joseph, Jr. & Rebecca, b. Apr. 4, 1759	1	64
Elisha, m. Lucretia WEBSTER, Jan. 8, 1785, by Rev. Judah Champion	1	189
Elisha, m. Lucretia WEBSTER, Jan. 8, 1785, by Rev. Judah Champion	2	261
Elisha, s. Elisha & Lucretia, d. Apr. 7, 1790	1	188
Elisha, s. Elisha & Lucretia, b. June 5, 1795	1	229
Elisha, s. Elisha & Lucretia, b. June 5, 1795; d. [ ], 1817*		
*(Note says "d. Apr. 7, 1790")	2	261
Elisha, m. Emeline A. PECK, b. of Litchfield, Oct. 13, 1851, by William		
B. Hoyt	TM49	65
Everitt, s. Jonathan & Sally, b. Sept. 6, 1797; d. Feb. 3, 1801	2	22
George, s. Joseph, Jr. & Rebecca, b. Feb. 5, 1763	1	64
George William, s. Benjamin W. & Susan, b. Feb. 24, 1833	2	316
Hannah, d. Joseph & Mary, b. Jan. 6, 1719/20	1	25
Hannah, m. Ephraim COLVER, b. of Litchfield, Jan. 24, 1739/40	1	47
Hannah, d. John & Lidia, b. Feb. 12, 1745/6	1	107
Hannah, m. Ambrose GRANT, Nov. 20, 1771, by Rev. Judah Champion	1	136-8
Isaac, of South Britain, ae 25, m. Mrs. Amy BRADLEY, of Bantam, ae		
37, Dec. 26, 1753, by Rev. Daniel E. Brown, of Bantam. Witnesses		
Marcelus Judd, of Litchfield & H. M. Pratt, of Bantam	TM49	97
Jemima, d. John & Lidia, b. May 28, 1744	1	107
John, s. Joseph & Mary, b. Aug. 6, 1717	1	25
John, m. Lidia COOK, Jan. 20, 1743/4, by Rev. Timothy Collens	1	107
John, s. John & Lidia, b. Sept. 10, 1747	1	107
John, d. Jan. 26, 1753	1	64
Jonathan, s. Joseph & Mary, b. Mar. 24, 1733	1	25
Jonathan, s. Jonathan & Susanah, b. Aug. 4, 1764; m. Sally ORTON, d.		
Samuel & Mary, Feb. 4, 1790, by Rev. Judah Champion	2	22
Joseph, s. Joseph & Mary, b.Nov. 17, 1725	1	25
Joseph, Jr., m. Rebecca SKINNER, of Hartford, June 4, 1734*, by Rev.		
Mr. Dorr, of Hartford *(correction: date crossed out, "1754"		
written over it in original manuscript)	1	65
Joseph, Jr., m. Patience ROSSETTER, Nov. 16, 1749, by Ebenezer		
Marsh, J.P.	1	107
Joseph, s. Joseph, Jr. & Rebecca, b. Apr. 26, 1755	1	64
Joseph William, s. Elisha & Lucretia, b. May 5, 1801	1	229

	Vol.	Page
MASON, (cont.)		
Joseph W[illia]m, s. Elisha & Lucretia, b. May 5, 1801	2	261
Joshua, s. Joseph & Mary, b. July 19, 1736	1	25
Joshua, m. Anne **WEBSTER,** June 1, 1763, by Rev. Judah Champion	2	107
Joshua, s. Elisha & Lucretia, b. Feb. 18, 1807	2	261
Joshua, s. Mary, d. Nov. 17, 1813, ae 77	1	24
Julia, d. Jonathan & Sally, b. Mar. 14, 1804	2	22
Lucina, d. John & Lidia, b. Oct. 18, 1749	1	65
Lucretia, d. Elisha & Lucretia, b. Nov. 1, 1790	1	189
Lucretia, d. Elisha & Lucretia, b. Nov. 1, 1790	2	261
Lidia, d. Joseph & Mary, b. Apr. 13, 1728	1	25
Lidia, wid. John, d. Mar. 4, 1753	1	64
Mary, d. Joseph & Mary, b. Aug. 30, 1715	1	25
Mary, m. William **HORSFORD,** Mar. 14, 1736	1	56
Mary, wid. Joseph, d. Feb. 10, 1787, ae 94 y.	1	24
Mary, d. Jonathan & Sally, b. Feb. 28, 1802	2	22
Mary, had s. Joshua, d. Nov. 17, 1813, ae 77	1	24
Patience, [twin with Prudence], d. Joseph, Jr. & Patience, b. Nov. 13, 1750	1	107
Patience, w. Joseph, Jr. d. Nov. 17, 1750, ae about 24 y.	1	106
Phineas, m. Sarah **REED,** b. of New Hartford, Mar. 30, 1834, by Rev. Samuel Fuller	TM49	37
Prudence, [twin with Patience], d. Joseph, Jr. & Patience, b. Nov. 13, 1750	1	107
Rachel, m.Charles **BALDWIN,** [ ], 1791, by Rev. Judah Champion	2	56
Ruth, d. Joseph & Mary, b. June 22, 1730	1	25
Ruth, m. Samuel **ORTON, Jr.,** [, 17], by Rev. Timothy Collens	1	69
Sally, d. Jonathan & Sally, b. Nov. 28, 1792; d. July 6, 1794	2	22
Sally, 2nd, d. Jonathan & Sally, b. June 14, 1795	2	22
Stephen, s. Joseph, Jr. & Rebecca, b. Aug. 10, 1761	1	64
Stephen, s. Elisha & Lucretia, b. Apr. 11, 1787	1	189
Stephen, s. Elisha & Lucretia, b. Apr. 11, 1787; d. May 17, 1787	2	261
Stephen, s. Elisha & Lucretia, d. May 17, 1787	1	188
Stephen, s. Elisha & Lucretia, d. May 17, 1787	2	261
Stephen, 2nd, s. Elisha & Lucretia, b. May 31, 1788	1	189
Stephen, 2nd, s. Elisha & Lucretia, b. May 31, 1788	2	261
Susanna, m. John **WEED,** Oct. 3, 1780, by Rev. Judah Champion	1	165
Thomas, m. Mary Ann **WILLIAMS,** b. of Litchfield, May 3, 1847, by Rev. Samuel Fuller	TM49	38
William, Jr., m. Polly **BENTON,** Mar. 19, 1822, by Rev. Morris Woodruff, J.P.	2	110
MASTERS, Nicholas, m. Hortensia **HUBBARD,** b. of Litchfield, Oct. 11, 1846, by Rev. Samuel Fuller	TM49	38
MATHER, Sarah, d. Timothy & Sarah, b. Nov. 24, 1737	1	25
MATTHEWS, MATHEWS, Albert, [s. Charles & Mary K.], b. Sept. 12, 1845	2	322
Annah, of Bristol, m. John **CARRIER,** of Canton, July 21, 1830, by Rev. L. P. Hickok	2	285
Betsey, d. [Robert & Orpah], b. Jan. 25, 1811	2	287
Charles, s. Robert & Orpah, b. Mar. 12, 1805	2	287
Charles, m. Sarah M. **HOYT,** Mar. 12, 1829	2	322
Charles, m. Mary **WILLIAMS,** Dec. 4, 1837, by Truman Marsh	2	315

	Vol.	Page
MATTHEWS, MATHEWS, (cont.),		
Charles, m. Mary K. **WILLIAMS,** Dec. 4, 1837	2	322
Charles, Sr., d. Aug. 6, 1850	2	322
Charles Henry, s. [Charles & Mary K.], b. Mar. 6, 1842	2	322
David, of Bristol, m. Polly E. **PLATT,** of Plymouth, May 7, 1835, by Rev. L. P. Hickok	2	296
David, of Bristol, m. Sally **LAW,** of Litchfield, Dec. 4, 1836, by Rev. Samuel Fuller, Jr.	2	296
George, s. [Robert & Orpah], b. Aug. 29, 1807	2	287
George, m. Luraney **HART,** Dec. 21, 1834	TM49	13
George, m. Lurania **HART,** Dec. 21, 1834, by Rev. L. P. Hickok	2	296
Hiram,s. [George & Luraney], b. Apr. 7, 1836	TM49	13
James William, s. [Charles & Sarah M.], b. Feb. 17, 1832	2	322
Janette, d. [Charles & Mary K.], b. Oct. 28, 1838	2	322
Julia, d. [George & Luraney], b. Mar. 9, 1842	TM49	13
Lyman, s. [Robert & Orpah], b. Oct. 21, 1821	2	287
Martha Maria, d. [Charles & Mary K.], b. Sept. 17, 1847	2	322
Mary Ann, d. [Charles & Mary K.], b. June 12, 1840	2	322
Nancy, of Bristol, m. William **HALE,** of Weathersfield, July 21, 1830, by Rev. L. P. Hickok	2	285
Rebecca, d. [Robert & Orpah], b. May 27, 1809	2	287
Rebecca, m. Oliver **CRAWFORD,** of Newburgh, N.Y., Jan. 18, 1835, by Rev. L. P. Hickok	2	296
Robert, b. Dec. 18, 1775, at New Haven; m. Orpah **PLANT,** May 18, 1804	2	287
Sarah M., w. Charles, d. Apr. 14, 1837	2	322
Sarah Maria, d. [Charles & Sarah M.], b. Dec. 27, 1836	2	322
Seth, s. [Charles & Mary K.], b. Nov. 18, 1849	2	322
Warren, [s. Charles & Mary K.], b. Nov. 8, 1843	2	322
MATTOCKS, MATTOCK, Anne, d. James & Sarah, b. Dec. 5, 1763	1	64
Anne, m. Elnathan **HOLLEY,** Sept. 28, 1783, by Rev. Mr. Nichols	1	181
Edna, d. James & Sarah, b. Sept. 16, 1767	1	64
Luce, d. James & Sarah, b. Jan. 30, 1762	1	64
Sarah, m. Jesse **KILBORN,** Feb. 24, 1765, by Rev. Judah Champion	1	61
Sarah, d. James & Sarah, b. June 29, 1765	1	64
Sarah, m. Andrew **PALMER,** July 24, 1783, by Andrew Adams	1	155
Sarah, m. Andrew **PALMER,** July 24, 1783, by Elisha Sheldon	2	172
MATTOON, Asenath, d. Samuel & Martha, b. May 25, 1782	1	149
Asenath, d. Samuel & Martha, b. May 25, 1782	1	188
Hannah M., of Plymouth, m. Joel A. **THORP,** of Litchfield, Jan. 21, 1838, by Rev. Lewis Gunn	2	315
Patty, d. Samuel & Martha, b. Oct. 1, 1783	1	149
Patty, d. Samuel & Martha, b. Oct. 1, 1783; d. Dec. 18, 1783	1	188
Patty, d. Dec. 18, 1783	1	148
MAXHY, Jane A., of Litchfield, m. Ambrose **KNAPP,** of North Canaan, July 20, 1841, by William Payne	2	334
MAZUZEN, MAZUZAN, John, s. Mark & Ama, b. Dec. 1, 1771	1	106
Mark, m. Ama **PALMER,** Apr. 6, 1769, by Rev. Solomon Palmer	1	106
Mark W., m. Maria **GOODWIN,** b. of Litchfield, June 25, 1837, by Rev. H. Bryant	2	314
MEADE, MEAD, Desire, m. Abraham **BENTON,** Mar. 18, 1790, by John Whittlesey, J.P.	1	249
William D., m. Eliza L. **HUBBARD,** Sept. 14, 1836, b. of New Haven,		

	Vol.	Page
MEADE, MEAD, (cont.),		
by Isaac Jones	2	299
MERCHANT, [see under **MARCHANT**]		
MERIET, [see under **MERRIT**]		
MERRIAM, MERIAM, [see also **MERRIMAN**], Honor, m. Benoni		
OLCOTT, Jan. 18, 1804, by Rev. Alex V. Griswould	2	146
Sally, m. Robert **CATLIN**, Nov. 9, 1800, by Rev. Truman Marsh	2	6
MERRILL, MERELL, MERRELS, MERRIL, [see also **MORRIL**], Ann,		
m. Joseph **GILLOT**, Jan. 23, 1727/8, by Rev. Benjamin Catlin	1	15
Fanny, m. James **BEACH**, Sept. [ ], 1810, by Rev. Truman Marsh	2	41
Hannah, m. Ebenezer **SPENCER**, Mar. 4, 1823, by Rev. Isaac Jones	2	118
MERRIMAN, MERIMAN, MARRIMAN, [see also **MERRIAM**],		
Alanson Hall, s. George & Mary, b. Apr. 24, 1827	2	97
Asahel, of Bristol, m. Eunice **PLATT**, of Litchfield, June 13, 1825, by		
Rev. Henry Robinson	2	7
Clarinda J., m. Hervey V. **STONE**, b. of Litchfield, May 8, 1843, by		
Rev. Ralph Smith	2	412
Clarinda Jane, d. George & Mary, b. May 20, 1822	2	97
Electa, d. Joseph & Betsey, b. June 25, 1803	1	228
Eliza, d. Joseph & Betsey, b. May 26, 1797	1	228
Eliza, m. Ephraim **SHERMAN**, June 7, 1821, by Rev. Joseph E. Camp	2	107
Emily, d. Joseph & Betsey, b. June 7, 1807	1	228
Emily, m. Norman **HALL**, b. of Litchfield, Dec. 6, 1829, by Rev.		
Birdsey Sillick	2	283
George, s. Joseph & Betsey, b. Sept. 24, 1799	1	228
George, m. Mary **CABLE**, b. of Litchfield, Nov. 30, 1820, by Morris		
Woodruff, J.P.	2	97
John A., m. Esther **CABLE**, Jan. 25, 1821, by Moses Woodruff, J.P.	2	98
Joseph, s. Joseph & Rachel, b. Nov. 3, 1772	1	24
Joseph, d. Oct. 21, 1775	1	106
Joseph, m. Betsey **SWIFT**, May 8, 1796, by Rev. James Noyce	1	228
Joseph, s. Joseph & Betsey, b. Apr. 8, 1810	1	228
Joseph, s. Joseph & Betsey, b. Apr. 12, 1815	1	228
Joseph, Sr., d. Nov. 15, 1829, ae 57	1	228
Joseph, m. Abigail **JOHNSON**, June 16, 1833, by Rev. L. P. Hickok	2	288
Julia, d. Joseph & Betsey, b. Aug. 27, 1801	1	228
Julia, d. Joseph & Betsey, d. Nov. 3, 1816	1	228
Julia L., m. Samuel **McNEILE, 2nd**, b. of Litchfield, Mar. 14, 1849, by		
Joseph Henson	TM49	36
Lucy A., m. Charles L. **PERKINS**, b. of Litchfield, Dec. 28, 1845, by		
Rev. William Dixon	TM49	12
Mary, d. Joseph & Betsey, b. May 8, 1805	1	228
Robert D., of Litchfield, m. Sarah **MILLER**, of Troy, N.Y., Sept. 29,		
1851, by N. C. Lewis	TM49	65
Sabra, m. Jeremiah **RANNEY**, June 16, 1822, by Rev. Isaac Jones	2	112
Samuel A., m. Mary **JOHNSON**, b. of Litchfield, Apr. 16, 1843, by		
Rev. Jason Wells	2	339
Sarah, m. Roswell **HARRISON**, Dec. 1, 1841, by J. Brace	2	335
Silas, s. Joseph & Rachel, b. Sept. 18, 1774	1	24
MERRIT, MERIET, Abner, his w. [ ]	1	31
Betsey, m. Norman **BARNES**, Jan. [ ], 1815	2	87
Hannah, m. Ebenezer **SPENCER**, Mar. 4, 1823, by Rev. Isaac Jones	2	253
MERWIN, MERVIN, MARWIN, Synthia, d. Samuel M. & Eunice, b. Oct.		

	Vol.	Page
MERWIN, MERVIN, MARWIN, (cont.),		
2, 1802	2	144
Emele Esther, d. Samuel M. & Eunice, b. Mar. 19, 1810	2	144
Eunice, d. Samuel M. & Eunice, b. Aug. 22, 1812	2	144
Frederick, s. Samuel M. & Eunice, b. Oct. 8, 1823	2	144
Frederick L., m. Mary A. **EDWARDS,** b. of Litchfield, Oct. 10, 1849, by Benjamin L. Swan	TM49	43
Jonathan, of Cornwall, m. Lorana **BUEL,** of Litchfield, Nov. 7, 1822, by Rev. Joseph Harvey, of Goshen	2	115
Marina, d. Samuel M. & Eunice, b. Sept. 1, 1804	2	144
Mariana, m. William S. **HOPKINS,** Aug. 13, 1830, by Frederick Holcomb	2	285
Myron, m. Abby P. **MARSH,** Apr. 8, 1851, by Rev. David L. Parmelee	TM49	62
Phebe, d. Samuel M. & Eunice, b. Apr. 20, 1807	2	144
Phebe, m. Dewey E. **PRESTON,** May 5, 1830, by Fred Holcomb	2	285
Samuel Andrew, s. Samuel M. & Eunice, b. Oct. 28, 1818	2	144
Samuel M., m. Eunice **SMITH,** May 10, 1801, by Rev. Noah Williston	2	144
MIDDLEBROOKS, Henry B., of Bridgeport, m. Lois M. **HAYDON,** of Litchfield, Nov. 29, 1849, by Rev. William B. Hoyt	TM49	44
MIGEON, Arsena, of Litchfield, m. Henry **MUNSON,** of East Bloomfield, Ontario Cty., N.Y., Feb. 26, 1849, by Rev. Samuel Fuller	TM49	36
Florentine, of Litchfield, m. Frederick J. **SEYMOUR,** of Waterbury, Aug. 28, 1849, by J. D. Berry	TM49	43
MILES, George, m. Charlotte **BALDWIN,** Oct. 3, 1825, by Rev. Truman Marsh	2	256
Nancy, m. Zachariah **SPENCER, Jr.,** Sept. 1, 1808, by Rev. Judah Champion	2	13
MILLARD, Amanda, m. Benjamin **KILBORN,** July 1, 1821, at Cornwall, by Rev. Wallter Smith	2	272
Josiah, Dr., of Manlius, N.Y., m. Rosamond **HINSDALE,** of Litchfield, Jan. 7, 1822, by Rev. Amos Pettingill	2	106
MILLER, Ann Maria, m. Nehemiah C. **EDWARDS,** b. of Litchfield, Apr. 8, 1845, by George H. Hastings. Int. Pub.	TM49	9
Anna, b. Nov. 13, 1733; m. Leaming **BRADLEY,** Nov. 15, 1759	2	68
Grant, s. Ichabod & Sarah, b. May 15, 1769	1	106
Harriet Abigail, m. David Collins **BULKLEY,** b. of Litchfield, Apr. 12, 1848, by Rev. Samuel Fuller	TM49	38
John H., m. Harriet **HILLS,** June 20, 1832, by Rev. Mr. Taylor, of South Farms	2	289
Sarah, of Troy, N.Y., m. Robert D. **MARRIMAN,** of Litchfield, Sept. 29, 1851, by N. C. Lewis	TM49	65
Thalia, of Litchfield, m. Burton **GILBERT,** of Warren, Feb. 21, 1848, by Rev. Samuel Fuller	TM49	38
William Guy, m. Julia Maria **SPRAGUE,** b. of Litchfield, Nov. 7 1847, by Rev. Samuel Fuller	TM49	38
MINOR, MINER, Alma Ruth, m. Reuben **TURRILL,** Aug. 20, 1816, by Rev. Mr. Welton, of Woodbury	2	76
Anna, m. Elisha **TROWBRIDGE,** Feb. 4, 1819, by John Jewett, 2nd,of Dutchess Cty., N.Y.	2	94
Burke, m. Eliza **TURNER,** Sept. 3, 1834, by Rev. Joseph E. Camp	2	297
Eliza, of Litchfield, m. Terties **WADMOUTH,** of New Hartford, Sept. 21, 1843, by Jonathan Brace	2	413
Gary H., representative Apr. 1856	2	1558

	Vol.	Page
MINOR, MINER, (cont.),		
Phinehas, representative May 1823, May 1827, May 1829, May 1835	2	1555-6
Sarah M., of Litchfield, m. George W. **BEACH**, of Litchfield, Nov. 25,		
1852, by Rev. Lewis Jessup	TM49	77
MITCHELL, Nathan, of Litchfield, m. Hannah **HEALY**, of Killingsworth,		
Aug. 30, 1738, by Rev. Timothy Collens	1	65
Nathan, s. Nathan & Hannah, b. Aug. 9, 1739	1	65
MONROE, Hannah, of Warren, m. Albert **BLAKE**, of Cornwall, Sept. 5,		
1854, by Rev. H. N. Weed	TM49	103
Leavitt, of Mindeth, N.Y., m. Diantha **STODDARD**, of Litchfield, Nov.		
6, 1836, in Bradleyville, by Rev. A. Billings Beach	2	284
MOODEY, Adonijah, of Litchfield, m. Sarah **SMITH**, of New Hartford,		
Nov. 9, 1742, by Rev. Jonathan Marsh	1	107
Ebenezer, s. Adonijah & Sarah, b. Jan. 9, 1743/4	1	107
MOON*, Thomas, m. Wealthy **GRISWOULD**, [ ], 1820, by Lyman		
Beecher *("**MOORE**"?)	2	98
-----, Arnold Copy says "(Probably this name is "Moore")"	1	228
MOORE, MORE, Alethea, d. Joshua & Phebe, b. May 1, 1798	1	228
Anna, d. Joshua & Phebe, b. Sept. 18, 1794	1	228
Benjamin, s. David & Polly, b. Dec. 28, 1786, at Norwich	1	108
Benjamin, m. Pierce **STOCKING**, Feb. 14, 1811, by Rev. Lyman		
Beecher	2	1
Benjamin, s. Benjamin & Pierce, b. July 31, 1813	2	1
Caleb, s. Joshua & Phebe, b. Aug. 6, 1809	1	228
Daniel Hartshorn, s. Joshua & Phebe, b. Mar. 26, 1807	1	228
David, m. Polly **COLLIER**, May 6, 1784, by Rev. Mr. Strong, of		
Norwich	1	108
David, s. David & Polly, b. July 27, 1795	1	108
David, m. Harriet A. **TROWBRIDGE**, Nov. 28, 1844, by Rev. D. L.		
Marks	TM49	7
Delight, d. David & Polly, b. Aug. 12, 1793	1	108
Elizabeth Collier, d. David & Polly, b. Oct. 23, 1801	1	108
Fanny Kirby, d. David & Polly, b. May 7, 1805	1	108
Harriet, d. David & Polly, b. Nov. 10, 1799	1	108
Harriet, d. David & Polly, b. Nov. 10, 1799; m. Horace **JOHNSON**, s.		
Benjamin & Lucretia, June 13, 1819, by Rev. Isaac Jones	2	120
Jane E. W., m. Homer **STODDARD**, Mar. 12, 1845, by Rev. D. L.		
Marks	TM49	8
Jemima, m. Enoch **PALMER**, July 10, 1746, by Joseph Bird, J.P.	1	30
John, s. Samuel & Rachel, b. May 7, 1739	1	65
Joseph, s. David & Polly, b. May 10, 1791	1	108
Joshua, m. Phebe **HARTSHORN**, Aug. 18, 1791	1	228
Keturah, m. William **CHURCHILL**, Dec. 24, 1800, by Rev. Joseph E.		
Camp	2	7
Laura, of Bradleyville, m. William L. **HUMISTON**, of Winsted, Nov.		
24, 1845, by Rev. William Dixon	TM49	12
Lavinia K., m. Tracy L. **BARNES**, Sept. 11, 1853, by Rev. H. N. Weed	TM49	91
Lemuel, s. Joshua & Phebe, b. June 8, 1792	1	228
Mary, d. Benjamin & Pierce, b. Oct. 26, 1811	2	1
Mary, m. James **STONE**, Dec. 17, 1814	2	49
Matilda, d. Joshua & Phebe, b. July 25,1796	1	228
Moses, m. Fanny **HART**, Mar. 30, 1835, by Rev. L. P. Hickok	2	296
Nelson A., m. Ann Maria **PICKETT**, Jan. 25, 1853, by Rev. David L.		

	Vol.	Page
MOORE, MORE, (cont.),		
Parmelee	TM49	78
Polly, d. David & Polly, b. Dec. 31, 1788	1	108
Rachal, d. Samuell & Rachal, b. Dec. 28, 1741	1	65
Richard, s. David & Polly, b. Dec. 20, 1784, at Norwich	1	108
Samuel, m. Rachel LANDON, Oct. 9, 1735, by Rev. Nathaniell Mather	1	65
Samuel, s. Samuel & Rachal, b. Oct. 27, 1736	1	65
Sarah, m. Samuel BROWN, Oct. 13, 1847, by Joseph Henson	TM49	23
Sidney D., m. Charlotte A. LANDON, b. of Bantam Falls, May 9, 1849, by J. D. Berry	TM49	41
Thomas Collier, s. David & Polly, b. Sept. 14, 1797	1	108
Willliam, of Plymouth, m. Harriet BUMAN, Jan. 11, 1848, by Joseph Henson	TM49	23
MOREHOUSE, Joel, of Woodbury, m. Altha M. THROOP, of Litchfield, May 12, 1847, by Rev. William Dixon	TM49	19
MORGAN, Ira, of Warren, m. Mrs. Margary STONE, of Litchfield, May 5, 1833, by Rev. Hart Talcott	2	293
John, of Kent, m. Cornelia Eliza BISSELL, of Milton, Nov. 3, 1831, by Rev. H. S. Atwater, of New Preston	2	290
MORELY, Clarissa, m. Ephraim BIDWELL, Oct. 9, 1825, by Rev. Truman Marsh	2	257
MORRIL, [see also MERRILL], Mary, m. William A. HART, Nov. 26, 1803, by Rev. Judah Champion	2	7
MORRIS, Abigail, d. Capt. James & Elizabeth, b. Aug. 2, 1783	1	149
Alanson Lewis, of Torringford, m. Mary Ann HART, of Litchfield, Sept. 17, 1835, by Rev. Samuel Fuller, Jr.	2	296
Asa, m. Ann RIGGS, Mar. 20, 1818, at Woodbridge, by Rev. Jason Allen	2	143
Catharine, m. Lorenzo MUNGER, b. of Litchfield, Jan. 2, 1853, by Rev. John J. Brandegee	TM49	77
Frances P., of Warren, m. Seabury WELLS, of Cornwall, Nov. 20, 1850, by H. L. Vaill	TM49	40
George M., of Litchfield, m. Harriet A. GRISWOLD, of Bantam Falls, May 1 [probably 1853], by Rev. Daniel E. Brown, of Bantam Falls	TM49	93
James, m. Phebe BARNES, Apr. 11, 1751, by Thomas Harrison, J.P.	1	107
James, s. James & Phebe, b. Jan. 8, 1752	1	107
James, Jr., m. Elizabeth HUBBARD, Dec. 20, 1781, by Hon. Jabez Hamlin	1	149
James, s. James & Elizabeth, b. Dec. 4, 1784	1	149
James, representative May 1802, Oct. 1800, May & Oct. 1803, May & Oct. 1804, May & Oct. 1805	2	1553
James, m. Rhoda FARNUM, Mar. 6, 1815, by Rev. Lyman Beecher	2	22
Jane Elizabeth, d. James & Rhoda, b. Jan. 30, 1816	2	22
Joseph Riggs, s. Asa & Ann, b. Apr. 26, 1822	2	143
Luce, d. James & Phebe, b. Aug. 14, 1754	1	107
Lucy, m. James WOODRUFF, Oct. 25, 1775	1	124
Mary Ann, d. Asa & Ann, b. Apr. 3, 1819	2	143
Reuben Smith, s. James & Elizabeth, b. May 23, 1786	1	149
Rhoda D., m. Samuel WHEELER, of Monroe, Feb. 17, 1824, by Rev. Henry Robinson, of South Farms	2	95
Robbert Hubbard, s. James & Elizabeth, b. July 20, 1789	1	149
Samuel B., s. Asa & Ann, b. May 29, 1824	2	143
Samuel Hubbard, s. James & Elizabeth, b. Feb. 6, 1788	1	149

	Vol.	Page
MORRIS, (cont.),		
Sarah Jane, d. Asa & Ann, b. Dec. 28, 1821	2	143
Sidney W., of Canaan, m. Esther A **NICKERSON**, of Litchfield, July 4, [1852], by N. C. Lewis	TM49	76
Timothy Dwight, s. James & Rhoda, b. Nov. 22, 1817	2	22
MORSE, MORS, [see also **MOSS**], Abby J., of Litchfield, m. Stephen **BECKWITH**, of Lyme, Nov. 7, 1853, by Rev. H. N. Weed	TM49	92
Abigail, m. Isaac **BALDWIN, Jr.**, b. of litchfield, Oct. 1, 1846, by Rev. William Dixon	TM49	16
Alvin, m. Esther **JOHNSON**, May 29, 1810, by Rev. Joseph E. Camp	2	54
Alvira, d. Caleb & Content, b. July 12, 1818	2	77
Augustus, s. Caleb & Content, b. Feb. 6, 1816	2	77
Belinda, d. Alvin & Esther, b. Feb. 6, 1817	2	54
Belinda, d. Alvin & Esther, d. Sept. 13, 1818	2	54
Benjamin Hart, m. Emiline Maria **CARRINGTON**, b. of Litchfield, Apr. 20, 1836, by Rev. Samuel Fuller, Jr.	2	296
Berthena, m. Harvey **PERKINS**, June 24, 1821, by Rev. Joseph E. Camp	2	106
Bethiah J., of Litchfield, m. Zelotes C. **GRANT**, of East Winsor, Apr. 30, 1832, by Levi Peck	2	290
Betsey M., of Litchield, m. Edward A. **DEMING**, of Berlin, Jan. 10, 1850, by Rev. William B. Hoyt	TM49	53
Caroline, d. Harley & Susan, b. July 2, 1821	2	134
Charles, s. Caleb & Content, b. May 15, 1814	2	77
David, s. Caleb & Content, b. Jan. 15, 1809	2	77
David, m. Delia **FRENCH**, Sept. 1, 1833, by Rev. Joseph E. Camp, of Northfield	2	292
Delia, d. Alvin & Esther, b. Mar. 24, 1818	2	54
Edwin R., s. [Orrin], b. Aug. 26, 1834	2	26
Eliza, of Litchfield, m. David P. **PARDY**, of Plymouth, Mar. 20, 1848, by Joseph Henson	TM49	23
Emeline, m. Francis **PRATT**, Sept. 10, 1832, by Rev. Joseph E. Camp, of Northfield	2	292
Emily A., m. Holmes O. **MORSE**, b. of Litchfield, Apr. 16, 1845, by G. C. V. Eastman	TM49	9
Esther Hart, d. Alvin & Esther, b. Oct. 24, 1813	2	54
Frederick, m. Mary Ann **TOMPKINS**, Mar. 19, 1848, by Rev. David L. Parmelee	TM49	22
George Eliakim, s. Harley [& Susan], b. Oct. 27, 1827	2	134
George Wyllys, s. Alvin & Esther, b. Mar. 2, 1811	2	54
George Wyllys, s. Alvin & Esther, d. Feb. 28, 1820	2	54
Harley, m. Susan **HALL**, Feb. 15, 1817, by Rev. James Noyce	2	134
Harley, of Wallingford, m. Harriet **MORSE**, May 9, 1821, by Rev. Joseph E. Camp	2	106
Harley, m. Harriet E. **ENSIGN**, Oct. 21, 1845, by Rev. David L. Parmelee	TM49	11
Harriet, m. Jacob **MORSE**, Mar. 14, 1821, by Rev. Joseph E. Camp	2	106
Harriet, m. Harley **MORSE**, of Wallingford, May 9, 1821, by Rev. Joseph E. Camp	2	106
Henry, m. Martha E. **JOHNSON**, Nov. 27, 1850, by Rev. David L. Parmelee	TM49	55
Holmes, s. Harley & Susan, b. Feb. 14, 1818	2	134
Holmes O., m. Emily A. **MORSE**, b. of Litchfield, Apr. 16, 1845, by		

	Vol.	Page
MORSE, MORS, [see also **MOSS**], (cont.),		
G. C. V. Eastman	TM49	9
Huldah, m. Hull **CHURCHILL**, Mar. 11, 1807, by Daniel Potter, J.P.	2	144
Jacob, m. Harriet **MORSE**, Mar. 14, 1821, by Rev. Joseph E. Camp	2	106
Jacob, Jr., m. Mary Jane **WHEELER**, b. of Litchfield, Oct. 16, 1848, by [Joseph Henson]	TM49	27
James M., m. Lucia A. **EMMONS**, b. of Litchfield, Mar. 25, 1839, by Rev. Richard Woodruff	2	324
John N., s. [Orrin], b. May 13, 1831	2	26
Joseph S., Rev., m. Jane **JOHNSON**, b. of Litchfield, May 6, 1845, by Rev. D. L. Marks	TM49	9
Julia Maria, d. Alvin & Esther, b. Aug. 7, 1812	2	54
Leander, s. Alvin & Esther, b. Sept. 20, 1815	2	54
Lemuel D., of Harwinton, m. Mary Ann **CHASE**, of Litchfield, Oct. 10, 1837, by Rev. Lewis Gunn	2	315
Lewis, m. Lydia **RHODEN**, Oct. 19, 1830, by Rev. William Lucas	2	286
Lucretia, d. Jacob & Harriet, b. Aug. 23, 1823	2	106
Lucretia Hall, d. Harley [& Susan], b. Jan. 18, 1834	2	134
Lurena E., m. Ezra H. **CHURCHILL**, b. of Litchfield, May 11, 1845, by Rev. Joel L. Dickinson, of Northfield	TM49	10
Mariann, d. Harley & Susan, b. Dec. 14, 1819	2	134
Mary Ann, Mrs., of Milton, m. Lewis **BAKER**, of La Fayette, N.Y., Nov. 23, 1841, by Ralph Smith	2	335
Mary Ann, of Litchfield, m. Dr. Timothy **LANGDON**, of Naugatuc, Dec. 21, 1841, by Jonathan Brace	2	320
Merret, s. Caleb & Content, b. Sept. 20, 1813	2	77
Munson, s. Caleb & Content, b. Apr. 4, 1820	2	77
Orrila, m. Lewis **PERKINS**, Aug. 16, 1826, by Joseph E. Camp	2	266
Patty, of Litchfield, m. Edward **CHURCHILL**, of Canojahary, Oct. 31, 1822, by Rev. William Bentley	2	116
Philena, m. Linus **MARSH**, Nov. 28, 1821, by Rev. Joseph E. Camp	2	107
Riley, s. Caleb & Content, b. Apr. 7, 1806	2	77
Roxania, m. Herman B. **MOSS**, b. of Litchfield, Oct. 18, 1840, at Waterbury, by Rev. Charles Chittenden	2	325
Sally, m. John **COLEBEY**, Sept. 2, 1832, by Truman Kilborn, J.P.	2	292
Samuel, s. Caleb & Content, b. Nov. 25, 1811	2	77
Sidney J., s. Orin, b. July 25, 1828	2	26
Susan, m. Nathan **FRENCH**, Dec. 27, 1826, by Rev. Joseph E. Camp, of Northfield	2	292
Susan S., of Litchfield, m. Thomas W. **WELLS**, of Plymouth, May 7, 1840, by Jonathan Brace	2	318
MOSES, Richard, of Torrington, m. Emeliza **PRITCHARD**, of Litchfield, Apr. 12, 1835, by Truman Kilborn, J.P.	2	298
MOSS, [see also **MORSE**], Aaron, s. Amos & Elizabeth, b. Sept. 26, 1794	2	19
Abraham, s. Amos & Elizabeth, b. Apr. 25, 1786	2	19
Abraham, m. Elizabeth **MARSH**, Nov. 10, 1807, by Rev. J. E. Camp	2	35
Amasa, m. Eleanor **COLVER**, Nov. 17, 1768	1	107
Amos, m. Rachel* **CULVER**, Dec. 13, 1777 *(In the births of the children the name is given "Elizabeth")	2	19
Amy, d. Isaac, b. July 6, 1812	2	128
Amy, m. George **JOHNSON**, Dec. 7, 1831, by Rev. Mr. Taylor, of South Farms	2	289
Amy, m. George **JOHNSON**, Dec. 7, 1831, by Rev. Mr. Taylor, of		

	Vol.	Page
MOSS, [see also **MORSE**], (cont.),		
South Farms	2	326
Anna, d. Philo & Rachel, b. June 11, 1796	2	71
Asahel H., m. Lucinda E. **BALDWIN**, b. of Litchfield, Apr. 19, 1848,		
by Benjamin L. Swan	TM49	24
Asahel Hall, s. John & Mehetabel, b. Apr. 7, 1786	1	189
Aurelia, d. Levi, Jr. & Thala, b. Oct. 19, 1806	2	79
Barthena, d. Levi, Jr. & Thala, b. Sept. 16, 1797	2	79
Barthena, m. Harvey **PERKINS**, June 24, 1821, by Rev. Joseph E. Camp	2	122
Bethiah F., d. Stephen & Lovisa, b. Dec. 27, 1811	2	35
Betsey Maria, d. John, Jr. & Sally, b. Jan. 12, 1815	2	39
Caleb, s. David & Eunice, b. Sept. 4, 1783	1	189
Caleb, m. Content **SUTLEFF**, [ ], 1803, by Daniel Potter, J.P.	2	77
Caroline Amanda, d. Moses & Caroline, b. Mar. 27, 1824	2	134
Charles Emory, s. Moses & Caroline, b. Dec. 11, 1818	2	134
Cynthia, d. Isaac, b, July 15, 1803	2	128
Damy, d. Isaac, b. June 23, 1814	2	128
David & Eunice, had d. [ ], b. Apr. 7, 1786; d. Oct. 7, 1792	1	189
Elizabeth, d. Amos & Elizabeth, b. Aug. 3, 1778	2	19
Elizabeth, d. Ives & Elizabeth, b. Dec. 23, 1788	1	189
Elizabeth, m. Reuben **SMITH, 3rd**, Dec. 10, 1795, by Rev. J. E. Camp	2	30
Elizabeth, d. Abraham & Elizabeth, b. Feb. 17, 1820	2	35
Ephraim Hall, s. David & Eunice, b. Sept. 13, 1778	1	107
Esther, d. Philo & Rachel, b. July 28, 1798	2	71
Eunice, d. David & Eunice, b. Oct. 10, 1791	1	189
Fanny, d. Isaac, b. Oct. 19, 1810	2	128
Fanny, m. George **ADDIS**, Nov. 29, 1832, by Rev. Mr. Taylor, of South		
Farms	2	289
Harley, s. John & Mehitabel, b. Oct. 6, 1792	1	189
Hariet, d. Levi, Jr. & Thala, b. Mar. 17, 1800	2	79
Harriet, d. Philo & Rachel, b. July 1, 1803	2	71
Herman B., m. Roxania **MORSE**, b. of Litchfield, Oct. 18, 1840, at		
Waterbury, by Rev. Charles Chittenden	2	325
Huldah, d. Ives & Elizabeth, b. Aug. 1, 1790	1	189
Isaac, s. Amos & Elizabeth, b. Apr. 20, 1784	2	19
Isaac, s. Isaac, b. July 1, 1806	2	128
Isaac, Jr., m. Nancy **BALDWIN**, b. of Litchfield, Jan. 7, 1830, by Rev.		
Bradley Sillick	2	284
Isaac, m. [ ]	2	128
Ives, s. Amos & Elizabeth, b. Mar. 9, 1767	1	107
Ives, s. Amos & Elizabeth, b. Mar. 9, 1769	1	189
Ives, m. Elizabeth **LORD**, Dec. 20, 1787, by Rev. Judah Champion	1	189
Jacob, s. Amos & Elizabeth, b. Mar. 6, 1792	2	19
Jacob, m. Lucretia **GILBERT**, Nov. 8, 1813, by Rev. Mr. Wheeler, of		
Watertown	2	40
James Harvey, s. Stephen & Lovisa, b. June 26, 1817	2	35
James Marsh, s. Abraham & Elizabeth, b. [ ], 1815	2	35
John, m. Mehetable **HALL**, May 14, 1773, by Rev. Mr. Waterman	1	189
John, s. John & Mahetabel, b. Mar. 27, 1784	1	189
John, Jr., m. Sally **LUWIN** (?), Mar. 20, 1810 by [ ] Patterson	2	39
John Sherman, s. Levi & Martha, b. Feb. 10, 1774	1	24
John Sherman, s. Levi & Martha, b. Feb. 10, 1774	2	30
Joseph Lee, s. John, Jr. & Sally, b. Dec. 15, 1810	2	39

	Vol.	Page
MOSS, [see also **MORSE**], (cont.),		
Katurah, d. David & Eunice, b. Feb. 20, 1785	1	189
Ketura, m. William **CHURCHILL**, Dec. 24, 1800, by Rev. Joseph E. Camp	2	3
Laura, d. Levi & Martha, b. Oct. 15, 1791	2	30
Laura, m. John **GARNSEY**, May 28, 1817, by Rev. Joseph E. Camp	2	88
Levi, m. Martha **SHERMAN**, Jan. 14, 1773, by Rev. David Judson, of Newtown	1	24
Levi, m. Martha **SHERMAN**, Jan. 14, 1773, by Rev. Mr. Judson, of Newtown	2	30
Levi, s. Levi & Martha, b. Sept. 19, 1775	1	107
Levi, s. Levi & Martha, b. Sept. 19, 1775	2	30
Levi, Jr., m. Thala **SANFORD**, Oct. 26, 1796, by Rev. Joseph E. Camp	2	79
Levi, s. Levi, Jr. & Thala, b. Mar. 14, 1822	2	79
Levi Andrus, s. Levi, Jr. & Thala, b. July 14, 1814	2	79
Lewis A., s. Jacob & Lucretia, b. Feb. 16, 1817	2	40
Linus G., s. Jacob & Lucretia, b. June 28, 1814	2	40
Linus G., m. Angeline H. **HUBBARD**, b. of Litchfield, Feb. 26, 1838, by Rev. Lewis Gunn	2	315
Louiza, d. Philo & Rachel, b. Mar. 17, 1810	2	71
Louisa, of Litchfield, m. Oman **MOSS**, of Harwinton, Feb. 27, 1828, at the house of Philo Moss, by Rev. Seth Higby	2	276
Lucretia, of Litchfield, m. Samuel P. **WHITING**, of Plymouth, May 28, 1845, by Rev. D. L. Marks	TM49	10
Lucy, d. John & Mahetabel, b. Dec. 12, 1781	1	189
Margary, d. Levi & Martha, b. May 19, 1778	2	30
Martha, d. John & Mahetabel, b. July 5, 1776	1	189
Martha, d. Levi & Martha, b. Mar. 24, 1785	2	30
Martha, m. Eldad **SMITH**, Dec. 12, 1792, by James Morris	1	201
Mathew, s. Isaac, b. Nov. 4, 1804	2	128
Matthew, m. Minerva **WHEELER**, Mar. 31, 1839, by Rev. Gad N. Smith	2	319
Mehetabel, d. John & Mehetabel, b. Jan. 24, 1790	1	189
Miles, s. David & Eunice, b. May 7, 1782	1	189
Monson, s. Isaac, b. Dec. 10, 1821	2	128
Moses, s. Amos & Elizabeth, b. Sept. 3, 1796	2	19
Moses, m. Caroline **CATLIN**, Feb. 18, 1818, by Rev. Elisha P. Jacobs	2	134
Olive, d. Levi & Martha, b. Aug. 24, 1789	2	30
Oman, of Harwinton, m. Louisa **MOSS**, of Litchfield, Feb. 27, 1828, at the house of Philo Moss, by Rev. Seth Higby	2	276
Orelia, d. Levi & Martha, b. Jan. 15, 1781	2	30
Orson, s. Solomon, Jr. & Hannah, b. Mar. 20, 1804	2	6
Orson, m. Laura **EMONS**, Jan. 16, 1837, by Dan Catlin	2	297
Orson M., s. Abraham & Elizabeth, b. Nov. 15, 1810	2	35
Philena, d. Levi, Jr. & Thala, b. Oct. 13, 1803	2	79
Philo, m. Rachel **WEBSTER**, Apr. 24, 1794, by Rev. Judah Champion	2	71
Philo, s. Philo & Rachel, b. Apr. 15, 1801	2	71
Polly, d. Levi & Martha, b. Dec. 1, 1786	2	30
Polly, m. Erastus **HALL**, [ ], 1796, by Rev. James Noyes	2	76
Polly, d. Solomon, Jr. & Hannah, b. Nov. 2, 1805	2	6
Polly, d. Levi, Jr. & Thala, b. Nov. 25, 1817	2	79
Polly, m. Hull **CHURCHILL**, Feb. 11, 1819	2	144
Rachel, d. Amos & Elizabeth, b. Jan. 29, 1780	2	19

	Vol.	Page
MOSS, [see also **MORSE**], (cont.),		
Rachel, d. Philo & Rachel, b. Sept. 19, 1805	2	71
Rachel, d. Abraham & Elizabeth, b. May 29, 1823	2	35
Rachel, m. Isaac **BALDWIN, Jr.,** [ ], by Rev. Mr. Camp	2	412
Roxanna, d. Isaac, b. Nov. 24, 1816	2	128
Sabra, d. Amos & Elizabeth, b. May 21, 1789	2	19
Sally, d. Philo & Rachel, b. Dec. 21, 1807	2	71
Sally, m. Senetor **BLAKESLEE,** Mar. 23, 1825, by Rev. Seth Higbey	2	139
Sarah, d. John & Mahitabel, b. Feb. 17, 1774	1	189
Solomon, Jr., m. Huldah **GILBERT,** Dec. 31, 1800, by Daniel Catlin	2	6
Sophira, d. Abraham & Elizabeth, b. July 25, 1808	2	35
Sophia, d. Abraham, m. George **NEWTON,** b. of Litchfield, June 28, 1827, by Rev. Frederick W. Sizer	2	271
Spelman, s. Solomon, Jr. & Hannah, b. Aug. 27, 1802	2	6
Stephen, s. Levi & Martha, b. Nov. 26, 1782	2	30
Stephen, m. Lovisa **SMITH,** Dec. 25, 1810, by Rev. Mr. Scranton	2	35
Susan, d. Caleb & Content, b. May 15, 1804	2	77
Susan S., d. Stephen & Lovisa, b. Feb. 1, 1814	2	35
Susanna, d. Ives & Elizabeth, b. Aug. [ ], 1792	1	189
Thala Ann, d. Levi, Jr. & Thala, b. June 19, 1811	2	79
Thankfull, d. Amos & Elizabeth, b. Mar. 4, 1782	2	19
William Edwin, s. Moses & Caroline, b. Nov. 1, 1821	2	134
W[illia]m W., m. Abigail **PERKINS,** Mar. 12, 1834, by Rev. L. P. Hickok	2	288
William Wyllys, s. John, Jr. & Sally, b. Sept. 2, 1812	2	39
MOULBECBIER, Alonzo, of Batavia, N.Y., m. Caroline **BROWN,** of Litchfield, Apr. 25, 1830, by Rev. L. P. Hickok	2	285
MOULTHROP, MOUTHROP, MOULTHOP, MOUNTHOP, Alvira, d. Solomon & Polly, b. Mar. 8, 1815	2	259
Anna, d. William & Mary, b. Nov. 23, 1804	2	25
Anna, d. William & Mary, d. Aug. 28, 1805	2	25
Erastus P., s. William & Mary, b. Dec. 6, 1815	2	25
Harriet, d. William & Mary, b. May 30, 1818	2	25
Harriet, m. Hiram **KILBORN,** b. of Litchfield, [Dec.] 24, [1840], by G. C. V. Eastman, in Milton Soc.	2	332
Jacob, s. William & Mary, b. Apr. 7, 1797	2	25
Jacob, s. William & Mary, d. Sept. 4, 1800	2	25
Jemima, d. Solomon & Polly, b. June 22, 1804	2	259
Jemima, of Litchfield, m. Samuel Hobson **WESTON,** of Warren, Apr. 26, 1829, by I. Jones	2	280
Lucy Ann, of Litchfield, m. Sylvanus M. **TODD,** of Warren, Jan. 30, 1848, by John F. Norton	TM49	22
Luman, s. Solomon & Polly, b. Sept. 3, 1809	2	259
Luzerne, m. Margarette **ANDREWS,** Nov. 10, 1844, by Rev. D. L. Parmelee	TM49	6
Lyman, s. Solomon & Polly, b. Apr. 25, 1811	2	259
Marian, d. William & Mary, b. Jan. 6, 1807	2	25
Melinda, d. William & Mary, b. Apr. 27, 1809	2	25
Orrin, s. William & Mary, b. Jan. 8, 1795	2	25
Orrin, s. William & Mary, d. Nov. 7, 1806	2	25
Polly, m. Jesse **OSBORN,** Mar. 12, 1807, by Rev. Truman Marsh	2	4
Solomon, m. Polly **STONE,** July 11, 1797, by John Welch, J.P.	2	259
Solomon, s. Solomon & Polly, b. Nov. 6, 1801	2	259

	Vol.	Page
MOULTHROP, MOUTHROP, MOULTHOP, MOUNTHOP, (cont.),		
Thala, d. William & Mary, b. Sept. 3, 1799	2	25
Thala, d. William & Mary, d. Sept. 3, 1800	2	25
Thala, 2nd, d. William & Mary, b. July 14, 1801	2	25
Thalia, of Litchfield, m. Benjamin **SACKETT**, of Warren, Oct. 31,		
1827, by Rev. Hart Talcott	2	273
Truman, s. Solomon & Polly, b. July 21, 1807	2	259
William, m. Mary **PAGE**, Nov. 27, 1793, by John Welsh	2	25
William, s. William & Mary, b. Sept. 26, 1812	2	25
William, s. William & Mary, d. Jan. 19, 1819	2	25
MOUNTHOP, [see under **MOULTHROP**]		
MUCLESTONE*, Lucia, m. David **BEECH**, Jan. 24, 1765, by Rev. Judah		
Champion *("**MUDESTONE**" in Woodruff's)	1	126
MUNGER, MONGER, Abigail, d. Julius & Mary*, b. Jan. 18, 1821		
*("Anna"?)	2	147
Abigail E., m. John C. **FULLER**, b. of Litchfield, Mar. 1, 1841, by Rev.		
Thomas Ellis	2	333
Amey, d. Joel, b. June 10, 1795	2	263
Asahel, s. Daniel & Eunice, b. June 3, 1770	1	149
Betsey, d. Joel, b. Apr. 1, 1789	2	263
Calvin, s. Daniel & Eunice, b. Nov. 12, 1776	1	149
Charles T., s. Julius & Mary*, b. Jan. 18, 1819 *("Anna"?)	2	147
Charlotte, d. Elisha S. & Polly, b. June 25, 1784	1	189
Charlotte, m. William **WARD, Jr.**, Mar. [ ], 1803	2	37
Clarinda, d. Julius & Mary*, b. Sept. 5, 1823 *("Anna"?)	2	147
Cornelia, d. Joel & Hannah, b. Feb. 8, 1819	2	263
Cinthia, d. Joel, b. Aug. 22, 1803	2	263
Daniel, s. Daniel & Eunice, b. Aug. 12, 1765	1	149
Elisha, s. Elisah S. & Polly, b. Oct. 26, 1790	1	189
Elisha S., m. Polly **KILBORN**, Oct. 29, 1783, by Rev. James Nichols	1	189
Eunice, m. Abijah **WARREN**, Dec. 11, 1777, by Rev. George Beckwith	1	165
George Miles, s. Julius [& Anna], b. Feb. 9, 1826	2	147
Hinman, s. Joel & [ ], b. July 22, 1792	2	263
James C., s. Julius [& Anna], b. Dec. 3, 1831	2	147
Joel, m. [ ], Nov. 4, 1783, by Rev. James Nichols	2	263
Joel, his w. [ ], d. Sept. 3, 1807, ae 43 y.	2	263
Joel, m. Hanna **INGRAHAM**, Mar. 1, 1812, by William Cogswell, J.P.	2	263
Julia A., m. James **TROWBRIDGE**, b. of Litchfield, June 20, 1852, by		
N. C. Lewis	TM49	76
Julius, s. Elisha S. & Polly, b. July 12, 1785	1	189
Julius, m. Mary* **WOODCOCK**, Sept. 24, 1809, by Rev. [ ]		
*(Arnold Copy says "Anna")	2	147
Lanman, s. Joel, b. Nov. 22, 1786	2	263
Lanman, s. Joel, d. Oct. 8, 1807, ae 21 y.	2	263
Lorenzo, m. Catharine **MORRIS**, b. of Litchfield, Jan. 2, 1853, by Rev.		
John J. Brandegee	TM49	77
Lorian, d. Julius & Mary*, b. Nov. 28, 1814 *("Anna"?)	2	147
Mary Kerwin, m. William **FISHER**, June 3, 1810, by Rev. Truman		
Marsh	2	0
Nelson, s. Julius & Mary*, b. Sept. 30, 1810 *("Anna"?)	2	147
Ozias, s. Julius & Mary*, b. Feb. 17, 1817 *("Anna"?)	2	147
Pamela, of Litchfield, m. Levi **PLATT**, of Winchester, Nov. [ ], 1823,		
by Rev. Lyman Beecher	2	127

	Vol.	Page
MUNGER, MONGER, (cont.),		
Polly, d. Elisha S. & Polly, b. May 26, 1787	1	189
Polly, d. Joel, b. July 27, 1791	2	263
Rachel A., d. Samuel & Rhoda, b. May 2, 1819	2	33
Rachel H., of Litchfield, m. [ ] **RUSSELL**, of Torrington, Dec. 13, 1840, by J. Brace	2	320
Rhoda, d. Daniel & Eunice, b. May 20, 1768	1	149
Rufus Elisha, s. Samuel & Rhoda, b. Apr. 2, 1821	2	33
Sabra, of Litchfield, m. Jane **BENTON**, of Bainbridge, N.Y., Mar. 24, 1849, by Rev. Isaac Jones	TM49	42
Samuel, m. Rhoda **SIMONS**, Apr. 30, 1818, by Seth Landon, J.P.	2	33
Sarah, d. Samuel & Rhoda, b. Oct. 5, 1822	2	33
Sarah Ann, d. Julius & Mary *, b. Aug. 22, 1812 *("Anna"?)	2	147
Sarah Ann, m. James **SMITH**, b. of Litchfield, [Nov.] 12, [1843], by Jonathan Brace	2	413
Sheldon, m. Jane **CASKEY**, b. of Litchfield, July 8, 1849, by Samuel Fuller	TM49	42
Susan, d. Joel & Hannah, b. May 7, 1815	2	263
Truman, s. Joel, b. Dec. 29, 1799	2	263
William, s. Joel, d. Jan. 30, 1788	2	263
William, s. Joel, b. July 30, 1802	2	263
William, 2nd, s. Joel, d. Feb. [ ], 1805	2	263
William, s. Joel & Hannah, b. Dec. 20, 1812	2	263
William, s. Joel, b. [ ]	2	263
MUNSON, MONSON, Alice, [w. William], d. May 6, 1821	2	269
Benjamin, m. Minerva **BEACH**, Aug. 21, 1821, by Rev. Isaac Jones	2	103
Charles, s. William & Olive, b. Jan. 8, 1799	2	86
Charles Bradley, s. W[illia]m & Alice, b. Jan. 6, 1821; d. Sept. 14, 1825	2	269
Clarissa, d. William & Olive, b. Feb. 18, 1803	2	86
Cornelia, d. W[illia]m & Polly, b. Mar. 22, 1825	2	269
Cornelia A., m. William L. **WOODRUFF**, Sept. 6, 1846, by Rev. David L. Parmelee	TM49	14
Delia, Mrs. of Cheshire, m. David W. **WOOD**, of Litchfield, Oct. 26, [1851], by N. C. Lewis	TM49	66
Garit, s. William & Olive, b. July 27, 1791, at Plymouth	2	86
George W., s. William & Olive, b. May 9, 1807	2	86
Henry, of East Bloomfield, Ontario Cty., N.Y., m. Arsena **MIGEON**, of Litchfield, Feb. 26, 1849, by Rev. Samuel Fuller	TM49	36
Julius, s. W[illia]m & Alice, b. Feb. 17, 1818	2	269
Levitt, s. William & Olive, b. Apr. 4, 1795, at Plymouth	2	86
Leavitt, m. Mrs. Almira **HALLOCK**, Jan. 4, 1852, by Rev. David L. Parmelee	TM49	66
Lucius E., s. William & Olive, b. Mar. 27, 1810* *(Followed by "1809")	2	86
Michael D., s. William & Olive, b. Feb. 15, 1805	2	86
Olive, d. William & Olive, b. Feb. 21, 1801	2	86
Phebe A., m. Elias C. **WOODRUFF**, May 8, 1845, by Rev. David L. Parmelee	TM49	10
Phebe Ann, d. W[illia]m & Polly, b. Apr. 5, 1823	2	269
Ransom, s. William & Olive, b. Jan. 9, 1797	2	86
Salena, d. Feb. 19, 1819	2	269
William, m. Olive **DAYTON**, Mar. 30, 1790, by Rev. Mr. Gridley	2	86
William, s. William & Olive, b. Jan. 10, 1793, at Plymouth	2	86

	Vol.	Page

MUNSON, MONSON, (cont.),

William, Jr., m. Alice **EMMONS**, Sept. 5, 1815 — 2 — 269

W[illia]m, Jr., m. Polly **BENTON**, Mar. 19, 1822 — 2 — 269

William, m. Elizabeth **FORD**, Sept. 6, 1835, by Rev. Rufus Babcock — 2 — 86

William, of New York State, m. Elizabeth **FORD**, of Litchfield, Sept. 22, 1835, by Rev. Rufus Babcock — 2 — 298

William Elijah, of New Haven, m. Hannah Roxana **FISHER**, of Litchfield, June 15, 1835, by Rev. Samuel Fuller, Jr. — 2 — 296

William H., s. W[illia]m & Alice, b. Aug. 1, 1816 — 2 — 269

[MURDOCK], MARDOCK, Anna, m. David **MARSH**, Jan. 19, 1809, by Rev. William Andrews — 2 — 32

MURPHY, W[illia]m, m. Ellenor **CARROLL**, Sept. 24, 1854, by Thomas H. Hendricken — TM49 — 100

MURRAY, MURRY, Esther, d. Hezekiah & Eunice, b. May 8, 1797 — 2 — 85

Esther, of Litchfield, m. Orlando F. **CRANE**, of Litchfield, Feb. 22, 1832, by Rev. Mr. Taylor, of South Farms — 2 — 289

Eunice Hotchkiss, w. Hezekiah, d. Oct. 19, 1813, ae 59 — 2 — 85

George M., m. Phebe M. **THOMAS**, b. of Litchfield, Jan. 1, 1828, by Rev. Henry Robinson, of South Farms — 2 — 274

George Marsh, s. Hezekiah & Eunice, b. May 17, 1803 — 2 — 85

Henry Augustus, s. Hezekiah & Eunice, b. Apr. 6, 1805 — 2 — 85

Hezekiah, m. Eunice **CAMP**, May 29, 1796, by Rev. Amos Chase — 2 — 85

Hezekiah, m. Huldah **HOTCHKISS**, [ ], 1815 — 2 — 85

Lucy, d. Hezekiah & Huldah, b. Sept. [ ], 1816 — 2 — 85

Philemon, s. Hezekiah & Eunice, b. May 6, 1801 — 2 — 85

Rufus, Rev., of Ridgeville, O., m. Martha Brooks **ROUSE**, of Woodbury, Nov. 17, 1822, in St Michaels Church, by Rev. Isaac Jones — 2 — 111

Sarah Hotchkiss, d. Hezekiah & Eunice, b. Mar. 9, 1799 — 2 — 85

Silas Hays, m. Sylena Ann **SCOTT**, b. of Woodbury, Nov. 27, 1848, at Bantam Falls, by Rev. F. D. Harriman — TM49 — 39

NASH, Henry, of Canton, m. Eleanora Louisa **FRISBIE**, of Washington, Oct. 15, 1834, by Rev. Samuel Fuller — TM49 — 37

Henry, of Canton, m. Eleanor L. **FRISBIE**, of Washington, Oct. 15, 1834, by Rev. Samuel Fuller — 2 — 289

Lydia, m. James **KELLOGG**, Nov. [ ], 1779, by Mr. Mather — 2 — 91

NEAL, Dama M., m. Robert **STEVENS**, b. of Litchfield, Nov. 26, [1851], by N. C. Lewis — TM49 — 66

Mary Ann, m. Samuel **BISHOP**, Oct. 30, 1828, by W. Clark, in New York State — 2 — 24

NEGUS, Alanson A., s. John & Harriet, b. Apr. 14, 1824 — 2 — 110

Ambrose Norton, s. John & Harriet, b. July 23, 1826 — 2 — 110

Amelia P., of Litchfield, m. John N. **ENSIGN**, of Watertown, Nov. 1, 1853, by Rev. H. N. Weed — TM49 — 92

Benjamin, s. John [& Harriet], b. Sept. 3, 1831 — 2 — 110

Eliza, d. John & Harriet, b. Nov. 9, 1828 — 2 — 110

Harriet, d. John & Harriet, b. Apr. 2, 1822 — 2 — 110

Harriet, Mrs., m. Henry **WOOD**, b. of Litchfield, Nov. 21, 1847, by Joseph Henson — TM49 — 23

Harriet P., m. Charles T. **WHAPLES**, Nov. 28, 1839, by Rev. Jonathan Brace — 2 — 318

John, m. Harriet Wait **PILGER**, Sept. 1, 1816, by Rev. Joseph Vaill — 2 — 110

John P., s. John & Harriet, b. Dec. 14, 1819 — 2 — 110

	Vol.	Page
NEGUS, (cont.),		
Joseph, m. Mary Ann **PLANT**, June 24, 1829, by I. Jones	2	281
Lydia J., m. John L. **VAN SICKLES**, June 30, 1850, by William B. Hoyt	TM49	54
Phebe Ann, m. Henry M. **JOHNSON**, b. of Litchfield, Sept. 1, 1844, by Rev. Johnson Howard, of Northfield & South Dover, N.Y.	TM49	55
William C., s. John & Harriet, b. Sept. 23, 1817	2	110
NEILE, Henry, of Litchfield, m. Abby J. **WILLIAMS**, of Watertown, Mar. 26, 1848, by Rev. Isaac Jones	TM49	24
NETTLETON, Laura, m. Asa **HOPKINS**, Nov. 7, 1811, by Rev. Luke Wood	2	80
Naomi, m. Hiram **CHURCHILL**, Nov. 25, 1830, by Rev. Joseph E. Camp, of Northfield	2	292
NEVINS, NIVINS, Anna, d. Samuel & Elizabeth, b. Mar. 24, 1811	2	26
Birdsey, s. Samuel & Elizabeth, b. Oct. 22, 1802	2	26
Birdsey, m. Jane F. **STARR**, Sept. 1, 1834, by Rev. L. P. Hickok	2	288
Elizabeth, d. Samuel & Elizabeth, b. Mar. 8, 1808	2	26
George Whitfield, s. Samuel & Elizabeth, b. Feb. 17, 1814	2	26
James, s. Samuel & Elizabeth, b. Apr. 14, 1805	2	26
Samuel, m. Elizabeth **SEYMOUR**, [ ]	2	26
Ursula B., of Litchfield, m. Horace **HOLISTER**, of Farmington, Feb. 18, 1823, by Rev. Truman Marsh	2	118
Ursula Bull, d. Samuel [& Elizabeth], b. Jan. 5, 1797	2	26
William Seymour, s. Samuel & Elizabeth, b. Feb. 7, 1800	2	26
NEWBURY, NEWBRE, Ama, d. John & Prudence, b. Feb. 15, 1752/3	1	67
Elias, s. John & Prudence, b. Apr. 20, 1751	1	67
John, of Middletown, m. Prudence **STONE**, of Guilford, May 10, 1750	1	67
Joseph A., m. Paulena M. **WILCOX**, Apr. 11, 1838, by Rev. Stephen Hubbell	2	320
Lidia, d. John & Prudence, b. Nov. 30, 1755	1	67
NEWCOMB, Alexander R., m. Rebecca R. **BEEBE**, Apr. 6, 1835, by Rev. L. P. Hickok	2	296
Clarissa, d. James C. & Mary, b. Oct. [ ], 1823	2	146
Clarissa A., of Litchfield, m. James **SCOTT, Jr.**, of Falls Villiage, Oct. 1, 1848, by John F. Norton	TM49	26
Clark, of Williamstown, Vt., m. Julia Ann **BUEL**, of Litchfield, Apr. 22, 1833, by Rev. Samuel Fuller	TM49	37
Clark, m. Julia Ann **BUEL**, Apr. 22, 1833, by Rev. Samuel Fuller	2	289
James B., s. James C. & Mary, b. Sept. 5, 1820	2	146
James B., m. Rosanna **KEELER**, b. of Litchfield, Apr. 17, 1849, by Rev. F. D. Harriman, of Bantam Falls	TM49	36
James C., m. Mercey **BURCH**, July 4, 1819, by Rev. Isaac Jones	2	146
Phebe, m. Jedediah **GUILD**, Aug. 31, 1823, by Rev. Isaac Jones	2	122
NEWELL, Franklin, m. Esther **BRISTOL**, Mar. 18, 1846, by Rev. David L. Parmelee	TM49	14
Mary, m. Timothy **GRISWOLD**, Mar. 18, 1771, by Rev. Mr. Hawley, of Farmington	1	136-8
NEWTON, NUTON, Emily, d. Isaac & Polly, b. June 6, 1816	2	132
Frederick, of Washington, m. S. Minerva **ODELL**, of Litchfield, Jan. 16, 1839. by G. C. V. Eastman	2	314
George, s. Isaac & Polly, b. Apr. 25, 1807	2	132
George, m. Sophia **MOSS**, d. Abraham, b. of Litchfield, June 28, 1827, by Rev. Frederick W. Sizer	2	271

	Vol.	Page
NEWTON, NUTON, (cont.),		
Harriet, m. James **GUANN** (?), b. of Litchfield, Jan. 1, 1851, by Rev.		
Benjamin W. Stone	TM49	61
Isaac, m. Polly **CURTISS**, Nov. 2, 1800, by Daniel Potter	2	132
Isaac, b. Dec. 14, 1801. "Given to Jeremiah **OSBORN** and bp. Jan. 2,		
1803".	1	67
Isaac, d. Sept. 21, 1803, ae 1 y. 9 m.	1	66
Lois, d. Isaac & Polly, b. Sept. 2, 1804	2	132
Lois, m. David **TURNEY**, Sept. 12, 1821, by Rev. Rodney Rossiter, of		
Plymouth	2	104
Mary, d. Isaac & Polly, b. Jan. 29, 1820	2	132
Ranson, s. Isaac & Polly, b. July 4, 1802	2	132
William, s. Isaac & Polly, b. Nov. 26, 1810	2	132
William, representative Apr. 1852, Apr. 1853	2	1558
NICHOLS, Horace, m. Abigail **PARSONS**, of Milton, Jan. 31, 1836, in		
Milton, by Rev. Isaac Jones	2	298
Mary, of Woodbury, m. William **GIBBS**, of Litchfield, Dec. 4, 1745, by		
Rev. Anthony Stoddard, of Woodbury	1	19
Miles, m. Harriet **LAMPMAN**, b. of Litchfield, Dec. 17, 1850, by		
Benjamin L. Swan	TM49	53
Sarah Ann, of Sharon, m. Charles **FREEMAN**, of Litchfield, Aug. 9,		
1848, by Benjamin L. Swan	TM49	24
Silas, m. Emily **COLVER**, July 3, 1835, by Rev. L. P. Hickok	2	296
NICKERSON, Esther A., of Litchfield, m. Sidney W. **MORRIS**, of Canaan,		
July 4, [1852], by N. C. Lewis	TM49	76
NIVINS, [see under **NEVINS**]		
NOBLE, Betsey, m. Aaron C. **GILBERT**, Nov. 22, 1802, by Rev. Joseph E.		
Camp	2	147
NORTH, Louisa, m. Samuel **TAYLOR**, Oct. 11, 1835, by Rev. L. P. Hickok	2	296
Polly, b. Jan. 6, 1785; m. Elisha **STONE**, July 10, 1804	2	28
Sally, m. Ira **BUEL**, Oct. 1, 1809, by Rev. Truman Marsh	2	125
NORTHROP, Abner, m. Ruth **TRUMBULL**, Sept. 14, 1814, by Morris		
Woodruff, J.P.	2	132
Chester L., m. Polly L. **ISBELL**, b. of Litchfield, Oct. 31, 1841, by Rev.		
Jason Wells	2	335
Dewitt Clinton, s. Abner & Ruth, b. Sept. 4, 1817	2	132
Elizabeth Ann, m. Job **SMITH**, Jan. 6, 1803, by Rev. B. Rine (?)	2	83
Ezekiel Trumbull, s. Abner & Ruth, b. July 23, 1819	2	132
Rachel, m. John **CLEMENS, Jr.**, Nov. 20, 1759, by Bushnel Bostwick,		
J.P.	1	46
NORTON, [see also **ORTON**], Ambrose, m. Clarissa **BALDWIN**, Oct. 8,		
1809, by Rev. Judah Champion	2	26
Ambrose, his Gr. Gr. mother & Mary **BAKER**, were sisters and came		
from Stratford & Woodbury	1	0
Betsey E., of Litchfield, m. Thomas P. **POTTER**, of Naugatuck, Nov.		
26, 1846, by Rev. William Dixon	TM49	16
Betsey Stewart, d. Birdsey & Luna, b. June 7, 1810	2	29
Betsey Stewart, d. Birdsey & Luna, d. Mar. 29, 1812	2	29
Birdsey, m. Luna **STEWART**, Sept. 14, 1806, by Rev. Asahel Hooker	2	29
Clarissa Maria, d. Ambrose & Clarissa, b. July 23, 1819	2	26
Dorcas, m. Joseph **BIRD**, Oct. 4, 1721, by Rev. Samuell Whitman	1	45
Ebenezer Miles, s. Miles & Lois, b. Nov. 21, 1799	1	67
Harriet Luna, d. Birdsey & Luna, b. Oct. 1, 1815	2	29

	Vol.	Page
NORTON, [see also **ORTON**], (cont.),		
James Shaw, s. Birdsey & Luna, b. Sept. 8, 1808	2	29
Jane, m. Henry **HALL**, Dec. 23, 1838, by Rev. Stephen Hubbell	2	320
Jeremiah, m. Mary Ann **PECK**, Nov. 18, 1823, by Rev. Lyman Beecher	2	129
Lucius Stewart, s. Birdsey & Luna, b. Feb. 20, 1812	2	29
Lucy Elvira, of Litchfield, m. Edward Arnold **SMITH**, of Naugatuck, Oct. 1, 1848, by Rev. Samuel Fuller	TM49	26
Mariette, of Litchfield, m. Lovett **STIMPSON**, of Norfolk, July 29, 1849, by Rev. William B. Hoyt	TM49	42
Mary, m. Benjamin **TROOP**, Dec. 25, 1813, by Rev. Amos Chase	2	43
Miles, m. Lois **McNEIL**, June 1, 1797, by Rev. Judah Champion	1	67
William, s. Ambrose & Clarissa, b. Mar. 25, 1811	2	26
William, m. Susan **GAYLORD**, May 1, 1845, by George Hastings	TM49	10
William David, s. Miles & Lois, b. Nov. 20, 1798	1	67
NOTT, Charles D., of Hartford, m. Irene **BEACH**, of Milton, Nov. 28, 1844, by Rev. Samuel Tomkins Carpenter, of Milton	TM49	7
Leonard Hartwell, m. Electa **BEACH**, Apr. 13, 1848, by Rev. Samuel Fuller	TM49	38
NOYES, NOYCE, Samuel Murhed, m. Nancy **TRYON**, b. of Wolcottville, Torrington, Aug. 3, 1828, by Rev. W[illia]m R. Gould	2	279
William Franklin, of Stonington, m. Julia Elizabeth **KING**, of Litchfield, Apr. 9, 1837, by Rev. Samuel Fuller	TM49	37
OAKES, Ebenezer, of Gloucester, Mass., m. Eunice M. **TYRRELL**, of Litchfield, Nov. 11, 1838, by William Payne	2	328
O'BRIEN, James, m. Mary **McNEIL**, Oct. 28, 1832, by Rev. L. P. Hickok	2	288
John, m. Emily **McNEILE**, Feb. 7, 1836, by Rev. L. P. Hickok	2	296
ODELL, Martha J., m. Henry **McNEILE**, b. of Litchfield, Oct. 21, 1840, by Rev. William Payne	TM49	18
Martha J., m. Henry L. **McNEILE**, Oct. 21, 1840, by Witlam Payne	2	331
Perry, m. Emily W. **LOOMIS**, Nov. 28, 1849, by Rev. D. L. Parmelee	TM49	44
S. Minerva, of Litchfield, m. Frederick **NEWTON**, of Washington, Jan. 16, 1839, by G. C. V. Eastman	2	314
OLCOTT, Barthena, d. Benoni & Honor, b. July 1, 1809	2	146
Benoni, m. Honor **MERRIAM**, Jan. 18, 1804, by Rev. Alex V. Griswould	2	146
Daniel, s. Benoni & Honor, b. Apr. 17, 1818	2	146
George, s. Benoni & Honor, b. Jan. 16, 1805	2	146
James, s. James & Mary, b. July 23, 1780	1	69
James, s. Benoni & Honor, b. Mar. 5, 1815	2	146
Joel White, s. James & Mary, b. Oct. 23, 1786	1	69
Mary, d. Benoni & Honor, b. June 28, 1806	2	146
Simeon, s. James & Mary, b. June 21, 1784	1	69
OLDS, Aaron, s. Caleb & Abigail, b. May 28, 1751	1	29
OLMSTEAD, David, m. Rachel **WOODRUFF**, Feb. 7, 1771	1	69
Mary, m. Jonah **WOODRUFF**, Nov. 27, 1769	1	125
ORTON, [see also **NORTON**], Abigail, d. Samuel, Jr. & Ruth, b. Apr. 19, 1752	1	29
Abigail, d. Samuel & Ruth, b. Mar. 26, 1771	1	29
Abigail, d. Samuel & Ruth, d. May 6, 1771	1	28
Abigail, wid. Samuel, d. Mar. 25, 1779	1	68
Abigail, d. John & Ruth, b. Apr. 21, 1794	1	153
Ama, d. Lemuel & Mary b. Mar. 22, 1779	1	110-11
Anne, d. Hezekiah & Anne, b. Dec. 1, 1752	1	29

	Vol.	Page
ORTON, [see also **NORTON**], (cont.),		
Anne, m. Jacob **WOODRUFF, Jr.**, Jan. 1, 1772, by Rev. Judah		
Champion	1	124
Anne, d. Lemuel & Mary, b. Jan. 20, 1776	1	110-11
Araunah, s. Samuel & Ruth, d. June 21, 1766	1	28
Araunah, s. Samuel & Ruth, b. June 24, 1769	1	69
Aruna*, m. Lois **GIBBS**, Sept. 1, 1793 *("Araunah")	2	10
Aurora, s. John & Ruth, b. June 22, 1796	1	153
Azariah, s. Samuel & Abigail, b. Aug. 18, 1729	1	29
Azariah, s. Hezekiah & Ann, b. Sept. 25, 1757	1	29
Azariah, s. Samuel & Ruth, b. Dec. 19, 1765	1	29
Azariah, m. Sibel **CLEAVELAND**, Feb. 3, 1780, by Rev. George		
Beckwith	1	110-11
Betsey, d. John & Ruth, b. Jan. 10, 1790	1	153
Betsey, d. Hezekiah & Hannah, b. Aug. 11, 1792	1	153
Betsey M., d. Miles & Lydia, b. Apr. 13, 1805	2	10
Clarissa, d. John & Ruth, b. Feb. 23, 1787	1	153
Damaris, d. Samuel & Ruth, b. July 15, 1767	1	69
Darius, s. Hezekiah & Anne, b. May 18, 1760	1	69
Demas, s. John & Ruth, b. Jan. 25, 1788	1	153
Dennis, s. Azariah & Sarah*, b. Nov. 7, 1781 *("Sybil"?)	1	110-11
Edward S., s. Miles & Lydia, b. Dec. 25, 1809	2	10
Eleanor, d. Hezekiah & Ann, b. July 28, 1758	1	29
Eleanor, m. Charles **WOODRUFF, Jr.**, Aug. 17, 1775, by Rev. George		
Beckwith	1	124
Eliada, s. Hezekiah & Ann, b. May 29, 1748	1	29
Eliada, m. Lucina **HUNGERFORD**, Jan. 10, 1770, by Rev. Mr.		
Chapman, of Farmington	1	69
Eliada, s. Eliada & Lucey, b. Aug. 16, 1775	1	110-11
Elizabeth M., d. Aruna & Lois, b. Jan. 17, 1804	2	10
Esther, d. Samuel, Jr. & Ruth, b. Aug. 22, 1763	1	29
Esther R., d. Aruna & Lois, b. Dec. 6, 1796	2	10
Giddeon, s. Samuel & Abigail, b. Aug. 18, 1732	1	29
Gideon, s. Samuel, Jr. & Ruth, b. Aug. 26, 1753	1	29
Gideon, s. Samuell, Jr. & Ruth, d. Sept. 9, 1753	1	28
Gideon, s. Samuel, Jr. & Ruth, b. July 19, 1754	1	69
Gideon, s. Lemuel & Mary, b. Dec. 31, 1768	1	110-11
Gideon, d. Sept. 29, 1778	1	68
Heman H., m. Mary Ann S. **THOMPSON**, Feb. 24, 1831, by Rev. L. P.		
Hickok	2	286
Hezekiah, s.Samuel & Abigail, b. Apr. 29, 1727	1	29
Hezekiah, m. Anne **SEDGWICK**, Sept. 2, 1745	1	69
Hezekiah, s. Hezekiah & Ann, b. Dec. 2, 1745	1	69
Hezekiah, Jr., m. Phebe **JOHNSON**, July 25, 1767, by Rev. Judah		
Champion	1	69
Hezekiah, s. Hezekiah, Jr. & Phebe, b. June 5, 1768	1	69
Hezekiah, Jr., d. May 25, 1770	1	68
Horatio, s. John & Ruth, b. Nov. 2, 1798	1	153
Huldah, d. Samuel, Jr. & Ruth, b. Apr. 9, 1758	1	69
Huldah, m. Philo **WOODRUFF**, Nov. 3, 1779, by Rev. George Beckwith	2	5
Irene G., d. Aruna & Lois, b. Oct. 13, 1795	2	10
James M., s. Aruna & Lois, b. Oct, 5, 1802	2	10
Jemima, d. Samuel & Abigail, b. Nov. 11, 1740	1	29

	Vol.	Page
ORTON, [see also **NORTON**], (cont.),		
Jemima, m. Archibald **McNEILE, Jr.**, Dec. 31, 1764, by Rev. Judah		
Champion	1	24
John, s. Samuel & Abigail, b. Mar. 4, 1744	1	29
John, s. Samuel & Ruth, b. Mar. 24, 1764	1	69
John, s. Lemuel & Mary, b. Dec. 4, 1770	1	110-11
Leman, s. Eliada & Lucy, b. Sept. 10, 1779	1	110-11
Lemon G., s. Aruna & Lois, b. June 22, 1805	2	10
Lemuel, s. Samuell & Abigail, b. Mar. 24, 1735	1	29
Lemuel, s. Lemuel & Mary, b. Mar. 5, 1761	1	29
Levi, s. Samuell & Ruth, b. Nov. 6, 1750	1	69
Levi, d. May 1, 1776	1	68
Lucia, d. Eliada & Lucie, b. June 29, 1772	1	110-11
Lucy S., d. Aruna & Lois, b. Oct. 22, 1808	2	10
Lucy Smedley, d. Arnah, b. Oct. 22, 1808	1	68
Lydia, m. Horace **PECK**, Jan. [ ], 1821, by Rev. Lyman Beecher	2	99
Maranda, d. Samuel, Jr. & Ruth, b. Apr. 17, 1761	1	29
Marian, d. Lemuel & Mary, b. Jan. 2, 1784	1	110-11
Marian, m. Louden **WEBSTER**, Feb. 14, 1804, by Rev. Dan		
Huntington	1	209
Mary, d. Lemuel & Mary, b. June 21, 1762	1	29
Mary, m. Ephraim **BURTON**, July 10, 1788	1	213
Mary, m. Marshall **TOMPKINS**, Feb. [ ], 1821, by Rev. Lyman		
Beecher	2	100
Mary A., d. Aruna & Lois, b. Feb. 25, 1801	2	10
Miles, s. Samuel & Ruth, b. Mar. 21, 1774	1	69
Miles, m. Lidia **GIBBS**, Jan. 22, 1795	2	10
Miles M., s. Miles & Lydia, b. June 4, 1799	2	10
Naby Morris, d. Miles & Lydia, b. July 1, 1807	2	10
Olive, d. Hezekiah & Anne, b. Mar. 17, 1765	1	69
Olive, d. Samuel & Ruth, b. May 12, 1777	1	69
Olive, d. Sept. 14, 1778	1	68
Olive, d. Azariah & Sarah*, b. Nov. 10, 1788 *("Sybil"?)	1	110-11
Orin A., s. Aruna & Lois, b. Nov. 25, 1806	2	10
Phebe, d. Hezekiah, Jr. & Phebe, b. Jan. 23, 1770	1	69
Phebe, d. Hezekiah & Hannah, b. Aug. 16, 1800	1	153
Phebe W., d. Aruna & Lois, b. May 27, 1810	2	10
Phebe Woodruff, d. Arunah, b. May 27, 1810	1	68
Polly, m. James **WEBSTER, 3rd**, Apr. 17, 1792, by Rev. Judah		
Champion	1	206
Polly Ann, d. John & Ruth, b. Mar. 12, 1791	1	153
Rachel R., d. Aruna & Lois, b. Sept. 18, 1798	2	10
Rhoda, d. Hezekiah & Anne, b. May 21, 1763	1	69
Rhoda, m. Nathaniel **GOODWIN**, Mar. 3, 1785, by Rev. Judah		
Champion	2	42
Rhoda, d. Azariah & Sarah*, b. Apr. 17, 1786 *("Sybil"?)	1	110-11
Rhoda T., d. Aruna & Lois, b. July [ ], 1812	2	10
Ruame, b. Mar. 22, 1779; m. John **CHURCHIL, Jr.**, Dec. 16, 1801	2	11
Ruth, w. Samuel, d. Nov. 10, 1798, ae 67	1	68
Ruth, d. John & Ruth, b. Mar. 3, 1802	1	153
Ruth G., d. Miles & Lydia, b. Mar. 19, 1803	2	10
Ruth M., d. Aruna & Lois, b. Nov. 15, 1799	2	10
Sally, d. Samuel & Mary, b. Dec. 14, 1765; m. Jonathan **MASON**,		

	Vol.	Page

ORTON, [see also **NORTON**], (cont.),

s. Johnathan & Susanah, Feb. 4, 1790, by Rev. Judah Champion	2	22
Sally, d. Hezekiah & Hannah, b. Nov. 21, 1790	1	153
Samuel, m. Abigail **SMEDLE**, Oct. 26, 1723, by Capt. Joseph Minor, J.P.	1	29
Samuel, s. Samuell & Abigail, b. Oct. 18, 1724	1	29
Samuel & Abigail, had child b. Sept. 28, 1736; d. same day	1	29
Samuel, s. Samuel, Jr. & Ruth, b. Dec. 27, 1759	1	69
Samuel, Jr., m. Ruth **MASON**, [, 17], by Rev. Timothy Collens	1	69
Samuel G., s. Miles & Lydia, b. June 6, 1797	2	10
Sedgewick, s. Hezekiah & Anne, b. Aug. 11, 1750	1	29
Sedgwick, m. Sarah **TUCKER**, May 6, 1778, by Rev. Judah Champion	1	110-11
Sherman, s. Azariah & Sarah*, b. Apr. 17, 1783 *("Sybil"?)	1	110-11
Solomon, s. Hezekiah, Jr. & Phebe, b. June 5, 1768	1	69
Thomas, s. Eliada & Lucey, b. Dec. 26. 1773	1	110-11
William, s. Lemuel & Mary, b. June 22, 1772	1	110-11
William H., s. Miles & Lydia, b. Mar. 20, 1801	2	10
Zenas, s. Eliada & Lucy, b. Oct. 13, 1777	1	110-11
OSBORN, OSBORNE, Almida, d. Eliada & Sally, b. Sept. 7, 1791	1	153
Almeda, m. Asahel **BEACH**, July 4, 1822, by Rev. Lyman Beecher	2	113
Almeda Mariah, m. Ferdinand **BUEL**, b. of Litchfield, Feb. 14, 1843, by Rev. Jason Wells	2	337
Amos, m. Laura **MARSH**, May 23, 1821, by Rev. Joseph E. Camp	2	106
Anna, of Litchfield, m. Timothy **WADHAMS**, of Goshen, May 5, 1836, by Rev. Samuel Fuller, Jr.	2	296
Anna, m. James **RILEY**, [ ]	2	10
Anna Julia, adopted d. Jacob & Anna, b. Oct. 17, 1812	1	68
Anne, d. Capt. John & Lois, b. June 16, 1773	1	68
Anne, d. John, Jr. & Olive, b. Nov. 4, 1795	1	110-11
Benjamin, of Litchfield, m. Elizabeth **WEBSTER**, of Hartford, Dec. 29, 1739, by Rev. Mr. Whiteman, of Hartford	1	69
Benjamin, s. Benjamin & Elizabeth, b. Nov. 5, 1751	1	29
Benjamin, m. Dorothy **BIRGE**, Sept. 27, 1758, by Rev. Judah Champion	1	29
Benjamin, d. July 26, 1762, in the 70th y. of his age	1	28
Benjamin, s. Isaac, Jr. & Lucy, b. Oct. 17, 1810	1	153
Betsey, m. Medad **GIBBS**, June 20, 1805, by Rev. Truman Marsh	2	126
Caroline M., m. George **KENNY**, b. of Litchfield, Oct. 12, 1846, by Rev. Benjamin L. Swan	TM49	16
Charles, s. Isaac, Jr. & Lucy, b. Feb. 13, 1817	1	153
Chauncey Smith, s. Heman & Sally, b. Sept. 29, 1809	2	34
Chauncey Smith, s. Heman & Sally, d. June 21, 1816, in the 7th y. of his age	2	34
Clarissa, 2nd w. Jesse, d. Nov. 13, 1826	2	4
Cornelia L., of Litchfield, m. Charles **WILCOX**, of Harwinton, June 4, 1839, by William Payne	2	328
Cornelius Elvin, s. Heman & Sally, b. Apr. 22, 1817	2	34
Curtiss L., m. Nancy D. **KILBORN**, June 4, 1839, by William Payne	2	328
Curtiss Landon, s. Heman & Sally, b. Mar. 9, 1814	2	34
David S., of Litchfield, m. Celina D. **WRIGHT**, of Goshen, Oct. 27, 1844, by Rev. S. T. Carpenter, of Milton	TM49	6

	Vol.	Page
OSBORN, OSBORNE, (cont.),		
David Sylvanus, s. Jesse & Clarissa, b. Dec. 5, 1824	2	4
Elado*, m. Sally **SACKE***, Nov. 28, 1788, by Rev. Judah Champion		
*("Eliada m. Sally **PECK**" in Woodruff's)	1	153
Eliada, s. John & Lois, b. Mar. 15, 1761	1	69
Eliada, m. Abigail **MARSH**, May 31, 1794/5, by Rev. Judah Champion	1	153
Eliada, s. Eliada & Abigail, b. Aug. 1, 1810	1	153
Elisha Marsh, s. Eliada & Abigail, b. May 4, 1804	1	153
Elizabeth, d. Benjamin & Elizabeth, b. May 24, 1748	1	29
Elizabeth, d. John & Lois, b. July 30, 1766	1	29
Ellen Aurene, of Litchfield, m. Benjamin **WEBSTER**, of Terryville, Oct.		
1, 1850, by Rev. William B. Hoyt	TM49	55
Ethan, s. John & Lois, b. Aug. 21, 1758	1	29
Heman, s. John & Lois, b. Apr. 19, 1755	1	69
Heman, s. Capt. John & Lois, d. June 2, 1773	1	68
Heman, s. John, Jr. & Olive, b. June 12, 1786	1	110-11
Heman, m. Sally **SMITH**, Nov. 6, 1808, by Rev. Truman Marsh	2	34
Heman, m. Abigail **STODDARD**, Sept. 9, 1827, by Rev. Isaac Jones	2	272
Hepzibah, m. Moses **BARNES**, Sept. 3, 1769, by David Welch, J.P.	1	84
Isaac, s. Benjamin & Elizabeth, b. July 22, 1744	1	69
Isaac, m. Submit **PALMER**, Feb. 3, 1780, by Rev. Judah Champion	1	110-11
Isaac, s. Isaac & Submit, b. June 29, 1781	1	110-11
Isaac, Jr., m. Lucy **BARBER**, May 15, 1802, by Rev. Truman Marsh	1	153
Isaac, d. Mar. 25, 1826	1	28
Jacob, s. Benjamin & Dorothy, b. July 15, 1759	1	29
James, m. Hester **BALDWIN**, b. of Litchfield, Dec. 19, 1847, by Joseph		
Henson	TM49	23
James Heman, s. Heman & Sally, b. Dec. 4, 1822	2	34
Jeremiah, s. Benjamin & Elizabeth, b. Apr. 23, 1741	1	69
Jesse, s. John, Jr. & Olive, b. Sept. 6, 1783	1	110-11
Jesse, m. Polly **MOULTHOP**, Mar. 12, 1807, by Rev. Truman Marsh	2	4
Jesse, m. Clarissa **GRISWOLD**, Sept. 22, 1822, by Rev. Isaac Jones	2	4
Jesse, m. Clarissa **GRISWOLD**, Sept. 22, 1822, by Rev. Isaac Jones	2	114
Jesse, m. Abigail **BALDWIN**, b. of Litchfield, July 1, 1827, by Rev.		
John S. Stone	2	271
John, m. Lois **PECK**, Dec. 18, 1751, by Rev. Timothy Collens	1	28
John, s. John & Lois, b. Aug. 22, 1752	1	29
John, Jr., m. Olive **PALMER**, Nov. 11, 1779, by Rev. Judah Champion	1	110-11
John, s. Eliada & Abigail, b. Dec. 25, 1799	1	153
John, 2nd, m. Abigail **GOODWIN**, Oct. 16, 1822, by Rev. Isaac Jones	2	115
Joseph, m. Anne **WOLF**, Aug. 26, 1777, by Rev. Judah Champion	1	110-11
Leman, of Utica, N.Y., m. Charlotte **HUBBARD**, of Litchfield, Feb. 24,		
1839, by Rev. Gad N. Smith	2	319
Lois, d. John & Lois, b. Aug. 24, 1769	1	69
Lois, d. John & Olive, b. Oct. 20, 1780	1	110-11
Lois, m. Norman **BARBER**, Mar. 12, 1805, by Rev. Judah Champion	2	33
Lois, wid. Capt. John, d. Nov. 28, 1819, ae 87 y.	1	28
Lois, w. Jeremiah, d. Mar. 28, 1826, ae 70 y.	1	28
Louisa M., m. Benjamin **WEBSTER, Jr.**, b. of Litchfield, Apr. 11,		
1849, by John F. Norton	TM49	36
Lucinda, d. Heman & Sally, b. May 22, 1811	2	34
Lucinda, d. Heman & Sally, d. Dec. 12, 1824	2	34
Mary, d. Benjamin & Elizabeth, b. Nov. 30, 1754	1	29

	Vol.	Page

OSBORN, OSBORNE, (cont.),

Mary, m. John **RALPH***, Apr. 29, 1781, by Rev. Judah Champion
    *("**ROLPH**" in Woodruff's book)   1   117

Mary, d. Isaac & Lucy, b. Dec. 13, 1807   1   153

Myron, s. Eliada & Abigail, b. Sept. 28, 1796   1   153

Myron, m. Emeline **GOODWIN**, Dec. 22, 1824, by Rev. Henry
    Robinson   2   138

Nathan Landon, s. Eliada & Abigail, b. July 27, 1807   1   153

Olive, d. Isaac & Submit, b. Feb. 20, 1783   1   110-11

Polly, w. Jesse, d. Aug. 18, 1819, ae 36 y.   2   4

Rachel, d. John, Jr. & Olive, b. Feb. 26, 1790   1   110-11

Rachel, m. David **MARSH**, Mar. 3, 1825, by Rev. Isaac Jones   2   32

Rebecca, d. John & Lois, b. Oct. 11, 1763   1   69

Rebecca, m. Samuel **SEYMOUR**, June 20, 1788, by Rev. Judah
    Champion   1   122

Rebecca, d. Eliada & Abigail, b. Apr. 28, 1801   1   153

Sally, w. Eliada, d. Aug. 28, 1792   1   152

Sally, d. John, Jr. & Olive, b. Sept. 11, 1793   1   110-11

Sally Maria, d. Heman & Sally, b. Sept. 2, 1820   2   34

Samuel, m. Hepsibah **PECK**, b. of Litchfield, Nov. 8, 1739, by Rev.
    Timothy Collens   1   69

Submit, w. Isaac, d. Dec. 24, 1785   1   28

Thalia, d. Capt. John & Lois, b. Oct. 18, 1776   1   110-11

Thala, m. Whitman **KILBORN**, Apr. 7, 1800, by Rev. Judah Champion   2   42

William, s. Isaac & Lucy, b. Dec. 17, 1804   1   153

-----, of Woodbury, m. Sally Ann **WEED**, of Litchfield, Nov. 30, 1837,
    by Truman Marsh   2   315

OVIATT, OVIAT, Elizabeth M., m. Rufus G. **REYNOLD**, Mar. 27, 1844,
    by Rev. David Parmelee   TM49   2

H. A., m. C. E. **CLARK**, May 31, 1847, by Rev. David L. Parmelee   TM49   19

John A., m. Caroline **MASON**, Nov. [ ], 1821, by Rev. Lyman Beecher   2   107

John A., of Washington, m. Elizabeth **COE**, of Litchfield, Jan. 11, 1837,
    by Gordon Hayes   2   297

OWEN, Easton, s. Phinehas & Rachal, b. July 5, 1785   1   68

Phinehas, m. Rachal **SMITH**, Mar. 24, 1784, by Rev. James Nichols   1   68

Phinehas Smith, s. Phinehas & Rachal, b. Feb. 20, 1787   1   68

Tubal, s. Phinehas & Rachal, b. Mar. 4, 1791   1   68

OXX, William, of New York, m. Diantha **VAILL**, of Litchfield, Nov. 13,
    1837, by Rev. Herman L. Vaill   2   314

PAGE, Charles, s. David, Jr. & Rhoda, b. May 10, 1812   2   96

Daniel, Jr., m. Ursula **SMITH**, Feb. 11, 1821, by Rev. Isaac Jones   2   99

David, Jr., s. David & Anna, b. July 8, 1777; m. Rhoda **GIBBS**, d.
    Benjamin & Thankfull, Mar. 12, 1801   2   96

Horatio, s. David, Jr. & Rhoda, b. Jan. 14, 1817   2   96

Ira, m. Elizabeth A. **KNAPP**, b. of Litchfield, Oct. 29, 1854, by Rev.
    H. N. Weed   TM49   103

Ithamer, m. Jenette **BIRGE**, Feb. 10, 1828, by E. B. Kellogg   2   275

Jeremiah, m. Sally **HUBBARD**, Aug. 26, 1822, by Rev. Lyman Beecher   2   113

Lois, d. David, Jr. & Rhoda, b. Jan. 26, 1802   2   96

Lois, m. Albert H. **BIRGE**, Dec. 28, 1819, by Rev. Isaac Jones   2   255

Lidia, m. Edward **LINLEY**, Sept. 27, 1771   1   62

Marcelia Ward, of Litchfield, m. N. Wilson **PARKER**, of Hamilton,
    N.Y., May 28, 1849, by Rev. F. D. Harriman, of Bantam Falls &

	Vol.	Page
PAGE, (cont.),		
Milton	TM49	41
Mary, m. William MOUNTHOP, Nov. 27, 1793, by John Welsh	2	25
Susan, d. David, Jr. & Rhoda, b. Mar. 12, 1807	2	96
Susan, m. Jarvis GRISWOULD, Jan. 1, 1826, by Rev. Isaac Jones	2	259
Thermer, s. David, Jr. & Rhoda, b. Jan. 21, 1804	2	96
Tryphena, m. Edward LINSLEY, Apr. 12, 1778, by Rev. Samuel Ellis, of Branford	1	105
William, of Salisbury, m. Ursula EMMONS, of Litchfield, June 7, 1835, by Rev. Samuel Fuller	TM49	37
William, of Salisbury, m. Ursula EMONS, of Litchfield, June 7, 1835, by Rev. Samuel Fuller	2	289
PAINE, PAYNE, Eliza, m. Josiah PARKS, Oct. 12, 1817	2	127
Harriet, m. Benjamin C. HALL, Jan. 9, 1822, by Rev. Rodney Rossiter, of Plymouth	2	110
Sally, m. John M. PECK, May 8, 1809, by Rev. Amos Chase	1	194
PALMER, PARMER, Almira S., m. Andrew J. PIERPOINT, Oct. 30, 1843, by Rev. D. L. Marks	TM49	1
Ama, m. Mark MAZUZEN, Apr. 6, 1769, by Rev. Solomon Palmer	1	106
Ambrose, s. Job & Rachel, b. Dec. 8, 1744	1	70
Ambrose, m. Cybel LONG, Jan. 14, 1766, by Timothy Collens, J.P.	1	73
Ambrose, m. Susanna CLARK, Sept. 15, 1774, by Thomas Matthews, J.P., of Waterbury	1	113
Amelia, d. Andrew & Sarah, b. Feb. 1, 1805	2	172
Andrew, m. Sarah MATTOCKS, July 24, 1783, by Andrew Adams	1	155
Andrew, m. Sarah MATTOCK, July 24, 1783, by Elisha Sheldon	2	172
Anne, d. Job & Rachal, b. Sept. 28, 1736	1	70
Anne, m. Solomon KILBORN, Apr. 8, 1756, by Rev. Judah Champion	1	60
Appolos Harrison, s. Simeon, Jr. & Statira, b. Sept. 24, 1815	2	37
Augustus Henry, s. Simeon, Jr. & Statira, b. Jan. 15, 1806	2	37
Bathsheba, d. Job & Rachal, b. May 2, 1742	1	70
Bathsheba, m. William LEWIS, Dec. [ ], 1773, by Rev. Judah Champion	1	104
Benjamin, s. Enoch & Jemima, b. May 17, 1747	1	30
Benjamin, m. Lydia KILBORN, Mar. 25, 1778, by Rev. Judah Champion	1	112
Benjamin, d. Mar. 9, 1780	1	112
Charles, s. Lyscomb & Charlotte, b. Aug. 16, 1823	2	83
Charles Alexander, s. Simeon, Jr. & Statira, b. Sept. 17, 1817	2	37
Chloe, of Branford, m. Barnias BEECH, May last day, 1759, by Rev. Judah Champion	1	43
Christopher C., s. John & Sally, b. Jan. 30, 1809	2	105
Clarinda, d. John & Sally, b. Sept. 20, 1806	2	105
Cornelia, d. John & Sally, b. Sept. 23, 1813	2	105
Cyrel, w. Ambrose, d. Dec. 3, 1771	1	72
Dennis Clark, s. Ambrose & Susanna, b. Mar. 16, 1775	1	73
Edwin, s. John & Sally, b. May 20, 1804	2	105
Eliza, d. Andrew & Sarah, b. Aug. 2, 1802	2	172
Elizabeth, d. Enoch & Jemima, b. Oct. 25, 1753	1	30
Elizabeth, m. Arthur EMONS, Jr., Nov. 6, 1777, by Jacob Woodruff, J.P.	1	50-1
Elizabeth, m. Isaac STONE, of Milford, Apr. 23, 1835, by Rev. L. P. Hickok	2	296

	Vol.	Page
PALMER, PARMER, (cont.),		
Elizabeth Baker, d. Simeon, Jr. & Statira, b. June 1, 1810	2	37
Enoch, m. Jemima **MORE,** July 10, 1746, by Joseph Bird, J.P.	1	30
Frederick Henry, s. Simeon, Jr. & Statira, b. Jan. 18, 1808	2	37
George, s. Andrew & Sarah, b. Nov. 25, 1799	2	172
George Henry, s. Simeon, Jr. & Statira, b. Oct. 7, 1804	2	37
Horace Long, s. Ambrose & Cybel, b. Oct. 23, 1771	1	73
Irene, d. John & Sally, b. Jan. 14, 1816	2	105
James F., s. John & Sally, b. July 24, 1811	2	105
Jemima, d. Enoch & Jemima, b. June 5, 1750	1	71
Jemima, m. Russel **EMONS,** Sept. 21, 1774, by Rev. Mr. Knap, of Winchester	1	50-1
Job, m. Sarah **BISSELL,** Nov. 13, 1788, by Rev. Judah Champion	1	112
John, m. Sally **KILBON,** Aug. 16, 1801, by Rev. Truman Marsh	2	105
Junius, s. Simeon, Jr. & Statira, b. Jan. 27, 1820	2	37
Kezia, d. Enoch & Jemima, b. Mar. 20, 1752	1	30
Keziah, d. Enoch & Jemiman, b. Mar. 20, 1752	1	71
Kezia, m. Phinehas **EMON,** July 18, 1776	1	50-1
Laura, d. John & Sally, b. Aug. 9, 1802	2	105
Lazaris, s. Enoch & Jemima, b. Oct. 9, 1757	1	30
Lucia, m. Russell **STONE,** May 13, 1821, by Rev. Isaac Jones	2	102
Lucy, d. Andrew & Sarah, b. Jan. 26, 1794	2	172
Lyman, m. Maria **BISSELL,** Oct. 16, 1825, by Rev. Truman Marsh	2	257
Liscome, s. Simeon & Mary, b. Apr. 20, 1797	1	156
Lyscomb, m. Charlotte **GATTE,** Nov. 5, 1819, by Rev. Isaac Jones	2	83
Marinda, m. Darrick V. S. **SANFORD,** Nov. 1, 1827, by Rev. Isaac Jones	2	273
Mary, d. Enoch & Jemima, b. Dec. 13, 1755	1	71
Mary, d. Andrew & Sarah, b. Feb. 13, 1786	2	172
Mary Ann, of Harwinton, m. Roswell **SCOVILLE, Jr.,** of Litchfield, Apr. 4, 1852, by Rev. John J. Brandegee	TM49	67
Mary Mattocks, d. Andrew & Sarah, b. Feb. 13, 1786	1	155
Mary R., m. Homer S. **PRATT,** b. of Litchfield, May 23, 1848, by John F. Norton	TM49	25
Nancy, d. Simeon, Jr. & Statira, b. Nov. 14, 1812	2	37
Nathan, of Stamford, m. Sally Ann **JUNE,** of New Fairfield, Mar. 23, 1834, by Daniel Wooster, Dea.	2	294
Olive, d. Job & Rachal, b. June 13, 1755	1	30
Olive, m. John **OSBORN, Jr.,** Nov. 11, 1779, by Rev. Judah Champion	1	110-11
Orestes, m. Elizabeth Ann **TERRELL,** Sept. 21, 1842, by Ralph Smith	2	411
Phares S., m. Mary **CLARK,** b. of Litchfield, Oct. 23, 1826, by John Welch, J.P.	2	266
Polly, m. Jason **WALKER,** Feb. 19, 1812, by Rev. Asa Tallmadge	2	50
Rachal, d. Job & Rachel, b. Aug. 5, 1747	1	71
Rachal, w. Job, d. Aug. 10, 1787	1	112
Reuben, s. Enoch & Jemima, b. Sept. 1, 1760	1	71
Reuben, m. Palmyra E. **ABBOTT,** b. of Litchfield, Mar. 10, 1847, by John F. Norton	TM49	18
Rhoda, m. Lyman **WOODWORTH,** Dec. 23, 1823, by Rev. Lyman Beecher	2	133
Sally, m. James **BIRGE,** Oct. 29, 1780, by Rev. James Nichols	2	145
Sally, d. Andrew & Sarah, b. May 25, 1791	2	172
Samuel, twin s. Andrew & Sarah, b. Dec. 31, 1783	1	155

	Vol.	Page
PALMER, PARMER, (cont.),		
Samuel, twin with [ ], s. Andrew & Sarah, b. Dec. 31, 1783	2	172
Samuel Edward, s. Andrew & Sarah, b. Nov. 17, 1811	2	172
Sarah, of Sheffield, Cty., of Yorkshire, Eng., m. John **EADON**, Jan. 25,		
1829, by Isaac Jones	2	279
Simeon, Jr., m. Statira **LINSLEY**, Nov. 24, 1803, by Rev.Mr. Chase	2	37
Submit, m. Isaac **OSBORN**, Feb. 3, 1780, by Rev. Judah Champion	1	110-11
Susanna, d. Andrew & Sarah, b. Oct. 8, 1788	1	155
Susana, d. Andrew & Sarah, b. Oct. 8, 1788	2	172
Susanna, d. Andrew & Sarah, b. July 29, 1808	2	172
Theodosia, d. Andrew & Sarah, b. Dec. 5, 1796	2	172
Walter C., s. Lyscomb & Charlotte, b. Aug. 27, 1820	2	83
Walter C., m. Elizabeth **FRISBIE**, b. of Litchfield, Apr. 20, 1847, by		
John F. Norton	TM49	19
Warren, s. Ambrose & Susanna, b. July 7, 1776	1	155
William, s. Simeon & Statira, b. Sept. 23, 1822	2	37
PALMETER, [see also **PARMELEE**], Abbe, m. Sherman **FRISBIE**, Oct.		
14, 1821, by Rev. Asa Tallmadge	2	104
Albert Ozias, s. David & Lucy, b. Dec. 9, 1806	2	44
Caroline, d. David & Lucy, b. Apr. 15, 1803	2	44
Celestia, d. David & Lucy, b. Mar. 18, 1809	2	44
David*, m. Lucy **LEWIS**, Jan. 22, 1795 *("David **PARMELEE**" in		
Woodruff's book)	2	44
David Lewis, s. David & Lucy, b. Nov. 11, 1795	2	44
Julia, d. David & Lucy, b. Dec. 23, 1797	2	44
Thomas Jefferson, s. David & Lucy, b. July 22, 1800	2	44
PALMS, Mary, m. Samuel G. **BRAMAN**, b. of Litchfield, Oct. 15, 1827, by		
Rev. John S. Stone	2	272
Sally Ann, m. Newton **GIBBS**, b. of Litchfield, Jan. 4, 1830, by Rev.		
Isaac Jones	2	283
PARDEE, PARDY, Almaran, s. Eli & Sarah, b. Mar. 4, 1798	1	156
Clarissa, d. Eli & Sarah, b. Oct. 11, 1795	1	156
Clarissa, d. Eli & Sarah, d. Nov. 2, 1795	1	154
David P., of Plymouth, m. Eliza **MORSE**, of Litchfield, Mar. 20, 1848,		
by Joseph Henson	TM49	23
Eli, m. Martha **MARSH**, Apr. 24, 1781, by Rev. Judah Champion	1	155
Eli, m. Sarah **LYMAN**, Feb. 24, 1791, by Samuel Darrow, J.P.	1	156
George, s. Eli & Sarah, b. Apr. 4, 1802	1	156
Isaac Lyman, s. Eli & Sarah, b. Feb. 20, 1800	1	156
John, s. Eli & Martha, b. Dec. 20, 1783	1	155
Martha, d. Eli & Sarah, b. June 28, 1791	1	156
Mary, d. Eli & Martha, b. Feb. 2, 1782	1	155
Samuel, s. Eli & Sarah, b. May 1, 1794	1	156
Samuel, s. Eli & Sarah, d. Aug. 4, 1796	1	154
Samuel, s. Eli & Martha, d. [ ]	1	154
Samuel Porter, s. Eli & Sarah, b. Oct. 27, 1796	1	156
Samuel Porter, s. Eli & Sarah, b. Mar. 10, 1797	1	154
Sarah, d. Eli & Sarah, b. Sept. 22, 1792	1	156
Sarah, d. Eli & Sarah, d. Feb. 16, 1795	1	154
Stephen, s. Eli & Martha, b. [ ], 1787	1	156
PARISH (?), Jabez M., see under Jabez M. **CARISH**	2	292
PARKER, Abner, m. Mary **SPERRY**, Dec. 22, 1785, by Rev. Noah Merwin,		
of Washington	2	15

	Vol.	Page
PARKER, (cont.),		
Amanda, d. Joseph & Lydia, b.Sept. 28, 1793	2	84
Amanda, of Litchfield, m. Charles B. **PHELPS**, of Woodbury, Jan. 28,		
1827, by Rev. Henry Robinson, of South Farms	2	268
Anson, s. Abner & Mary, b. May 31, 1789	2	15
Anson, s. Abner & Mary, d. Feb. 27, 1813	2	15
Edward, of Plymouth, m. Sarah Ann **WEBSTER**, May 17, 1837, by		
R. M. Chipman	2	313
Edward, of Plymouth, m. Adaline M. **WHAPLES**, of Litchfield, Oct. 22,		
1845, by Rev. David L. Marks	TM49	13
Frederick Sheldon, s. Joseph & Lydia, b. Oct. 24, 1798	2	84
Horatio S., s. Abner & Mary, b. Apr. 9, 1795	2	15
Horatio S., s. Abner & Mary, d. Mar. 8, 1813	2	15
Joseph, Dr., m. Lydia **HARRISON**, Jan. 2, 1786, by James Morris	2	84
Joseph, m. Sarah **BLACKMAN**, July 12, 1809, by Rev. Azel Backus,		
of Bethlem	2	84
Joseph, s. Joseph & Sarah, b. July 19, 1810	2	84
Julia, d. Abner & Mary, b.Apr. 4, 1806	2	15
Lamira Ann, d. Joseph & Sarah, b. Aug. 29, 1814	2	84
Lucy B., d. Abner & Mary, b. Feb. 25, 1802	2	15
Lydia, w. Joseph, d. Sept. 17, 1806	2	84
Lydia Maria, d. Joseph & Lydia, b. Dec. 28, 1795	2	84
Mary Ann, d. Abner & Mary, b. June 21, 1787	2	15
N. Wilson, of Hamilton, N.Y., m. Marcelia Ward **PAGE**, of Litchfield,		
May 28, 1849, by Rev. F. D. Harriman, of Bantam Falls & Milton	TM49	41
Nancy, d. Joseph & Lydia, b. July 6, 1788	2	84
Nancy, m. Jabez **WHITTLESEY**, Sept. 27, 1809, by Rev. Samuel		
Whittlesey	2	83
Polly, d. Abner & Mary, b. July 28, 1792	2	15
Rebecca, d. Abner & Mary, b. Jan. 5, 1814	2	15
Roswell H., s. Abner & Mary, b. Feb. 17, 1804	2	15
Sarah, d. Joseph & Lydia, b. Sept. 27, 1786	2	84
Simeon B., s. Abner & Mary, b. Mar. 9, 1798	2	15
PARKHURST, PACKHURST, Julia Rosella, d. [Prentice & Emeline], b.		
May 4, 1844	TM49	14
Prentice, m. Emeline **WILLMOTT**, Dec. 8, 1839	TM49	14
Prentice, of Woodville, Washington, Conn., m. Emeline **WILLMOTT**,		
of Litchfield, Dec. 8, 1839, by Rev. Isaac Jones	2	327
PARKS, PARKE, Edward J., of Plymouth, m. Eliza **BALL**, of Waterbury,		
Oct. 8, 1829, by Rev. L. P. Hickok	2	282
Elizabeth, d. Josiah & Eliza, b. July 23, 1818	2	127
Emily, d. Josiah & Eliza, b. Nov. 22, 1821	2	127
Josiah, m. Eliza **PAINE**, Oct. 12, 1817, by Rev. [ ]	2	127
Mary M., d. Josiah & Eliza, b. Feb. 5, 1820	2	127
PARMELEE, PARMALEE, PALMALEE, PARMELE, PALMERLY,		
PARMALY, PARMELEY, [see also **PALMETER**], Abbey, d. Amos, b.		
Apr. 23, 1801; m. Sherman **FRISBIE**, s. Friend H., Oct. 14, 1821,		
by Rev. Asa Tallmadge	2	321
Abby, d. Amos & Elizabeth, b. Apr. 29, 1801	2	135
Amos, s. David & Patience, b. July 24, 1734	1	31
Amos, s. Amos & Sarah, b. July 27, 1763	1	73
Amos, Jr., m. Elizabeth **GRACE**, May 27, 1786, by Rev. Judah		
Champion	2	135

	Vol.	Page
PARMELEE, PARMALEE, PALMALEE, PARMELE, PALMERLY, PARMALY, PARMELEY, [see also **PALMETER**], (cont.),		
Amos, Jr., m. Betsey **CARTER**, Sept. 12, 1814, by [ ]	2	135
Ann, d. David & Pacience, b. May 9, 1736	1	31
Anne, d. Amos & Sarah, b. July 13, 1759	1	73
Anne, m. Noah **BISHOP**, May [ ], 1762, by Rev. Judah Champion	2	24
Anne, d. Thomas & Sarah, b. Jan. 20, 1763	1	113
Anne, m. Louis **KILBORN**, Jan. 30, 1782, by Rev. James Nichols	1	145
Asa, s. Amos & Elizabeth, b. Apr. 23, 1803	2	135
Benjamin, s. Thomas & Sarah, d. Apr. 12, 1752	1	112
Briant, s. Jonathan & Sary, b. Aug. [ ], 1730	1	30
Briant, s. Jonathan & Sary, b. July 31, 1732	1	31
Deidamia, d. Thomas & Sary, b. Feb. 16, 1745/6	1	71
Desire, d. David & Patience, b. Feb. last, 1740/1	1	70
Desire, d. Amos, b. Oct. 6, 1765, at Litchfield; m. Partridge **PARSONS**, s. Eliphaz & Abigail, Jan. 18, 1792, by Rev. Judah Champion	2	57
Desire, d. Amos & Sarah, b. Oct. 6, 1765	1	73
Dolly, d. John Gold & Anne, b. July 22, 1774	1	113
Elizabeth, d. Thomas & Sary, b. Feb. 5, 1753	1	71
Elizabeth, w. Amos, d. Apr. 11, 1813	2	135
Esther, d. John Gould & Anne, b. June 26, 1772	1	33
Eunice, d. Thomas, Jr. & Elizabeth, b. Dec. 30, 1763	1	113
Gennet, m. Clark O. **GUILD**, b. of Litchfield, Sept. 1, 1837, by Rev. H. Bryant	2	314
Heman, s. Amos & Elizabeth, b. Sept. 25, 1786	2	135
Herman, s. Amos & Sarah, b. Sept. 12, 1769	1	73
Howell, s. Amos & Elizabeth, b. Mar. 24, 1794	2	135
Jenett, d. Amos & Betsey, b. Sept. 20, 1816	2	135
John, s. Amos & Sarah, b. May 15, 1757	1	73
John, m. Elizabeth **TRAVIS**, Jan. 18, 1782, by David Welch	1	155
John Gould, s. Thomas & Sary, b. Feb. 3, 1743/4	1	71
John Gould, m. Ann **HUIRD**, July 25, 1766, by Increase Mosely, J.P.	1	30
John Gould, s. John Gould & Ann, b. Feb. 27, 1768	1	113
John Gould, d. Sept. 7, 1776	1	112
John Gould, d. Apr. 21, 1777, ae 9 y.	1	112
Jonathan, m. Sary **TAYLOR**, Dec. [ ], 1728, by Rev. Mr. Marsh, of Windsor	1	31
Julia, of Litchfield, m. Hosea **WEBSTER**, of Augusta, Ga., Sept. 18, 1820, in St. Michaels Church, by Rev. Isaac Jones	2	96
Levi, of Litchfield, m. Sarah **SWAN**, of Kent, Feb. 18, 1775, by Rev. Peter Starr	1	113
Lucia Anne, d. John Gould & Anne, b. Mar. 25, 1770	1	33
Lucy, d. Amos & Elizabeth, b. Dec. 27, 1796	2	135
Lucy, m. James **TROWBRIDGE**, Apr. 22, 1818, by Rev. Lyman Beecher	2	126
Lynde, s. Amos & Elizabeth, b. Apr. 12, 1799	2	135
Lynde, m. Anna **TOMKINS**, Jan. [ ], 1821, by Rev. Lyman Beecher	2	100
Mary, d. David & Pacienes, b. Sept. 9, 1738	1	30
Oliver, s. Jonathan, & Sarah, b. Oct. [ ], 1734	1	70
Philethea, d. Thomas & Sarah, b. Apr.11, 1765	1	113
Polly, d. Amos & Sarah, b. Oct. 5, 1761	1	73
Polly, m. Thomas **STONE**, Jan. 14, 1782, by Rev. Judah Champion	2	59
Polly, d. Amos & Elizabeth, b. Apr. 1, 1792	2	135

	Vol.	Page
PARMELEE, PARMALEE, PALMALEE, PARMELE, PALMERLY, PARMALY, PARMELEY, [see also **PALMETER**], (cont.),		
Polly, of Bristol, m. Benjamin **HUBBARD**, of Litchfield, Aug. 24, 1841, in Watertown	TM49	54
Reuben, s. Thomas & Sary, b. Mar. 1, 1755	1	71
Rhoda, m. Chester **FERVER**, Mar. 13, 1831, by Rev. William Lucas	2	286
Ruth, d. Thomas & Sarah, b. May 21, 1759	1	113
Sally, m. Richard **BROWN**, [ ], 1801, by David Whittlesey	2	89
Samuel, s. Amos & Sarah, b. Oct. 24, 1771	1	73
Sarah, d. Jonathan & Sary, b. Apr. 22, 1730	1	31
Sary, d. Jonathan & Sary, d. May 8, 1730	1	30
Sarah, m. John **CATLIN**, Jan. 8, 1769, by Cyrus Marsh, J.P.	1	130
Sheldon, s. Thomas, Jr. & Elizabeth, b. Mar. 16, 1770	1	70
Solomon, s. John & Elizabeth, b. Mar. 30, 1783	1	155
Thomas, s. Thomas & Sary, b. July 31, 1742	1	71
Thomas, Jr., m. Elizabeth **ROOTS**, of Woodbury, Sept. 15, 1762, by Rev. Mr. Brinsmade, at Judah, Woodbury	1	33
Thomas Truman, s. Thomas, Jr. & Elizabeth, b. Apr. 6, 1767	1	113
Timothy E., of Warren, m. Alvinia **SHOWERS**, of Litchfield, June 7, 1829, by Hart Talcott	2	281
Timothy J., m. Mahala **STONE**, Oct. 19, 1828, by I. Jones	2	278
Truman, s. John & Elizabeth, b. Oct. 19, 1787	1	154
PARMER, [see under **PALMER**]		
PARRISH, PARISH, William, m. Eliza **WAUGH**, Oct. 27, 1824, by Rev. Henry Robinson	2	137
PARSONS, Abigail, d. Partridge & Desire, b. Apr. 22, 1793	2	57
Abigail, of Milton, m. Horace **NICHOLS**, Jan. 31, 1836, in Milton, by Rev. Isaac Jones	2	298
Asahel, s. John & Sarah, b. Sept. 23, 1783	1	155
Charles, s. Eliphaz & Lois, b. Mar. 12, 1812	2	23
Eliphaz, s. Eliphaz & Abigail, b. Feb. 12, 1770	1	30
Eliphaz, Jr., m. Lois **BISHOP**, May 6, 1797, by Rev. Mr. Butler	2	23
Eliphaz Turner, s. Eliphaz & Lois, b. Nov. 19, 1807	2	23
Eunice, d. John & Sarah, b. Aug. 5, 1781	1	155
George, s. John & Sarah, b. Nov. 8, 1773	1	155
Huldah, d. Eliphaz & Lois, b. Mar. 27, 1802	2	23
Irene, d. Partridge & Desire, b. Aug. 18, 1802	2	57
John, m. Sarah **WRIGHT**, Oct. 13, 1772, by Rev. Judah Champion	1	155
John Brainard, s. Eliphaz & Abigail, b. June 11, 1776	1	30
John Brainard, s. Eliphaz & Lois, b. Mar. 28, 1810	2	23
Lucretia, d. Eliphaz & Lois, b. Mar. 27, 1798	2	23
Lucretia, m. Lyman **CARTER**, July 7, 1822, by Rev. Isaac Jones	2	113
Mehetabel, d. Eliphaz & Lois, b. Sept. 25, 1805	2	23
Mehetable, m. Charles **FERRIS**, b. of Litchfield, Mar. 16, 1831	TM49	17
Mahitabel, m. Charles **FERRIS**, Mar. 28, 1831, by I. Jones	2	288
Mila, of Litchfield, m. David **BALDWIN**, of Goshen, Mar. 26, 1823, by Rev. Josiah Dickerson	2	119
Mirza, d. Partridge & Desire, b. Aug. 1, 1797	2	57
Nabby, d. Eliphaz & Lois, b. July 25, 1814	2	23
Partridge, s. Eliphaz & Abigail, b. Aug. 22, 1763, at Middletown; m. Desire **PALMALEE**, d. Amos, Jan. 18, 1792, by Rev. Judah Champion	2	57
Phebe, d. Eliphaz & Lois, b. May 24, 1800	2	23

	Vol.	Page
PARSONS, (cont.),		
Sabury E., m. Markus PRINCE, Jan. 2, 1844, by Rev. D. L. Marks	TM49	1
Sophia, d. Partridge & Desire, b. Dec. 20, 1795	2	57
William Catlin, s. Partridge & Desire, b. May 16, 1808	2	57
PATMOR, Milton Andrews, of Penn., m. Amanda Elizabeth BROWN, of		
Litchfield, June 23, 1836, by Rev. Samuel Fuller, Jr.	2	296
PATTERSON, PATERSON, Ruth, m. Judah* STRONG, Apr. 17, 1774,		
by Rev. Judah Champion *("Jedediah" in Woodruff's)	1	161
Sarah, of Litchfield, m. Truman H. JUDSON, of Woodbury, [June] 16,		
1841, by G. V. C. Eastman	2	334
PAYNE, [see under PAINE]		
PEARS, [see also PIER], Mary, of Litchfield, m. Broughton [ ]		
JOHNSON, of Shuffield, in Boston Colony, Dec. 31, 1740, by		
Capt. John Buell, J.P.	1	58
PEASE, Deziah, m. Abel CAMP, Jr., Feb. 22, 1808, by Nathaniel Stepens	2	47
Rensellaer, of Bridgeport, m. Caroline JACKSON, of Litchfield,		
(colored), Oct. 10, 1850, by Benjamin L. Swan	TM49	55
PECK, PACK, Abigail, m. James STODDOR, June 22, 1738	1	77
Abijah, s. Elisha & Sarah, b. Oct. [ ], 1733	1	70
Abijah, m. Rhoda FITCH, June 6, 1773, by Rev. Judah Champion	1	113
Abijah, s. Abijah & Rhoda, b. Feb. 5, 1776	1	33
Abraham, s. Abraham & Hannah, b. Nov. 15, 1763	1	33
Abraham, m. Honor DEWOLF, [ ], 1787, by Rev. Judah		
Champion	1	195
Abraham, d. Aug. 26, 1801, in the 91st y. of his age	1	194
Alanson Ami, s. Abraham & Honor, b. Feb. 4, 1790	1	195
Albert A., m. Adeline THOMAS, b. of Litchfield, Mar. 25, 1850, by		
Rev. William B. Hoyt	TM49	53
Alfred, s. Philo & Hannah, b. Feb. 26, 1779	2	49
Alfred, m. Susan BALDWIN, May 14, 1807, by Rev. Dan Huntington	2	124
Alvin, s. Alfred & Susan, b. Feb. 16, 1815	2	124
Ama, d. Thomas & Sary, b. Apr. 12, 1745	1	71
Ama, m. Israel HUNTINGTON, June 7, 1764, by Rev. Judah		
Champion	1	98
Amy, m. William GIBBS, Jr., Sept. [ ], 1769, by Mr. Hart, J.P.	2	7
Ann, d. Thomas & Sarah, b. Feb. 7, 1734/5	1	31
Ann, d. Reeve & Rachal, b. Jan. 27, 1757	1	113
Anna, m. Titus HARRISON, Feb. 18, 1756, by Thomas Harrison, J.P.	1	57
Anna, d. Benjamin, b. July 17, 1763	1	30
Anna, d. Asahel & Anna, b. Apr. 18, 1801	2	82
Anna, m. Herman BISSELL, Dec. [ ], 1820, by Rev. Lyman Beecher	2	99
Anne, d. Timothy & Sarah, b. Mar. 21, 1755	1	71
Anne, of Litchfield, m. Nathaniel Little WALLACE, of Middletown,		
Feb. 20, 1777, by A. Adams	1	207
Asa, m. Hannah FARNAM, June 15, 1786, by Rev. Judah Champion	1	195
Asa, d. May 17, [ ]	1	194
Asahel, s. Reeve & Rachal, b. Aug. 13, 1762	1	33
Asahel, m. Anna MARSH, Feb. [ ], 1789	2	82
Asahel, s. Asahel & Anna, b. Apr. 29, 1792	2	82
Asahel, Jr., m. Abba CATLIN, Feb. 18, 1816, by Rev. Mr. Beecher	2	80
Benjamin, m. Mary FRISBIE, Oct. 22, 1755, by Rev. Judah Champion	1	71
Benjamin, s. Benjamin & Mary, b. Dec. 28, 1756	1	71
Benjamin, d. Dec. 1, 1788	1	112

	Vol.	Page
PECK, PACK, (cont.),		
Benjamin, s. Eliada & Sally, b. Nov. 7, 1799	2	14
Biah, d. Elisha, decd. & Sarah, b. Sept. 20, 1738	1	70
Caty, m. Caleb **BACON,** Apr. 17, 1799, by Rev. Dan Huntington	2	4
Chauncey, s. Asahel & Anna, b. Aug. 25, 1789	2	82
Chauncey, m. Minerva **BIDWELL,** Apr. 22, 1812	2	66
Clarissa, m. Isaac **WOODRUFF,** June 22, 1797, by Rev. Amos Chase	1	245
Clarrissa, m. Henry **STARR,** May 1, 1808, by Rev. Dan Huntington	2	11
Cornelia, d. Chauncey & Minerva, b. Dec. 9, 1814	2	66
Cornelius, m. Bethiah **BEEBE,** Feb. 5, 1748/9, by Rev. Timothy Collens	1	30
Cornelius, s. Cornelius & Bethiah, b. Mar. 26, 1753	1	30
Daniel M., m. Harriet **MARVIN,** Nov. 7, 1843	TM49	93
Daniel M., of Woodbury, m. Harriet **MARVIN,** of Litchfield, [Nov.] 7, [1843]*, by Jonathan Brace *(Note says, "Nov. 10, 1843")	2	413
David, s. Abram & Honor, b. Dec. 8, 1794	1	195
David, s. Abraham, Jr., d. Feb. 18, 1796	1	194
Deliverance, m. William **GREEVES,** June 14, 1759, by Ebenezer Marsh	1	139
Dille, d. Elisha & Sarah, b. Jan. 25, 1735	1	70
Earl, m. Nancy **BEECHER,** Mar. [ ], 1825, by Rev. J. E. Camp	2	265
Edmond, s. Asahel & Anna, b. Aug. 14, 1799	2	82
Edmond, s. Alfred & Susan, b. June 12, 1812	2	124
Eli Payne, s. John M. & Sally, b. July 28, 1810	1	194
Eli Payne, s. John M. [& Sally], d. Oct. 5, 1820, in Missouri, Territorie	1	194
Eliada, s. Benjamin & Mary, b. July 16, 1770	1	113
Eliada, m. Sally **BECKWITH,** Oct. 28, 1798	2	14
Eliada, m. Abigail **WHITTLESEY,** June 4, 1806	2	14
Eleada, m. Julia **SHERMAN,** May 7, 1826, by Joseph E. Camp	2	266
Elijah, s. Thomas & Sarah, b. Oct. 27, 1754	1	30
Elijah, s. Asahel & Anna, b. Oct. 29, 1794	2	82
Elijah, of Flushing, L.I., m. Amelia **LEWIS,** of Litchfield, Mar. 31, 1845, by William Payne	TM49	9
Elisha, s. Elisha & Sary, b. July 10, 1731	1	31
Elisha, m. Sarah **GRANT,** Jan. [ ], 1770*, by Rev. Timothy Collens *(1730/1" in Woodruff's)	1	31
Elizabeth, d. Cornelius & Bethiah, b.Mar. 9, 1750	1	30
Elizabeth, m. Abel **ATWATER,** May 15, 1776, by Rev. Judah Champion	1	210-11
Elizur, s. Reeve & Sarah, b. Feb. 24, 1776	1	155
Emeline A., m. Elisha **MASON,** b. of Litchfield, Oct. 13, 1851, by William B. Hoyt	TM49	65
Epaphraditus, s. Abraham & Honor, b. July 6, 1791	1	195
Eunis, d. William & Lois, b. Sept. [ ], 1736	1	70
Frederick D., of Banbury, m. Lucy D. **HALL,** of Milton, Dec. 28, 1836, by Rev. P. Teller Babbit	2	298
George, s. Reeve & Rachel, b. Nov. 17, 1765	1	113
George Henry, [s. Daniel M. & Harriet], b. Sept. 3, 1849	TM49	93
Hannah, d. Abraham & Honor, b. Apr. 22, 1788	1	195
Hannah, m. David **KING,** Jan. 25, 1821, by Rev. Amos Pettingill	2	98
Hannah Farnam, d. John M. & Sally, b. June 10, 1812	1	194
Harriet, d. Asahel & Anna, b. June 10, 1806	2	82
Harriet, of Litchfield, m. Elijah **ROUSE,** of Cornwall, June 8, 1836, by		

	Vol.	Page
PECK, PACK, (cont.),		
Rev. Isaac Jones	2	298
Helen Antoinette, d. Asahel, Jr. & Abba, b. Jan. 9, 1823	2	80
Henry Catlin, s. Asahel, Jr. & Abba, b. Jan. 11, 1817	2	80
Henry W., s. Eliada & Abigail, b. May 23, 1807	2	14
Hepsibah, m. Samuel **OSBORN**, b. of Litchfield, Nov. 8, 1739, by Rev.		
Timothy Collens	1	69
Hiram, m. Frances **WHAPLES**, Dec. 16, 1840, by William Payne	2	332
Hiram Daniel, s. [Daniel M. & Harriet], b. Aug. 9, 1847	TM49	93
Hiram W., s. Chauncey & Minerva, b. Apr. 9, 1818	2	66
Horace, s. Asahel & Anna, b. June 10, 1791	2	82
Horace, m. Lydia **ORTON**, Jan. [ ], 1821, by Rev. Lyman Beecher	2	99
Horace, m. Almedia **DOOLITTLE**, b. of Litchfield, Apr. 30, 1837, by		
Rev. Samuel Fuller	TM49	37
Horatio, s. Reeve, Jr. & Sarah, b. Sept. 26, 1799	1	156
Ireaneus S., s. [Chauney & Minerva], b. Apr. 27, 1825	2	66
Isaac, m. Ruth **TOMBELSON**, May 20, 1735, by Rev. Timothy		
Collens	1	70
Isaac, s. Abraham & Honor, b. July 27, 1800	1	195
James, s. Eliada & Abigail, b. Feb. 5, 1812; d. Mar. 21, 1813	2	14
James B., s. [Chaunce & Minerva], b. Sept. 4, 1828	2	66
James B., m. Amanda **KILBORN**, Sept. 9, 1840, by Jonathan Brace	2	319
James Baldwin, s. Alfred & Susan, b. Jan. 28, 1808	2	124
Jerusha, d. William & Lois, b. Sept. [ ], 1727	1	70
Jerusha, m. Joseph **VAILL**, Feb. 2, 1744, by Rev. Timothy Collens	1	123
Jesse, of Farmington, m. Margarett **BALDWIN**, of Litchfield, Nov. 29,		
1826, by Rev. Epaprus Goodman	2	267
John M., m. Sally **PAYNE**, May 8, 1809, by Rev. Amos Chase	1	194
John Mason, s. Asa & Hannah, b. Oct. 31, 1789	1	195
Julius, s. Asahel & Anna, b. July 29, 1804	2	82
Keturah*, w. Abijah, d. Sept. 1, 1772, in the 44th y. of her age		
*(Arnold Copy has "Thedurah")	1	32
Keturah, d. Abijah & Rhoda, b. Jan. 22, 1774	1	113
Leah, m. Benjamin **BISSELL**, Nov. 6, 1740, by Rev. Timothy Collens	1	129
Leah, wid. Paul, d. June 5, 1767, in the 86th y. of her age	1	32
Levi, s. Thomas & Sary, b. June 23, 1748	1	71
Lois, d. William & Lois, b. Sept. [ ], 1732	1	70
Lois, m. John **OSBORN**, Dec. 18, 1751, by Rev. Timothy Collens	1	28
Lucius B., [s. Daniel M. & Harriet], b. May 18, 1858	TM49	93
Lucretia, d. Abraham & Honor, b. Apr. 22, 1798	1	195
Lucy, m. Norman **KILBORN**, Sept. 12, 1810, by Rev. Truman Marsh	2	67
Luman O., m. Almira **FOSTER**, b. of Watertown, Sept. 26, 1854, by		
Rev. H. N. Weed	TM49	103
Mahola, m. John **HARRISON**, June 23, 1800, by Rev. Amos Chase	1	181
Margaret, m. Harris **HOPKINS**, Apr. 4, 1764, by Rev. [ ]	2	78
Maria Emeline, d. Asahel, Jr. & Abba, b. Sept. 22, 1820	2	80
Mary, d. Cornelius & Bethiah, b. July 27, 1754	1	30
Mary, d. Benjamin & Mary, b. July 12, 1759	1	71
Mary, m. Richard **WALLACE**, Apr. 27, 1780, by Rev. Judah Champion	1	165
Mary, m. Richard **WALLACE**, Apr. 27, 1780, by Rev. Judah Champion	1	207
Mary, d. Abram & Honor, b. Mar. 6, 1796	1	195
Mary, m. Dr. Abel **CATLIN, 2nd**, Mar. 20, 1808, by Rev. Dan		
Huntington	2	33

	Vol.	Page
PECK, PACK, (cont.),		
Mary, of Litchfield, m. Edward D. **MANSFIELD**, of Cincinnati, O.,		
Apr. 25, 1827, by Rev. John J. Stone	2	269
Mary A., m. John H. **LEAVENWORTH**, Apt. 13, 1852, by Rev. David		
L. Parmelee	TM49	74
Mary Ann, d. Philo & Hannah, b. Nov. 20, 1795	2	49
Mary Ann, m. Jeremiah **NORTON**, Nov. 18, 1823, by Rev. Lyman		
Beecher	2	129
Mary Ann, of Litchfield, m. Hiram H. **BLISH**, of Marlborough, Apr. 30,		
1839, by Rev. Gad N. Smith	2	319
Mindwell, d. Thomas & Sarah, b. Oct. 26, 1737	1	70
Minerva, m. Leonard **AMES**, Jan. 1, 1796, by Rev. Daniel Catlin, of		
Harwinton	1	210-11
Moses, s. Reeve & Rachal, b. Jan. 19, 1754	1	30
Nancy, m. Chebor **EMONS**, Nov. 17, 1814	2	21
Ozias, s. Asahel & Anna, b. May 17, 1797	2	82
Ozias, m. Mahola **HUBBARD**, Oct. 21, 1823, by Rev. Henry Robinson,		
of South Farms	2	129
Paul, d. Dec. 21, 1751, ae 85 y.	1	32
Paul, d. Apr. 28, 1777, ae about 75 y. Killed by the British at the		
Danbury alarm	1	112
Philo, m. Hannah **HICKS**, Feb. 26, 1778, by Rev. Judah Champion	2	49
Philosibbius, s.Timothy & Sarah, b. Oct. 3, 1752 ("Philo Eusebius")	1	71
Polly, d. Philo & Hannah, b. Apr. 29, 1785	2	49
Polly, d. Philo & Hannah, d. Aug. 26, 1793	2	49
Rachal, m. Reuben **HEBBARD**, b. of Litchfield, Oct. 14, 1740, by Rev.		
Timothy Collens	1	57
Rachal, d. Thomas & Sarah, b. Oct. 7, 1752	1	30
Rachal, d. Reeve & Rachel, b. Feb. 18, 1769	1	113
Rebecka, d. Isaac & Ruth, b. Dec. 15, 1736	1	70
Reene*, s. John & Mehetiable, b. Mar. 3, 1723 *("Reeve **PECK**"		
written over)	1	31
Reeve, Jr., m. Sarah **BUTTES***, Apr. 17, 1774 *("BUTLER" mar.		
"Apr. 14" in Woodruff's)	1	155
Reeve, s. Reeve, Jr & Sarah, b. Nov. 4, 1782	1	155
Reuben, s. Reeve & Rachal, b. Jan. 24, 1760	1	33
Rhoda, d. Timothy & Sarah, b. Mar. 21, 1758	1	71
Rhoda, d. Benjamin & Mary, b. Oct. 8, 1766	1	70
Rhoda, d. Philo & Hannah, b. Sept. 25, 1782	2	49
Rhoda, m. Lot **CHASE**, Apr. 3, 1783, by Rev. Judah Champion	2	40
Rhoda, m. Truman **CLINTON**, June 22, 1797, by Rev. Amos Chase	1	215
Sally, m. Thomas **TROWBRIDGE**, Dec. 29, 1785, by Rev. Mr.		
Whittlesey, of New Haven	2	41
Sally*, m. Eliada **OSBORN**, Nov. 28, 1788, by Rev. Judah Champion		
*(Arnold Copy has "Sally **SACKE**, m. Elado **OSBORN**")	1	153
Sally, w. Eliada, d. Nov. 29, 1799	2	14
Samuel, s. Reeve & Sarah, b. Mar. 20, 1778	1	155
Sarah, wid., m. Joshua **SMITH**, Nov. 15, 1739, by Rev. Timothy		
Collens	1	35
Sarah, m. Benjamin **STONE**, b. of Litchfield, Feb. 28, 1739/40, by Rev.		
Timothy Collens	1	77
Sary, d. Thomas & Sary, b. Aug. 18, 1742	1	30
Sarah, d. Timothy & Sary, b. Jan. 3, 1762	1	71

	Vol.	Page
PECK, PACK, (cont.)		
Sarah, m. Zacharias **JOHNSON**, July 20, 1765, by Jacob Woodruff,		
J.P.	1	59
Sarah, d. Reeve, Jr. & Sarah, b. Sept. 22, 1780	1	155
Sarah Maria, d. Eliada, m. Joseph **WHITTLESEY**, of Berlin, May 22,		
1849, by Benjamin L. Swan	TM49	41
Sheldon W., s. Eliada & Abigail, b. Aug. 31, 1809	2	14
Sheldon W., m. Olive G. **BEEBE**, Aug. 30, 1841, by Jonathan Brace	2	334
Sidney, m. Catharine **COLLIN***, b. of Litchfield, Dec. 2, 1829, by		
Morris Woodruff, J.P. ***("CATLIN"?)**	2	283
Sybel, d. Abraham & Hannah, b. Aug. 9, 1765	1	73
Thedurah*, w. Abijah, d. Sept. 1, 1772, in the 44th y. of her age		
*("Keturah")	1	32
Thomas, m. Sarah **SMITH**, Aug. 27, 1733, by Capt. [ ] Buel,		
J.P.	1	31
Thomas, s. Thomas & Sarah, b. Apr. 24, 1741	1	70
Timothy, s. William & Lois, b. Mar. [ ], 1730/1	1	70
Timothy, m. Sarah **PLUMB**, Dec. 18, 1751, by Rev. Timothy Collens	1	71
Timothy, s. Timothy & Sarah, b. Aug. 26, 1765	1	113
Virgil, s. Timothy & Sarah, b. Sept. 4, 1768	1	33
Walter, s. Alfred & Susan, b. Jan. 16, 1810	2	124
Walter, [s. Daniel M. & Harriet], b. Sept. 16, 1860	TM49	93
William, s. Asahel & Anna, b. Mar. 14, 1808	2	82
William Guy, s. Alfred & Susan, b. Oct. 16, 1820	2	124
PEEBLES*, Rosetta, m. John **WELCH**, Nov. 8, 1784, by Rev. [ ]		
Dempster *(Arnold Copy has "PEOPLES")	2	50
PELET*, Abigail, m. Abial **SMITH**, Sept. 24, 1729, by Rev. Benjamin Alton		
*(Arnold Copy has "JELET")	1	37
PELTON, Lucy, m. Thomas **ADDIS**, Nov. 27, 1814, by Rev. Isaac Jones	2	137
PENDLETON, Benjamin N., m. Seraphine **WHEELER**, b. of Litchfield,		
Jan. 8, 1851, by Rev. Benjamin W. Stone	TM49	61
Margaret, of Litchfield, m. Henry B. **CHAPIN**, of Sheffield, Mass., Jan.		
26, 1848, by Joseph Henson	TM49	23
PENFIELD, Abigial, m. Ebenezer **BOLLS**, Dec. 20, 1789, by Rev. Mr.		
Austin	2	26
Laura E., of Northfield, m. Reuben H. **ROOT**, of Waterbury, Apr. 12,		
1852, by Lewis Jessup, of Northfield	TM49	75
Mary J., of Northfield, m. William F. **CLARK**, of Orange, Sept. 1,		
1852, by Rev. Lewis Jessup	TM49	76
PENNOCK, Polly, of Warren, m. Charles **DeFOREST**, of Goshen, Nov. 22,		
1835, by Charles Chittenden	2	298
PEOPLES*, Rosetta, m. John **WELCH**, Nov. 8, 1784, by Rev. [ ]		
Dempster *("PEEBLES")	2	50
PERKINS, Abigail, d. Harvey & Abigail, b. May 8, 1813	2	122
Abigail, w. Harvey, d. June [ ], 1819	2	122
Abigail, m. W[illia]m W. **MOSS**, Mar. 12, 1834, by Rev. L. P. Hickok	2	288
Anna, of Litchfield, m. Charles F. **CLARK**, of Bethany, Dec. 25, 1853,		
by S. T. Seelye	TM49	94
Beecher, m. Mary Ann **WRIGHT**, Dec. 24, 1833, by Rev. David G.		
Tomlinson	2	293
Betsey, m. Luther **JOHNSON**, [ ], by Mr. Bronson, of		
Waterbury	2	142
Charles Daniel, of Oxford, m. Lydia Ann **WHITTLESEY**, of South		

	Vol.	Page
PERKINS, (cont.),		
Farms, Nov. 5, 1835, by Rev. Samuel Fuller, Jr.	2	296
Charles L., m. Lucy A. **MERRIMAN**, b. of Litchfield, Dec. 28, 1845, by Rev. William Dixon	TM49	12
Delia A., m. Merret **WOODRUFF**, Dec. 20, 1843, by Rev. D. L. Marks	TM49	1
Delia A., [d. Harvey & Barthena], [ ]	2	122
Edwin, s. Harvey & Abigail, b. Jan. 5, 1809	2	122
Eliza, d. Harvey & Abigail, b. July 24, 1816	2	122
Eliza, of Litchfield, m. Frederic P. **AUTEN**, of Haslingen, N.J., Nov. 1, 1837, by R. M. Chipman	2	314
Eliza Ann, m. Elihu **HOTCHKISS**, b. of Litchfield, Oct. 10, 1838, by Rev. Gad. N. Smith	2	319
Frederick, of Torrington, m. Juliaette M. **SPENCER**, of Litchfield, Jan. 11, 1845, by Charles L. Webb, J.P.	TM49	7
Hannah, m. Moses **WHEELER**, May [ ], 1795, by Rev. Mr. Holley, at Woodbridge	2	123
Harvey, m. Abigail **RUSSELL**, of Woodbridge, [ ], 1802, by Rev. Mr. Holley	2	122
Harvey, m. Berthena **MORSE**, June 24, 1821, by Rev. Joseph E. Camp	2	106
Harvey, m. Barthena **MOSS**, June 24, 1821, by Rev. Joseph E. Camp	2	122
Harvey B., [s. Harvey & Barthena], [ ]	2	122
Henry, s. Harvey & Abigail, b. Jan. 27, 1807	2	122
Henry, m. Harriet **McNEILE**, Mar. 12, 1834, by Rev. L. P. Hickok	2	288
Julia, d. Harvey & Abigail, b. Oct. 6, 1803, at Woodbridge	2	122
Lewis, s. Harvey & Abigail, b. Apr. 1, 1804	2	122
Lewis, m. Orrila **MORSE**, Aug. 16, 1826, by Joseph E. Camp	2	266
Louisa, m. James T. **CABLE**, b. of Litchfield, Apr. 1, 1838, by Enos Stoddard, J.P.	2	317
Mary A., of Litchfield, m. John T. **COLBY**, of Norwalk, Apr. 7, 1845, by Rev. D. L. Marks	TM49	9
Mary Deming, of Litchfield, m. Rev. James Mason **HOPPIN**, of Salem, Mass., June 13, 1850, by Benjamin L. Swan	TM49	54
Nancy, of Cornwall, m. Henry S. **GRISWOLD**, of Litchfield, Mar. 12, 1829, by Rev. Silas Ambler	2	280
Newton, m. Mary **HUMPERVILLE**, Aug. 13, 1832, by Frederick Holcomb	2	291
Norman, m. Sarah **DAVIS**, b. of Litchfield, Nov. 25, 1847, by Joseph Henson	TM49	23
Norman B., s. Harvey & Barthena, b. June 3, 1822	2	122
Orrin, s. Harvey & Abigail, b. July 27, 1805	2	122
Orrin, m. Lucinda **WHEELER**, b. of Litchfield, Sept. 14, 1829, by L. P. Hickok	2	281
PERRY, Sally, m. Amos **DICKINSON**, Aug. 6, 1819, by Rev. Mr. Hubbard	2	141
PETERS, Catharine E., m. W[illia]m **ROGERS**, June 1, 1831, by Gordon Hayes	2	287
Eber, m. Mrs. Anne **STEWART**, Oct. 22, 1836, by Rev. E. Washburn	2	299
John Thompson, m. Lucy **CLEMMENS**, June 25, 1828, by I. Jones	2	277
Lauren L., m. Harriet **WADHAMS**, Feb. 29, 1836, by Rev. L. P. Hickok	2	296
PETTIBONE, Sary, m. Joel **CLEMENS**, Mar. 23, 1757, by Rev. Abel Newell, of Goshen	1	46
PETTIS, George, m. Sally **FORD**, Sept. 7, 1828, by Rev. Joseph E. Camp, of Northfield	2	292

	Vol.	Page
PETTITT, Catharine, d. Samuel & Elizabeth, b. June 22, 1739	1	30
PHELPS, Abigail, m. Jeheil GRANT, Feb. last day, 1743/4, by Rev. Mr. Tudor, of Windsor	1	99
Abigail, d. Joshua & Hannah, b. Dec. 25, 1759	1	71
Anne, d. Edward, Jr. & Hannah, b. Jan. 2, 1754	1	71
Augustus, m. Deziah CAMP, Nov. 22, 1848, by Rev. David L. Parmelee	TM49	39
Caleb, of Troy, m. Clarissa GOODWIN, Sept. 22, 1806, by Rev. Dan Huntington	1	195
Charles B., of Woodbury, m. Amanda PARKER, of Litchfield, Jan. 28, 1827, by Rev. Henry Robinson, of South Farms	2	268
Deborah, d. Edward & Deborah, b. Sept. 15, 1725	1	31
Deborah, d. Edward & Deborah, b. Sept. 15, 1725	1	112
Deborah, m. Alexander McNIELE, Oct. 28, 1747, by Timothy Collens	1	107
Deborah, d. Edward, Jr. & Hannah, b. Dec. 24, 1759	1	71
Deborah, w. Capt. Edward, d. Jan. 18, 1771, in the 73rd y. of her age	1	32
[Deborah], w. Edward, d. Jan. 18, 1771, in the 73rd y. of her age	1	112
Deborah, m. Eli SMTIH, Mar. 24, 1779, by Rev. Judah Champion	2	28
Edward, m. Deborah GRISWOLD, June 18, 1723, by Rev. Mr. Marsh, of Windsor	1	31
Edward, m. Deborah GRISWOLD, June 18, 1723, by Rev. Mr. Marsh, of Windsor	1	112
Edward, s. Edward & Deborah, b. Dec. 25, 1727	1	31
Edward, s. Edward & Deborah, b. Dec. 25, 1727	1	112
Edward, representative Oct. 1744, May & Oct. 1745	2	1545-6
Edward, Jr., m. Hannah MARSH, Dec. 21, 1752, by Ebenezer Marsh, J.P.	1	71
Edward, s. Edward, Jr. & Hannah, b. Apr. 19, 1758	1	71
Edward, s. John & Sally, b. Dec. 17, 1782	2	40
Edward, d. May 3, 1790, in the 93rd y. of his age	1	112
Edward, s. Edward & Deborah, d. Mar. 26, 1797, in the 70th y. of his age	1	112
Edward, m. Lavinia FORBES, Jan. 3, 1806, by Rev. Mr. Backus	2	41
Edward, s. Edward & Lavinia, b. July 14, 1809	2	41
Elijah, m. Lucy IVES, Feb. 9, 1812, by Rev. Mr. Mills	2	57
Elizabeth Whiting, m. Rev. Dan HUNTINGTON, Jan. 1, 1800, by Rev. Dr. Parsons	1	222-3
Esther Bishop, d. Elijah & Lucy, b. Feb. 5, 1813	2	57
Eunice, d. Joshua, b. Aug. 30, 1766	1	113
Hannah, d. Joshusa & Hannah, b. Apr. 20, 1753	1	71
Hannah, d. Edward, Jr. & Hannah, b. Apr. 21, 1764	1	71
Hannah, m. Mark PRINDLE, Nov. 7, 1796, by Moses Seymour, J.P.	1	156
Henry, of Albany, m. Louisa C. LEWIS, of Litchfield, Sept. 16, 1829, by L. P. Hickok	2	281
James Shether, s. John, Jr. & Abby, b. Nov. 9, 1823	2	136
James Shether, m. Seraphina WHEELER, b. of Litchfield, May 20, 1847, by Rev. Samuel Fuller	TM49	38
John, s. Edward, Jr. & Hannah, b. Mar. 3, 1756	1	71
John, m. Sally SHETHER, Oct. 24, 1780, by Rev. Judah Champion	2	40
John, s. John & Sally, b. Sept. 9, 1784	2	40
John, s. Edward & Lavinia, b. Dec. 28, 1807	2	41
John, Jr., m. Abby SMITH, May 24, 1817, by Rev. Isaac Jones	2	136
John, 2nd, of Litchfield, m. Martha S. FRENCH, of New Hampshire,		

	Vol.	Page
PHELPS, (cont.),		
Mar. 6, 1842, at Charlestown, N.H.	TM49	25
Joshua, m. Hannah **BIRGE**, July 8, 1752, by Rev. Mr. Russell, of		
Windsor	1	71
Joshua, s. Joshua & Hannah, b. Aug. 27, 1762	1	71
Julia Maria, d. John, Jr. & Abby, b. Dec. 12, 1820	2	136
Lucretia Maria, d. [John, 2nd & Martha S.], b. Feb. 4, 1843	TM49	25
Leucy, d. Edward & Deborah, b. Mar. 28, 1741	1	32
Lucy, d. Edward & Deborah, b. Mar. 28, 1741	1	112
Lucy, m. Ebenezer **MARSH, Jr.**, Apr. 15, 1763, by Ebenezer Marsh,		
J.P.	1	149
Lucy Marsh, d. Edward & Deborah, d. [ ], 1772	1	112
Maria P., d. John, Jr. & Abby, b. Apr. 29, 1818	2	136
Maria P., d. John, Jr. & Abby, d. May 6, 1822	2	136
Martha Elizabeth, d. [John, 2nd & Martha S.], b. May 2, 1847	TM49	25
Mary, d. Joshua & Hannah, b. July 24, 1756	1	71
Mindwell, d. Edward & Deborah, b. Feb. 17, 1732. "Geo. **COTHIER's**		
wife" *("**CATLIN**" in Woodruff's book)	1	31
Mindwell, d. Edward & Deborah, b. Feb. 17, 1732	1	112
Nathan, s. Elijah & Lucy, b. Dec. 12, 1814	2	57
Ozias, s. Edward, Jr. & Hannah, b. May 2, 1760	1	71
Polly, d. John & Sally, b. Aug. 21, 1781	2	40
Rhoda, d. Joshua & Hannah, b. Jan. 31, 1758	1	71
Rosel, s. Edward & Deborah, b. Dec. 8, 1738; d. Nov. 18, 1739	1	32
Roswell, s. Edward & Deborah, b. Dec. 8, 1738	1	112
Roswell, s. Edward & Deborah, d. Nov. 8, 1739	1	112
Sally, d. John & Sally, b. July 4, 1787	2	40
Sally A., of Litchfield, m. Homer B. **RICHARDS**, of Goshen, Sept. 5,		
1841, by William Payne	2	335
Sally Ann, d. [Edward & Lavinia], b. Sept. 3, 1819	2	41
Samuel Shether, s. John & Sally, b. May 13, 1793	2	40
Sarah, d. Edward, Jr. & Hannah, b. Oct. 4, 1766	1	113
Sarah, m. David **PEIRPOINT**, June 20, 1787, by Rev. Judah		
Champion	2	40
Titus, s. Elijah & Lucy, b. Dec. 26, 1816	2	57
PHILLEY, Benjamin, s. Gurdon [& Polly], b. Apr. 29, 1823	2	109
Elizabeth, d. Gurdon [& Polly], b. Feb. 3, 1828	2	109
Gurdon, m. Polly **CRAMTON**, Feb. 1, 1818, by Rev. Lyman Beecher	2	109
Walter, s. Gurdon & Polly, b. Sept. 8, 1821; d. Apr. 6, 1825	2	109
Walter, s. Gurdon [& Polly], b. Nov. 9, 1826	2	109
PHILLIPS, PHILIPS, Gideon, s. Gideon & Temperance, b. Apr. 21, 1761	1	33
Lura, m. Nathan **AVERY**, Feb. 22, 1825, by Rev. Isaac Jones	2	86
Temperance, m. Nathan **SWAN**, Oct. 4, 1770, by Rev. Judah Champion	1	159
PICKETT, PICKET, Alanson J., m. Marietta **SMITH**, Dec. 8, 1829	TM49	64
Alanson J., m. Marietta **SMITH**, b. of Litchfield, Dec. 8, 1829, by Rev.		
Abraham Browne	2	283
Alanson J., m. Nancy **WARREN**, Mar. 27, 1842	TM49	64
Alanson J., m. Nancy **WARREN**, Mar. 27, 1842, by Jonathan Brace	2	336
Alanson Jasper, s. Rufus & Paulina, b. Oct. 16, 1808	2	91
Ann Maria, d. [Alanson J. & Marietta], b. June 3, 1832	TM49	64
Ann Maria, m. Nelson A. **MOORE**, Jan. 25, 1853, by Rev. David L.		
Parmelee	TM49	78
Birdsey, s. Caleb & Sarah, b. Dec. 4, 1811	2	21

	Vol.	Page
PICKETT, PICKET, (cont.),		
Caleb, of Danbury, m. Sally **STEWART**, of Litchfield, Sept. 16, 1801,		
by Rev. Judah Champion	2	21
Caleb, m. Avis **CRAMPTON**, June 21, 1818	2	21
Edwin Clark, s. [Alanson J. & Marietta], b. Aug. 15, 1834	TM49	64
Edwin Nelson, s. Caleb & Sally, b. Jan. 10, 1805, in Danbury	2	21
Eli K., m. Malinda **GRISWOLD**, Sept. 22, 1811, by Rev. Truman		
Marsh	2	57
Eliza, d. Caleb & Sally, b. Sept. 4, 1802, in Danbury	2	21
Frederick, s. Caleb & Avis, b. July 22, 1821	2	21
Henry S., s. Caleb & Sally, b. Mar. 22, 1816	2	21
Henry Spencer, s. Eli K. & Melinda, b. July 14, 1816	2	57
Hulda Marinda, d. Rufus & Paulina, b. Dec. 17, 1811	2	91
John, s. Caleb & Sally, b. July 19, 1807	2	21
Julia Belden, d. [Alanson J. & Marietta], b. Apr. 7, 1838	TM49	64
Laury Julia, d. Rufus & Paulina, b. Aug. 17, 1810	2	91
Marietta, d. [Alanson J. & Marietta], b. Apr. 1, 1840; d. Dec. 10, 1840	TM49	64
Marietta, w. Alanson J., d. July 12, 1840	TM49	64
Marinda H., m. William H. **FARNUM**, Sept. 6, 1837	TM49	98
Martha Shaw, d. Caleb & Sally, b. July 21, 1809	2	21
Minerva, m. Newton **SMITH**, May 17, 1843, by Rev. David L.		
Parmelee	2	411
Paulina, d. Rufus & Paulina, b. Mar. 19, 1815	2	91
Rufus, m. Paulina **TURREL**, Jan. 3, 1808, in New Fairfield	2	91
Rufus S., m. Sarah Ann **SMITH**, b. of Litchfield, May 7, 1840, by		
Richard Woodruff	2	327
Rufus Seymour, s. Rufus & Paulina, b. May 6, 1817	2	91
Sally, w. Caleb, d. Feb. 13, 1817	2	21
Sarah J., m. David A. **McCORD**, Jan. 1, 1845, by Rev. David L.		
Parmelee	TM49	7
Seth Griswould, s. Eli K. & Melinda, b. Aug. 5, 1814	2	57
William Seymour, s. Eli K. & Melinda, b. Aug. 12, 1812	2	57
PIER, PYER, [see also **PEARS**], John, s. Thomas & Margret, b. Dec. 14,		
1728	1	31
Lucy, d. Thomas & Margret, b. July 30, 1727	1	31
Pachence, d. Thomas & Dorothy, b. Aug. 10, 1722; d. Sept. 4, 1722	1	31
Sarah, d. Thomas & Dorothy, b. May 19, 1719	1	31
Thomas, s. Thomas & Margaret, b. Apr. 6, 1730	1	31
PIERCE, PEARCE, George, of Bristol, m. Emily **STONE**, of Litchfield,		
Oct. 10, 1838, by Rev. Gad N. Smith	2	319
Mary, m. Adonijah **STRONG**, June 28, 1774, by Andrew Adams, J.P.	1	161
Susan, m. James **BRACE**, Jan. 11, 1792, by Rev. Judah Champion	2	87
PIERPOINT, PEIRPOINT, Abby, d. James & Elizabeth, b. Oct. 13, 1797	2	144
Abby, m. Rev. John **LANGDON**, Dec. 9, 1824, by Rev. Henry		
Robinson	2	134
Andrew J., s. Edward & Olive, b. Feb. 11, 1821	2	249
Andrew J., m. Almira S. **PALMER**, Oct. 30, 1843, by Rev. D. L. Marks	TM49	1
Charles, s. David & Sarah, b. May 22, 1802	2	40
Cornelius, s. James M. [& Sila], b. Aug. 15, 1829	2	130
David, m. Sarah **PHELPS**, June 20, 1787, by Rev. Judah Champion	2	40
David, s. David & Sarah, b. Dec. 19, 1788	2	40
Edward, s. David & Sarah, b. July 1, 1793	2	40
Edward, m. Olive **BLAKESLEE**, Apr. 14, 1815, by Rev. [ ]	2	249

	Vol.	Page
PIERPOINT, PEIRPOINT, (cont.),		
Elizabeth, d. James & Elizabeth, b. May 28, 1792	2	144
Elizabeth, w. James, d. July 28, 1815	2	144
Elizabeth Langdon, d. James & Elizabeth, d. [ ], 1823	2	144
Elvira J., d. Andrew J. & Almira S., b. Aug. 30, 1844	TM49	0
George, s. Sherman & Sidney, b. May 21, 1819	2	133
George B., s. Edward & Olive, b. Nov. 1, 1818	2	249
Henry, s. James M. [& Sila], b. Apr. 30, 1831	2	130
James, m. Elizabeth **COLLINS**, Sept. 28, 1782, by Rev. Judah Champion	2	144
James, m. Lucy **CROSSMAN**, Dec. 16, 1817, at Salsbury, by Rev. John Langdon	2	144
James E., s. Edward & Olive, b. Aug. 21, 1816	2	249
James M., s. James & Elizabeth, b. June 23, 1800	2	144
James M., m. Sila M. **HARRISON**, Nov. 5, 1823, by Rev. Henry Robinson	2	130
James Morris, [s. James M. & Sila], b. Sept. 29, 1839	2	130
John, s. James & Elizabeth, b. Apr. 6, 1785	2	144
John, s. David & Sarah, b. Sept. 10, 1805	2	40
John, m. Mary L. **LORD**, Sept. 23, 1810, by Rev. Lyman Beecher	2	16
Katie S., d. [Andrew J. & Almira S.], b. Sept. 11, 1855	TM49	0
Laura, d. David & Sarah, b. Sept. 12, 1808	2	40
Leonard, s. James & Lucy, b. Oct. 28, 1819	2	144
Leonard, m. Cynthia **TURNER**, b. of Litchfield, [Jan.] 28, [1841], by Jonathan Brace	2	332
Lucy M., [d. James M. & Sila], b. Oct. 13, 1835	2	130
Mary Ann, of Northfield, m. Oliver A. G. **TODD**, of Plymouth, June 29, 1834, by Rev. Fosdic Harrison, of Roxbury	2	295
Mary Elizabeth, d. John & Mary S., b. Sept. 18, 1812	2	16
Minerva, d. Sherman & Sidney, b. Sept. 4, 1809	2	133
Minerva, m. Sherman P. **WOODWARD**, Nov. 29, 1827, by Fred Holcomb	2	273
Robert, s. David & Sarah, b. May 4, 1791	2	40
Robert, s. James M. [& Sila], b. Oct. 16, 1827	2	130
Sarah, d. David & Sarah, b. Aug. 21, 1797	2	40
Sarah, d. James M. & Sila, b. Oct. 11, 1824	2	130
Sherman, s. James & Elizabeth, b. June 29, 1783	2	144
Sherman, m. Sidney **HAMASTON**, Dec. 1, 1807, by Rev. Joseph E. Camp	2	133
Warren, s. David & Sarah, b. June 7, 1795	2	40
William, s. David & Sarah, b. Jan. 31, 1800	2	40
William Alston, s. John & Mary S., b. July 11, 1811	2	16
PILGER, Harriet Wait, m. John **NEGUS**, Sept. 1, 1816, by Rev. Joseph Vaill	2	11
PILGRIM, Charles L., of New York, m. Almira **THOMAS**, of Litchfield, Sept. 10, 1837, by Rev. Lewis Gunn	2	313
Rodman, of Brooklyn, Conn., m. Mary A. **CLOCK**, of Litchfield, Jan. 24, 1848, by Benjamin L. Swan	TM49	21
PITCHER, William, m. Mary Ann **WADSWORTH**, Oct. 4, 1834, by Rev. L. P. Hickok	2	288
PLANT, Abigail, d. Ruel & Phebe, b. Oct. 21, 1828	2	110
Abigail, of Litchfield, m. Aaron **BALDWIN**, of Harwinton, Feb. 20, 1848, by Rev. Joseph Henson	TM49	23
Ammi, s. Stephen & Rebecca, b. Nov. 5, 1789	1	155

	Vol.	Page
PLANT, (cont.),		
Ammi, m. Mary **BARNEY**, Dec. 7, 1820, by Rev. Isaac Jones	2	97
Benet, s. Stephen & Rebecca, b. Mar. 21, 1785	1	155
Charlotte, d. Ruel & Phebe, b. July 1, 1826	2	110
David, s. Ruel & Phebe, b. Jan. 30, 1821	2	110
Harriet, d. Ruel & Phebe, b. Mar. 16, 1814	2	110
Isaac, s. Stephen & Rebecca, b. Mar. 31, 1793	1	156
Isaac, s. Ruel & Phebe, b. Aug. 13, 1808	2	110
Jane, d. Ruel & Phebe, b. Feb. 4, 1819	2	110
Jerusha, d. Stephen & Rebecca, b. May 17, 1778	1	73
Jerusha, d. Stephen & Rebecca, b. May 17, 1778	1	113
Joel, s. Timothy & Mary, b. Aug. 22, 1776	1	155
Joel, s. Timothy & Mary, b. Aug. 24, 1776	1	70
Lucy Parish, d. Timothy & Mary, b, Nov. 6, 1774	1	155
Margaret, d. Timothy & Mary, b. Dec. 11, 1771	1	70
Maryan, d. Ruel & Phebe, b. Feb. 7, 1811	2	110
Mary Ann, m. Joseph **NEGUS**, June 24, 1829, by I. Jones	2	281
Naomi, d. Stephen & Rebecca, b. Sept. 2, 1776	1	113
Orpah, d. Stephen & Rebecca, b. July 24, 1780	1	113
Orpah, b. July 25, 1780, at Litchfield; m. Robert **MATTHEWS**, May 18, 1804	2	287
Phebe, d. Ruel & Phebe, b. Sept. 1, 1823	2	110
Rebecca, d. Stephen & Rebecca, b. May 21, 1787	1	155
Ruel, m. Phebe **SPRINGER**, Sept. 18, 1807, by Rev. Truman Marsh	2	110
Ruel, m. Huldah **WILLIAMS**, Oct. 30, 1842, by Jason Wells	2	337
Stephen, m. Rebecca **WEBSTER**, Sept. 16, 1773, by Rev. Judah Champion	1	30
Stephen, s. Stephen & Rebecca, b. Jan. 25, 1782	1	113
Stephen, s. Ruel & Phebe, b. Jan. 31, 1817	2	110
Timothy, m. Mary **COLDBREATH**, May 10, 1771, by Rev. Job Prudden, of Milford	1	30
Timothy, s. Timothy & Mary, b. Jan. 3, 1773	1	70
PLATT, Curtiss F., of Warren, m. Cynthia J. **SMITH**, of Litchfield, Feb. 4, 1841, by Rev. Harley Goodwin, of Warren	2	332
David M., m. Elmina M. **POTTER**, b. of Litchfield, Jan. 24, 1845, by John F. Norton	TM49	7
Eunice, of Litchfield, m. Asahel **MERRIMAN**, of Bristol, June 13, 1825, by Rev. Henry Robinson	2	7
Hannah J., m. Isaac **STEVENS**, Sept. 7, 1814, at New Haven, by Rev. Mr. Taylor	2	272
Levi, of Winchester, m. Pamela **MUNGER**, of Litchfield, Nov. [ ], 1823, by Rev. Lyman Beecher	2	127
Mary S., of Warren, m. William M. **WHEELER**, of Litchfield, Feb. 25, 1849, by Rev. F. D. Harriman	TM49	39
Polly E., of Plymouth, m. David **MATTHEWS**, of Bristol, May 7, 1835, by Rev. L. P. Hickok	2	296
PLUMB, PLUMBE, Amanda E., of Litchfield, m. Joseph **STOCKBRIDGE**, of New York, Jan. 19, 1847, by Rev. Benjamin L. Swan	TM49	17
Amelia C., m. Thomas H. **RICHARDS**, July 23, 1849, by Benjamin L. Swan	TM49	42
Anne, d. Ebenezer & Deborah, b. May 23, 1784	1	156
Betsey, d. Ebenezer & Deborah, b. June 19, 1782	1	156
Caroline, d. Henry & Caroline, b. Sept. 20, 1777	1	155

	Vol.	Page
PLUMB, PLUMBE, (cont.),		
Charity, d. Friend & Mary, b. Oct. 5, 1793	1	195
Charles, s. Ebenezer & Deborah, b. July 28, 1789	1	156
Charlotte, of Litchfield, m. Asa **SLADE**, of Kent, Aug. 4, 1845, by John F. Norton	TM49	11
David, s. Ezra & Sarah, b. Mar. 4, 1778	1	155
David, Rev. of Stratford, m. Lucy Ann **STONE**, of Litchfield, July 7, 1835, by Rev. Chester W[illia]m Turney	2	298
Deborah, d. Ebenezer & Deborah, b. Feb. 26, 1772	1	156
Deborah, m. James **TRAVIS**, Sept. 30, 1773, by Rev. Judah Champion	1	121
Ebenezer, s. Ezra & Elizabeth, b. Jan. 27, 1746/7	1	71
Ebenezer, m. Deborah **GRISWOULD**, Mar. 24, 1768, by Rev. Solomon Palmer	1	156
Ebenezer, s. Ebenezer & Deborah, b. Feb. 8, 1774	1	156
Elijah, s. Ebenezer & Deborah, b. Mar. 26, 1780	1	156
Elizabeth, d. Ezra & Elizabeth, b. May 9, 1742	1	113
Elizabeth, m. Jacob **HARRISON**, Feb. 3, 1762, by Rev. Judah Champion	1	141
Elizabeth, d. Ezra, Jr. & Sarah, b. Nov. 17, 1779	1	155
Ezra, m. Elizabeth **BUELL**, Mar. 29, 1739, by Rev. Timothy Collens	1	113
Ezra, s. Ezra & Elizabeth, b. May 10, 1755	1	30
Ezra, Jr., m. Sarah **WOODRUFF**, June 8, 1775, by Elisha Sheldon	1	113
Ezra, Jr., m. Sarah **GRISWOLD**, Dec. 4, 1783, by Rev. Judah Champion	1	155
Ezra, s. Ezra, Jr. & Sarah, b. Dec. 25, 1786	1	155
Ezra, Jr. d. July 1, 1787	1	154
Ezra, d. Oct. 17, 1787	1	154
Frederick W., m. Hannah H. **LANDON**, b. of Litchfield, Dec. 8, 1828, by Rev. John S. Stone	2	279
Friend, s. Ebenezer & Deborah, b. Apr. 2, 1769	1	156
Friend, m. Mary **SMITH**, [　　　　]	1	195
Grace C., of Litchfield, m. Jesse C. **PUSHA**, of Hartford, Aug. 31, 1846, at the house of wid. Plumb, by Rev. Benjamin L. Swan	TM49	14
Hannah, d. Ezra & Elizabeth, b. Nov. 24, 1749	1	71
Hannah, m. Ebenezer **BUELL, Jr.**, Nov. 24, 1768	1	169
Henry, s. Henry & Caroline, b. Sept. 17, 1775	1	70
Horatio, s. Friend & Mary, b. Oct. 14, 1798	1	195
John, s. Ezra, Jr. & Sarah, b. July 6, 1776	1	155
Joseph, d. Dec. 31, 1768, ae about 73 y.	1	70
Mariah, d. Friend & Mary, b. Mar. 23, 1795	1	195
Maria B., of Litchfield, m. Wallace W. **WADHAMS**, of Goshen, Mar. 27, 1850, by Benjamin L. Swan	TM40	53
Orrin, s. Friend & Mary, b. Aug. 23, 1801	1	195
Rachel, d. Ebenezer & Deborah, b. June 14, 1770	1	156
Reuben, s. Ebenezer & Deborah, b. Jan. 14, 1778	1	156
Samuel, s. Ebenezer & Deborah, b. Dec. 9, 1775	1	156
Samuel, s. Friend & Mary, b. Sept. 17, 1796	1	195
Sarah, m. Timothy **PECK**, Dec. 18, 1751, by Rev. Timothy Collens	1	71
Sarah, w. Ezra, Jr., d. Feb. 8, 1781	1	154
Sarah, d. Ezra, Jr. & Sarah, b. Oct. 19, 1784	1	155
William, s. Friend & Mary, b. Apr. 12, 1800	1	195
POND, Asa, s. Beriah & Sylvia, b. Feb. 13, 1795	2	75
Beriah, m. Sylvia **SANFORD**, [　　　　], 1787, at Plymouth	2	75

	Vol.	Page
POND, (cont.),		
Beriah, s. Beriah & Sylvia, b. May 3, 1807	2	75
David Wyllys, s. Wyllys & Hannah, b. Feb. 3, 1815	2	63
Elizabeth, d. Wyllys & Hannah, b. Feb. 3, 1817	2	63
Hiram Lord, s. Wyllys & Hannah, b. July 4, 1813	2	63
Laurena Selina, d. Beriah & Sylvia, b. Jan. 31, 1809	2	75
Lucy, d. Beriah & Sylvia, b. Nov. 17, 1798	2	75
Lyman, s. Beriah & Sylvia, b. Nov. 13, 1796	2	75
Miles, s. Beriah & Sylvia, b. May 15, 1801	2	75
Pliney Bartholomew, s. Beriah & Sylvia, b. July 18, 1811	2	75
Rhoda, m. Truman M. **CATLIN**, Apr. 12, 1829, at Camden, Oneida Cty., N.Y.	2	248
Riley, s. Beriah & Sylvia, b. Dec. 6, 1802	2	75
Ruth C., of Washington, m. David P. **WETMORE**, of Litchfield, June 26, 1853, by Hugh P. Welch, J.P.	TM49	91
Wyllys, m. Hannah **LORD**, Dec. 29, 1811, by Rev. Truman Marsh	2	63
PORTER, John, m. Rachel **POTTER**, May 4, 1826, by Rev. Truman Marsh	2	263
Milcent, m. Abel **CAMP**, May 29, 1808	2	48
POST, Melissa, m. Benjamin **BISSELL**, Jr., Feb. 6, 1822, by Rev. Charles Prentice	2	148
Sally T., m. Elisha P. **CORNING**, June 14, 1820, by Lyman Beecher	2	95
POTTER, Adeline, d. Orrin & Rhoda, b. May 6, 1815	2	46
Albert, m. Mary **STONE**, [June 25, 1828], by I. Jones	2	277
Almeda, d. Joel & Thankfull, b. Feb. 21, 1792	2	39
Almida, m. Horace **SMITH**, Apr. 7, 1811, by Rev. Mr. Fowler	2	23
Bela, s. Joel & Thankfull, b. June 16, 1785	2	39
Curtiss, s. Joel & Thankfull, b. July 26, 1800	2	39
Curtiss, m. Abby **SEELEY**, Sept. 23, 1821, by Rev. Asa Tallmadge	2	104
Elmina M., m. David M. **PLATT**, b. of Litchfield, Jan. 24, 1845, by John F. Norton	TM49	7
G[ ], Dr. of Prospect, m. Mrs. Mary A. **SMITH**, of Litchfield, Dec. 31, 1848, by Joseph Henson	TM49	40
Garey Gray, s. Miner & Polly, b. July 2, 1818	2	128
Harriet, of Orange Cty., N.Y., m. Horace **SEELEY**, of Goshen, May 26, 1839, by Rev. H. Bryant	2	325
Henry A., m. Julia E. **GRISWOLD**, Oct. 3, 1853, by Rev. David L. Parmelee	TM49	92
Herman, s. Joel & Thankfull, b. Apr. 5, 1787	2	39
Herman, m. Pamela **EMONS**, Feb. 24, 1813, by Nathan Bassett	2	46
Joel, m. Thankful **STONE**, Sept. [ ], 1784, in Bradford, by Rev. Mr. Eells	2	39
Laura, d. Joel & Thankfull, b. Oct. 2, 1794	2	39
Lydia A., of Litchfield, m. George W. **COGSWELL**, of New Preston, Sept. 7, 1846, by Rev. William Dixon	TM49	15
Lydian, d. Minor & Polly, b. Sept. 26, 1820	2	128
Minor, m. Polly **GRAY**, Feb. 26, 1817, by Rev. Lyman Beecher	2	128
Miner, s. Miner & Sally, b. July 31, 1823	2	128
Minor R., m. Julia P. **STONE**, of Litchfield, Sept. 16, 1844, by G. C. V. Eastman	TM49	5
Newton, s. Herman & Pamela, b. Dec. 11, 1813	2	46
Orrin, s. Joel & Thankfull, b. Apr. 21, 1789	2	39
Orrin, m. Rhoda **EMONS**, Sept. 24, 1812, by Rev. Amos Chase	2	46
Rachel, m. John **PORTER**, May 4, 1826, by Rev. Truman Marsh	2	263

	Vol.	Page

POTTER, (cont.),

Ranson S., m. Rhoda M. **WOODWORTH**, Apr. 14, 1831, by Rev.
    William Lucas   2   287

Raphael, m. Diana **LANDON**, b. of Litchfield, May 22, 1834, by Enos
    Stoddard, J.P.   2   295

Sally, d. Miner & Polly, b. Dec. 15, 1821   2   128

Sally J., m. Asa L. **GRANNISS**, b. of Litchfield, Mar. 11, 1849, by John
    F. Norton   TM49   36

Thomas P., of Naugatuck, m. Betsey E. **NORTON**, of Litchfield, Nov.
    26, 1846, by Rev. William Dixon   TM49   16

POTTS, Mary Jane, of Stamford, m. John Jenkinson **GARNSEY**, of
    Watertown, June 25, 1837, by Rev. Charles Rockwell   2   313

POWERS, Elvira Menarch, m. George Washington **FISH**, b. of Litchfield,
    Aug. 31, 1845, by Rev. Samuel Fuller   TM49   37

PRATT, PRAT, Francis, m. Emeline **MORSE**, Sept. 10, 1832, by Rev.
    Jospeh E. Camp, of Northfield   2   292

Henry, m. Jane **HORNBECK**, Jan. 12, 1824, by Rev. Isaac Jones   2   131

Henry M., of Bradleyville, m. Abby L. **LAW**, of Litchfield, Jan. 28,
    1846, by Rev. J. L. Dickinson, of Northfield   TM49   13

Homer S., m. Mary R. **PALMER**, b. of Litchfield, May 23, 1848, by
    John F. Norton   TM49   25

Martin, of Cornwall, m. Harriet **BEACH**, of Litchfield, Dec. 25, 1820,
    by Joseph Harvey   2   98

Mary L., of Litchfield, m. Myron J. **THRALL**, of Barrington, Nov. 16,
    1853, by Rev. H. N. Weed   TM49   92

Susannah, m. Isaac **MARSH**, Dec. 23, 1735, by Rev. Mr. Wadsworth   1   64

PRESCOTT, PRESCOT, George R., m. Elizabeth R. **FISH**, Dec. 13, 1842,
    by J. Brace   2   411

Harriet Arabella, m. Lovel **BEACH**, Nov. 5, 1822, by Rev. Isaac Jones   2   115

PRESTON, Asa, m. Ruhamah **TAYLOR**, Dec. 24, 1755, by Rev. Judah
    Champion   1   71

Asa, s. Asa & Ruhamah, b. Oct. 13, 1758   1   30

Dewey E., m. Phebe **MERWIN**, May 5, 1830, by Fred Holcomb   2   285

Deidannia, d. John & Ruhamah, b. Mar. 6, 1778   1   155

Jehiel, s. Asa & Rhuhamah, b. May 22, 1756   1   71

John, m. Susanna **ANDREWS**, Nov. 6, 1776, by Rev. Judah Champion   1   155

John S., Jr., of Harwinton, m. Hannah **CHURCHILL**, of Litchfield,
    [, 1832], by Rev. Levi Peck   2   291

Noah, m. Lucy **MARSH**, May [ ], 1823, by Rev. Joseph E. Camp   2   265

Ruhamah, d. Asa & Ruhamah, b. Oct. 22, 1761   1   113

Ruth, m. Tahan **TAYLOR**, Feb. 10, 1757, by Rev. Judah Champion   1   121

Susanna, d. John & Susanna, b. Apr. 17, 1776   1   155

Ursula, m. Lemuel **HUMPHERVILLE**, Jan. 1, 1800, by Daniel Catlin,
    J.P.   2   142

PRICE, Lucretia J., of Milton, m. Alson **SANFORD**, of Goshen, Mar. 11,
    1849, by John F. Norton   TM49   36

PRINCE, Markus, m. Sabury E. **PARSONS**, Jan. 2, 1844, by Rev. D. L.
    Marks   TM49   1

PRINDLE, Charles, s. Mark & Lois, b. Aug. 12, 1756   1   113

Hannah, w. Mark, d. [   ], in the 86th y. of her age   1   112

Lois, d. Mark & Lois, b. Oct. 16, 1759   1   113

Mark, m. Lois **MARSH**, Nov. 3, 1755, by Ebenezer Marsh   1   113

Mark, m. Hannah **PHELPS**, Nov. 7, 1796, by Moses Seymour, J.P.   1   156

	Vol.	Page
PRINDLE, (cont.),		
Mark, d. May 28, 1804, in the 71st y. of his age	1	112
Rachel, of Cornwall, m. Lyman L. **GRISWOLD**, of Litchfield, Mar. 24, 1844	TM49	67
Sarah, m. Jacob **TURNER**, May 13, 1799, by Rev. Chauncey Prindle	2	36
PRITCHARD, Darling, m. Nancy F. **GLOVER**, May 28, 1809, by Rev. Truman Marsh	2	45
Elizabeth, m. Ebenezer **CLARK**, Mar. 15, 1795, in Waterbury	2	74
Emeliza, d. Darling & Nancy, b. May 21, 1815	2	45
Emeliza, of Litchfield, m. Richard **MOSES**, of Torrington, Apr. 12, 1835, by Truman Kilborn, J.P.	2	298
Frederick G., s. Darling & Nancy, b. Nov. 29, 1812	2	45
Polly, m. Judd **GRISWOLD**, b. of Litchfield, Jan. 31, 1830, by Enos Stoddard, J.P.	2	284
Polly G., d. Darling & Nancy G., b. Nov. 24, 1810	2	45
PRUDDEN, PRUDEN, Mary, m. Dr. Gurdon **HUNTINGTON**, of Cairo, Nov. 10, 1821, by Rev. Amos Pettingill, of South Farms Soc.	2	104
PUSHA, Jesse C., of Hartford, m. Grace C. **PLUMB**, of Litchfield, Aug. 31, 1846, at the house of wid. Plumb, by Rev. Benjamin L. Swan	TM49	14
PYER, [see under **PIER**]		
QUANN, John, m. Mary **HICKEY**, b. of Ireland, Feb. 29, [1852], by N. C. Lewis	TM49	74
QUIN, Peter, d. Mar. 31, 1776	1	114
RADCLIFFE, James Buel, s. Jere & Arianda, b. Aug. 13, 1808	2	2
Jane Ellen, of Litchfield, m. Walter **JOY**, of Buffalo, N.Y., Jan. 22, 1833, by Rev. Samuel Fuller	TM49	37
Jane Ellen, m. Walter **JOY**, Jan. 22, 1833, by Rev. Samuel Fuller	2	289
Jerry, m. Arianda **WEBSTER**, Apr. 27, 1806, by Rev. Truman Marsh	2	2
William Kilsall, twin with Woolsey Webster, s. Jerry & Arianda, b. Jan. 5, 1807	2	2
Woolsey Webster, twin with William Kilsall, s. Jerry & Arianda, b. Jan. 5, 1807	2	2
RALPH, Jacob Osborn, s. John & Mary, b. Feb. 17, 1788	1	117
John, m. Mary **OSBORN**, Apr. 29, 1781, by Rev. Judah Champion *("ROLPH" in Woodruff's book)	1	117
Polly, d. John & Mary, b. Apr. 23, 1786	1	117
Stephen, s. John & Mary, b. Jan. 20, 1784	1	117
RANKIN, Robert G., of New York, m. Laura M. **WOLCOTT**, of Litchfield, Mar. 30, 1831, by Rev. Lawrence P. Hickok	2	286
RANNEY, Jeremiah, m. Sabra **MERRIMAN**, June 16, 1822, by Rev. Isaac Jones	2	112
RAY, Adaline E., of Litchfield, m. Andrew J. **WHEELER**, of New Haven, June 1, 1840, by Rev. Fosdic Harrison, of Bethlehem	2	320
Adaline Eliza, d. William & Nancy, b. Feb. 24, 1820	2	258
Eliza W., d. William & Nancy, b. Jan. 17, [1817]; d. Jan. 19, 1817	2	258
Henry Rowland, s. William & Nancy, b. July 24, 1823	2	258
Henry Roland, m. Lydia Ann **KILBORN**, b. of Litchfield, May 4, 1846 by Rev. Samuel Fuller	TM49	37
Julia A., m. Nathan B. **HINMAN**, Apr. 14, 1852, by Rev. David L. Parmelee	TM49	74
Lemuel Blackman, s. William & Nancy, b. Aug. 3, 1825	2	258
Lucius Edwin, s. William & Nancy, b. Nov. 15, 1821	2	258
Mary, m. Hiram **GRISWOLD**, of Goshen, [Mar.] 27, 1834, by Rev.		

	Vol.	Page
RAY, (cont.),		
James F. Warner, of South Farms	2	289
William, m. Nancy **BLACKMAN**, Jan. 29, 1816, by Rev. Lyman Beecher	2	258
William, representative Apr. 1838, Apr. 1839	2	1557
William M., s. William & Nancy, b. Apr. 29, 1818	2	258
RAYMOND, Amy, m. Charles **JACKSON**, b. of Bethleman, Oct. 9, 1836, by Rev. Fosdic Harrison, of Bethleham	2	297
Diana, m. Horace **WAUGH**, Feb. [ ], 1816, by George D. Kasson, J.P.	2	90
REA, RHEA, Abby, m. Henry **WHITTLESEY**, July 20, 1815, by Rev. Samuel Whittlesey	2	84
Abigail, d. William & Hannah, b. Dec. 5, 1790	2	5
Adaline E., d. William & Nancy, b. Feb. 24, 1820	2	82
Anna, d. William & Hannah, b. Apr. 12, 1796	2	5
Anna, m. Erastus **BENTON**, Apr. 22, 1819, by Rev. Amos Pettingill	2	146
David, s. William & Hannah, b. Oct. 17, 1781	2	5
David, m. Phebe **WOODRUFF**, July 2, 1814, by Morris Woodruff	2	82
Eliza, d. William & Nancy, b. Jan. 2, 1817	2	82
Eliza, d. William & Nancy, d. Jan. 17, 1817	2	82
Elizabeth, d. William & Hannah, b. Mar. 12, 1785	2	5
Elizabeth, m. Benton **BARNARD**, Jan. 24, 1811, by James Morris, J.P.	2	141
Ezra Camp, s. John & Charlotte, b. Nov. 11, 1817	2	81
Hannah, d. William & Hannah, b. Jan. 8, 1789	2	5
Hannah, m. Frederick **WHITTLESEY**, July 20, 1815, by Rev. Samuel Whittlesey	2	84
Henry Rowland, s. William & Nancy, b. July 24, 1823	2	82
Israel, s. William & Hannah, b. June 3, 1794	2	5
James Henry, s. John & Charlotte, b. Mar. 27, 1819	2	81
John, s. William & Hannah, b. Dec. 14, 1786	2	5
John, m. Charlotte **CAMP**, Dec. 19, 1816, by Rev. Amos Pettingill	2	81
Julian, d. John & Charlotte, b. Jan. 17, 1824	2	81
Lemuel Blackman, s. William & Nancy, b. Aug. 3, 1825	2	82
Lucius Edwin, s. William & Nancy, b. Nov. 15, 1822	2	82
Lucy M., of South Farms, m. Noah S. **WADHAMS**, of Goshen, July 9, 1838, by Rev. Thomas Savage, of Bedford, N.H.	2	316
Lucy Matilda, d. David & Phebe, b. Mar. 26, 1819	2	82
Morris Woodruff, s. David & Phebe, b. Apr. 24, 1817	2	82
Polly, d. William & Hannah, b. June 4, 1798	2	5
Sally, d. William & Hannah, b. June 3, 1783	2	5
Susan Camp, d. John & Charlotte, b. Feb. 1, 1822	2	81
William, m. Hannah **GIBBS**, Nov. 9, 1780, by Esquire Averit, J.P.	2	5
William, s. William & Hannah, b. Oct. 15, 1792	2	5
William, m. Nancy **BLACKMAN**, Jan. 29, 1816, by Rev. Lyman Beecher	2	82
William M., s. William & Nancy, b. Apr. 29, 1818	2	82
REDDAN, Hugh, m. Betsey **SHEPARD**, Nov. 27, 1820, by Lyman Beecher	2	98
REDFIELD, Isaac B., of Fairfield, m. Ann **MARSH**, of Litchfield, South Farms, Apr. 8, 1827, by Rev. John J. Stone	2	270
REED, Sarah, m. Phineas **MASON**, b. of New Hartford, Mar. 30, 1834, by Rev. Samuel Fuller	TM49	37
REEVE, Aaron B., s. Tapping & Sally, b. Oct. 3, 1780	1	117
Tapping, m. Sally **BURR**, June 24, 1773, by Rev. Mr. Hubbard, of Fairfield	1	117

	Vol.	Page
REEVE, (cont.),		
Tapping, m. Betsey **THOMSON,** Apr. 30, 1798, by Rev. Mr. Backus	1	117
REYNOLD, Rufus G., m. Elizabeth M. **OVIATT,** Mar. 27, 1844, by Rev.		
David Parmelee	TM49	2
RHEA, [see under **REA**]		
RHODEN, Lydia, m. Lewis **MORSE,** Oct. 19, 1830, by Rev. William Lucas	2	286
RICE, David, m. Saloame **TAYLOR,** July 16, 1811	2	82
RICHARDS, Delia Maria, m. Garwood Hawley **BECKWITH,** Jan. 29,		
1826, by Rev. Daniel Coe, of Winchester	2	260
Homer B., of Goshen, m. Sally A. **PHELPS,** of Litchfield, Sept. 6, 1841,		
by William Payne	2	335
Nancy E., of Goshen, m. John B. **ROBERTSON,** of Hartland, Sept. 6,		
1837, by Rev. John Lucky	2	315
Sally, m. David Clinton **DICKINSON,** of Torrington, Sept. 14, 1823,		
by Rev. Epaphras Goodman, of Torrington	2	51
Thomas H., m. Amelia C. **PLUMB,** July 23, 1849, by Benjamin L.		
Swan	TM49	42
RICHARDSON, Henry, of Somers, m. Verona **LANDON,** of Litchfield,		
Mar. 27, 1836, by Rev. Samuel Fuller, Jr.	2	296
RICHMOND, Ephraim, s. Silus & Hannah, b. June 15, 1734	1	37
Phebe, d. Silas & Hannah, b. Oct. 29, 1736	1	35
Silus, m. Hannah **EMONS,** Dec. 19, 1733, by Capt. John Buel, J.P.	1	37
RIGGS, Ann, m. Asa **MORRIS,** Mar. 20, 1818, at Woodbridge, by Rev.		
Jason Allen	2	143
Esther, d. Jeremiah & Anne, b. Apr. 15, 1770	1	75
Jeremiah, s. Jeremiah & Anne, b. Mar. 2, 1778	1	75
Mary Ann, of Milton, m. John **CARTER,** June 16, 1831, by Rev.		
William Lucas	2	287
Samuel, s. Jeremiah & Anne, b. Jan. 18, 1769	1	75
Samuel, s. Jeremiah & Anne, d. Feb. 15, 1769	1	74
Samuel, s. Jeremiah & Anne, b. Oct. 1, 1773	1	75
Susannah, d. Jeremiah & Anne, b. Mar. 21, 1776	1	75
Susannah, d. Jeremiah & Anne, d. Sept. 21, 1777	1	74
RIGHT, [see under **WRIGHT**]		
RILEY, Aaron, s. James & Anna, b. Nov. 11, 1806	2	10
Dayton, s. James & Anna, b. Mar. 2, 1797	2	10
James, s. James & Anna, b. Mar. 12, 1800	2	10
James, m. Anna **OSBORN,** [ ]	2	10
John O., s. James & Anna, b. Aug. [ ], 1814	2	10
Joseph, s. James & Anna, b. Sept. 25, 1804	2	10
Philip Dare, s. James & Anna, b. Apr. 24, 1810	2	10
RING, Catharine, m. Conrad **BAKER,** b. of Germany, Dec. 19, 1852, by		
Rev. John J. Brandegee	TM49	77
RIPNER, Samuel, m. Mary **LEE,** Feb. 7, 1771	1	75
Samuel, s. Samuel & Mary, b. Feb. 7, 1772	1	75
Stephen Lee, s. Samuel & Mary, b. Feb. 11, 1774	1	75
ROBBINS, Abigail, m. Minias **TURNAY,** Nov. 2, 1823, by Rev. Isaac Jones	1	129
ROBERTS, ROBBERTS, Albert, s. Daniel & Mabel, b. July 17, 1804	2	59
Albert, m. Sally M. **STEVENS,** Oct. 31, 1827, by Rev. Joseph E. Camp,		
of Northfield	2	292
Almond Peck, s. Daniel & Mabel, b. July 9, 1798	2	59
Charlotte, m. Charles **MARSH,** June 16, 1793, by Rev. David Butler	1	229
Clark W., s. Joel G. & Mehetabel, b. Oct. 3, 1810	2	12

	Vol.	Page
ROBERTS, ROBBERTS, (cont.),		
Daniel, m. Mabel **EASTON**, July 7, 1794, by Rev. Mr. Wathams	2	59
David C., s. Joel G. & Mehetabel, b. Nov. 2, 1817	2	12
Elizabeth N., d. Joel G. & Mehetabel, b. June 28, 1808	2	12
George Pratt, s. Daniel & Mabel, b. Apr. 18, 1811	2	59
Harriet Newel, d. Daniel & Mabel, b. Feb. 16, 1815	2	59
Helen Maria, of Litchfield, m. Hubbel **WEST, Jr.**, of Wis., Oct. 1, 1850,		
by Benjamin W. Stone	TM49	55
Henry G., s. Joel G. & Mehetabel, b. Oct. 20, 1812	2	12
Henry Mason, s. Daniel [& Mabel], b. [ ]	2	59
J. D., of Pardeeville, Wis., m. Louisa **COE**, of Litchfield, Oct. 13, 1851		
by Rev. Benjamin L. Swan	TM49	66
Jesse, s. Daniel & Mabel, b. June 23, 1807	2	59
Joel G., m. Mehetabel **COUCH**, Oct. 28, 1802	2	12
Joseph W., d. Joel G. & Mehetabel, b. Mar. 21, 1806	2	12
Julia Ann, d. Daniel & Mabel, b. June 3, 1802	2	59
Julia Ann, m. John R. **BRADLEY**, Dec. 27, 1824, by Rev. Lyman		
Beecher	2	139
Julia Ann, m. John R. **BRADLEY**, Dec. 27, 1824, by Rev. Lyman		
Beecher	2	278
Norman Easton, s. Daniel & Mabel, b. Apr. 28, 1809	2	59
Rumina, d. Daniel & Mabel, b. Mar. 5, 1800	2	59
Rumina, m. Leonard **BLAKESLEE**, Nov. 14, 1821, by Rev. Joseph E.		
Camp	2	107
Sally G., d. Joel G. & Mehetabel, b. Sept. 20, 1804	2	12
Susanna, d. Daniel & Mabel, b. Apr. 8, 1796	2	59
William Edwin, s. Daniel & Mabel, b. Jan. 21, 1813	2	59
ROBERTSON, Daniel, m. Mary Jane **SEYMOUR**, Aug. 23, 1838, by Rev.		
Stephen Hubbell	2	320
John B., of Hartland, m. Nancy E. **RICHARDS**, of Goshen, Sept. 6,		
1837, by Rev. John Lucky	2	315
ROBEY, Thomas R., of Brockport, Monroe Cty., N.Y., m. Clarissa		
SEYMOUR, of Litchfield, Oct. 22, 1828, by Rev. Isaac Jones	2	278
ROBINSON, Elizabeth L., m. Cornelius L. **WETMORE**, [ ], in		
Mass.	2	248
Lydia, m. Elihu **HOTCHKISS**, [ ], 1769, by Rev. Mr. Halley	2	79
Mehetable, m. Nathan **FARNUM**, Dec. 14, 1796, by Rev. Mr. Collin, of		
Lanesborough	1	92-5
ROCKWELL, Abigail, m. Rollin **HOYT**, Apr. 8, 1830, by Rev. William		
Lucas	2	286
Betty, m. Samuel **GUNN**, Nov. 26, 1793, by David Whittlesey	2	55
ROGERS, ROGER, Anne, d. Joseph & Susanna, b. Jan. 1, 1762, at Hartford	1	75
Daniel, m. Peggy **SMITH**, Apr. [ ], 1798, by Henry Rowland, of Windsor	2	76
Daniel Smith, s. Daniel & Peggy, b. Dec. 9, 1804	2	76
David, of Warren, m. Elizabeth **SHOWERS**, of Litchfield, Aug. 30,		
1829, by Enos Stoddard, J.P.	2	282
Fanny Malina, d. Daniel & Peggy, b. Sept. 15, 1821	2	76
Hulda, d. Joseph & Susanna, b. Sept. 10, 1764	1	75
Joseph, m. Susanna **FLOWER**, Jan. 31, 1759, by Rev. Elnathan		
Whitman, of Hartford	1	74
Joseph, s. Joseph & Susanna, b. Mar. 3, 1770	1	75
Lucia, d. Joseph & Susanna, b. June 14, 1768	1	75
Lydia, d. Daniel & Peggy, b. June 7, 1814	2	76

	Vol.	Page
ROGERS, ROGER, (cont.),		
Meletiah, d. Joseph & Susanna, b. Feb. 21, 1773	1	75
Nancy, d. Daniel & Peggy, b. Oct. 9, 1799	2	76
Nancy, of Litchfield, m. John **CLARK**, of Brooklyn, N.Y., Sept. 4,		
1828, by Rev. John S. Stone	02	278
Orilla, d. Daniel & Peggy, b. Jan. 3, 1811	2	76
Polly, m. David **BUELL**, Mar. 22, 1800, by Rev. Dan Huntington	2	148
Ruth, d. Joseph & Susanna, b. Jan. 21, 1766	1	75
Samuel, s. Daniel & Peggy, b. Feb. 2, 1817	2	76
Sary, d. Joseph & Susanna, b. Feb. 22, 1763, at Hartford	1	75
William, s. Jonathan, d. July 31, 1805, ae 38 y.	1	238
William, s. Daniel & Peggy, b. July 15, 1807	2	76
W[illlia]m, m. Catharine E. **PETERS**, June 1, 1831, by Gordon Hayes	2	287
ROLPH, [see under **RALPH**]		
ROOSECRAFT, William, m. Almira **WHEELER**, b. of Litchfield, Feb. 14,		
1848, by Joseph Henson	TM49	23
ROOT, ROOTS, Elizabeth, of Woodbury, m. Thomas **PARMELE, Jr.,**		
Sept. 15, 1762, by Rev. Mr. Brinsmade, at Judah Woodbury	1	33
Laura, m. Jonah **ALLEN**, Jan. 31, 1825, by Rev. George E. Pierce	2	37
Louisa P., of Litchfield, m. William **LIDDECOTT**, of Northampton,		
Dec. 26, 1852, by Rev. Charles R. Adams, of West Goshen	TM49	78
Mabel, m. Dinnis **BRADLEY**, [ ], 1796, by Rev. Noah Benedict	2	94
Mary E., m. Charles **CULVER**, b. of Litchfield, July 1, 1853, by Rev.		
H. N. Weed	TM49	91
Mary H., m. Luke Lewis, Dec. 27, 1795, by Rev. Mr. Cowles	2	34
Polly, m. Jason **WALLACK**, Dec. 20, 1844, by Rev. D. L. Marks	TM49	7
Reuben H., of Waterbury, m. Laura E. **PENFIELD**, of Northfield, Apr.		
12, 1852, by Lewis Jessup, of Northfield	TM49	75
ROSS, Asher, s. Simeon & Mary, b. Jan. 20, 1754	1	75
Asher, s. Simeon & Mary, b. Jan. 20, 1755	1	35
Elizabeth, d. Simeon & Mary, b. Jan. 12, 1765	1	34
Mary, d. Simeon & Mary, b. May 6, 1761	1	34
Sarah, d. Simeon & Mary, b. July 8, 1758	1	34
Simeon, s. Simeon & Mary, b. June 29, 1753	1	75
ROSSITER, ROSSETTER, ROSETTER, Ama, d. Stephen & Ann, b. July,		
11, 1743	1	35
Ama, d. Stephen & Ann, d. Aug. 18, 1743	1	34
Amos, s. Stephen & Ann, b. Mar. 10, 1746/7	1	35
Ann, m. Stephen **BIDWELL**, June 5, 1748, by Rev. Timothy Collens	1	85
Anna, d. Jonathan & Millecent, d. Feb. 15, 1760	1	74
Anne, d. Jonathan & Millecent, b. Oct. 13, 1762	1	75
Anne, d. Jonathan & Millecent, b. Jan. 23, 1763	1	75
Anne, wid., d. July 20, 1772, in the 75th y. of her age	1	34
Hannah, d. Jonathan & Millicent, b. July 18, 1764	1	75
Honour, [twin with Olive], d. Jonathan & Millecent, b. May 28, 1766	1	75
Huldah, d. Jonathan & Mellecent, b. Feb. 17, 1700	1	75
Jonathan, d. Feb. 20, 1752	1	34
Jonathan, m. Millecent **CATLING**, Nov. 15, 1757, by Rev. Andrew		
Bartholomew, at Harwington	1	75
Jonathan, s. Jonathan & Millecent, b. Dec. 25, 1761	1	75
Lucia, d. Apr. 9, 1738, in th 19th y. of her age	1	34
Millecent, d. Jonathan & Mellecent, b. Jan. 9, 1757	1	75
Oliver, [twin with Honour], d. Jonathan & Millecent, b. May 28, 1766	1	75

	Vol.	Page
ROSSITER, ROSSETTER, ROSETTER, (cont.),		
Patience, m. Joseph **MASON, Jr.**, Nov. 16, 1749; by Ebenezer Marsh, J.P.	1	107
Rachal, d. Stephen & Ann, b. Dec. 1, 1751	1	35
Sabra, d. Jonathan & Millecent, b. Feb. 8, 1768	1	75
Samuel, m. Tryphene **SMITH**, Nov. 12, 1775, by Rev. Judah Champion	1	34
Samuel, s. Samuel & Tryphena, b. Dec. 25, 1775	1	75
Samuel, s. Samuel & Tryphena, d. June 18, 1778	1	74
Sary, d. Stephen & Ann, b. Nov. 19, 1744	1	35
ROUSE*, Daniel, s. Daniel & Lucretia, b. Feb. 7, 1773 *("ROWE" in Woodruff's book)	1	34
Elijah, of Cornwall, m. Harriet **PECK**, of Litchfield, June 8; 1836, by Rev. Isaac Jones	2	298
Martha Brooks, of Woodbury, m. Rev. Rufus **MURRAY**, of Ridgeville, O., Nov. 17, 1822, in St. Michaels Church, by Rev. Isaac Jones	2	111
ROWE*, Daniel, s. Daniel & Lucretia, b. Feb. 7, 1773 *(Arnold copy has "ROUSE")	1	34
ROWLAND, Andrew, m. Anna **MARSH**, d. John, 3rd & Rhoda [ ]	2	93
Andrew, Jr., of Fairfield, m. Anne **MARSH**, of Litchfield, Mar. 26, 1799, by Rev. Judah Champion	1	117
Anna, [w. Andrew], d. Feb. 18, 1819, in the 40th y. of her age	2	93
Eliza, d. Andrew & Anna, b. Oct. 2, 1802	2	93
Elizabeth, d. Andrew & Anna, b. Oct. 2, 1802	1	117
ROWLESON, Hannah, m. Chene **AMES**, Feb. 23, 1775, by Leah Hart, J.P.	1	166
ROWLEY, Ann Belinda, d. [Loomis & Rachel], b. Dec. 4, 1835	TM49	12
Charles M., s. [Loomis & Rachel], b. May 14, 1840	TM49	12
Loomis, m. Rachel **McNEILE**, Mar. 2, 1825	TM49	12
Loomis, m. Rachel **McNEILE**, Mar. 2, 1825, by Rev. Lyman Beecher	2	139
Mary Abigail, d. [Loomis & Rachel], b. July 1, 1838; d. July 25, 1838	TM49	12
Orton L., s. [Loomis & Rachel], b. Apr. 24, 1831	TM49	12
Orton Loomis, s. [Loomis & Rachel], b. Aug. 20, 1829; d. Aug. 31, 1830	TM49	12
Rachel Eliza, d. [Loomis & Rachel], b. Nov. 4, 1833	TM49	12
Ruth Belinda, d. Loomis & Rachel, b. Sept. 21, 1826; d. Dec. 6, 1833	TM49	12
RUSSELL, RUSSEL, Abigail, of Woodbridge, m. Harvey **PERKINS,** [ ], 1802, by Rev. Mr. Holley	2	122
Benjamin, s. Stephen & Margaret, b, July 16, 1778	1	117
Catharine, d. Emanuel & Betsey, b. Apr. 8, 1811	2	28
Catharine, m. William **SCOFIELD**, Nov. 23, 1851, by Rev. David L. Parmelee	TM49	65
Christania M., d. Emanuel & Betsey, b. Sept. 22, 1824	2	28
David, s. Stephen & Margaret, b. Oct. 22, 1790	1	117
Elijah, s. Stephen & Margaret, b. Mar. 13, 1773	1	75
Elijah, s. Stephen & Margaret, d. Oct. 1, 1777	1	74
Elijah, s. Stephen & Margaret, b. Aug. 18, 1787	1	117
Eliza Emeline, d. Emanuel & Betsey, b. Mar. 22, 1803, in Amenia, N.Y.	2	28
Emanuel, m. Betsey **WILLIAMS**, Nov. 2, 1801	2	28
George W., s. Emanuel & Betsey, b. [ ], 1819	2	28
Harriet C., d. Emanuel & Betsey, b. May 31, 1817	2	28
Henry, s. Emanuel & Betsey, b. Apr. 6, 1815	2	28
Isaac, s. Emanuel & Betsey, b. May 2, 1807, in Sharon	2	28
Isaac, s. Stephen & Sally, b. Mar. 4, 1810	2	56
John, m. Mary **WOODRUFF**, Sept. 1, 1777	1	115-6

	Vol.	Page
RUSSELL, RUSSEL, (cont.),		
John & Mary, had child b. Sept. 17, 1777 & Apr. 13, 1778	1	115-6
John W., s. Stephen & Sally, b. Jan. 28, 1804	2	56
John W., Dr., m. Eliza BEEBEE, June 2, 1828, by Daniel L. Carroll	2	276
Joseph, s. Emanuel & Betsey, b. July 15, 1809	2	28
Leonard, of Tond-du-Lac, Wis., m. Cornelia KENNEY, of Litchfield, Oct. 24, 1853, by Rev. Benjamin L. Swan	TM49	92
Lois, m. John WESTOVER, May 20, 1820, by Rev. Isaac Jones	2	255
Lucy, d. Stephen & Margaret, b. May 7, 1782	1	117
Margaret, d. Stephen & Margaret, b. Aug. 12, 1784	1	117
Mary Ann, d. Stephen & Margaret, b. Oct. 13, 1774	1	75
Mary Ann, d. Stephen & Margaret, d. Sept. 18, 1777	1	74
Stephen, m. Margaret ANDRUS, Dec. 20, 1772, by Rev. Andrew Storrs, of Waterbury	1	74
Stephen, m. Sally WADHAMS, Apr. 17, 1803, by Rev. Mr. Hooker, of Goshen	2	56
Stephen, m. Anne BUEL, Dec. 25, 1820, by Rev. Isaac Jones	2	98
Stephen, representative May 1830, May 1831, May 1834	2	1556
Thaddeus, of North Bremford, Mass,, m. Eliza HARRISON, of North Bremford, Mass., [May] 28, 1843, by Jonathan Brace	2	339
Thankful, m. Charles GOODWIN, Mar. 7, 1754, by Rev. Mr. Hemingway, of East Haven	1	14
Ursula, d. Stephen & Margaret, b. Sept. 9, 1776	1	75
Ursula, d. Stephen & Margaret, d. Sept. 25, 1777	1	74
Ursula, d. Stephen & Margaret, b. Aug. 5, 1780	1	117
William, s. Emanuel & Betsey, b. [ ] 1, 1805	2	28
William, s. Emanuel & Betsey, b. Mar. 29, 1813	2	28
William E., m. Emeline BRADLEY, b. of Torrington, May 24, 1827, by Rev. John J. Stone	2	270
——, of Torrington, m. Rachel H. MUNGER, of Litchfield, Dec. 13, 1840, by J. Brace	2	320
SACKE*, Sally, m. Elado OSBORN, Nov. 28, 1788, by Rev. Judah Champion *("Sally PECK m. Eliada OSBORN")	1	153
SACKETT, SAKET, Aaron, m. Phebe HART, July 6, 1786	1	201
Amanda, d. Aaron & Phebe, b. Aug. 23, 1795	1	201
Benjamin, of Warren, m. Thalia MOUNTHROP, of Litchfield, Oct. 31, 1827, by Rev. Hart Talcott	2	273
Charles, s. Aaron & Phebe, b. May 23, 1793	1	201
Clarissa, d. Aaron & Phebe, b. May 26, 1791	1	201
Eliza, m. Charles WADHAM, Feb. 6, 1826, by Rev. Levi Smith	2	260
Elizabeth, d. Aaron & Phebe, b. Apr. 8, 1789	1	201
Huldah, d. Aaron & Phebe, b. June 25, 1787	1	201
Phebe Hart, d. Aaron & Phebe, b. May 27, 1798	1	201
SAGE, Roswell, of Cornwall, m. Philomela HOSFORD, Feb. 5, 1824, by Rev. Isaac Jones	2	132
SALISBURY, Philip, m. Marinda BONNEY, b. of Litchfield, Oct. 18, 1839, by Rev. H. Bryant	2	325
SALTONSTALL, Thomas, m. Mary ANDREWS, b. of Litchfield, Aug. 10, 1854, by Rev. Lewis Gunn	TM49	111-½
SANFORD, Abby, d. Asa & Susanna, b. June 3, 1809	2	34
Abigail, d. Truman & Dina, b. July 10, 1808	2	35
Alson, of Goshen, m. Lucretia J. PRICE, of Milton, Mar. 11, 1849, by John F. Norton	TM49	36

	Vol.	Page
SANFORD, (cont.),		
Amanda, d. Asa & Susanna, b. Feb. 26, 1796	2	34
Amos, of Goshen, m. Huldah McNEILE, of Litchfield, Apr. 29, 1852, by H. L. Vaill	TM49	74
Anna, d. Truman & Dina, b. Apr. 12, 1811	2	35
Anna M., d. Ozias & Eunice, b. Feb. 10, 1818	2	88
Asa, m. Susanna **BALDWIN**, Sept. 15, 1790, by David Welch	2	34
Barzillai, s. Elias & Alice, b. July 7, 1786	1	163
Benjamin, s. Elias & Ellis, b. Apr. 18, 1784	1	163
Birdsey, s. Levi & Elizabeth, May 29, 1815	2	51
Catherine, d. Asa & Susanna, b. Sept. 9, 1791	2	34
Catharine, b. Sept. 9, 1791; m. Elias McNEILE, s. Samuell & Sina, Oct. 11, 1813 (Chenango Broome Cty., N.Y.)	1	109
Catharine, m. Elias McNEIL, b. of Litchfield, Oct. 11, 1813	TM49	18
Clarissa, m. William **BEEBEE**, Jan. 17, 1807	2	85
Clarissa, m. William **HARRISON**, Nov. 12, 1823, by Rev. Henry Robinson	2	130
Clark, s. Jonah & Rhoda, b. July 10, 1764	1	76
Daniel, s. Elias & Ellis, b. Mar. 3, 1780	1	159
Derick Rollin, s. Garwood & Diantha, b. Sept. 16, 1822	2	103
Darrich V. S., s. Asa & Susanna, b. July 9, 1801	2	34
Darrick V. S., m. Marinda **PALMER**, Nov. 1, 1827, by Rev. Isaac Jones	2	273
David, s. Truman & Dina, b. May 30, 1800	2	35
David C., m. Amelia S. **SEYMOUR**, May 25, 1830, by Rev. William Lucas	2	286
Deidamia, d. Stephen & Abigail, b. Sept. 11, 1774	1	157-8
Dina*, m. Truman **WEBSTER**, Oct. 8, 1795, by Rev. E. Camp *("Dima" in Woodruff's)	2	35
Dorcas, d. Asa & Susanna, b. Mar. 28, 1807	2	34
Elias, m. Alice **FULLER**, Jan. 23, 1776, by Rev. Mr. Backues	1	161
Esther R., d. Asa & Susanna, b. Jan. 20, 1804	2	34
Esther R., m. William **HAMMILL**, Oct. 8, 1824, by Rev. Lyman Beecher	2	136
Frances W., of Litchfield, m. Edward F. **ATWATER**, of New Haven, Oct. 20, 1846, by Rev. William Dixon	TM49	16
Garwood, s. Asa & Susanna, b. Dec. 14, 1793	2	34
Garwood, m. Diantha **BISSELL**, [ ], 1820, by Lyman Beecher	2	98
Garwood, m. Diantha **BISSELL**, [ ], 1820, by Rev. Lyman Beecher	2	103
Hannah, m. Ephraim **HARRISON**, Feb. 15, 1751, by Thomas Harrison, J.P.	1	57
Hannah, m. John **HUMASTON, Jr.**, Dec. 14, 1769, by Timothy Collens, J.P.	1	98
Harriet, m. Eliot **MASON**, Jan. 28, 1822, by Rev. Isaac Jones	2	109
James Harvey, s. Levi & Elizabeth, b. Oct. 7, 1816	2	51
Joel, m. Charity **WHEELER**, Oct. 8, 1832, by Rev. L. P. Hickok	2	288
John, s. Charles & Ellis, b. Mar. 20, 1782	1	161
John, of Hartford, m. Ann **BARNARD**, of Litchfield, Sept. 6, 1837, by Rev. Fosdic Harrison, of Bethlehem	2	317
John S., m. Sally **WHEELER**, Oct. 8, 1832, by Rev. L. P. Hickok	2	288
Jonah, m. Rhoda **WOODRUFF**, Dec. 7, 1757, by Thomas Harrison, J.P.	1	76
Jonah, s. Jonah & Rhoda, b. Jan. 27, 1773	1	118
Joseph, s. Capt. Joseph & Mary, b. July 28, 1745	1	35

	Vol.	Page
SANFORD, (cont.),		
Joseph, representative May & Oct. 1747	2	1546
Joseph, s. Jonah & Rhoda, b. Apr. 17, 1758	1	76
Joseph, 2nd, m. Chloe **GOODWIN**, Jan. 1, 1784, by Rev. Judah Champion	1	163
Joseph, s. Ozias & Eunice, b. May 1, 1820	2	88
Joseph Fuller, s. Elias & Ellis, b. Mar. 13, 1777	1	163
Levi, m. Elizabeth **TERREL**, Jan. 12, 1812	2	51
Lucinda, d. Elias & Alice, b. Aug. 14, 1778	1	163
Lucy, d. Ozias & Lydia, b. May 6, 1811	2	88
Lueza, of Litchfield, m. Richard **FOWLER**, of New Haven, Sept. 14, 1847, by Joseph Henson	TM49	23
Lydia, w. Ozias, d. Apr. 13, 1815, ae 27	2	88
Lyman, s. Truman & Dina, b. Nov. 7, 1805	2	35
Lynus, s. Solomon & Thankful, b. Sept. 22, 1776	1	163
Lynus, s. Solomon & Thankful, d. Feb. [ ], 1777	1	162
Marian, d. Levi & Elizabeth, b. Oct. 7, 1812	2	51
Marvin, s. Oliver & Elizabeth, b. Oct. 2, 1771	1	120
Mary, of New Haven, m. John **HUMISTON**, of Litchfield, June 5, 1738, by Rev. Isaac Hilles	1	16
Mary, d. Joseph & Mary, b. Oct. 4, 1739	1	35
Mary, d. Oliver & Elizabeth, b. June 4, 1762	1	120
Mary, d. Moses & Mary, b. Mar. 10, 1768	1	118
Mary A., of Litchfield, m. Edwin A. **BULKELEY**, of New Haven, Feb. 5, 1850, by Rev. William B. Hoyt	TM49	53
Mary Ann G., d. Asa & Susanna, b. June 11, 1811	2	34
Nathaniel, s. Joseph & Chloe, b. Oct. 27, 1784	1	163
Olive, m. Erastus **GOODWIN**, Jan. 30, 1799, by Rev. Judah Champion	2	262
Oliver, m. Elizabeth **LYON**, Feb. 8, 1762, by Jacob Woodruff, J.P.	1	161
Orinda, d. Oliver & Elizabeth, b. Jan. 27, 1769	1	120
Ozias, m. Lydia **BROWN**, May 24, 1810, by Isaac Aliton	2	88
Ozias, m. Eunice **HANDS**, Feb. 4, 1816, by Rev. Isaac Jones	2	88
Rhoda, d. Joseph & Chloe, b. Jan. 23, 1786	1	163
Rhoda, m. William Henry **HARRISON**, b. of Litchfield, Nov. 6, 1822, by Morris Woodruff, J.P.	2	115
Rhoda Pamela, d. Jonah & Rhoda, b. Apr. 27, 1768	1	159
Rollin, m. Maria **SEYMOUR**, b. of Litchfield, May 25, 1835, by Rev. Samuel Fuller	TM49	37
Rollin, m. Maria **SEYMOUR**, May 25, 1835, by Rev. Samuel Fuller	2	289
Roxanne, d. Oliver & Elizabeth, b. Dec. 10, 1766	1	120
Sally, d. Solomon & Thankful, b. June 29, 1778	1	163
Sally, d. Truman & Dina, b. Apr. 12, 1814	2	35
Saphira, d. Truman & Dina, b. May 18, 1802	2	35
Sarah, d. Oliver & Elizabeth, b. Sept. 15, 1764	1	120
Sarah, m. Ephraim S. **HALL**, [ ], 1785, by Rev. Joseph Bellamy	2	55
Simeon, s. Jonah & Rhoda, b. May 6, 1775	1	20
Solomon, m. Thankful **SPERRY**, Nov. 24, 1774, by Rev. Andrew Storrs, of Northbury, Waterbury	1	161
Stephen, m. Abigail **FULLER**, Jan. 6, 1774, by Rev. Andrew Storrs, of Waterbury	1	161
Susan, d. Asa & Susanna, b. Oct. 5, 1797	2	34
Susan Luissa, d. Garwood & Diantha, b. Mar. 4, 1821	2	103
Sylvia, m. Beriah **POND** [ ], 1787, at Plymouth	2	75

	Vol.	Page
SANFORD, (cont.),		
Thala, m. Levi **MOSS, Jr.**, Oct. 26, 1796, by Rev. Joseph E. Camp	2	79
SAUNDERS, Abigail, m. Bernard **McCONNELL**, Sept. 6, 1847, by Rev.		
Benjamin L. Swan	TM49	19
Mary Ann, m. James P. **TOMKINS**, June 27, 1824, by Rev. Isaac		
Jones	2	123
Orra, m. Philander **WESTOVER**, b. of Litchfield, Apr. 5, 1827, by		
Rev. Henry Robinson, of South Farms	2	269
Polly* R., m. James **TRYON**, June [ ], 1797 *("Patty"in Woodruff's)	2	31
Wealthy M., m. Horace L. **DEAN**, July 1, 1830, by Rev. L. P. Hickok	2	285
SAWYER, Henry W., m. Julia **AMES**, July 4, 1841, [by] J. Brace	2	334
SAXTON, Sylvester, m. Sophronia **HART**, June 24, 1840, at Wolcottville	2	249
SCOFIELD, Amanda M., m. Amza L. **STEPHENS**, June 29, 1832, by Rev.		
Mr. Taylor, of South Farms	2	289
William, m. Catharine **RUSSELL**, Nov. 23, 1851, by Rev. David L.		
Parmelee	TM49	65
SCOTT, James, Jr., of Falls Villiage, m. Clarissa A. **NEWCOMB**, of		
Litchfield, Oct. 1, 1848, by John F. Norton	TM49	26
Mary Ann, of Woodbury, m. John W. **WILMOTT**, of Litchfield, Mar.		
20, 1848, by Rev. Samuel Fuller	TM49	38
Sylena Ann, m. Silas Hays **MURRAY**, b. of Woodbury, Nov. 27, 1848,		
at Bantam Falls, by Rev. F. D. Harriman	TM49	39
SCOVILLE, SCOVIL, SCOVILL, Adna, [d. Roswell & Anne], b. July 18,		
1815	2	266
Ameret, d. [Roswell & Anne], b. Mar. 15, 1824	2	266
Hannah, of Litchfield, m. David L. **WOODRUFF**, of New Hartford,		
Feb. 13, 1823, by Rev. Epaphras Goodwin, of Torringford	2	118
Henry, s. [Roswell & Anne], b. July 30, 1826	2	266
James, twin with Julius, s. [Roswell & Anne], b. Dec. 1, 1818	2	266
Julius, twin with James, s. [Roswell & Anne], b. Dec. 1, 1818	2	266
Julius, m. Caroline N. **BUTTON**, Sept. 17, 1845, by Rev. Jno Morrison		
Ried, of Wolcottville	TM49	11
Lucius, [s. Roswell & Anne], b. Mar. 19, 1810	2	266
Palaski, s. Roswell & Anne, b. Jan. 28, 1808	2	266
Ransby, of Cornwall, m. Mary **BUEL**, of Litchfield, Mar. 9, 1831, by		
Rev. L. P. Hickok	2	287
Roswell, s. [Roswell & Anne], b. Dec. 31, 1820	2	266
Roswell, Jr., of Litchfield, m. Mary Ann **PALMER**, of Harwinton, Apr.		
4, 1852, by Rev. John J. Brandegee	TM49	67
Sally, m. Samuel **CATLIN**, of Harwinton, Dec. 8, 1824, by Rev.		
George E. Dumas	2	34
Squire, s. [Roswell & Anne], b. Feb. 16, 1822	2	266
SEDGWICK, Anne, m. Hezekiah **ORTON**, Sept. 2, 1745	1	69
Catharine Louisa, d. [Frederic] R. & Mary A., b. July 7, 1840	2	323
Frederic R., m. Mary Ann **STODDARD**, Sept. 18, 1836	2	323
Philo C., m. Eliza **ADAM**, Oct. 2, 1833, by Rev. David G. Tomlinson	2	293
Ruel, m. Harriet J. **BIRGE**, b. of Litchfield, Nov. 15, 1853, by Rev.		
John J. Brandegee	TM49	94
Theodore R., m. Mary Ann **STODDARD**, Sept. 18, 1836, by Rev. R. S.		
Crampton	2	299
Theodore Stoddard, s. [Frederic] R. & Mary Ann, b. Mar. 18, 1837	2	323
SEELEY, SEELYE, Abby, m. Curtiss **POTTER**, Sept. 23, 1821, by Rev.		
Asa Tallmadge	2	104

	Vol.	Page
SEELEY, SEELYE, (cont.),		
Horace, of Goshen, m. Harriet **POTTER**, of Orange Cty., N.Y., May 26, 1839, by Rev. H. Bryant	2	325
Luman, s. Justus & Sarah, b. Nov. 5, 1776	1	161
Mary R., of Goshen, m. George H. **WESTOVER**, of Litchfield, Jan. 19, 1843, by Rev. Ralph Smith	2	411
Sarah, m. Jobeas **LANSON** (colored), b. of Litchfield, Feb. 3, 1828, by Rev. John S. Stone	2	274
Thomas T., Dr., of Woodbury, m. Sarah **DEMING**, of Litchfield, Jan. 13, 1846, by Rev. Jno Churchill, of Woodbury	TM49	13
Truman, s. Justus, Jr. & Sarah, b. June 25, 1780	1	159
SEIMMAY*, Clarissa Irene, m. Thomas Sheldon **GRANNISS**, June 29, 1828, by I. Jones *("**SEYMOUR**")	2	277
SELKRIGG, SELKRIG, SILKRIGG, Hannah, m. Levi **WOODRUFF**, Oct. 1, 1787, by James Merret, J.P.	1	207
Lucy, m. Elijah **WAY**, Apr. 24, 1783, by Rev. James Nichols	1	204-5
SEPSON, Levi, s. Pomp & Clarry Davis, b. Jan. 28, 1801 (Probably colored)	1	151
SEYMOUR, SEYMORE, Aaron, s. Moses & Rachel, b. Mar. 4, 1749, at Hartford	1	241
Aaron, [s. Moses & Rachel], d. Sept. [ ], 1820, ae 71 y. 6 m.	1	241
Abigail, m. Peter **BUELL**, Jr., Dec. 25, 1766, by Rev. Judah Thompson	1	43
Amelia S., m. David C. **SANFORD**, May 25, 1830, by Rev. William Lucas	2	286
Amelia Selinna, d. Ozias & Selinna, b. Mar. 6, 1809	1	241
Amelia Selina, d. Ozias & Selina, b, Mar. 6, 1809	2	20
Anna, m. John **WETMORE**, Mar. 16, 1806, by Rev. Dan Hudon	2	61
Catharine, d. Moses & Rachel, b. Aug. 29, 1756	1	241
Catharine, [d. Moses & Rachel], d. Mar. 19, 1814, in the 58th y. of her age	1	241
Charles, s. Samuel & Rebecca, b. Mar. 13, 1793	1	122
Clarissa, d. Moses & Molly, b. Aug. 3, 1772	1	200
Clarissa, d. Moses & Molly, b. Aug. 3, 1772	2	248
Clarissa, d. Samuell & Rebecca, b. July 23, 1780	1	122
Clarissa, m. Truman **MARSH**, Oct. 22, 1791, by Rev. Ashbel Baldwin	2	20
Clarissa, m. Rev. Truman **MARSH**, Oct. 22, 1791, by Rev. Ashbel Baldwin	2	67
Clarissa, of Litchfield, m. Thomas R. **ROBEY**, of Brockport, Monroe Cty., N.Y., Oct. 22, 1828, by Rev. Isaac Jones	2	278
Clarissa Irene*, m. Thomas Sheldon **GRANNISS**, June 29, 1828, by I. Jones *(Arnold Copy has "Clarissa Irene **SEIMMAY**")	2	277
Delia Starr, d. Moses, Jr. & Mabel, b. Nov. 25, 1806	2	20
Dorothy, d. Moses & Rachel, b. Oct. 13, 1746, at Hartford	1	241
Dorothy, m. Abel **CATLIN**, Nov. 20, 1776	1	132
Dorothy, [d. Moses & Rachel], d. June 5, 1819, in the 73rd y. of her age	1	241
Edward, of Torrington, m. Harriet **JOHNSON**, of Bristol, Nov. 26, 1829, by Isaac Jones	2	282
Elizabeth, m. Samuel **NIVINS**, [ ]	2	26
Epaphraditus, s. Moses & Molly, b. July 8, 1783	1	200
Epaphraditas, s. Moses & Molly, b. July 8, 1783	2	248
Epaphras, s. Moses & Mabel, b. Aug. 7, 1812	2	20
Eunice, d. Moses & Rachel, b. Aug. 7, 1751, at Hartford	1	241
Eunice, m. Seth **LANDON**, Nov. 23, 1801, by Rev. Truman Marsh	2	25
Frederick J., of Waterbury, m. Florentine **MIGEON**, of Litchfield. Aug.		

	Vol.	Page
SEYMOUR, SEYMORE, (cont.),		
28, 1849, by J. D. Berry	TM49	43
George, s. Moses, Jr. & Mabel, b. Dec. 27, 1816	2	20
George, representative Apr. 1846, Apr. 1847	2	1557
Harriet, d. Samuel & Rebecca, b. Mar. 24, 1789	1	122
Harriet, m. Harry **FITCH**, colored, b. Mar. 13, 1826, by Rev. Seth Higby	2	27
Harriette Sophronia, d. Ozias & Selina, b. Oct. 25, 1806	2	20
Henrietta S., m. George C. **WOODRUFF**, Sept. 28, 1829, by Rev. Truman Marsh	2	77
Henrietta Sophronia, d. Ozias & Salinna, b. Oct. 25, 1806	1	241
Henry, s. Moses & Molly, b. Mar. 30, 1780	1	200
Henry, s. Moses & Molly, b. May 30, 1780	2	248
Henry, s. Moses, Jr. & Mabel, b. Nov. 25, 1808	2	20
Horatio, s. Moses & Molly, b. May 30, 1778	2	248
Horatio, s. Moses & Molly, b. May 31, 1778	1	200
James, s. Samuel & Rebecca, b. Apr. 20, 1791	1	122
James, representative May 1798	2	1552
Jane Maria, d. Moses, Jr. & Mabel, b. Mar. 7, 1811	2	20
John, m. Rachel E. **WETMORE**, Dec. 26, 1853, by Rev. John J. Brandegee	TM49	94
John Strong, s. Moses, Jr. & Mabel, b. May 15, 1803	1	241
John Strong, s. Moses, Jr. & Mabel, b. May 15, 1803	2	20
Loisa, d. Moses, Jr. & Mabel, b. May 12, 1801	2	20
Louisa, d. Moses, Jr. & Mabel, b. May 12, 1801	1	241
Luisa, of Litchfield, m. Stanley G. **LOCKWOOD**, of New Milford, Feb. 9, 1823, by Rev. Truman Marsh	2	118
Margaret, m. John **CATLING**, Aug. 25, 1731, by Nathaniell Stanley	1	7
Maria, m. Rollin **SANFORD**, b. of Litchfield, May 25, 1835, by Rev. Samuel Fuller	TM49	37
Maria, m. Rollin **SANFORD**, May 25, 1835, by Rev. Samuel Fuller	2	289
Maria S., d. Ozias & Selina, b. Mar. 8, 1813	2	20
Marana Norton, d. Moses, Jr. & Mabel, b. Feb. 13, 1805	2	20
Mary Jane, m. Daniel **ROBERTSON**, Aug. 23, 1838, by Rev. Stephen Hubbell	2	320
Moses, s. Moses & Rachel, b. July 23, 1742	1	200
Moses, s. Moses & Rachel, b. July 23, 1742, at Hartford	1	241
Moses, m. Molly **MARSH**, Nov. 7, 1771, by Rev. Judah Champion	1	159
Moses, m. Molly **MARSH**, Nov. 7, 1771, by Rev. Judah Champion	1	200
Moses, m. Molly **MARSH**, Nov. 7, 1771, by Rev. Judah Champion	2	248
Moses, s. Moses & Molly, b. June 30, 1774	1	200
Moses, s. Moses & Molly, b. June 30, 1774	2	248
Moses, Sr., d. Sept. 24, 1795, ae 85 y.	1	241
Moses, representative Oct. 1795, May & Oct. 1796, May & Oct. 1797, Oct. 1798, May 1799, May & Oct. 1801, Oct. 1802, May 1806, May & Oct. 1810, Oct. 1811, May 1811, May 1812	2	1552-4
Moses, Jr., m. Mabel **STRONG**, Feb. 23, 1800, by Seth Storrs, in Addison, Vt.	1	241
Moses, Jr., of Litchfield, m. Mabel **STRONG**, of Addison, Vt., Feb. 23, 1800, by Seth Storrs, J.P., in Addison, Vt.,	2	20
Moses McCure, s. Moses, Jr. & Mabel, b. July 31, 1814	2	20
Moses, Jr., s. Moses & Molly, d. May 8, 1826, ae 52 y.	2	248
Origin S., representative Apr. 1842, Apr. 1843, Apr. 1849, Apr. 1850	2	1557-8

	Vol.	Page
SEYMOUR, SEYMORE, (cont.),		
Orrigin Storrs, s. Ozias & Selinna, b. Feb. 9, 1804	1	241
Origin Storrs, s. Ozias & Selina, b. Feb. 9, 1804	2	20
Ozias, s. Moses & Molly, b. July 8, 1776	1	200
Ozias, s. Moses & Molly, b. July 8, 1776	2	248
Ozias, m. Selinna **STORRS**, Mar. 3, 1803, by Rev. John Sherman	1	241
Ozias, of Litchfield, m. Salina **STORRS**, of Mansfield, Mar. 3, 1803, by		
Rev. John Sherman	2	20
Rachel, d. Moses & Rachel, b. Dec. 17, 1744, at Hartford	1	241
Rachal, w. Moses, d. July 23, 1763, ae 47 y.	1	241
Rachel, [d. Moses & Rachel], d. July 24, 1794, in the 50th y. of her age	1	241
Rachel, m. Stephen **COGSWELL**, Dec. 21, 1823, by Rev. Lyman		
Beecher	2	133
Samuel, s. Moses & Rachel, b. Jan. 21, 1754, at Hartford	1	241
Samuel, m. Rebecca **OSBORN**, June 20, 1788, by Rev. Judah Champion	1	122
Samuell & Rebecca, had s. [ ], b. Mar. 13, 1794; d. Sept. 30,		
1794	1	122
Sarah, d. Moses & Rachel, b. Feb. 16, 1740, at Hartford, West Soc.,		
d. [ ], 1799, in the 59th y. of her age	1	241
Selina, w. Moses, d. Nov. 2, 1814, in the 29th y. of her age	2	20
Titus, s. Abel & Damaris, b. July 6, 1774	1	120
William Strong, s. Samuell & Rebecca, b. July 19, 1802	1	122
SHARP, Alva, m. Lucy **BISSELL**, Nov. 15, 1830, by Rev. William Lucas	2	286
Homer, m. Nabby Catlin **STODDARD**, Nov. 13, 1825, by Rev. Isaac		
Jones	2	258
SHARPLESS, Stephen, of Connellsville, Pa., m. Hulda **KELLOGG**, of		
Litchfield, Aug. 21, 1828, by D. L. Carroll	2	278
SHAW, Martha, m. Nathan **STEWARD**, Mar.* 11, 1760, by Rev. Hobert		
Easterbrook, of East Haddam *("Dec." in Woodruff's)	1	163
SHEARES, Joseph W., m. Charlotte S. **HUGHES**, Mar. 28, 1852, by Rev.		
David L. Parmelee	TM49	67
SHELDON, Daniel, m. Huldah **STONE**, May 13, 1784, by James Morris	1	200
Elisha, representative Oct. 1755, Oct. 1757, May & Oct. 1758, May &		
Oct. 1759, May & Oct. 1760, May 1761	2	1547-8
Elisha, s. Samuel & Elizabeth, b. July 15, 1782	1	161
Frederick, s. Daniel & Huldah, b. Mar. 2, 1785	1	200
Hannah, m. Dr. Seth **BIRD**, Feb. 8, 1768, by W[illia]m Pullen, V.D.M.,		
at Hartford	1	44
Harry, s. Daniel & Huldah, b. Oct. 18, 1790	1	200
Lois, m. Lynde **LORD**, July 7, 1757, by Rev. Judah Champion	1	63
Lucy, d. Daniel & Huldah, b. June 27, 1788	1	200
Lucy, of Litchfield, m. Theron **BEACH**, of Goshen, Jan. 9, 1832, by		
Rev. L. P. Hickok	2	288
Ruth, d. Feb. 21, 1818	1	37
Samuel, m. Elizabeth **BALDWIN**, July 31, 1780, by Rev. Judah		
Champion	1	161
Samuel, s. Samuel & Elizabeth, b. Dec. 28, 1784	1	163
William, s. Daniel & Huldah, b. Apr. 5, 1802	1	200
SHEPARD, SHEPHERD, Aaron, m. Susanna **CHAMBERLAIN**, Nov. 1,		
1759, by Jacob Woodruff, J.P.	1	118
Betsey, m. Hugh **REDDAN**, Nov. 27, 1820, by Lyman Beecher	2	98
Ezekiel, s. Ezekiel & Thankful, of Westfield, b. Dec. 12, 1743	1	77
Huldah, m. Philander **WESTOVER**, Mar. 27, 1823, by Rev. Lyman		

	Vol.	Page
SHEPARD, SHEPHERD, (cont.),		
Beecher	2	118
Huldah, m. Philander **WESTOVER,** Mar. 27, 1823	2	135
Lydia, m. David **BOOTH,** Mar. 4, 1821, by Rev. Lyman Beecher	2	251
Thankful, m. Alexander **THOMSON,** Aug. 17, 1747, by Rev. Timothy Collens	1	27
SHERMAN, Amos C., m. Minerva A. **SMITH,** Oct. 18, 1840, by Rev. Thomas Ellis	2	331
Ephraim, m. Eliza **MERRIMAN,** June 7, 1821, by Rev. Joseph E. Camp	2	107
Julia, m. Eleada **PECK,** May 7, 1826, by Joseph E. Camp	2	266
Martha, m. Phenias **BRADLEY,** Apr. 24, 1740, by Rev. Joseph Noyce, of New Haven	1	129
Martha, m. Levi **MOSS,** Jan. 14, 1773, by Rev. David Judson, of Newtown	1	24
Martha, m. Levi **MOSS,** Jan. 14, 1773, by Rev. Mr. Judson of Newtown	2	30
Polly Matilda, m. Ariel **BRADLEY,** Jan. 26, 1809, by Rev. Judah Champion	2	42
William, s. Ephraim & Eliza, b. Dec. 13, 1825	2	107
SHERWOOD, Cynthia, m. William **ELIOTT,** Mar. 13, 1824, at Southbury, by John Pearce	2	274
Samuel, of Manchester, m. Sarah **GIBBS,** of Litchfield, Aug. 3, 1845, by Rev. William Dixon	TM49	11
SHETHER, James, s. John & Sarah, b. Aug. 28, 1775	1	34
John, m. Sarah **SMITH,** Jan. 27, 1773, by Rev. Richard Moseley	1	34
Sally, m. John **PHELPS,** Oct. 24, 1780, by Rev. Judah Champion	2	40
Sarah Smith, d. John & Sarah, b. Apr. 20, 1774	1	34
SHORES, Heman K., m. Olive M. **BLAKESLEE,** Jan. [ ], 1822, by Rev. Lyman Beecher	2	108
SHOWERS, Alvinia, of Litchfield, m. Timothy E. **PARMELEE,** of Warren, June 7, 1829, by Hart Talcott	2	281
Elizabeth, of Litchfield, m. David **ROGERS,** of Warren, Aug. 30, 1829, by Enos Stoddard, J.P.	2	282
SHUMWAY, Sibel, m. Thomas **HARRISON,** Sept. 20, 1764, by Elisha Stoddard	1	99
SILKRIGG, [see under **SELKRIGG**]		
SILL, Sedley, of Sporta, N.Y., m. Abby M. **BARBOUR,** of Litchfield, Sept. 10, 1820, by Rev. Isaac Jones	2	96
SIMESON, Robert, m. Ann Eliza **CAMP,** b. of Litchfield, Oct. 16, 1851, by Rev. Benjamin L. Swan	TM49	66
SIMMONS, [see also **SIMONDS & SIMONS**], Rachel, m. Norman **STODDARD,** Apr. 28, 1822, by Rev. Isaac Jones	2	111
Rhoda, had d. Harriet McClemon, b. Jan. 16, 1810	2	3
SIMONDS, [see also **SIMMONS & SIMONS**], George, of New York, m. Venetta **WHETNEY,** of Litchfield, Mar. 28, [1852], by N. C. Lewis	TM49	74
SIMONS, [see also **SIMONDS & SIMMONS**], Mary, m. Seyming **BRADLEY,** b. of Litchfield, Sept. 19, 1830, by Rev. Bradley Sillick	2	286
Rhoda, m. Samuel **MUNGER,** Apr. 30, 1818, by Seth, Landon, J.P.	2	33
SIMPSON, Grace, m. James **WINSHIP,** Nov. 12, 1832, by Rev. L. P. Hickok	2	288
Robert D., m. Mary Jane **FOSTER,** Nov. 24, 1853, by David L. Parmelee	TM49	94

	Vol.	Page
SIPEON Celinda Elizabeth, d. [Levi & Mariah (colored)], b. Dec. 30, 1829	2	118
Charles, s. [Levi & Mariah (colored)], b. July 6, 1835	2	118
Henry, s. [Levi & Mariah (colored)], b. Aug. 3, 1833;d. Oct. 23, 1834	2	118
John, s. Levi & Mariah (colored), b. June 29, 1828	2	118
Mary Henrietta, [d. Levi & Mariah (colored)], b. Mar. 1, 1832	2	118
William, s. Levi & Mariah (colored), b. May 16, 1827	2	118
SISCO, Elizabeth, d. Jacob & Eliza, b. May 12, 1745	1	119
Hannah, d. Jacob & Eliza, b. July 7, 1739	1	119
Mary, d. Jacob & Eliza, b. Mar. 13, 1736/7	1	119
SKEEL, SKEELES, Patience, m. Moore GIBBS, June 29, 1786, by Rev.		
John Miner, of South Britain	2	15
Thresa Maria, m. Lyman BESSELL, [ ]	2	114
SKELTON, Mary M., of Litchfield, m. Hubbell B. CONE, of Wetumpka,		
Ala., Nov. 17, 1836, by Rev. Alpheas Geer, of Hebron	2	299
Millesent Parthenia, of Watertown, m. Rev. Ebenezer O. BEERS, of the		
New York Annual Conference, Dec. 27, 1842, by Jason Wells	2	337
Phila M., of South Farms, m. Welles D. DAVIS, of Portland, Jan. 18,		
1853, by Rev. Alpheas Geers, of North Guilford	TM49	78
SKINNER, Abigail, w. Gen Timothy, d. May 16, 1806	1	162
Alma, d. Timothy & Susanna, b. June 4, 1780	1	161
Alma, d. Timothy & Susanna, d. Sept. 4, 1797	1	120
Alma, d. Gen. Timothy & Susanna, d. Sept. 5, 1797, ae 18 y.	1	162
James, s. Timothy & Susanna, b. Sept. 24, 1784	1	161
John W., of St. Louis, Mo., m. Mary E. BRACE, of Litchfield, Dec. 8,		
1852, by Rev. Benjamin L. Swan	TM49	77
Oliver, s. Timothy & Susanna, b. July 18, 1782	1	161
Rebecca, of Hartford, m. Joseph MASON, Jr., June 4, 1734* by Rev.		
Mr. Dorr of Hartford *(correction: crossed out with 1754 written		
above)	1	65
Richard, s. Timothy & Susanna, b. May 30, 1778	1	157-8
Roger, s. Timothy & Susanna, b. June 10, 1773	1	157-8
Susanna, d. Timothy & Susanna, b. Nov. 25, 1775	1	161
Susanna, d. Timothy & Susanna, d. Aug. 17, 1798	1	120
Susanna, w. Gen. Timothy, d. Jan. 29, 1801	1	120
Timothy, m. Susanna MARSH, Nov. 15, 1770	1	120
Timothy, s. Timothy & Susanna, b. Aug. 18, 1771	1	120
Timothy, s. Timothy & Susanna, d. Nov. 3, 1790	1	120
Timothy, Gen., m. Abigail BALDWIN, May 17, 1801, by Rev. Judah		
Champion	1	122
SLADE, [see also SLATE], Asa, m. Susan MANSFIELD, May 17, 1826, by		
Rev. Henry Robinson	2	262
Asa, of Kent, m. Charlotte PLUMB, of Litchfield, Aug. 4, 1845, by		
John F. Norton	TM49	11
SLATE, [see also SLADE], Aaron, s. Samuell & Mary, b. Feb. 2, 1748	1	76
Ann, d. Samuell & Mary, b. Mar. 26, 1740/1	1	77
Eleanor, d. Samuell & Mary, b. June 2, 1746	1	119
Elizabeth, d. Samuell & Mary, b. Sept. 14, 1756	1	76
Ezekiel, s. Samuell & Mary, b. Jan. 15, 1752	1	35
Lemuel, s. Samuell & Mary, b. Sept. 10, 1759	1	76
Mary, d. Samuell & Mary, b. July 19, 1743	1	77
Samuel, s. Samuell & Mary, b. Nov. 14, 1743	1	77
SLOCUM, Mary, m. Charles GRISWOLD, Oct. 15, 1852, by Rev. David L.		
Parmelee	TM49	76

	Vol.	Page
SMEDLEY, SMEDLE, SMEDLYE, Aaron, s. Samuell & Esther, b. Mar. 9, 1750	1	119
Abigail, m. Samuel **ORTON**, Oct. 26, 1723, by Capt. Joseph Minor, J.P.	1	29
Abigail, d. Ephraim & Anna, b. Feb. 12, 1774	1	200
Abigail, d. Chester & Clarissa, b. [ ] 16, 1818	2	89
Ann, d. Samuell & Esther, b. Apr. 10, 1748	1	119
Anna, w. Chester, d. Apr. 14, 1809	2	89
Anne, d. John & Deliverance, b. June 7, 1760	1	76
Anne, w. Chester, b. Sept. 13, 1786	2	4
Anne, d. Chester & Anna, b. Aug. 28, 1818 (Arnold Copy says, "this entry is in the original book")	2	89
Aphelia M., m. William H. **LAWRENCE**, Oct. 26, 1854, by Rev. David L. Parmelee	TM49	105
Chester, s. Ephraim & Anna, b. Feb. 17, 1783	1	200
Chester, s. Ephraim, b. Feb. 17, 1783; m. Anne **LANDON**, Feb. 6, 1805	2	4
Chester, m. Anna **LANDON**, Feb. 6, 1805	2	89
Chester, m. Clarissa **LANDON**, Mar. 22, 1810	2	89
Clarinda, d. Chester & Clarissa, b. Jan. 17, 1811	2	89
Concurrance, d. Ephraim & Concurrance, b. Nov. 2, 1740	1	35
Concurrance, d. Nathan & Phebe, b. [ ]	1	122
Damaris, d. Ephraim & Concurrance, b. Feb. 4, 1747	1	35
Damaris, m. Richard **BLAKE**, July 6, 1769	1	127
Deliverance, d. John & Deliverance, b. Mar. 14, 1756	1	76
Edward, s. Chester & Anne, b. July 22, 1807	2	4
Edward, s. Chester & Anna, b. July 22, 1807	2	89
Edward, s. Chester & Anna, d. Dec. 6, 1808	2	89
Ephraim, s. Ephraim & Concurrance, b. July 14, 1742	1	35
Ephraim, Jr., m. Anne **GIBBS**, Jan. 28, 1767, by Rev. Judah Champion	1	76
Ephraim, Jr., s. Chester & Clarissa, b. Aug. 25, 1812	2	89
Ephraim, Jr., d. May 20, 1821, in the 79th y. of his age	1	34
Ephraim, Jr., d. May 20, 1821, in the 79th y. of his age	1	76
Eunice, d. Ephraim & Concurrance, b. Aug. 12, 1751	1	35
Eunice, d. Ephraim, Jr. & Anne, b. Oct. 27, 1767	1	76
Eunice, d. Chester & Anne, b. Nov. 8, 1805	2	4
Eunice, d. Chester & Anna, b. Nov. 8, 1805	2	89
Frederick, s. Nathan & Phebe, b. Nov. 25, 178[ ]	1	122
Gideon, s. Ephraim & Concurrance, b. Mar. 30, 1745	1	35
Gideon, m. Sarah **GIBBS**, Nov. 17, 1768, by Rev. Judah Champion	1	34
Gideon, s. Ephraim & Anna, b. Sept. 20, 1788	1	200
Gideon, s. Ephraim & Anna, b. Sept. 20, 1788	2	121
Gideon, m. Tryphena **STONE**, Feb. 15, 1808, by Rev. Truman Marsh	2	121
Gideon Lindorf, s. Chester & Clarissa, b. Sept. 12, 1823	2	89
Hannah, m. Josiah **STRONG**, Sept. 22, 1734, by Rev. Anthony Stoddard	1	37
Hannah, d. Ephraim & Concurrance, b. Mar. 1, 1756	1	35
Irene, d. Gideon & Sarah, b. June 8, 1776	1	159
James, s. Ephraim & Concurrance, b. Dec. 25, 1754	1	35
James, s. Ephraim & Concurrance, d. Jan. 20, 1755	1	34
James, s. Nathan & Phebe, b. June [ ], 1774	1	122
James, s. Nathan & Phebe, d. June [ ], 1776	1	122
James, s. Nathan & Phebe, b. Feb. [ ], 1790	1	122
James, m. Lydia G. **WAUGH**, Apr. 30, 1845, by Rev. David L. Parmelee	TM49	9

	Vol.	Page
SMEDLEY, SMEDLE, SMEDLYE, (cont.),		
Jemima, d. Samuel & Esther, b. Dec. 25, 1739	1	119
John, s. Sam[ue]ll & Esther, b. Jan. 4, 1730/1	1	37
John, s. Chester & Clarissa, b. Aug. 20, 1815	2	89
John, s. Chester & Clarissa, d. Mar. 12, 1816	2	89
Joseph, s. Chester & Clarissa, b. Nov. 18, 1821	2	89
Joshua, s. Samuell & Esther, b. Mar. 1, 1755	1	119
Lucina, d. Samuell & Esther, b. May 29, 1753	1	119
Lucy, d. Ephraim & Anna, b. May 29, 1785	1	200
Mary, m. William **HALL, Jr.**, Feb. 9, 1758, by Thomas Harrison, J.P.	1	17
Moses, s. Samuell & Esther, b. Jan. 23, 1746	1	119
Moses, s. Gideon & Sarah, b. Apr. 13, 1769; d. Sept. 6, 1770	1	36
Nathan, s. Ephraim & Concurrance, b. Apr. 12, 1749	1	35
Nathan, s. Nathan & Phebe, b. [ ]	1	122
Nathan, m. Phebe **DOOLITTLE**, [ ], by Rev. Judah		
Champion	1	122
Olive, d. Ephraim & Anna, b. Sept. 29, 1780	1	200
Olive, m. Ebenezer **BURGISS**, Mar. 20, 1804, by Rev. Amos Chase	2	54
Olive Birge, d. Chester & Clarissa, b. Feb. 26, 1820	2	89
Phebe, d. Nathan & Phebe, b. [ ], 1780	1	122
Phebe, m. David **HALL**, Mar. 4, 1802, by James Morris	2	72
Rachel, d. Chester & Clarissa, b. July 28, 1814	2	89
Sabra, d. Nathan & Phebe, b. Aug. [ ], 1776	1	122
Sally, d. Gideon & Sarah, b. Mar. 23, 1771	1	36
Sally, d. Chester & Clarissa, b. Jan. 15, 1817	2	89
Sam[ue]ll, Jr., m. Esther **KILLBORN**, Feb. 1, 1729, by Rev. Timothy		
Collens	1	37
Samuel, s. Samuell & Esther, b. Jan. 3, 1742	1	119
Samuel, d. Feb. 16, 1756, in the 54th y. of his age	1	76
Tryphena, d. John & Deliverance, b. May 20, 1738	1	35
William L., m. Julia C. **MARK**, May 9, 1836, by Rev. R. S. Crampton	2	299
William L., representative Apr. 1848	2	1558
SMITH, Aaron, representative May & Oct. 1808, May & Oct. 1809, May		
1811, Oct. 1811, May & Oct. 1812, May & Oct. 1813, May 1814	2	1554
Aaron Curtis, s. Horace & Almida, b. Sept. 8, 1812	2	23
Abby, m. John **PHELPS, Jr.**, May 24, 1817, by Rev. Isaac Jones	2	136
Abby J., m. James D. **CHAPMAN**, b. of Litchfield, Aug. 24, 1828, by		
Rev. Henry Robinson, of South Farms	2	277
Abel, s. Stephen & Ruhamah, b. Sept. 14, 1768	1	157-8
Abial, m. Abigail **JELET***, Sept. 24, 1729, by Rev. Benjamin Alton		
*("PELET" in Woodruff's book)	1	37
Abial, Jr., s. Abial & Abigail, b. Jan. 10, 1734/5	1	37
Abiel, m. Joanna **GOODWIN**, Apr. 19, 1739, by John Marsh, J.P.	1	119
Abiel, Jr., m. Hannah **BEACH**, Apr. 2, 1758, by Rev. Solomon Palmer	1	76
Abigail, d. Abial & Abigail, b. July 15, 1730	1	37
Abigail, w. Abial, d. July 12, 1738, in the 33rd y. of her age	1	36
Abigail, d. Josiah & Abigail, b. Aug. 12, 1743	1	119
Abigail, m. Zebulon **BISSELL**, May 21, 1749, by Rev. Mr. Gibbs	1	83
Abigail, d. Reuben & Abigail, b. Oct. 19, 1775	1	36
Abigail, m. David J. **THOMAS**, Dec. 26, 1830, by Rev. Joseph E.		
Camp, of Northfield	2	292
Abraham, s. Reuben & Elizabeth, b. Dec. 5, 1804	2	30
Abram C., m. Elizabeth **HARRISON**, b. of Litchfield, Dec. 5, 1838, by		

	Vol.	Page
SMITH, (cont.),		
Rev. Richard Woodruff, of South Farms	2	316
Alban, s. Eldad & Martha, b. Feb. 19, 1799	1	201
Alban, s. Eldad & Martha, d. Apr. 10, 1799	1	200
Almira, d. Horace & Almida, b. Apr. 26, 1815	2	23
Almira, m. Erastus L. **WEDGE**, b. of Litchfield, Mar. 23, 1834, by Hugh P. Welch, J.P.	2	294
Almira C., of Plymouth, m. Curtis P. **BLAKESLEE**, of Northfield, Sept. 24, 1848, by Rev. Joel L. Dickinson, of Northfield	TM49	26
Amasa, of Harwinton, m. Phebe Ann **WHEELER**, of Litchfield, Aug. 16, 1838, by Rev. Gad N. Smith	2	319
Ann, d. Abiel & Joanna, b. Apr. 20, 1740	1	119
Anner, m. Girdon **GRANNISS**, Mar. 3, 1808	2	71
Anna, m. Nathaniel **BISSELL**, Jan. 2, 1811, by Rev. Mark Mead, of Middlebury	2	148
Anna A., m. Merrett A. **CLARK**, b. of Northfield, Sept. 6, 1847, by Rev. J. L. Dickinson	TM49	19
Anna Amanda, d. [David & Anna], b. Sept. 4, 1828	2	66
Anna Harrison, d. Nathan D. & Marian, b. Dec. 1, 1821	2	121
Anne, twin with Elizabeth, d. Stephen & Ruhamah, b. July 20, 1773	1	157-8
Anson C., m. Clarinda F. **BURGE**, Nov. 27, 1836, by Rev. A. Billings Beach	2	299
Bateman, s. David & Mary, b. Jan. 21, 1792	2	1
Bateman, m. Julia **BISHOP**, Nov. 25, 1816, by Ephraim Depew, J.P., of Rochester, N.Y.	2	113
Benjamin, s. David & Anna, b. June 7, 1816	2	66
Benjamin F., m. Frances E. **WINSHIP**, July 15, 1830, by Rev. L. P. Hickok	2	285
Betsey, m. Leverett **DARROW**, Oct. 18, 1821, by Rev. Mr. Pettingill	2	104
Betsey, of Litchfield, m. Leverett **DARROW**, of Plymouth, Oct. 18, 1821, by Rev. Amos Pettingill	2	111
C. F., of Woodbury, m. M. **BRYANT**, of South Farms, May 30, 1852, by Lewis Jessup, of Northfield	TM49	75
Caroline, d. Hick & Hannah, d. [ ]	2	59
Catherine, m. Ira **BROWN**, Sept. 30, 1807	2	39
Charles, s. David & Mary, b. Mar. 12, 1804	2	1
Charles, s. David & Anna, b. Dec. 6, 1810	2	66
Charles, m. Susan **GUNN**, b. of Litchfield, Feb. 23, 1844, by Charles S. Webb, J.P.	TM49	2
Chester F., m. Dian C. **GRISWOLD**, Oct. 30, 1836, in Milton, by Rev. Amos B. Buel	2	299
Chloe, d. Stephen & Mary, b. Mar. 23, 1735	1	77
Chloe, m. Daniel **LANDON**, Jr., Nov. 9, 1755	1	105
Cloe, m. Samuel **SWEET**, Oct. 19, 1828, by Rev. Joseph E. Camp	2	292
Clarissa, d. Noah & Eleanora, b. June 13, 1786	1	157-8
Clarissa, d. Eli & Deborah, b. May 25, 1800	2	28
Clarissa, m. Sylvester **GALPIN**, Oct. 9, 1831, at West Haven, by Rev. S. William Stebbins	2	324
Cynthia J., of Litchfield, m. Curtiss F. **PLATT**, of Warren, Feb. 4, 1841, by Rev. Harley Goodwin, of Warren	2	332
Cynthia J., m. Sylvester **GALPIN**, May 2, 1841, at New Haven, by Rev. T. B. Truesdale	2	324
Daniel, s. Daniel & Mary, d. June 4, 1783	2	0

	Vol.	Page

SMITH, (cont.),

	Vol.	Page
David, m. Mary **BACKMAN***, Jan. 20, 1780, by Rev. Judah Champion *("BATEMAN" in Woodruff's. Residents of Litchfield)	2	1
David, s. David & Mary, b. Oct. 31, 1780	2	1
David, s. David & Mary, b. Feb. 26, 1784	2	1
David, s. Eli & Deborah, b. Feb. 8, 1788	2	28
David, s. Eli & Deborah, d. Mar. 2, 1788	2	28
David, d. Apr. 21, 1805	2	0
David, m. Anna **BARTHOLOMEW**, June 2, 1808, by Rev. Mr. Camp	2	66
David, s. David & Anna, b. Apr. 16, 1822	2	66
Deidamia, d. Josiah & Abigail, b. Jan. 1, 1732	1	119
Deidamia, m. Beriah **STONE**, Feb. 18, 1750, by Mr. Gibbs	1	119
Deidama, d. Supreme & Jerusha, b. Feb. 21, 1772	1	118
Deidamia, d. Jonathan, Jr. & Bethia, b. Mar. 1, 1776	1	157-8
Diantha, d. Nathaniel, Jr., b. Jan. 10, 1778; m. James **KILBORN**, Dec. 25, 1795, by Rev. Mr. Botts	2	16
Diantha P., m. William H. **TEMMINS**, b. of Bantam Falls, Feb. 14, 1849, by Joseph Henson	TM49	40
Dotha, d. David & Mary, b. Feb. 12, 1800	2	1
Ebenezer, s. Abial & Abigail, b. Feb. 14, 1736/7	1	35
Ebenezer, m. Hannah **BUELL**, Sept. 9, 1762, by Rev. Judah Champion	1	139
Ebenezer, m. Hann[nah] **BUELL**, Sept. 9, 1762	1	157-8
Edward, s. David & Anna, b. July 8, 1820	2	66
Edward Arnold, of Naugatuck, m. Lucy Elvira **NORTON**, of Litchfield, Oct. 1, 1848, by Rev. Samuel Fuller	TM49	26
Eldad, s. Jonathan, Jr. & Behtiah, b. July 23, 1768	1	157-8
Eldad, m. Martha **MOSS**, Dec. 12, 1792, by James Morris	1	201
Eleanor, m. Noah **SMITH**, Nov. 15, 1772, by Rev. Judah Champion	1	120
Electa, m. Tomlinson **WILLS**, Jan. 16, 1823, by Rev. Isaac Jones	2	117
Eli, m. Deborah **PHELPS**, Mar. 24, 1779, by Rev. Judah Champion	2	28
Eli, s. Eli & Deborah, b. Nov. 12, 1783	2	28
Elias, s. Stephen & Mary, b. May 20, 1739	1	77
Elias, s. Supreme & Jerusha, b. Feb. 20, 1766	1	118
Elihu Hubbard, s. Reuben & Abigail, b. Sept. 4, 1771	1	36
Elihu Hubbard, s. Dr. Reuben & Abigail, b. Sept. 4, 1771	1	159
Elihu Hubbard, d. Sept. 19, 1798	1	36
Elisha Hervey, s. Noah & Eleanor, b. May 26, 1780	1	120
Eliza E., of Litchfield, m. J. J. **LESCHER**, of Mt. Carmel, Ill., Nov. 12, 1851, by Rev. Benjamin L. Swan	TM49	66
Eliza Emmeline, d. Lyman T. [& Julia], b. Dec. 10, 1825	2	139
Eliza R., d. Lemuel & Nancy, b. May 7, 1806	2	92
Elizabeth, twin with Anne, d. Stephen & Ruhamah, b. July 20, 1773	1	157-8
Elizabeth, m. Lyman **WEBSTER**, Aug. 28, 1828, by Rev. Joseph E. Camp, of Northfield	2	292
Elizabeth, of Litchfield, m. George N. **ATWOOD**, of Bethlem, Dec. 8, 1847, by Rev. Philo R. Hurd, of Watertown	TM49	20
Elizabeth, of Litchfield, m. George W. **TILESTON**, of Williamsburg, Mass., Feb. 2, 1851, by Rev. William B. Hoyt	TM49	61
Elizur B., m. Almira **BISSELL**, Jan. [ ], 1821, by Rev. Lyman Beecher	2	100
Esther, d. Abial & Abigail, b. July 12, 1738	1	35
Esther, m. John **TRYON**, Sept. 22, 1755	1	79
Esther, m. Joseph **BISSELL**, Sept. 5, 1774, by David Welch, J.P.	1	43
Esther, m. Joseph **BISSELL**, Sept. 5, 1774, by David Welch, J.P.	1	167

	Vol.	Page
SMITH, (cont.),		
Esther, d. Stephen & Ruhamah, b. Oct. 19, 1774	1	157-8
Eunice, d. Eli & Deborah, b. Nov. 11, 1791	2	28
Eunice, m. Samuel M. **MERWIN,** May 10, 1801, by Rev. Noah Williston	2	144
Experience, m. Benjamin **HORSFORD,** May 9, 1723, by Capt. John Marsh, J.P.	1	16
Experience, d. Abiel, Jr. & Hannah, b. May 16, 1760	1	76
Fanny, d. Reuben & Abigail, b. Feb. 3, 1780	1	36
Finette, of Litchfield, m. Henry B. **FISKE,** of Waterbury, Aug. 22, 1849, by Rev. William B. Hoyt	TM49	42
Frederick, m. Triphena **STODDARD,** Mar. 14, 1827, by T. Marsh	2	269
Frederick Russell, s. Eli & Deborah, b. Mar. 3, 1796	2	28
George, m. Ellen **STONE,** Oct. [ ], 1824, by Rev. Isaac Jones	2	136
George Augustus E., s. Bateman & Julia, b. Aug. 23, 1819	2	113
George W., s. Lemuel & Nancy, b. Mar. 3, 1811	2	92
George Washington, s. Eli & Deborah, b. Mar. 20, 1798	2	28
Gideon, s. Abiel & Joanna, b. July 29, 1743	1	119
Hannah, d. Nathaniell & Mehetabel, b. Nov. 14, 1761	1	76
Hannah M., d. Lemuel & Nancy, b. Oct. 15, 1813	2	92
Hannah Maria, d. Hick & Hannah, b. Aug. 30, 1805	1	62
Hannah Maria, d. Hick & Hannah, b. Aug. 30, 1805	2	59
Hariette, d. David & Mary, b. July 18, 1782	2	1
Henry, m. Mabel **TAYLOR,** Aug. 2, 1773, by Rev. Judah Champion	1	161
Henry, m. Mabel **TAYLOR,** Aug. 2, 1773	1	161
Herman Landon Vaill, s. Reuben & Elizabeth, b. Oct. 18, 1815	2	30
Hezekiah, s. Jonathan, Jr. & Bethiah, b. July 13, 1766	1	157-8
Hick, m. Hannah **FORBES,** Sept. 11, 1799, by Rev. Joshua Knap	1	62
Hick, m. Hannah **FORBES,** Sept. 11, 1799, by Rev. Joshua Knap	2	59
Hiram, s. Eldad & Martha, b. Oct. 6, 1793	1	201
Hiram, s. David & Anna, b. Apr. 9, 1809	2	66
Horace, s. Eli & Deborah, b. July 13, 1789	2	28
Horace, m. Almida **POTTER,** Apr. 7, 1811, by Rev. Mr. Fowler	2	23
Huldah, d. Joshua & Sarah, b. Sept. 6, 1746	1	163
Huldah, d. Simeon & Rachal, b. June 8, 1763	1	76
Huldah, m. Daniel **GARRIT,** Nov. 12, 1794	2	94
Huldah D., m. Chester **BROOKEIR,** Mar. 27, 1831, by I. Jones	2	288
Ira, s. Hick & Hannah, b. June 16, 1800	1	62
Ira, s. Hick & Hannah, b. June 16, 1800	2	59
Ira, m. Sally M. **STONE,** Dec. 26, 1822, by Rev. Isaac Jones	2	116
Isaac Sanford, s. Stephen S. & Lucretia H., b. July 28, 1828	2	277
Isaiah H., s. Job & Elizabeth Ann, b. June 17, 1809, in Milford	2	83
Israel, m. Caroline **CATLIN,** Nov. 21, 1832, by Rev. L. P. Hickok	2	288
Israel H., m. Julia B. **HAND,** Nov. 21, 1848, by Rev. David L. Parmelee	TM49	39
J. Edward, M.D., of Kent, m. Octavia K. **BATES,** of Litchfield, May 2, 1853, by Rev. Benjamin L. Swan	TM49	93
Jacob, s. Abiel & Joanna, b. Nov. 3, 1747	1	119
Jacob, Jr., m. Mary **LEWIS,** Jan. 13, 1763, by Rev. Judah Champion	1	118
Jacob, s. Jacob, Jr. & Mary, b. Oct. 3, 1768	1	157-8
James, s. Jacob, Jr. & Mary, b. Feb. 25, 1772	1	157-8
James, s. [David & Anna], b. Apr. 6, 1826	2	66
James, m. Sarah Ann **MUNGER,** b. of Litchfield, [Nov.] 12, [1843], by Jonathan Brace	2	413

	Vol.	Page
SMITH, (cont.),		
James Fenn, s. Reuben & Elizabeth, b. Oct. 27, 1812	2	30
Job, m. Elizabeth Ann **NORTHROP**, Jan. 6, 1803, by Rev. B. Rine (?)	2	83
John, s. Josiah & Abigail, b. Nov. 1, 1735	1	119
John, Capt., d. Feb. 16, 1807, in the 69th y. of his age	1	162
Jonathan, s. Stephen & Mary, b. Nov. 6, 1747	1	119
Jonathan, Jr., m. Bethiah **DOOLITTLE**, Apr. 25, 1765, by Rev. Judah Champion	1	157-8
Jonathan, s. Jonathan, Jr. & Bethia, b. Feb. 1, 1778	1	157-8
Jonathan, s. Eldad & Martha, b. June 9, 1797	1	201
Joseph, s. Supream, b. Jan. 30, 1768	1	163
Joshua, m. wid. Sarah **PECK**, Nov. 15, 1739, by Rev. Timothy Collens	1	35
Joshua, s. Joshua & Sarah, b. July 17, 1754	1	163
Josiah, s. Josiah & Abigail, b. July 20, 1754	1	119
Julia, m. Jacob D. **STONE**, b. of Washington, Feb. 14, 1848, by Joseph Henson	TM49	23
Julia M., m. George H. **BALDWIN**, b. of Litchfield, Sept. 18, 1849, by Benjamin L. Swan	TM49	43
Julia Maria, d. Lyman T. [& Julia], b. Mar. 7, 1828	2	139
Kate, d. Henry & Mabel, b. Feb. 17, 1782	1	161
Lemuel, s. Jacob, Jr. & Mary, b. July 18, 1774; m. Nancy **JONES**, Nov. 17, 1797	2	92
Lemuel & Nancy, had infant b. June 5, 1818	2	92
Lester N., s. Job & Elizabeth Ann, b. Dec. 27, 1803, in Milford	2	83
Lester N., m. Abby **CATLIN**, Apr. 26, 1826, by Rev. Henry Robinson	2	262
Levi, s. Stephen & Ruhamah, b. Sept. 16, 1771	1	157-8
Levi, m. Polly **FENN**, Dec. 7, 1809, by Rev. Joseph E. Camp	2	126
Lewis, s. Eldad & Martha, b. July 19, 1795	1	201
Lorenda, d. Eli & Deborah, b. Oct. 11, 1779	2	28
Lorinda, m. Elijah **LYMAN**, Nov. 18, 1798, by John Welch, J.P.	1	62
Lovisa, m. Stephen **MOSS**, Dec. 25, 1810, by Rev. Mr. Scranton	2	35
Lovisa, m. Lewis **HUBBARD**, Jan. 10, 1813, by Rev. Mr. Ives, of Cheshire	2	121
Lucretia, m. Herman **BIRD**, Nov. 24, 1823, by Rev. Truman Marsh	2	131
Lucy, d. Reuben & Elizabeth, b. May 7, 1807	2	30
Lucy Ann, d. Hick & Hannah, b. Sept. 21, 1808	1	62
Lucy Ann, d. Hick & Hannah, b. Sept. 21, 1808	2	59
Lyman J., s. Lemuel & Nancy, b. Dec. 22, 1798	2	92
Lyman V., m. Julia **BISSELL**, Feb. 23, 1825, by Rev. Lyman Beecher	2	139
Mabel, d. Henry & Mabel, b. July 18, 1779	1	161
Madeira, d. Noah & Eleanor, b. June 25, 1778	1	120
Margaretta, m. William A. **HART**, July 5, 1787, by Judah Holcomb, J.P.	2	7
Maria Louisa, d. Stephen S. & Lucretia H., b. Oct. 27, 1826	2	277
Maria Theresa, d. David & Mary, b. May 8, 1786	2	1
Marian, d. David & Mary, b. Nov. 14, 1795	2	1
Marian, d. David & Mary, d. Jan. 18, 1798, ae 2 m.	2	0
Marian, d. David & Mary, b. Feb. 19, 1802	2	1
Maryan, d. Lemuel & Nancy, b. Jan. 15, 1816	2	92
Marietta, m. Alanson J. **PICKETT**, Dec. 8, 1829	TM49	64
Marietta, m. Alanson J. **PICKETT**, b. of Litchfield, Dec. 8, 1829, by Rev. Abraham Browne	2	283
Martha, d. Nathan D. & Mary Ann, b. Mar. 27, 1827	2	121

	Vol.	Page
SMITH, (cont.),		
Mary, d. Jacob, Jr. & Mary, b. Nov. 30, 1766	1	157-8
Mary, d. Supreme & Jerusha, b. Dec. 10, 1769	1	118
Mary, d. Jonathan, Jr. & Bethiah, b. May 24, 1773	1	157-8
Mary, d. David & Anna, b. Dec. 14, 1814	2	66
Mary, m. Joseph **TRYON**, May 23, 1817, by Rev. Lyman Beecher	2	140
Mary, m. Friend **PLUMB**, [ ]	1	195
Mary A., m. George **BROWN**, b. of Litchfield, June 25, 1848, by		
[Joseph Henson]	TM49	27
Mary A., Mrs, of Litchfield, m. Dr. G[ ] **POTTER**, of Prospect,		
Dec. 31, 1848, by Joseph Henson	TM49	40
Mary Ann, m. Daniel **GARRETT**, Jr., Sept. 24, 1841, by Jonathan		
Brace	2	335
Mary Sheldon, d. Reuben & Abigail, b. Oct. 29, 1773	1	36
Matilda, m. Lambert **JOHNSON**, Sept. 20, 1785	2	7
Mehetabel, d. Abiel & Joanna, b. Jan. 16, 1741/2	1	119
Mehetabel, of Wallingford, m. Josiah **BENTON**, Aug. 20, 1765, by		
Rev. James Dana, of Wallingford	1	84
Mercy, m. Nathaniel **GILLOT**, of Litchfield, Apr. 6, 1727, by Rev.		
Timothy Collens	1	15
Meriam, d. Joshua & Sarah, b. Nov. 6, 1752	1	163
Meriam, d. Noah & Eleanora, b. Sept. 21, 1788	1	157-8
Merrit, s. Lemuel & Nancy, b. July 18, 1801	2	92
Merrit, s. Lemuel & Nancy, d. Jan. 22, 1804	2	92
Meret, s. Lemuel & Nancy, b. Aug. 20, 1808	2	92
Minas, of Watertown, m. Emma **BLACKMAN**, of Litchfield, Jan. 24,		
1828, by Rev. Henry Robinson, of South Farms	2	275
Minerva, d. Noah & Eleanor, b. Feb. 18, 1776	1	120
Minerva A., m. Amos C. **SHERMAN**, Oct. 18, 1840, by Rev. Thomas		
Ellis	2	331
Moses, s. David & Mary, b. Mar. 31, 1788	2	1
Nathan D., m. Marian **HARRISON**, Mar. 19, 1818	2	121
Nathaniel, s. Abial & Abigail, b. Nov. 2, 1731	1	37
Nathaniel, m. Mehetable **GOODWIN**, Feb. 2, 1758, by Rev. Jonathan		
Marsh, of New Hartford	1	76
Newton, m. Minerva **PICKETT**, May 17, 1843, by Rev. David L.		
Parmelee	2	411
Noah, m. Eleanor **SMITH**, Nov. 15, 1772, by Rev. Judah Champion	1	120
Ogden, of Elizabethtown, N.J., m. Julia **KELLOGG**, of Litchfield, Nov.		
5, 1828, by Frederick Holcomb	2	278
Olive, d. Stephen & Mary, b. Oct. 20, 1733	1	77
Olive, d. Stephen & Ruhamah, b. May 11, 1770	1	157-8
Olive, d. Supreme & Jerusha, b. Jan. 25, 1774	1	118
Olive, d. David & Mary, b. Nov. 3, 1797	2	1
Olive, m. Dan **TROOP**, Jan. 1, 1818, by Rev. Lyman Beecher	2	112
Orange, s. Simeon & Rachel, b. June 4, 1765	1	76
Origin Charles, s. Charles & Susan, b. May 4, 1844	TM49	21
Peggy, m. Daniel **ROGER**, Apr. [ ], 1798, by Henry Rowland, of		
Windsor	2	76
Phebe, d. Joshua & Sarah, b. June 16, 1743	1	35
Phelps, s. Eli & Deborah, b. Jan. 4, 1794	2	28
Philo, s. Noah & Eleanor, b. Feb. 28, 1774	1	120
Phinehas, s. Nathaniel & Mehitable, b. Oct. 27, 1759	1	76

	Vol.	Page
SMITH, (cont.),		
Polly, d. David & Mary, b. Mar. 7, 1790	2	1
Polly, d. Reuben & Elizabeth, b. Jan. 17, 1798	2	30
Polly, d. Reuben & Elizabeth, d. Mar. 29, 1799	2	30
Polly Lewis, d. Reuben & Elizabeth, b. June 10, 1800	2	30
Prosper Wells, s. Nathan D. & Mary Ann, b. Mar. 11, 1825	2	121
Rachel, d. Nathaniell & Mehetabel, b. June 16, 1762	1	76
Rachal, m. Phinehas **OWEN**, Mar. 24, 1784, by Rev. James Nichols	1	68
Rachel Moss, d. Reuben & Elizabeth, b. Sept. 5, 1802	2	30
Rebecca, d. Jacob & Elizabeth, b. Dec. 25, 1756	1	163
Reuben, [twin with Simeon], s. Josiah & Abigail, b. Aug. 6, 1741	1	119
Reuben, s. Jacob, Jr. & Mary, b. Apr. 19, 1770	1	157-8
Reuben, of Litchfield, m. Abigail **HUBBARD**, of Middletown, Oct. 23, 1770, by Rev. Enoch Huntington	1	36
Reuben, Dr., m. Mrs. Abigail **HUBBARD**, Oct. 23, 1770, by Rev. Mr. Huntington, of Middletown	1	163
Reuben, 3rd, m. Elizabeth **MOSS**, Dec. 10, 1795, by Rev. J. E. Camp	2	30
Reuben, s. Reuben & Elizabeth, b. May 17, 1810	2	30
Reuben, s. Hick & Hannah, d. [ ]	2	59
Rhoda, d. Abial & Abigail, b. June 23, 1733	1	37
Rhoda, d. Josiah & Abigail, b. Jan. 10, 1756	1	119
Rhoda, alias **HUNGERFORD**, m. Milo **BEACH**, of Cornwall, Nov. 18, 1823, by Rev. Isaac Jones	2	130
Rosanna, m. Ezra **BURGESS**, Sept. 8, 1771, by Increase Moseley, J.P.	1	84
Rufus, s. Nathan D. & Marian, b. Sept. 25, 1819	2	121
Rufus, m. Mary Ann **McNEILE**, May 13, 1845, by George Hastings	TM49	10
Ruhamah, m. Stephen **SMITH**, Sept. 12, 1767, by Rev. Judah Champion	1	157-8
Ruth, d. Josiah & Abigail, b. Oct. 7, 1750	1	119
Sabra, d. Josiah & Abigail, b. Apr. 11, 1740	1	119
Sally, d. Noah & Eleanor, b. Aug. 21, 1782	1	120
Sally, d. Eli & Deborah, b. Sept. 10, 1785	2	28
Sally, m. Heman **OSBORN**, Nov. 6, 1808, by Rev. Truman Marsh	2	34
Sally J., m. William C. **WAKEFIELD**, b. of Litchfield, Sept. 12, 1842, by Rev. Isaac Jones	2	336
Sally Jennet, d. Ira & Sally M., b. June 23, 1824	2	116
Samuel, s. David & Anna, b. July 7, 1818	2	66
Samuel L., m. Jane M. **WICKWIRE**, Oct. 4, 1848, by Rev. David L. Parmelee	TM49	26
Sarah, m. Thomas **PECK**, Aug. 27, 1733, by Capt. [ ] Buel, J.P.	1	31
Sarah, d. Joshua & Sarah, b. Sept. 5, 1740	1	35
Sarah, of New Hartford, m. Adonijah **MOODEY**, of Litchfield, Nov. 9, 1742, by Rev. Jonathan Marsh	1	107
Sarah, d. Joshua & Sarah, b. May 4, 1749	1	163
Sarah, d. Stephen & Mary, b. Dec. 7, 1749	1	35
Sarah, m. John **SHETHER**, Jan. 27, 1773, by Rev. Richard Moseley	1	34
Sarah, m. Nathan **LANDON**, Feb. 13, 1788, by Rev. Judah Champion	2	88
Sarah Ann, m. Rufus S. **PICKETT**, b. of Litchfield, May 7, 1840, by Richard Woodruff	2	327
Sarah Ann, m. John **MARSH**, Apr. 19, 1853, by Rev. David L. Parmelee	TM49	93
Sidney, s. Hick & Hannah, d. [ ]	2	59

	Vol.	Page
SMITH, (cont.),		
Simeon, [twin with Reuben], s. Josiah & Abigail, b. Aug. 6, 1741	1	119
Stephen, m. Mary **STODDER**, Jan. 25, 1732/3, by Rev. Timothy		
Collens	1	77
Stephn, s. Stephen & Mary, b. Mar. 2, 1741	1	77
Stephen, m. Lidia **HALL**, Mar. 26, 1764, by Jacob Woodruff, J.P.	1	118
Stephen, s. Stephen & Lidia, b. Sept. 23, 1764	1	118
Stephen, m. Ruhamah **SMITH**, Sept. 12, 1767, by Rev. Judah		
Champion	1	157-8
Submit, d. Josiah & Abigail, b. Oct. 15, 1733	1	119
Submit, m. Jonathan **BISHOP, Jr.**, Dec. 18, 1753, by Rev. Mr.		
Mansfield	1	44
Supream, s. Stephen & Mary, b. Aug. 16, 1737	1	77
Supreme, m. Jerusha **KILBURN**, Nov. 25, 1764, by Rev. Thomas		
Davies	1	118
Thankful, b. Aug. 28, 1778, at West Haven; m. Benedict A. **LAW**, Apr.		
6, 1797	2	294
Thomas, s. Eli & Deborah, b. Oct. 22, 1781	2	28
Truman, s. David & Anna, b. Nov. 19, 1812	2	66
Truman, representative May 1821, May 1832, May 1834	2	1556
Truman, m. Julia A. **FOX**, Nov. 4, 1833, by Rev. Joseph E. Camp, of		
Northfield	2	292
Tryphena, d. Jonathan & Esther, b. Aug. 22, 1754	1	76
Tryphene, m. Samuel **ROSSETTER**, Nov. 12, 1775, by Rev. Judah		
Champion	1	34
Ursula, d. David & Mary, b. Nov. 3, 1793	2	1
Ursula, m. Daniel **PAGE, Jr.**, Feb. 11, 1821, by Rev. Isaac Jones	2	99
Wait, s. Josiah & Abigail, b. Nov. 13, 1737	1	119
Walter Edwin, s. [Charles & Susan], b. Sept. 17, 1845	TM49	21
Whiting, s. Phineas & Anna, b. Sept. 16, 1780	1	163
Whiting P., m. Catharine **GOODWIN**, Feb. 20, 1839, by Rev. Jonathan		
Brace	2	318
William, s. Stephen & Mary, b. Aug. 16, 1745	1	119
William, s. Jonathan, Jr. & Bethiah, b. Feb. 8, 1771	1	157-8
William, s. Henry & Mabel, b. Sept. 8, 1774	1	120
William, s. Henry & Mabel, b. Sept. 8, 1774	1	161
William, s. Lemuel & Nancy, b. Nov. 3, 1803	2	92
SPARKS, Osborn, of Sheffield, Mass., m. Sarah M. **TAYLOR**, of Litchfield,		
Sept. 2, 1846, by Rev. William Dixon	TM49	15
SPAULDING, SPALDEN, Frederick A., of Norfolk, m. Mary **GOODWIN**,		
May 1, 1836, by Rev. L. P. Hickok	2	296
Nancy, m. Joseph **HODGEE**, July 10, 1825, by Rev. Isaac Jones	2	143
SPENCER, Aaron, s. Ephraim & Sarah, b. Jan. 19, 1783	2	60
Aaron, s. Ephraim & Sarah, b. Oct. 29, 1806	2	60
Aaron, s. Alban & Abigail, b. July 23, 1808	2	70
Alban, s. Ephraim & Sarah, b. Jan. 13, 1785	2	60
Alban, m. Abigail **STODDARD**, Jan. 19, 1807	2	70
Anna, d. Zachariah & Mary, b. Apr. 16, 1783	2	9
Anna Maria, d. Alban & Abigail, b. Oct. 27, 1812	2	70
Clarissa, d. Ephraim & Sarah, b. Aug. 25, 1790	2	60
Clarissa, d. Ephraim & Sarah, d. Sept. 29, 1793	2	60
Clarissa, d. Henry & Rachel, b. Nov. 15, 1806	2	61
Clarissa, m. Artemus **WRIGHT**, of Winchester, Dec. 17, 1823, by Enos		

	Vol.	Page
SPENCER, (cont.),		
Stoddard, J.P.	2	78
Clarissa, d. Ebenezer & Hannah, b. May 3, 1824	2	253
Cornelia E., of Litchfield, m. William ANDRUS, of Hartford, Jan. 19, 1848, by Rev. Benjamin L. Swan	TM49	21
Ebenezer, s. Ephraim & Sarah, b. Aug. 16, 1801	2	60
Ebenezer, m. Hannah MERRIL, Mar. 4, 1823, by Rev. Isaac Jones	2	118
Ebenezer, m. Hannah MERRIT, Mar. 4, 1823, by Rev. Isaac Jones	2	253
Elias, s. Ephraim & Sarah, b. Mar. 22, 1795	2	60
Elias, s. Ephraim, Jr. & Cordelia, b. Sept. 25, 1824	2	253
Ephraim, m. Sarah STODDARD, June 4, 1782	2	60
Ephraim, s. Ephraim & Sarah, b. Feb. 15, 1793	2	60
Ephraim, Jr., m. Cordelia WOODEN, Oct. 26, 1822, by Rev. [ ]	2	253
Ercintha, m. Levi Scovil HOW, of Cornwall, Oct. 27, 1823, by Rev. Isaac Jones	2	94
Eunice, m. Warham GIBBS, Mar. 4, 1756, by Rev. John Graham, of Suffield	1	139
George, s. Ephraim, Jr. & Cordelia, b. Nov. 27, 1822	2	253
Hannah, d. Henry & Rachel, b. Sept. 1, 1802	2	61
Hariet, d. Henry & Rachel, Oct. 7, 1798	2	61
Henry, m. Rachel GATE, Oct. 31, 1797, by Rev. Mr. Blakeslee	2	61
Henry, s. Zachariah & Nancy, b. June 18, 1814	2	13
Henry, s. Alban & Abigail, b. Apr. 30, 1815	2	70
Henry, s. Alban & Abigail, d. July 22, 1816	2	70
Juliet, d. Ebenezer & Hannah, b. June 8, 1825	2	253
Juliaette M., of Litchfield, m. Frederjck PERKINS, of Torrington, Jan. 11, 1845, by Charles L. Webb, J.P.	TM49	7
Lemuel Johnson, s. Dyer & Triphena, b. May 9, 1808	2	272
Lucia, d. Henry & Rachel, b. Nov. 8, 1804	2	61
Lucius Wilder, s. Henry & Rachel, b. Apr. 24, 1813	2	61
Mary, d. Henry & Rachel, b. Jan. 26, 1809	2	61
Mary, d. Henry & Rachel, d. Aug. 21, 1809	2	61
Medad Gates, s. Henry & Rachel, b. May 24, 1800	2	61
Melinda, d. Alban & Abigail, b. Aug. 2, 1810	2	70
Michael, s. John & Elizabeth, b. May 26, 1761	1	118
Polly, d. Zachariah & Mary, b. Apr. 19, 1781	2	9
Polly Mary, d. Henry & Rachel, b. Aug. 7, 1810	2	61
Rebecca Ann, d. Henry & Rachel, b. Oct. 29, 1815	2	61
Rodman, s. John & Elizabeth, b. Feb. 19, 1759	1	118
Sally, d. Ephraim & Sarah, b. Nov. 14, 1796	2	60
Sally, m. Noah BEACH, Aug. 21, 1808, by Rev. Truman Marsh	2	29
Sally, m. Truman WESTOVER, Mar. 6, 1820, by Rev. Isaac Jones	2	138
Samuel Miles, s. Zachariah, Jr. & Nancy, b. Mar. 27, 1816	2	13
Solon, s. Ephraim & Sarah, b. Oct. 11, 1810	2	60
Sylvester, s. Ephraim & Sarah, b. Jan. 3, 1799	2	60
Truman, s. Ephraim & Sarah, b. Jan. 3, 1806	2	60
Tryphena, m. Labon BEACH, Jr., June 6, 1815, by Morris Woodruff	2	36
William Stoddard, s. Ephraim & Sarah, b. July 18, 1803	2	60
Zachariah, s. Zachariah & Mary, b. May 20, 1785	2	9
Zachariah, Jr., m. Nancy MILES, Sept. 1, 1808, by Rev. Judah Champion	2	13
SPERRY, Anna, m. Roswell HARRISON, May [ ], 1796, by Rev. Nathaniel Taylor	2	139

	Vol.	Page

SPERRY, (cont.),

Eliza M., m. John R. **COLT**, May 21, 1854, by Rev. David L. Parmelee — TM49 — 101

Hull, m. Ann Louisa P. **THRALL**, Apr. 10, 1834, by Rev. L. P. Hickok — 2 — 288

Mary, m. Abner **PARKER**, Dec. 22, 1785, by Rev. Noah Merwin, of Washington — 2 — 15

Sarah Ann, of Litchfield, m. John William **COOK**, of New York City, July 19, 1848, by Rev. Samuel Fuller — TM49 — 38

Thaddeus, of Goshen, m. Sylvia M. **LANDON**, of Litchfield, Dec. 28, 1826, at the house of Heman Beach, by Rev. Frances H. Case, of Goshen — 2 — 268

Thankful, m. Solomon **SANFORD**, Nov. 24, 1774, by Rev. Andrew Storrs, of Northbury, Waterbury — 1 — 161

SPOONER, Elkanah, of Woodbury, m. Mrs. Lucia **STONE**, of Litchfield, Jan. 29, 1838, by Enos Stoddard, J.P. — 2 — 315

SPRAGUE, Julia Maria, m. William Guy **MILLER**, b. of Litchfield, Nov. 7, 1847, by Rev. Samuel Fuller — TM49 — 38

SPRINGER, Phebe, m. Ruel **PLANT**, Sept. 18, 1807, by Rev. Truman Marsh — 2 — 110

STAMFORD, Caroline Elizabeth, d. David & Eliza, b. Sept. 2, 1820 — 2 — 117

David, m. Eliza **BURNHAM**, Dec. 12, 1812, by Rev. Isaac Jones — 2 — 117

STANLEY, Abigail, d. Timothy, Jr. & Mary, b. Mar. 21, 1762 — 1 — 34

Eunice, d. Timothy, Jr. & Mary, b. Feb. 19, 1764 — 1 — 34

Frederic, s. Timothy, Jr. & Mary, b. Apr. 15, 1758 — 1 — 34

Frederick, m. Sabra **BISHOP**, Sept. 25, 1781 — 1 — 162

Henry, s. Frederick & Sabra, b. Feb. 9, 1783 — 1 — 162

Mary, d. Timothy, Jr. & Mary, b. June 10, 1756 — 1 — 34

Pamela, d. Timothy, Jr. & Mary, b. Feb. 25, 1760 — 1 — 34

Timothy, 3rd, m. Lucy **WOODRUFF**, Dec. 22, 1775, by Rev. Abel Newell, of Goshen — 1 — 161

Timothy, s. Timothy & Lucy, b. Apr. 6, 1777 — 1 — 161

STANTON, Mary Ann, of Litchfield, m. William **GIBSON**, of New Marlborough, Mass., Nov. 23, 1842, by Jonathan Brace — 2 — 411

STARR, STAR, Ann Eliza, d. Henry & Clarissa, b. Dec. 2, 1814 — 2 — 11

Caroline, d. Daniel & Rachel, b. Nov. 8, 1803 — 1 — 201

Daniel, m. Rachel **BUELL**, Apr. 20, 1784, by Rev. Judah Champion — 1 — 201

Harriet, d. Daniel & Rachel, b. Jan. 27, 1801 — 1 — 201

Harry, s. Daniel & Rachel, b. Jan. 12, 1785 — 1 — 201

Henry, m. Clarrissa **PECK**, May 1, 1808, by Rev. Dan Huntington — 2 — 11

Henry Daniel, s. Henry & Clarissa, b. Nov. 20, 1810 — 2 — 11

Jane, d. Daniel & Rachel, b. Jan. 20, 1807 — 1 — 201

Jane F., m. Birdsey **NEVINS**, Sept. 1, 1834, by Rev. L. P. Hickok — 2 — 288

Jerusha, d. Daniel & Rachel, b. Apr. 5, 1789 — 1 — 201

Julia Anne Belle, d. Henry & Clarrissa, b. Mar. 11, 1809 — 2 — 11

Lucy, d. Daniel & Rachel, b. Jan. 27, 1792 — 1 — 201

Nancy, d. Daniel & Rachel, b. Jan 12, 1787 — 1 — 201

Sally M., m. Daniel L. **BENTON**, b. of Litchfield, Nov. 30, 1829, by Morris Woodruff, J.P. — 2 — 283

Thomas, of Washington, m. Anna **STODDARD**, of Litchfield, May 8, 1823, by Morris Woodruff, J.P.   (Perhaps "Starr **THOMAS**") — 2 — 102

STEARNS, Josiah L., Dr. of New York City, m. Louisa C. **JUDD**, of Litchfield, May 1, 1839, by Rev. Richard Woodruff — 2 — 324

STEBBINS, Luther Holcomb, of Hartland, m. Julia **WEBSTER**, of Litchfield, Sept. 30, 1845, by Rev. Samuel Fuller — TM49 — 37

	Vol.	Page
STEDMAN, Almorian, s. Ebenezer & Thankfull, b. Aug. 2, 1800	2	18
Amanda, d. Ebenezer & Thankfull, b. Nov. 18, 1805	2	18
Amanda, m. James **TRYON,** Mar. [ ], 1824, by Rev. Joseph E. Camp	2	265
Artimitia, d. Ebenezer & Thankfull, b. Oct. 9, 1807	2	18
Ebenezer, s. Ebenezer & Thankfull, b. Dec. 9, 1801	2	18
Isaac, s. Ebenezer & Thankfull, b. July 21, 1810	2	18
Ives M., s. Ebenezer & Thankfull, b. Jan. 26, 1813	2	18
Ruby, d. Ebenezer & Thankfull, b. July 24, 1804	2	18
Ruby, m. Merret N. **WOODRUFF,** Oct. 9, 1825, by Rev. Frederick Holcomb	2	257
STEEL, Charles, m. Sally **CABLE,** Jan. 15, 1822, by Morris Woodruff, J.P.	2	109
Rosamond, m. Nathan **FARNUM,** Dec. 22, 1762, by Rev. Joseph Bellamy, of Woodbury	1	13
Wealthy, m. Samuel **BARNARD,** Sept. 30, 1787	2	62
STEPHENS, [see also **STEVENS**], Amza L., m. Amanda M. **SCOFIELD,** June 29, 1832, by Rev. Mr. Taylor, of South Farms	2	289
W[illia]m A., m. Mary A. **BEACH,** Feb. 14, 1844, by Rev. D. L. Marks	TM49	4
STEVENS, [see also **STEPHENS**], Amelia, m. Frederick **BEACH,** Nov. 7, 1828, by Rev. I. Jones	2	278
Angeline, m. Newton **ENSIGN,** b. of Litchfield, Mar. 29, 1829, by Rev. Henry Robinson, of South Farms	2	280
Charles Edwin, s. Isaac & Hannah J., b. Feb. 17, 1827	2	272
Henry W., m. Jane **WADHAMS,** Oct. 21, 1845, by Rev. David L. Parmelee	TM49	11
Isaac, m. Hannah J. **PLATT,** Sept. 7, 1814, at New Haven, by Rev. Mr. Taylor	2	272
James, m. Mary Irene **GUILD,** Feb. 1, 1837, by Rev. A. Billings Beach	2	299
John, s. Isaac & Hannah J., b. Sept. 10, 1823, at Plymouth	2	272
John, m. Sarah Ann **BARNES,** b. of Litchfield, Aug. 2, 1846, by Rev. Samuel Fuller	TM49	38
Margaret, m. Hezekiah **THOMAS, Jr.,** May 10, 1821, by Rev. Isaac Jones	2	102
Robert, s. Isaac [& Hannah J.], b. Dec. 21, 1829, at South Farms	2	272
Robert, m. Dama M. **NEAL,** b. of Litchfield, Nov. 26, [1851], by N. C. Lewis	TM49	66
Sally M., m. Albert **ROBERTS,** Oct. 31, 1827, by Rev. Joseph E. Camp, of Northfield	2	292
Seymour, m. Emeline Letitia **GOULD,** b. of Litchfield, Feb. 19, 1829, by Rev. Harry Finch	2	280
Thomas B., m. Emeline A. **WHEELER,** May 7, 1845, by Rev. D. L. Marks	TM49	10
Ursula, m. Dan J. **JUDD,** Apr. 23, 1828, by Rev. Joseph E. Camp, of Northfield	2	292
STEWARD, [see under **STEWART**]		
STEWART, STEWARD, Alice, d. Nathan & Martha, b. Jan. 10, 1776	1	161
Anne, Mrs., m. Eber **PETERS,** Oct. 22, 1836, by Rev. E. Washburn	2	299
Betsey, d. Nathan & Martha, b. May 1, 1784	1	157-8
Betsey, m. Julius **GRISWOULD,** June 1, 1808	2	66
Daniel, m. Phebe **CHAPMAN,** Jan. 11, 1762, by Rev. Joseph Fowler, of East Haddam	1	159
Daniel, s. Daniel & Phebe, b. Nov. 18, 1762	1	159
George, m. Ann **HUNTER,** Sept. 10, 1843, by Rev. David S. Marks	2	413
Hannah, d. Nathan & Martha, b. July 6, 1763	1	163

	Vol.	Page
STEWART, STEWARD, (cont.),		
Jared, s. Nathan & Martha, b. June 4, 1761	1	163
Jared, s. Nathan & Martha, b. June 22, 1779	1	157-8
John L., m. Betsey L. **ANDREWS**, June 30, 1833, by Rev. L. P. Hickok	2	288
Luna, d. Nathan & Martha, b. Sept. 3, 1786	1	157-8
Luna, m. Birdsey **NORTON**, Sept. 14, 1806, by Rev. Asahel Hooker	2	29
Marjory, m. Caleb **GIBBS**, June 30, 1757, by Rev. Judah Champion	1	139
Martha, d. Nathan & Martha, b. July 30, 1771	1	34
Martha, d. Nathan & Martha, b. July 30, 1771	1	159
Martha, w. Nathan, d. Nov. 27, 1786	1	157-8
Molly, d. Nathan & Martha, b. June 17, 1769	1	159
Nathan, m. Martha **SHAW**, Mar. 11, 1760, by Rev. Hobert Easterbrook, of East Haddam	1	163
Nathan, s. Nathan & Martha, b. Apr. 27, 1765	1	163
Phebe, d. Daniel & Phebe, b. Dec. 21, 1766	1	159
Sally, of Litchfield, m. Caleb **PICKET**, of Danbury, Sept. 16, 1801, by Rev. Judah Champion	2	21
Sarah, d. Nathan & Martha, b. May 24, 1773	1	34
Sarah, d. Nathan & Martha, b. Sept. 1, 1781	1	157-8
William, s. Nathan & Martha, b. June 5, 1767	1	159
STILES, Richard W., m. Elizabeth **COOK**, Aug. 31, 1824, by Rev. Lyman Beecher	2	13
STILSON, STILLSON, Eunice, m. William **THROOP**, Apr. 27, 1775, by Daniel Everitt, J.P.	1	121
Samuel H., m. Clarinda **WICKWIRE**, Mar. 4, 1844, by Rev. David L. Parmelee	TM49	4
STIMPSON, Lovett, of Norfolk, m. Mariette **NORTON**, of Litchfield, July 29, 1849, by Rev. William B. Hoyt	TM49	42
STOCKBRIDGE, Joseph, of New York, m. Amanda E. **PLUMB**, of Litchfield, Jan. 19, 1847, by Rev. Benjamim L. Swan	TM49	17
STOCKER, Betsey, m. Ebenezer **JOHNSON**, June 20, 1821, by Ozias Lewis, J.P.	2	103
Hannah, m. Daniel **KEELER**, Oct. [ ], 1809, by Rev. Truman Marsh	2	48
STOCKING, STOCKIN, Pierce, m. Benjamin **MOORE**, Feb. 14, 1811, by Lyman Beecher	2	1
Rachel, m. Senier **BEACH**, Mar. 12, 1781, by Rev. Mr. Champion	1	249
STOCKMAN, Silas, m. Sarah E. **WHITTLESEY**, Nov. 25, 1847, by Rev. David L. Parmalee	TM49	20
STOCKWELL, Abigail, m. Joseph **KILBORN, Jr.**, Nov. 12, 1723	1	21
Hannah, m. Abraham **HASKIN**, Feb. 10, 1774, by Rev. Judah Champion	1	17
Sarah, m. Joshua **BORDMAN**, Feb. 14, 1724/5, by Rev. Timothy Collens	1	5
STODDARD, STODDER, STODDOR, Aron, s. Moses & Ruth, b. July 15, 1739	1	77
Aaron, d. Jan. 12, 1777, in captivity in New York	1	162
Abigail, d. James & Abigail, b. Oct. 2, 1743	1	119
Abigail, d. James & Abigail, b. Mar. 22, 1749	1	119
Abigail, m. Abel **BARNES**, Jan. 19, 1752, by Thomas Harrison, J.P.	1	128
Abigail, m. Edward **JOHNSON, Jr.**, Nov. 13, 1760	1	59
Abigail, d. Moses, Jr. & Abigail, b. Nov. 7, 1768	1	159
Abigail, m. Timothy **FOOT**, Oct. 2, 1791, by Rev. Amos Chase	1	176-7
Abigail, m. Alban **SPENCER**, Jan. 19, 1807	2	70

	Vol.	Page
STODDARD, STODDER, STODDOR, (cont.),		
Abigail, d.Jasper & Sophia, b. Sept. 21, 1815	2	251
Abigail, m. Heman **OSBORN**, Sept. 9, 1827, by Rev. Isaac Jones	2	272
Alanson, s. Enos & Aurelia, b. Dec. 31, 1813	2	100
Alanson, m. Wealth S. **BARNARD**, b. of Litchfield, Aug. 17, 1837, by		
Enos Stoddard, J.P.	2	313
Alanson, m. Wealthy S. **BARNARD**, Aug. 17, 1837, by Enos Stoddard	2	327
Albert, s. Enos & Aurillia, b. Nov. 20, 1801	2	100
Albert, m. Delia E. **McCALL**, b. of Litchfield, May 21, 1851, by		
William B. Hoyt	TM49	63
Anna, d. Enos & Aurillia, b. Nov. 11, 1805	2	100
Anna, of Litchfield, m. Thomas **STARR***, of Washington, May 8, 1823,		
by Morris Woodruff, J.P. *(Perhaps "Starr **THOMAS**")	2	102
Anthy, d. Enos & Aurillia, b. June 24, 1808	2	100
Asa B., s. Enos & Aurillia, b. Aug. 28, 1800	2	100
Azel, s. Obed & Susan, b. Jan. 25, 1800	2	8
Betsey, d. Obed & Susan, b. June 6, 1808	2	8
Briant, s. James & Abigail, b. Nov. 16, 1739	1	119
Briant, m. Phebe **BARNES**, Apr. 21, 1763, by Jacob Woodruff, J.P.	1	118
Catharine, d. Levi & Patty, b. Apr. 30, 1801	2	53
Catharine, d. Jasper & Sophia, b. Oct. 25, 1827	2	251
Charles, s. Enos & Aurelia, b. Mar. 17, 1818	2	100
Chester, s. Enos & Aurilia, b. Nov. 23, 1810	2	100
Chesterfield Valentine, s. Obed & Susan, b. July 16, 1810	2	8
Clarissa, d. Briant & Phebe, b. June 24, 1774	1	120
Cynthia, d. Enos & Aurillia, b. Apr. 18, 1799	2	100
Daniel, s. John & Eunice, b. Apr. 29, 1760	1	159
Daniel, m. Lorana **STONE**, Oct. 2, 1783	2	66
Daniel, m. Lucretia **BISHOP**, Apr. 29, 1797	2	66
Daniel B., m. Maria D. **COE**, May 31, 1831, by Rev. L. P. Hickok	2	287
Daniel Bradley, s. Daniel & Lucretia, b. Mar. 5, 1808	2	66
David, s. Moses & Ruth, b. Aug. 8, 1747	1	35
David Camp, s. Samuel & Sarah, b. Jan. 26, 1821; d. Nov. 13, 1822	2	93
Dewitt, s. Jasper & Sophia, b. Aug. 6, 1838	2	251
Diantha, of Litchfield, m. Leavitt **MONROE**, of Mindeth, N.Y., Nov. 6,		
1836, in Bradleyville, by Rev. A. Billings Beach	2	284
Eliza, d. Jasper & Sophia, b. Oct. 27, 1823	2	251
Ellen, d. Jasper & Sophia, b. Sept. 17, 1835	2	251
Emily, d. Obed & Susan, b. May 20, 1806	2	8
Enoch, s. Moses & Abigail, b. Apr. 24, 1767	1	120
Enos, s. Moses & Abigail, b. July 23, 1777	1	120
Enos, m. Aurillia **BACON**, May 14, 1798, by [ ]	2	100
Enos, s. Enos & Aurelia, b. Feb. 23, 1812	2	100
Enos, Jr., m. Catharine C. **MARSH**, Mar. 24, 1837, by Rev. A. Billings		
Beach	2	298
Enos, representative Apr. 1842, Apr. 1843	2	1557
Enos, farmer, ae 39, m. Hannah **KEELER**, ae 29, b. of Litchfield, May		
31, 1853, by Rev. Daniel E. Brown, of Bantam. Witnesses Daniel		
Keeler & Sherman Keeler	TM49	94
Erastus, s. Briant, b. Sept. 4, 1766; d. Feb. 14, 1767	1	36
Eunice, d.Jesse & Anne, b. Feb. 2, 1792	1	201
Eunice, m. Guy **HAND**, Dec. 26, 1812, by Rev. Truman Marsh	2	15
Eunice, d. Samuel & Sarah, b. May 17, 1816	2	93

	Vol.	Page
STODDARD, STODDER, STODDOR, (cont.),		
Everretta Elizabeth, d. [Alanson & Wealthy S.], b. June 7, 1848	2	326
Frederick, m. Jenette **WILMOTT**, b. of Litchfield, Dec. 31, 1844, by		
G. C. V. Eastman	TM49	8
Frederick Samuel, s. Harmon & Nancy, b. Sept. 20, 1825	2	131
Frederick Sam[ue]ll, s. Herman & Nancy, b. Sept. 20, 1825	2	259
Freeman, s. Herman & Nancy, b. July 29, 1829	2	259
George, s. Jasper & Sophia, b. Mar. 11, 1833	2	251
George, m. Julia E. **HAYES**, Apr. 9, 1854, by Rev. David L. Parmelee	TM49	85
Gideon, s. Obed & Mary, b. Feb. 2, 1768	1	159
Gideon, m. Anna **KILBORN**, Feb. 28, 1790	2	87
Hannah, d. Moses & Ruth, b. Mar. 24, 1733	1	37
Hannah, d. John & Eunice, b. July 25, 1756	1	159
Henry, s. Gideon & Anna, b. Dec. 5, 1806	2	87
Henry Alanson, s. Alanson & Wealthy S., b. Aug. 15, 1843	2	326
Herman, s. Jesse & Anna, b. Apr. 11, 1797	1	201
Herman, m. Nancy **KILBORN**, Jan. 3, 1819, by Rev. Isaac Jones	2	259
Homer, s. Harmon & Nancy, b. July 2, 1822	2	131
Homer, s. Herman & Nancy, b. July 2, 1822	2	259
Homer, m. Jane E. W. **MOORE**, Mar. 12, 1845, by Rev. D. L. Marks	TM49	8
Irene, d. John & Eunice, b. Sept. 6, 1764	1	159
James, m. Abigail **PECK**, June 22, 1738	1	77
James, s. James & Abigail, b. Sept. 13, 1747	1	119
James, d. Mar. 28, 1749	1	118
Jasper, s. Moses & Abigail, b. June 20, 1793	2	251
Jasper, m. Sophia **HUBBARD**, July 11, 1813, by Rev. Amos Chase	2	251
Jenett, d. Jasper & Sophia, b. Apr. 10, 1831	2	251
Jerusha, d. John & Sarah, d. July 26, 1728	1	37
Jerusha, d. Moses & Ruth, b. Nov. 18, 1734	1	37
Jerusha, m. Justus **WEBSTER**, Nov. 29, 1750, by Thomas Harrison, J.P.	1	83
Jerusha, d. John & Eunice, b. Mar. 16, 1758	1	159
Jesse, s. John & Euncie, b. Sept, 17, 1762	1	159
Jesse, s. Obed & Mary, b. Dec. 2, 1769	1	159
Jesse, s. Obed & Mary, d. Sept. 24, 1771	1	157-8
Jesse, m. Anne **CATLIN**, May [ ], 1791, by Rev. Ashbel Baldwin	1	201
Jesse, s. Gideon & Anna, b. July 3, 1792	2	87
Jesse, s. Samuel & Sarah, b. Mar. 29, 1818	2	93
Jesse, d. Jan. 23, 1846, ae 83 y.	1	201
John, s. John & Sary, d. Dec. [ ], 1735, in the 26th y. of his age	1	36
John, s. Moses & Ruth, b. July 12, 1736	1	77
John, s. Levi & Patty, b. June 4, 1804	2	53
John, Capt. John, d. Mar. 20, 1818, in the 82nd y. of his age	1	162
John, Ens., d. [ ]	1	37
Lavatith(?), s. Jasper & Sophia, b. Dec. 13, 1816	2	251
Leonard, s. Gideon & Anna, b. Oct. 20, 1801	2	87
Leonard, m. Lucy A. **TROWBRIDGE**, Sept. 3, 1854, by Rev. Horatio		
N. Weed	TM49	103
Levi, s. John & Eunice, b. Jan. 27, 1771	1	159
Levi, s. John, b. Jan. 27, 1771; m. Patty **BENNET**, Apr. 27, 1794	2	53
[Levi & Patty], had child b. Feb. 20, 1796; d. Feb. 24, 1796	2	53
Lois, d. Obed & Mary, b. July 17, 1771	1	159
Lois, m. John **KILBORN**, Apr. 26, 1790	2	60
Lorana, d. Daniel & Lucretia, b. Aug. 24, 1798	2	66

	Vol.	Page
STODDARD, STODDER, STODDOR, (cont.),		
Lorana, w. Daniel, d. [ ]	2	66
Lucia, d. Jasper & Sophia, b. Oct. 26, 1829	2	251
Lucretia, d. Daniel & Lucretia, b. Oct. 3, 1800	2	66
Lucy, m. Joseph **BRADLEY**, May 24, 1798	2	68
Lidia, d. Briant & Phebe, b. Apr. 11, 1770	1	118
Lydia, d. Jasper & Sophia, b. June 15, 1814	2	251
Lydia P., m. Ephraim **HARRISON**, Oct. 6, 1833, by Rev. L. P. Hickok	2	288
Mariana, d. Gideon & Anna, b. June 6, 1810	2	87
Mariana, d. Jasper & Sophia, b. Jan. 31, 1822	2	251
Marietta, m. Eli **BENEDICT**, Nov. 29, 1818	2	261
Marrella, d. Levi & Patty, b. Feb. 11, 1798	2	53
Mary, m. Stephen **SMITH**, Jan. 25, 1732/3, by Rev. Timothy Collens	1	77
Mary, d. Aaron & Philena, b. Jan. 10, 1778	1	163
Mary Ann, d. Jasper & Sophia, b. Dec. 19, 1818	2	251
Mary Ann, m. David C. **BUCKLEY**, May 2, 1831, by Rev. William Lucas	2	287
Mary Ann, m. Theodore R. **SEDGWICK**, Sept. 18, 1836, by Rev. R. S. Crampton	2	299
Mary Ann, m. Frederic R. **SEDGWICK**, Sept. 18, 1836	2	323
Mary Elizabeth, d. [Alanson & Wealthy], b. Apr. 24, 1841; d. Apr. 24, 1844	2	327
Mary Maria, d. Obed & Susan, b. Feb. 4, 1802	2	8
Merret, s. Jasper & Sophia, b. Dec. 21, 1824	2	251
Minerva, d. Samuel & Sarah, b. Mar. 13, 1823	2	93
Moses, m. Ruth **GOODWIN**, May 18, 1732, by Capt. John Marsh, J.P., of Hartford	1	37
Moses, s. Moses & Ruth, b. May 14, 1741; d. Dec. 21,1831	1	77
Moses, Jr., m. Abigail **BARNES**, Apr. 23, 1766, by Jacob Woodruff	1	120
Moses, s. Moses & Abigail, b. Sept. 15, 1773	1	34
Moses, Capt., d. Sept. 2, 1777	1	162
Moses, s. Enos & Aurelia, b. Oct. 15, 1815	2	100
Moses, m. Harriet **CHACE**, Jan. 4, 1837, by Rev. A. Billings Beach	2	299
Nabby, d. Gideon & Anna, b. Aug. 29, 1794	2	87
Naby Catlin, d. Jesse & Anna, b. Oct. 20, 1805	1	201
Nabby Catlin, m. Homer **SHARP**, Nov. 13, 1825, by Rev. Isaac Jones	2	258
Neri, s. Obed & Mary, b. Oct. 28, 1773	1	34
Norman, m. Rachel **SIMMONS**, Apr. 28, 1822, by Rev. Isaac Jones	2	111
Obed, s. Moses & Ruth, b. Apr. 5, 1743	1	77
Obed, m. Mary **HARRISON**, Mar. 4, 1767, by Rev. Judah Champion	1	159
Obed, d. Dec. 3, 1777	1	157-8
Obed, s. Obed, decd. & Mary, b. Feb. 19, 1778	1	157-8
Obed, s. Obed, b. Feb. 19, 1778; m. Susanna **STODDARD**, Dec. [ ], 1799	2	8
Olive, d. Briant & Phebe, b. Dec. 31, 1767	1	118
Olive Jane, d. Truman & Lois Clarissa, b. Sept. 28, 1845	TM49	27
Orange, s. James & Abigail, b. May 18, 1741	1	119
Orange, s. Enos & Aurillia, b. Apr. 18, 1804	2	100
Orson, s. Obed & Susan, b. Jan. 1, 1804	2	8
Phebe, m. James **WAUGH**, b. of Litchfield, Dec. 17, 1829, by Morris Woodruff, J.P.	2	283
Prudence, m. Charles **WOODRUFF**, Nov. [ ], 1744	1	41
Rachal, d. John & Eunice, b. Aug. 29, 1768	1	159

	Vol.	Page
STODDARD, STODDER, STODDOR, (cont.),		
Rachel, d. Jesse & Anna, b. May 27, 1800	1	201
Rhoda, d. Briant & Phebe, b. Sept. 22, 1764	1	118
Rhoda, d. John & Eunice, b. Dec. 29, 1766	1	159
Rhoda, m. David **WESTOVER**, Feb. [ ], 1795, by Rev. Judah		
Champion	2	143
Ruth, w. Dea. Moses, d. Aug. 19, 1777	1	162
Ruth, m. James **TRYON**, [ ], 1788	2	31
Sally, d. Gideon & Anna, b. Nov. 15, 1796	2	87
Samuel, s. Jesse & Anna, b. Feb. 18, 1794	1	201
Samuel, m. Sarah **CAMP**, Apr. 13, 1815, by Rev. Roger Searl	2	93
Sarah, d. James & Abigail, b. July 25, 1745	1	119
Sarah, m. Ephraim **SPENCER**, June 4, 1782	2	60
Solomon, s. Gideon & Anna, b. Nov. 1, 1799	2	87
Susan, b. May 20, 1778; m. Obed **STODDARD**, Dec. [ ], 1799	2	8
Triphena, m. Frederick **SMITH**, Mar. 14, 1827, by T. Marsh	2	269
Truman, s. Jasper & Sophia, b. July 6, 1820	2	251
Truman, m. Lois Clarissa **BARBER**, Sept. 9, 1843, by Rev. William		
Payne	TM49	27
Whitman, s. Gideon & Anna, b. Dec. 9, 1790	2	87
William, s. Levi & Patty, b. Mar. 11, 1799	2	53
William, s. Levi & Patty, d. Oct. 11, 1802	2	53
William, s. Gideon & Anna, b. Oct. 3, 1804	2	87
William Benton, s. Alanson & Wealthy, b. Sept. 20, 1839	2	327
STONE, Abigail, m. Jerome **JOHNSON**, b. of Litchfield, Oct. 29, 1838, by		
Rev. Jonathan Brace	2	318
Abram D., m. Maranda **BISSELL**, b. of Litchfield, Feb. 27, 1828, by		
Rev. John S. Stone	2	275
Alfred, s. Benjamin & Pamela, b. Jan. 28, 1813	2	12
Almira, d. Israel & Abby, b. July 30, 1812	2	58
Alvah, s. Thomas & Polly, b. June 20, 1797	2	59
Alvah, m. Army **GRANNIS**, b. of Litchfield, Oct. 5, 1834, by Truman		
Kilborn, J.P.	2	295
Alva, m. Cordelia M. **BUELL**, Nov. 1, 1840, by William Payne	2	331
Alvira, d. Benjamin & Pamela, b. Jan. 23, 1811	2	12
Ann, d. Silvanus & Ann, b. Nov. 2, 1747	1	119
Anna, d. Seth, b. Jan. 5, 1787; m. Lewis **STONE**, s. Jonah, Dec. 15,		
1806, by Rev Truman Marsh	2	94
Anne, d. Silvanus & Ann, b. Jan. 14, 1752	1	76
Anne, d. Reuben & Rachel, b. Mar. 22, 1770	1	76
Anne, d. James & Anne, b. Jan. 12, 1786	1	163
Antha, d. Israel & Abby, b. Mar. [ ], 1807	2	58
Antha, m. Lorenzo **WHEELER**, June 17, 1828, by I. Jones	2	277
Appollos, m. Eunice **TROOP**, [ ], 1799, by James Morris	2	58
Arme, m. Rufus **AMES**, Apr. 27, 1851, by Rev. David L. Parmelee	TM49	62
Asahel, s. Enos & Mary, b. Oct. 6, 1742	1	35
Asahel, s. Beriah & Deidamia, b. Apr. 3, 1763	1	118
Augustus, s. Benjamin & Pamela, b. Sept. 5, 1808	2	12
Augustus Baldwin, s. Thomas & Polly, b. Dec. 30, 1807	2	59
Belamy Robinson, s. [James & Mary], b. July 5, 1829	2	49
Benjamin, m. Sarah **PECK**, b. of Litchfield, Feb. 28, 1739/40, by Rev.		
Timothy Collens	1	77
Benjamin, s. Benjamin & Sarah, b. July 6, 1745	1	35

	Vol.	Page
STONE, (cont.),		
Benjamin, s. Reuben & Rachel, b. Feb. 13, 1777	1	76
Benjamin, s. Reuben & Rachel, b. Feb. 13, 1777	2	12
Benjamin, m. Pamela **WEBB**, Mar. [ ], 1797, by Rev. B. Judd of Litchfield	2	12
Beriah, m. Deidamia **SMITH**, Feb. 18, 1750, by Mr. Gibbs	1	119
Betsey, d. Benjamin & Pamela, b. May 3, 1806	2	12
Betty, d. Josiah & Hannah, b. Feb. 19, 1747/8	1	119
Caroline, m. Charles **WRIGHT**, Oct. 20, 1816, by Rev. Isaac Jones	2	260
Caroline L., d. James & Mary, b. June 8, 1821	2	49
Charles, s. John & Lowly, b. Aug. [ ], 1792	2	50
Charles, m. Phebe **GIBB**, Sept. 17, 1822, by Rev. Isaac Jones	2	114
Charles Abram, s. Hiram, b. Apr. 6, 1829	2	114
Charles Larabee, s. James & Mary, b. Apr. 17, 1819	2	49
Charlotte, d. James & Anne, b. Feb. 9, 1796	1	162
Clarissa, d. Thomas & Polly, b. Dec. 9, 1803	2	59
Clarissa, m. Wyllys **STONE**, Dec. 10, 1821, by Rev. Truman Marsh	2	109
Cornelia, d. Appolos & Eunice, b. May 2, 1811	2	58
Cornelia, m. Ephraim R. **BUNNEL**, Mar. 6, 1828, by I. Jones	2	274
David, s. Jonah & Ruth, b. July 12, 1771	1	120
David, s. Israel & Abby, b. Mar. [ ], 1815	2	58
Desire, m. Wyllys **STONE**, Dec. 11, 1821, by Rev. Truman Marsh	2	250
Dolle, [twin with Hannah], d. Stephen & Rebecca, b. Dec. 25, 1758	1	120
Dorcas, d. Reuben & Rachel, b. June 6, 1768	1	76
Dorcas, d. Reuben & Rachel, b. June 9, 1768	1	159
Dotha L., m. William R. **BUEL**, May 2, 1832, by Rev. L. P. Hickok	2	288
Edwin, s. Wyllys & Clarissa, b. Mar. 8, 1823	2	250
Edwin, s. Lewis & Anna, b. Oct. 5, 1823	2	94
Edwin, m. Hellen R. **CHACE**, Sept. 30, 1846, by John F. Norton	TM49	15
Eli C., s. Solomon & Rebecca, b. Nov. 26, 1797	2	92
Eli C., m. Eliza **GRANNIS**, Apr. 2, 1832, by Rev. David S. Tomlinson, of Bradleyville	2	290
Elisha, b. Mar. 20, 1784; m. Polly **NORTH**, July 10, 1804	2	28
Eliza, d. Lewis & Anna, b. July 7, 1807	2	94
Eliza, m. Bissell **BLAKESLEE**, Sept. 7, 1823, by Rev. Isaac Jones	2	124
Eliza A., m. Reynolds C. **CRANDALL**, b. of Litchfield, Dec. 13, 1840, by Rev. Thomas Ellis	2	331
Ellen, m. George **SMITH**, Oct. [ ], 1824, by Rev. Isaac Jones	2	136
Emeline, of Litchfield, m. Henry **GUY**, of Middlefield, Sept. 25, 1831, by Rev. William Lucas	2	287
Emily, of Litchfield, m. George **PEARCE**, of Bristol, Oct. 10, 1838, by Rev. Gad N. Smith	2	319
Enos, s. Enos & Mary, b. Aug. 5, 1744	1	35
Ephraim K., s. Israel & Abby, b. Nov. 10, 1804, in Litchfield	2	58
Ephraim K., m. Almira J. **WRIGHT**, b. of Litchfield, Oct. 14, 1834, by Truman Kilborn, J.P.	2	295
Erwin, s. Lewis & Anna, b. Aug. 7, 1818	2	94
Erwin, of Bradleyville, m. Ann Maria **CHASE**, of Milton, Sept. 27, 1843, by Ralph Smith	2	340
Evelyna, d. Solomon & Rebecca, b. Feb. 27, 1796	2	92
Fanny, d. Thomas & Mary*, b. July 9, 1784 *(Probably "Polly")	2	59
Frederick, s. Solomon & Rebecca, b. Oct. 3, 1802	2	92
Frederick, s. Wyllys & Clarissa, b. Feb. 2, 1825	2	250

	Vol.	Page
STONE, (cont.),		
Hannah, d. Josiah, Jr. & Hannah, b. Oct. 16, 1743	1	77
Hannah, [twin with Dolle], d. Stephen & Rebecca, b. Dec. 25, 1758	1	120
Harriet, d. James & Anne, b. Apr. 16, 1792	1	162
Harriet, d. James & Mary, b. Sept. 12, 1822	2	49
Harriet, of Litchfield, m. Heman WADHAMS, of Goshen, Feb. 9, 1830, by Enos Stoddard, J.P.	2	284
Harry, b. Feb. 12, 1815; m. Matilda BUNNELL, Feb. 13, 1842	TM49	15
Harry, s. Appolos & Eunice, b. Feb. 12, 1815	2	58
Harry Merrett, s. [Harry & Matilda], b. Mar. 23, 1845	TM49	15
Heber, s. Beriah & Deidamia, b. Mar. 8, 1751	1	119
Heber, m. Sarah BISSELL, Jan. 1, 1772, by Timothy Collens, J.P.	1	34
Helen A., m. Anthony G. DAVIS, Mar. 15, 1831, by Rev. W. Lucas	2	287
Heman, s. Reuben & Rachal, b. June 18, 1764	1	76
Henry, s. Elisha [& Polly], b. July 5, 1811	2	28
Hervey V., m. Clarinda J. MERRIMAN, b. of Litchfield, May 8, 1843, by Rev. Ralph Smith	2	412
Homer B., m. Lucy LINSLEY, b. of Litchfield, Mar. 2, 1828, by Enos Stoddard, J.P.	2	275
Horace, s. Lewis & Anna, b. Feb. 10, 1813	2	94
Horatio, s. Benjamin & Pamela, b. Nov. 15, 1798	2	12
Huldah, d. Enos & Mary, b. Apr. 23, 1746	1	35
Hulda, d. Stephen & Rebecca, b. Nov. 11, 1759	1	120
Huldah, m. William GOLD, Mar. 5, 1767, by Rev. Judah Champion	1	136-8
Huldah, m. Daniel SHELDON, May 13, 1784, by James Morris	1	200
Huldah, m. Francis TOMPKINS, Jan. 23, 1806, by Rev. Truman Marsh	2	3
Ira, s. Beriah & Deidamia, b. June 18, 1758	1	118
Irene, d. Josiah & Hannah, b. Aug. 24, 1756	1	76
Irene, d. Lewis & Anna, b. July 16, 1820	2	94
Isaac, of Milford, m. Elizabeth PALMER, Apr. 23, 1835, by Rev. L. P. Hickok	2	296
Israel, s. Jonah & Ruth, b. June 5, 1775	1	161
Israel, m. Abby GATES, June 23, 1795	2	58
Israel, m. Mrs. Barbara ISBEL, of Litchfield, Feb. 16, 1830, by Enos Stoddard, J.P.	2	284
Jabes, s. Thomas & Polly, b. Nov. 12, 1794	2	59
Jacob D., m. Julia SMITH, b. of Washington, Feb. 14, 1848, by Joseph Henson	TM49	23
James, s. Beriah & Deidamia, b. Aug. 22, 1760	1	118
James, s. John & Lowly, b. [ ], 1790	2	50
James, m. Mary MOORE, Dec. 17, 1814	2	49
James, s. James & Mary, b. Apr. 28, 1815	2	49
Jarvis, s. Benjamin & Pamela, b. Apr. 15, 1801	2	12
Joel, s. Stephen & Rebecca, b. Aug. 7, 1749	1	120
John, s. John & Lowly, b. [ ], 1787	2	50
John, of Bethlem, m. Mary N. LINSLEY, of Litchfield, Sept. 27, 1829, by Rev. Henry Robinson, of South Farms	2	282
John, m. Lowly WATKINS, [ ], by Cyprian Webster	2	50
Jonah, s. Silvanus & Anne, b. Nov. 3, 1747	1	76
Josiah, Jr., m. Hannah BURRUS, of Windsor, Sept. 14, 1738, by Rev. Timothy Collens	1	77
Josiah, s. Josiah & Hannah, b. Mar. 4, 1749/50	1	119

	Vol.	Page
STONE, (cont.),		
Josiah, s. Josiah & Elizabeth, b. Apr. 27, 1776	1	163
Josiah, d. Nov. 10, 1777	1	162
Julia, m. Erastus LANDON, May 20, 1832, by Rev. Luther Mead	2	290
Julia A., m. Reynold C. CRANDALL, Sept. 13, 1838, by Rev. Gad N. Smith	2	319
Julia P., m. Minor R. POTTER, b. of Litchfield, Sept. 16, 1844, by G. C. V. Eastman	TM49	5
Laura Matilda, d. [Harry & Matilda], b. July 30, 1843; d. Apr. 5, 1844	TM49	15
Leman, s. Stephen & Rebecca, b. Dec. 29, 1750	1	120
Leaman, s. Thomas & Polly, b. Feb. 20, 1793	2	59
Leman, s. Appolos & Eunice, b. Mar. 28, 1813	2	58
Leonard, m. Sarah JACKSON, b. of Litchfield, Oct. 22, 1849, by Rev. W. B. Hoyt	TM49	43
Levi, s. Beriah & Deidamia, b. July 1, 1753	1	119
Levi, s. Elisha [& Polly], b. Dec. 19, 1808	2	28
Levi, m. Harriet HINMAN, b. of Litchfield, Nov. 19, 1840, by William Payne	2	332
Lewis, s. Jonah, b. Nov. 14, 1778; m. Anna STONE, d. Seth, Dec. 15, 1806, by Rev. Truman Marsh	2	94
Liza, d. Stephen & Rebecca, b. Feb. 13, 1753	1	120
Lorain, d. Silvanus & Anne, b. Feb 19, 1763	1	76
Lorana, m. Daniel STODDARD, Oct. 2, 1783	2	66
Lucia, Mrs. of Litchfield, m. Elkanah SPOONER, of Woodbury, Jan. 29, 1838, by Enos Stoddard, J.P.	2	315
Lucina, d. Beriah & Deidamia, b. Aug. 14, 1755	1	118
Lucy, d. Stephen & Rebecca, d. Feb. 25, 1768	1	36
Lucy, d. John & Lowly, b. June 1798	2	50
Lucy, d. Appolos & Eunice, b. Oct. 6, 1805	2	58
Lucy, m. Elijah BUNNEL, May 28, 1826, by Rev. Truman Marsh	2	263
Lucy Ann, d. Solomon & Rebecca, b. Feb. 7, 1811	2	92
Lucy Ann, of Litchfield, m. Rev. David PLUMB, of Stratford, July 7, 1835, by Rev. Chester William Turney	2	298
Lurinda, d. Benjamin & Pamela, b. July 23, 1803	2	12
Lydia, d. Silvanus & Lydia, b. Dec. 23, 1734	1	37
Lidia, d. Noah & Sarah, b. Feb. 21, 1762	1	118
Lydia, m. Solomon GOSLIE, June 10, 1784	2	60
Mabel, d. Silvanus & Anne, b. Oct. 28, 1768	1	159
Mehala, d. Appolos & Eunice, b. June 12, 1807	2	58
Mahola, m. Abel H. CLEMENCE, b. of Litchfield, Feb. 13, 1828, by Rev. John Stone	2	275
Mahala, m. Timothy J. PARMALEE, Oct. 19, 1828, by I. Jones	2	278
Margary, Mrs. of Litchfield, m. Ira MORGAN, of Warren, May 5, 1833, by Rev. Hart Talcott	2	293
Maria, d. Lewis & Anna, b. July 21, 1816	2	94
Maria, d. James & Mary, b. Apr. 24, 1817	2	49
Marillia, d. Israel & Abby, b. Nov. 20, 1802, in Ridgefield	2	58
Mary, m. Ebenezer COLVER, Oct. 24, 1745, by Rev. Timothy Collens	1	131
Mary, m. Albert POTTER, [June 25, 1828], by I. Jones	2	277
Mary Jane, d. [Hiram], b. Apr. 30, 1831	2	114
Minerva, m. Abner LANDON, Apr. 24, 1822, by Rev. Isaac Jones	2	111
Molly, m. Eli WILLMOTT, Sept. 28, 1802, by Rev. Dan Huntington	2	140
Morgan, s. Israel & Abby, b. Jan. 17, 1801, in Symsbury	2	58

	Vol.	Page
STONE, (cont.),		
Moses, s. Reuben & Rachel, b. July 5, 1782	1	201
Nabby, d. Heber & Sarah, b. Mar. 19, 1773	1	34
Nabby, d. Heber & Sarah, d. Dec. 24, 1775	1	162
Nabby, d. Heber & Sarah, b. Sept. 22, 1777	1	163
Nabby, d. Heber & Sarah, d. Mar. 2, 1780	1	162
Noah, s. Silvanus & Lydia, b. Oct. 13, 1736	1	77
Noah, m. Sarah **CLARK**, Dec. 24, 1758, by Rev. Judah Champion	1	118
Noah, 3rd s. Solomon & Rebecca, b. Dec. 24, 1806	2	92
Noah, m. Margary **FRISBIE**, b. of Litchfield, Jan. 21, 1829, by Rev. Hart Talcott	2	279
Norman, s. Noah & Sarah, b. Jan. 25, 1771	1	118
Norman, s. Thomas & Mary*, b. May 19, 1787 *(Probably "Polly")	2	59
Olive, d. Reuben & Rachel, b. Aug. 18, 1766	1	76
Olive, d. Reuben & Rachel, b. Aug. 15, 1767	1	163
Olive, m. John **WAUGH**, Oct. 17, 1787, by Rev. Amos Chase	1	206
Oran, s. James & Anne, b. Mar. 1, 1784	1	163
Orange, s. Thomas & Polly, b. July 2, 1789	2	59
Orris, s. Heber & Sarah, b. Mar. 28, 1775	1	163
Polly, d. John & Lowly, b. Sept. 26, 1783	2	50
Polly, m. Solomon **MOULTHROP**, July 11, 1797, by John Welch, J.P.	2	259
Polly, m. Zachariah **BOSTWICK**, May 16, 1826, by Rev. Truman Marsh	2	264
Prudence, of Guilford, m. John **NEWBRE**, of Middletown, May 10, 1750	1	67
Rachal, d. Benjamin & Sarah, b. Oct. 24, 1741	1	35
Rachel, d. Stephen & Rebecca, b. Nov. 22, 1761	1	120
Rachel, m. Reuben **STONE**, Dec. 24, 1762, by Rev. Judah Champion	1	76
Rachel, m. Truman **STONE**, Feb. 6, 1822, by Rev. Isaac Jones	2	109
Rebecca, w. Stephen, d. Nov. 9, 1767	1	36
Rebecca, d. Appolos & Eunice, b. May 12, 1809	2	58
Rebecca Beebe, m. David Wessells **HAND**, b. of Litchfield, Mar. 1, 1836, by Rev. Samuel Fuller, Jr.	2	296
Rene, d. Stephen & Rebecca, b. Jan. 9, 1755	1	120
Reuben, s. Silvanus & Lidia, b. Jan. 18, 1740/1	1	119
Reuben, m. Rachel **STONE**, Dec. 24, 1762, by Rev. Judah Champion	1	76
Rhoda, d. Silvanus & Lidia, b. Jan. 22, 1738/9	1	119
Rhoda, d. Noah & Sarah, b. Mar. 4, 1764	1	118
Rhoda, m. Horace **CLARK**, Nov. 1, 1831, by Rev. L. P. Hickok	2	288
Russell, s. Thomas & Polly, b. Nov. 26, 1798	2	59
Russell, m. Lucia **PALMER**, May 13, 1821, by Rev. Isaac Jones	2	102
Ruth, d. Silvanus & Anne, b. July 14, 1755	1	76
Ruth, m. Thomas **GRANNISS**, Nov. 21, 1799	2	54
Sabra, d. Noah & Sarah, b. Sept. 21, 1773	1	118
Sabra, d. John & Lowly, b. Aug. [ ], 1782	2	50
Sally, d. Heber & Sarah, b. Nov. 1, 1779	1	163
Sally, d. John & Lowly, b. Mar.. [ ], 1785	2	50
Sally, m. Hiram B. **WOODCOCK**, May 21, 1821, by Rev. Isaac Jones	2	103
Sally M., m. Ira **SMITH**, Dec. 26, 1822, by Rev. Isaac Jones	2	116
Sarah, d. Enos & Mary, b. June 13, 1739	1	35
Sarah, m. Isaac **BISSELL**, Oct. 1, 1746, by Rev. Timothy Collens	1	85
Sarah, m. Abraham **BUELL**, May 20, 1759, by Rev. Judah Champion	1	85
Sarah, d. Noah & Sary, b. July 7, 1760	2	118

	Vol.	Page
STONE, (cont.),		
Sarah, m. Zadock, **GIBBS, Jr.**, Apr. 22, 1779, by Rev. Judah Champion	1	179
Sarah C., m. Abraham B. **EVERETT**, Jan. 14, 1830, by Rev. William		
Lucas	2	286
Sarah J., m. Nathaniel G. **LOVELAND**, Nov. 29, 1838, by Rev.		
Jonathan Brace	2	318
Sarah Jane, d. Chester* & Phebe, b. Dec. 20, 1825 *("Charles"?)	2	114
Seth, s. Benjamin & Sarah, b. Oct. 28, 1743	1	35
Seth, s. Reuben & Rachel, b. Oct. 6, 1763	1	76
Sheldon, s. Lewis & Anna, b. May 17, 1809	2	94
Silvanus, m. Lydia **RIGHT**, Mar. 12, 1733/4, by Rev. Mr. Doolittle, of		
Northfield	1	37
Silvanus, s. Silvanus & Anne, b. July 22, 1765	1	159
Silvanus, s. Elisha [& Polly], b. May 28, 1805	2	28
Simeon, m. Cornelia **HAND**, b. of Litchfield, May 17, 1838, by Rev.		
Fosdic Harrison, of Bethlehem	2	317
Sina, m. Samuel **McNEILE**, Jan. 4, 1766, by Rev. Judah Champion	1	108
Sina, d. Heber & Sarah, b. Sept. 28, 1781	1	163
Solomon, s. Noah & Sarah, b. Sept. 4, 1768	1	118
Solomon, m. Rebecca **BEEBEE**, Jan. 20, 1794, by Rev. Mr. Faren	2	92
Stephen, s. Stephen & Rebecca, b. Jan. 1, 1746/7	1	120
Stephen, s. Stephen & Rebecca, d. May 22, 1765	1	36
Stephen, m.Deliverance **CHAPMAN**, May 12, 1768, by Jacob		
Woodruff, J.P.	1	120
Stephen, s. Stephen & Deliverance, b. Apr. 21, 1769	1	120
Temperance, d. Josiah, Jr. & Hannah, b. Nov. 2, 1739	1	77
Thankful, d. Josiah, Jr. & Hannah, b. Sept. 21, 1745	1	77
Thankful, m. Joel **POTTER**, Sept. [ ], 1784, in Bradford, by Rev. Mr.		
Eells	2	39
Thomas, m. Polly **PALMELY**, Jan. 14, 1782, by Rev. Judah Champion	2	59
Truman, s. Noah & Sarah, b. May 8, 1766	1	118
Truman, s. Beriah & Deidamia, b. July 19, 1766	1	76
Truman, s. Appolos & Eunice, b. Oct. 12, 1800	2	58
Truman, m. Rachel **STONE**, Feb. 6, 1822, by Reb. Isaac Jones	2	109
Tryphena, m. Gideon **SMEDLEY**, Feb. 15, 1808, by Rev. Truman		
Marsh	2	121
Warren, s. Reuben & Rachel, b. Apr. 4, 1772	1	76
William, s. Silvanus & Anne, b. Oct. 4, 1760	1	76
William, s. John & Lowly, b. Mar. [ ], 1795	2	50
William, s. Elisha [& Polly], b. Aug. 23, 1813	2	28
William, s. Appolos & Eunice, b. Jan. 14, 1819	2	58
Wyllys, m. Clarissa **STONE**, Dec. 10, 1821, by Rev. Truman Marsh	2	109
Wyllys, m. Desire **STONE**, Dec. 11, 1821, by Rev. Truman Marsh	2	250
STORRS, Salina, of Mansfield, m. Ozias **SEYMOUR**, of Litchfield, Mar. 3,		
1803, by Rev. John Sherman	2	20
Selinna, m. Ozias **SEYMOUR**, Mar. 3, 1803, by Rev. John Sherman	1	241
STOUGHTON, Sarah, m. Roger **BISSELL**, Oct. 25, 1743, by Rev. Jonathan		
Marsh, of Windsor	1	85
STRONG, Abigail, d. Josiah & Hannah, b. Aug. 22, 1739	1	35
Abigail, d. Supply & Anne, b. Sept. 28, 1743	1	119
Abijah, d. Supply & Lois, b. June 25, 1727	1	36
Adonijah, m. Mary **PIERCE**, June 28, 1774, by Andrew Adams, J.P.	1	161
Anne, d. Supply & Anne, b. Aug. 23, 1741	1	119

	Vol.	Page
STRONG, (cont.),		
Anne, w. Supply, d. May 25, 1783	1	160
Asahel, s. Supply & Anne, b. Dec. 30, 1736	1	119
Asahel, d. Apr. 21, 1782	1	160
David, s. Josiah & Hannah, b. July 6, 1744	1	35
Elijah, s. Josiah & Hannah, b. Mar. 10, 1727	1	35
Hannah, d. Josiah & Hannah, b. June 22, 1735	1	37
Idea, d. Jedidiah & Ruth, b. Oct. 25, 1775	1	161
Idia, d. Sept. 25, 1804, in the 29th y. of her age, at Newport, Vt.	1	160
Jedidiah, s. Supply & Anne, b. Nov. 7, 1738	1	119
Jedidiah, representative Oct. 1771, May & Oct. 1772, May & Oct. 1773, May & Oct. 1774, May & Oct. 1775, May & Oct. 1776, May & Oct. 1777, May & Oct. 1778, May & Oct. 1779, May 1780, Oct. 1781, May & Oct. 1782, May 1783, May & Oct. 1789, Oct. 1785, May & Oct. 1786, Oct. 1787, May 1788	2	1549-51
Jedediah*, m. Ruth PAT[T]ERSON, Apr. 17, 1774, by Rev. Judah Champion *(Arnold Copy has "Judah")	1	161
Jedediah, m. Susanna WYLLYS, Jan. 22, 1788, by Rev. Judah Champion	1	201
Jedediah, d. Aug. 21, 1802, ae 64 y.	1	160
Joseph, s. Josiah & Hannah, b. Sept. 15, 1747	1	35
Josiah, m. Hannah SMEDLE, Sept. 22, 1734, by Rev. Anthony Stoddard	1	37
Judah, m. Ruth PATERSON, Apr. 17, 1774, by Rev. Judah Champion	1	161
Lois, d. Supply & Lois, b. Nov. 15, 1723	1	36
Lois, d. Supply & Lois, d. Dec. 28, 1724	1	36
Lovis, w. Supply, d. Apr. 26, 1730, ae [ ]	1	36
Lydia A., m. Ebenezer W. BOLLES, Oct. 18, 1832, by Rev. L. P. Hickok	2	288
Mabel, m. Moses SEYMOUR, Jr., Feb. 23, 1800, in Addison, Vt., by Seth Storrs	1	241
Mabel, of Addison, Vt., m. Moses SEYMOUR, Jr., of Litchfield, Feb. 23, 1800, in Addison, Vt., by Seth Storrs, J.P.	2	20
Martha, m. Nathaniel HOSFORD, Oct. 2, 1746, by Rev. Jonathan Marsh, of Windsor	1	17
Rachal, d. Supply & Lois, b. Aug. 1, 1729	1	36
Rachel, m. Samuel BEECH, Jr., Sept. 7, 1749, by Ebenezer Marsh, J.P.	1	129
Ruth, d. Eleazer & Jemima, b. Mar. 17, 1723	1	36
Ruth, d. Josiah & Hannah, b. May 12, 1749	1	35
Ruth, d. Oct. 3, 1777	1	160
Solomon, s. Josiah & Hannah, b. Sept. 26, 1741	1	35
Supply, m. Lowese BUELL, Jan. 16, 1722/3, by John Marsh, J.P.	1	37
Supply, d. Nov. 26, 1786, ae 90 y.	1	160
Thankfull, d. Supply & Lois, b. Sept. 7, [1725], d. [Sept.] 17, 1725	1	36
Theodore J., m. Eliza A. HINMAN, Apr. 28, 1847, by John R. Keep	TM49	19
William, s. Josiah & Hannah, b. Sept. 20, 1745	1	77
STUDLEY, Calvin H., of Sharon, m. Mary S. HOTCHKISS, of Litchifield, Apr. 13, 1854, by Rev. Horatio N. Weed	TM49	85
STURTEVANT, Ruth, m. William DICKINSON, May 19, 1774, by Daniel Lee, J.P.	1	49
SUTLEFF, Content, m. Caleb MOSS, [ ], 1803, by Daniel Potter, J.P.	2	77
Eliza, m. Hiram BROOKS, Jan. 4, 1835, by Joseph E. Camp	2	297
SWAN, Abigail, d. Alanson & Chary, b. July 30, 1822	2	129

	Vol.	Page
SWAN, (cont.)		
Alanson, m. Charey **BARNEY**, Sept. [ ], 1815, by Ebenezer Tanner	2	129
Alvira, d. Alanson & Chary, b. Feb. 28, 1817	2	129
Levi, s. Alanson & Chary, b. Jan. 12, 1820	2	129
Lucia, d. Nathan & Temperance, b. Aug. 5, 1771	1	159
Nathan, m. Temperance **PHILLIPS**, Oct. 4, 1770, by Rev. Judah Champion	1	159
Olive, d. Nathan & Temperance, b. June 16, 1773	1	159
Sarah, of Kent, m. Levi **PARMELE**, of Litchfield, Feb. 18, 1775, by Rev. Peter Starr	1	113
Temperance, d. Nathan & Temperance, b. Jan. 15, 1778	1	163
SWEET, Samuel, m. Cloe **SMITH**, Oct. 19, 1828, by Rev. Joseph E. Camp, of Northfield	2	292
SWIFT, Betsey, m. Joseph **MERRIMAN**, May 8, 1796, by Rev. James Noyce	1	228
Catharine Ward, m. Rev. George Henry **HASTINGS**, b. of New York City, Aug. 26, 1847, by Rev. Samuel Fuller	TM49	38
Chandler, of Cornwall, m. Anna **MANSFIELD**, May 28, 1822, by Morris Woodruff, J.P.	2	111
TALLAND, Benjamin, Col., m. Mary **FLOYD**, Mar. 16, 1784, in Brookline, N.Y., by Rev. B. Tallmadge	1	242-3
TALLMADGE, Benjamin*, Col., m. Mary **FLOYD**, Mar. 16, 1784, in Brookline, N.Y., by Rev. B. Tallmadge *(Arnold Copy has "Benjamin TALLAND")	1	242-3
Benjamin, s. Benjamin & Mary, b. Sept. 10, 1794	1	242-3
David, of Torringford, m. Emeline **BUELL**, of Litchfield, Nov. 28, 1833, by Rev. Aaron S. Hill	2	294
Elliott C., m. Rhoda E. **TURNER**, Apr. 6, 1830, by Rev. William Lucas	2	286
Frederick Augustus, s. Benjamin & Mary, b. Aug. 29, 1792	1	242-3
George Washington, s. Benjamin & Mary, b. Sept. 13, 1800	1	242-3
Hannah, m. Joseph **HUBBARD**, Jr., Aug. 7, 1813, by Rev. Mr. Ives	2	51
Harriet, m. John **DELAFIELD**, Dec. [ ], 1821, by Rev. Lyman Beecher	2	107
Harriet Wadsworth, d. Benjamin & Mary, b. Apr. 3, 1797	1	242-3
Henry Floyd, s. Benjamin & Mary, b. June 11, 1787	1	242-3
Maria, d. Benjamin & Mary, b. Mar. 25, 1790	1	242-3
Selah W., of Southwick, Mass., m. Mrs. Adaline M. **HURD**, July 2, 1854, by Rev. H. A. Weed	TM49	85
Sybel, m. Amos **GALPIN**, Jan. 31, 1785, by Rev. Mr. Foot, of Cheshire	1	221
William Smith, s. Benjamin & Mary, b. Oct. 20, 1785	1	242-3
TANNER, Hannah, d. Thomas & Martha, b. June last 1735	1	39
Jane, of Poughkeepsie, m. Phillip **HUBBARD**, of Litchfield, Dec. 25, 1827, by Rev. John S. Stone	2	273
John, s. Thomas & Martha, b. Feb. 4, 1732/3	1	39
Ruth, d. Thomas & Martha, b. Sept. 28, 1740	1	79
Sarah, d. Thomas & Martha, b. Feb. 8, 1737/8	1	39
TARKINGTON (?)*, Willliam H., m. Julia M. **DALEY**, Oct. 8, 1854, by Rev. David L. Parmelee *(Arnold Copy has "TURKINGTON")	TM49	105
TAYLOR, TALER, TAYLER, Alaner*, m. Zebulon **COLVER**, July 30, 1740, by Rev. Timothy Collens *("Eleanor")	1	47
Alanson, of Danbury, m. Rebecca **FARNAM**, of Litchfield, Oct. 9, 1822, by Morris Woodruff	2	114
Ambrose, s. Zebulon & Sarah, b. July 15, 1744	1	78
Ame, d. Zebulon & Sarah, b. Aug. 26, 1738	1	27

	Vol.	Page
TAYLOR, TALER, TAYLER, (cont.),		
Anne, d. Zebulon & Sarah, b. Mar. 15, 1734/5	1	39
Anne, m. Joshua **GARRITT**, Dec. 11, 1735, by Rev. Timothy Collens	1	97
Avis, d. Zebulon & Sarai, b. July 30, 1733	1	39
Benjamin, s. Ebenezer & Zerviah, b. Mar. 10, 1756	1	79
Charity, m. Silas W. **WHEELER**, Nov. 15, 1823, by Rev. Isaac Jones	2	129
Ebenezer, s. Ebenezer & Elener, b. July 14, 1721	1	39
Ebenezer, Jr., m. Zerviah **COLVER**, Jan. 17, 1749/50, by Capt. Joseph		
Bird, J.P.	1	79
Ebenezer, s. Ebenezer, Jr. & Zerviah, b. Jan. 22, 1751/2	1	79
Elener, d. Ebenezer & Elener, b. May 5, 1723	1	39
Eleanor, see also Alaner		
Elias, s. Simeon & Olive, b. May 8, 1792	2	266
Elizabeth, d. Ebenezer & Elener, b. Aug. 24, 1729	1	39
Elizabeth, d. Tahan & Ruth, b. Apr. 28, 1775	1	121
Epaphro, s. Simeon & Olive, b. June 2, 1790	2	82
Friend, s.Tahan & Ruth, b. Mar. 7, 1764	1	121
Hannah, m. John **FARNAM**, Nov. 29, 1795, by James Morris	2	63
Hiram, of Salisbury, m. Melinda **BEACH**, of Litchfield, June 12, 1831,		
by Rev. L. P. Hickok	2	287
Horace, s. Simeon & Olive, b. May 8, 1792	2	82
Ira, m. Lucinda **BEACH**, Dec. [ ], 1823, by Rev. Isaac Jones	2	130
J. Lewis, of New York, m. Mary E. **GOODWIN**, of Litchfield, Aug. 9,		
1842, by Jonathan Brace	2	336
Joanna, d. Ebenezer, Jr. & Zerviah, b. Oct. 6, 1750	1	79
Joel, s. Ebenezer & Elener, b. Sept. 3, 1732	1	39
Joel, of Litchfield, m. Eleanor **GOODELL**, of Pomfret, July 5, 1758, by		
Timothy Sabin, J. P.	1	79
John, s. Zebulon & Sarah, b. Nov. 14, 1736	1	39
John, s. Ebenezer, Jr. & Zerviah, b. Oct. 4, 1760	1	79
Joseph, s. Ebenezer, Jr. & Zerviah, b. Nov. 29, 1753	1	27
Mable, d. Ebenezer & Elner, b. Aug. 28, 1739	1	79
Mabel, m. Henry **SMITH**, Aug. 2, 1773, by Rev. Judah Champion	1	161
Margret, d. Tahan & Ruth, b. Nov. 15, 1759	1	121
Mary, d. Ebenezer & Elener, b. Jan. 27, 1735	1	39
Mary, d. Tahan & Ruth, b. Dec. 11, 1757	1	121
Moses, s. Ebenezer & Zerviah, b. Jan. 13, 1758	1	79
Neri, s. Tahan & Ruth, b. Sept. 29, 1772	1	121
Phinehas B., m. Sedina **BLAKESLEE**, Apr. 13, 1828, by F. Holcomb	2	276
Polly, m. Eben **JUDSON**, Nov. 23, 1807, by Rev. Dan Huntington	2	75
Rhoda, d. Capt. Zebulon & Thankful, b. Sept. 7, 1781	1	121
Ruhame, d. Ebenezer & Elener, b. June 26, 1725	1	39
Ruhamah, m. Asa **PRESTON**, Dec. 24, 1755, by Rev. Judah Champion	1	71
Saloame, d. Simeon & Olive, b. Apr. 22, 1788; m. David **RICE**, July		
16, 1811	2	82
Samuel, m. Louisa **NORTH**, Oct. 11, 1835, by Rev. L. P. Hickok	2	296
Sary, m. Jonathan **PARMALEE**, Dec. [ ], 1728, by Rev. Mr. Marsh, of		
Windsor	1	31
Sarah, d. Zebulon & Sarah, b. Oct. 21, 1730	1	39
Sarah, of London, Eng., m. Gad **GUILD**, of Litchfield, Nov. 4, 1810, by		
Rev. Truman Marsh	TM49	27
Sarah, m. Gad **GUILD**, Nov. 4, 1810, by Rev. Truman Marsh	2	146
Sarah M., of Litchfield, m. Osborn **SPARKS**, of Sheffield, Mass., Sept.		

	Vol.	Page
AYLOR, TALER, TAYLER, (cont.),		
2, 1846, by Rev. William Dixon	TM49	15
Seth Minor, of Collinsville, m. Anna Miranda **TRYON**, of Litchfield,		
Nov. 20, 1836, by Rev. Samuel Fuller, Jr.	2	296
Tabitha, d. Tahan & Ruth, b. Oct. 25, 1770	1	121
Tahan, s. Ebenezer & Elener, b. June 14, 1727	1	39
Tahan, m. Ruth **PRESTON**, Feb. 10, 1757, by Rev. Judah Champion	1	121
Tahan, s. Tahan & Ruth, b. Nov. 25, 1761	1	121
Thaddeus, s. Tahan & Ruth, b. June 18, 1766	1	121
Thomas Grant, s. Tahan Taylor, b. Aug. 21, 1768	1	79
Veron D., Rev. m. Catharine M. **WOODRUFF**, May 2, 1831, by Rev.		
D. C. Griswold, of Watertown	2	290
Veron D. & Catharine M., had s. [ ], b. Mar. 14, 1832	2	290
Zebulon, m. Sarah **HOSFORD**, Dec. 20, 1727, by Rev. Timothy Collens	1	39
Zebulon, s. Zebulon & Sarah, d. June 17, 1746	1	38
Zebulon, s. Zebulon & Sarah, b. Mar. 25, 1747	1	79
Zebulon, Sergt., d. Jan. 1, 1763, in the 61st y. of his age	1	38
Zebulon, m. Rhoda **GRANT**, Jan. 19, 1775, by Rev. Judah Champion	1	121
Zebulon, Capt., m. Thankful **WOODRUFF**, Nov. 23, 1780, by Rev.		
Judah Champion	1	121
Zenas, of Warren, m. Mary Ann **GRANNIS**, of Litchfield, Oct. 25,		
1832, by Rev. Hart Talcott, of Warren	2	291
EMMINS, William H., m. Diantha P. **SMITH**, b. of Bantam Falls, Feb. 14,		
1849, by Joseph Henson	TM49	40
ERRILL, TERRIL, TERRELL, TYRRELL, TERREL, TURRELL,		
Darius, of Winchester, m. Ann **KILLBORN**, Feb. 6, 1823, by Ozias		
Lewis	2	117
Darius, of Winchester, m. Susan **BROWN**, of Litchfield, May 25, 1829,		
by Rev. Henry Robinson, of South Farms	2	281
Elizabeth, m. Levi **SANFORD**, Jan. 12, 1812	2	51
Elizabeth Ann, m. Orestes **PALMER**, Sept. 21, 1842, by Rev. Ralph		
Smith	2	411
Eunice M., of Litchfield, m. Ebenezer **OAKES**, of Gloucester, Mass.,		
Nov. 11, 1838, by William Payne	2	328
George, s. Reuben & Alma Ruth, b. Jan. 6, 1817, in Woodbury	2	76
Paulina, m. Rufus **PICKET**, Jan. 3, 1808, in New Fairfield	2	91
Polly Maria, m. Orman **GILBERT**, Mar. 12, 1815, by Rev. Isaac Jones	2	49
Reuben, m. Alma Ruth **MINOR**, Aug. 20, 1816, by Rev. Mr. Welton,		
of Woodbury	2	76
Sidney, m. Lucinda **McNEILE**, Apr. 9, 1838, by Rev. Stephen Hubbell	2	320
W. W., m. Mary A. **FISHER**, b. of Litchfield, Jan. 6, 1839, by William		
Payne	2	328
ETHER, George, m. Margaret **HUGHES**, b. formerly of England, now of		
Litchfield, Aug. 28, 1853, by Rev. Horatio N. Weed	TM49	91
HOMAS, Adeline, m. Albert A. **PECK**, b. of Litchfield, Mar. 25, 1850, by		
Rev. William B. Hoyt	TM49	53
Almira, of Litchfield, m. Charles L. **PILGRIM**, of New York, Sept. 10,		
1837, by Rev. Lewis Gunn	2	313
Charlotte, m. Edward **BLAKESLEE**, Feb. 17, 1822, by Rev. Joseph		
Perry, at New Haven	2	148
David J., m. Abigail **SMITH**, Dec. 26, 1830, by Rev. Joseph E. Camp,		
of Northfield	2	292
Eliza, m. Herman **BEACH, Jr.**, b. of Litchfield, Jan. 16, 1837, by Rev.		

	Vol.	Page
THOMAS, (cont.),		
E. Washburn	2	297
Eunice, m. David D. **GUILD**, Dec. 24, 1834, by Rev. David G. Tomlinson, of Milton	2	295
Harriet, m. Thomas W. **CROSBIE**, Oct. 4, 1814, by Amasa Porter, of Darby	2	256
Hezekiah, Jr., m. Margaret **STEVENS**, May 10, 1821, by Rev. Isaac Jones	2	102
James M., m. Cornelia R. **WHITTLESEY**, b. of Litchfield, July 6, 1837, by Rev. Fosdic Harrison, of Bethlehem	2	313
John, s. Joseph & Anne, b. May 9, 1769	1	79
Joseph, s. Joseph & Anne, b. May 27, 1764	1	79
Laura C., of Litchfield, m. Henry S. **JENNINGS**, of Fairfield, May 6, 1827, by Rev. Henry Robinson, of South Farms	2	270
Maria, of Bethlem, m. Leonard L. **WILKINSON**, of Harwinton, May 29, 1848, by Joseph Henson	TM49	24
Mary, d. Joseph & Anne, b. Oct. 4, 1762	1	79
Phebe M., m. George M. **MURRAY**, b. of Litchfield, Jan. 1, 1828, by Rev. Henry Robinson, of South Farms	2	274
Rhoda Ann, m. Job **CLARK**, Apr. 25, 1841, by Rev. David L. Parmelee	2	333
Samuel, s. Joseph & Anne, b. July 21, 1779	1	79
Sarah C., of South Farms, m. Eben S. **JOHNSON**, of Litchfield, Nov. 28, 1844, by Gordon Hayes	TM49	6
Starr, of Washington, m. Anna **STODDARD**, of Litchfield, May 8, 1823, by Morris Woodruff, J.P. (Perhaps "Thomas **STARR**")	2	102
Tabitha, m. Rev. Isaac **JONES**, Oct. 17, 1804, by Rev. James Dana, D.D., at New Haven	2	93
Theba, m. Erastus **GOODWIN**, Mar. 21, 1821, at Salisbury, by Rev. Mr. Hide	2	262
THOMPSON, THOMSON, Alexander, m. Mary **BALDWIN**, July 2, 1744, by Rev. Timothy Collens	1	27
Alexander, m. Thankful **SHEPHERD**, Aug. 17, 1747, by Rev. Timothy Collens	1	27
Alexander, s. Alex[ander] & Thankful, b. Apr. 3, 1748	1	27
Artemesia, m. James Helleger **JOHNSON**, b. of Litchfield (colored), July 4, 1833, by Rev. Samuel Fuller	TM49	38
Augustus, m. Polly **JOHNSON**, Dec. 14, 1834, by Rev. Joseph E. Camp	2	297
Betsey, m. Tapping **REEVE**, Apr. 30, 1798, by Rev. Mr. Backus	1	117
Edward P., m. Jane H. **WEBSTER**, b. of Litchfield, Apr. 7, 1851, by Benjamin L. Swan	TM49	62
Eliza R., of Lyons, N.Y., m. Dr. R. M. **WOODRUFF**, of Litchfield, Oct. 13, 1842, by Jonathan Brace	2	337
Irene, m. Cromwell **GOODWIN**, Sept. 24, 1804, by Rev. Dan Huntington	1	220
James, s. Alexander & Thankful, b. May 29, 1753	1	79
John Young, s. Alexander & Thankful, b. Sept. 5, 1758	1	79
Mary, w. Alexander, d. Feb. 12, 1745/6, ae 22 y. 10 m. 21 d.	1	38
Mary, m. Charles **BUTLER**, May 9, 1790, by Rev. Stephen Stebbins	1	249
Mary Ann S., m. Heman H. **ORTON**, Feb. 24, 1831, by Rev. L. P. Hickok	2	286
Molly, d. Alexander, Jr. & Phebe, b. Nov. 19, 1770	1	27
Simeon, s. Alexander & Thankful, b. Nov. 3, 1762	1	79

	Vol.	Page
THOMPSON, THOMSON, (cont.),		
Simeon, s. Alexander & Thankful, d. Mar. 7, 1768	1	38
Thomas, s. Alexander & Thankful, b. Apr. 26, 1750	1	79
THORPE, THORP, Amos M., m. Mary Catharine **LATCHFORD**, Feb. 9,		
1851, by Rev. Benjamin W. Stone	TM49	61
Joel A., of Litchfield, m. Hannah M. **MATTOON**, of Plymouth, Jan. 21,		
1838, by Rev. Lewis Gunn	2	315
Rufus C., m. Julia **LITTLE**, of Northfield, Nov. 11, 1849, by Rev.		
Benjamin W. Stone	TM49	54
THRALL, Ann Louisa P., m. Hull **SPERRY**, Apr. 10, 1834, by Rev. L. P.		
Hickok	2	288
Luke, of Torrington, m. Harriet A. **WOOSTER**, of Litchfield, Feb. 21,		
1830, by Rev. L. P. Hickok	2	284
Myron J., of Barrington, m. Mary L. **PRATT**, of Litchfield, Nov. 16,		
1835, by Rev. H. N. Weed	TM49	92
THROOP, THROOPE, TROOP, Abigail, d. Benj[ami]n & Mary, b. June 8,		
1798	1	203
Altha, d. Dan & Olive, b. Aug. 21, 1820	2	112
Altha M., of Litchfield, m. Joel **MOREHOUSE**, of Woodbury, May 12,		
1847, by Rev. William Dixon	TM49	19
Benjamin, s. Joseph & Deborah, b. Sept. 13, 1752	1	79
Benjamin, m. Mary **BURGISS**, Nov. 16, 1775, by Increase Moseley,		
J.P.	1	121
Benjamin, s. Benjamin & Mary, b. Dec. 19, 1784	1	203
Benjamin, m. Mary **NORTON**, Dec. 25, 1813, by Rev. Amos Chase	2	43
Calvin, s. Benjamin & Mary, b. Sept. 19, 1779	1	203
Dan, m. Ama **BARNES**, Apr. 25, 1771, by Rev. Judah Champion	1	121
Dan, s. Benjamin & Mary, b. Apr. 28, 1796	1	203
Dan, m. Olive **SMITH**, Jan. 1, 1818, by Rev. Lyman Beecher	2	112
Deborah, twin with Joseph, d. Benjamin & Mary, b. Apr. 8, 1788	1	203
Eli, s. William & Eunice, b. Aug. 17, 1787	1	203
Elizabeth, m. Alexander **WAUGH**, Feb. 12, 1766, by Increase Moseley	1	125
Elizabeth M., m. William R. **KEELER**, b. of Litchfield, May 12, 1847,		
by Rev. William Dixon	TM49	19
Eunice, d. William & Eunice, b. June 4, 1781	1	121
Eunice, m. Appollos **STONE**, [ ], 1799, by James Morris	2	58
Irene, d. Benjamin & Mary, b. Jan. 14, 1778	1	203
James, s. Benjamin & Mary, b. Jan. 19, 1791	1	203
Joseph, s. William & Sarah, b. Apr. 19, 1772	1	78
Joseph, twin with Deborah, s. Benjamin & Mary, b. Apr. 8, 1788	1	203
Julina, d. Benj[ami]n & Mary, b. Nov. 29,1793	1	203
Leman, s. William & Eunice, b. Dec. 18, 1779	1	121
Lucy, d. William & Eunice, b. Oct. 19, 1784	1	203
Marian, d. William & Eunice, b. Oct. [ ], 1790	1	78
Martha, d. Joseph & Deborah, b. July 12, 1753	1	79
Mary, 1st w. Benjamin, d. May 27, 1818	2	43
Monroe, s. Dan & Olive, b. July 22, 1818	2	112
Polly, d. Benjamin & Mary, b. Dec. 8, 1782	1	203
Rhoda, d. Joseph & Deborah, b. June 10, 1758	1	79
Samuel, s. Joseph & Deborah, b. Nov. 8, 1761	1	79
Samuel, s. Benjamin & Mary, b. Aug. 12, 1 776	1	203
Sarah, w. William, d. Jan. 17, 1774	1	78
Sarah, d. William & Eunice, b. June 12, 1776	1	121

	Vol.	Page
THROOP, THROOPE, TROOP, (cont.),		
Sarah, m. Grant **WICKWIRE**, Apr. 12, 1791, by Rev. Ashbel Baldwin	2	53
Sheldon, s. William & Eunice, b. Dec. 29, 1788	1	203
William, m. Sarah **HAND**, Nov. 19, 1767, by Rev. Jonathan Todd, of East Guilford	1	121
William, s. William & Sarah, b. Aug. 15, 1768	1	121
William, s. William & Sarah, d. May 4, 1770	1	78
William, s. William & Sarah, b. Sept. 15, 1770	1	78
William, m. Eunice **STILLSON**, Apr. 27, 1775, by Daniel Everitt, J.P.	1	121
TIBBALS, Richard, of Norfolk, m. Harriet M. **CAMP**, of Litchfield, Mar. 6, 1837, by B. Y. Messenger, V.D.M.	2	313
TIERNAY, Jane L., of Litchfield, m. Edwin **BLAKESLEE**, of New Haven, Oct. 6, 1851, by N. C. Lewis	TM49	65
TILER, [see under **TYLER**]		
TILESTON, George W., of Williamsburg, Mass., m. Elizabeth **SMITH**, of Litchfield, Feb. 2, 1851, by Rev. William B. Hoyt	TM49	61
TILFORD, Huldah, had s. Obed Bissell Wing, b. Mar. 1, 1800	1	204-5
Huldah, m. Reuben **BISSELL,** [ ], by Rev. Truman Marsh	2	2
TINGER, Matilda, m. Almon **BALDWIN**, May 14, 1815	2	64
TITUS, John G., m. Mary **HARTSHORN**, Apr. 8, 1852, by Rev. David L. Parmelee	TM49	67
William, of Litchfield, m. Diadamia **VAN HOOSEN**, of Watertown, Nov. 7, 1841, by Rev. Jason Wells	2	335
TODD, Emeline A., of Northfield, m. Edmund **JORDAN**, of Waterbury, Jan. 26, 1851, in Northfield, by Rev. Ruel H. Tuttle	TM49	61
Julius, m. Caroline **BASSETT**, Jan. 10, 1827, by Rev. Joseph E. Camp, of Northfield	2	292
Oliver A. G., of Plymouth, m. Mary Ann **PIERPOINT**, of Northfield, June 29, 1834, by Rev. Fosdic Harrison, of Roxbury	2	295
Polly, m. John S. **HARRISON**, Oct. 16, 1822, by Rev. Joseph E. Camp, of Northfield	2	292
Sylvanus M., of Warren, m. Lucy Ann **MOUTHROP**, of Litchfield, Jan. 30, 1848, by John F. Norton	TM49	22
TOLLES, Maria, of Woodbury, m. Linus **GILBERT**, of Litchfield, Feb. 9, 1821, by Rev. Frederick Holcomb, of Watertown	2	148
TOMLINSON, TOMBELSON, Nelson, of Plymouth, m. Mariah **CHURCHILL**, of Litchfield, [ ] 25, 1841, by G. C. V. Eastman	2	335
Ruth, m. Isaac **PECK**, May 20, 1735, by Rev. Timothy Collens	1	70
TOMPKINS, TOMKINS, THOMPKINS, Almira Caroline, d. [Lucius & Betsey Ann], b. Aug. 21, 1843	TM49	3
Anna, m. Lynde **PALMELEE**, Jan. [ ], 1821, by Rev. Lyman Beecher	2	100
Egbert W., s. Lucius & Betsey Ann, b. Apr. 7, 1829	2	62
Egbert Wheeler, s. Lucius & Betsey Ann, b. Apr. 7, 1829	TM49	3
Elizabeth, m. Ira **BROWN**, Nov. 27, 1810	2	39
Emeline Amanda, d. [Lucius & Betsey Ann], b. Apr. 12, 1840	TM49	3
Francis, m. Huldah **STONE**, Jan. 23, 1806, by Rev. Truman Marsh	2	3
Garrett, m. Martha **DUNBAR**, Aug. 14, 1825, by Rev. J. E. Camp	2	265
George Hobart, s. [Lucius & Betsey Ann], b. Sept. 30, 1844	TM49	3
Harriet Artemesia, d. [Lucius & Betsey Ann], b. Oct. 14, 1837	TM49	3
Helen Irene, d. [Lucius & Betsey Ann], b. Mar. 26, 1842	TM49	3
James P., m. Mary Ann **SAUNDERS**, June 27, 1824, by Rev. Isaac Jones	2	123
Julia Elizabeth, d. [Lucius & Betsey Ann], b. Nov. 26, 1834	TM49	3

	Vol.	Page
TOMPKINS, TOMKINS, THOMPKINS, (cont.),		
Julia Elizabeth, d. Lucius & Betsey Ann, b. Nov. 26, 1834	2	62
Lucius, b. Mar. 2, 1799; m. Betsey Ann **CARTER**, Aug. 5, 1827	TM49	3
Lucius, m. Betsey Ann **CARTER**, b. of Litchfield, Aug. 5, 1827	TM49	3
Lucius, m. Ann* **CARTER**, b. of Litchfield, Aug. 5, 1827, by Rev. John		
S. Stone *(Arnold Copy says "Betsey Ann **CARTER** was name		
by which she was baptized")	2	271
Lucius Marshall, s. [Lucius & Betsey Ann], b. Jan. 22, 1839	TM49	3
Marshall, m. Mary **ORTON**, Feb. [ ], 1821, by Rev. Lyman Beecher	2	100
Mary, m. Ebenezer **CLARK**, Nov. 10, 1790, in Waterbury	2	74
Mary Ann, d. [Lucius & Betsey Ann], b. Apr. 13, 1831	TM49	3
Mary Ann, d. Lucius & Betsey Ann, b. Apr. 13, 1831	2	62
Mary Ann, m. Frederick **MORSE**, Mar. 19, 1848, by Rev. David L.		
Parmelee	TM49	22
Mary Jane, d. Enos & Phebe, b. Mar. 13, 1838	2	322
Polly, m. Sherman **HAMASTON**, Dec. 28, 1812, by Rev. Joseph E.		
Camp	2	69
Samuel Carter, s. [Lucius & Betsey Ann], b. Mar. 4, 1836	TM49	3
Samuel Carter, s. Lucius & Betsey Ann, b. Mar. 4, 1836	2	62
Sarah Jennet, d. [Lucius & Betsey Ann], b. Sept. 1, 1832	TM49	3
Sarah Jennett, d. Lucius & Betsey Ann, b. Sept. 1, 1832	2	62
Uriah Tracy, s. Francis & Huldah, b. June 21, 1807	2	3
TOOLEY, Joseph H., of Mereden, m. Dotha **BUNNEL**, of Litchfield, Nov.		
27, 1834, by Rev. David G. Tomlinson, of Milton	2	295
TOREY*, Rhoda, d. Ripley & Mindwell, b. Feb. 7, 1771 *(Arnold Copy		
has "**TOUCEY**")	1	121
TOUCY*, Rhoda, d. Ripley & Mindwell, b. Feb. 7, 1771 *("**TOREY**" in		
Woodruff's book)	1	121
TOWNSEN, Huldah, d. Richard & Nancy, b. Dec. 31, 1752	1	79
Huldah, d. Richard & Nancy, b. June 26, 1754	1	79
TRACY, Caroline, d. Uriah & Susannah, b. Dec. 26, 1792	1	203
Ferebe, m. John **McNEILE, Jr.**, Feb. 27, 1837, by Rev. Charles		
Chittenden	2	297
George Manning, s. Uriah & Susanna, b. Dec. 24, 1790	1	203
Julia, d. Uriah & Susanna, b. Nov. 25, 1786	1	203
Sally M.C., m. James **GOULD**, Oct. 21, 1798	2	115
Sally McCandy, d. Uriah & Susanna, b. Feb. 14, 1783	1	203
Susan, of Washington, m. Asal **HUBBARD**, of Warren, Feb. 4, 1839,		
by Rev. H. Bryant	2	325
Susanna, d. Uriah & Susanna, b. Jan. 18, 1785	1	203
Tryphena, see Tryphena **TRAY**	1	209
Uriah, m. Susanna **BULL**, May 1, 1782, by Rev. Judah Champion	1	203
Urial, representative Oct. 1788, May & Oct. 1789, May & Oct. 1790,		
May & Oct. 1791, May 1792, May 1793	2	1551-2
TRAVIS, TRAVIE, Elizabeth, d. James & Deborah, b. Dec. 13, 1776	1	121
Elizabeth*, m. John **PALMELY**, Jan. 18, 1782, by David Welch		
*("Elizabeth **TRAVIS**")	1	155
Isaac, s. James & Deborah, b. July 19, 1774	1	121
James, m. Deborah **PLUMBE**, Sept. 30, 1773, by Rev. Judah Champion	1	121
TRAY, Tryphena [**TRACY**], d. Nehemiah, m. Jonathan **WRIGHT**, June 27,		
1784, by Rev. Mr. Parsons, of East Haddam	1	209
TREADWAY, TREADAWAY, Eunis, d. Thomas & Sarah, b. Apr. 19, 1738	1	79
John Hurlburt, s. George & Mary, b. June 31, 1828	2	279

	Vol.	Page
TREADWAY, TREADAWAY, (cont.),		
Mary, w. George, d. June 16, 1828	2	279
Sarah, d. Thomas & Sarah, b. Aug. 30, 1736	1	39
Sarah, w. Thomas, d. Dec. 18, 1738, in the 38th y. of her age	1	38
Thomas, of Litchfield, m. Sarah **BUCK**, of New Milford, Oct. 8, 1735,		
by Roger Brownson, J.P.	1	39
TREAT, Deborah Emily, d. Eli & Urana, b. Apr. 15, 1813	2	264
Eli, m. Urana **BALDWIN**, [　　　], by Rev. [　　　]	2	264
George Donald, s. Eli & Urana, b. Aug. 9, 1806	2	264
Hannah Catharine, d. Eli & Urana, b. Oct. 10, 1808	2	264
Jane Emele, d. Eli & Urana, b. Aug. 22, 1804	2	264
M[　　] Esther, d. Eli & Urana, b. Apr. 26, 1801	2	264
Robert, of Middlebury, m. Hannah M. **WHITTLESEY**, of Litchfield,		
Nov. 28, 1837, by Rev. Fosdic Harrison, of Bethlehem	2	317
Sally, m. Junius **BURGISS**, Nov. 19, 1821, by Rev. John Langdon, of		
Bethlem	2	110
Sally Eliza, d. Eli & Urana, b. Nov. 18, 1802	2	264
Sophronia A., of Litchfield, m. Henry F. **FAIRBANKS**, of New York,		
Aug. 27, 1837, by Enos Stoddard, J.P.	2	313
Sophronia Adeline, d. Eli & Urana, b. Mar. 8, 1811	2	264
TROOP, [see under **THROOP**]		
TROWBRIDGE, Aden, m. Robert **WILLIAMS**, Oct. 11, 1840, by Rev.		
William Payne	2	331
Charles, s. Thomas & Sally, b. Feb. 1, 1801	2	41
Cornelia, of Litchfield, m. George B. **COOK**, of Winsted, Nov. 24,		
1851, by Benjamin L. Swan	TM49	66
Elisaha, s. Thomas & Sally, b. Apr. 22, 1789	2	41
Elisha, m. Anna **MINER**, Feb. 4, 1819, by John Jewett, 2nd, of		
Dutchess Cty., N.Y.	2	94
Elizabeth, d. Thomas & Sally, b. Aug. 2, 1805	2	41
Frederick Hart, s. Stephen [& Eliza], b. July 31, 1828	2	146
Harriet A., m. David **MOORE**, Nov. 28, 1844, by Rev. D. L. Marks	TM49	7
Helen Elizabeth, d. James & Lucy, b. Dec. 29, 1821	2	126
Henry J., s. Thomas & Sally, b. July 29, 1803	2	41
Henry P., m. Muna **KILBORN**, b. of Litchfield, July 12, 1841, by		
William Payne	2	334
James, s. Thomas & Sally, b. Oct. 1, 1794	2	41
James, m. Lucy **PALMALEE**, Apr. 22, 1818, by Rev. Lyman Beecher	2	126
James, s. James & Lucy, b. May 11, 1819	2	126
James, m. Julia A. **MUNGER**, b. of Litchfield, June 20, 1852, by N. C.		
Lewis	TM49	76
John P., m. Laura M. **CROSSMAN**, b. of Litchfield, July 3, 1851, by		
Benjamin L. Swan	TM49	63
Julia C., d. Thomas & Sally, b. Dec. 29, 1810	2	41
Lucy A., m. Leonard **STODDARD**, Sept. 3, 1854, by Rev. Horatio N.		
Weed	TM49	103
Maria H., d. Stephen, of Litchfield, m. Frederick **GOODWIN**, of		
Stockbridge, May 18, 1848, by Rev. Truman Marsh	TM49	24
Maria Hall, d. Stephen & Eliza, b. Oct. 29, 1824	2	146
Sally, d. Thomas & Sally, b. Nov. 11, 1791	2	41
Sarah Elizabeth, d. Stephen [& Eliza], b. Oct. 12, 1834	2	146
Stephen, s. Thomas & Sally, b. Feb. 13, 1798	2	41
Thomas, m. Sally **PECK**, Dec. 29, 1785, by Rev. Mr. Whittlesey, of		

	Vol.	Page
TROWBRIDGE, (cont.),		
New Haven	2	41
Thomas, s. Thomas & Sally, b. Apr. 16, 1787	2	41
TRUMAN, Elizabeth, m. Daniel **JOHNSON,** b. of Torrington, Nov. 18, 1840, by William Payne	2	332
TRUMBULL, Ruth, m. Abner **NORTHROP,** Sept. 14, 1814, by Morris Woodruff, J.P.	2	132
TURNER, Rhoda, m. Rev. Joseph E. **CAMP,** Dec. 3, 1795, by Rev. Judah Champion	2	264
TRYON, Almira, d. James & Ruth, b. Oct. 4, 1791	2	31
Almira, d. James & Jane, b. Oct. 4, 1809	1	203
Anna Miranda, d. Joseph & Mary, b. June 21, 1818	2	140
Anna Miranda, of Litchfield, m. Seth Minor **TAYLOR,** of Collinsville, Nov. 20, 1836, by Rev. Samuel Fuller, Jr.	2	296
Clarissa, d. Joseph & Sally, b. July 11, 1791	1	203
Clarrisa, had s. Isaac Gates, b. June 4, 1809	1	203
Cornelia, d. James & Polly R., b. Mar. 4, 1812	2	31
David, s. James & Polly R., b. Aug. 4, 1803	2	31
Eliza, d. James & Polly R., b. July 27, 1801	2	31
Esther, d. James & Polly R., b. Oct. 6, 1807	2	31
Friend Joseph, s. Joseph & Mary, b. Apr. 14, 1824	2	140
James, m. Ruth **STODDARD,** [ ], 1788	2	31
James, m. Polly* R. **SAUNDERS,** June [ ], 1797 *("Patty" in Woodruff's)	2	31
James, s. James & Polly R., b. June 23, 1799	2	31
James, m. Lucinda **FRISBIE,** Jan. 11, 1814	2	31
James, m. Amanda **STEDMAN,** Mar. [ ], 1824, by Rev. Joseph E. Camp	2	265
James, d. Nov. 23, 1825, ae 59 y.	2	31
Jeremiah, s. James & Polly R., b. Jan. 16, 1810	2	31
John, m. Esther **SMITH,** Sept. 22, 1755	1	79
John, s. John & Esther, b. Feb. 20, 1756	1	79
John, d. May 19, 1816, in the 88th y. of his age	1	78
John Smith, s. Joseph & Mary, b. May 26, 1822	2	140
Joseph, s. John & Esther, b. Jan. 11, 1759	1	79
Joseph, s. Joseph & Sarah, b. Nov. 29, 1788	1	203
Joseph, d. Nov. 15,1798	1	202
Joseph, m. Mary **SMITH,** May 23, 1817, by Rev. Lyman Beecher	2	140
Maria, m. Joseph Lynde **LORD,** May 10, 1812, by Rev. Lyman Beecher	2	17
Marianda, d. Joseph & Sarah, b. July 2, 1784	1	203
Mary, d. James & Polly R., b. July 9, 1805	2	31
Mary, m. Phillip C. **FENN,** Sept. 1, 1824, by Rev. Isaac Jones	2	134
Mary Ann, m. Eben **HULL,** b. of Litchfield, Apr. 7, 1839, by Rev. Gad N. Smith	2	319
Mary Anner, d. Joseph & Mary, b. Sept. 13, 1819	2	140
Nancy, m. Samuel Murhed **NOYCE,** b. of Wolcottville, Torrington, Aug. 3, 1828, by Rev. W[illia]m R. Gould	2	279
Polly R., w. James, d. Mar. [ ], 1813	2	31
Ruth, w. James, d. June [ ], 1795	2	31
Ruth, d. James & Polly* R., b. Mar. [ ], 1798 *("Patty)	2	31
Ruthy, d. James & Patty, b. Mar. 19, 1798	1	203
Sally, d. Joseph & Sarah, b. Oct. 19, 1787	1	203
Sarah, w. Joseph, d. Dec. 13, 1798	1	202
TUCKER, Sarah, m. Sedgwick **ORTON,** May 6, 1778, by Rev. Judah		

	Vol.	Page
TUCKER, (cont.),		
Champion	1	110-11
TUMA, Clarissa, m. Joseph **ISAAC**, (colored), May 10, 1812, by Rev.		
Truman Marsh	2	101
TURKINGTON*, William H., m. Julia M. **DALEY**, Oct. 8, 1854, by Rev.		
David L. Parmelee *("**TARKINGTON**"?)	TM49	105
TURNAY, [see under **TURNEY**]		
TURNER, Abner Manning, s. Eber & Matilda, b. July 27, 1824	2	13
Allison, s. Jacob & Sarah, b. Apr. 16, 1800	2	36
Allison, m. Sarah **MERCHANT**, June 22, 1820, by Frederick Holcomb	2	96
Betsey, d. Eber & Matilda, b. June 6, 1821	2	13
Bille, m. Philena **CURTISS**, Jan. [ ], 1796, by Daniel Potter, J.P.	2	5
Cynthia, d. Isaac & Cynthia, b. Sept. 20, 1815	2	38
Cynthia, Mrs., m. Jonathan **CARRINGTON**, b. of Litchfield, Apr. 18,		
1838, by G. C. V. Eastman	2	317
Cynthia, m. Leonard **PIERPOINT**, b. of Litchfield, [Jan.] 28, [1841],		
by Jonathan Brace	2	332
David Pindle, s. Jacob & Sarah, b. Jan. 11, 1815	2	36
Eber, s. Titus & Sarah, b. Oct. 13, 1782	1	203
Eber, m. Matilda **WILMOT**, Jan. 9, 1809, by Rev. Joseph E. Camp	2	13
Edward Thomas, s. Eber &Matilda, b. Mar. 21, 1835	2	13
Elisha Mason, s. Isaac & Cynthia, b. June 18, 1822	2	38
Eliza, d. Eber & Matilda, b. May 24, 1815	2	13
Eliza, m. Burke **MINOR**, Sept. 3, 1834, by Rev. Joseph E. Camp	2	297
Elizabeth, d. Titus & Sarah, b. Aug. 4, 1767	1	121
Elizabeth, d. Titus & Sarah, b. Aug. 4, 1767	1	203
Elizabeth C., m. Joseph H. **GARNSEY**, Nov. 26, 1829, by Fred Holcomb	2	283
Elizabeth Caroline, d. Jacob & Sarah, b. Nov. 26, 1812	2	36
Esther, d. Eber & Matilda, b. Dec. 6, 1812	2	13
Esther, m. Canfield **CHURCHILL**, Apr. 14, 1834, by Rev. Joseph E.		
Camp	2	297
Harriet, d. Bille & Philena, b. July 18, 1796	2	5
Isaac, s. Titus & Sarah, b. May 13, 1780	1	203
Isaac, m. Cynthia **MASON**, Jan. 15, 1810, by Rev. Joseph E. Camp	2	38
Israel, s. Allison & Sarah, b. Feb. 26, 1823	2	96
Jacob, s. Titus & Sarah, b. Apr. 22, 1778	1	203
Jacob, m. Sarah **PRINDLE**, May 13, 1799, by Rev. Chauncey Prindle	2	36
Jacob, m. Fanny **FOX**, July 1, 1827, by Fred Holcomb	2	272
Lewis, Wilmot, s. Eber & Matilda, b. Jan. 27, 1818	2	13
Lucius J., m. Nancy E. **FOX**, July 28, 1833, by Rev. Joseph E. Camp, of		
Northfield	2	292
Lucius Sherman, s. Eber & Matilda, b. Mar. 16, 1811	2	13
Lucretia M., d. Isaac & Cynthia, b. Apr. 8, 1811	2	38
Maria, d. Isaac & Cynthia, b. Dec. 25, 1817	2	38
Maria, of Litchfield, m. John **HUMPHREY**, of Norfolk, Oct. 30, 1845,		
by Rev. Samuel Fuller	TM49	37
Pamela, d. Allison & Sarah, b. Aug. 7, 1821	2	96
Phebe, d. Titus & Sarah, b. June 11, 1769	1	121
Phebe, d. Titus & Sarah, b. June 11, 1769	1	203
Phebe, m. Joseph Harris **HOPKINS**, Mar. 3, 1790, by Daniel Potter, J.P.	2	79
Phebe, d. Bille & Philena, b. Aug. 19, 1801	2	5
Phebe, m. Jason **CURTISS**, [ ], 1820, by Lyman Beecher	2	98
Phebe Hopkins, d. Isaac & Cynthia, b. Mar. 12, 1813	2	38

	Vol.	Page
TURNER, (cont.),		
Rachel, d. Jacob & Sarah, b. Oct. 18, 1817	2	36
Rhoda, d. Titus & Sarah, b. May 22, 1772	1	121
Rhoda, d. Titus & Sarah, b. May 22, 1772	1	203
Rhoda Adeline, d. Jacob & Sarah, b. Mar. 8, 1807; d. May 4, 1810	2	36
Rhoda E., m. Elliot C. **TALLMADGE,** Apr. 6, 1830, by Rev. William Lucas	2	286
Rhoda Emeline, twin with Ruth Adaline, d. Jacob & Sarah, b. Jan. 24, 1810	2	36
Rhoda M., m. George **BARNES,** b. of Litchfield, Northfield Parish, June 4, 1849, by Rev. Joseph D. Hall, of Plymouth	TM49	41
Rhoda Maria, d. Eber & Matilda, b. Nov. 23, 1827	2	13
Rosetta, d. Bille & Philena, b. June 27, 1807	2	5
Rosetta, of Litchfield, m. Rufus **LEWIS,** of Hartford, Sept. 13, 1829, by Rev. L. P. Hickok	2	281
Ruth Adaline, twin with Rhoda Emeline, d. Jacob & Sarah, b. Jan. 24, 1810	2	36
Sarah, d. Thomas & Anna, b. Apr. 19, 1805	2	85
Tertius, m. Abigail **WEBSTER,** Jan. 23, 1828, by Rev. Joseph E. Camp, of Northfield	2	292
Turtius Witman, s. Jacob & Sarah, b. Apr. 27, 1805, in Plymouth	2	36
Thomas, s. Titus & Sarah, b. Oct. 24, 1765	1	79
Thomas, s. Titus & Sarah, b. Oct. 24, 1765	1	203
Thomas, m. Anna **MERCHANT,** July [ ], 1791, by David Potter, J.P.	2	85
Titus, m. Sarah **BLAKELEY,** Jan. 27, 1765, by Rev. Mr. Scovell, of Waterbury	1	79
Titus, s. Jacob & Sarah, b. Feb. 10, 1802, in Plymouth	2	36
Titus, 2nd, m. Sophia **WEBSTER,** Oct. 11, 1827, by Rev. Joseph E. Camp, of Northfield	2	292
TURNEY, TURNAY, Abigail Mariah, d. Manias & Abigail, b. May 25, 1824	2	129
David, m. Lois **NEWTON,** Sept. 12, 1821, by Rev. Rodney Rossiter, of Plymouth	2	104
Minias, m. Abigail **ROBBINS,** Nov. 2, 1823, by Rev. Isaac Jones	2	129
Minias, s. Minias & Abigail, b. July 22, 1826	2	129
Myron, s. Minias & Abigail, b. Aug. 29, 1827	2	129
TURRILL, [see under **TERRILL**]		
TUTHILL, [see under **TUTTLE**]		
TUTTLE, TUTHILL, Cornelia, m. Addison **JOHNSON,** Feb. 8, 1838, by Rev. Stephen Hubbell	2	320
Cornelia Loiza, d. William & Hannah, b. Sept. 22, 1813	2	64
Ellen, m. Chauncey **WARNER,** Mar. 30, 1841, by Rev. Harvey D. Kitchel	2	333
Esther, m. Nathaniel **LEWIS,** Jan. 16, 1767, by Timothy Collens, J.P.	1	63
Harriet, of Litchfield, m. Elias **FRINK,** of Cornwall, Nov. 27, 1844, by Rev. John F. Norton	TM49	7
Henry Williams, s. William & Polly, b. Aug. 13, 1808	2	64
Jennett, m. George **BIDWELL,** b. of Northfield, Oct. 8, 1848, by J. L. Dickinson	TM49	27
Levi, s. Eliphalet & Desire, b. Apr. 3, 1751	1	27
Levi, d. Apr. 19, 1778, in the Continental Army	1	78
Mary L., of Litchfield, m. Edwin **WADHAMS,** of Goshen, May 22, 1828, by Rev. Frances H. Case, of Goshen	2	277
Mary Lewis, d. William & Polly, b. Oct. 20, 1806	2	64

	Vol.	Page
TUTTLE, TUTHILL, (cont.),		
Polly, w. William, d. Dec. 16, 1811	2	64
Rhoda, d. Eliphalet & Desire, b. Sept. 11, 1753	1	27
Sally E., m. Buel **BLAKE**, May 8, 1842	TM49	75
Sally E., of Milton, m. Buel **BLAKE**, of Cornwall, May 8, 1842, by		
Ralph Smith	2	410
Sally Eleanor, d. William & Polly, b. Nov. 28, 1811	2	64
Sarah, m. Billy **WAY**, Nov. 15, 1813, by Rev. Joseph E. Camp	2	18
Sherman Everest, s. William & Hannah, b. Apr. 4, 1816	2	64
Submit, d. Eliphalet & Desire, b. Feb. 12, 1756	1	27
William, m. Polly **LEWIS**, Oct. 6, 1805, by Rev. Uriel Gridley	2	64
William, m. Hannah **AVEREST**, Sept. 12, 1812, by Rev. Mr. Stone, of		
Cornwall	2	64
William G., m. Maria C. **BUEL**, Sept. 16, 1832, at Bradleyville, by Rev.		
D. E. Tomlinson	2	291
TYLER, TILER, Hannah, m. Charles **KELCEY**, Nov. 8, 1770	1	103
Jesse, m. Julia **CHURCHILL**, Apr. 28, 1832, by Rev. George E. Pierce	2	291
Thankful, m. John **HAMASTON**, June 21, 1770, by Rev. Mr. Steeres,		
of Northbury	1	16
William, m. Almada **BEACH**, May 25, 1824, by Rev. Lyman Beecher	2	136
UPSON, John, m. Anna **BARNES**, Jan. 14, 1836, by Rev. Charles Chittenden	2	298
Maria, m. Curtiss **BLAKESLEE**, Feb. 23, 1834, by Rev. Joseph E.		
Camp	2	297
VAIL, VAILL, Almira, d. Benjamin & Sylva, b. Aug. 10, 1801	2	9
Ama, d. Joseph & Jerusha, b. Apr. 2, 1749	1	81
Anna, d. Benjamin & Sylva, b. Jan. 9, 1796	2	9
Benjamin, s. Joseph & Jerusha, b. Mar. 23, 1772	1	81
Benjamin, m. Sylva **LANDON**, Nov. 11, 1793, by Rev. Judah		
Champion	2	9
Benjamin Lyman, s. Benjamin & Sylva, b. Feb. 21, 1811	2	9
Charles, s. Benjamin & Sylva, b. Dec. 30, 1803	2	9
Charles, m. Cornelia A. **GRISWOLD**, Apr. 19, 1832, by Rev. L. P.		
Hickok	2	288
Diantha, d. Benjamin & Sylva, b. Mar. 7, 1807	2	9
Diantha, of Litchfield, m. William **OXX**, of New York, Nov. 13, 1837,		
by Rev. Herman L. Vaill	2	314
Hannah, m. Ozias **GOODWIN**, Oct. 26, 1761, by Timothy Collens, J.P.	1	139
Herman Landon, s. Benjamin & Sylva, b. Dec. 7, 1794	2	9
Huldah, d. Joseph & Jerusha, b. May 26, 1762	1	81
Jerusha, d. Joseph & Jerusha, b. Oct. 17, 1746	1	123
Jerusha, d. Feb. 1, 1781	1	80
Joseph, m. Jerusha **PECK**, Feb. 2, 1744, by Rev. Timothy Collens	1	123
Joseph, s. Joseph & Jerusha, b. July 3, 1753	1	81
Lois, d. Joseph & Jerusha, b. Mar. 20, 1756	1	81
Lidia, d. Joseph & Jerusha, b. Apr. 15, 1759	1	81
Sarah, d. Joseph & Jerusha, b. Feb. 12, 1769	1	81
Urana, d. Joseph & Jerusha, b. Dec. 6, 1765	1	81
VAN HOOSEN, Diadamia, of Watertown, m. William **TITUS**, of Litchfield,		
Nov. 7, 1841, by Rev. Jason Wells	2	335
VAN SICKLES, John L., m. Lydia J. **NEGUS**, June 30, 1850, by William B.		
Hoyt	TM49	54
VAN WINKLE, Edgar S., of New York, m. Hannah **BEACH**, Nov. 11,		
1835, by Rev. L. P. Hickok	2	296

	Vol.	Page
WADHAMS, WADSHAMS, WADHAM, Ann, m. Samuel **BUELL, 2nd,** Jan. 30, 1811, by Rev. Joseph Harvey	2	135
Anna, m. Harvey **BIRGE,** b. of Litchfield, Sept. 28, 1840, by Seth W. Scofield	2	327
Birdsey, of Goshen, m. Elizabeth Eliza **MARSH,** of Litchfield, Oct. 9, 1820, by Lyman Beecher	2	97
Charles, m. Eliza **SAKET,** Feb. 6, 1826, by Rev. Levi Smith	2	260
Charles D., m. Mary **HALL,** b. of Milton, Sept. 14, 1843, by Rev. E. M. Porter	2	412
Edwin, of Goshen, m. Mary L. **TUTTLE,** of Litchfield, May 22, 1828, by Rev. Frances H. Case, of Goshen	2	277
Elizabeth*, m. Zopher **BEECH,** Dec. 10, 1741, by John Beech, J.P. *("Elizabeth **WOODDAMS**")	1	129
George D., of Wolcottville, m. Eliza R. **WOODRUFF,** of Litchfield, Apr. 10, 1854, by Rev. B. L. Swan	TM49	101
Harriet, m. Lauren L. **PETERS,** Feb. 29, 1836, by Rev. L. P. Hickok	2	296
Heman, of Goshen, m. Harriet **STONE,** of Litchfield, Feb. 9, 1830, by Enos Stoddard, J.P.	2	284
Jane, m. Henry W. **STEVENS,** Oct. 21, 1845, by Rev. David L. Parmelee	TM49	11
Martha A., of Litchfield, m. George E. **BIDWELL,** of Terryville, Dec. 17, 1749*, by Benjamin L. Swan *(Probably "1849")	TM49	44
Minerva, m. Samuel **BUELL,** June 29, 1819, by Rev. Joseph Harvey, of Goshen	2	119
Noah S., of Goshen, m. Lucy M. **RHEA,** of South Farms, July 9, 1838, by Rev. Thomas Savage, of Bedford, N.H.	2	316
Norman, of Goshen, m. Philinda **HUNGERFORD,** of Litchfield, Aug. 17, 1822, by Rev. Isaac Jones	12	113
Norman T., m. Mary R. **WHITTLESEY,** Apr. 16, 1851, by Rev. David L. Parmelee	TM49	62
Sally, m. Stephen **RUSSELL,** Apr. 17, 1803, by Rev. Mr. Hooker, of Goshen	2	56
Timothy, of Goshen, m. Anna **OSBORN,** of Litchfield, May 5, 1836, by Rev. Samuel Fuller, Jr.	2	296
Wallace W., of Goshen, m. Maria B. **PLUMB,** of Litchfield, Mar. 27, 1850, by Benjamin L. Swan	TM49	53
Walstein C., of Goshen, m. Mary A. **BISHOP,** of Litchfield, Dec. 29, 1850, by Rev. H. L. Vaill	TM49	40
WADMOUTH, Terties, of New Hartford, m. Eliza **MINOR,** of Litchfield, Sept. 21, 1843, by Jonathan Brace	2	413
WADSWORTH, Charles, s. Henry & Mary Ann, b. May 8, 1814	2	69
Elijah, s. Joseph & Elizabeth, b. Nov. 14, 1747	1	206
Elijah, m. Rhoda **HOPKINS,** Feb. 16, 1780, by Rev. Judah Champion	1	165
Elijah, m. Rhoda **HOPKINS,** Feb. 16, 1780	1	206
Elijah, Capt., had negro Prium, s. Nancy, b. Feb. 9, 1801	1	151
Epaphras, m. Clara **CATLIN,** Mar. 23, 1780, by Rev. Judah Champion	1	165
Frederick, s. Elijah & Rhoda, b. Mar. 7, 1786	1	206
Henry, s. Elijah & Rhoda, b. Oct. 11, 1782	1	206
Henry, m. Mary Ann **BRADLEY,** Mar. 19, 1811, by Rev. Truman Marsh	2	69
James Leaming, s. Henry & Mary Ann, b. Feb. 26, 1820	2	69
Jane Elizabeth, d. Henry & Mary Ann, b. Apr. 15, 1817	2	69
Mary Ann, d. Henry & Mary Ann, b. Dec. 1, 1811	2	69

	Vol.	Page
WADSWORTH, (cont.),		
Mary Ann, m. William **PITCHER,** Oct. 4, 1834, by Rev. L. P. Hickok	2	288
Mary Ann, m. Abel **HAMIAKS,** of Columbia, N.Y., Dec. 10, 1834, by		
Rev. L. P. Hickok	2	296
Rhoda, d. Elijah & Rhoda, b. Feb. 13, 1784	1	206
WAGONER, Wilson D., m. Malinda L. **HARRISON,** Oct. 18, 1843, by Rev.		
David L. Parmelee	2	340
WALEFIELD, William C., m. Sally J. **SMITH,** b. of Litchfield, Sept. 12,		
1842, by Rev. Isaac Jones	2	336
WALKER, David, s. Josiah & Phebe, b. Dec. 26, 1735	1	41
Jason, m. Polly **PALMER,** Feb. 19, 1812, by Rev. Asa Tallmadge	2	50
Jason, d. Oct. 6, 1823	2	50
Josiah, s. Josiah & Febe, b. Oct. 8, 1723	1	41
Phebe, w. Josiah, d. Sept. 26, 1738	1	40
Polly Esther, m. Samuel **JOHNSON,** b. of Litchfield, Apr. 27, 1828, by		
David Bird, J.P.	2	276
Zachariah, s. Josiah & Phebe, b. July 16, 1738	1	41
WALLACE, Elizabeth, d. Richard & Mary, b. May 28, 1788	1	207
Elizabeth, of Bradleyville, m. Samuel **WALLACE,** of Orange Cty.,		
N.Y., Jan. 2, 1840, by Rev. Jonathan Brace	2	318
Hiram, twin with Huran, s. Richard & Mary, b. Apr. 16, 1792	1	206
Huran, twin with Hiram, s. Richard & Mary, b. Apr. 16, 1792	1	206
Matthew, s.Nathaniel & Anne, b. Apr. 12, 1781	1	207
Nathaniel, s. Nathaniel & Anne, b. Apr.13, 1779	1	207
Nathaniel Little, of Middletown, m. Anne **PECK,** of Litchfield, Feb. 20,		
1777, by A. Adams	1	207
Polly, d. Richard & Mary, b. Apr. 13, 1781	1	207
Reuben, s.Nathaniel & Anne, b. Apr. 22, 1783	1	207
Rhoda, d. Richard & Mary, b. Mar. 14, 1783	1	207
Richard, m. Mary **PECK,** Apr. 27, 1780, by Rev. Judah Champion	1	165
Richard, m. Mary **PECK,** Apr. 27, 1780, by Rev. Judah Champion	1	207
Richard, s. Richard & Mary, b. May 20, 1790	1	207
Sally, d. Richard & Mary, b. Feb. 20, 1785	1	207
Samuel, of Orange Cty., N.Y., m. Elizabeth **WALLACE,** of		
Bradleyville, Jan. 2, 1840, by Rev. Jonathan Brace	2	318
WALLACK, Jason, m. Polly **ROOT,** Dec. 20, 1844, by Rev. D. L. Marks	TM49	7
WALLER, Abigal, d. Joseph & Hanah, b. Oct. 1, 1727	1	41
Joseph, m. Hannah **BUELL,** Dec. 8, 1726, by Rev. Timothy Collens	1	41
WALLON, James, m. Abigail **KILBORN,** Sept. 11, 1823, by Rev. Truman		
Marsh	2	131
WARD, Abigail, d. William, Jr. & Charlotte, b. [ ], 1806	2	37
Abigail, d. David & Rhoda, b. Dec. 10, 1808	2	145
Ambros, s. William, Jr. & Charlotte, b. [ ], 1816	2	37
Augustus, s. David & Rhoda, b. Mar. 12, 1797	2	145
Caroline, d. William, Jr. & Charlotte, b. [ ], 1810	2	37
Caroline, of Litchfield, m. Judson **WOOSTER,** of Bridgeport, Jan. 26,		
1845, by G. C. V. Eastman	TM49	8
Clarissa, d. David & Rhoda, b. Oct. 26, 1799	2	145
Clarissa, d. David & Rhoda, d. May 1, 1821	2	145
David, m. Rhoda **COE,** Jan. 14, 1788, by Rev. Mr. Huntington, of		
Middletown	2	145
David Coe, s. David & Rhoda, b. June 16, 1815	2	145
Diantha, d. David & Rhoda, b. Feb. 5, 1793	2	145

	Vol.	Page
WARD, (cont.),		
Elias, s. William, Jr. & Charlotte, b. [ ], 1814	2	37
Elizabeth, d. David & Rhoda, b. June 5, 1791	2	145
Grace, m. Ashbel WESSELL, May 8, 1808, by Rev. Truman Marsh	2	22
Harriet, d. William, Jr. & Charlotte, b. [ ], 1807	2	37
Henry, s. William, Jr. & Charlotte, b. Feb. [ ], 1805	2	37
Jane Antoinette, m. Herman WARNER, Jr., b. of Litchfield, May 1, 1836, by Rev. Samuel Fuller, Jr.	2	296
John, s. William, Jr. & Charlotte, b. [ ], 1808	2	37
John, m. Eunice BUCKLEY, May 21, 1833, by Rev. L. P. Hickok	2	288
Julian, d. William, Jr. & Charlotte, b. Mar. [ ], 1804	2	37
Loren, d. David & Rhoda, b. July 14, 1789	2	145
Maria, m. Alexander CADY, Aug. 28, 1849, by Rev. David L. Parmelee	TM49	42
Marietta, m. Joseph BIRGE, Apr. 2, 1786, by Rev. Ashbel Baldwin	2	252
Marietta, m. Joseph BIRGE, Apr. 2, 1789, by Rev. Ashbel Baldwin	1	250
Mary Charlotte, m. Frederick Augustus GRANNIS, b. of Litchfield, Dec. 24, 1845, by Rev. Samuel Fuller	TM49	37
Nathan, s. David & Rhoda, b. Mar. 16, 1795	2	145
Rachal, m. Benjamin GIBBS, May 18, 1729	1	15
Roswell B., of Hartford, m. Catharine M. WEBB, Mar. 12, 1832, by Rev. L. P. Hickok	2	288
William, Jr., m. Charlotte MUNGER, Mar. [ ], 1803	2	37
William, s. William, Jr. & Charlotte, b. [ ], 1812	2	37
WARDEN, Amelia, m. Lorenzo HART, Oct. [Nov.] 11, 1821, by Rev. Isaac Jones	2	252
WARNER, Chauncey, m. Ellen TUTTLE, Mar. 30, 1841, by Rev. Harvey D. Kitchel	2	333
Esther B., m. Marshall F. WHITNEY, of Washington, Apr. 12, 1826, by Rev. Isaac Jones	2	262
Herman, Jr., m. Jane Antoinette WARD, b. of Litchfield, May 1, 1836; by Rev. Samuel Fuller, Jr.	2	296
John S., of Plymouth, m. Emily LORD, Feb. 18, 1824, by Rev. Isaac Jones	2	132
Lucetta, of Plymouth, b. June 6, 1785; m. Jacob HUBBARD, Nov. 8, 1815, by Rev. Luther Hart	2	254
Miranda, m. Elihu HARRISON, Apr. 20, 1820, by Rev. Frederick Holcomb	2	101
Pernal, m. Harriet L. WEBSTER, Nov. 6, 1831, by Rev. L. P. Hickok	2	288
Sarah, d. Reuben, b. May 17, 1767	1	82
WARREN, Abijah, m. Eunice MUNGER, Dec. 11, 1777, by Rev. George Beckwith	1	165
Althashtruty (?), d. Harris & Sarah Ann, b. Jan. 20, 1822	2	149
Belah, s. Abijah & Eunice, b. Jan. 28, 1783	1	124
Charlotte Ann, d. Harris & Sarah Ann, b. Mar. 4, 1820	2	149
Christian, d. Abijah & Eunice, b. Oct. 26, 1778	1	165
Harris, m. Sarah Ann WICKWIRE, Sept. 12, 1813, by Rev. Amos Chase	2	149
Henry Alexander, s. Harris & Sarah, b. May 3, 1825	2	149
Jane Elizabeth, d. Harris & Sarah Ann, b. June 22, 1816	2	149
Juliet, d. Harris & Sarah Ann, b. Nov. 3, 1814, at New Milford	2	149
Margaret Ann, m. Augustus C. BUELL, Jan. 12, 1829, by Rev. Joseph E. Camp, of Northfield	2	292
Mary, of Plymouth, m. David C. LORD, of Litchfield, Apr. 28, 1828, at		

	Vol.	Page
WARREN, (cont.),		
Plymouth	2	322
Nancy, m. Alanson J. **PICKETT**, Mar. 27, 1842	TM49	64
Nancy, m. Alanson J. **PICKETT**, Mar. 27, 1842, by Jonathan Brace	2	336
Reuben, s. Reuben & Phebe, b. Feb. 1, 1769	1	125
Riley, m. Eunice P. **DAY**, Apr. 29, 1849, by Rev. David L. Parmelee	TM49	36
Sally Maria, d. Harris & Sarah Ann, b. Feb. 5, 1818	2	149
WASHBURN, Elizabeth S., m. Virgillius G. **COOKE**, Sept. 23, 1840, by		
Jonathan Brace	2	327
WATKINS, WADKIER, Annis, m. Midian **GRISWOULD**, [ ],		
1784, by David Catlin	2	58
Elizabeth, m. Calvin **COMSTOCK**, Nov. 27, 1771, by Daniel Catlin,		
J.P.	1	88
Lowly, m. John **STONE**, [ ], by Cyprian Webster	2	50
Sarah, m. Zebulon **BISSELL**, Jr., Jan. 13, 1774, by Rev. Andrew		
Bartholomew	1	167
WATSON, Anne, m. Hugh **HANNA**, Apr. 18, 1765	1	99
WAUGH, Alexander, m. Elizabeth **THROOP**, Feb. 12, 1766, by Increase		
Moseley	1	125
Chloe, d. Samuel & Elizabeth, b. Jan. 29, 1807	2	55
Cloe, d. Samuel & Elizabeth, d. Jan. 13, 1808	2	55
Clarence Henry, s. Leverett J. & Lucy, b. Dec. 15, 1845	TM49	3
Dan, s. Alexander & Elizabeth, b. Nov. 12, 1767	1	125
Dorcas, d. John & Olive, b. Oct. 17, 1792	1	206
Eliza, d. Sam[ue]ll & Elizabeth, b. Nov. 1, 1798	1	245
Eliza, d. Samuel & Elizabeth, b. Nov. 1, 1798	2	55
Eliza, m. William **PARISH**, Oct. 27, 1824, by Rev. Henry Robinson	2	137
Elizabeth, d. Joseph & Elizabeth, b. Oct. 26, 1772	1	40
Harvey, s. Horace [& Diana], b. Mar. 4, 1828	2	90
Henry H., m. Martha **FAIRCHILD**, June 20, 1848, by Rev. David L.		
Parmelee	TM49	22
Horace, s. John & Olive, b. Mar. 6, 1791	1	206
Horace, m. Diana **RAYMOND**, Feb. [ ], 1816, by George D. Kasson,		
J.P.	2	90
James, m. Hannah **BRADLEY**, Oct. 10, 1786, by Rev. Mr. Damins, of		
Salisbury	1	207
James, m. Phebe **STODDARD**, b. of Litchfield, Dec. 17, 1829, by		
Morris Woodruff, J.P.	2	283
John, m. Olive **STONE**, Oct. 17, 1787, by Rev. Amos Chase	1	206
John, d. Apr. 23, 1813	1	206
Joseph, s. Joseph & Elizabeth, b. Dec. 4, 1763	1	125
Julian, d. John & Olive, b. Oct. [ ], 1806	1	206
Julia Ann, m. Isaac **BRISTOL**, June 12, 1848, by Rev. David L.		
Parmelee	TM49	22
Leman, s. Joseph & Elizabeth, b. Aug. 4, 1774	1	40
Leverett, s. Horace & Diana, b. Mar. 4, 1817	2	90
Lowdon B., s., Sam[ue]ll & Elizabeth, b. May 6, 1794	1	245
Louden B., s. Samuel & Elizabeth, b. May 6, 1794	2	55
Loudon B., d. Sept. 12, 1796, ae 2 y. 5 m.	1	244
Loudon B., s. Samuel & Elizabeth, d. Sept. 12, 1796	2	55
Lucy, d. John & Olive, b. Sept. 4, 1796	1	206
Lydia G., d. Samuel & Elizabeth, b.May 20, 1804	2	55
Lydia G., d. Sam[ue]l & Elizabeth, b. May 16, 1804	1	245

	Vol.	Page
WAUGH, (cont.),		
Lydia G., m. James **SMEDLEY,** Apr. 30, 1845, by Rev. David L. Parmelee	TM49	9
Minerva, d. John & Olive, b. June 26, 1803	1	206
Minerva, of Litchfield, m. Philo **FAIRCHILD,** of Watertown, Dec. 5, 1822, by Morris Woodruff	2	116
Moses, s. John & Olive, b. Nov. 13, 1788	1	206
Polly, d. John & Olive, b. Mar. 26, 1794	1	206
Rachel, d. Joseph & Elizabeth, b. Apr. 8, 1766	1	125
Rebecca, d. Joseph & Eliza, b. Mar. 13, 1768	1	125
Robert, m. Ruth **GUITTEAU,** of Bethlem, Nov. 28, 1758, by Daniel Everest, J.P.	1	82
Ruth, d. Robert & Ruth, b. Dec. 21, 1759	1	83
Samuell, m. Elizabeth **GOODWIN,** Dec. 2, 1784, by Rev. Mr. Brinsmade	1	245
Samuel, m. Elizabeth **GOODWIN,** Dec. [ ], 1784, by Rev. Mr. Brinsmade	2	55
Samuel, s. Samuel & Elizabeth, b. Nov. 1, 1802	2	55
Samuel, Jr., m. Caroline **MARSH,** b. of Litchfield, Jan. 28, 1829, by Rev. Henry Robinson, of South Farms	2	279
Sam[ue]l W., s. Sam[ue]l & Elizabeth, b. Apr. 9, 1802	1	245
Sophrona, d. Sam[ue]l & Elizabeth, b. Oct. 15, 1791	1	245
Sophronia, d. Samuel & Elizabeth, b. Oct. 15, 1791	2	55
Thaddeus, s. Joseph & Elizabeth, b. Jan. 3, 1759	1	125
Thenina*, d. Samuel & Elizabeth, b. Nov. 3, 1785 *("Therina" in Woodruff's book)	1	245
Therina, d. Samuel & Elizabeth, b. Nov. 3, 1785	2	55
Theron Leverett, s. Leverett J. & Lucy, b. July 6, 1843	TM49	3
WAY, Allithea, m. Isaac **BISSELL, Jr.,** Dec. 13, 1770, by Rev. Judah Champion	1	44
Alvin, s. Asa & Lydia, b. Mar. 25, 1799	2	1
Avis, of Goshen, m. Bostwick **HURD,** of Marlborough, Jan. 14, 1827, by Hugh P. Welch	2	268
Billy, s. Elijah & Lucy, b. Dec. 14, 1787	1	204-5
Billy, m. Sarah **TUTTLE,** Nov. 15, 1813, by Rev. Joseph E. Camp	2	18
Edwin, s. Elijah & Lucy, b. Apr. 10, 1802	1	204-5
Elijah, m. Lucy **SELKRIG,** Apr. 24, 1783, by Rev. James Nichols	1	204-5
Jared, s. Thomas, Jr. & Mary, b. June 28, 1809	2	12
Norris, s. Asa & Lydia, b. Sept.1, 1801	2	1
Orill, d. Thomas, Jr. & Mary, b. June 15, 1819	2	12
Philomela, d. Elijah & Lucy, b. Oct. 24, 1783	1	204-5
Thomas, Jr., m. Mary **WILLIAMS,** Oct. [ ], 1805, by Rev. Mr. Benendict, of Woodbury	2	12
Tryphena, d. Elijah & Lucy, b. Apr. 24, 1796	1	204-5
WEBB, Catharine M., m. Roswell B. **WARD,** of Hartford, Mar. 12, 1832, by Rev. L. P. Hickok	2	288
Pamela, m. Benjamin Stone, Mar. [ ], 1797, by Rev. B. Judd, of Litchfield	2	12
Zephaniah, s. Charles & Catharine, b. Sept. 11, 1824	2	135
WEBSTER, Abigail, m. Tertius **TURNER,** Jan. 23, 1828, by Rev. Joseph E. Camp, of Northfield	2	292
Abner, s. Timothy, Jr. & Mabel, b. Jan. 13, 1777	1	165
Ann, m. Laban **BEACH, Jr.,** Mar. 9, 1823, by Rev. Isaac Jones	2	118

	Vol.	Page
WEBSTER, (cont.),		
Anna, d. Elijah & Martha, b. Mar. 9, 1789	1	164
Anna, d. Orange & Dianthe, b. Sept. 28, 1802	2	21
Anna, m. Abner G. FOX, Mar. 2, 1829, by Rev. Joseph E. Camp, of		
Northfield	2	292
Anne, m. Joshua MASON, June 1, 1763, by Rev. Judah Champion	1	107
Arianda, d. Reuben & Anne, b. Jan. 12, 1782	1	204-5
Aranda, d. Claudiaus & Margaret, b. Sept. 16, 1796	1	204-5
Arianda, m. Jerry RADCLIFFE, Apr. 27, 1806, by Rev. Truman Marsh	2	2
Asa, s. Justus & Jerusha, b. May 1, 1764	1	82
Ashbel Wheeler, s. Louden & Marian, b. Jan. 8, 1807	1	209
Augustine, s. Reuben & Anne, b. May 22, 1791	1	204-5
Avis, d. Benjamin & Lucretia, b. Apr. 20, 1763	1	125
Avis, m. Elen CRAMPTON, Jan. 1, 1783, by Rev. Judah Champion	1	171
Avis Eliza, d. Louden & Maryan, b. Sept. 8, 1813	1	209
Belinda, d. Reuben & Anne, b. Sept. 23, 1787	1	204-5
Belinda, m. Seth P. BEERS, Sept. 12, 1807, by Rev. Truman Marsh	2	31
Benjamin, s. Benjamin & Elizabeth, b. Dec. 8, 1736	1	41
Benjamin, representative Oct. 1752, May & Oct. 1753, May 1754, May		
1755	2	1547
Benjamin, Dea., d. July 10, 1755	1	40
Benjamin, s. Benjamin & Lucretia, b. Feb. 10, 1769	1	82
Benjamin, d. Oct. 29, 1782	1	82
Benjamin, Jr., m. Louisa M. OSBORN, b. of Litchfield, Apr. 11, 1849,		
by John F. Norton	TM49	36
Benjamin, of Terryville, m. Ellen Aurene OSBORN, of Litchfield, Oct.		
1, 1850, by Rev. William B. Hoyt	TM49	55
Centhian, d. Louden & Marian, b. May 12, 1805	1	209
Charles, s. Benjamin & Elizabeth, b. Mar. 19, 1743/4	1	41
Charles B., m. Lucinda BALDWIN, b. of Litchfield, Nov. 4, 1849, by		
Rev. William B. Hoyt	TM49	44
Clark, s. Michael & Elizabeth, b. Dec. 10, 1774	1	124
Claudius, s. Benjamin & Lucretia, b. Aug. 27, 1772	1	125
Claudiaus, m. Margaret BUEL, Feb. 1, 1795, by Rev. Judah Champion	1	204-5
Claudius, s. Louden & Maryan, b. Aug. 11, 1817	1	209
Cynthia Ann, m. Nehemiah Clark EDWARDS, Oct. 1, 1823, by Rev.		
Isaac Jones	2	124
Dan, s. Benjamin & Lucretia, b. Jan. 23, 1776	1	165
Daniel, s. Michael & Elizabeth, b. Mar. 24, 1776	1	124
David, s. Orange & Dianthe, b. June 22, 1804	2	21
Dennis, s. Timothy, Jr. & Mabel, b. Aug. 29, 1779	1	165
Dianthe Belinda, d. Orange & Dianthe, b. Oct. 31, 1815	2	21
Edwin, s. Reuben & Anna, b. May 8, 1803	1	204-5
Elihu, m. Sally MARSH, Nov. [ ], 1823, by Rev. Joseph E. Camp	2	265
Elijah, s. Benjamin & Elizabeth, b. Dec. 28, 1732	1	41
Elijah, s. Dea. Benjamin & Eliza, d. Aug. 18, 1754	1	40
Elijah, s. Benjamin & Lucretia, b. Mar. 19, 1761	1	83
Elijah, m. Martha CLARK, Oct. 18, 1780, by [ ]	1	165
Elijah, s. Timothy & Sarah, b. Mar. 29, 1755	1	83
Elizabeth, of Hartford, m. Benjamin OSBORN, of Litchfield, Dec. 29,		
1739, by Rev. Mr. Whiteman, of Hartford	1	69
Elizabeth, d. Benjamin & Elizabeth, b. Jan. 23, 1741	1	41
Elizabeth, d. Michael & Elizabeth, b. Nov. 5, 1777	1	165

	Vol.	Page
WEBSTER, (cont.),		
Elizabethm, see Elizabeth **MARSH**	1	148
Emily, m. Kirby **MARSH**, Apr. 29, 1833, by Rev. L. P. Hickok	2	288
Fanny, d. Claudiaus & Margaret, b. Dec. 23, 1799	1	204-5
George, s. Reuben & Anna, b. Sept. 8, 1796	1	204-5
Harriet Buel, of Brooklyn, N.Y., m. Charles Ogilvie **BELDEN**, of		
Milwaukie, Wis., July 13, 1852, by Rev. John Bandegee	TM49	75
Harriet L., m. Pernal **WARNER**, Nov. 6, 1831, by Rev. L. P. Hickok	2	288
Harriet Lucretia, d. Louden & Mary Ann, b. Sept. 4, 1811	1	209
Hosea, s. Reuben & Anne, b. Dec. 14, 1789	1	204-5
Hosea, of Augusta, Ga., m. Julia **PARMELEE**, of Litchfield, Sept. 18,		
1820, by Rev. Isaac Jones, in St. Michaels Church	2	96
Huldah, d. Timothy & Sarah, b. Feb. 21, 1767	1	40
Huldah, d. Elijah & Martha, b. Mar. 20, 1797	1	164
James, s. Benjamin & Elizabeth, b. June 2, 1734	1	41
James, s. Dea. Benjamin & Elizabeth, d. July 30, 1754	1	40
James, s. Justus & Jerusha, b. July 19, 1755	1	41
James, s. Timothy & Sarah, b. May 17, 1759	1	83
James, 3rd, m. Polly **ORTON**, Apr. 17, 1792, by Rev. Judah Champion	1	206
James Kilborn, s. Orange & Dianthe, b. May 26, 1811	2	21
Jane H., m. Edward P. **THOMPSON**, b. of Litchfield, Apr. 7, 1851, by		
Benjamin L. Swan	TM49	62
Jennet, d. Claudiaus & Margaret, b. Nov. 1, 1809	1	204-5
Jerusha, d. May 29, 1777	1	82
John, s. Benjamin & Elizabeth, b. Apr. 3, 1747	1	41
Julia, of Litchfield, m. Henry H. **FOX**, of Woodbury, Nov. 8, 1835, by		
R. S. Crampton	2	298
Julia, of Litchfield, m. Luther Holcomb **STEBBINS**, of Hartland, Sept.		
30, 1845, by Rev. Samuel Fuller	TM49	37
Justus, m. Jerusha **STODDOR**, Nov. 29, 1750, by Thomas Harrison,		
J.P.	1	83
Justus, d. May 23, 1777	1	82
Lamira, d. White & Phebe, b. Jan. 19, 1809	1	164
Leman, s. Michael & Elizabeth, b. June 16, 1782	1	207
Levi, s. Elijah & Martha, b. July 10, 1787	1	164
Levi, s. Elijah & Martha, d. Sept. 4, 1792	1	164
Louden, s. Benjamin & Lucretia, b. Mar. 3, 1780	1	207
Louden, m. Marian **ORTON**, Feb. 14, 1804, by Rev. Dan Huntington	1	209
Lucretia, d. Benjamin & Lucretia, b. Feb. 14, 1766	1	125
Lucretia, m. Elisha **MASON**, Jan. 8, 1785, by Rev. Judah Champion	1	189
Lucretia, m. Elisha **MASON**, Jan. 8, 1785, by Rev. Judah Champion	2	261
Lucretia, m. William **BUELL, 2nd**, Nov. 27, 1816, by Rev. Lyman		
Beecher	2	126
Lucy, d. White & Phebe, b. Sept. 5, 1805	1	164
Luman, s. Michael & Elizabeth, b. Feb. 5, 1781	1	165
Luther, s. Orange & Dianthe, b. Mar. 8, 1809	2	21
Lyman, m. Elizabeth **SMITH**, Aug. 28, 1828, by Rev. Joseph E. Camp,		
of Northfield	2	292
Mana, m. Lucius P. **WOODRUFF**, Feb. 28, 1844, by Rev. D. L. Marks	TM49	4
Margaret, d. Louden & Maryan, b. Nov. 15, 1815	1	209
Mariah, d. Elijah & Martha, b. Jan. 14, 1800	1	164
Marina, m. Norman **BUEL**, Dec. 28, 1812, by Rev. Lyman Beecher	2	127
Mary Ann, d. Louden & Mary, b. Mar. 15, 1809	1	209

	Vol.	Page
WEBSTER, (cont.),		
Mary Ann, of Litchfield, m. Daniel S. **EDWARDS**, of Roxbury, Apr. 15, 1829, by Rev. Isaac Jones	2	280
Michael, s. Timothy & Sary, b. May 8, 1748	1	41
Michael, m. Elizabeth **CLARK**, July 10, 1774, by Rev. Judah Champion	1	124
Michael, s. Michael & Elizabeth, b. Mar. 10, 1779	1	165
Olive, d. Elijah & Martha, b. Oct. 15, 1791	1	164
Olive, d. Elijah & Martha, d. Nov. 8, 1792	1	164
Olive, d. Elijah & Martha, b. Feb. 13, 1794	1	204-5
Orange, s. Stephen & Honor, b. Dec. 28, 1780	2	21
Orange, m. Dianthe **CATLIN**, June 17, 1801, by Rev. Judah Champion	2	21
Orange, s. Orange & Dianthe, b. Nov. 10, 1813	2	21
Osman, s. Timothy, Jr. & Mabel, b. Oct. 18, 1774	1	82
Peter Buel, s. Claudiaus & Margaret, b. Nov. 4, 1805	1	204-5
Polly, d. Benjamin & Lucretia, b. Feb. 11, 1783	1	207
Rachel, m. Philo **MOSS**, Apr. 24, 1794, by Rev. Judah Champion	2	71
Rebecka, m. Ebenezer **BEEBE**, Feb. 28, 1735/6, by Rev. Timothy Collens	1	87
Rebecca, d. Justus & Jerusha, b. Sept. 17, 1751	1	83
Rebecca, m. Stephen **PLANT**, Sept. 16, 1773, by Rev. Judah Champion	1	30
Reuben, s. Timothy & Sary, b. Feb. 7, 1757	1	41
Reuben, m. Anna **BUEL**, June 2, 1781, by Rev. Judah Champion	1	204-5
Reuben, representative May 1826	2	1556
Ruth, d. Timothy & Sarah, b. Mar. 2, 1762	1	82
Sally, m. A. Watson **FOX**, July 1, 1832, by Rev. Joseph E. Camp of Northfield	2	292
Sary, d. Timothy & Sary, b. Sept. 24, 1751	1	41
Sarah, d. Stephen & Honor, b. Sept. 8, 1765	1	125
Sarah, w. Timothy, d. Oct. 7, 1814, ae 90 y.	1	164
Sarah Ann, m. Edward **PARKER**, of Plymouth, May 17, 1837, by R.M. Chipman	2	313
Smith, s. Elijah & Martha, b. July 13, 1785	1	164
Sophia, m. Titus **TURNER, 2nd,** Oct. 11, 1827, by Rev. Joseph E. Camp, of Northfield	2	292
Stephen, s. Benjamin & Elizabeth, b. May 21, 1739	1	41
Stephen, s. Orange & Dianthe, b. Mar. 9, 1807	2	21
Susanah, m. William **MARSH**, Nov. 9, 1733, by Rev. Daniel Wadsworth	1	25
Timothy, m. Sary **WHITE**, Aug. 15, 1745	1	41
Timothy, s. Timothy & Sary, b. Jan. 12, 1747	1	41
Timothy & Sarah, had child b. Feb. 26, 1763; d. [same day]	1	40
Timothy, Jr., m. Mabel **BIDWELL**, Aug. 23, 1770, by Rev. Judah Champion	1	125
Timothy, s. Timothy, Jr. & Mabel, b. Nov. 10, 1772	1	125
Timothy, d. Apr. 30, 1803, in the 80th y. of his age	1	164
Truman, m. Dina* **SANFORD**, Oct. 8, 1795, by Rev. E. Camp *("Dima"?)	2	35
Waite, s. Elijah & Martha, b. Sept. 7, 1781	1	207
White, s. Elijah & Martha, b. Sept. 7, 1781	1	164
White, m. Phebe **HART**, Jan. 6, 1803, by Rev. Joseph E. Camp, of Northfield	1	164
William M., of Litchfield, m. Jane **BALDWIN**, of Milton, May 17, 1852, by N. C. Lewis, in Milton	TM49	74

	Vol.	Page
WEDGE, Erastus L., m. Almira **SMITH,** b. of Litchfield, Mar. 23, 1824, by		
Hugh P. Welch, J.P.	2	294
Maria A., m. Loran **HALLOCK,** b. of Litchfield, Dec. 26, 1852, by		
Rev. Charles R. Adams, of West Goshen	TM49	77
Ruthy, m. Elisha **GLOVER,** Apr. 27, 1815, by E. Tanner	2	45
WEED, John, m. Susanna **MASON,** Oct. 3, 1780, by Rev. Judah Champion	1	165
Juliett, m. Horatio **BENTON,** Oct. 3, 1832, by Rev. Mr. Taylor, of		
South Farms	2	289
Merinda P., m. Solomon P. **ANDREWS,** Oct. 17, 1844, by Rev. David		
L. Parmelee	TM49	6
Sally Ann, of Litchfield, m. [ ] **OSBORNE,** of Woodbury, Nov.		
30, 1837, by Truman Marsh	2	315
WEEKS, Abel, s. Ezra & Esther, b. June 10, 1820	2	14
Anna, d. Holand & Hannah, b. Sept. 23, 1782	1	207
Ebenezer, s. Holand & Hannah, b. July 16, 1784	1	207
Esther, d. Holland & Hannah, d. Dec. 3, 1787	1	164
Ezra, m. Esther **BEACH,** Dec. 12, 1812, by Rev. Mr. Gillet, of		
Torrington	2	14
Frederick, s. Ezra & Esther, b. Mar. 14, 1818	2	14
Sally, m. Enos **EMONS,** Apr. 29, 1800	2	57
Sally, d. Ezra & Esther, b. Dec. 2, 1813	2	14
Samuel Beach, s. Ezra & Esther, b. Sept. 30, 1815	2	14
Sarah, d. Holand & Hannah, b. Dec. 29, 1785	1	207
WELCH, Anne, had d. Mary, b. Feb. 5, 1769	1	40
David, m. Irene **MARSH,** Dec. 6, 1758, by Judah Champion, V.D.M.	1	83
David, representative May 1770, May & Oct. 1773, Oct. 1774, May		
1775, Oct. 1780	2	1549-50
David, had negroes Jesse, s. Phillis, b. Feb. 6, 1776 & Frank, s. Phillis, b.		
Feb. 2, 1785	1	151
David, Major, had negro Louisa, b. Mar. 4, 1789	1	151
David, had negro Hosea, b. June 29, 1796	1	151
David, d. Mar. 26, 1815, in the 91st y. of his age	1	82
David F., s. John & Rosetta, b. Apr. 27, 1791	2	50
Delia E., of Litchfield, ae 24, m. William E. **DICKINSON,** of		
Ontenagen, Mich., ae 39, Sept. 8, 1853, by Rev. David E. Brown,		
of Milton. Witnesses Hon. O. P. Seymour, Mrs. Delia Barnes, of		
Buffalo, N.Y.	TM49	91
Eliza, d. John & Rosetta, b. Aug. 30, 1804	2	50
Elizabeth, Mrs., of New Milford, m. Rev. Judah **CHAMPION,** of		
Litchfield, Jan. 4, 1758, by Rev. Nathaniel Taylor, of New Milford	1	131
Garret P., m. Clarissa **MARSH,** Sept. 10, 1823, by Rev. Truman Marsh	2	131
Gerret Peoples, s. John & Rosetta, b. May 18, 1795	2	50
Hugh P., m. Helen M. **WILLIAMS,** b. of Litchfield, Sept. 22, 1845, by		
Rev. Isaac Jones	TM49	11
Hugh Peoples*, s. John & Rosetta, b. July 20, 1793 *("Peebles"?)	2	50
Irene, d. John & Rosetta, b. Feb. 23, 1787	1	207
Irene, d. John & Rosetta, b. Feb. 23, 1787	2	50
Irene, w. David, d. May 4, 1814, in the 76th y. of her age	1	82
John, s. David & Irene, b. Sept. 23, 1759	1	83
John, m. Rosetta **PEOPLES*,** Nov. 8, 1784, by Rev. [ ]		
Dempster *("PEEBLES")	2	50
John, s. John & Rosetta, b. Feb. 6, 1798	2	50
John, representative Oct. 1799, May 1800, Oct. 1801, May 1819, May		

	Vol.	Page
WELCH, (cont.),		
1820, May 1821, May 1822	2	1552-5
John, s. John & Rosetta, d. Mar. 11, 1815	2	50
Mary, d. Anne, b. Feb. 5, 1769	1	40
Ruth, Mrs., m. Reynold **MARVIN**, Feb. 23, 1763, by Rev. Nathaniell		
Taylor	1	107
William, s. John & Rosetta, b. Aug. 6, 1785	1	207
William, s. John & Rosetta, b. Aug. 6, 1785	2	50
William, s. John & Rosetta, d. Aug. 25, 1811	2	50
William Henry, s. John & Rosetta, b. June 1, 1805	2	50
WELLS, Pina, of Cornwall, m. Henry **FITCH**, of Litchfield (colored), Nov.		
5, 1835, by Rev. Samuel Fuller, Jr.	2	296
Seabury, of Cornwall, m. Frances P. **MORRIS**, of Warren, Nov. 20,		
1850, by H. L. Vaill	TM49	40
Thomas W., of Plymouth, m. Susan S. **MORSE**, of Litchfield, May 7,		
1840, by Jonathan Brace	2	318
WELMOT, [see under **WILMOTT**]		
WELTON, Albert, of Bristol, m. Susan A. **BIDWELL**, of Litchfield, Jan. 26,		
1842, by Jason Wells	2	336
WESSELLS, WESSELL, Abigail, d. Lawrence & Abigail, b. Mar. 28, 1768	1	125
Ashbel, s. Lawrence & Abigail, b. Mar. 14, 1771	1	125
Ashbel, m. Grace **WARD**, May 8, 1808, by Rev. Truman Marsh	2	22
George Baldwin, s. Lawrence & Abigail, b. Dec. 30, 1774	1	124
Henry Walton, s. Ashbel & Grace, b. Feb. 20, 1809	2	22
John Lorence, s. Ashbel & Grace, b. Jan. 8, 1813	2	22
Lawrence, m. Abigail **BALDWIN**, Nov. 10, 1761, by Rev. Judah		
Champion	1	125
Leverett Ward, s. Ashbel & Grace, b. July 28, 1819	2	22
WEST, Andrew Jackson, s. Hubbel & Sarah, b. Jan. 8, 1816, at Colebrook	2	149
Barbara, m. Samuel **ADDIS**, Sept. 3, 1821, by Rev. Isaac Jones	2	104
Hubbel, m. Sarah **CHAMBERLAIN**, June 8, 1814, at Colebrook, by		
Rev. Rufus Babcock	2	149
Hubbel, s. Hubbel & Sarah, b. May 9, 1824	2	149
Hubbel, Jr., of Wis., m. Helen Maria **ROBBERTS**, of Litchfield, Oct. 1,		
1850, by Benjamin W. Stone	TM49	55
Samuel Chamberlain, s. Hubbel & Sarah, b. June 26, 1818, at Colebrook	2	149
Sarah Jane, d. Hubbel & Sarah, b. Feb. 13, 1821	2	149
WESTON, Polly C., of Woodville, m. Samuel Clark **GOSLEE**, of Litchfield,		
May 2, 1849, at Woodville, by Rev. F. D. Harriman, of Bantam		
Falls & Milton	TM49	41
Samuel Hobson, of Warren, m. Jemima **MOULTHROP**, of Litchfield,		
Apr. 26, 1829, by I. Jones	2	280
WESTOVER, Amey, d. Joseph & Mehetabel, b. June 2, 1812	2	149
Amy, m. John W. **FISH**, b. of Litchfield, Apr. 22, 1838, by Rev. Lewis		
Gunn	2	317
Clarinda, d. David & Rhoda, b. June 10, 1798	2	143
Clarinda, m. Sylvanus **BISHOP**, Dec. 16, 1830, by Rev. William Lucas	2	286
Dame, d. Joseph & Mahitabel, b. Oct. [ ], 1797	2	149
David, m. Rhoda **STODDARD**, Feb. [ ], 1795, by Rev. Judah Champion	2	143
David, m. Lavina **WOODRUFF**, b. of Litchfield, Oct. 28, 1828, by		
Rev. Henry Robinson, of South Farms	2	278
David Russell, s. John & Lois, b. Sept. 29, 1826	2	255
David Russell, s. John & Lois, d. July 2, 1833	2	255

	Vol.	Page
WESTOVER, (cont.),		
David S., s. David & Rhoda, b. Aug. 8, 1800	2	143
David S., s. David & Rhoda, d. Aug. 27, 1805	2	143
Elizabeth, w. Philander, d. Aug. 26, 1822	2	135
George H., of Litchfield, m. Mary R. SEELEY, of Goshen, Jan. 19, 1843, by Rev. Ralph Smith	2	411
George Henry, s. Truman & Sally, b. Dec. 2, 1820	2	138
Helen M., m. Joseph KENNEY, b. of Litchfield, Oct. 3, 1849, by B. L. Swan	TM49	43
Hephzibah, d. Joseph & Mehetebel, b. Nov. 12, 1802	2	149
Hepzibah, m. Orson CURTISS, Mar. 23, 1825, by Rev. Seth Higbey	2	139
Huldah, w. Philander, d. Sept. 29, 1824	2	135
Ira, s. Joseph & Rebecca, b. Jan. 3, 1790	2	149
John, s. David & Rhoda, b. Mar. 5, 1797	2	143
John, m. Lois RUSSELL, May 20, 1820, by Rev. Isaac Jones	2	255
Joseph, m. Rebecca KILBORN, Sept. [ ], 1787, by Rev. Ashbel Baldwin	2	149
Joseph, m. Mehetabel KILBORN, Sept. [ ], 1796, by Rev. Amos Chase	2	149
Leman, s. Joseph & Rebecca, b. July 31, 1791	2	149
Levi John, s. John & Lois, b. Jan. 7, 1829	2	255
Lewis, m. Mary WHEELER, Jan. 1, 1837, by Rev. A. Billings Beach	2	299
Linus, s. David & Rhoda, b. Aug. 17, 1804	2	143
Lois, d. Joseph & Mehetabel, b. July 7, 1805	2	149
Lucius, s. Joseph & Mehetabel, b. July 11, 1817	2	149
Lyman Elbert, s. John & Lois, b. May 6, 1834	2	255
Lyman Lewis, s. John & Lois, b. July 19, 1831	2	255
Maria, d. Philander & Elizabeth, [ ], Oct. 10, 1810	2	135
Maria, m. Lewis HOTCHKISS, Mar. 23, 1834, by Rev. James F. Warner, of South Farms	2	289
Martha*, d. Joseph & Rebecca, d. June 24, 1817 *("Martia" in Woodruff's book)	2	149
Martia, d. Joseph & Rebecca, b. Mar. 24, 1789	2	149
Mary, d. David & Rhoda, b. Nov. 9, 1807	2	143
Mary, m. Rufus AMES, Jan. 10, 1832, by Rev. Mr. Taylor, of South Farms	2	289
Mary, m. Rufus AMES, Jan. 10, 1832, by Rev. Vernon D. Taylor	2	316
Mary, m. William CURTISS, Jan. 11, 1846, by Rev. David L. Parmelee	TM49	13
Mehetabel, d. Joseph & Mehetabel, b. Dec. 16, 1809	2	149
Philander, m. Elizabeth KILBORN, Dec. 10, 1795, by Rev. [ ] Butler	2	135
Philander, m. Huldah SHEPARD, Mar. 27, 1823, by Rev. Lyman Beecher	2	118
Philander, m. Huldah SHEPARD, Mar. 27, 1823	2	135
Philander, m. Orra SAUNDERS, b. of Litchfield, Apr. 5, 1827, by Rev. Henry Robinson, of South Farms	2	269
Polly, d. Joseph & Mahetabel, b. Mar. 19, 1801	2	149
Polly, d. Joseph & Rebecca, d. Sept. 1, 1819	2	149
Rachel, m. Jeremiah KILBORN, b. of Litchfield, [Mar.] 14, 1844, by G. C. V. Eastman	TM49	2
Rachel C., d. John & Lois, b. Jan. 11, 1824	2	255
Rebecca, w. Joseph, d. [ ], 1795	2	149
Rebecca, d. Joseph & Rebecca, d. Aug. 20, 1815	2	149
Rebecca Birge, d. Joseph & Rebecca, b. Oct. [ ], 1793	2	149
Rhoda S., d. John & Lois, b. Apr. 10, 1821	2	255

	Vol.	Page
WESTOVER, (cont.),		
Sally, Mrs., m. Eli **WILLMOTT**, Aug. 17, 1828, by Rev. Isaac Jones	2	277
Truman, s. Philander & Elizabeth, b. Aug. 28, 1797	2	135
Truman, m. Sally **SPENCER**, Mar. 6, 1820, by Rev. Isaac Jones	2	138
Welthy, d. Joseph & Mahetabel, b. July 22, 1798	2	149
Wealthy, d. Joseph & Mehetabel, d. July 22, 1821	2	149
WETMORE, WETTMORE, Anna, w. John, d. Mar. 10, 1804	1	208
Anna, w. John, d. Mar. 10, 1804	2	61
Anna Emeline, m. Cyrus **CATLIN**, Sept. 14, 1824	2	112
Anna Minerva, d. Edward, b. Feb. 9, 1850	TM49	17
Beatia, m. Hiram **BISSELL**, [ ], 1805	2	114
Bradley, s. David & Sena, b. Dec. 8, 1809	2	286
Cornelius L., s. David & Sena, b. Dec. 16, 1806	2	286
Cornelius L., m. Elizabeth L. **ROBINSON**, [ ], in Mass.	2	248
David, d. June 15, 1774	1	82
David, m. Sena **BRONSON**, May 5, 1805	2	286
David, 2nd, s. David & Sena, b. Dec. 19, 1807	2	286
David P., of Litchfield, m. Ruth C. **POND**, of Washington, June 26,		
1853, by Hugh P. Welch, J.P.	TM49	91
Delia E., d. Cornelius L. & Elizabeth L., b. Feb. 14, 1830	2	248
Ebenezer Brown, s. John & Anna, b. June 2, 1798	1	208
Ebenezer Brown, s. John & Anna, b. June 2, 1798	2	61
Edward F., s. Cornelius L. & Elizabeth L., b. June 26, 1832	2	248
Emeline, d. John & Anna, b. Dec. 30, 1806	2	61
Emeline, m. Cyrus **CATLIN**, Sept. [ ], 1824, by Rev. Joseph E. Camp	2	265
Emeline, twin with Jane Stanley, d. Edward, b. Feb. 28, 1852	TM49	17
Emeline Anna, m. Cyrus **CATLIN**, Sept. 14, 1824, by Rev. Josep E.		
Camp	2	275
Frederick, s. John & Anna, b. Feb. 23, 1800	1	208
Frederick, s. John & Anna, b. Feb. 23, 1800	2	61
Henry, s. John & Anna, b. Feb. 23, 1812	2	61
Jane Stanley, twin with Emeline, d. Edward, b. Feb. 28, 1852	TM49	17
John, m. Anna **HAMLIN**, [ ], 1795, by Rev. Mr. Grann	1	208
John, m. Anna **HAMLIN**, [ ], 1795, at Middletown, by Rev. Mr.		
Graves	2	61
John, m. Anna **SEYMOUR**, Mar. 16, 1806, by Rev. Dan Hudon	2	61
John, s. John & Anna, b. May 22, 1814	2	61
John, d. Mar. 31, 1815, in the 81st y. of his age	1	82
Joseph Sylvester, s. David & Sena, b. Mar. 19, 1814	2	286
Julia A., of Litchfield, m. Hiram **GRITMAN**, of Warren, July 2, 1843,		
by Rev. Ralph Smith	2	412
Julia Josephine, d. Cornelius L. & Elizabeth L., b. Oct. 8, 1834	2	248
Juliana, d. David & Sena, b. Dec. 3, 1820	2	286
Lucy J., of Milton, m. George G. **GRISWOLD**, of Plymouth, Jan. 3,		
1842, by S. W. Scofield	2	336
Mary Ann, d. John & Anna, b. Nov. 2, 1808	2	61
Mary Eliza, d. David & Sena, b. Mar. 3, 1817	2	286
Norman, s. David & Sena, b. Sept. 18, 1811	2	286
Norman, m. Slina **BIRGE**, Feb. 21, 1836, by Rev. Isaac Jones	2	298
Peleg, s. Joseph & Beaty, b. Mar. 23, 1782	1	207
Rachel E., m. John **SEYMOUR**, Dec. 26, 1853, by Rev. John J.		
Brandegee	TM49	94
Rhoda, m. John **GRISWOULD**, Aug. 23, 1782	2	6

	Vol.	Page
WETMORE, WETTMORE, (cont.),		
Sally, m. Joseph **BARNES**, Dec. 5, 1793, by Rev. James Morris	2	4
Sarah, d. David & Sarah, b. Apr. 12, 1772	1	82
Timothy Seymour, s. John & Anna, b. July 16, 1810	2	61
WHAPLES, Adaline M., of Litchfield, m. Edward **PARKER**, of Plymouth,		
Oct. 22, 1845, by Rev. David L. Marks	TM49	13
Charles T., m. Harriet P. **NEGUS**, Nov. 28, 1839, by Rev. Jonathan		
Brace	2	318
Frances, m. Hiram **PECK**, Dec. 16, 1840, by William Payne	2	332
WHEELER, Albert, m. Miranda S. **BEACH**, Dec. 25, 1832, by Rev. L. P.		
Hickok	2	288
Almira, m. William **ROOSECRAFT**, b. of Litchfield, Feb. 14, 1848, by		
Joseph Henson	TM49	23
Andrew J., of New Haven, m. Adaline E. **RAY**, of Litchfield, June 1,		
1840, by Rev. Fosdic Harrison, of Bethlehem	2	320
Anna, d. Moses & Anna, b. May 8, 1812	2	123
Anna, of Litchfield, m. Amasa **BLANCHARD**, of Monson, Apr. 10,		
1839, by Rev. Jonathan Brace	2	318
Ansel C., m. Lucy M. **BARNES**, b. of Litchfield, Oct. 12, 1845, by Rev.		
Daniel L. Marks	TM49	13
Charity, m. Joel **SANFORD**, Oct. 8, 1832, by Rev. L. P. Hickok	2	288
Charles, m. Elizabeth **GILES***, b. of Litchfield, Nov. 10, 1841, by		
G. C. V. Eastman *("GUILD")	2	335
Ch[arle]s, representative Apr. 1849, Apr. 1850	2	1558
Charles Gilbert, s. [Peleg & Eliza], b. Mar. 27, 1832	2	338
Clarissa, of Litchfield, m. Hiram W. **HUBBARD**, of Plymouth, Oct. 4,		
1840, by Jonathan Brace	2	330
Edmin, s. [Peleg & Eliza], b. Jan. 26, 1834	2	338
Eliza O., of Litchfield, m. Lucius D. **ALLEN**, of Goshen, May 30, 1838,		
by Rev. Grant Powers, of Goshen	2	317
Emeline A., m. Thomas B. **STEVENS**, May 7, 1845, by Rev. D. L.		
Marks	TM49	10
George, s. Moses & Anna, b. Jan. 29, 1808	2	123
Hannah, d. Moses & Hannah, b. May 29, 1799, at Oxford	2	123
Hannah, w. Moses, d. Apr. 24, 1804	2	123
Hannah, m. Alva **BUNNEL**, May 2, 1823, by Rev. Isaac Jones	2	120
Henry William, s. [Peleg & Eliza], b. May 9, 1836	2	338
Lorenzo, of Litchfield, m. Antha **STONE**, June 17, 1828, by I. Jones	2	277
Lucinda, d. Moses & Anna, b. July 15, 1806	2	123
Lucinda, m. Orrin **PERKINS**, b. of Litchfield, Sept. 14, 1829, by L. P.		
Hickok	2	281
Maria, d. Moses & Hannah, b. Apr. 18, 1804, at Litchfield	2	123
Mary, d. Moses & Anna, b. Mar. 30, 1810	2	123
Mary, m. Lewis **WESTOVER**, Jan. 1, 1837, by Rev. A. Billings Beach	2	299
Mary Jane, m. Jacob **MORSE, Jr.**, b. of Litchfield, Oct. 16, 1848, by		
[Joseph Henson]	TM49	27
Mary Susan, d. [Peleg & Eliza], b. Apr. 10, 1838	2	338
Mary T., of Bantam Falls, m. James **HOAR**, May 18, 1851, by J. D.		
Berry	TM49	62
Matilda, m. Charles **McNEILE**, b. of Litchfield, Apr. 25, 1841, by		
William Payne	2	333
Mynerva, d. Moses & Hannah, b. Feb. 14, 1802, at Oxford	2	123
Minerva, m. Matthew **MOSS**, Mar. 31, 1839, by Rev. Gad N. Smith	2	319

	Vol.	Page
WHITTLESEY, (cont.),		
Henry, m. Abby **REA**, July 20, 1815, by Rev. Samuel Whittlesy	2	84
Henry Rea, s. Henry & Abby, b. Apr. 26, 1816	2	84
Jabez, s. Roger N. & Anna, b. Feb. 8, 1786	2	83
Jabez, m. Nancy **PARKER**, Sept. 27, 1809, by Rev. Samuel Whittlesey	2	83
Joseph, of Berlin, m. Sarah Maria **PECK**, d. Eliada, May 22, 1849, by		
Benjamin L. Swan	TM49	41
Lucy, m. Stephen **COGSWELL, Jr.**, Apr. 12, 1824, by Rev. Henry		
Robinson, of South Farms Soc.	2	85
Lydia Ann, d. Jabez & Nancy, b. Jan. 14, 1816	2	83
Lydia Ann, of South Farms, m. Charles Daniel **PERKINS**, of Oxford,		
Nov. 5, 1835, by Rev. Samuel Fuller, Jr.	2	296
Mary R., m. Norman T. **WADHAMS**, Apr. 16, 1851, by Rev. David L.		
Parmelee	TM49	62
Mary Rea, d. Frederick & Hannah, b. Nov. 28, 1820	2	84
Newton, s. Roger & Anne, b. Oct. 31, 1777	1	165
Newton, s. Roger N. & Anna, b. Oct. 31, 1777	2	83
Newton Parker, s. Jabez & Nancy, b. Apr. 22, 1812	2	83
Roger Newton, m. Anne **WOODRUFF**, Apr. 20, 1775	1	165
Roger Newton, m. Anna **WOODRUFF**, Apr. 20, 1775	2	83
Samuel, s. Roger N. & Anne, b. Dec. 18, 1775	1	165
Samuel, s. Roger N. & Anna, b. Dec. 18, 1775	2	83
Sarah E., m. Silas **STOCKMAN**, Nov. 25, 1847, by Rev. David L.		
Parmelee	TM49	20
Sarah Elizabeth, d. Frederick [& Hannah], b. May 13, 1828	2	84
Susanna, d. Roger N. & Anna, b. Feb. 13, 1784	2	83
William, s. Roger N. & Anna, b. July 28, 1788	2	83
William Henry, s. Jabez & Nancy, b. July 1, 1810	2	83
WICKWIRE, Almena, m. Benjamin **DUNING**, Jan. 27, 1812	2	69
Atheta, d. Grant & Sarah, b. Oct. 23, 1797	2	53
Catharine, d. Grant & Sarah, b. Mar. 21, 1809	2	53
Catharine L., of Litchfield, m. Charles **FOSTER**, of Bethlem, Dec. 17,		
1829, by Rev. Abraham Browne	2	283
Charles, s. Grant & Sarah, b. June 28, 1805	2	53
Charles, m. Balinda **GRISWOULD**, of Washington, Nov. 10, 1828, by		
Rev. I. Jones	2	278
Clarinda, m. Samuel H. **STILSON**, Mar. 4, 1844, by Rev. David L.		
Parmelee	TM49	4
Syntha, d. Grant & Sarah, b. Nov. 22, 1799	2	53
Cynthia, m. Ephraim **HAY**, of Bethlem, Dec. 21, 1820, by Rev. John		
Langman, of Bethlem	2	102
Frederick Wolcott, s. Grant & Sarah, b. Mar. 7, 1807	2	53
Grant, m. Sarah **TROOP**, Apr. 12, 1791, by Rev. Ashbel Baldwin	2	53
James, m. Sarah **BARNES**, Aug. 25, 1779, by Rev. George Beckwith	1	165
Jane M., m. Samuel L. **SMITH**, Oct. 4, 1848, by Rev. David L.		
Parmelee	TM49	26
Lucy, d. Grant & Sarah, b. Apr. 2, 1802	2	53
Lucy, m. Samuel **CATLIN**, May 1, 1825, by Morris Woodruff	2	139
Mary, d. Grant & Sarah, b. Aug. 17, 1814	2	53
Sally, d. James & Sarah, b. Mar. 12, 1780	1	165
Sarah Ann, d. Grant & Sarah, b. June 21, 1793	2	53
Sarah Ann, m. Harris **WARREN**, Sept. 12, 1813, by Rev. Amos Chase	2	149
Sheldon, s. Grant & Sarah, b. Mar. 22, 1795	2	53

	Vol.	Page
WILCOX, Charles, of Harwinton, m. Cornelia L. **OSBORN,** of Litchfield,		
June 4, 1839, by William Payne	2	328
Paulena M., m. Joseph A. **NEWBURY,** Apr. 11, 1838, by Rev. Stephen		
Hubbell	2	320
WILKINSON, Leonard L., of Harwinton, m. Maria **THOMAS,** of Bethlem,		
May 29, 1848, by Joseph Henson	TM49	24
WILLIAMS, Abby J., of Watertown, m. Henry **NEILE,** of Litchfield, Mar.		
26, 1848, by Rev. Isaac Jones	TM49	24
Betsey, m. Emanuel **RUSSELL,** Nov. 2, 1801	2	28
Charles, m. Huldah **KILBORN,** Oct. 27, 1805, by Rev. Amos Chase	2	92
Charles K., s. Charles & Huldah, b. Jan. 5, 1809	2	92
Edward, m. Betsey **BRADLEY,** Nov. 26, 1820, by James Birge, J.P.	2	101
George Clinton, s. Charles & Huldah, b. Mar. 17, 1820	2	92
Helen M., m. Hugh P. **WELCH,** b. of Litchfield, Sept. 22, 1845, by Rev.		
Isaac Jones	TM49	11
Huldah, m. Ruel **PLANT,** Oct. 30, 1842, by Jason Wells	2	337
Jeremiah, m. Lavina **HALLOT,** Jan. 16, 1823, by Rev. Ananias		
Dathick	2	80
Lucia P., d. Charles & Huldah, b. May 1, 1818	2	92
Maria, d. Charles & Huldah, b. Feb. 18, 1816	2	92
Mary, m. Thomas **WAY, Jr.,** Oct. [ ], 1805, by Rev. Benedict, of		
Woodbury	2	12
Mary, d. Charles & Huldah, b. Jan. 11, 1813	2	92
Mary, m. Charles **MATTHEWS,** Dec. 4, 1837, by Truman Marsh	2	315
Mary Ann, m. Thomas **MASON,** b. of Litchfield, May 3, 1847, by Rev.		
Samuel Fuller	TM49	38
Mary J., of Bethlem, m. James **CANFIELD,** of Litchfield, Apr. 21,		
1835, by R. S. Crampton, V.D.M.	2	298
Mary K., m. Charles **MATTHEWS,** Dec. 4, 1837	2	322
Robert, m. Aden **TROWBRIDGE,** Oct. 11, 1840, by Rev. William		
Payne	2	331
Sally, d. Charles & Huldah, b. Sept. 18, 1806	2	92
Warner W., s. Charles & Huldah, b. Feb. 17, 1811	2	92
William, m. Lydia **AMES,** Jan. 10, 1832, by Rev. Mr. Taylor, of South		
Farms	2	289
WILLS, Abby Jane, d. Tomlinson & Electa, b. Oct. 21, 1826	2	117
Frank Smith, s. Tomlinson & Electa, b. Sept. 2, 1841	2	117
Mary Ann Smith, d. Tomlinson & Electa, b. Oct. 22, 1839	2	117
Phillip, s. Tomlinson & Electa, b. Dec. 20, 1823	2	117
Susannah Augusta, d. Tomlinson & Electa, b. Nov. 2, 1828	2	117
Tomlinson, m. Electa **SMITH,** Jan. 16, 1823, by Rev. Isaac Jones	2	117
Virginia Maria, d. Tomlinson & Electa, b. May 20, 1835	2	117
WILMOTT, WELMOT, WILLMOTT, WILMOT, Emeline, d. Eli &		
Mary, b. Jan. 19, 1816	2	140
Caroline Matilda, d. John, Jr. & Caroline, b. Feb. 11, 1802	2	54
Eli, m. Molly **STONE,** Sept. 28, 1802, by Rev. Dan Huntington	2	140
Eli, m. Mrs. Sally **WESTOVER,** Aug. 17, 1828, by Rev. Isaac Jones	2	277
Eli Taylor, s. John, Jr. & Caroline, b. Sept. 26, 1800	2	54
Emeline, m. Prentice **PARKHURST,** Dec. 8, 1839	TM49	14
Emeline, of Litchfield, m. Prentice **PACKHURST,** of Woodville,		
Washington, Conn., Dec. 8, 1839, by Rev. Isaac Jones	2	327
Hiram, s. Eli & Mary, b. Aug. 29, 1803	2	140
Hiram, s. Eli & Mary, d. Aug. 25, 1825	2	140

	Vol.	Page
WILMOTT, WELMOT, WILLMOTT, WILMOT, (cont.),		
Jenette, m. Frederick **STODDARD**, b. of Litchfield, Dec. 31, 1844, by		
G. C. V. Eastman	TM49	8
John, Jr., m. Caroline **JOHNSON**, Oct. 18, 1797	2	54
John, Jr., d. Jan. 7, 1810	2	54
John W., of Litchfield, m. Mary Ann **SCOTT**, of Woodbury, Mar. 20,		
1848, by Rev. Samuel Fuller	TM49	38
John Wyllys, s. John, Jr. & Caroline, b. Sept. 3, 1798	2	54
Julia, d. Eli & Mary, b. Feb. 17, 1812	2	140
Julia, m. Osander **BISHOP**, Sept. 15, 1833, by Rev. John Dowdney	2	294
Lucius, s. Eli & Mary, b. July 11, 1808	2	140
Lucius, m. Mary Ann **KILBORN**, Sept. 15, 1833, by Rev. David G.		
Tomlinson, of Bradleyville	2	294
Mary, d. Eli & Mary, b. May 15, 1810	2	140
Mary, m. Luman **BISHOP**, Sept. 25, 1831, by Rev. Mr. Taylor, of South		
Farms	2	289
Mary M., m. Loyal W. **ALLIN**, Jan. 24, 1826, by Rev. Isaac Jones	2	260
Matilda, m. Eber **TURNER**, Jan. 9, 1809, by Rev. Joseph E. Camp	2	13
Nelson, s. Eli & Mary, b. Feb. 10, 1806	2	140
Oliver Johnson, s. John, Jr. & Caroline, b. July 28, 1807	2	54
Polly Maria, d. John, Jr. & Caroline, b. Nov. 16, 1803	2	54
Willis, of Waterbury, m. Sally O. **GIBBS**, of South Farms, Sept. 25,		
1843, by Rev. Fosdic Harrison, of Bethleham	2	340
WILSON, Virgil, of Harwinton, m. Minerva W. **BUTTON**, Apr. 19, 1848,		
by Rev. S. T. Seeley	TM49	24
WING, Obed Bissell, s. Huldah Tilford , b. Mar. 1, 1800	1	204-5
WINSHIP, Charles, s. James & Emily, b. July [ ], 1825	2	38
Chloe Maria, d. James & Emily, b. Nov. 12, 1816	2	38
Cornelia A., m. Walter **FILLEY**, b. of Litchfield, June 12, 1854, by		
Rev. Benjamin L. Swan	TM49	101
Elizabeth Ann, d. James & Emily, b. Apr. 8, 1819	2	38
Emeline, d. James & Emily, b. Feb. 10, 1818	2	38
Frances E., m. Benjamin F. **SMITH**, July 15, 1830, by Rev. L. P.		
Hickok	2	285
James, m. Emily **CLAP**, Feb. 14, 1813, by Rev. Abel Flint	2	38
James, s. James & Emily, b. Aug. 7, 1821	2	38
James, m. Grace **SIMPSON**, Nov. 12, 1832, by Rev. L. P. Hickok	2	288
Julia C., of Litchfield, m. Asa J. **FRENCH**, of Plymouth, Feb. 7, 1844,		
by Rev. Isaac Jones	TM49	2
Leonard, s. James & Emily, b. May 1, 1823	2	38
Marian, m. Benjamin **FILLEY**, b. of Litchfield, Dec. 24, 1845, by Rev.		
Joel Dickinson, of Northfield	TM49	12
WOLCOTT, WOLCOT, Betsey, w. Frederick, d. Apr. 2, 1812	2	17
Charles Moseley, s. Frederick & Sally, b. Nov. 20, 1816	2	17
Chauncey Goodrich, s. Frederick & Sally, b. Mar. 15, 1819	2	17
Chauncey Goodrich, s. Frederick & Sally, d. Oct. 28, 1820	2	17
Elizabeth, d. Frederick & Betsey, b. Mar. 6, 1806	2	17
Elizabeth, of Litchfield, m. John P. **JACKSON**, of Newark, N.J., May		
22, 1827, by Rev. John J. Stone	2	270
Frederick, m. Betsey **HUNTINGTON**, Oct. 12, 1800, by Rev. Mr.		
Strong, of Norwich	1	245
Frederick, m. Betsey **HUNTINGTON**, Oct. 12, 1800, by Rev. Mr.		
Strong, of Norwich	2	17

	Vol.	Page
WOLCOTT, WOLCOT, (cont.),		
Frederick, representative May 1802, May 1803	2	1553
Frederick, m. Sally W. **COOKE**, June 21, 1815, by Rev. William Andrews, of Danbury	2	17
Frederick Henry, s. Frederick & Betsey, b. Aug. 19, 1808	2	17
Hannah H., m. Rev. Fred **FREEMAN**, Apr. 21, 1834, by Rev. L. P. Hickok	2	288
Hannah Huntington, d. Frederick & Betsey, b. Jan. 14, 1803	2	17
Hannah Huntington, d. Frederick & Hannah, b. July 14, 1803	1	245
Henry*, s. Frederick & Sally, b. Nov. 24, 1820 *(Should be "Henry **GRISWOLD**" and is corrected May 28, 1842, by S. P. Bolles, T. C.)	2	17
Henry **GRISWOLD**, see Henry **WOLCOTT**	2	17
Jedediah, had negro Hebe William, d. Apr. 11, 1803	1	150
Joshua Huntington, s. Frederick & Betsey, b. Aug. 29, 1804	2	17
Laura M., of Litchfield, m. Robert G. **RANKIN**, of New York, Mar. 30, 1831, by Rev. Lawrence P. Hickok	2	286
Laura Maria, d. Frederick & Betsey, b. Aug. 14, 1811	2	17
Mary Ann, d. Frederick & Hannah, b. Aug. 9, 1801	1	245
Mary Ann Goodrich, d. Frederick & Betsey, b. Aug. 9, 1801	2	17
Mary Frances, d. Frederick & Sally, b. July 9, 1823	2	17
Oliver, representative May 1767, Oct. 1768, Oct. 1770, Oct. 1764,	2	1548-9
Oliver, Hon., had negroes Juba, b. Mar. 7, 1780 & Cloe, b. Oct. 6, 1791	1	151
Oliver, Hon., had negroes Peggy Zillah, b. Oct. 7, 1786 & Chloe, b. July 25, 1788	1	151
Oliver, s. Oliver S. & Jane C. (Law), b. Sept. 14, 1823	2	98
Oliver S., m. Jane C*. **CONRAD**, Mar. 9, 1820, by Lyman Beecher *("Law" written over C.)	2	98
WOLF, WOLFF, Abigail D., m. Thomas **ADDIS**, Oct. 1, 1790, by Rev. [ ]	2	137
Anne, m. Joseph **OSBORN**, Aug. 26, 1777, by Rev. Judah Champion	1	110-11
WOOD, David, of Warren, m. Bula **BEACH**, of Litchfield, June 12, 1822, by Rev. Isaac Jones	2	112
David W., of Litchfield, m. Mrs. Delia **MONSON**, of Cheshire, Oct. 26, [1851], by N. C. Lewis	TM49	66
Henry, m. Mrs. Harriet **NEGUS**, b. of Litchfield, Nov. 21, 1847, by Joseph Henson	TM49	23
Lois L., m. Frederick J. **BRAMIN**, b. of Litchfield, Oct. 11, 1849, by Rev. William B. Hoyt	TM49	43
Maria A., m. Edmund **GUILD**, b. of Litchfield, May 19, 1850, by Rev. William B. Hoyt	TM49	54
WOODCOCK, Albert, m. Polly **BLAKESLEE**, Aug. 1, 1817, by Mr. Searls	2	126
Comfort, m. Jonathan **CHURCHILL**, [ ]	1	132
Frederick Swartz, s. Hiram B. & Sally, b. Sept. 1, 1833	2	103
Hiram B., m. Sally **STONE**, May 21, 1821, by Rev. Isaac Jones	2	103
Louisa, d. Hiram B. & Sally, b. May 22, 1825	2	103
Mary*, m. Julius **MUNGER**, Sept. 24, 1809, by Rev. [ ] *(Arnold Copy says "Anna")	2	147
Ozias Stone, s. Hiram B. & Sally, b. Dec. 1, 1822	2	103
WOODDAMS, [see under **WADHAMS**]		
WOODEN, [see under **WOODIN**]		
WOODIN, WOODEN, Cordelia, m. Ephraim **SPENCER, Jr.**, Oct. 26,		

	Vol.	Page
WOODIN, WOODEN, (cont.),		
1822, by Rev. [ ]	2	253
Helen Almeda, m. David Merritt **CANDACE**, b. of Litchfield, Jan. 3,		
1854, by Rev. Benjamin Swan	TM49	101
William, m. Phebe **JACKSON**, Dec. 31, 1823, by Rev. Isaac Jones	2	131
WOODRUFF, Abigail, d. Nathaniel B. & Beda, b. Feb. 8, 1786	1	207
Abigail, d. Salmon & Lavina, b. Aug. 26, 1815	2	62
Abigail E., m. Murray **KENNEY**, Aug. 25, 1835, by Rev. L. P. Hickok	2	296
Abraham, s. Wright & Thankfull, b. Sept. 10, 1771	1	125
Abraham, s. Wright & Thankful, d. Jan. 6, 1780	1	164
Amanda, d. Philo & Huldah, b. Nov. 5, 1794	2	5
Ann, d. Jacob & Lucy, b. Apr. 5, 1756	1	83
Ann, d. [John A. & Lavina], b. Dec. 9, 1827	2	293
Ann, d. [John A. & Lavina], b. Dec. 9, 1827	2	325
Anna, m. Roger Newton **WHITTLESEY**, Apr. 20, 1775	2	83
Anna Maria, d. Salmon & Lavina, b. Aug. 4, 1818	2	62
Anne, w. Jacob, d. May 27, 1754	1	40
Anne, m. Roger Newton **WHITTLESEY**, Apr. 20, 1775	1	165
Anne, d. Jacob, Jr. & Anne, b. June 16, 1778	1	165
Asenath, see under Senath		
Benjamin, of Litchfield, m. Eunis **MARTEN**, of Woodbury, Nov. 20,		
1739, by Capt. Joseph Miner, J.P.	1	83
Benjamin, s. Benjamin & Eunice, b. Nov. 1, 1752	1	83
Benjamin, m. Hannah **BALDWIN**, July 2, 1759, by Rev. Samuel		
Whittlesey, of Milford	1	83
Birdsey, s. Oliver & Annis, b. Mar. 3, 1791	1	245
Catharine, d. Philo & Huldah, b. July 6, 1786	2	5
Catharine, w. Enoch J., d. Sept. 8, 1823	2	140
Catharine M., m. Rev. Veron D. **TAYLOR**, May 2, 1831, by Rev.		
D. C. Griswold, of Watertown	2	290
Charles, m. Prudence **STODDER**, Nov. [ ], 1744	1	41
Charles, s. Charles & Prudence, b. May 5, 1752	1	83
Charles, Jr., m. Eleanor **ORTON**, Aug. 17, 1775, by Rev. George		
Beckwith	1	124
Chauncey, s. Benjamin & Hannah, b. Aug. 27, 1766	1	125
Clark, s. James & Sally, b. Aug. 23, 1791	1	207
Daniel Webster, s. [John A. & Lavina], b. Sept. 14, 1840	2	293
Daniel Webster, s. [John A. & Lavina], b. Sept. 14, 1840	2	325
David, s. Philo & Huldah, b. May 13, 1790	2	5
David L., of New Hartford, m. Hannah **SCOVIL**, of Litchfield, Feb. 13,		
1823, by Rev. Epaphras Goodwin, of Torringford	2	118
Denman, m. Naomi **GILLET**, Feb. 1, 1813, by Asa Tallmadge	2	32
Edward, s. Salmon & Lavina, b. Nov. 7, 1820	2	62
Edward, m. Hannah **KILBOURNE**, d. Norman, b. of Bantam Falls,		
Sept. 28, 1846, by Joshua D. Berry, at his house	TM49	16
Edwin, s. Jacob, Jr. & Anne, b. Oct. 24, 1782	1	207
Edwin, s. James & Sally, b. Dec. 3, 1797	1	164
Electa, d. Charles & Prudence, b. Sept. 8, 1747	1	41
Electa, m. Levi **HARRISON**, Oct. 21, 1766, by Rev. Judah Champion	1	99
Elias C., m. Phebe A. **MONSON**, May 8, 1845, by Rev. David L.		
Parmelee	TM49	10
Eliza R., of Litchfield, m. George D. **WADHAM**, of Wolcottville, Apr.		
10, 1854, by Rev. B. L. Swan	TM49	101

	Vol.	Page
WOODRUFF, (cont.),		
Elizabeth, d. Benjamin & Hannah, b. Mar. 29, 1764	1	125
Emily, d. John A. & Lavina, b. Apr. 16, 1824	1	120
Emily, d. John A. & Lavina, b. May 7, 1824	2	293
Emily, d. John A. & Lavina, b. May 7, 1824	2	325
Emily, d. John A., of Litchfield, m. James **HALIN**, of Harwinton, May 2, 1849, by Benjamin L. Swan	TM49	41
Emily B., m. Samuel R. **ENSIGN**, b. of Litchfield, Nov. 16, 1826, by Rev. Henry Robinson, of South Farms	2	267
Enoch J., m. Catharine M. **ENSIGN**, Dec. 31, 1808, by Rev. Amos Chase	2	140
Enoch J., m. Huldah Maria **GARRET**, May 4, 1826, by Joseph E. Camp	2	266
Esther Ann, d. Oliver & Annis, b. Dec. 27, 1800	1	245
Eunis, m. Zebulon **GIBBS**, Jan. 22, 1733/4, by Capt. John Buel, J.P.	1	55
Eunice, d. Benjamin & Eunice, b. Feb. 16, 1754	1	41
Eunice, w. Benjamin, d. Oct. 30, 1758	1	40
Eunice, m. Henry **GIBBS**, Dec. 25, 1772	1	136-8
Ezekiel, m. Sally **HALL**, June 30, 1782, by Rev. Enoch Huntington, of Middletown	1	207
Fanny Maria, d. Denman & Naomi, b. May 31, 1815	2	32
Francis M., m. George W. **LOCKWOOD**, Nov. 10, 1842, by Jason Wells	2	337
George C., m. Henrietta S. **SEYMOUR**, Sept. 28, 1829, by Rev. Truman Marsh	2	77
George C., representative Apr. 1851	2	1558
George Catlin, s. Morris & Candace, b. Dec. 1, 1805	2	77
George Morris, s. George C. & Herietta S., b. Mar. 3, 1836	2	77
Hannah, d. Benjamin & Hannah, b. May 11, 1760	1	125
Hannah, m. Enos **BARNS**, Jr., Mar. 11, 1782, by Rev. Judah Champion	1	213
Hannah, d. Nathaniell & Mary, b. Dec. 8, [ ]	1	83
Hardy, s. Oliver & Annis, b. July 16, 1786	1	245
Harriet L., d. John A. & Lavina, b. Feb. 20, 1832*; d. Nov. 1, 1837 *(Date conflicts with birth of Walter. Probably "1834")	2	325
Harriet L., d. [John A. & Lavina], b. Feb. 20, 1834; d. Nov. 1, 1837	2	293
Henriety, d. Levi & Hannah, b. Dec. 15, 1788	1	207
Henrietta Selina, d. George C. & Henrietta S., b. Apr. 11, 1831; d. July 30, 1834	2	77
Henry Clay, s. [John A. & Lavina], b. Mar. 4, 1838	2	293
Henry Clay, s. [John A. & Lavina], b. Mar. 4, 1838	2	325
Himan, s. Isaac & Clarissa, b. Apr. 24, 1800	1	245
Huldah, d. Jacob & Lucia, b. Sept. 16, 1765	1	82
Isaac, s. Wright & Thankful, b. Oct. 2, 1775	1	125
Isaac, m. Clarissa **PECK**, June 22, 1797, by Rev. Amos Chase	1	245
Isaac B., of Watertown, m. Sarah Ann **GILBERT**, of Litchfield, Oct. 7, 1841, by Rev. Philo R. Hurd, of Watertown	2	328
Jacob, m. Anne **GRISWOLD**, Dec. 31, 1741, by Rev. Mr. Collens	1	83
Jacob, s. Jacob & Ann, b. Feb. 2, 1746/7	1	83
Jacob, Ens., m. Luce **FARNUM**, May 22, 1755, by Rev. Judah Champion	1	83
Jacob, representative May 1759, Oct. 1768	2	1547-9
Jacob, Jr., m. Anne **ORTON**, Jan. 1, 1772, by Rev. Judah Champion	1	124
Jacob, s. Salmon & Lavina, b. Oct. 17, 1813	2	62

	Vol.	Page
WOODRUFF, (cont.),		
James, s. Jacob & Ann, b. Aug. 21, 1749	1	41
James, m. Lucy **MORRIS**, Oct. 25, 1775	1	124
James, s. James & Lucy, b. May 20, 1786	1	207
James, m. Sally **BARTHOLOMEW**, Aug. 1, 1790, by Rev. Mr. Chase,		
of South Farms Soc.	1	207
James, m. Lucretia **CATLIN**, Nov. 17, 1812, by Rev. Joseph E. Camp	2	56
James, s. Morris & Candace, b. July [ ], 1813; d. Dec. 15, 1813	2	77
James, s. James & Lucretia, b. Aug. 27, 1815	2	56
Jerome B., m. Rachel **BARBER**, June 5, 1833, by Rev. David G.		
Tomlinson, of Bradleyville	2	293
Jerusha, d. Charles & Prudence, b. Feb. 20, 1745/6	1	41
John, s. Charles & Prudence, b. Nov. 11, 1749	1	41
John A., b. Sept. 24, 1797; m. Lavina **HOSFORD**, Apr. 16, 1823	2	293
John A., b. Sept. 24, 1797; m. Lavina **HOSFORD**, Apr. 16, 1823	2	325
John A., m. Lavina **HOSFORD**, Apr. 16, 1823, by Rev. Isaac Jones	2	120
John A., m. Nicy M. **HOPKINS**, b. of Litchfield, June 9, 1853, by Rev.		
Lewis Jessup	TM49	91
John Newton, s. [John A. & Lavina], b. June 4, 1830	2	293
John Newton, s. [John A. & Lavina], b. June 4, 1830	2	325
Jonah, s. Benjamin & Eunice, b. Feb. 8, 1747/8	1	83
Jonah, m. Mary **OLMSTEAD**, Nov. 27, 1769	1	125
Lavina, m. David **WESTOVER**, b. of Litchfield, Oct. 28, 1828, by Rev.		
Henry Robinson, of South Farms	2	278
Lemming, s. Jacob, Jr. & Anne, b. Feb. 21, 1773	1	124
Levi, s. Philo & Huldah, b. May 17, 1784	2	5
Levi, m. Hannah **SILKRIGG**, Oct. 1, 1787, by James Merret, J.P.	1	207
Lewis Bartholomew, s. Morris & Candace, b. Jan. 19, 1809	2	77
Louis D., s. Denman & Naomi, b. Dec. 3, 1824	2	32
Luanna, d. Jacob, Jr. & Anne, b. Jan. 14, 1776	1	124
Lucius, see Lucretia **WOODRUFF**	2	56
Lucius Denman, of Litchfield, m. Mary Ann **FERNOLD**, of Penfield,		
Charlotte Cty., N.B., Oct. 7, 1846, by Rev. Samuel Fuller	TM49	38
Lucius P., m. Mana **WEBSTER**, Feb. 28, 1844, by Rev. D. L. Marks	TM49	4
Lucretia*, d. James & Lucretia, b. Nov. 30, 1813 *(Note reads:		
"Should be Lucius son of")	2	56
Luce, d. Jacob & Luce, b. Dec. 30, 1758	1	83
Lucy, m. Timothy **STANLEY, 3rd**, Dec. 22, 1775, by Rev. Abel		
Newell, of Goshen	1	161
Lucy, m. Enos **BARNS, Jr.**, Dec. 11, 1783, by Rev. Judah Champion	1	213
Lucy, d. James & Lucy, b. Aug. 9, 1789	1	207
Lucy, w. James, d. Apr. 28, 1790	1	206
Lucy Morris, d. Morris & Candace, b. July 1, 1807	2	77
Lydia, d. Jacob & Ann, b. Aug. 7, 1751	1	83
Maria C., d. Enoch J. & Catharine, b. July 31, 1809	2	140
Mary, m. John **RUSSELL**, Sept. 1, 1777	1	115-16
Mary, d. John A. & Lavina, b. Jan. 1, 1778	2	120
Mary, d. [John A. & Lavina], b. Jan. 17, 1826	2	293
Mary, d. [John A. & Lavina], b. Jan. 17, 1826	2	325
Merret, m. Delia A. **PERKINS**, Dec. 20, 1843, by Rev. D. L. Marks	TM49	1
Merret N., m. Ruby **STEDMAN**, Oct. 9, 1825, by Rev. Frederick		
Holcomb	2	257
Morris, s. James & Lucy, b. Sept. 3, 1777	1	165

	Vol.	Page

WOODRUFF, (cont.),

	Vol.	Page
Morris, m. Candace **CATLIN**, Nov. 21, 1804, by Rev. Joshua Williams	2	77
Morris, representative May 1824, May 1825, May 1826, May 1829		
May 1830, May 1836, May 1837	2	1555-7
Moses, representative Oct. 1812, May & Oct. 1813, May & Oct. 1814,		
May 1815	2	1554
Nathaniel, s. Nathaniel & Thankfull, b. May 3, 1728	1	41
Nathaniel, m. Mary **KILBORN**, Nov. 5, 1749	1	83
Nathaniel, Capt., d. Nov. 13, 1758, in the 73rd y. of his age	1	40
Nathaniel Baldwin, s. Benjamin & Hannah, b. Jan. 17, 1762	1	125
Olive, d. Oliver & Annis, b. Aug. 7, 1795	1	245
Oliver, s. Charles & Prudence, b. Apr. 30, 1755	1	82
Oliver, m. Annis **KNAP**, Dec. 5, 1785	1	245
Orange, s. Charles & Prudence, b. Oct. 7, 1765	1	82
Patience, d. Benjamin & Eunice, b. Nov. 3, 1745	1	41
Phebe, d. Wright, b. Oct. 22, 1769	1	125
Phebe, d. James & Lucy, b. Sept. 26, 1780	1	207
Phebe, d. Isaac & Clarissa, b. Sept. 26, 1798	1	245
Phebe, m. David **REA**, July 2, 1814, by Morris Woodruff	2	82
Philo, m. Huldah **ORTON**, Nov. 3, 1779, by Rev. George Beckwith	2	5
Philo, s. Philo & Huldah, b. May 4, 1788	2	5
R.M., Dr. of Litchfield, m. Eliza R. **THOMPSON**, of Lyons, N.Y., Oct.		
13, 1842, by Jonathan Brace	2	337
Rachal, d. Benjamin & Eunice, b. Aug. 31, 1750	1	83
Rachel, m. David **OLMSTEAD**, Feb. 7, 1771	1	69
Reuben Morris, s. Morris & Candace, b. May 8, 1811	2	77
Rhoda, d. Benjamin & Eunis, b. May 26, 1742	1	83
Rhoda, d. Charles & Prudence, b. Nov. 5, 1757	1	83
Rhoda, m. Jonah **SANFORD**, Dec. 7, 1757, by Thomas Harrison, J.P.	1	76
Ruth, d. Jacob & Luce, b. Dec. 7, 1761	1	83
Ruth, d. Jacob, Jr. & Anna, b. Feb. 1, 1785	1	124
Salmon, s. Jacob & Anne, b. Nov. 3, 1787	1	207
Salmon, m. Lavina **ENSIGN**, Oct. 10, 1811, by Rev. Amos Chase	2	62
Samuel, s. Nathaniell & Mary , b. Aug. 9, 1753	1	83
Samuel, m. Sarah **JOHNSON**, Jan. 10, 1776, by Rev. Judah Champion	1	124
Sarah, d. Nathaniel & Thankful, b. Dec. 27, 1725	1	41
Sarah, m. Gideon **HARRISON**, Feb. 11, 1746/7 by Timothy Collens	1	57
Sarah, m. Ezra **PLUMBE, Jr.**, June 8, 1775, by Elisha Sheldon	1	113
Sarah, d. Nathaniell & Mary, b. July 13, [ ]	1	83
Sarah Jane, d. Denman & Naomi, b. Nov. 4, 1822	2	32
Sarah Jane, of Litchfield, m. Joseph **DENISON**, of Newton, Mass., July		
8, 1845, by Rev. William Dixon	TM49	11
Seneth*, m. Daniel **MARSH**, Dec. 23, 1798, by James Morris		
*("Asenath")	2	14
Sidney, s. Oliver & Annis, b. Feb. 2, 1787	1	245
Simeon, s. Benjamin & Eunis, b. Sept. 9, 1740	1	83
Simeon, s. Benjamin & Eunis, d. Oct. 10, 1740	1	82
Simeon, s. Benjamin & Eunice, b. Jan. 30, 1743/4	1	83
Simeon, s. Jonah & Mary, b. June 8, 1773	1	40
Simeon, s. Philo & Huldah, b. July 26, 1782	2	5
Solomon, s. Charles & Prudence, b. Oct. 3, 1759	1	82
Steph[en], s. Oliver & Annis, b. Sept. 15, 1802	1	245
Thankfull, d. Benjamin & Eunice, b. May 31, 1747	1	41

	Vol.	Page
WOODRUFF, (cont.),		
Thankful, m. Capt. Zebulon **TAYLOR**, Nov. 23, 1780, by Rev. Judah Champion	1	121
Theede, d. Joel & Anne, b. Oct. 8, 1742	1	83
Theda, m. Elihu **HARRISON**, Jan. 19, 1764, by Rev. Judah Champion	1	99
Theada, d. Philo & Huldah, b. June 13, 1780	2	5
Ursula, d. Jonah & Mary, b. May 8, 1771	1	125
Walter, s. [John A. & Lavina], b. July 2, 1832	2	293
Walter, s. [John A. & Lavina], b. July 2, 1832	2	325
Weight*, s. Jacob & Ann, b. Aug. 10, 1744 *("Wright" in Woodruff's book)	1	41
William E., s. Enoch & Catharine, b. Apr. 30, 1814* *("1815" in a previous entry but it should be "1814" as stated by his father)	2	140
William E., s. Enoch J. & Catharine, b. Apr. 30, 1815	2	140
William L., m. Cornelia A. **MUNSON**, Sept. 6, 1846, by Rev. David L. Parmelee	TM49	14
Wright*, s. Jacob & Ann, b. Aug. 10, 1744 *("Weight" in Arnold Copy)	1	41
Wright, s. Isaac & Clarissa, b. Apr. 1, 1802	1	245
WOODWARD, Mary J., of Litchfield, m. Horace **HUBBARD**, of Watertown, Dec. 31, 1854, at the house of H. B. Woodward, by Rev. Frederick Holcomb	TM49	105
Sherman P., m. Minerva **PIERPOINT**, Nov. 29, 1827, by Fred Holcomb	2	273
WOODWORTH, Charles, s. Jonathan & Sarah, b. Oct. 4, 1790	1	206
Jonathan, m. Sarah **CULVER**, Nov. 27, 1788, by Rev. Judah Champion	1	206
Lyman, m. Rhoda **PALMER**, Dec. 23, 1823, by Rev. Lyman Beecher	2	133
Mary Ann, of Litchfield, m. Samuel **BALDWIN**, of Hunter, N.Y., Mar. 17, 1830, by Rev. Lawrence P. Hickok	2	285
Rhoda M., m. Ranson S. **POTTER**, Apr. 14, 1831, by Rev. William Lucas	2	287
WOOSTER, Anna, d. Lemuel & Levina, b. Mar. 17, 1795	2	124
Clarissa, d. Lemuel & Rebecca, b. Nov. 13, 1782	2	124
Elizabeth Marsh, d. Henry & Olive Maria, b. [ ], 1813	2	31
Fanny, d. Lemuel & Levina, b. Oct. 9, 1806	2	124
Frances J., m. David J. **McEWEN**, Mar. 16, 1829, by Mr. Jones	2	280
Harriet, d. Lemuel & Levina, b. Aug. 23, 1800	2	124
Harriet A., of Litchfield, m. Luke **THRALL**, of Torrington, Feb. 21, 1830, by Rev. L. P. Hickok	2	284
Henry, s. Lemuel & Rebecca, b. Nov. 25, 1786	2	124
Henry, m. Olive Maria **GARRIT**, Sept. 2, 1809, by Rev. Truman Marsh	2	31
Jeremiah, s. Lemuel & Rebecca, b. Feb. 21, 1785	2	124
Judson, s. Lemuel & Levina, b. May 13, 1803	2	124
Judson, of Bridgeport, m. Caroline **WARD**, of Litchfield, Jan. 26, 1845, by G. C. V. Eastman	TM49	8
Lemuel, m. Rebecca **GILLET**, Jan. [ ], 1782, by Rev. Judah Champion	2	124
Lemuel, m. Levina **JUDSON**, July 20, 1789	2	124
Lewis, s. Lemuel & Levina, b. Apr. 13, 1793	2	124
Lyman, s. Lemuel & Levina, b. Mar. 9, 1798	2	124
Lyman, m. Mary C. **McNEILE**, June 4, 1834, by Rev. L. P. Hickok	2	288
Mary Maria, d. Henry & Olive Maria, b. Apr. 7, 1812	2	31
Rebecca, w. Lemuel, d. Dec. [ ], 1786	2	124
Rebecca, d. Lemuel & Levina, b. Apr. 17, 1791	2	124

	Vol.	Page
WOOSTER, (cont.),		
Thankful, m. Charles **McNEILE**, Feb. 3, 1773, by Rev. Judah Champion	1	189
Truman, m. Anner **FORD**, b. of Litchfield, Mar. 31, 1850, by Rev. William B. Hoyt	TM49	53
WORDEN, Amelia, m. Lorenzo **HART**, Nov. 11, 1821, by Rev. Isaac Jones	2	105
WORKMAN, ——, of Winton Hampton Gloucestershire, Eng., m. William **DEWS**, of Wakefield, York Cty., Sept. 9, 1849, by Rev. Isaac Jones	TM49	42
WRIGHT, RIGHT, Adelia Teressa, d. [Jonathan, 2nd & Betsey], b. Nov. 5, 1837	2	132
Allice, d. Jonathan & Thankful, b. Aug. 7, 1795	1	209
Alice, of Milton, m. Robert **FERRIS**, of New Milford, Sept. 13, 1843, by Rev. E. M. Porter	2	412
Almira J., m. Ephraim K. **STONE**, b. of Litchfield, Oct. 14, 1834, by Truman Kilborn, J.P.	2	295
Almira Jennett, d. Jonathan, 2nd & Almira, b. Aug. 28, 1816	2	132
Artemus, of Winchester, m. Clarissa **SPENCER**, Dec. 17, 1823, by Enos Stoddard, J.P.	2	78
Benjamin Franklin, s. [Jonathan, 2nd & Betsey], b. Jan. 2, 1835	2	132
Celina D., of Goshen, m. David S. **OSBORN**, of Litchfield, Oct. 27, 1844, by Rev. S. T. Carpenter, of Milton	TM49	6
Charles, s. Jonathan & Thankful, b. June 10, 1791	1	209
Charles, m. Caroline **STONE**, Oct. 20, 1816, by Rev. Isaac Jones	2	260
Charles Belden Carroll, s. [Jonathan, 2nd & Betsey], b. Oct. 22, 1831	2	132
Clarinda* Maria, d. Samuel & Desdimona, b. Sept. 25, 1818 *(Written over "Clarissa")	2	17
Clarissa Maria, see Clarinda Maria **WRIGHT**	2	17
Eliza, m. Newton B. **ABBOT**, May 25, 1844, by Rev. D. L. Marks	TM49	4
Elizabeth, d. James & Elizabeth, b. May 28, 1791* *("1771" in Woodruff's)	1	82
Ellis, d. Samuel & Disdamona, b. Mar. 12, 1817	2	17
Everett H., m. Louisa **LANDON**, b. of Litchfield, Sept. 22, 1852, by Rev. John J. Brandegee	TM49	76
Everett Hale, s. Samuel & Desdamona, b. Nov. 21, 1821	2	17
Frederick, s. Charles & Caroline, b. May 22, 1817	2	260
George Frederick, s. Jonathan, 2nd & Betsey, b. Dec. 19, 1824, in Warren	2	132
Gustavus Adolphus, s. [Jonathan, 2nd & Betsey], b. Nov. 4, 1826, in Washington	2	132
Henry Stanton, s. Jonathan, 2nd & Almira, b. Aug. 2, 1820	2	132
Honor, d. Jonathan & Leah, b. Dec. 9, 1767	1	165
Huldah, d. Jonathan & Leah, b. Sept. 27, 1771	1	165
Huldah, d. James & Elizabeth, b. June 18, 1786	1	207
Huldah, d. Jonathan, m. Rosier **FREAY***, May [ ], 1789, by Rev. Judah Champion *("Roger **FRY**". Corrected by Mrs. Bissell)	1	176-7
James, m. Elizabeth **LEE**, Dec. 13, 1768, by Rev. Judah Champion	1	125
James, s. Jonathan & Leah, b. Aug. 19, 1769	1	165
James, s. James & Elizabeth, b. Oct. 6, 1769	1	82
John, s. James & Elizabeth, b. Feb. 17, 1773	1	82
John, s. Jonathan & Leah, b. Jan. 4, 1776	1	165
Jonathan, m. Leah **BISSELL**, Apr. 6, 1767, by Rev. Judah Champion	1	165
Jonathan, m. Tryphena **TRAY** [**TRACY**], d. Nehemiah, June 27, 1784,		

	Vol.	Page
WRIGHT, RIGHT, (cont.),		
by Rev. Mr. Parsons, of East Haddam	1	209
Jonathan, m. Thankful **LANDON,** d. David, May 15, 1788, by David Welch	1	209
Jonathan, 2nd, s. Jonathan, Jr. & Honor, b. Dec. 18, 1790	2	132
Jonathan, 2nd, m. Betsey **GRISWOULD,** Jan. 25, 1824, by Rev. Isaac Jones	2	132
Lydia, m. Silvanus **STONE,** Mar. 12, 1733/4, by Rev. Mr. Doolittle, of Northfield	1	37
Marian, d. Jonathan & Thankful, b. Jan. 24, 1794	1	209
Marian, d. Samuel & Disdamona, b. June 19, 1815 *("Mary Ann")	2	17
Marian, d. Charles & Caroline, b. Oct. 6, 1823	2	260
Martha, d. James & Elizabeth, b. Feb. 24, 1775	1	82
Mary, d. James & Elizabeth, b. Mar. 18, 1777	1	124
Mary Ann, m. Beecher **PERKINS,** Dec. 24, 1833, by Rev. David G. Tomlinson	2	293
Mary Ann, see also Marian		
Polly, d. Jonathan & Leah, b. June 18, 1780	1	165
Rebecca, m. Jacob S. **BLACKMAN,** May 10, 1823, by Rev. Reuben Sherwood, of Norwalk	2	256
Richard Corbet, s. [Jonathan, 2nd & Betsey], b. Jan. 6, 1839	2	132
Sally, twin with Sina, d. Jonathan & Leah, b. Oct. 18, 1773	1	165
Sally, m. Benjamin **GRISWOULD,** Aug. 5, 1799, by Rev. Dan Huntington	2	72
Samuel, s. Jonathan & Thankful, b. Mar. 1, 1789	1	209
Samuel, m. Disdamona **GUILDS,** May 29, 1814, by Rev. Isaac Jones	2	17
Sarah, m. John **PARSON,** Oct. 13, 1772, by Rev. Judah Cahmpion	1	155
Sina, twin with Sally, d. Jonathan & Leah, b. Oct. 18, 1773	1	165
Sina, d. Jonathan & Sarah, d. Mar. [ ], 1774	1	164
Sina, d. Jonathan & Leah, b. June 12, 1778	1	165
Sina, d. Jonathan & Leah, d. Nov. 22, 1793	1	164
Susannah, d. Jonathan & Tryphena, b. Mar. 31, 1785	1	209
Thomas, s. James & Elizabeth, b. Sept. 24, 1783	1	207
Tryphena, w. Jonathan, d. Nov. 20, 1785 (probably 1786)	1	208
Tryphena, d. Jonathan & Tryphena, b. Nov. 16, 1786	1	209
Washington Irving, s. [Jonathan, 2nd & Betsey], b.Nov. 30, 1828	2	132
William Henry, s. Charles & Caroline, b. Nov. 11, 1821	2	260
WYANT, Jane, of New Milford, m. Enos **CARPENTER,** of Litchfield, Aug. 23, 1852, by Rev. Lewis Gunn	TM49	77
WYLLYS, Susanna, m. Jedediah **STRONG,** Jan. 22, 1788, by Rev. Judah Champion	1	201
YOUNG, YOUNGS, Elizabeth, m. Elijah **GRISWOLD,** Feb. 21, 1739/40, by Rev. Timothy Collens	1	99
Martha, m. Daniel **LANDON,** May 22, 1736, by Rev. Jared Eliot	1	23
Polly, m. Silas E. **CHENEY,** May 18, 1807, by Rev. Mr. Barber	2	12
NO SURNAME, Betsey, m. Appleton **MARSH,** Feb. [ ], 1801, by James Morris, J.P.	2	258
Desire, m. Asahel **GRISWOULD,** Jr., Aug. 17, 1797	2	3

Printed in the USA
CPSIA information can be obtained
at www.ICGtesting.com
LVHW010713020224
770740LV00006B/87

9 780806 316000